PELICAN BOOKS

AN ANTHOLOGY OF INDIAN LITERATURE

Dr John B. Alphonso-Karkala, Professor of Literature at the State University of New York at New Paltz, has taught Indian and comparative Asian literature since 1964. He has also taught Oriental humanities at Columbia University and the City College, New York. Prior to teaching, he was in the Indian Foreign Service, stationed at Geneva, London, and at the United Nations in New York from 1953 to 1960.

Dr Karkala was born in South Kanara, Mysore State, in India. He graduated from Bombay University with degrees in literature and philosophy, and from Columbia University with a Ph.D. in English and comparative literature. He is active in research and in teaching Indian and comparative literature. He has chaired group and seminar meetings of the Modern Language Association, examining problems related to the teaching of Indian literature in colleges and schools, and has presented a number of papers in Europe and America. His publications include articles such as *World Humanities in Undergraduate Curriculum* and *The Beginnings of the Asian Novel*, and he has written *Indo-English Literature in the Nineteenth Century* (1970).

Dr Karkala is currently working on a critical study of Jawaharlal Nehru as a writer, and is engaged on a research project supported by the State University of New York, on a comparative approach to South Asian literature.

AN ANTHOLOGY OF
INDIAN LITERATURE

Edited by
JOHN B. ALPHONSO-KARKALA

May we attain that excellent glory of Savitar
(God of Light)
So may he stimulate our thoughts.

– 'Gayatri', *Rig Veda*, III.62.10

PENGUIN BOOKS

Penguin Books Ltd, Harmondsworth, Middlesex, England
Penguin Books Inc., 7110 Ambassador Road, Baltimore, Maryland 21207, U.S.A.
Penguin Books Australia Ltd, Ringwood, Victoria, Australia

—

First published 1971
SBN 021 248 5
This collection copyright © Penguin Books, Inc., 1971

—

Made and printed in Great Britain
by Hazell Watson & Viney Ltd, Aylesbury, Bucks
Set in Monotype Ehrhardt

CONTENTS

Contents

Contents

PREFACE

THE sub-Himalayan region, in spite of the present political demar-
cations, can be regarded as a single geographical unit, presenting a
multi-foliate culture of peoples with a diversity of languages, attitudes,
and ways of life, yet with a fundamental underlying cultural unity.
However, presently available anthologies or studies of Indian literature generally deal with literature in a single language (for example
Sanskrit literature, Pali literature, Tamil literature), or give some
account of literature in a modern Indian language (for example
Bengali literature). Such presentations are, no doubt, valuable in the
study and appreciation of a particular language and its literature. But
there is a need for a composite presentation of Indian literature to
give an over-all picture of the literary tradition of the sub-continent,
as well as to relate the literary movements permeating different
languages of the region. This anthology is a modest attempt in that
direction.

The literature of India can be regarded as emerging in a few large
and sweeping movements, affecting the whole region, and expressing
the sensibilities of the people around some spiritual explosions during
long periods of history. Such waves of aesthetic activities may be
recognized in a few broad strands, namely:

    I. Age of Rishis [Seers], 3000–100 B.C.
   II. Age of Gurus [Teachers], 600 B.C.–A.D. 500
  III. Age of Acharyas [Scholars], 400 B.C.–A.D. 1000
  IV. Age of Bhaktas [Mystics], A.D. 700–1800
   V. Age of Mahatma [Great Soul], A.D. 1800–

My undertaking to present a composite anthology of Indian literature was made possible by, among other things, several important
sources of inspiration. My former and present students, especially
those in the courses in Oriental Humanities at Columbia University,
Asian Literature at City College, New York, and Comparative Literature and Indian Literature at the State University of New York,
New Paltz, have helped me to consider Indian classics over and over

again from different points of view, and to place them in comparison with literary works from other parts of the world. A list of texts for such comparison is included in the Appendix. Beyond this daily confrontation, there are generations of translators and scholars who by their extreme devotion to Sarasvati (goddess of Learning), and dedication to Indology, have bequeathed to us the fruits of their labours in various translations and literary studies.

New Paltz, New York   JOHN B. ALPHONSO-KARKALA
31 March 1969

❧

Part One

AGE OF RISHIS
[SEERS]
3000–100 B.C.

❧

A. SRUTI [Revealed]

Vedas (Sanskrit, *c.* 3000–1200 B.C.)

1. Hymns from the *Rig Veda*

Upanishads (Sanskrit, *c.* 1200–600 B.C.)

2. *Katha Upanishad*
3. *Isa Upanishad*
4. *Chandogya Upanishad*
5. *Brihad-aranyaka Upanishad*

B. ITHIHASA [Heroic Epic]

Krishna Dwaipayana Vyasa, *Mahabharata* (Sanskrit, *c.* 900–500 B.C.)

6. Pativrata Mahatmya: The Story of Savitri
7. The Bhagavad Gita

C. KAVYA [Literary Epic]

8. Valmiki, *Ramayana* (Sanskrit, *c.* 600–300 B.C.)
9. Ilango Adigal, *Shilappadikaram* (Tamil, *c.* 200 B.C.–A.D. 100)

Vedas

(Sanskrit, *c.* 3000–1200 B.C.)

In explaining the existential situation in which they found themselves, the ancient Indians personified natural phenomena and bestowed upon them an essence of spirituality. The elemental forces of nature which they encountered in their daily lives were named and deified in hymns. For example, the phenomenon of fire is called Agni; the phenomenon of wind is Vayu; the phenomenon of the sun is Surya; the phenomenon of the appearance of the colourful dawn is the coming of the beautiful goddess Ushas; the phenomenon of clouds breaking into rain is the work of Indra, the god of atmosphere. Thus, it was easy to explain what was unexplainable. Using a kind of symbolic logic, or the dramatic shorthand of myths, Vedic poets established emotional and prayerful relations with different aspects of nature through a series of hymns, in what amounted to a kind of naturalistic polytheism. In this process, almost every natural aspect acquired a spiritual name and deified form, and merited praise or worship. These poetic apprehensions of some aspects of Reality or its attributes, these visionary testaments of the *rishis*, or seers, evoked in their naïve simplicity, a child-like faith. The Vedic hymns express this exuberant rapture and bold adventure of the human spirit in its earliest attempt to establish a communication with the unknown spirit of the universe.

In the course of over a thousand years, during which the hymns of the *Rig Veda* (the earliest of the four *Vedas*) seem to have evolved, there appear a number of broad strata of development. The first is the naturalistic polytheism, giving poetic birth to the anthropomorphic divinities (Agni, Ushas, Vayu, Ratri, Indra); second, polytheism developing into henotheism, when one among the many gods is extolled as the highest at a time, without any one of them reaching the position of the supreme deity (Varuna, Vishnu, Rudra); third, the development of abstract ideas and the emergence of monotheism in the form of a supreme god, conceived in terms of functions or qualities, as the upholder of the law, the preserver of the universe, regulator of other gods and forces, the lord of beings, creator, or maker (Prajapati, Visvakarman; Faith, Knowledge, Speech); fourth, and what is unique in the Indian search for the Ultimate, the Vedic Indians develop a kind of monism, where the whole cosmos is conceived as a unitary principle or energy, manifesting itself in infinite variety (Purusha); finally, towards the end of the Vedic period, there emerges a spirit of critical inquiry, when men question their own earlier poetic explanations about the universe and, in fact, their own concepts about gods; however, they leave these questions unanswered (Song of Creation). This line of reasoned inquiry into the nature of things, the law of the universe, the way of the cosmos, and man's place in it becomes the subject of investigation of the later philosophical speculations called the *Aranyakas, Upanishads*, or *Vedanta*.

A study of the hymns of the *Vedas* is indispensable for any understanding of the multi-foliate Indian culture and traditions. Obviously, these hymns are poetic compositions of highly gifted, perhaps divinely inspired, sages, and, in fact, they are held by millions to be *sruti*, or revealed texts, and therefore scriptural. But more important than this is the fact that they are the earliest gropings of mankind towards understanding man's essence and his existence. Because these gropings into the inexhaustible mysteries of life are dressed in allegorical, mythical, and symbolic forms, their meanings become unfolded in every age like fresh waves upon the surface of the ocean. During India's long history of over 3,000 years, these hymns not only have remained the bedrock of thought and expression, and ways of life of the Indian people, but they also continue to be the fountainhead of spiritualities, and the living faith and consolation of a large part of mankind. A study of these hymns, even as literature, will be revealing in some sense.

There are four *Vedas*: the *Rig Veda*, the *Sama Veda*, the *Yajur Veda*, and the *Atharva Veda*. Each of the *Vedas* contains three sections: the *Samhitas* (collection of hymns); *Brahmanas* (prose treatise explaining sacrificial rituals and formulas); *Aranyakas* and *Upanishads* (metaphysical speculations, explaining the hymns).

The dates of the composition and collection of the *Vedas* are uncertain. However, it is reckoned that long periods of time must have elapsed between the first composition of the hymns and their subsequent compilation. It is established with some certainty that the hymns were current in India about 1500 B.C. in the arrangement in which they have come down to the present day. These works, no doubt, synthesize and embody the thoughts and visions of several generations of poets and seers, at different levels of spiritual and intellectual sophistication, and with different cultural and racial backgrounds, until they were finally expressed and formally recorded in Vedic Sanskrit. This explains both the heterogeneity and the multiple strata of thought.

The *Rig Veda*, the oldest and the most important of the four *Vedas*, consists of 1,017 hymns, arranged in 10 books, perhaps covering a period of over 1,000 years, during which time they may have been composed.

The hymns included in this section are taken from the translation by Ralph T. H. Griffith, *The Hymns of the Rig Veda*, 2 vols., Benares: E. J. Lazarus & Co., 3rd ed. 1920–6; reprinted, Chowkamba Sanskrit Studies Series, Vol. XXXV (2 vols.), Varanasi, 1963. (First published in 1889 and 1896.)

HYMNS FROM THE
RIG VEDA

I.1   *To AGNI (the god of Fire)*

1. I laud Agni, the chosen priest, god, minister of sacrifice,
   The hotar, lavishest of wealth.

2. Worthy is Agni to be praised by living as by ancient seers:
   He shall bring hitherward the gods.

3. Through Agni man obtaineth wealth, yea, plenty, waxing day by
   day,
   Most rich in heroes, glorious.

---

1. *Agni:* cf. Latin *ignitus*, past participle of *ignire*, to ignite. As sacrificial
fire, Agni is the messenger carrying the oblations of the worshippers to the
gods: at the same time, he is the herald who brings the gods to the place of
sacrifice. Consequently, the correct worship of Agni was of prime importance
and was developed to an extraordinary degree in the *Rig Veda.*

Hotar: an invoking priest, a herald who calls the gods to receive the
offerings.

4. Agni, the perfect sacrifice which thou encompassest about
   Verily goeth to the gods.

5. May Agni, sapient-minded priest, truthful, most gloriously great,
   The god, come hither with the gods.

6. Whatever blessing, Agni, thou wilt grant unto thy worshipper,
   That, Angiras, is indeed thy truth.

7. To thee, dispeller of the night, O Agni, day by day with
      prayer
   Bringing thee reverence, we come;

8. Ruler of sacrifices, guard of law eternal, radiant one,
   Increasing in thine own abode.

9. Be to us easy of approach, even as a father to his son;
   Agni, be with us for our weal.

X.16   *To AGNI (Fire)*

1. Burn him not up, nor quite consume him, Agni: let not his body or
      his skin be scattered.
   O Jatavedas, when thou hast matured him, then send him on his
      way unto the fathers.

2. When thou hast made him ready, Jatavedas, then do thou give him
      over to the fathers.
   When he attains unto the life that waits him, he shall become the
      deities' controller.

----

6. *Angiras:* another name for Agni, or the first sacrificer.

1. Stanzas 1–5 are repeated while the body of the departed is being
partially consumed on the funeral pile.

Jatavedas: another name for Agni.

3. The sun receive thine eyes, the wind thy spirit; go, as thy merit is, to earth or heaven.

   Go, if it be thy lot, unto the waters; go, make thine home in plants with all thy members.

4. Thy portion is the goat: with heat consume him; let thy fierce flame, thy glowing splendour, burn him.

   With thine auspicious forms, O Jatavedas, bear this man to the region of the pious.

5. Again, O Agni, to the fathers send him who, offered in thee, goes with our oblations.

   Wearing new life let him increase his offspring: let him rejoin a body, Jatavedas.

I.50   *To SURYA (the Sun god)*

1. His bright rays bear him up aloft, the god who knoweth all that lives,

   Surya, that all may look on him.

2. The constellations pass away, like thieves, together with their beams,

   Before the all-beholding Sun.

3. His herald rays are seen afar refulgent o'er the world of men,

   Like flames of fire that burn and blaze.

4. Swift and all beautiful art thou, O Surya, maker of the light,

   Illuming all the radiant realm.

---

4. Agni is addressed. *The goat* was sacrificed on the funeral pyre. Since Agni as sacrificial fire transmutes material objects cast into it by the worshippers to the non-material world of the gods, Agni as fire of the funeral pyre is the transporter of the dead from the corporeal to the non-corporeal world.

5. Thou goest to the hosts of gods, thou comest hither to mankind,
   Hither all light to behold.

6. With that same eye of thine wherewith thou lookest, brilliant Varuna,
   Upon the busy race of men,

7. Traversing sky and wide mid-air, thou metest with thy beams our days,
   Sun, seeing all things that have birth.

8. Seven bay steeds harnessed to thy car bear thee, O thou far-seeing one,
   God, Surya with the radiant hair.

9. Surya hath yoked the pure bright seven, the daughters of the car; with these,
   His own dear team, he goeth forth.

10. Looking upon the loftier light above the darkness, we have come
    To Surya, god among the gods, the light that is most excellent.

11. Rising this day, O rich in friends, ascending to the loftier heaven,
    Surya, remove my heart's disease, take from me this my yellow hue.

12. To parrots and to starlings let us give away my yellowness
    Or this my yellowness let us transfer to Haritala trees.

13. With all his conquering vigour, this Aditya hath gone up on high,
    Giving my foe into mine hand: let me not be my foeman's prey.

---

6. *Varuna.* Used here as an appellative (the encompasser) and applied to the Sun. See later Varuna is the god of Natural Order of the Universe.

8–9. *Seven bay steeds.* The sun is conceived as riding in a chariot drawn by seven horses (seven days of the week). Since the days are generated by the riding Sun, they are also referred to as the 'seven daughters of the car'.

11–12. Surya, as curative minister, is invoked to restore vigour to the living and to cast off paleness from human beings.

13. *Aditya:* son of Aditi (Infinity, Infinite Nature), Surya or Sun.

I.113 *To USHAS (the goddess of Dawn)*

1. This light is come, amid all lights the fairest; born is the brilliant, far-extending brightness.

   Night, sent away for Savitar's uprising, hath yielded up a birth-place for the morning.

2. The fair, the bright is come with her white offspring; to her the dark one hath resigned her dwelling.

   Akin, immortal, following each other, changing their colours, both the heavens move onward.

3. Common, unending is the sisters' pathway: taught by the gods, alternately they travel.

   Fair-formed, of different hues and yet one-minded, Night and Dawn clash not, neither do they tarry.

4. Bright leader of glad sounds, our eyes behold her: splendid in hue she hath unclosed the portals.

   She, stirring up the world, hath shown us riches: Dawn hath awakened every living creature.

5. Rich Dawn, she sets afoot the coiled-up sleeper, one for enjoyment, one for wealth or worship,

   Those who saw little for extended vision: all living creatures hath the Dawn awakened.

---

1. *Savitar:* the sun.
2. *White Offspring:* the white clouds.
Dark one: Ratri, the goddess of Night.
Both the heavens: Day and Night.
4. *Leader of glad sounds.* Dawn awakens the early singing birds and other living things.
5. *Those who saw little,* during the darkness of the night.

6. One to high sway, one to exalted glory, one to pursue his gain and one his labour;
   All to regard their different vocations, all moving creatures hath the Dawn awakened.

7. We see her there, the child of heaven, apparent, the young maid, flushing in her shining raiment.
   Thou sovran lady of all earthly treasure, flush on us here, auspicious Dawn, this morning.

8. She, first of endless morns to come hereafter, follows the path of morns that have departed.
   Dawn, at her rising, urges forth the living: him who is dead she wakes not from his slumber.

9. As thou, Dawn, hast caused Agni to be kindled, and with the sun's eye hast revealed creation,
   And hast awakened men to offer worship, thou hast performed, for gods, a noble service.

10. How long a time, and they shall be together. – Dawns that have shone and dawns to shine hereafter?
    She yearns for former dawns with eager longing, and goes forth gladly shining with the others.

11. Gone are the men who in the days before us looked on the rising of the earlier morning.
    We, we the living, now behold her brightness, and they come nigh who shall hereafter see her.

12. Foe-chaser, born of Law, the law's protectress, joy-giver, waker of all pleasant voices,
    Auspicious, bringing food for gods' enjoyment, shine on us here, most bright, O Dawn, this morning.

---

6. This verse alludes to basically four broad divisions of functions in a society: the thinker and legislator, the administrator, the trader, and the labourer.

9. *Hast caused Agni to be kindled*: the daybreak being the proper time for lighting household and sacrificial fire.

12. Evil spirits vanish when the Dawn appears.

13. From days eternal hath Dawn shone, the goddess, and shows this light today, endowed with riches.
    So will she shine on days to come; immortal she moves on in her own strength, undecaying.

14. In the sky's borders hath she shone in splendour: the goddess hath thrown off the veil of darkness.
    Awakening the world with purple horses, on her well-harnessed chariot Dawn approaches.

15. Bringing all life-sustaining blessings with her, showing herself, she sends forth brilliant lustre.
    Last of the countless mornings that have vanished, first of bright morns to come hath Dawn arisen.

16. Arise! the breath, the life, again hath reached us: darkness hath passed away, and light approacheth.
    She for the sun hath left a path to travel: we have arrived where men prolong existence.

17. Singing the praises of refulgent mornings with his hymn's web, the priest, the poet, rises.
    Shine then today, rich maid, on him who lauds thee, shine down on us the gift of life and offspring.

18. Dawns giving sons all heroes, kine and horses, shining upon the man who brings oblations, –
    These let the soma-presser gain when ending his glad songs louder than the voice of Vayu.

19. Mother of gods, Aditi's form of glory, ensign of sacrifice, shine forth exalted.
    Rise up, bestowing praise on our devotion: all-bounteous, make us chief among the people.

---

18. *Soma-presser:* one who presses soma, a juice of a milky climbing plant (*Asclepias acida*), extracted and fermented, forming a beverage offered in libations to the gods and drunk by people in communion.
Voice of Vayu: roaring of the god of Wind.

19. *Aditi.* Infinity is considered the mother of everything, and Dawn is her special form of glory.

20. Whatever splendid wealth the dawns bring with them to bless
    the man who offers praise and worship,
    Even that may Mitra, Varuna vouchsafe us, and Aditi and Sindhu,
    earth and heaven.

X.168   *To VAYU (the god of Wind)*

1. O the Wind's chariot, O its power and glory! Crashing it goes and
   hath a voice of thunder.
   It makes the regions red and touches heaven, and as it moves the
   dust of earth is scattered.

2. Along the traces of the Wind they hurry, they come to him as dames
   to an assembly.
   Borne on his car with these for his attendants, the god speeds forth,
   the universe's monarch.

3. Travelling on the paths of air's mid-region, no single day doth he
   take rest or slumber.
   Holy and earliest-born, friend of the waters, where did he spring
   and from what region came he?

4. Germ of the world, the deities' vital spirit, this god moves ever as
   his will inclines him.
   His voice is heard, his shape is ever viewless. Let us adore this
   Wind with our oblation.

X.127   *To RATRI (the goddess of Night)*

1. With all her eyes the goddess Night looks forth approaching many
   a spot:
   She hath put all her glories on.

---

20. *Mitra, Varuna:* deities.
Sindhu: the river Indus.

2. Immortal, she hath filled the waste, the goddess hath filled height
   and depth:
   She conquers darkness with her light.

3. The goddess as she comes hath set the Dawn her sister in her place:
   And then the darkness vanishes.

4. So favour us this night, O thou whose pathways we have visited
   As birds their nest upon the tree.

5. The villagers have sought their homes, and all that walks and all
   that flies,
   Even the falcons fain for prey.

6. Keep off the she-wolf and the wolf; O Urmya, keep the thief away;
   Easy be thou for us to pass.

7. Clearly hath she come nigh to me who decks the dark with richest
   hues:
   O morning, cancel it like debts.

8. These have I brought to thee like kine. O Night, thou child of
   heaven, accept
   This laud as for a conqueror.

I.32   *To INDRA (the god of Atmosphere)*

1. I will declare the manly deeds of Indra, the first that he achieved,
   the thunder-wielder.
   He slew the dragon, then disclosed the waters, and cleft the
   channels of the mountain torrents.

---

1. *Indra:* the most prominent god in the *Rig Veda*. With his weapon
vajra (thunderbolt), fashioned by Tvashtar (artist of the gods), Indra slays
the dragons (clouds), and liberates the waters which come down the mountain slopes as rain. This elemental conflict of heat and moisture attempting
to overtake one another in a continuous cycle is allegorically represented in
this hymn as Indra's fight with the dragons and their mother Vritra (Drought).

2. He slew the dragon lying on the mountain: his heavenly bolt of
   thunder Tvashtar fashioned.
   Like lowing kine in rapid flow descending, the waters glided
   downward to the ocean.

3. Impetuous as a bull, he chose the soma, and in three sacred
   beakers drank the juices.
   Maghavan grasped the thunder for his weapon, and smote to
   death this firstborn of the dragons.

4. When, Indra, thou hadst slain the dragon's firstborn, and overcome the charms of the enchanters,
   Then, giving life to Sun and Dawn and Heaven, thou foundest
   not one foe to stand against thee.

5. Indra, with his own great and deadly thunder, smote into pieces
   Vritra, worst of Vritras.
   As trunks of trees, what time the axe hath felled them low on the
   earth, so lies the prostrate dragon.

6. He, like a mad, weak warrior, challenged Indra, the great, impetuous, many-slaying hero.
   He, brooking not the clashing of the weapons, crushed – Indra's
   foe – the shattered forts in falling.

7. Footless and handless still, he challenged Indra, who smote him
   with his bolt between the shoulders.
   Emasculate yet claiming manly vigour, thus Vritra lay with
   scattered limbs dissevered.

8. There, as he lies like a bank-bursting river, the waters taking
   courage flow above him.
   The dragon lies beneath the feet of torrents which Vritra with his
   greatness had encompassed.

---

3. *Bull:* Indra.
Maghavan: Indra, the Lord Bountiful.
5. *Vritra:* dragon of Drought, whose children are the clouds.
6. *Forts:* the clouds conceived as dragons, as well as the forts within which
moisture is imprisoned.

9. Then humbled was the strength of Vritra's mother: Indra hath cast his deadly bolt against her.

The mother was above, the son was under, and like a cow beside her calf lay Danu.

10. Rolled in the midst of never-ceasing currents flowing without a rest for ever onward,

The waters bear off Vritra's nameless body: the foe of Indra sank too during darkness.

11. Guarded by Ahi stood the thralls of Dasas, the waters stayed like kine held by the robber.

But he, when he had smitten Vritra, opened the cave wherein the floods had been imprisoned.

12. A horse's tail wast thou when he, O Indra, smote on thy bolt; thou, god without a second,

Thou has won back the kine, hast won the soma; thou hast let loose to flow the seven rivers.

13. Nothing availed him lightning, nothing thunder, hailstorm or mist which he had spread around him:

When Indra and the dragon strove in battle, Maghavan gained the victory for ever.

14. Whom sawest thou to avenge the dragon, Indra, that fear possessed thy heart when thou hadst slain him;

That, like a hawk affrighted through the regions, thou crossedst nine-and-ninety flowing rivers?

---

9. *Danu:* the mother of dragons, the Drought.

11. *Ahi:* mother of dragons.

Dasas. Dragons.

12. *A horse's tail.* The destruction of the dragons by Indra was as easily done as the horse sweeps away the flies by its tail.

Seven rivers. Probably the five branches of the Indus river, and two branches of the Ganges river, all of which flow from the Himalaya mountains.

14. Indra's fight against Vritra or Drought is a prolonged one because the clouds gather together after a long journey across many rivers.

Nine-and-ninety: a great many.

15. Indra is king of all that moves and moves not, of creatures tame
    and horned, the thunder-wielder.
    Over all living men he rules as sovran, containing all as spokes
    within the felly.

I.159 *To DYAVA-PRTIVI (Heaven and Earth)*

1. I praise with sacrifices mighty Heaven and Earth at festivals, the
   wise, the strengtheners of Law.
   Who, having gods for progeny, conjoined with gods, through
   wonder-working wisdom bring forth choicest boons.

2. With invocations, on the gracious Father's mind, and on the
   Mother's great inherent power I muse.
   Prolific Parents, they have made the world of life, and for their
   brood all around wide immortality.

3. These sons of yours well skilled in work, of wondrous power,
   brought forth to life the two great Mothers first of all.
   To keep the truth of all that stands and all that moves, ye guard the
   station of your Son who knows no guile.

4. They with surpassing skill, most wise, have measured out the
   twins united in their birth and in their home.
   They, the refulgent sages, weave within the sky, yea, in the depths
   of seas, a web for ever new.

5. This is today the goodliest gift of Savitar: this thought we have
   when now the god is furthering us.
   On us with loving kindness, Heaven and Earth, bestow riches and
   various wealth and treasure hundredfold!

---

3. *These sons of yours:* Ribhus and Surya, who restored their parents'
youth.
Two great Mothers: the parents of all, Heaven and Earth.
Your son who knows no guile: Surya, the sun, who is regarded as the symbol
of Truth.

4. *The twins:* Heaven and Earth.

V.85 *To VARUNA (the god of Natural Order)*

1. Sing forth a hymn sublime and solemn, grateful to glorious
    Varuna, imperial ruler,
   Who hath struck out, like one who slays the victim, earth as a skin
    to spread in front of Surya.

2. In the tree-tops the air he hath extended, put milk in kine and
    vigorous speed in horses,
   Set intellect in hearts, fire in the waters, Surya in heaven and
    Soma on the mountain.

3. Varuna lets the big cask, opening downward, flow through the
    heaven and earth and air's mid-region.
   Therewith the universe's sovran waters earth as the shower of rain
    bedews the barley.

4. When Varuna is fain for milk, he moistens the sky, the land, and
    earth to her foundation.
   Then straight the mountains clothe them in the raincloud: the
    heroes, putting forth their vigour, loose them.

5. I will declare this mighty deed of magic, of glorious Varuna, the
    lord immortal,
   Who, standing in the firmament, hath meted the earth out with the
    sun as with a measure.

6. None, verily, hath ever let or hindered this the most wise god's
    mighty deed of magic,
   Whereby with all their flood, the lucid rivers fill not one sea wherein
    they pour their waters.

7. If we have sinned against the man who loves us, have ever wronged
    a brother, friend, or comrade,
   The neighbour ever with us, or a stranger, O Varuna, remove
    from us the trespass.

8. If we, as gamesters cheat at play, have cheated, done wrong unwittingly or sinned of purpose,
   Cast all these sins away like loosened fetters, and, Varuna, let us be
   thine own beloved.

I.154 *To VISHNU (the All-Pervading god)*

1. I will declare the mighty deeds of Vishnu, of him who measured
   out the earthly regions,
   Who propped the highest place of congregation, thrice setting
   down his footstep, widely striding.

2. For this his mighty deed is Vishnu lauded, like some wild beast,
   dread, prowling, mountain roaming;
   He within whose three wide-extended paces all living creatures
   have their habitation.

3. Let the hymn lift itself as strength to Vishnu, the bull, far-striding,
   dwelling on the mountains,
   Him who alone with triple step hath measured this common
   dwelling-place, long, far extended,

4. Him whose three places that are filled with sweetness, imperishable, joy as it may list them,
   Who verily alone upholds the threefold, the earth, the heaven, and
   all living creatures.

5. May I attain to that his well-loved mansion where men devoted
   to the gods are happy.
   For there springs, close akin to the wide-strider, the well of meath
   in Vishnu's highest footstep.

---

1. *Vishnu* is striding through the regions of the universe in three steps,
explained as three-fold manifestation of birth, growth, and decay.
   Highest place of congregation. Sky or heaven where gods assemble.
   5. *Meath:* nectar, or the celestial soma.

6. Fain would we go unto your dwelling-places where there are many
horned and nimble oxen,
For mightily, there, shineth down upon us the widely-striding
Bull's sublimest mansion.

I.43   *To RUDRA (the Terrible god)*

1. What shall we sing to Rudra, strong, most bounteous, excellent
wise,
That shall be dearest to his heart?

2. That Aditi may grant the grace of Rudra to our folk, our kine,
Our cattle and our progeny;

3. That Mitra and that Varuna, that Rudra may remember us,
Yea, all the gods with one accord.

4. To Rudra, Lord of sacrifice, of hymns and balmy medicines,
We pray for joy and health and strength.

5. He shines in splendour like the Sun, refulgent as bright gold is he,
The good, the best among the gods.

6. May he grant health into our steeds, well-being to our rams and
ewes,
To men, to women, and to kine.

---

6. *Many horned and nimble oxen:* stars with twinkling light.

1. *Rudra.* The terrible or fiery god appears in this hymn as a gentle and
beneficent god of healing. Rudra causes destruction through decay and
disease. He is prayed to prevent such disease and decay through his healing
powers. Rudra is called the Maha-deva in the *Yajur Veda.* Rudra is identified with the earliest god Shiva, the presiding god of Kasi, or Benaras, or
Varnasi, the holy of holies of India, somewhat similar to Rome of Europe,
or Mecca of Arabia.

2. *Aditi:* Infinity, or boundless heaven and earth.

3. *Mitra, Varuna.* Mitra, a god, is generally associated with Varuna, being
rulers of the day and the night. They together uphold the Law of Nature.

6. Rudra is addressed as *Pasupati*, Lord and guardian of cattle.

7. O Soma, set thou upon us the glory of a hundred men,
   The great renown of mighty chiefs.

8. Let not malignities, nor those who trouble Soma, hinder us.
   Indu, give us a share of strength.

9. Soma! head, central point, love these; Soma! know these as serving
     thee,
   Children of thee Immortal, at the highest place of holy law.

X.14   *To YAMA (the god of Death)*

1. Honour the king with thine oblations, Yama, Vivasvan's son, who
     gathers men together,
   Who travelled to the lofty heights above us, who searches out and
     shows the path to many.

2. Yama first found for us a place to dwell in: this pasture never can
     be taken from us.
   Men born on earth tread their own paths that lead them whither
     our ancient fathers have departed.

3. Matali prospers there with Kavyas, Yama with Angiras' sons,
     Brihaspati with Rikvans:
   Exalters of the gods, by gods exalted, some joy in praise and some
     in our oblations.

------

8. *Indu:* literally, 'drop'. The name also refers to the Moon, the Soma
juice, and also the river Indus.

9. *At the highest place of holy law:* the place where sacrifice is performed.

1. The hymn is partly addressed to Yama, the god of death, and partly to
the departed spirit whose body is consumed on the funeral pyre. Yama, the
son of Vivasvan (Sun), and his twin sister Yami are the first human pair, the
originators of mankind (X.10). Yama is the first of men that died and found
a place where the departed could go.

4. Come, seat thee on this bed of grass, O Yama, in company with Angirases and fathers.

   Let texts recited by the sages bring thee: O king, let this oblation make thee joyful.

5. Come, Yama, with the Angirases the holy, rejoice thee here with children of Virupa.

   To sit on sacred grass at this our worship, I call Vivasvan, too, thy father hither.

6. Our fathers are Angirases, Navagvas, Atharvans, Bhrigus who deserve the soma.

   May these, the holy, look on us with favour, may we enjoy their gracious loving kindness.

7. Go forth, go forth upon the ancient pathways whereon our sires of old have gone before us.

   There shalt thou look on both the kings enjoying their sacred food, god Varuna and Yama.

8. Meet Yama, meet the fathers, meet the merit of free or ordered acts, in highest heaven.

   Leave sin and evil, seek anew thy dwelling, and bright with glory wear another body.

9. Go hence, depart ye, fly in all directions: this place for him the fathers have provided.

   Yama bestows on him a place to rest in adorned with days and beams of light and waters.

10. Run and outspeed the two dogs, Sarama's offspring, brindled, four-eyed, upon thy happy pathway.

    Draw nigh then to the gracious-minded fathers where they rejoice in company with Yama.

7–12. Addressed to the spirit of the dead whose funeral rites are being celebrated.

10. *Two Dogs:* offspring of Sarama, the hound of Indra.

11. And those two dogs of thine, Yama, the watchers, four-eyed, who
    look on men and guard the pathway, –
    Entrust this man, O king, to their protection, and with prosperity
    and health endow him.

12. Dark-hued, insatiate, with distended nostrils, Yama's two envoys
    roam among the people;
    May they restore to us a fair existence here and today, that we may
    see the sunlight.

13. To Yama pour the soma, bring to Yama consecrated gifts:
    To Yama sacrifice prepared and heralded by Agni goes.

14. Offer to Yama holy gifts enriched with butter, and draw near:
    So may he grant that we may live long days of life among the gods.

15. Offer to Yama, to the king, oblation very rich in meath:
    Bow down before the rishis of the ancient times, who made this
    path in days of old.

16. Into the six expanses flies the great one in Trikadrukas.
    The Gayatri, the Trishtup, all metres in Yama are contained.

X.141   *To VISVEDEVAS (All gods)*

1. Turn hither, Agni, speak to us: come to us with a gracious mind.
   Enrich us, master of the house: thou art the giver of our wealth.

2. Let Aryaman vouchsafe us wealth, and Bhaga, and Brihaspati.
   Let the gods give their gifts, and let Sunrita, goddess, grant us
   wealth.

All the gods are addressed collectively.

2. *Aryaman:* an Aditya, son of Aditi (Infinity), a celestial god.

Bhaga: an Aditya, a celestial god who presides over marriage.

Brihaspati. The name alternates with Brahmanaspati, personification or
deification of the action of worship at sacrifice: sometimes Agni.

Sunrita: goddess Pleasantness; sometimes also *Vagdevata*, goddess of
Speech.

3. We call king Soma to our aid, and Agni with our songs and hymns,
   Adityas, Vishnu, Surya, and the Brahman priest Brihaspati.

4. Indra, Vayu, Brihaspati, gods swift to listen, we invoke,
   That in the synod all the folk may be benevolent to us.

5. Urge Aryaman to send us gifts, and Indra, and Brihaspati,
   Vata, Vishnu, Sarasvati and the strong courser Savitar.

6. Do thou, O Agni, with thy fires strengthen our prayer and sacrifice:
   Urge givers to bestow their wealth to aid our service of the gods.

X.121   *To KA (WHO?), the Unknown god [Prajapati]*

1. In the beginning rose Hiranyagarbha, born only lord of all created
   beings.
   He fixed and holdeth up this earth and heaven. What god shall we
   adore with our oblation?

2. Giver of vital breath, of power and vigour, he whose commandments all the gods acknowledge:
   The lord of death, whose shade is life immortal. What god shall
   we adore with our oblation?

---

3. *Soma:* god of Soma juice.
5. *Vata:* god of Wind.
Sarasvati: river goddess; also later the goddess of Learning, and Speech.
Savitar: the sun god, an Aditya.
1. This hymn addressed to Ka, meaning Who?, has given rise to various
interpretations. Some commentators have suggested that this hymn is
addressed to the Unknown God. Man usually worships the gods he knows;
but there could be gods that he does not know. Apparently there is an
attempt to accept and understand the limitation of man's capacity to know,
and his capacity to conceive what is inconceivable. The refrain, therefore,
seems to be saying: Prajapati (Lord of Beings), in what other names (what
other gods) shall we adore you with our oblations?
Hiranyagarbha: 'the golden germ', the first source of life.

3. Who by his grandeur hath become sole ruler of all the moving
   world that breathes and slumbers:
   He who is lord of men and lord of cattle. What god shall we adore
   with our oblation?

4. His, through his might, are these snow-covered mountains, and
   men call sea and Rasa his possession:
   His arms are these, his are these heavenly regions. What god shall
   we adore with our oblation?

5. By him the heavens are strong and earth is stedfast, by him light's
   realm and sky-vault are supported:
   By him the regions in mid-air were measured. What god shall we
   adore with our oblation?

6. To him, supported by his help, two armies embattled look with
   trembling in their spirit,
   When over them the risen sun is shining. What god shall we adore
   with our oblation?

7. What time the mighty waters came, containing the universal germ,
   producing Agni,
   Thence sprang the gods' one spirit into being. What god shall we
   adore with our oblation?

8. He in his might surveyed the floods containing productive force
   and generating worship.
   He is the god of gods, and none beside him. What god shall we
   adore with our oblation?

9. Ne'er may he harm us who is earth's begetter, nor he whose laws
   are sure, the heavens' creator,
   He who brought forth the great and lucid waters. What god shall
   we adore with our oblation?

10. Prajapati! thou only comprehendest all these created things, and
    none beside thee.
    Grant us our hearts' desire when we invoke thee: may we have
    store of riches in possession.

X.81 *To VISVAKARMAN (the Maker of the Universe)*

1. He who sate down as Hotar-priest, the Rishi, our father, offering up all things existing –

   He, seeking through his wish a great possession, came among men on earth as archetypal.

2. What was the place whereon he took his station? What was it that supported him? How was it?

   Whence Visvakarman, seeing all, producing the earth, with mighty power disclosed the heavens.

3. He who hath eyes on all sides round about him, a mouth on all sides, arms and feet on all sides,

   He, the sole god, producing earth and heaven, weldeth them, with his arms as wings, together.

4. What was the tree, what wood in sooth produced it, from which they fashioned out the earth and heaven?

   Ye thoughtful men inquire within your spirit whereon he stood when he established all things.

5. Thine highest, lowest, sacrificial natures and these thy midmost here, O Visvakarman,

   Teach thou thy friends at sacrifice, O Blessed, and come thyself, exalted, to our worship.

6. Bring thou thyself, exalted with oblation, O Visvakarman, earth and heaven to worship.

   Let other men around us live in folly: here let us have a rich and liberal patron.

7. Let us invoke today, to aid our labour, the lord of speech, the thought-swift Visvakarman.

   May he hear kindly all our invocations who gives all bliss for aid, whose works are righteous.

---

1. Visvakarman is represented as the universal creator, *omnificent* or unlimited in creative power, prime mover, the architect of the worlds, and the universal mind.

X.90   *To PURUSHA (the Universal Spirit)*

1. A thousand heads hath Purusha, a thousand eyes, a thousand feet.
   On every side pervading earth he fills a space ten fingers wide.

2. This Purusha is all that yet hath been and all that is to be,
   The lord of immortality which waxes greater still by food

3. So mighty is his greatness; yea, greater than this is Purusha.
   All creatures are one-fourth of him, three-fourths eternal life in
   heaven.

4. With three-fourths Purusha went up: one-fourth of him again was
   here.
   Thence he strode out to every side over what eats not and what
   eats.

5. From him Viraj was born; again Purusha from Viraj was born.
   As soon as he was born he spread eastward and westward o'er the
   earth.

6. When gods prepared the sacrifice with Purusha as their offering,
   Its oil was spring; the holy gift was autumn; summer was the
   wood.

7. They balmed as victim on the grass Purusha born in earliest time.
   With him the deities and all Sadhyas and Rishis sacrificed.

8. From that great general sacrifice the dripping fat was gathered up.
   He formed the creatures of the air, and animals both wild and
   tame.

---

1. *Purusha:* the all-pervading universal spirit, cosmic energy, the life-giving principle in animated things, conceived as a person having innumerable eyes, heads, and feet. Although as Purusha it pervades the universe, as individual spirit it is enclosed in the tiniest of space. Purusha is the sacrificer and the sacrifice itself.

5. *Viraj:* primeval germ.

6–7. The cosmic action of the Purusha is allegorically conceived in different imageries of sacrifice: life process as a sacrifice in terms of seasons and the passage of time; man sacrificing a lamb to the god.

9. From that great general sacrifice Richas and Sama-hymns were
   born:
   Therefrom were spells and charms produced; the Yajus had its
   birth from it.

10. From it were horses born, from it all cattle with two rows of teeth:
    From it were generated kine, from it the goats and sheep were born.

11. When they divided Purusha, how many portions did they make?
    What do they call his mouth, his arms? What do they call his
    thighs and feet?

12. The Brahman was his mouth, of both his arms was the Rajanya
    made.
    His thighs became the Vaisya, from his feet the Sudra was pro-
    duced.

13. The moon was gendered from his mind, and from his eye the sun
    had birth;
    Indra and Agni from his mouth were born, and Vayu from his
    breath.

---

9. *Yajus:* Yajur Veda, i.e. the spells and charms of *Yajur Veda*.

11–16. Purusha is conceived as a whole man with various functions
divided among various limbs. This imagery is allegorically used to explain
the functioning of the organized society, the functioning of natural and
supernatural processes.

12. The *Brahamins* are like the speech that comes from the mouth,
reflecting the thought of the mind; that is, the thinking and legislating
element, or the cream of the society. The Rajanya (Kshatriyas), or regal or
ruling and administering group, is like the arms that protect and defend the
society. The Vaisyas or traders, artisans and craftsmen, are like the thighs
that support and sustain the society. The Sudras, or workers of all kinds, are
like the feet that provide locomotion or move the society. This hymn in which
human society is conceived in terms of human organism becomes the basis
for the subsequent elaborate classification of society, first on the basis of
function or occupation, and later degenerating into hereditary class, called
the Caste system.

14. Forth from his navel came mid-air; the sky was fashioned from his head;
    Earth from his feet, and from his ear the regions. Thus they formed the worlds.

15. Seven fencing-sticks had he, thrice seven layers of fuel were prepared,
    When the gods, offering sacrifice, bound, as their victim, Purusha.

16. Gods, sacrificing, sacrificed the victim: these were the earliest holy ordinances.
    The mighty ones attained the height of heaven, there where the Sadhyas, gods of old, are dwelling.

X.129   *To CREATION*

1. Then was not non-existent nor existent: there was no realm of air, no sky beyond it.
   What covered in, and where? and what gave shelter? Was water there, unfathomed depth of water?

2. Death was not then, nor was there aught immortal: no sign was there, the day's and night's divider.
   That one thing, breathless, breathed by its own nature: apart from it was nothing whatsoever.

3. Darkness there was: at first concealed in darkness, this All was indiscriminated chaos.
   All that existed then was void and formless: by the great power of warmth was born that unit.

4. Thereafter rose desire in the beginning, Desire, the primal seed and germ of spirit.
   Sages who searched with their heart's thought discovered the existent's kinship in the non-existent.

5. Transversely was their severing line extended: what was above it
   then, and what below it?
   There were begetters, there were mighty forces, free action here
   and energy up yonder.

6. Who verily knows and who can here declare it, whence it was born
   and whence comes this creation?
   The gods are later than this world's production. Who knows, then,
   whence it first came into being?

7. He, the first origin of this creation, whether he formed it all or did
   not form it,
   Whose eye controls this world in highest heaven, he verily knows it,
   or perhaps he knows not.

IX.1   *To SOMA PAVAMANA*

1. In sweetest and most gladdening stream flow pure, O Soma, on
   thy way,
   Pressed out for Indra, for his drink.

2. Fiend-queller, friend of all men, he hath with the wood attained
   unto
   His place, his iron-fashioned home.

3. Be thou best Vritra-slayer, best granter of bliss, most liberal:
   Promote our wealthy princes' gifts.

4. Flow onward with thy juice unto the banquet of the mighty gods;
   Flow hither for our strength and fame.

5. O Indu, we draw nigh to thee, with this one object day and day:
   To thee alone our prayers are said.

---

1. Nearly all the hymns in Book IX are addressed to the personified or
deified soma juice offered as libation during the sacrifice. The juice is
addressed as Soma, or Indu (the drop), or Soma Pavamana (moon) which,
containing the celestial nectar, the drink of the gods, is identified with the
soma plant and its exhilarating juice.

6. By means of this eternal fleece may Surya's daughter purify
   Thy Soma that is foaming forth.

7. Ten sister maids of slender form seize him within the press and
   hold
   Him firmly on the final day.

8. The virgins send him forth: they blow the skin musician-like, and
   fuse
   The triple foe-repelling meath.

9. Inviolable milch-kine round about him blend for Indra's drink,
   The fresh young soma with their milk.

10. In the wild raptures of this draught, Indra slays all the Vritras: he
    The Hero, pours his wealth on us.

X.151   *To SRADDHA (Faith)*

1. By Faith is Agni kindled, through Faith is oblation offered up.
   We celebrate with praises Faith upon the height of happiness.

2. Bless thou the man who gives, O Faith; Faith, bless the man who
   fain would give.
   Bless thou the liberal worshippers: bless thou the word that I have
   said.

3. Even as the deities maintained Faith in the mighty Asuras,
   So make this uttered wish of mine true for the liberal worshippers.

---

   6. *Surya's daughter:* Surya (sun) being considered the Truth or Law, his
daughter is Faith, or Sraddha.

   7. *Ten sister maids:* ten fingers of the juice presser.

   8. *Virgins:* fingers.

In this hymn faith is deified.

   3. *Asuras:* primeval gods.

4. Guarded by Vayu, gods and men who sacrifice draw near to Faith.
Man winneth Faith by yearnings of the heart, and opulence by
Faith.

5. Faith in the early morning, Faith at noonday will we invocate,
Faith at the setting of the Sun. O Faith, endow us with belief.

X.71   *To JNANAM (Knowledge)*

1. When men, Brihaspati, giving names to objects, sent out Vak's
first and earliest utterances,
All that was excellent and spotless, treasured within them, was
disclosed through their affection.

2. Where, like men cleansing corn flour in a cribble, the wise in spirit
have created language,
Friends see and recognize the marks of friendship: their speech
retains the blessed sign imprinted.

3. With sacrifice the trace of Vak they followed, and found her
harbouring within the Rishis.
They brought her, dealt her forth in many places: seven singers
make her tunes resound in concert.

---

4. *Vayu:* god of Wind.

Jnanam, or Knowledge, addressed in this hymn, is of *Paramabrahmanam*
(Supreme Reality), or of higher Truth, which teaches man his own nature
and how he may be reunited to the Supreme Self.

The hymn deals with the problem of understanding the higher knowledge
enclosed in language, or the symbolical or allegorical meaning of the words
and images in the *Vedas.*

1. *Vak:* voice or speech, the sacred word, a means of communication
between man and god.

3. *Harbouring within the Rishis.* They discovered, in the course of sacrifice,
that the inspired Rishis alone understood Speech as required for spiritual
purposes.

Seven singers: seven metres, the Gayatri, etc.

4. One man hath ne'er seen Vak, and yet he seeth: one man hath hearing but hath never heard her.

   But to another hath she shown her beauty as a fond well-dressed woman to her husband.

5. One man they call a laggard, dull in friendship: they never urge him on to deeds of valour.

   He wanders on in profitless illusion: the Voice he heard yields neither fruit nor blossom.

6. No part in Vak hath he who hath abandoned his own dear friend who knows the truth of friendship

   Even if he hears her still in vain he listens: naught knows he of the path of righteous action.

7. Unequal in the quickness of their spirit are friends endowed alike with eyes and hearing.

   Some look like tanks that reach the mouth or shoulder, others like pools of water fit to bathe in.

8. When friendly Brahmans sacrifice together with mental impulse which the heart hath fashioned,

   They leave one far behind through their attainments, and some who count as Brahmans wander elsewhere.

9. Those men who step not back and move not forward, nor Brahmans nor preparers of libations,

   Having attained to Vak in sinful fashion spin out their thread in ignorance like spinsters.

10. All friends are joyful in the friend who cometh in triumph, having conquered in assembly.

    He is their blame-averter, food-provider: prepared is he and fit for deed of vigour.

11. One plies his constant task reciting verses: one sings the holy psalm in Sakvari measures.

    One more, the Brahman, tells the lore of being and one lays down the rules of sacrificing.

Upanishads

(Sanskrit, *c.* 1200–600 B.C.)

The *Upanishads*, or the metaphysical speculations forming the concluding portions of the *Vedas* (also called *Vedanta*), are the most outstanding and the oldest philosophical works now extant in the world. They are older than the works of Plato or the Book of Lao Tzu. In the body of world literature, therefore, the *Upanishads*, having seldom, if ever, been surpassed for profundity of thought or poetic beauty, occupy a unique place.

The source of the seminal thoughts in the *Upanishads* can be traced to the spirit of inquiry of the ancient Indians – Dravidians or Aryans – who, inheriting influences from earlier civilizations, such as that of the Indus valley, remained somewhat outside or alien to the ritualistic life that evolved from the hymns dedicated to various Vedic divinities. When the ritual life became too formalized and, to some extent, fossilized, as could be expected during the course of a millennium, streams of thought that were dormant, or concurrently smouldering, seem to have found their expression in the form, first, of protest against organized religion. The rational inquiry, some elements of which could be found in the later Vedic hymns (for example X.129), subordinated many of the earlier myths to an abstract, higher, unitary principle. This reduced the ceremonials to allegorical or symbolical explanations, thus shifting the emphasis from the performance of the rituals to the realization of their meaning. In this process, the first reformation gave birth from about 1200 B.C. to some remarkable philosophical dialogues between *rishis*, or sages, and their disciples in the calm seclusion of the forest. For this reason, the *Upanishads* are also sometimes referred to as *Aranyakas* or the 'Forest Books' (for example *Brihad-aranyaka Upanishad*).

One of the messages of the *Upanishads* is that immortality is not what one gains after death but what one becomes conscious of in life (*Katha Upanishad*). It teaches that the individual essence or self (called for name's sake *atman*), if it is immortal, never dies; nor is it born, but it always is. Consequently, mortal life is but an existential

44

expression of that eternal essence, bracketed by a series of the phenomena of birth and death, or great transitions. For example, we may
popularly recognize water as liquid; it exists in other states of tension
or existential forms as solid ice, soft snow, gaseous steam, or cloud.
When the form changes by the transitions, the essence of water is not
lost. So is the essence of life in relation to existence and transitions. It
is only when man becomes conscious of himself as embodying the
eternal essence that he achieves immortality, and thereafter acts in the
light of that consciousness.

Another, yet more fundamental message of the *Upanishads* is that
the individual essence or self (*atman*) is the same as the Universal
Essence or Self (called for name's sake *Brahman*), of which the
individual self is only a part. In other words, man is not outside the
Absolute Reality but is a part of it in a manifested form (*Brihad-
aranyaka Upanishad*). However, man sees everywhere multiplicity,
mainly because he recognizes the existential forms and conceives in
terms of *nama-rupa* (name and form) some aspects of the manifested
Universal Self. On account of this limitation in the process of human
knowledge, man cannot know the Reality but can know only Conceptual Reality, or Reality conceived in name and form. Nevertheless,
because man embodies the eternal essence within him, he can come to
understand it by yoking his body-apparatus (Yoga) to realize that the
self within (microcosm) is the same thing as the Self without, or the
Universal Self (Macrocosm); or that *atman* is the same thing as or a
part of *Brahman*. This self-realization then becomes the basis for
action of the enlightened man who can see and recognize Universal
Self everywhere. The unitive knowledge helps him to reconcile the
diversity of manifestations, multiplicity of perceptions, and infinite
variety of interpretations of what is perceived. The unitary principle,
or the Universal Essence, or Energy (somewhat similar to Spinoza's
'metaphysical substance' or Lao Tzu's 'Tao'), is explained by a
series of examples, comparing *Brahman* and *atman* to the ocean and
the waves, ocean and the rivers, honey, or salt, etc. (*Chandogya
Upanishad*).

Since the unknown, unknowable, eternal, non-theistic Absolute
cannot be completely enclosed in definitive statements, positive or
negative, *Brahman* is referred to as 'That', being neither masculine

nor feminine or neuter, but rather neutral. However, it is difficult to establish prayerful relations between the individual and the Universal, and ethical relations among the individuals, through vague and abstract concepts. It becomes necessary to conceive *Brahman* in existential humanistic experience. The Absolute thus becomes limited by a concept in a language and meaning in a culture, and particularized through aesthetic and visual artifacts. Such Conceptual Reality, or personalized representation of the Universal Self (called for name's sake *Isvara*, or god), though a kind of 'vanity of vanities', is necessary, but not necessarily absolute. For there could be as many concepts as there are languages and speakers. All such personalized concepts about the Universal Self that man makes in the world in different cultures, and in different times in history, are true and not true (like the blind man's concepts upon seeing the elephant within his limited experience). The difficulty, therefore, is not in forming the concepts, but in asserting that one particular concept is the only one and the true one – an assertion of a kind of 'monopolistic view of Truth'. It would be an absurdity, from the Upanishadic point of view, to state that there is only one way of looking at a large mountain. Since the Absolute Reality is somewhat larger than a mountain, the limited faculties of man cannot exhaust the possibilities of making concepts about *Brahman* inasmuch as a shell cannot empty the ocean (*Isa Upanishad*). As an example, one could say the present-day 'death-of-God-theology' seems to be attacking a particularized concept about god in terms of medieval and Renaissance European aesthetic expression, and not the principle of god itself.

Finally, in emphasizing the possibility of plurality of concepts about the Absolute, the *Upanishads* reduce the tyranny of contrary concepts and the rigidity about the dualism involved in 'either-or' – the Absolute Good (god) against Absolute Evil (devil) – to simple relatives from a point of view. Thus, both the duality and the multiplicity are subordinated to the law of 'ends and means' within the generalized principle of unity in diversity, the crowning glory of the *Upanishads*.

The metaphysical ideas contained in the *Upanishads* have largely determined the world view of Indian philosophical systems and shaped the cultural and literary expressions. Besides, through the spread of Indian spiritualities and translations from the Sanskrit, the *Upanishads* have also influenced the world view of Buddhists in Asia, of Sufi and Christian mystics, and of transcendental idealists in Europe and America. Hegel and Schopenhauer, Emerson and T. S. Eliot, found in these works consolations of life and death. Upanishadic thought also influenced the early abstract painters; it is greatly agitating contemporary existentialists the world over. A study of these works, though basic to the appreciation of Indian literature, is no doubt germane to a better understanding of the concerns, thought, and action current in the present-day world.

Traditionally, there are about 150 *Upanishads*, of which about thirteen are considered the earliest and fundamental, often commented upon and translated. They are: *Brihad-aranyaka* (the longest and the most important), *Chandogya, Aitareya, Taittiriya, Prasna, Mundaka, Mandukya, Kausika, Maitria, Svetasvatara, Katha, Kena,* and *Isa* (shortest). The *Katha Upanishad* is here annotated in detail to enable the reader to study at least one *Upanishad* in depth.

The selections included here are taken from the translations by F. Max Müller, *The Upanishads*, Vols. I and XV, in the Sacred Books of the East Series, Oxford: Clarendon Press, 1879, 1884; republished, New York: Dover Publications, 1962 (T.992 and T.993).

Selections: *Isa Upanishad* (complete), and *Chandogya Upanishad*, sections VI. 8, 9, 10, 11, 12, and 13, from *Upanishads*, Vol. I. *Katha Upanishad* (complete), and *Brihad-aranyaka Upanishad*, sections I. 4, II. 4, and V. 2, from *Upanishads*, Vol. XV.

The *Katha Upanishad*, perhaps the most widely known among all the *Upanishads*, is considered to be one of the most complete, and most perfect, examples of the mystic, philosophic, and poetic document of ancient India.

Though the first mention of the story of Nachiketas is to be found in the *Rig Veda* (X.135), a fuller account of it appears in the *Brahmana* (III.1.8) of the Taittiriya School of *Yajur Veda*, where it is used to explain a certain ceremonial, called Nachiketas sacrifice. In the *Katha Upanishad* the story becomes a peg on which to hang the philosophic discourse on the question of immortality.

Vajasravasa, a pious man, performs a sacrifice and gives away as presents to the priests some old and barren cows. His son, Nachiketas, seeing the uselessness of the presents, is disturbed by the unreality of his father's formal observance of the ritual, and offers himself as a sacrificial present. The father ignores his son's offer for a while, until Nachiketas persistently asks him, 'To whom will you give me?' Vajasravasa in rage says 'Unto Yama [Death] I give you.' The spoken word is sacred and cannot be broken, so Nachiketas goes to the abode of Yama in accordance with his father's words. However, Yama is not there to receive this unexpected guest, and Nachiketas has to wait for three days without receiving the usual hospitality. Yama, arriving after three days, apologizes for his delay and inhospitality and offers the boy three boons in recompense. For the first boon, Nachiketas asks that his father's anger be allayed and that he be returned to him; for the second, he asks to know the fire-sacrifice by which one's good works (*ista-purta*) may not become exhausted; and for the third, he asks to know the truth about death – whether or not there is an immortal substance in man which is deathless.

In the *Katha Upanishad*, Nachiketas's third request is developed to give enlightenment on the great transition called death. Yama discusses the nature of *atman*, its origin, its destiny. He tells Nachiketas that self-knowledge alone is the Highest Knowledge and the Highest Good.

The *Upanishad* is in two Adhyayas (chapters), each of which contains three Vallis (sections). There are some passages common to the *Katha Upanishad* and the *Bhagavad Gita*.

The method of presenting a metaphysical argument through the medium of myth, drama, and poetry has also been followed in other cultures, especially in *The Book of Job*, which bears a considerable resemblance to the *Katha Upanishad*.

KATHA UPANISHAD

FIRST ADHYAYA

—

FIRST VALLI

1. Vajasravasa, desirous (of heavenly rewards), surrendered (at a sacrifice) all that he possessed. He had a son of the name of Nachiketas.

2. When the (promised) presents were being given (to the priests), faith entered into the heart of Nachiketas, who was still a boy, and he thought:

3. 'Unblessed, surely, are the worlds to which a man goes by giving (as his promised present at a sacrifice) cows which have drunk water, eaten hay, given their milk, and are barren.'

4. He (knowing that his father had promised to give up all that he possessed, and therefore his son also) said to his father: 'Dear father, to whom wilt thou give me?'

He said it a second and a third time. Then the father replied (angrily):

'I shall give thee unto Death.'

I.1. In this *Upanishad* Vajasravasa represents external ceremonialism of orthodoxy; Nachiketas (Na + chiketas, one who has no knowledge) represents the seeker of knowledge, or spiritual wisdom. The formalism and hypocrisy of the father disturbs the son.

I.4. *True to his word*: cf. consequence of the spoken word of Dasaratha, king of Ayodhya, and Rama, his son in the *Ramayana*; also Kunti's words to her five sons when they brought Draupadi to her cottage, during their days of exile, in the *Mahabharata*.

(The father, having once said so, though in haste, had to be true to his word and to sacrifice his son.)

5. The son said: 'I go as the first, at the head of many (who have still to die); I go in the midst of many (who are now dying). What will be the work of Yama (the ruler of the departed) which today he has to do unto me?

6. 'Look back how it was with those who came before, look forward how it will be with those who come hereafter. A mortal ripens like corn, like corn he springs up again.'

(Nachiketas enters into the abode of Yama Vaivasvata, and there is no one to receive him. Thereupon one of the attendants of Yama is supposed to say:)

7. 'Fire enters into the houses, when a Brahmana enters as a guest. That fire is quenched by this peace-offering – bring water, O Vaivasvata!

8. 'A Brahmana that dwells in the house of a foolish man without receiving food to eat, destroys his hopes and expectations, his possessions, his righteousness, his sacred and his good deeds, and all his sons and cattle.'

(Yama, returning to his house after an absence of three nights, during which time Nachiketas had received no hospitality from him, says:)

9. 'O Brahmana, as thou, a venerable guest, hast dwelt in my house three nights without eating, therefore choose now three boons. Hail to thee! and welfare to me!'

10. Nachiketas said: 'O Death, as the first of the three boons I choose that Gautama, my father, be pacified, kind, and free from anger towards me; and that he may know me and greet me, when I shall have been dismissed by thee.'

11. Yama said: 'Through my favour Auddalaki Aruni, thy father, will know thee, and be again towards thee as he was before. He shall sleep peacefully through the night, and free from anger, after having seen thee freed from the mouth of death.'

I.9. Cf. three boons granted by Yama to Savitri.

I.10. *Gautama*: Nachiketas's father, Vajasravasa, is also called Aruni Auddalaki Gautama.

12. Nachiketas said: 'In the heaven-world there is no fear; thou are not there, O Death, and no one is afraid on account of old age. Leaving behind both hunger and thirst, and out of the reach of sorrow, all rejoice in the world of heaven.

13. 'Thou knowest, O Death, the fire-sacrifice which leads us to heaven; tell it to me, for I am full of faith. Those who live in the heaven-world reach immortality – this I ask as my second boon.'

14. Yama said: 'I tell it thee, learn it from me, and when thou understandest that fire-sacrifice which leads to heaven, know, O Nachiketas, that it is the attainment of the endless worlds, and their firm support, hidden in darkness.'

15. Yama then told him that fire-sacrifice, the beginning of all the worlds, and what bricks are required for the altar, and how many, and how they are to be placed. And Nachiketas repeated all as it had been told to him. Then Mrityu, being pleased with him, said again:

16. The generous, being satisfied, said to him: 'I give thee now another boon; that fire-sacrifice shall be named after thee, take also this many-coloured chain.

17. 'He who has three times performed this Nachiketa rite, and has been united with the three (father, mother, and teacher), and has performed the three duties (study, sacrifice, almsgiving) overcomes birth and death. When he has learnt and understood this fire, which knows (or makes us know) all that is born of Brahman, which is venerable and divine, then he obtains everlasting peace.

18. 'He who knows the three Nachiketa fires, and knowing the three, piles up the Nachiketa sacrifice, he, having first thrown off the chains of death, rejoices in the world of heaven, beyond the reach of grief.'

I.13. *Fire-sacrifice:* symbolically spoken of the fire that brought forth creation, that sustains the universe, and all the living beings. Consequently, activity, or action, is a sacrifice.

I.17. *Three times:* study, meditate, understand; know, study, and practise.
United with the three: mother, father, teacher; Vedas, Brahmanas, Upanishads.
Three duties: study, sacrifice, charity.
Nachiketas's fire-sacrifice seems to be the fire of the seeker after Truth in which all his actions become a sacrifice.

19. 'This, O Nachiketas, is thy fire which leads to heaven, and which thou hast chosen as thy second boon. That fire all men will proclaim. Choose now, O Nachiketas, thy third boon.'

20. Nachiketas said: 'There is that doubt, when a man is dead – some saying, he is; others, he is not. This I should like to know, taught by thee; this is the third of my boons.'

21. Death said: 'On this point even the gods have doubted formerly; it is not easy to understand. That subject is subtle. Choose another boon, O Nachiketas, do not press me, and let me off that boon.'

22. Nachiketas said: 'On this point even the gods have doubted indeed, and thou, Death, hast declared it to be not easy to understand, and another teacher like thee is not to be found – surely no other boon is like unto this.'

23. Death said: 'Choose sons and grandsons, who shall live a hundred years, herds of cattle, elephants, gold, and horses. Choose the wide abode of the earth, and live thyself as many harvests as thou desirest.

24. 'If you can think of any boon equal to that, choose wealth, and long life. Be (king), Nachiketas, on the wide earth. I make thee the enjoyer of all desires.

25. 'Whatever desires are difficult to attain among mortals, ask for them according to thy wish; these fair maidens with their chariots and musical instruments – such are indeed not to be obtained by men – be waited on by them whom I give to thee, but do not ask me about dying.'

26. Nachiketas said: 'These things last till tomorrow, O Death, for they wear out this vigour of all the senses. Even the whole of life is short. Keep thou thy horses, keep dance and song for thyself.

27. 'No man can be made happy by wealth. Shall we possess wealth, when we see thee? Shall we live, as long as thou rulest? Only that boon (which I have chosen) is to be chosen by me.

28. 'What mortal, slowly decaying here below, and knowing, after having approached them, the freedom from decay enjoyed by the

---

I.23–5. Cf. the temptation of Gautama Siddhartha, the Buddha; Jesus the Christ. Yama, not being the evil, first tempts and, when he is convinced of the sincerity of the seeker, reveals to him the Knowledge.

immortals, would delight in a long life, after he has pondered on the pleasures which arise from beauty and love?

29. 'No, that on which there is this doubt, O Death, tell us what there is in that great hereafter. Nachiketas does not choose another boon but that which enters into the hidden world.'

SECOND VALLI

1. Death said: 'The good is one thing, the pleasant another; these two, having different objects, chain a man. It is well with him who clings to the good; he who chooses the pleasant, misses his end.

2. 'The good and pleasant approach man: the wise goes round about them and distinguishes them. Yea, the wise prefers the good to the pleasant, but the fool chooses the pleasant through greed and avarice.

3. 'Thou, O Nachiketas, after pondering all pleasures that are or seem delightful, hast dismissed them all. Thou hast not gone into the road that leadeth to wealth, in which many men perish.

4. 'Wide apart and leading to different points are these two, ignorance, and what is known as wisdom. I believe Nachiketas to be one who desires knowledge, for even many pleasures did not tear thee away.

5. 'Fools dwelling in darkness, wise in their own conceit, and puffed up with vain knowledge, go round and round, staggering to and fro, like blind men led by the blind.

6. 'The hereafter never rises before the eyes of the careless child, deluded by the delusion of wealth. "This is the world," he thinks, "there is no other" – thus he falls again and again under my sway.

7. 'He (the Self) of whom many are not even able to hear, whom many, even when they hear of him, do not comprehend; wonderful

---

2.1. Cf. Plato. In every one of us there are two ruling and directing principles, one being an innate device of pleasure, the other an acquired judgement which aspires after excellence (*Phaedrus*).

2.5. Cf. Matthew 25.14. If the blind lead the blind, both shall fall into the ditch.

2.7. *Bhagavad Gita*, 7.3.

is a man, when found, who is able to teach him (the Self); wonderful is he who comprehends him, when taught by an able teacher.

8. 'That (Self), when taught by an inferior man, is not easy to be known, even though often thought upon; unless it be taught by another, there is no way to it, for it is inconceivably smaller than what is small.

9. 'That doctrine is not to be obtained by argument, but when it is declared by another, then, O dearest, it is easy to understand. Thou hast obtained it now; thou art truly a man of true resolve. May we have always an inquirer like thee!'

10. Nachiketas said: 'I know that what is called a treasure is transient, for that eternal is not obtained by things which are not eternal. Hence the Nachiketa fire(-sacrifice) has been laid by me (first); then, by means of transient things, I have obtained what is not transient (the teaching of Yama).'

11. Yama said: 'Though thou hadst seen the fulfilment of all desires, the foundation of the world, the endless rewards of good deeds, the shore where there is no fear, that which is magnified by praise, the wide abode, the rest, yet being wise thou hast with firm resolve dismissed it all.

12. 'The wise who, by means of meditation on his Self, recognizes the Ancient, who is difficult to be seen, who has entered into the dark, who is hidden in the cave, who dwells in the abyss, as God, he indeed leaves joy and sorrow far behind.

13. 'A mortal who has heard this and embraced it, who has separated from it all qualities, and has thus reached the subtle Being, rejoices, because he has obtained what is a cause for rejoicing. The house (of Brahman) is open, I believe, O Nachiketas.'

14. Nachiketas said: 'That which thou seest as neither this nor that, as neither effect nor cause, as neither past nor future, tell me that.'

2.10. *By means of transient things*: cf. Blake's *Auguries of Innocence*:
>   To see a world in a grain of sand
>   And a heaven in a wild flower;
>   Hold infinity in the palm of your hand,
>   And eternity in an hour.

15. Yama said: 'That word (or place) which all the Vedas record, which all penances proclaim, which men desire when they live as religious students, that word I tell thee briefly, it is Om.

16. 'That (imperishable) syllable means Brahman, that syllable means the highest (Brahman); he who knows that syllable, whatever he desires, is his.

17. 'This is the best support, this is the highest support; he who knows that support is magnified in the world of Brahma.

18. 'The knowing (Self) is not born, it dies not; it sprang from nothing, nothing sprang from it. The Ancient is unborn, eternal, everlasting; he is not killed, though the body is killed.

19. 'If the killer thinks that he kills, if the killed thinks that he is killed, they do not understand; for this one does not kill, nor is that one killed.

20. 'The Self, smaller than small, greater than great, is hidden in the heart of that creature. A man who is free from desires and free from grief, sees the majesty of the Self by the grace of the Creator.

21. 'Though sitting still, he walks far; though lying down, he goes everywhere. Who, save myself, is able to know that God who rejoices and rejoices not?

2.15. *Bhagavad Gita*, 2.20.
Om, or Aum: the mystic syllable representing the essence of the universe, all knowledge. It is the symbol of the manifested as well as unmanifested Brahman.

2.18. *Bhagavad Gita*, 8.11.

2.19. *Bhagavad Gita*, 2.19. Answer to Nachiketas: Self does not die.

2.20. Through the tranquillity of the mind and the senses (he sees) the greatness of the self – Radhakrishnan. Cf. Christian *ataraxia*, the untroubled peace of true faith, of trust which leads to vision – Rawson. Cf. John 14, 'Let not your hearts be troubled'; Sermon on the Mount with its repeated warning against anxious striving as a hindrance in the way of entrance into the Kingdom of Heaven; Lao Tzu, *Tao Teh Ching*, 37.

2.21. By these contradictory predicates, the impossibility of conceiving Brahman through empirical determinations is brought out. Brahman has peaceful stability and active energy. In the former it is Brahman, in the latter Ishvara.

22. 'The wise who knows the Self as bodiless within the bodies, as unchanging among changing things, as great and omnipresent, does never grieve.

23. 'That Self cannot be gained by the Veda, nor by understanding, nor by much learning. He whom the Self chooses, by him the Self can be gained. The Self chooses him (his body) as his own.

24. 'But he who has not first turned away from his wickedness, who is not tranquil, and subdued, or whose mind is not at rest, he can never obtain the Self (even) by knowledge.

25. 'Who then knows where He is, He to whom the Brahmans and Kshatriyas are (as it were) but food, and death itself a condiment?

THIRD VALLI

1. 'There are the two, drinking their reward in the world of their own works, entered into the cave (of the heart), dwelling on the highest summit (the ether in the heart). Those who know Brahman call them shade and light; likewise, those householders who perform the Trinachiketa sacrifice.

2. 'May we be able to master that Nachiketa rite which is a bridge for sacrificers; also that which is the highest, imperishable Brahman for those who wish to cross over the fearless shore.

3. 'Know the Self to be sitting in the chariot, the body to be the chariot, the intellect (buddhi) the charioteer, and the mind the reins.

4. 'The senses they call the horses, the objects of the senses their roads. When he (the Highest Self) is in union with the body, the senses, and the mind, then wise people call him the Enjoyer.

5. 'He who has no understanding and whose mind (the reins) is never firmly held, his senses (horses) are unmanageable, like vicious horses of a charioteer.

6. 'But he who has understanding and whose mind is always firmly held, his senses are under control, like good horses of a charioteer.

3.3. *Chariot*. Cf. Plato, *Phaedo* (24–8); *Phaedrus* (246 f.); *Republic* (IV.433). Intelligence is considered as the ruling power of the self (called *buddhi* in the *Upanishad*, and *nous* by Plato). The concept of Yoga, meaning to yoke or harness the senses, is related to the symbolism of the chariot.

7. 'He who has no understanding, who is unmindful and always impure, never reaches that place, but enters into the round of births.

8. 'But he who has understanding, who is mindful and always pure, reaches indeed that place, from whence he is not born again.

9. 'But he who has understanding for his charioteer, and who holds the reins of the mind, he reaches the end of his journey, and that is the highest place of Vishnu.

10. 'Beyond the senses there are the objects, beyond the objects there is the mind, beyond the mind there is the intellect, the Great Self is beyond the intellect.

11. 'Beyond the Great there is the Undeveloped, beyond the Undeveloped there is the Person (purusha). Beyond the Person there is nothing – this is the goal, the highest road.

12. 'That Self is hidden in all beings and does not shine forth, but it is seen by subtle seers through their sharp and subtle intellect.

13. 'A wise man should keep down speech and mind; he should keep them within the Self which is knowledge; he should keep knowledge within the Self which is the Great; and he should keep that (the Great) within the Self which is the Quiet.

14. 'Rise, awake! having obtained your boons, understand them!

3.7. Cf. 5.7.

3.10–12. On the sea shore one can say: beyond the thin vapour is the water drop, beyond the drop is the foam, beyond the foam is the wave, beyond the wave is the sea, beyond the sea is the deep ocean. The water that is in the thinnest of vapour, or strongest wave, or the deepest ocean is the same and one but it appears different and is called differently, because of different states of existence or tension. Similarly the spirit in individual self (*atman*) is the same as the spirit in the universal Self (*Paramatman*, or *Purusha*), which is referred to as the *Hiranya Garbha* (*Rig Veda* X.121), the Golden Germ, or the Universal Soul.

3.11. *Nothing:* not negative, but positive; not one particularized thing, but one thing that is everything no-thing, for example a lump of uncarved clay. Cf. *kincit* (no-thing that can be known), with Buddhist *Sunyata* (Zero), or the unpredicated eternal subject, unknowable, beyond the description of unity, duality, multiplicity.

3.14. *Path:* cf. Matthew 7.14.

The sharp edge of a razor is difficult to pass over; thus the wise say the path (to the Self) is hard.

15. 'He who has perceived that which is without sound, without touch, without form, without decay, without taste, eternal, without smell, without beginning, without end, beyond the Great, and unchangeable, is freed from the jaws of death.

16. 'A wise man who has repeated or heard the ancient story of Nachiketas told by Death, is magnified in the world of Brahman.

17. 'And he who repeats this greatest mystery in an assembly of Brahmans, or full of devotion at the time of the Sraddha sacrifice, obtains thereby infinite rewards.'

SECOND ADHYAYA

—

FOURTH VALLI

1. Death said: 'The Self-existent pierced the opening (of the senses) so that they turn forward: therefore man looks forward, not backward into himself. Some wise man, however, with his eyes closed and wishing for immortality, saw the Self behind.

2. 'Children follow after outward pleasures, and fall into the snare of widespread death. Wise men only, knowing the nature of what is immortal, do not look for anything stable here among things unstable.

3. 'That by which we know form, taste, smell, sounds, and loving touches, by that also we know what exists besides. This is that (which thou hast asked for).

4. 'The wise, when he knows that that by which he perceives all objects in sleep or in waking is the great omnipresent Self, grieves no more.

5. 'He who knows this living soul which eats honey (perceives

---

4.1. Cf. Plato, *Republic* VII, the allegory of the cave; *Phaedo*, the body as an instrument of external perception and internal reflection. The *Upanishad* calls for restraint and direction and not suppression of the senses. 'Spiritual search has inward movement leading to revelation ... from intellection to insight' (Radhakrishnan).

objects) as being the Self, always near, the Lord of the past and the future, henceforward fears no more. This is that.

6. 'He who (knows) him who was born first from the brooding heat (for he was born before the water), who, entering into the heart, abides therein, and was perceived from the elements. That is that.

7. '(He who knows) Aditi also, who is one with all deities, who arises with Prana (breath of Hiranyagarbha), who, entering into the heart, abides therein, and was born from the elements. This is that.

8. 'There is Agni (fire), the all-seeing, hidden in the two fire-sticks, well-guarded like a child (in the womb) by the mother, day after day to be adored by men when they awake and bring oblations. This is that.

9. 'And that whence the sun rises and whither it goes to set, there all the Devas are contained, and no one goes beyond. This is that.

10. 'What is here (visible in the world), the same is there (invisible in Brahman); and what is there, the same is here. He who sees any difference here (between Brahman and the world), goes from death to death.

11. 'Even by the mind this (Brahman) is to be obtained, and then there is no difference whatsoever. He goes from death to death who sees any difference here.

12. 'The person (purusha), of the size of a thumb, stands in the middle of the Self (body?), as lord of the past and the future, and henceforward fears no more. This is that.

13. 'That person, of the size of a thumb, is like a light without smoke, lord of the past and the future, he is the same today and to-morrow. This is that.

14. 'As rain-water that has fallen on a mountain-ridge runs down the rocks on all sides, thus does he, who sees a difference between qualities, run after them on all sides.

15. 'As pure water poured into pure water remains the same, thus, O Gautama, is the Self of a thinker who knows.

4.13. cf. *Savitri:* Yama extracts the Purusha from Satyavan's body (*The Revelation* 1.8).

FIFTH VALLI

1. 'There is a town with eleven gates belonging to the Unborn (Brahman), whose thoughts are never crooked. He who approaches it, grieves no more, and liberated (from all bonds of ignorance) becomes free. This is that.

2. 'He (Brahman) is the swan (sun), dwelling in the bright heaven; he is the Vasu (air), dwelling in the sky; he is the sacrificer (fire), dwelling on the hearth; he is the guest (Soma), dwelling in the sacrificial jar; he dwells in men, in gods (vara), in the sacrifice (rita), in heaven; he is born in the water, on earth, in the sacrifice (rita), on the mountains; he is the True and the Great.

3. 'He (Brahman) it is who sends up the breath (prana), and who throws back the breath (apana). All the Devas (senses) worship him, the adorable (or the dwarf), who sits in the centre.

4. 'When that incorporated (Brahman), who dwells in the body, is torn away and freed from the body, what remains then? This is that.

5. 'No mortal lives by the breath that goes up and by the breath that goes down. We live by another, in whom these two repose.

6. 'Well then, O Gautama, I shall tell thee this mystery, the old Brahman, and what happens to the Self, after reaching death.

7. 'Some enter the womb in order to have a body, as organic beings, others go into inorganic matter, according to their work and according to their knowledge.

8. 'He, the highest Person, who is awake in us while we are asleep, shaping one lovely sight after another, that indeed is the Bright, that is Brahman, that alone is called the Immortal. All worlds are contained in it, and no one goes beyond. This is that.

5.1. *Town with eleven gates:* human body with eleven openings: two eyes, two ears, two nostrils, mouth, anus, generating organ, the navel, and the saggital suture (the opening at the top of the skull). Cf. *Bhagavad Gita*, 5.13, where the last two openings are omitted.

5.7. Cf. 3.7. Rebirth is determined by the Law of Karma, or Action and cumulative consequences. Though Karma acts in some sense as destiny in the new birth, yet the person is free to change his Karma by his actions.

9. 'As the one fire, after it has entered the world, though one, becomes different according to whatever it burns, thus the one Self within all things becomes different, according to whatever it enters, and exists also without.

10. 'As the one air, after it has entered the world, though one, becomes different according to whatever it enters, thus the one Self within all things becomes different, according to whatever it enters, and exists also without.

11. 'As the sun, the eye of the whole world, is not contaminated by the external impurities seen by the eyes, thus the one Self within all things is never contaminated by the misery of the world, being himself without.

12. 'There is one ruler, the Self within all things, who makes the one form manifold. The wise who perceive him within their Self, to them belongs eternal happiness, not to others.

13. 'There is one eternal thinker, thinking non-eternal thoughts, who, though one, fulfils the desires of many. The wise who perceive him within their Self, to them belongs eternal peace, not to others.

14. 'They perceive that highest indescribable pleasure, saying, This is that. How then can I understand it? Has it its own light, or does it reflect light?

15. 'The sun does not shine there, nor the moon and the stars, nor these lightnings, and much less this fire. When he shines, everything shines after him; by his light all this is lighted.

5.11. The suffering in the world is real but it does not touch the spirit; it only touches the psycho-physical vehicle in the body. The individual ego makes a confusion between the unsuffering self and the not-self. This false identification (Maya, or delusion) is due to non-knowledge of the true nature of Brahman.

5.14. Does the supreme shine in itself or does it shine in its expression?

5.15. *By his light all this is lighted:* cf. *Bhagavad Gita,* 10.41.

SIXTH VALLI

1. 'There is that ancient tree, whose roots grow upward and whose branches grow downward – that indeed is called the Bright, that is called Brahman, that alone is called the Immortal. All worlds are contained in it, and no one goes beyond. This is that.

2. 'Whatever there is, the whole world, when gone forth (from the Brahman), trembles in its breath. That Brahman is a great terror, like a drawn sword. Those who know it become immortal.

3. 'From terror of Brahman fire burns, from terror the sun burns, from terror Indra and Vayu, and Death, as the fifth, run away.

4. 'If a man could not understand it before the falling asunder of his body, then he has to take body again in the worlds of creation.

5. 'As in a mirror, so (Brahman may be seen clearly) here in this body; as in a dream, in the world of the fathers; as in the water, he is seen about in the world of the Gandharvas; as in light and shade, in the world of Brahma.

6. 'Having understood that the senses are distinct (from the Atman), and that their rising and setting (their waking and sleeping) belongs to them in their distinct existence (and not to the Atman), a wise man grieves no more.

7. 'Beyond the senses is the mind, beyond the mind is the highest (created) Being, higher than that Being is the Great Self, higher than the Great, the highest Undeveloped.

8. 'Beyond the Undeveloped is the Person, the all-pervading and entirely imperceptible. Every creature that knows him is liberated, and obtains immortality.

9. 'His form is not to be seen, no one beholds him with the eye. He is imagined by the heart, by wisdom, by the mind. Those who know this, are immortal.

6.1. Cf. *Bhagavad Gita*, 15.3. The tree of life with its unseen roots in Brahman.

6.4. Cf. Rebirth, 3.7 and 5.7.

6.7. Cf. 3.10–11.

10. 'When the five instruments of knowledge stand still together with the mind, and when the intellect does not move, that is called the highest state.

11. 'This, the firm holding back of the senses, is what is called Yoga. He must be free from thoughtlessness then, for Yoga comes and goes.

12. 'He (the Self) cannot be reached by speech, by mind, or by the eye. How can it be apprehended except by him who says: "He is"?

13. 'By the words "He is", is he to be apprehended, and by (admitting) the reality of both (the invisible Brahman and the visible world, as coming from Brahman). When he has been apprehended by the words "He is", then his reality reveals itself.

14. 'When all desires that dwell in his heart cease, then the mortal becomes immortal, and obtains Brahman.

15. 'When all the ties of the heart are severed here on earth, then the mortal becomes immortal – here ends the teaching.

16. 'There are a hundred and one arteries of the heart, one of them penetrates the crown of the head. Moving upwards by it, a man (at his death) reaches the Immortal; the other arteries serve for departing in different directions.

17. 'The Person not larger than a thumb, the inner Self, is always settled in the heart of men. Let a man draw that Self forth from his body with steadiness, as one draws the pith from a reed. Let him

---

6.10–11. Cf. Patanjali's *Yoga Sutra*. One requires vigilant earnestness to realize self is Self; This is That.

Cf. Jesus's Sermon on the Mount, regarding the Blessed Man who hungers for justice.

6.12–13. Way of faith proceeds from Word (conceptual), apprehension (rational), to understanding (visionary). When the self (like a radio) is tuned to the higher Self (transmitter), the realization of the Truth comes.

6.16. *Arteries of the heart:* there are many directions in which an individual could go; one of them leads to Brahman.

6.17. 'As one draws the wind from the reed' – Radhakrishnan. The wind is there in the flute (reed), but it is the blowing of wind that makes the sound, and a controlled blowing makes the music. Cf. Hamlet admonishing Guildenstern: 'Do you think I am easier to be played on than a pipe?' (III.2.390–6).

know that Self as the Bright, as the Immortal; yes, as the Bright, as the Immortal.'

18. Having received this knowledge taught by Death and the whole rule of Yoga (meditation), Nachiketas became free from passion and death, and obtained Brahman. Thus it will be with another also who knows thus what relates to the Self.

19. May He protect us both! May He enjoy us both! May we acquire strength together! May our knowledge become bright! May we never quarrel! Om! Peace! peace! peace! Hari, Om!

ISA UPANISHAD*

Sometimes called

VAJASANEYI-SAMHITA UPANISHAD

. All this, whatsoever moves on earth, is to be hidden in the Lord the Self). When thou hast surrendered all this, then thou mayest njoy. Do not covet the wealth of any man!

---

*This *Upanishad* belongs to the Vajasaneyi school of Yajur Veda. It is not so much concerned with the *Brahman* as the Absolute (*Para-brahman*), but the Absolute in relation to the world and the creation (*Paramesvara*). It teaches that life in the world and life in the divine Spirit are not incompatible (Radhakrishnan).

This *Upanishad*, though apparently simple and intelligible, is in reality one of the most difficult to understand properly. It begins by declaring that all has to be surrendered to the Lord. The name, lord, is peculiar, as having a far more personal colouring than Atman, Self, or Brahman, the usual names given by the *Upanishads* to what is the object of the highest knowledge.

Next follows a permission to continue the performance of sacrifices, provided that all desires have been surrendered. And here occurs our first difficulty, which has perplexed ancient as well as modern commentators.

I hold that the *Upanishad* wishes to teach the uselessness by themselves of all good works, whether we call them sacrificial, legal, or moral, and yet, at the same time, to recognize, if not the necessity, at least the harmlessness of good works, provided they are performed without any selfish motives, without any desire of reward, but simply as a preparation for higher knowledge, as a means, in fact, of subduing all passions, and producing that serenity of mind without which man is incapable of receiving the highest knowledge. From that point of view the *Upanishad* may well say, Let a man wish to live here his appointed time, let him even perform all works. If only he knows that all must be surrendered to the Lord, then the work done by him will not cling to him. It will not work on and produce effect after effect, nor will it involve him in a succession of new births in which to enjoy the reward of his works, but it will leave him free to enjoy the blessings of the highest knowledge. It will have served as a preparation for that higher knowledge which the *Upanishad* imparts, and which secures freedom from further births (F. Max Müller).

2. Though a man may wish to live a hundred years, performing works, it will be thus with him; but not in any other way: work will thus not cling to a man.

3. There are the worlds of the Asuras covered with blind darkness. Those who have destroyed their self (who perform works, without having arrived at a knowledge of the true Self), go after death to those worlds.

4. That one (the Self), though never stirring, is swifter than thought. The Devas (senses) never reached it, it walked before them. Though standing still, it overtakes the others who are running. Matarisvan (the wind, the moving spirit) bestows powers on it.

5. It stirs and it stirs not; it is far, and likewise near. It is inside of all this, and it is outside of all this.

6. And he who beholds all beings in the Self, and the Self in all beings, he never turns away from it.

7. When to a man who understands, the Self has become all things, what sorrow, what trouble can there be to him who once beheld that unity?

8. He (the Self) encircled all, bright, incorporeal, scatheless, without muscles, pure, untouched by evil; a seer, wise, omnipresent, self-existent, he disposed all things rightly for eternal years.

9. All who worship what is not real knowledge (good works), enter into blind darkness: those who delight in real knowledge, enter, as it were, into greater darkness.

10. One thing, they say, is obtained from real knowledge; another they say, from what is not knowledge. Thus we have heard from the wise who taught us this.

11. He who knows at the same time both knowledge and not-knowledge, overcomes death through not-knowledge, and obtains immortality through knowledge.

12. All who worship what is not the true cause, enter into blind darkness; those who delight in the true cause, enter, as it were, into greater darkness.

13. One thing, they say, is obtained from (knowledge of) the cause; another, they say, from (knowledge of) what is not the cause. Thus we have heard from the wise who taught us this.

14. He who knows at the same time both the cause and the destruc-

ion (the perishable body), overcomes death by destruction (the perishable body), and obtains immortality through (knowledge of) the true cause.

15. The door of the True is covered with a golden disk. Open that, O Pushan, that we may see the nature of the True.

16. O Pushan, only seer, Yama (judge), Surya (sun), son of Prajapati, spread thy rays and gather them! The light which is thy fairest form, I see it. I am what He is (viz. the person in the sun).

17. Breath to air, and to the immortal! Then this my body ends in ashes. Om! Mind, remember! Remember thy deeds! Mind, remember! Remember thy deeds!

18. Agni, lead us on to wealth (beatitude) by a good path, thou, O God, who knowest all things! Keep far from us crooked evil, and we shall offer thee the fullest praise!

The *Chandogya Upanishad*, the second longest *Upanishad* in eight chapters, belongs to the *Sama Veda*. The first two chapters of the *Upanishad* discuss the problems of liturgy and doctrine, such as the genesis and the significance of *Aum*. The remaining chapters discuss the nature of *Brahman*. Chapter VI, from which these extracts are taken, contains Uddalaka Aruni's teaching to his son Svetaketu, concerning the oneness of *Brahman*, illustrated by a number of examples.

EIGHTH KHANDA

1. Uddalaka Aruni said to his son Svetaketu: 'Learn from me the true nature of sleep (*svapna*). When a man sleeps here, then, my dear son, he becomes united with the True, he is gone to his own (Self). Therefore they say, svapiti, he sleeps, because he is gone (*apita*) to his own (*sva*).

2. 'As a bird when tied by a string flies first in every direction, and finding no rest anywhere, settles down at last on the very place where it is fastened, exactly in the same manner, my son, that mind (the *jiva*, or living Self in the mind), after flying in every direction, and finding no rest anywhere, settles down on breath; for indeed, my son, mind is fastened to breath.

3. 'Learn from me, my son, what are hunger and thirst. When a man is thus said to be hungry, water is carrying away (digests) what has been eaten by him. Therefore as they speak of a cow-leader (*go-naya*), a horse-leader (*asva-naya*), a man-leader (*purusha-naya*), so they call water (which digests food and causes hunger) food-leader (*asanaya*). Thus (by food digested, etc.), my son, know this offshoot (the body) to be brought forth, for this (body) could not be without a root (cause).

4. 'And where could its root be except in food (earth)? And in the same manner, my son, as food (earth) too is an offshoot, seek after its root, viz. water. And as water too is an offshoot, seek after its root, viz. fire. And as fire too is an offshoot, seek after its root, viz. the True.

es, all these creatures, my son, have their root in the True, they
dwell in the True, they rest in the True.

5. 'When a man is thus said to be thirsty, fire carries away what
has been drunk by him. Therefore as they speak of a cow-leader
(*go-naya*), of a horse-leader (*asva-naya*), of a man-leader (*purusha-naya*), so they call fire *udanya*, thirst, i.e. water-leader. Thus (by
water digested, etc.), my son, know this offshoot (the body) to be
brought forth: this (body) could not be without a root (cause).

6. 'And where could its root be except in water? As water is an
offshoot, seek after its root, viz. fire. As fire is an offshoot, seek after
its root, viz. the True. Yes, all these creatures, O son, have their root
in the True, they dwell in the True, they rest in the True.

'And how these three beings (*devata*), fire, water, earth, O son,
when they reach man, become each of them tripartite, has been said
before. When a man departs from hence, his speech is merged in his
mind, his mind in his breath, his breath in heat (fire), heat in the
highest Being.

7. 'Now that which is that subtle essence (the root of all), in it all
that exists has its self. It is the True. It is the Self, and thou, O
Svetaketu, art it.'

'Please, Sir, inform me still more,' said the son.

'Be it so, my child,' the father replied.

NINTH KHANDA

1. 'As the bees, my son, make honey by collecting the juices of
distant trees, and reduce the juice into one form.

2. 'And as these juices have no discrimination, so that they might
say, I am the juice of this tree or that, in the same manner, my son,
all these creatures, when they have become merged in the True
(either in deep sleep or in death), know not that they are merged in the
True.

3. 'Whatever these creatures are here, whether a lion, or a wolf,
or a boar, or a worm, or a midge, or a gnat, or a mosquito, that they
become again and again.

4. 'Now that which is that subtle essence, in it all that exists has its
self. It is the True. It is the Self, and thou, O Svetaketu, art it.'

'Please, Sir, inform me still more,' said the son.
'Be it so, my child,' the father replied.

TENTH KHANDA

1. 'These rivers, my son, run, the eastern (like the Ganga) toward the east, the western (like the Sindhu) toward the west. They go from sea to sea (i.e. the clouds lift up the water from the sea to the sky, and send it back as rain to the sea). They become indeed sea. And as those rivers, when they are in the sea, do not know, I am this or that river.

2. 'In the same manner, my son, all these creatures, when they have come back from the True, know not that they have come back from the True. Whatever these creatures are here, whether a lion, or a wolf, or a boar, or a worm, or a midge, or a gnat, or a mosquito, that they become again and again.

3. 'That which is that subtle essence, in it all that exists has its self. It is the True. It is the Self, and thou, O Svetaketu art it.'

'Please, Sir, inform me still more,' said the son.
'Be it so, my child,' the father replied.

ELEVENTH KHANDA

1. 'If someone were to strike at the root of this large tree here, it would bleed, but live. If he were to strike at its stem, it would bleed, but live. If he were to strike at its top, it would bleed, but live. Pervaded by the living Self that tree stands firm, drinking in its nourishment and rejoicing;

2. 'But if the life (the living Self) leaves one of its branches, that branch withers; if it leaves a second, that branch withers; if it leaves a third, that branch withers. If it leaves the whole tree, the whole tree withers. In exactly the same manner, my son, know this.' Thus he spoke:

3. 'This (body) indeed withers and dies when the living Self has left it; the living Self dies not.

'That which is that subtle essence, in it all that exists has its self. It is the True. It is the Self, and thou, Svetaketu, art it.'

'Please, Sir, inform me still more,' said the son.
'Be it so, my child,' the father replied.

TWELFTH KHANDA

1. 'Fetch me from thence a fruit of the nyagrodha tree.'

'Here is one, Sir.'

'Break it.'

'It is broken, Sir.'

'What do you see there?'

'These seeds, almost infinitesimal.'

'Break one of them.'

'It is broken, Sir.'

'What do you see there?'

'Not anything, Sir.'

2. The father said: 'My son, that subtile essence which you do not perceive there, of that very essence this great nyagrodha tree exists.

3. 'Believe it, my son. That which is the subtile essence, in it all that exists has its self. It is the True. It is the Self, and thou, O Svetaketu, art it.'

'Please, Sir, inform me still more,' said the son.

'Be it so, my child,' the father replied.

THIRTEENTH KHANDA

1. 'Place this salt in water, and then wait on me in the morning.'

The son did as he was commanded.

The father said to him: 'Bring me the salt, which you placed in the water last night.'

The son having looked for it, found it not, for, of course, it was melted.

2. The father said: 'Taste it from the surface of the water. How is it?'

The son replied: 'It is salt.'

'Taste it from the middle. How is it?'

The son replied: 'It is salt.'

'Taste it from the bottom. How is it?'

The son replied: 'It is salt.'

The father said: 'Throw it away and then wait on me.'

He did so; but salt exists for ever.

Then the father said: 'Here also, in this body, forsooth, you do not perceive the True (*Sat*), my son; but there indeed it is.

3. 'That which is the subtile essence, in it all that exists has its self. It is the True. It is the Self, and thou, O Svetaketu, art it.'

I.5 BRIHAD-ARANYAKA UPANISHAD

The *Brihad-aranyaka* (literally, Great Forest) *Upanishad*, the longest and the most important of the *Upanishads*, belongs to the *Yajur Veda*. It consists of six Adhyayas (chapters), each subdivided into Brahmanas or sections. The teaching of this *Upanishad* can be classified as falling into three sections: (a) *Madhu Kanda* teaches the basic identity of the individual self and the Universal Self; (b) *Muni Kanda* or *Yajnavalkya* provides the philosophical justifications; and (c) *Khila Kanda* deals with three modes of worship, roughly explaining the three stages of spiritual life: hearing the teaching, logical reflection, and contemplative meditation.

In every culture and civilization, man has tried to explain creation through some myth, and often imposed such a myth as the only and the absolute explanation. However, in the *Vedas* and the *Upanishads*, there is no one myth or theory of creation but several. The Indian *rishis* seem to discount the idea of a 'monopolistic view of truth', of one and the only explanation of the cosmic process about which man knows very little, if not nothing. Consequently, they seem to be saying that man could comprehend the unknown beginning of the world through existential experience only by means of visionary myths, symbols, parables, or allegories.

First Adhyaya · In the Beginning

FOURTH BRAHMANA

1. In the beginning this was Self alone, in the shape of a person (*purusha*). He looking round saw nothing but his Self. He first said, 'This is I'; therefore he became I by name. Therefore even now, if a man is asked, he first says, 'This is I,' and then pronounces the other name which he may have. And because before (*purva*) all this, he (the Self) burnt down (*ush*) all evils, therefore he was a person (*purusha*). Verily he who knows this, burns down everyone who tries to be before him.

2. He feared, and therefore anyone who is lonely fears. He thought, 'As there is nothing but myself, why should I fear?' Thence his fear passed away. For what should he have feared? Verily fear arises from a second only.

3. But he felt no delight. Therefore a man who is lonely feels no delight. He wished for a second. He was so large as man and wife together. He then made this his Self to fall in two (*pat*), and thence arose husband (*pati*) and wife (*patni*). Therefore Yajnavalkya said: 'We two are thus (each of us) like half a shell.' Therefore the void which was there, is filled by the wife. He embraced her, and men were born.

4. She thought, 'How can he embrace me, after having produced me from himself? I shall hide myself.'

She then became a cow, the other became a bull and embraced her, and hence cows were born. The one became a mare, the other a stallion; the one a male ass, the other a female ass. He embraced her, and hence one-hoofed animals were born. The one became a she-goat, the other a he-goat; the one became a ewe, the other a ram. He embraced her, and hence goats and sheep were born. And thus he created everything that exists in pairs, down to the ants.

5. He knew, 'I indeed am this creation, for I created all this.' Hence he became the creation, and he who knows this lives in this his creation.

6. Next he thus produced fire by rubbing. From the mouth, as from the fire-hole, and from the hands he created fire. Therefore both the mouth and the hands are inside without hair, for the fire-hole is inside without hair.

And when they say, 'Sacrifice to this or sacrifice to that god,' each god is but his manifestation, for he is all gods.

Now, whatever there is moist, that he created from seed; this is Soma. So far verily is this universe either food or eater. Soma indeed is food, Agni eater. This is the highest creation of Brahman, when he created the gods from his better part, and when he, who was (then) mortal, created the immortals. Therefore it was the highest creation. And he who knows this, lives in this his highest creation.

_____
3. Cf. Plato, *Symposium* 189c.

7. Now all this was then undeveloped. It became developed by form and name, so that one could say, 'He, called so and so, is such a one.' Therefore at present also all this is developed by name and form, so that one can say, 'He, called so and so, is such a one.'

He (Brahman or the Self) entered thither, to the very tips of the finger-nails, as a razor might be fitted in a razor-case, or as fire in a fire-place.

He cannot be seen, for, in part only, when breathing, he is breath by name; when speaking, speech by name; when seeing, eye by name; when hearing, ear by name; when thinking, mind by name. All these are but the names of his acts. And he who worships (regards) him as the one or the other, does not know him, for he is apart from this (when qualified) by the one or the other (predicate). Let men worship him as Self, for in the Self all these are one. This Self is the footstep of everything, for through it one knows everything. And as one can find again by footsteps what was lost, thus he who knows this finds glory and praise.

8. This, which is nearer to us than anything, this Self, is dearer than a son, dearer than wealth, dearer than all else.

And if one were to say to one who declares another than the Self dear, that he will lose what is dear to him, very likely it would be so. Let him worship the Self alone as dear. He who worships the Self alone as dear, the object of his love will never perish.

9. Here they say: 'If men think that by knowledge of Brahman they will become everything, what then did that Brahman know, from whence all this sprang?'

10. Verily in the beginning this was Brahman, that Brahman knew (its) Self only, saying, 'I am Brahman.' From it all this sprang. Thus, whatever Deva was awakened (so as to know Brahman), he indeed became that (Brahman); and the same with Rishis and men. The Rishi Vamadeva saw and understood it, singing, 'I was Manu (moon), I was the sun.' Therefore now also he who thus knows that he is Brahman, becomes all this, and even the Devas cannot prevent it, for he himself is their Self.

Now if a man worships another deity, thinking the deity is one and he another, he does not know. He is like a beast for the Devas. For verily, as many beasts nourish a man, thus does every man nourish the Devas. If only one beast is taken away, it is not pleasant; how much more when many are taken! Therefore it is not pleasant to the Devas that men should know this.

11. Verily in the beginning this was Brahman, one only. That being one, was not strong enough. It created still further the most excellent Kshatra (power), viz. those Kshatras (powers) among the Devas – Indra, Varuna, Soma, Rudra, Parjanya, Yama, Mrityu, Isana. Therefore there is nothing beyond the Kshatra, and therefore at the Rajasuya sacrifice the Brahmana sits down below the Kshatriya. He confers that glory on the Kshatra alone. But Brahman is (nevertheless) the birthplace of the Kshatra. Therefore though a king is exalted, he sits down at the end (of the sacrifice) below the Brahman, as his birthplace. He who injures him, injures his own birthplace. He becomes worse, because he has injured one better than himself.

12. He was not strong enough. He created the Vis (people), the classes of Devas which in their different orders are called Vasus, Rudras, Adityas, Visve Devas, Maruts.

13. He was not strong enough. He created the Sudra colour (caste), as Pushan (as nourisher). This earth verily is Pushan (the nourisher); for the earth nourishes all this whatsoever.

14. He was not strong enough. He created still further the most excellent Law (*dharma*). Law is the Kshatra (power) of the Kshatra, therefore there is nothing higher than the Law. Thenceforth even a weak man rules a stronger with the help of the Law, as with the help of a king. Thus the Law is what is called the true. And if a man declares what is true, they say he declares the Law; and if he declares the Law, they say he declares what is true. Thus both are the same.

15. There are then this Brahman, Kshatra, Vis, and Sudra. Among the Devas that Brahman existed as Agni (fire) only, among men as Brahmana, as Kshatriya through the (divine) Kshatriya, as Vaisya through the (divine) Vaisya, as Sudra through the (divine) Sudra. Therefore people wish for their future state among the Devas through Agni (the sacrificial fire) only; and among men through the Brahmana, for in these two forms did Brahman exist.

Now if a man departs this life without having seen his true future life (in the Self), then that Self, not being known, does not receive and bless him, as if the Veda had not been read, or as if a good work had not been done. Nay, even if one who does not know that (Self), should perform here on earth some great holy work, it will perish for him in the end. Let a man worship the Self only as his true state. If a man worships the Self only as his true state, his work does not perish, for whatever he desires that he gets from that Self.

16. Now verily this Self (of the ignorant man) is the world of all creatures. In so far as man sacrifices and pours out libations, he is the world of the Devas; in so far as he repeats the hymns, etc., he is the world of the Rishis; in so far as he offers cakes to the fathers and tries to obtain offspring, he is the world of the fathers; in so far as he gives shelter and food to men, he is the world of men; in so far as he finds fodder and water for the animals, he is the world of the animals; in so far as quadrupeds, birds, and even ants live in his houses, he is their world. And as everyone wishes his own world not to be injured, thus all beings wish that he who knows this should not be injured. Verily this is known and has been well reasoned.

17. In the beginning this was Self alone, one only. He desired, 'Let there be a wife for me that I may have offspring, and let there be wealth for me that I may offer sacrifices.' Verily this is the whole desire, and, even if wishing for more, he would not find it. Therefore now also a lonely person desires, 'Let there be a wife for me that I may have offspring, and let there be wealth for me that I may offer sacrifices.' And so long as he does not obtain either of these things, he thinks he is incomplete. Now his completeness (is made up as follows): mind is his Self (husband); speech the wife; breath the child; the eye all worldly wealth, for he finds it with the eye; the ear his divine wealth, for he hears it with the ear. The body (atman) is his work, for with the body he works. This is the fivefold sacrifice, for fivefold is the animal, fivefold man, fivefold all this whatsoever. He who knows this, obtains all this.

*

Second Adhyaya

FOURTH BRAHMANA

1. Now when Yajnavalkya was going to enter upon another state, he said: 'Maitreyi, verily I am going away from this my house (into the forest). Forsooth, let me make a settlement between thee and that Katyayani (my other wife).'

2. Maitreyi said: 'My lord, if this whole earth, full of wealth, belonged to me, tell me, should I be immortal by it?'

'No,' replied Yajnavalkya; 'like the life of rich people will be thy life. But there is no hope of immortality by wealth.'

3. And Maitreyi said: 'What should I do with that by which I do not become immortal? What my lord knoweth (of immortality), tell that to me.'

4. Yajnavalkya replied: 'Thou who art truly dear to me, thou speakest dear words. Come, sit down, I will explain it to thee, and mark well what I say.'

5. And he said: 'Verily, a husband is not dear, that you may love the husband; but that you may love the Self, therefore a husband is dear.

'Verily, a wife is not dear, that you may love the wife; but that you may love the Self, therefore a wife is dear.

'Verily, sons are not dear, that you may love the sons; but that you may love the Self, therefore sons are dear.

'Verily, wealth is not dear, that you may love wealth; but that you may love the Self, therefore wealth is dear.

'Verily, the Brahman-class is not dear, that you may love the Brahman-class; but that you may love the Self, therefore the Brahman-class is dear.

'Verily, the Kshatra-class is not dear, that you may love the Kshatra-class; but that you may love the Self, therefore the Kshatra-class is dear.

'Verily, the worlds are not dear, that you may love the worlds; but that you may love the Self, therefore the worlds are dear.

'Verily, the Devas are not dear, that you may love the Devas; but that you may love the Self, therefore the Devas are dear.

'Verily, creatures are not dear, that you may love the creatures; but that you may love the Self, therefore are creatures dear.

'Verily, everything is not dear, that you may love everything; but that you may love the Self, therefore everything is dear.

'Verily, the Self is to be seen, to be heard, to be perceived, to be marked, O Maitreyi! When we see, hear, perceive, and know the Self, then all this is known.

6. 'Whosoever looks for the Brahman-class elsewhere than in the Self, was abandoned by the Brahman-class. Whosoever looks for the Kshatra-class elsewhere than in the Self, was abandoned by the Kshatra-class. Whosoever looks for the worlds elsewhere than in the Self, was abandoned by the worlds. Whosoever looks for the Devas elsewhere than in the Self, was abandoned by the Devas. Whosoever looks for creatures elsewhere than in the Self, was abandoned by the creatures. Whosoever looks for anything elsewhere than in the Self, was abandoned by everything. This Brahman-class, this Kshatra-class, these worlds, these Devas, these creatures, this everything, all is that Self.

7. 'Now as the sounds of a drum, when beaten, cannot be seized externally (by themselves), but the sound is seized, when the drum is seized or the beater of the drum;

8. 'And as the sounds of a conch-shell, when blown, cannot be seized externally (by themselves), but the sound is seized, when the shell is seized or the blower of the shell;

9. 'And as the sounds of a lute, when played, cannot be seized externally (by themselves), but the sound is seized, when the lute is seized or the player of the lute;

10. 'As clouds of smoke proceed by themselves out of a lighted fire kindled with damp fuel, thus, verily, O Maitreyi, has been breathed forth from this great Being what we have as Rigveda, Yajur-veda, Sama-veda, Atharvagnirasas, Ithihasa (legends), Purana (cosmogonies), Vidya (knowledge), the Upanishads, Slokas (verses), Sutras (prose rules), Anuvyakhyanas (glosses), Vyakhyanas (commentaries). From him alone all these were breathed forth.

11. 'As all waters find their centre in the sea, all touches in the skin, all tastes in the tongue, all smells in the nose, all colours in the eye, all sounds in the ear, all percepts in the mind, all knowledge in the

heart, all actions in the hands, all movements in the feet, and all the Vedas in speech –

12. 'As a lump of salt, when thrown into water, becomes dissolved into water, and could not be taken out again, but wherever we taste (the water) it is salt – thus verily, O Maitreyi, does this great Being, endless, unlimited, consisting of nothing but knowledge, rise from out these elements, and vanish again in them. When he has departed, there is no more knowledge (name), I say, O Maitreyi.' Thus spoke Yajnavalkya.

13. Then Maitreyi said: 'Here thou has bewildered me, Sir, when thou sayest that having departed, there is no more knowledge.'

But Yajnavalkya replied: 'O Maitreyi, I say nothing that is bewildering. This is enough, O beloved, for wisdom.

'For when there is as it were duality, then one sees the other, one smells the other, one hears the other, one salutes the other, one perceives the other, one knows the other; but when the Self only is all this, how should he smell another, how should he see another, how should he hear another, how should he salute another, how should he perceive another, how should he know another? How should he know him by whom he knows all this? How, O beloved, should he know (himself), the Knower?'

*

Fifth Adhyaya

This section, called *Khila Kanda* (Supplementary Chapter), deals with various auxiliary means of arriving at a knowledge of *Brahman*. The parable points out that though the Truth is one its perceptions are many, depending upon the nature of the perceiver, while interpretations of what is perceived could be innumerable (for example, one mountain can be perceived from many points of view; yet each view is true and not completely true, and thus they apparently conflict with one another). Since the perceiver is conditioned by his nature, which is determined by the cumulative effect of the three gunas (qualities) – Satva (divine), Rajas (human), and Tamas (demonic) – it is necessary for man to exercise self-restraint in order to achieve the state of peace for the perception of Truth.

T. S. Eliot uses this parable of Prajapati teaching his students through one syllable in Part V, 'What the Thunder Said', of his poem *The Waste Land*. Since the wasteland in the human person is brought about by the lack of self-restraints, the spiritual waters for the resurrection of the spirit in man could come only by listening to the Thunder which sounds and echoes in the Universal Self as well as in the individual self, and practising the essential restraints.

Cf. Dante's classification of human actions in the *Inferno*: Upper Hell, sins of the misuse of appetites (sensuality); Middle Hell, sins of the misuse of strength (violence); Nether Hell, sins of the misuse of intelligence (fraud).

SECOND BRAHMANA

1. The threefold descendants of Prajapati, gods, men, and Asuras (evil spirits), dwelt as Brahmacharins (students) with their father Prajapati. Having finished their studentship the gods said: 'Tell us (something), Sir.' He told them the syllable da. Then he said: 'Did you understand?' They said: 'We did understand. You told us "Damyata", Be subdued.' 'Yes,' he said, 'you have understood.'

2. Then the men said to him: 'Tell us something, Sir.' He told them the same syllable da. Then he said: 'Did you understand?' They said: 'We did understand. You told us "Datta", Give.' 'Yes,' he said, 'you have understood.'

---

1. *Threefold descendants*. Human beings are distinguished in terms of their action as belonging to three classes: those emphasizing godly disposition (intelligence), human disposition (acquisitiveness), and demonic disposition (force). This corresponds to the predominance of one of the three gunas.

Damyata. Those who magnify in them the divine disposition (intelligence) are in danger of misusing that quality, resulting in fraud. To guard against such misuse, they should exercise self-restraint on their mind and practise the virtue of compassion or be subdued.

2. *Datta*. Those who magnify in them the human disposition (acquisitiveness) are in danger of misusing that quality, resulting in avariciousness. To guard against such misuse, they should exercise self-control on their desires, and practise the virtue of giving, or charity.

3. Then the Asuras said to him: 'Tell us something, Sir.' He told them the same syllable da. Then he said: 'Did you understand?' They said: 'We did understand. You told us "Dayadham", Be merciful.' 'Yes,' he said, 'you have understood.'

The divine voice of thunder repeats the same, Da da da, that is, Be subdued, Give, Be merciful. Therefore let that triad be taught, Subduing, Giving, and Mercy.

---

3. *Dayadham.* Those who magnify in them the demonic disposition (force) are in danger of misusing that quality, resulting in violence or cruelty. To guard against such misuse, they should exercise self-restraint on their strength and practise the virtue of kindness.

The first millennium B.C. can be regarded roughly as the epic period in India, during which time four epics gradually evolved and were finally compiled out of the myths, legends, and lore of the people of the sub-continent. Much of the folk culture which had existed in an oral tradition found sophisticated literary expression in the languages of culture of the time. Two of these epics were thus expressed in Sanskrit and two in Tamil. They are Krishna Dwaipayana Vyasa's *Mahabharata* (Sanskrit, *c*. 900–500 B.C.); Valmiki's *Ramayana* (Sanskrit, *c*. 600–300 B.C.); Ilango Adigal's *Shilappadikaram* (Tamil, *c*. 200 B.C.–A.D. 100); and Kulavanigan Cattanar's *Manimekhalai* (Tamil, 100 B.C.–A.D. 200). Of these four epics, only *Mahabharata*, the oldest and the greatest work, can properly be considered the heroic epic (or called *Ithihasa*), while the other three are basically literary, or artificial court epics (or called *Kavyas*).

The *Mahabharata*, consisting of about 220,000 lines (Homer's *Iliad* has 15,600 lines), is the longest epic poem in the world. It is also a store-house of Indian culture. The kernel of the epic deals with the story of the descendants of Bharata, son of King Dushyanta and Shakuntala (later, heroine of the play by Kalidasa, fifth century A.D.), namely, the Pandavas and their cousins, the Kauravas. The Kauravas, being envious of the prosperity of the Pandavas, fraudulently deprive them of their kingdom and send them into thirteen years of exile, at the end of which they engage them in a bitter and futile war at Kurukshetra (near Delhi) in order to retain their possessions. At the end of the war, the Kauravas are completely destroyed and the Pandavas rule the kingdom.

The epic story of the *Mahabharata* accounts for only one fifth of the poem. Woven into the fabric of this narrative are a great many works of philosophy, religion, astronomy, cosmology, polity, economics, sociology, as well as innumerable legends, anecdotes, and works of didactic intention. All these compositions, springing perhaps from different earlier cultural oases and having prior, independent existence in some form, are skilfully subordinated to the central plot structure of the epic, however loose it may be. Though the final work, by its very nature, is somewhat of anonymous authorship, it is generally regarded as being compiled or arranged by *rishi* Krishna Dwaipayana Vyasa during the period about 900–500 B.C.

Two selections from the *Mahabharata* are included here to give an example of an anecdote and a philosophical text. The first is from Book III, *Vana Parva*, concerning the chaste wife, Savitri, and the second is from Book VI, *Bhishma Parva*, containing the philosophical dialogue between the Pandava hero, Arjuna, and his princely charioteer, Krishna, before the beginning of the battle at Kurukshetra. This metaphysical moment in eighteen chapters is popularly known as the *Bhagavad Gita*, or 'The Lord's Song' or 'Song Celestial'.

I.6 KRISHNA DWAIPAYANA VYASA
MAHABHARATA

(Sanskrit, *c.* 900–500 B.C.)

BOOK III: VANA PARVA (SECTIONS 291–7)
THE STORY OF SAVITRI

Book III (*Vana Parva*) of the *Mahabharata* deals with the thirteen years of exile which the five Pandava brothers and their wife, Princess Draupadi, spend in the Kamayaka forest. Among the many relatives, friends, and sages who visit and console them in the forest is *rishi* Markandeya. Yudhishthir, the eldest of the Pandava brothers, asks Markandeya whether any one man has undergone as much undeserved suffering as he has. The *rishi* then tells him the story of Rama, the prince of Ayodhya; his fourteen years of exile with his wife Sita and brother Lakshman; the abduction of Sita by Ravana, the king of Lanka; the slaying of Ravana and the rescue of Sita; and the final return of Rama to his kingdom (Sections 271–90). This story later becomes the subject of Valmiki's epic *Ramayana* (50,000 lines). Though Yudhishthir is somewhat relieved by listening to Rama's story, he asks the sage once again whether there has been any woman as chaste and faithful as Draupadi who, having faithfully followed her husband, has endured so much misery. Markandeya then relates the story of Savitri, the chaste wife, and the power of her chastity, or *Pativrata Mahatmya* (Sections 291–7).

Savitri, along with other famous heroines in Indian literature (e.g. Sita in the epic *Ramayana*, Kannaki in the epic *Shilappadikaram*, and Shakuntala in the play *Shakuntala*), takes her place as an ideal woman, devoted to her husband like 'a shadow to the substance'. Yet of all these faithful and chaste women, Savitri alone wins her husband back from death, as if in a kind of success story wherein Love conquers Death. Her shrewd colloquy with Yama, the god of Death, projecting a kind of woman's logic, makes her even more magnificently woman-like, surpassing the faithful Achaian Alcestis, or Ithacan Penelope, or Hebraic Ruth.

The episode of Savitri included here is taken from the translation by Edwin Arnold, *Indian Idylls,* London: Trubner & Co., 1883.

I.6   PATIVRATA MAHATMYA:

THE STORY OF SAVITRI

> There was a Raja, pious-minded, just, –
> King of the Madras, – valiant, wise, and true;
> Victorious over sense, a worshipper;
> Liberal in giving, prudent, dear alike
> To peasant and to townsman; one whose joy
> Lived in the weal of all men – Aswapati –
> Patient, and free of any woe, he reigned,
> Save that his manhood passing, left him alone,
> A childless lord; for this he grieved; for this
> Heavy observances he underwent,
> Subduing needs of flesh, and oftentimes
> Making high sacrifice to Savitri;
> While, for all food, at each sixth watch he took
> A little measured dole; and thus he did
> Through sixteen years (most excellent of Kings!)
> Till at the last, divinest Savitri
> Grew well-content, and, taking shining shape,
> Rose through the flames of sacrifice and showed
> Unto that prince her heavenly countenance.
> 'Raja,' the Goddess said – the Gift-bringer –
> 'Thy piety, thy purity, thy fasts,
> The largesse of thy hands, thy heart's wide love,
> Thy strength of faith, have pleased me. Choose some boon.
> Thy dearest wish, Monarch of Madra, ask;
> It is not meet such merit go in vain.'
>
> The Raja answered: 'Goddess, for the sake
> Of children I did bear these heavy vows:
> If thou art well-content, grant me, I pray,

Fair babes, continuers of my royal line;
This is the boon I choose, obeying law;
For – say the holy seers – the first great law
Is that a man leave seed.'

        The Goddess said:
'I knew thine answer, Raja, ere it came;
And He, the Maker of all, hath heard my word
That this might be, The self-existent One
Consenteth. Born there shall be unto thee
A girl more sweet than any eyes have seen;
There is not found on earth so fair a maid!
I that rejoice in the Great Father's will
Know this and tell thee.'

        'Ah! so may it be!'
The Raja cried, once and again; and she,
The Goddess, smiled again, and vanished so;
While Aswapati to his palace went.
There dwelled he, doing justice to all folk;
Till, when the hour was good, the wise King lay
With her that was his first and fairest wife,
And she conceived a girl (a girl, my liege!
Better than many boys), which wonder grew
In darkness, – as the Moon among the stars
Grows from a ring of silver to a round
In the month's waxing days, – and when time came
The Queen a daughter bore, with lotus-eyes,
Lovely of mould. Joyous that Raja made
The birth-feast; and because the fair gift fell
From Savitri the Goddess, and because
It was her day of sacrifice, they gave
The name of 'Savitri' unto the child.
In grace and beauty grew the maid, as if
Lakshmi's own self had taken woman's form.

Lakshmi: goddess of Prosperity, spouse of Vishnu.

And when swift years her gracious youth made ripe,
Like to an image of dark gold she seemed
Gleaming, with waist so fine, and breasts so deep,
And limbs so rounded. When she moved, all eyes
Gazed after her, as though an Apsara
Had lighted out of Swarga. Not one dared,
Of all the noblest lords, to ask for wife
That miracle, with eyes purple and soft
As lotus-petals, that pure perfect maid,
Whose face shed heavenly light where she did go.

Once she had fasted, laved her head, and bowed
Before the shrine of Agni, – as is meet, –
And sacrificed, and spoken what is set
Unto the Brahmans – taking at their hands
The unconsumèd offerings, and so passed
Into her father's presence – bright as Sri,
If Sri were woman! – Meekly at his feet
She laid the blossoms; meekly bent her head,
Folded her palms, and stood, radiant with grace,
Beside the Raja. He, beholding her
Come to her growth, and thus divinely fair,
Yet sued of none, was grieved at heart and spake:
'Daughter, 'tis time we wed thee, but none comes
Asking thee; therefore, thou thyself some youth
Choose for thy lord, a virtuous prince: whoso
Is dear to thee, he shall be dear to me;
For this the rule is by the sages taught –
Hear the commandment, noble maid – "That sire
Who giveth not his child in marriage
Is blamable; and blamable that kin
Who weddeth not; and blamable that son
Who, when his father dieth, guardeth not

Apsara: celestial nymph.
Swarga: heaven.
Sri: Lakshmi.

His mother." Heeding this,' the Raja said,
'Haste thee to choose, and so choose that I bear
No guilt, dear child, before the all-seeing Gods.'

Thus spake he; from the royal presence then
Elders and ministers dismissing. She, –
Sweet Savitri, – low lying at his feet,
With soft shame heard her father, and obeyed.
Then, on a bright car mounting, companied
By ministers and sages, Savitri
Journeyed through groves and pleasant woodland-towns
Where pious princes dwelled, in every spot
Paying meet homage at the Brahmans' feet;
And so from forest unto forest passed,
In all the Tirthas making offerings:
Thus did the Princess visit place by place.

The King of Madra sat among his lords
With Narada beside him, counselling:
When – (son of Bharat!) entered Savitri;
From passing through each haunt and hermitage,
Returning with those sages. At the sight
Of Narad seated by the Raja's side,
Humbly she touched the earth before their feet
With bended forehead.

                    Then spake Narada:
'Whence cometh thy fair child? and wherefore, King,
Being so ripe in beauty, giv'st thou not
The Princess to a husband?'

                         'Even for that
She journeyed,' quoth the Raja; 'being come,
Hear for thyself, great Rishi, what high lord
My daughter chooseth.' Then, being bid to speak

Tirthas: pilgrimage centres.

Of Narad and the Raja, Savitri
Softly said this: 'In Chalva reigned a prince,
Lordly and just, Dyumutsena named,
Blind, and his only son not come to age;
And this sad king an enemy betrayed
Abusing his infirmity, whereby
Of throne and kingdom was that king bereft;
And with his queen and son, a banished man,
He fled into the wood; and, 'neath its shades,
A life of holiness doth daily lead.
This Raja's son, born in the court, but bred
'Midst forest peace, – royal of blood, and named
Prince Satyavan, – to him my choice is given.'

'Aho!' cried Narad, 'evil is this choice
Which Savitri hath made, who, knowing not,
Doth name the noble Satyavan her lord:
For, noble is the Prince, sprung of a pair
So just and faithful found in word and deed
The Brahmans styled him "Truth-born" at his birth.
Horses he loved, and ofttimes would he mould
Coursers of clay, or paint them on the wall;
Therefore "Chitraswa" was he also called.'

Then spake the King: 'By this he shall have grown –
Being of so fair birth – either a prince
Of valour, or a wise and patient saint.'

Quoth Narad: 'Like the sun is Satyavan
For grace and glory; like Vrihaspati
For counsel; like Mahendra's self for might;
And hath the patience of th' all-bearing earth.'

'Is he a liberal giver?' asked the King;
'Loveth he virtue? Wears he noble airs?
Goeth he like a prince, with sweet proud looks?'

'He is as glad to give, if he hath store,
As Rantideva,' Narada replied.
'Pious he is; and true as Shivi was,
The son of Usinara; fair of form
(Yayati was not fairer); sweet of looks
(The Aswins not more gracious); gallant, kind,
Reverent, self-governed, gentle, equitable,
Modest, and constant. Justice lives in him,
And Honour guides. Those who do love a man
Praise him for manhood; they that seek a saint
Laud him for purity, and passions tamed.'

'A prince thou showest us,' the Raja said,
'All virtues owning. Tell me of some faults,
If fault he hath.'

                        'None lives,' quoth Narada,
'But some fault mingles with his qualities;
And Satyavan bears that he cannot mend.
The blot which spoils his brightness, the defect
Forbidding yonder Prince, Raja, is this, –
'Tis fated he shall die after a year:
Count from today one year, he perisheth!'

'My Savitri,' the King cried; 'go, dear child,
Some other husband choose. This hath one fault;
But huge it is, and mars all nobleness:
At the year's end he dies; – 'tis Narad's word,
Whom the gods teach.'

                        But Savitri replied:
'Once falls a heritage; once a maid yields
Her maidenhood; once doth a father say,
"Choose, I abide thy choice." These three things done,
Are done forever. Be my Prince to live
A year, or many years; be he so great
As Narada hath said, or less than this;

Once have I chosen him, and choose not twice!
My heart resolved, my mouth hath spoken it,
My hand shall execute; – this is my mind!'

Quoth Narad: 'Yea, her mind is fixed, O King,
And none will turn her from the path of truth!
Also the virtues of Prince Satyavan
Shall in no other man be found. Give thou
Thy child to him. I gainsay not.'

                                   Therewith
The Raja sighed: 'Nay, what must be, must be.
She speaketh sooth: and I will give my child,
For thou our Guru art.'

                    Narada said:
'Free be the gift of thy fair daughter, then;
May happiness yet light! – Raja, I go.'
So went that sage, returning to his place;
And the King bade the nuptials be prepared.
He bade that all things be prepared, – the robes,
The golden cups; and summoned priest and sage,
Brahman and Rity-yaj and Purohit;
And, on a day named fortunate, set forth
With Savitri. In the mid-wood they found
Dyumutsena's sylvan court: the King,
Alighting, paced with slow steps to the spot
Where sat the blind lord underneath a sal,
On mats woven of kusa grass. Then passed
Due salutations; worship, as is meet: –
All courteously the Raja spake his name,
All courteously the blind King gave to him
Earth, and a seat, and water in a jar;
Then asked, 'What, Maharaja, bringeth thee?'
And Aswapati, answering, told him all.

Brahman, Rity-yaj, Purohit: learned men, sacrificer, priest.

With eyes fixed full upon Prince Satyavan
He spake: 'This is my daughter, Savitri;
Take her from me to be wife to thy son,
According to the law; thou know'st the law.'
Dyumutsena said: 'Forced from our throne,
Wood-dwellers, hermits, keeping state no more,
We follow right, and how would right be done
If this most lovely lady we should house
Here, in our woods, unfitting home for her?'
Answered the Raja: 'Grief and joy we know,
And what is real and seeming, – she and I;
Nor fits this fear with our unshaken minds.
Deny thou not the prayer of him who bows
In friendliness before thee; put not by
His wish who comes well-minded unto thee;
Thy stateless state shows noble; thou and I
Are of one rank; take then this maid of mine
To be thy daughter, since she chooseth me
Thy Satyavan for son.'

        The blind lord spake:
'It was of old my wish to grow akin,
Raja, with thee, by marriage of our blood;
But ever have I answered to myself,
"Nay, for thy realm is lost; – forgo this hope!"
Yet now, so let it be, since so thou wilt;
My welcome guest thou art. Thy will is mine.'

Then gathered in the forest all those priests,
And with due rites the royal houses bound
By nuptial tie. And when the Raja saw
His daughter, as befits a princess, wed,
Home went he, glad. And glad was Satyavan,
Winning that beauteous spouse, with all gifts rich;
And she rejoiced to be the wife of him,
So chosen of her soul. But when her sire
Departed, from her neck and arms she stripped

Jewels and gold, and o'er her radiant form
Folded the robe of bark and yellow cloth
Which hermits use; and all hearts did she gain
By gentle actions, soft self-government,
Patience, and peace. The Queen had joy of her
For tender services and mindful cares;
The blind King took delight to know her days
So holy, and her wise words so restrained;
And with her lord in sweet converse she lived
Gracious and loving, dutiful and dear.

But while in the deep forest softly flowed
This quiet life of love and holiness,
The swift moons sped; and always in the heart
Of Savitri, by day and night, there dwelt
The words of Narada, – those dreadful words!

Now, when the pleasant days were passed, which brought
The day of Doom, and Satyavan must die
(For hour by hour the Princess counted them,
Keeping the words of Narada in heart),
Bethinking on the fourth noon he should die,
She set herself to make the 'Threefold Fast',
Three days and nights forgoing food and sleep;
Which, when the King Dyumutsena heard,
Sorrowful he arose, and spake her thus;
'Daughter, a heavy task thou takest on;
Hardly the saintliest soul might such abide.'
But Savitri gave answer: 'Have no heed:
What I do set myself I will perform;
The vow is made, and I shall keep the vow.'
'If it be made,' quoth he, 'it must be kept;
We cannot bid thee break thy word, once given.'
With that the King forbade not, and she sat
Still, as though carved of wood, three days and nights.
But when the third night passed, and brought the day
Whereon her lord must die, she rose betimes,

Made offering on the altar flames, and sang
Softly the morning prayers; then, with clasped palms
Laid on her bosom, meekly came to greet
The King and Queen, and lowlily salute
The grey-haired Brahmans. Thereupon those saints –
Resident in the woods – made answer mild
Unto the Princess: 'Be it well with thee,
And with thy lord, for these good deeds of thine.'
'May it be well!' she answered; in her heart
Full mournfully that hour of fate awaiting
Foretold of Narad.

        Then they said to her:
'Daughter, thy vow is kept. Come, now, and eat.'
But Savitri replied: 'When the sun sinks
This evening, I will eat, – that is my vow.'

So when they could not change her, afterward
Came Satyavan, the Prince, bound for the woods,
An axe upon his shoulder; unto whom
Wistfully spake the Princess: 'Dearest Lord,
Go not alone today; let me come too;
I cannot be apart from thee today.'
'Why not "today"?' quoth Satyavan. 'The wood
Is strange to thee, Beloved, and its paths
Rough for thy tender feet; besides, with fast
Thy soft limbs faint; how wilt thou walk with me?'

'I am not weak nor weary,' she replied,
'And I can walk. Say me not nay, sweet Lord,
I have so great a heart to go with thee.'

'If thou hast such good heart,' answered the Prince,
'I shall say yea; but first entreat the leave
Of those we reverence, lest a wrong be done.'

So, pure and dutiful, she sought that place
Where sat the King and Queen, and, bending low,
Murmured request: 'My husband goeth straight
To the great forest, gathering fruits and flowers;
I pray your leave that I may be with him.
To make the Agnihotra sacrifice
Fetcheth he those, and will not be gainsaid,
But surely goeth. Let me go. A year
Hath rolled since I did fare from th' hermitage
To see our groves in bloom. I have much will
To see them now.'

            The old King gently said:
'In sooth it is a year since she was given
To be our son's wife, and I mind me not
Of any boon the loving heart hath asked,
Nor any one untimely word she spake;
Let it be as she prayeth. Go, my child;
Have care of Satyavan, and take thy way.'

So, being permitted of them both, she went, –
That beauteous lady, – at her husband's side,
With aching heart, albeit her face was bright.
Flower-laden trees her large eyes lighted on,
Green glades where pea-fowl sported, crystal streams,
And soaring hills whose green sides burned with bloom,
Which oft the Prince would bid her gaze upon;
But she as oft turned those great eyes from them
To look on him, her husband, who must die
(For always in her mind were Narad's words).
And so she walked behind him, guarding him,
Bethinking at what hour her lord must die,
Her true heart torn in twain, one half to him
Close-cleaving, one half watching if Death come.

Then, having reached where woodland fruits did grow,
They gathered those, and filled a basket full;

And afterwards the Prince plied hard his axe,
Cutting the sacred fuel. Presently
There crept a pang upon him; a fierce throe
Burned through his brows, and, all asweat, he came
Feebly to Savitri, and moaned: 'O wife,
I am thus suddenly too weak for work;
My veins throb, Savitri; my blood runs fire;
It is as if a threefold fork were plunged
Into my brain. Let me lie down, fair Love!
Indeed, I cannot stand upon my feet.'

Thereon that noble lady, hastening near,
Stayed him, that would have fallen, with quick arms;
And, sitting on the earth, laid her lord's head
Tenderly in her lap. So bent she, mute,
Fanning his face, and thinking 'twas the day –
The hour – which Narad named – the sure fixed date
Of dreadful end – when, lo! before her rose
A shade majestic. Red his garments were,
His body vast and dark, like fiery suns
The eyes which burned beneath his forehead-cloth;
Armed was he with a noose, awful of mien.
This Form tremendous stood by Satyavan,
Fixing its gaze upon him. At the sight
The fearful Princess started to her feet.
Heedfully laying on the grass his head,
Up started she, with beating heart, and joined
Her palms for supplication, and spake thus
In accents tremulous: 'Thou seem'st some god;
Thy mien is more than mortal; make me know
What god thou art, and what thy purpose here.'

And Yama said (the dreadful God of death);
'Thou art a faithful wife, O Savitri,
True to thy vows, pious, and dutiful;
Therefore I answer thee. Yama I am!
This Prince, thy lord, lieth at point to die;

Him will I straightway bind and bear from life;
This is my office, and for this I come.'

Then Savitri spake sadly: 'It is taught,
Thy messengers are sent to fetch the dying;
Why is it, Mightiest, thou art come thyself?'

In pity of her love, the Pitiless
Answered, – the King of all the Dead replied:
'This was a Prince unparalleled, thy lord;
Virtuous as fair, a sea of goodly gifts,
Not to be summoned by a meaner voice
Than Yama's own: therefore is Yama come.'

With that the gloomy God fitted his noose,
And forced forth from the Prince the soul of him –
Subtile, a thumb in length – which being reft,
Breath stayed, blood stopped, his body's grace was gone,
And all life's warmth to stony coldness turned.
Then, binding it, the Silent Presence bore
Satyavan's soul away toward the South.

But Savitri the Princess followed him:
Being so bold in wifely purity,
So holy by her love: and so upheld,
She followed him.

                Presently Yama turned.
'Go back,' quoth he; 'pay him the funeral dues.
Enough, O Savitri! is wrought for love;
Go back! too far already hast thou come.'

Then Savitri made answer: 'I must go
Where my lord goes, or where my lord is borne;
Nought other is my duty. Nay, I think,
By reason of my vows, my services
Done to the Gurus, and my faultless love,

Grant but thy grace, I shall unhindered go.
The sages teach that to walk seven steps,
One with another, maketh good men friends;
Beseech thee, let me say a verse to thee: –

> Be master of thyself, if thou wilt be
> Servant of Duty. Such as thou shalt see
> Not self-subduing, do no deeds of good
> In youth or age, in household or in wood.
> But wise men know that virtue is best bliss,
> And all by some one way may reach to this.
> It needs not men should pass through orders four
> To come to knowledge: doing right is more
> Than any learning; therefore sages say
> Best and most excellent is Virtue's way.'

Spake Yama then: 'Return! yet I am moved
By those soft words; justly their accents fell,
And sweet and reasonable was their sense.
See, now, thou faultless one. Except this life
I bear away, ask any boon from me;
It shall not be denied.'

Savitri said:

'Let, then, the King, my husband's father, have
His eyesight back, and be his strength restored,
And let him live anew, strong as the sun.'

'I give this gift,' Yama replied: 'thy wish,
Blameless, shall be fulfilled. But now go back;
Already art thou wearied, and our road
Is hard and long. Turn back, lest thou, too, die.'

The Princess answered: 'Weary am I not,
So I walk nigh my lord. Where he is borne,
Thither wend I. Most mighty of the gods,
I follow whereso'er thou takest him.
A verse is writ on this, if thou wouldst hear:

> There is nought better than to be
> With noble souls in company:
> There is nought dearer than to wend
> With good friends faithful to the end.
> This is the love whose fruit is sweet;
> Therefore to bide therein is meet.'

Spake Yama, smiling: 'Beautiful! Thy words
Delight me; they are excellent, and teach
Wisdom unto the wise, singing soft truth.
Look, now! except the life of Satyavan,
Ask yet another – any – boon from me.'

Savitri said: 'Let, then, the pious King,
My husband's father, who hath lost his throne,
Have back the Raj; and let him rule his realm
In happy righteousness. This boon I ask.'

'He shall have back the throne,' Yama replied,
'And he shall reign in righteousness: these things
Will surely fall. But thou, gaining thy wish,
Return anon; so shalt thou 'scape sore ill.'

'Ah, awful God! who hold'st the world in leash,'
The Princess said, 'restraining evil men,
And leading good men, – even unconscious, – there
Where they attain, hear yet these famous words:

The constant virtues of the good are tenderness and love
To all that lives – in earth, air, sea – great, small – below, above,
Compassionate of heart, they keep a gentle thought for each,

Kind in their actions, mild in will, and pitiful of speech;
Who pitieth not he hath not faith; full many an one so lives,
But when an enemy seeks help the good man gladly gives.'

'As water to the thirsting,' Yama said,
'Princess, thy words melodious are to me.
Except the life of Satyavan thy lord,
Ask one boon yet again, for I will grant.'
Answer made Savitri: 'The King, my sire,
Hath no male child. Let him see many sons
Begotten of his body, who may keep
The royal line long regnant. This I ask.'

'So it shall be!' the Lord of death replied;
'A hundred fair preservers of his race
Thy sire shall boast. But this wish being won,
Return, dear Princess; thou hast come too far.'

'It is not far for me,' quoth Savitri,
'Since I am near my husband; nay, my heart
Is set to go as far as to the end;
But hear these other verses, if thou wilt:

  By that sunlit name thou bearest,
  Thou, Vaivaswata! art dearest;
  Those that as their Lord proclaim thee,
  King of Righteousness do name thee;
  Better than themselves the wise
  Trust the righteous. Each relies
  Most upon the good, and makes
  Friendship with them. Friendship takes
  Fear from hearts; yet friends betray,
  In good men we may trust alway.'

'Sweet lady,' Yama said, 'never were words
Spoke better; never truer heard by ear;
Lo! I am pleased with thee. Except this soul,
Ask one gift yet again, and get thee home.'

'I ask thee, then,' quickly the Princess cried,
'Sons, many sons, born of my body: boys;
Satyavan's children; lovely, valiant, strong.
Continuers of their line. Grant this, kind God.'

'I grant it,' Yama answered; 'thou shalt bear
Those sons thy heart desireth, valiant, strong.
Therefore go back, that years be given thee.
Too long a path thou treadest, dark and rough.'
But, sweeter than before, the Princess sang:
  'In paths of peace and virtue
   Always the good remain;
  And sorrow shall not stay with them,
   Nor long access of pain;
  At meeting or at parting
   Joys to their bosom strike;
  For good to good is friendly,
   And virtue loves her like.
  The great sun goes his journey
   By their strong truth impelled;
  By their pure lives and penances
   Is earth itself upheld;
  Of all which live or shall live
   Upon its hills and fields,
  Pure hearts are the "protectors",
   For virtue saves and shields.

  'Never are noble spirits
   Poor while their like survive;
  True love has gems to render,
   And virtue wealth to give.
  Never is lost or wasted

The goodness of the good;
Never against a mercy,
Against a right, it stood;
And seeing this, that virtue
Is always friend to all,
The virtuous and true-hearted,
Men their "protectors" call.'

'Line for line, Princess! as thou sangest so,'
Quoth Yama, 'all that lovely praise of good,
Grateful to hallowed minds, lofty in sound,
And couched in dulcet numbers – word by word –
Dearer thou grew'st to me. O thou great heart,
Perfect and firm! ask any boon from me, –
Ask an incomparable boon!'

                    She cried
Swiftly, no longer stayed: 'Not heaven I crave,
Nor heavenly joys, nor bliss incomparable,
Hard to be granted even by thee; but *him*,
My sweet lord's life, without which I am dead;
Give me that gift of gifts! I will not take
Aught less without him, – not one boon, – no praise,
No splendours, no rewards, – not even those sons
Whom thou didst promise. Ah, thou wilt not, now,
Bear hence the father of them, and my hope!
Make thy free word good; give me Satyavan
Alive once more.'

                    And thereupon the God –
The Lord of Justice, high Vaivaswata –
Loosened the noose and freed the Prince's soul,
And gave it to the lady, saying this,
With eyes grown tender: 'See, thou sweetest queen
Of women, brightest jewel of thy kind!
Here is thy husband. He shall live and reign
Side by side with thee, – saved by thee, – in peace,

And fame, and wealth, and health, many long years;
For pious sacrifices world-renowned.
Boys shalt thou bear to him, as I did grant, –
Kshatriya kings, fathers of kings to be,
Sustainers of thy line. Also, thy sire
Shall see his name upheld by sons of sons,
Like the immortals, valiant, Malavas.'

These gifts the awful Yama gave, and went
Unto his place; but Savitri – made glad,
Having her husband's soul – sped to the glade
Where his corse lay. She saw it there, and ran,
And, sitting on the earth, lifted its head,
And lulled it on her lap full tenderly.
Thereat warm life returned: the white lips moved;
The fixed eyes brightened, gazed, and gazed again;
As when one starts from sleep and sees a face –
The well-belovèd's – grow clear, and, smiling, wakes,
So Satyavan. 'Long have I slumbered, Dear,'
He sighed, 'why didst thou not arouse me? Where
Is gone that gloomy man that haled at me?'
Answered the Princess: 'Long, indeed, thy sleep,
Dear Lord, and deep; for he that haled at thee
Was Yama, God of Death; but he is gone;
And thou, being rested and awake, rise now,
If thou canst rise; for, look, the night is near!'

Thus, newly living, newly waked, the Prince
Glanced all around upon the blackening groves,
And whispered: 'I came forth to pluck the fruits,
O slender-waisted, with thee: then, some pang
Shot through my temples while I hewed the wood,
And I lay down upon thy lap, dear wife,
And slept. This do I well remember. Next –
Was it a dream, – that vast, dark, mighty One
Whom I beheld? Oh, if thou saw'st and know'st,
Was it in fancy, or in truth, he came?'

Softly she answered: 'Night is falling fast;
Tomorrow I will tell thee all, dear Lord.
Get to thy feet, and let us seek our home.
Guide us, ye Gods! the gloom spreads fast around;
The creatures of the forest are abroad,
Which roam and cry by night. I hear the leaves
Rustle with beasts that creep. I hear this way
The yells of prowling jackals; beasts do haunt
In the southern wood; their noises make me fear.'

'The wood is black with shadows,' quoth the Prince;
'You would not know the path; you could not see it;
We cannot go.'

        She said: 'There was today
A fire within this forest, and it burned
A withered tree; yonder the branches flame.
I'll fetch a lighted brand and kindle wood:
See! there is fuel here. Art thou so vexed
Because we cannot go? Grieve not. The path
Is hidden, and thy limbs are not yet knit.
Tomorrow, when the ways grows clear, depart;
But, if thou wilt, let us abide tonight.'
And Satyavan replied: 'The pains are gone
Which racked my brow; my limbs seem strong again;
Fain would I reach our home, if thou wilt aid.
Ever betimes I have been wont to come
At evening to the place where those we love
Await us. Ah, what trouble they will know,
Father and mother, searching now for us!
They prayed me hasten back. How they will weep,
Not seeing me; for there is none save me
To guard them. "Quick return," they said; "our lives
Live upon thine; thou art our eyes, our breath,
Our home of lineage; unto thee we look
For funeral cakes, for mourning feasts, for all."
What will these do alone, not seeing me,

Who am their stay? Shame on the idle sleep
And foolish dreams which cost them all this pain!
I cannot tarry here. My sire belike,
Having no eyes, asks at this very hour
News of me from each one that walks the wood.
Let us depart. Not, Savitri, for us
Think I, but for those reverend ones at home,
Mourning me now. If they fare well, 'tis well
With me; if ill, nought's well; what would please them
Is wise and good to do.'

                    Thereat he beat
Faint hands, eager to go; and Savitri,
Seeing him weeping, wiped his tears away,
And gently spake: 'If I have kept the fast,
Made sacrifices, given gifts, and wrought
Service to holy men, may this black night
Be bright to those and thee; for we will go.
I think I never spoke a false word once
In all my life, not even in jest; I pray
My truth may help tonight them, thee, and me!'

'Let us set forth,' he cried; 'if any harm
Hath fallen on those so dear, I could not live;
I swear it by my soul! As thou art sweet,
Helpful, and virtuous, aid me to depart.'
Then Savitri arose, and tied her hair,
And lifted up her lord upon his feet;
Who, as he swept the dry leaves from his cloth,
Looked on the basket full of fruit. 'But thou,'
The Princess said, 'tomorrow shalt bring these;
Give me thine axe, the axe is good to take.'
So saying, she hung the basket on a branch,
And in her left hand carrying the axe,
Came back, and laid his arm across her neck,
Her right arm winding round him. So they went.

The *Bhagavad Gita*, a philosophical poem of extraordinary beauty, perhaps having a prior, independent existence in some form, has been incorporated into the *Mahabharata* in Book VI, *Bhishma Parva* (Sections 25–42). The poem is in the form of a dialogue between the Pandava hero, Arjuna, and his charioteer, Krishna (man-divine or *avatara* of God Vishnu), on the battlefield of Kurukshetra (near Delhi). In the epic, this metaphysical dialogue in eighteen chapters is a part of a longer narrative in which Sanjaya, counsellor to the blind king Dhritarashtra, relates to him the entire battle between his sons (Kauravas) and his brother's children (Pandavas).

It is obvious from the text of the poem that the reference to the war at Kurukshetra is only peripheral and not central to it. After the first two chapters, the war is almost completely forgotten until the end. What is essential and most significant in the poem, however, is the discussion of the important ideas and doctrines relating to the individual self (*atman*), the Universal Self (*Brahman*), the nature of human action, the problem of evil in society, the phenomenon of *avatara* (incarnation of divine energy to uphold the moral law whenever evil predominates), the beatic vision of the Cosmic Form (*Vishwarupa*), and the nature of Bhakti or loving-faith. In the light of these discussions, the battle symbolically becomes, in the opening line of the poem, a *Dharmakshetre* or a field of battle for upholding the (*Dharma*): for the individual, the war is against the world and against his own senses, so that he may reach the divine self within by transcending conscious and sub-conscious mind into an electrifying vision.

The compressed text of the poem has as many contradictions as can be found in life itself. Yet it has been the living fountainhead of faith for Indian spiritualities throughout the ages, in the same sense as 'the Way of Life' enunciated by Moses (prophet of God Jehovah) in the Hebrew epic (Pentateuch, Book II, 20:1–17) became the foundation of faith for Semitic spiritualities, namely Judaism, Christianity, and Islam. The references to the war at Kurukshetra or the wanderings in the Sinai desert are, no doubt, marginal to the teachings of the man-divine (*avatara* or prophet), while the teachings themselves are of universal significance.

The conflict of the epic hero Arjuna in the *Mahabharata* somewhat resembles the conflict of Achilles in Homer's *Iliad*. Both heroes refuse to fight at a critical point in a great war, not because they are cowards or are afraid of death, but for other reasons. Both of them live through a period of confusion, mental darkness, and emotional crisis until some light prompts them to return to the battlefield. The reasons for their sudden withdrawal from conflict, their gradual awakening or growing up to their perception of their own sense of identity and their role in society, and the purpose of their final return to action dramatically contrast the cultural values and attitudes of two great ancient civilizations.

The selections included here are taken from the translation by Juan Mascaró, *The Bhagavad Gita*, Baltimore, Maryland: Penguin Books, 1962, Chapters 1–4, 9–11, 17–18.

I.7   THE BHAGAVAD GITA

Arjuna's Despair

[1]

DHRITA-RASHTRA

1. On the field of Truth, on the battle-field of life, what came to pass, Sanjaya, when my sons and their warriors faced those of my brother Pandu?

---

1. *Dhrita-rashtra.* After the death of King Pandu, his blind brother Dhrita-rashtra succeeds to the throne. Because of jealousy and rivalry between his one hundred sons (Kauravas, eldest son Duryodhana) and the five sons of Pandu (Pandavas: Yudhishthir, Bhima, Arjuna, Nakula, and Sahadeva), the kingdom is divided. However, in a fraudulent game of dice, the Kauravas cheat Pandavas of their kingdom and send them into thirteen

SANJAYA

2. When your son Duryodhana saw the armies of the sons of Pandu he went to his master in the art of war and spoke to him these words:

3. See there, master, the vast army of the Pandavas well set in order of battle by the son of Drupada, your own wise pupil.

4. There can we see heroic warriors, powerful archers, as great as Bhima and Arjuna in battle: Yuyudhana and Virata and king Drupada of the great chariot of war.

5. And Dhrishta-ketu of the steadfast banner, and Chekitana, the king of the Chedis. We see the heroic king of Kasi, and Purujit the conqueror, and his brother Kunti-bhoja, and Saibya mighty among men.

6. And victorious Yudhamanyu, and powerful Uttamaujas; and Saubhadra, the son of Arjuna, and the five princes of queen Draupadi. See them all in their chariots of war.

7. But hear also the names of our greatest warriors, the leaders of my own army. I will bring them to your memory.

8. There is yourself, my master in war, and also Bhishma, old and wise. There is Karna, the enemy of Arjuna, his half-brother; and Kripa, victor of battles. There is your own son Asvatthama, and also my brother Vikarna. There is Saumadatti, king of the Bahikas.

---

years of exile. At the end of this period, Krishna pleads for the restoration of the rights of Pandavas, but Duryodhana refuses to yield anything. Finally both sides prepare for war at Kurukshetra. At that time rishi Vyasa grants a boon of vision to Sanjaya, a courtier, so that he could see the whole battlefield and relate the events to the blind king. The *Bhagavad Gita* begins at this point.

The opening line, *Dharmakshetre Kurukshetre*, symbolically refers to the battlefield at Kurukshetra as Dharmakshetre or a battlefield for upholding the moral law (Dharma). Cf. Dante's journey in the *Divine Comedy* symbolizing the mental quest for the 'Kingdom of Heaven' within.

3. *Drupada:* king of Panchala, and father of Draupadi, wife of the Pandavas.

3–11. Cf. the epic convention of listing heroes and ships in Homer.

9. And many other heroic warriors ready to give their lives for me; all armed with manifold weapons, and all of them masters of war.

10. We can number our armies led by Bhishma, but innumerable seem their armies led by Bhima.

11. Stand therefore all firm in the line of battle. Let us all defend our leader Bhishma.

12. To encourage Duryodhana, Bhishma, the glorious old warrior of the Kurus, sounded loud his war-cry like the roar of a lion, and then blew his far-sounding conch-shell.

13. Then the rumbling of war drums, the stirring sound of cymbals and trumpets, and the roaring of conch-shells and horns filled the sky with a fearful thunder.

14. Thereupon Krishna of Madhava and Arjuna, the son of Pandu, standing in their glorious chariot drawn by white horses, answered the challenge and blew their divine conch-shells.

15. Krishna, the Lord of the soul, blew his conch-shell Pancha-janya. Arjuna, the winner of treasure, sounded forth his own Deva-datta. His brother Bhima, of tremendous feats, blew his great conch-shell the Paundra.

16. Their eldest brother, king Yudhishthira, sounded his Eternal-Victory; and Nakula and Sahadeva the Sweet-sounding and the Jewel-blossom.

17. And the king of Kasi of the powerful bow, and Sikhandi of the great war chariot, Dhrishta-dyumna and Virata, and Satyaki the never-conquered;

18. And king Drupada and the sons of his daughter Draupadi; and Saubhadra, the heroic son of Arjuna, sounded from all sides their conch-shells of war.

---

14. Both Krishna and Arjuna are referred to in this poem by various epithets.

Krishna: *Hrsikesa* (lord of senses); *Govinda* (lord of cattle); *Vasudeva* (son of Vasudeva); *Narayana* (Man-divine); *Madhusudana* (slayer of demon Madhu); *Janardhana* (liberator of man); *Achyuta* (immovable, imperishable); *Partha-sarathi* (charioteer of Partha or Arjuna), etc.

Arjuna: *Pandava* (son of Pandu); *Bharata* (descendant of Bharata); *Partha* (son of Pritha or Kunti); *Gudakesha* (having long hair tied like a ball); *Dhanamjaya* (winner of wealth), etc.

19. At that fearful sound the earth and the heavens trembled, and also trembled the hearts of Duryodhana and his warriors.
20. The flight of arrows was now to begin, and Arjuna, on whose banner was the symbol of an ape, saw Duryodhana and his warriors drawn up in their lines of battle. He thereupon took up his bow.
21. And spoke these words to Krishna:

ARJUNA

Drive my chariot, Krishna immortal, and place it between the two armies.
22. That I may see those warriors who stand there eager for battle, with whom I must now fight at the beginning of this war.
23. That I may see those who have come here eager and ready to fight, in their desire to do the will of the evil son of Dhrita-rashtra.

SANJAYA

24. When Krishna heard the words of Arjuna he drove their glorious chariot and placed it between the two armies.
25. And facing Bhishma and Drona and other royal rulers he said: 'See, Arjuna, the armies of the Kurus, gathered here on this field of battle.'
26. Then Arjuna saw in both armies fathers, grandfathers, sons,
27. grandsons; fathers of wives, uncles, masters; brothers, companions
28. and friends.
    When Arjuna thus saw his kinsmen face to face in both lines of battle, he was overcome by grief and despair and thus he spoke with a sinking heart.

ARJUNA

When I see all my kinsmen, Krishna, who have come here on this field of battle,
29. Life goes from my limbs and they sink, and my mouth is sear and dry; a trembling overcomes my body, and my hair shudders in horror;
30. My great bow Gandiva falls from my hands, and the skin over my

flesh is burning; I am no longer able to stand, because my mind is whirling and wandering.

31. And I see forebodings of evil, Krishna. I cannot foresee any glory if I kill my own kinsmen in the sacrifice of battle.

32. Because I have no wish for victory, Krishna, nor for a kingdom, nor for its pleasures. How can we want a kingdom, Govinda, or its pleasures or even life,

33. When those for whom we want a kingdom, and its pleasures, and the joys of life, are here in this field of battle about to give up their wealth and their life?

34. Facing us in the field of battle are teachers, fathers and sons; grandsons, grandfathers, wives' brothers; mothers' brothers and fathers of wives.

35. These I do not wish to slay, even if I myself am slain. Not even for the kingdom of the three worlds: how much less for a kingdom of the earth!

36. If we kill these evil men, evil shall fall upon us: what joy in their death could we have, O Janardhana, mover of souls?

37. I cannot therefore kill my own kinsmen, the sons of king Dhrita-rashtra, the brother of my own father. What happiness could we ever enjoy, if we killed our own kinsmen in battle?

38. Even if they, with minds overcome by greed, see no evil in the destruction of a family, see no sin in the treachery to friends;

39. Shall we not, who see the evil of destruction, shall we not refrain from this terrible deed?

40. The destruction of a family destroys its rituals of righteousness, and when the righteous rituals are no more, unrighteousness overcomes the whole family.

41. When unrighteous disorder prevails, the women sin and are impure; and when women are not pure, Krishna, there is disorder of castes, social confusion.

42. This disorder carries down to hell the family and the destroyers of the family. The spirits of their dead suffer in pain when deprived of the ritual offerings.

43. Those evil deeds of the destroyers of a family, which cause this social disorder, destroy the righteousness of birth and the ancestral rituals of righteousness.

44. And have we not heard that hell is waiting for those whose familiar rituals of righteousness are no more?

45. O day of darkness! What evil spirit moved our minds when for the sake of an earthly kingdom we came to this field of battle ready to kill our own people?

46. Better for me indeed if the sons of Dhrita-rashtra, with arms in hand, found me unarmed, unresisting, and killed me in the struggle of war.

SANJAYA

47. Thus spoke Arjuna in the field of battle, and letting fall his bow and arrows he sank down in his chariot, his soul overcome by despair and grief.

Krishna's Reply to Arjuna:
Relevance of human action on three levels: cosmic,
social, and individual

[2]

SANJAYA

1. Then arose the Spirit of Krishna and spoke to Arjuna, his friend, who with eyes filled with tears, thus had sunk into despair and grief.

KRISHNA

2. Whence this lifeless dejection, Arjuna, in this hour, the hour of trial? Strong men know not despair, Arjuna, for this wins neither heaven nor earth.

3. Fall not into degrading weakness, for this becomes not a man who is a man. Throw off this ignoble discouragement, and arise like a fire that burns all before it.

---

47. *Chariot:* symbol of the psychological body-apparatus of man. Cf. *Katha Upanishad* III.3–4; Plato, *Laws* 898C; *Milindapanha* II.1.1.

ARJUNA

4. I owe veneration to Bhishma and Drona. Shall I kill with my arrows my grandfather's brother, great Bhishma? Shall my arrows in battle slay Drona, my teacher?

5. Shall I kill my own masters who, though greedy of my kingdom, are yet my sacred teachers? I would rather eat in this life the food of a beggar than eat royal food tasting of their blood.

6. And we know not whether their victory or ours be better for us. The sons of my uncle and king, Dhrita-rashtra, are here before us: after their death, should we wish to live?

7. In the dark night of my soul I feel desolation. In my self-pity I see not the way of righteousness. I am thy disciple, come to thee in supplication: be a light unto me on the path of my duty.

8. For neither the kingdom of the earth, nor the kingdom of the gods in heaven, could give me peace from the fire of sorrow which thus burns my life.

SANJAYA

9. When Arjuna the great warrior had thus unburdened his heart, 'I will not fight, Krishna,' he said, and then fell silent.

10. Krishna smiled and spoke to Arjuna – there between the two armies the voice of God spoke these words:

KRISHNA

11. Thy tears are for those beyond tears; and are thy words words of wisdom? The wise grieve not for those who live; and they grieve not for those who die – for life and death shall pass away.

---

7. Arjuna not only is overcome by despair and anxiety, but also is driven by an ardent desire for certainty about his path of duty.

10. Krishna smiles at Arjuna's wishful thinking about human sorrow and suffering. He then explains the relevance of human action on cosmic (11–30), social (31–9), and individual (39–53) levels; and how a man of disciplined mind acts (54–72).

11–30. From the cosmic point of view, one who really understands does not grieve; for the essence (self, spirit, atman) within the individual, being

12. Because we all have been for all time: I, and thou, and those kings of men. And we all shall be for all time, we all for ever and ever.

13. As the Spirit of our mortal body wanders on in childhood, and youth and old age, the Spirit wanders on to a new body: of this the sage has no doubts.

14. From the world of the senses, Arjuna, comes heat and comes cold, and pleasure and pain. They come and they go: they are transient. Arise above them, strong soul.

15. The man whom these cannot move, whose soul is one, beyond pleasure and pain, is worthy of life in Eternity.

16. The unreal never is: the Real never is not. This truth indeed has been seen by those who can see the true.

17. Interwoven in his creation, the Spirit is beyond destruction. No one can bring to an end the Spirit which is everlasting.

18. For beyond time he dwells in these bodies, though these bodies have an end in their time; but he remains immeasurable, immortal. Therefore, great warrior, carry on thy fight.

19. If any man thinks he slays, and if another thinks he is slain, neither knows the ways of truth. The Eternal in man cannot kill: the Eternal in man cannot die.

20. He is never born, and he never dies. He is in Eternity: he is for evermore. Never-born and eternal, beyond times gone or to come, he does not die when the body dies.

21. When a man knows him as never-born, everlasting, never-changing, beyond all destruction, how can that man kill a man, or cause another to kill?

---

eternal, That was, is, and will be, while the existential phases like childhood, youth, manhood, age, or cycles of birth and death, pass away; the wise do not confuse the two nor grieve for the imperishable. One can only have a visionary understanding of the essence but cannot know That through learning.

19-20. Cf. *Katha Upanishad* II.18-19. Cf. Emerson's poem *Brahma*:

> If the red slayer thinks he slays,
> Or if the slain think he is slain,
> They know not well the subtle ways
> I keep and pass and turn again.

22. As a man leaves an old garment and puts on one that is new, the Spirit leaves his mortal body and wanders on to one that is new.

23. Weapons cannot hurt the Spirit and fire can never burn him. Untouched is he by drenching waters, untouched is he by parching winds.

24. Beyond the power of sword and fire, beyond the power of waters and winds, the Spirit is everlasting, omnipresent, never-changing, never-moving, ever One.

25. Invisible is he to mortal eyes, beyond thought and beyond change. Know that he is, and cease from sorrow.

26. But if he were born again and again, and again and again he were to die, even then, victorious man, cease thou from sorrow.

27. For all things born in truth must die, and out of death in truth comes life. Face to face with what must be, cease thou from sorrow.

28. Invisible before birth are all beings and after death invisible again. They are seen between two unseens. Why in this truth find sorrow?

29. One sees him in a vision of wonder, and another gives us words of his wonder. There is one who hears of his wonder; but he hears and knows him not.

30. The Spirit that is in all beings is immortal in them all: for the death of what cannot die, cease thou to sorrow.

31. Think thou also of thy duty and do not waver. There is no greater good for a warrior than to fight in righteous war.

---

22. Plato, *Crito*. Crito: 'In what way shall we bury you, Socrates?' Socrates: 'In any way you like, but first you must catch *me*, the real me. Be of good cheer, my dear Crito, and say that you are burying my body only, and do with *that* whatever is usual.'

27. Cf. Buddha's parable of the mustard seed to Kisa Gotami.

31–9. From the social point of view there is no greater duty for a warrior than to do battle in a war that is for the upholding of the moral law. In an organized society there is no one who has no duty, for the organism can be sustained only when all the elements function in a cooperative and cumulative way. A warrior who abandons his duty at the time of lawful war is like a carpenter who plays the fiddle when he should work on carpentry, or like a surgeon who begins to paint when he should perform an operation. Such abandonment of expected duty will bring about a collapse of the social organization. Disregarding the contraries of pleasure and pain, and con-

32. There is a war that opens the doors of heaven, Arjuna! Happy the warriors whose fate is to fight such war.

33. But to forgo this fight for righteousness is to forgo thy duty and honour: is to fall into transgression.

34. Men will tell of thy dishonour both now and in times to come. And to a man who is in honour, dishonour is more than death.

35. The great warriors will say that thou hast run from the battle through fear; and those who thought great things of thee will speak of thee in scorn.

36. And thine enemies will speak of thee in contemptuous words of ill-will and derision, pouring scorn upon thy courage. Can there be for a warrior a more shameful fate?

37. In death thy glory in heaven, in victory thy glory on earth. Arise therefore, Arjuna, with thy soul ready to fight.

38. Prepare for war with peace in thy soul. Be in peace in pleasure and pain, in gain and in loss, in victory or in the loss of a battle. In this peace there is no sin.

39. This is the wisdom of Sankhya – the vision of the Eternal. Hear now the wisdom of Yoga, path of the Eternal and freedom from bondage.

---

sequences of gain or loss, one who knows his place in society performs his duty. This is the wisdom one acquires from the discipline of knowledge or learning.

39. *Sankhya and Yoga* in the *Gita* does not mean the systems of philosophy known by that name; nor does Yoga mean Patanjaliyoga ... The dualism of the Sankhya-Yoga is transcended in the *Gita* which affirms the reality of the Supreme Self (S. Radhakrishnan).

In the *Gita* Sankhya refers to the intellectual account of the intuition of the Unchanging One; it is the discipline of knowledge. Yoga is the discipline of action. The *Gita* raises the question: How should one who discerns the eternal self in perishable body, and knows his moral duty in the events of the world, act?

39–53. From the individual's point of view, action (and not actionlessness) is the main office of life. The ideal action is that which frees the actor from the bondage of action, and is performed through a disciplined mental attitude (Yoga). Those who merely seek enjoyment of power through the words of Vedas and rituals, being robbed of insight, are fettered to

40. No step is lost on this path, and no dangers are found. And even a little progress is freedom from fear.

41. The follower of this path has one thought, and this is the End of his determination. But many-branched and endless are the thoughts of the man who lacks determination.

42. There are men who have no vision, and yet they speak many words. They follow the letter of the Vedas, and they say 'there is nothing but this.'

43. Their soul is warped with selfish desires, and their heaven is a selfish desire. They have prayers for pleasures and power, the reward of which is earthly rebirth.

44. Those who love pleasure and power hear and follow their words: they have not the determination ever to be one with the One.

45. The three Gunas of Nature are the world of the Vedas. Arise beyond the three Gunas, Arjuna! Be in Truth eternal, beyond earthly opposites. Beyond gains and possessions, possess thine own soul.

46. As is the use of a well of water where water everywhere overflows, such is the use of all the Vedas to the seer of the Supreme.

47. Set thy heart upon thy work, but never on its reward. Work not for a reward; but never cease to do thy work.

48. Do thy work in the peace of Yoga and, free from selfish desires, be not moved in success or in failure. Yoga is evenness of mind – a peace that is ever the same.

49. Work done for a reward is much lower than work done in the Yoga of wisdom. Seek salvation in the wisdom of reason. How poor those who work for a reward!

50. In this wisdom a man goes beyond what is well done and what is not well done. Go thou therefore to wisdom: Yoga is wisdom in work.

---

mortality. What profit there is in a tank of water when the whole valley is flooded, so much profit is in scriptures and rituals to a man of action with a disciplined mind (39–47). Seeking refuge in the stabilized mind and renouncing the fruits of action and not action itself, an enlightened one acts and in such action becomes one or submerged with the action of Universal self (48–53).

51. Seers in union with wisdom forsake the rewards of their work, and free from the bonds of birth they go to the abode of salvation.

52. When thy mind leaves behind its dark forest of delusion, thou shalt go beyond the scriptures of times past and still to come.

53. When thy mind, that may be wavering in the contradictions of many scriptures, shall rest unshaken in divine contemplation, then the goal of Yoga is thine.

ARJUNA

54. How is the man of tranquil wisdom, who abides in divine contemplation? What are his words? What is his silence? What is his work?

KRISHNA

55. When a man surrenders all desires that come to the heart and by the grace of God finds the joy of God, then his soul has indeed found peace.

56. He whose mind is untroubled by sorrows, and for pleasures he has no longings, beyond passion, and fear and anger, he is the sage of unwavering mind.

57. Who everywhere is free from all ties, who neither rejoices nor sorrows if fortune is good or is ill, his is a serene wisdom.

58. When in recollection he withdraws all his senses from the attractions of the pleasures of sense, even as a tortoise withdraws all its limbs, then his is a serene wisdom.

59. Pleasures of sense, but not desires, disappear from the austere soul. Even desires disappear when the soul has seen the Supreme.

60. The restless violence of the senses impetuously carries away the mind of even a wise man striving towards perfection.

61. Bringing them all into the harmony of recollection, let him sit in devotion and union, his soul finding rest in me. For when his senses are in harmony, then his is a serene wisdom.

62. When a man dwells on the pleasures of sense, attraction for them arises in him. From attraction arises desire, the lust of possession, and this leads to passion, to anger:

62-3. Evil in human society is caused by human actions, misguided by passions, and their cumulative consequences.

63. From passion comes confusion of mind, then loss of remembrance, the forgetting of duty. From this loss comes the ruin of reason, and the ruin of reason leads man to destruction.

64. But the soul that moves in the world of the senses and yet keeps the senses in harmony, free from attraction and aversion, finds rest in quietness.

65. In this quietness falls down the burden of all her sorrows, for when the heart has found quietness, wisdom has also found peace.

66. There is no wisdom for a man without harmony, and without harmony there is no contemplation. Without contemplation there cannot be peace, and without peace can there be joy?

67. For when the mind becomes bound to a passion of the wandering senses, this passion carries away man's wisdom, even as the wind drives a vessel on the waves.

68. The man who therefore in recollection withdraws his senses from the pleasures of sense, his is a serene wisdom.

69. In the dark night of all beings awakes to Light the tranquil man. But what is day to other beings is night for the sage who sees.

70. Even as all waters flow into the ocean, but the ocean never overflows, even so the sage feels desires, but he is ever one in his infinite peace.

71. For the man who forsakes all desires and abandons all pride of possession and of self reaches the goal of peace supreme.

72. This is the Eternal in man, O Arjuna. Reaching him all delusion is gone. Even in the last hour of his life upon earth, man can reach the Nirvana of Brahman – man can find peace in the peace of his God.

Discipline of Action

[3]

ARJUNA

1. If thy thought is that vision is greater than action, why dost thou enjoin upon me the terrible action of war?

2. My mind is in confusion because in thy words I find contra-

dictions. Tell me in truth therefore by what path may I attain the
Supreme.

KRISHNA

3. In this world there are two roads of perfection, as I told thee
before, O prince without sin: Jnana Yoga, the path of wisdom of
the Sankhyas, and Karma Yoga, the path of action of the Yogis.

4. Not by refraining from action does man attain freedom from
action. Not by mere renunciation does he attain supreme perfection.

5. For not even for a moment can a man be without action. Help-
lessly are all driven to action by the forces born of Nature.

6. He who withdraws himself from actions, but ponders on their
pleasures in his heart, he is under a delusion and is a false follower
of the Path.

7. But great is the man who, free from attachments, and with a
mind ruling its powers in harmony, works on the path of Karma
Yoga, the path of consecrated action.

8. Action is greater than inaction: perform therefore thy task in life.
Even the life of the body could not be if there were no action.

9. The world is in the bonds of action, unless the action is consecration. Let thy actions then be pure, free from the bonds of
desire.

10. Thus spoke the Lord of Creation when he made both man and
sacrifice: 'By sacrifice thou shalt multiply and obtain all thy
desires.

11. 'By sacrifice shalt thou honour the gods and the gods will then
love thee. And thus in harmony with them shalt thou attain the
supreme good.

12. 'For pleased with thy sacrifice, the gods will grant to thee the joy
of all thy desires. Only a thief would enjoy their gifts and not offer
them in sacrifice.'

13. Holy men who take as food the remains of sacrifice become free
from all their sins; but the unholy who have feasts for themselves
eat food that is in truth sin.

14. Food is the life of all beings, and all food comes from rain above.
Sacrifice brings the rain from heaven, and sacrifice is sacred action.

15. Sacred action is described in the Vedas and these come from the Eternal, and therefore is the Eternal everpresent in a sacrifice.

16. Thus was the Wheel of the Law set in motion, and that man lives indeed in vain who in a sinful life of pleasures helps not in its lutions.

17. But the man who has found the joy of the Spirit and in the Spirit has satisfaction, who in the Spirit has found his peace, that man is beyond the law of action.

18. He is beyond what is done and beyond what is not done, and in all his works he is beyond the help of mortal beings.

19. In liberty from the bonds of attachment, do thou therefore the work to be done: for the man whose work is pure attains indeed the Supreme.

20. King Janaka and other warriors reached perfection by the path of action: let thy aim be the good of all, and then carry on thy task in life.

21. In the actions of the best men others find their rule of action. The path that a great man follows becomes a guide to the world.

22. I have no work to do in all the worlds, Arjuna – for these are mine. I have nothing to obtain, because I have all. And yet I work.

23. If I was not bound to action, never-tiring, everlastingly, men that follow many paths would follow my path of inaction.

24. If ever my work had an end, these worlds would end in destruction, confusion would reign within all: this would be the death of all beings.

25. Even as the unwise work selfishly in the bondage of selfish works, let the wise man work unselfishly for the good of all the world.

26. Let not the wise disturb the mind of the unwise in their selfish work. Let him, working with devotion, show them the joy of good work.

27. All actions take place in time by the interweaving of the forces of Nature; but the man lost in selfish delusion thinks that he himself is the actor.

28. But the man who knows the relation between the forces of Nature and actions, sees how some forces of Nature work upon other forces of Nature, and becomes not their slave.

29. Those who are under the delusion of the forces of Nature bind themselves to the work of these forces. Let not the wise man who sees the All disturb the unwise who sees not the All.

30. Offer to me all thy works and rest thy mind on the Supreme. Be free from vain hopes and selfish thoughts, and with inner peace fight thou thy fight.

31. Those who ever follow my doctrine and who have faith, and have a good will, find through pure work their freedom.

32. But those who follow not my doctrine, and who have ill-will, are men blind to all wisdom, confused in mind: they are lost.

33. 'Even a wise man acts under the impulse of his nature: all beings follow nature. Of what use is restraint?'

34. Hate and lust for things of nature have their roots in man's lower nature. Let him not fall under their power: they are the two enemies in his path.

35. And do thy duty, even if it be humble, rather than another's, even if it be great. To die in one's duty is life: to live in another's is death.

ARJUNA

36. What power is it, Krishna, that drives man to act sinfully, even unwillingly, as if powerlessly?

KRISHNA

37. It is greedy desire and wrath, born of passion, the great evil, the sum of destruction: this is the enemy of the soul.

38. All is clouded by desire: as fire by smoke, as a mirror by dust, as an unborn babe by its covering.

39. Wisdom is clouded by desire, the everpresent enemy of the wise, desire in its innumerable forms, which like a fire cannot find satisfaction.

40. Desire has found a place in man's senses and mind and reason. Through these it blinds the soul, after having overclouded wisdom.

41. Set thou, therefore, thy senses in harmony, and then slay thou sinful desire, the destroyer of vision and wisdom.

42. They say that the power of the senses is great. But greater than

the senses is the mind. Greater than the mind is Buddhi, reason: and greater than reason is He – the Spirit in man and in all.

43. Know Him therefore who is above reason; and let his peace give thee peace. Be a warrior and kill desire, the powerful enemy of the soul.

Discipline of Visionary Knowledge

[4]

KRISHNA

1. I revealed this everlasting Yoga to Vivasvan, the sun, the father of light. He in turn revealed it to Manu, his son, the father of man. And Manu taught his son, king Ikshvaku, the saint.

2. Then it was taught from father to son in the line of kings who were saints; but in the revolutions of times immemorial this doctrine was forgotten by men.

3. Today I am revealing to thee this Yoga eternal, this secret supreme: because of thy love for me, and because I am thy friend.

ARJUNA

4. Thy birth was after the birth of the sun: the birth of the sun was before thine. What is the meaning of thy words: 'I revealed this Yoga to Vivasvan'?

KRISHNA

5. I have been born many times, Arjuna, and many times hast thou been born. But I remember my past lives, and thou hast forgotten thine.

6. Although I am unborn, everlasting, and I am the Lord of all, I

5-8. *Avatara*, the incarnation of divine energy in different times in history in different places, to uphold the Moral Law, when evil predominates. Consequently, the great spiritual leaders of the world can be regarded as *Avataras* or men-divine, who in their own times preached a way of life, none of them necessarily contradictory, but all leading to the same Supreme Self.

come to my realm of nature and through my wondrous power I am born.

7. When righteousness is weak and faints and unrighteousness exults in pride, then my Spirit arises on earth.

8. For the salvation of those who are good, for the destruction of evil in men, for the fulfilment of the kingdom of righteousness, I come to this world in the ages that pass.

9. He who knows my birth as God and who knows my sacrifice, when he leaves his mortal body, goes no more from death to death, for he in truth comes to me.

10. How many have come to me, trusting in me, filled with my Spirit, in peace from passions and fears and anger, made pure by the fire of wisdom!

11. In any way that men love me in that same way they find my love: for many are the paths of men, but they all in the end come to me.

12. Those who lust for earthly power offer sacrifice to the gods of the earth; for soon in this world for men success and power come from work.

13. The four orders of men arose from me, in justice to their natures and their works. Know that this work was mine, though I am beyond work, in Eternity.

14. In the bonds of works I am free, because in them I am free from desires. The man who can see this truth, in his work he finds his freedom.

15. This was known by men of old times, and thus in their work they found liberation. Do thou therefore thy work in life in the spirit that their work was done.

---

11. Also cf. 7.21 and 9.23. These verses of the *Gita* emphasize a great tolerance towards the many different approaches to the Absolute or God. Those who are vouchsafed the vision of Truth convey it symbolically through *Nama-rupa* (name-form) in a language with a meaning particular to a culture. These names and forms, consequently, are mere aids to help us to become conscious of our deepest self and through it the Universal Self. The *Gita* does not speak of this or that religion but of the impulse which is expressed in all forms and names, that is the desire to find the Absolute and understand our relation to That. In other words, the same God is worshipped by all under different *Nama-rupa*.

16. What is work? What is beyond work? Even some seers see this not aright. I will teach thee the truth of pure work, and this truth shall make thee free.

17. Know therefore what is work, and also know what is wrong work. And know also of a work that is silence: mysterious is the path of work.

18. The man who in his work finds silence, and who sees that silence is work, this man in truth sees the Light and in all his works find peace.

19. He whose undertakings are free from anxious desire and fanciful thought, whose work is made pure in the fire of wisdom: he is called wise by those who see.

20. In whatever work he does such a man in truth has peace: he expects nothing, he relies on nothing, and ever has fullness of joy.

21. He has no vain hopes, he is the master of his soul, he surrenders all he has, only his body works: he is free from sin.

22. He is glad with whatever God gives him, and he has risen beyond the two contraries here below; he is without jealousy, and in success or in failure he is one: his works bind him not.

23. He has attained liberation: he is free from all bonds, his mind has found peace in wisdom, and his work is a holy sacrifice. The work of such a man is pure.

24. Who in all his work sees God, he in truth goes unto God: God is his worship, God is his offering, offered by God in the fire of God.

25. There are Yogis whose sacrifice is an offering to the gods; but others offer as a sacrifice their own soul in the fire of God.

26. In the fire of an inner harmony some surrender their senses in darkness; and in the fire of the senses some surrender their outer light.

27. Others sacrifice their breath of life and also the powers of life in the fire of an inner union lighted by a flash of vision.

28. And others, faithful to austere vows, offer their wealth as a sacrifice, or their penance, or their practice of Yoga, or their sacred studies, or their knowledge.

29. Some offer their out-flowing breath into the breath that flows in;

16–18. Cf. T. S. Eliot, *The Four Quartets: The Dry Salvages*.

and the in-flowing breath into the breath that flows out: they aim at Pranayama, breath-harmony, and the flow of their breath is in peace.

30. Others, through practice of abstinence, offer their life into Life. All those know what is sacrifice, and through sacrifice purify their sins.

31. Neither this world nor the world to come is for him who does not sacrifice; and those who enjoy what remains of the sacrifice go unto Brahman.

32. Thus in many ways men sacrifice, and in many ways they go to Brahman. Know that all sacrifice is holy work, and knowing this thou shalt be free.

33. But greater than any earthly sacrifice is the sacrifice of sacred wisdom. For wisdom is in truth the end of all holy work.

34. Those who themselves have seen the Truth can be thy teachers of wisdom. Ask from them, bow unto them, be thou unto them a servant.

35. When wisdom is thine, Arjuna, never more shalt thou be in confusion; for thou shalt see all things in thy heart, and thou shalt see thy heart in me.

36. And even if thou wert the greatest of sinners, with the help of the bark of wisdom thou shalt cross the sea of evil.

37. Even as a burning fire burns all fuel into ashes, the fire of eternal wisdom burns into ashes all works.

38. Because there is nothing like wisdom which can make us pure on this earth. The man who lives in self-harmony finds this truth in his soul.

39. He who has faith has wisdom, who lives in self-harmony, whose faith is his life; and he who finds wisdom, soon finds the peace supreme.

40. But he who has no faith and no wisdom, and whose soul is in doubt, is lost. For neither this world, nor the world to come, nor joy is ever for the man who doubts.

41. He who makes pure his works by Yoga, who watches over his soul, and who by wisdom destroys his doubts, is free from the bondage of selfish work.

42. Kill therefore with the sword of wisdom the doubt born of

ignorance that lies in thy heart. Be one in self-harmony, in Yoga, and arise, great warrior, arise.

Discipline of Sovereign Mystery

[9]

KRISHNA

1. I will tell thee a supreme mystery, because thy soul has faith. It is vision and wisdom and when known thou shalt be free from sin.
2. It is the supreme mystery and wisdom and the purification supreme. Seen in a wonder of vision, it is a path of righteousness very easy to follow, leading to the highest End.
3. But those who have no faith in this Truth, come not unto me: they return to the cycles of life in death.
4. All this visible universe comes from my invisible Being. All beings have their rest in me, but I have not my rest in them.
5. And in truth they rest not in me: consider my sacred mystery. I am the source of all beings, I support them all, but I rest not in them.
6. Even as the mighty winds rest in the vastness of the ethereal space, all beings have their rest in me. Know thou this truth.
7. At the end of the night of time all things return to my nature; and when the new day of time begins I bring them again into light.
8. Thus through my nature I bring forth all creation, and this rolls round in the circles of time.
9. But I am not bound by this vast work of creation. I am and I watch the drama of works.
10. I watch and in its work of creation nature brings forth all that moves and moves not: and thus the revolutions of the world go round.
11. But the fools of the world know not me when they see me in my

---

7. *Night of time: Pralaya*, periods of cosmic dissolution, alternating with periods of creation.

own human body. They know not my Spirit supreme, the infinite God of this all.

12. Their hope is in vain, their works are in vain, their learning is vain, their thoughts are vain. They fall down to the nature of demons, towards the darkness of delusion of hell.

13. But there are some great souls who know me: their refuge is my own divine nature. They love me with a oneness of love: they know that I am the source of all.

14. They praise me with devotion, they praise me for ever and ever. Their vows are strong; their harmony is ever one; and they worship me with their love.

15. Others worship me, and work for me, with the sacrifice of spiritual vision. They worship me as One and as many, because they see that all is in me.

16. For I am the sacrifice and the offering, the sacred gift and the sacred plant. I am the holy words, the holy food, the holy fire, and the offering that is made in the fire.

17. I am the Father of this universe, and even the Source of the Father. I am the Mother of this universe, and the Creator of all. I am the Highest to be known, the Path of purification, the holy Om, the Three Vedas.

18. I am the Way, and the Master who watches in silence; thy friend and thy shelter and thy abode of peace. I am the beginning and the middle and the end of all things: their seed of Eternity, their Treasure supreme.

19. The heat of the sun comes from me, and I send and withhold the rain. I am life immortal and death; I am what is and I am what is not.

20. There are men who know the Three Vedas, who drink the Soma, who are pure from sin. They worship and pray for heaven. They

---

13-15. The idea is apparently that enlightened worshippers of Vasudeva assume at least the same physical refinement as the gods (by predominance of the mood of *Sattva*), and at the end of their present lives most of them rise at least to the paradise of the gods, while the most exalted of them are at once united with Vasudeva himself. Those of them that rise to paradise never lapse, but advance in successive births until they also reach Vasudeva (L. D. Barnett).

reach indeed the heaven of Indra, the king of the gods, and there
they enjoy royal pleasures.

21. They enjoy that vast world of heaven, but the reward of their
work comes to an end: they return to the world of death. They
follow the words of the Three Vedas, they lust for pleasures that
pass away: in truth they attain pleasures that pass away.

22. But to those who adore me with a pure oneness of soul, to those
who are ever in harmony, I increase what they have and I give
them what they have not.

23. Even those who in faith worship other gods, because of their love
they worship me, although not in the right way.

24. For I accept every sacrifice, and I am their Lord supreme. But
they know not my pure Being, and because of this they fall.

25. For those who worship the gods go to the gods, and those who
worship the fathers go to the fathers. Those who worship the
lower spirits go to the lower spirits; but those who worship me
come unto me.

26. He who offers to me with devotion only a leaf, or a flower, or a
fruit, or even a little water, this I accept from that yearning soul,
because with a pure heart it was offered with love.

27. Whatever you do, or eat, or give, or offer in adoration, let it be an
offering to me; and whatever you suffer, suffer it for me.

28. Thus thou shalt be free from the bonds of Karma which yield
fruits that are evil and good; and with thy soul one in renunciation
thou shalt be free and come to me.

29. I am the same to all beings, and my love is ever the same; but
those who worship me with devotion, they are in me and I am in
them.

30. For even if the greatest sinner worships me with all his soul, he
must be considered righteous, because of his righteous will.

31. And he shall soon become pure and reach everlasting peace. For
this is my word of promise, that he who loves me shall not perish.

32. For all those who come to me for shelter, however weak or

23. Plurality of spiritualities. Cf. 4.11 and 7.21.
29. God has no enemies, or there is no Absolute Evil.

humble or sinful they may be – women or Vaisyas or Sudras – they all reach the Path supreme.

33. How much more the holy Brahmins and the royal saints who love me! Having come to this world of sorrow, which is transient, love thou me.

34. Give me thy mind and give me thy heart, give me thy offerings, and thy adoration; and thus with thy soul in harmony, and making me thy goal supreme, thou shalt in truth come to me.

Discipline of Supernal Manifestations

[10]

KRISHNA

1. Hear again, mighty Arjuna, hear the glory of my Word again. I speak for thy true good, because thy heart finds joy in me.

2. The hosts of the gods know not my birth, nor the great seers on earth, for all the gods come from me, and all the great seers, all.

3. He who knows I am beginningless, unborn, the Lord of all the worlds, this mortal is free from delusion, and from all evils he is free.

4. Intelligence, spiritual vision, victory over delusion, patient

5. forgiveness, truth, self-harmony, peacefulness, joys and sorrows, to be and not to be, fear and freedom from fear, harmlessness and non-violence, an ever-quietness, satisfaction, simple austerity, generosity, honour and dishonour; these are the conditions of mortals and they all arise from me.

6. The seven seers of times immemorial, and the four founders of the human race, being in me, came from my mind; and from them came this world of men.

7. He who knows my glory and power, he has the oneness of un-wavering harmony. This is my truth.

8. I am the One source of all: the evolution of all comes from me. The wise think this and they worship me in adoration of love.

9. Their thoughts are on me, their life is in me, and they give light

to each other. For ever they speak of my glory; and they find peace and joy.

10. To those who are ever in harmony, and who worship me with their love, I give the Yoga of vision and with this they come to me.

11. In my mercy I dwell in their hearts and I dispel their darkness of ignorance by the light of the lamp of wisdom.

ARJUNA

12. Supreme Brahman, Light supreme, and supreme purification, Spirit divine eternal, unborn God from the beginning, omnipresent Lord of all.

13. Thus all the seers praised thee: the seer divine Narada; Asita, Devala and Vyasa. And this is now thy revelation.

14. I have faith in all thy words, because these words are words of truth, and neither the gods in heaven nor the demons in hell can grasp thy infinite vastness.

15. Only thy Spirit knows thy Spirit: only thou knowest thyself. Source of Being in all beings, God of gods, ruler of all.

16. Tell me in thy mercy of thy divine glory wherein thou art ever, and all the worlds are.

17. For ever in meditation, how shall I ever know thee? And in what manifestations shall I think of thee, my Lord?

18. Speak to me again in full of thy power and of thy glory, for I am never tired, never, of hearing thy words of life.

KRISHNA

19. Listen and I shall reveal to thee some manifestations of my divine glory. Only the greatest, Arjuna, for there is no end to my infinite greatness.

20. I am the soul, prince victorious, which dwells in the heart of all things. I am the beginning, the middle, and the end of all that lives.

21. Among the sons of light I am Vishnu, and of luminaries the radiant sun. I am the lord of the winds and storms, and of the lights in the night I am the moon.

22. Of the Vedas I am the Veda of songs, and I am Indra, the chief of the gods. Above man's senses I am the mind, and in all living beings I am the light of consciousness.

23. Among the terrible powers I am the god of destruction; and among monsters Vittesa, the lord of wealth. Of radiant spirits I am fire; and among high mountains the mountain of the gods.

24. Of priests I am the divine priest Brihaspati, and among warriors Skanda, the god of war. Of lakes I am the vast ocean.

25. Among great seers I am Bhrigu; and of words I am Om, the Word of Eternity. Of prayers I am the prayer of silence; and of things that move not I am the Himalayas.

26. Of trees I am the tree of life, and of heavenly seers Narada. Among celestial musicians, Chitra-ratha; and among seers on earth, Kapila.

27. Of horses I am the horse of Indra, and of elephants his elephant Airavata. Among men I am king of men.

28. Of weapons I am the thunderbolt, and of cows the cow of wonder. Among creators I am the creator of love; and among serpents the serpent of Eternity.

29. Among the snakes of mystery I am Ananta, and of those born in the waters I am Varuna, their lord. Of the spirits of the fathers I am Aryaman, and of rulers Yama, the ruler of death.

30. Of demons I am Prahlada their prince, and of all things that measure I am time. Of beasts I am the king of beasts, and of birds Vainateya who carries a god.

31. Among things of purification I am the wind, and among warriors I am Rama, the hero supreme. Of fishes in the sea I am Makara the wonderful, and among all rivers the holy Ganges.

32. I am the beginning and the middle and the end of all that is. Of all knowledge I am the knowledge of the Soul. Of the many paths of reason I am the one that leads to Truth.

33. Of sounds I am the first sound, A; of compounds I am coordination. I am time, never-ending time. I am the Creator who sees all.

34. I am death that carries off all things, and I am the source of things to come. Of feminine nouns I am Fame and Prosperity; Speech, Memory and Intelligence; Constancy and patient Forgiveness.

35. I am the Brihat songs of all songs in the Vedas. I am the Gayatri

of all measures in verse. Of months I am the first of the year, and of the seasons the season of flowers.

36. I am the cleverness in the gambler's dice. I am the beauty of all things beautiful. I am victory and the struggle for victory. I am the goodness of those who are good.

37. Of the children of Vrishni I am Krishna; and of the sons of Pandu I am Arjuna. Among seers in silence I am Vyasa; and among poets the poet Usana.

38. I am the sceptre of the rulers of men; and I am the wise policy of those who seek victory. I am the silence of hidden mysteries; and I am the knowledge of those who know.

39. And know, Arjuna, that I am the seed of all things that are; and that no being that moves or moves not can ever be without me.

40. There is no end of my divine greatness, Arjuna. What I have spoken here to thee shows only a small part of my Infinity.

41. Know thou that whatever is beautiful and good, whatever has glory and power is only a portion of my own radiance.

42. But of what help is it to thee to know this diversity? Know that with one single fraction of my Being I pervade and support the Universe, and know that I Am.

Discipline of the Vision of the Cosmic Form

[11]

ARJUNA

1. In thy mercy thou hast told me the secret supreme of thy Spirit, and thy words have dispelled my delusion.

2. I have heard in full from thee of the coming and going of beings, and also of thy infinite greatness.

---

41. Theory of aesthetics.

3. I have heard thy words of truth, but my soul is yearning to see: to see thy form as God of this all.

4. If thou thinkest, O my Lord, that it can be seen by me, show me, O God of Yoga, the glory of thine own Supreme Being.

KRISHNA

5. By hundreds and then by thousands, behold, Arjuna, my manifold celestial forms of innumerable shapes and colours.

6. Behold the gods of the sun, and those of fire and light; the gods of storm and lightning, and the two luminous charioteers of heaven. Behold, descendant of Bharata, marvels never seen before.

7. See now the whole universe with all things that move and move not, and whatever thy soul may yearn to see. See it all as One in me.

8. But thou never canst see me with these thy mortal eyes: I will give thee divine sight. Behold my wonder and glory.

SANJAYA

9. When Krishna, the God of Yoga, had thus spoken, O king, he appeared then to Arjuna in his supreme divine form.

10. And Arjuna saw in that form countless visions of wonder: eyes from innumerable faces, numerous celestial ornaments, numberless heavenly weapons;

11. Celestial garlands and vestures, forms anointed with heavenly perfumes. The Infinite Divinity was facing all sides, all marvels in him containing.

12. If the light of a thousand suns suddenly arose in the sky, that splendour might be compared to the radiance of the Supreme Spirit.

---

3. It is one thing to know that the Eternal Spirit dwells in all things and another to have the vision of it. . . . The vision is not a myth or a legend but a spiritual experience. Cf. the transfiguration of Jesus (Mark 9. 2–8); Dante's vision (*Paradise*, XXXIII).

8–9. The vision is not a mental construction but the disclosure of a truth from beyond the finite mind. The spontaneity and directness of the experience are brought out here. Cf. the Vision of Ezekiel; Exodus 33.18; Revelation 4; *Saddharmapundarika i*; Isaiah 60.1–5.

13. And Arjuna saw in that radiance the whole universe in its variety, standing in a vast unity in the body of the God of gods.

14. Trembling with awe and wonder, Arjuna bowed his head, and joining his hands in adoration he thus spoke to his God.

ARJUNA

15. I see in thee all the gods, O my God; and the infinity of the beings of thy creation. I see god Brahma on his throne of lotus, and all the seers and serpents of light.

16. All around I behold thy Infinity: the power of thy innumerable arms, the visions from thy innumerable eyes, the words from thy innumerable mouths, and the fire of life of thy innumerable bodies. Nowhere I see a beginning or middle or end of thee, O God of all, Form Infinite!

17. I see the splendour of an infinite beauty which illumines the whole universe. It is thee! with thy crown and sceptre and circle. How difficult thou art to see! But I see thee: as fire, as the sun, blinding, incomprehensible.

18. Thou art the Imperishable, the highest End of knowledge, the support of this vast universe. Thou, the everlasting ruler of the law of righteousness, the Spirit who is and who was at the beginning.

19. I see thee without beginning, middle, or end; I behold thy infinite power, the power of thy innumerable arms. I see thine eyes as the sun and the moon. And I see thy face as a sacred fire that gives light and life to the whole universe in the splendour of a vast offering.

20. Heaven and earth and all the infinite spaces are filled with thy Spirit; and before the wonder of thy fearful majesty the three worlds tremble.

21. The hosts of the gods come to thee and, joining palms in awe and wonder, they praise and adore. Sages and saints come to thee, and praise thee with songs of glory.

22. The Rudras of destruction, the Vasus of fire, the Sadhyas of

---

15-31. When the first atom bomb was tested in the Nevada desert, it seems Dr Robert Oppenheimer recited these verses.

prayers, the Adityas of the sun; the lesser gods Visve-Devas, the two Asvins charioteers of heaven, the Maruts of winds and storms, the Ushmapas spirits of ancestors; the celestial choirs of Gandharvas, the Yakshas keepers of wealth, the demons of hell and the Siddhas who on earth reached perfection: they all behold thee with awe and wonder.

23. But the worlds also behold thy fearful mighty form, with many mouths and eyes, with many bellies, thighs and feet, frightening with terrible teeth: they tremble in fear, and I also tremble.

24. When I see thy vast form, reaching the sky, burning with many colours, with wide open mouths, with vast flaming eyes, my heart shakes in terror: my power is gone and gone is my peace, O Vishnu!

25. Like the fire at the end of Time which burns all in the last day, I see thy vast mouths and thy terrible teeth. Where am I? Where is my shelter? Have mercy on me, God of gods, Refuge Supreme of the world!

26. The sons of Dhrita-rashtra, all of them, with other princes of this

27. earth, and Bhishma and Drona and great Karna, and also the greatest warriors of our host, all enter rushing into thy mouths, terror-inspiring with their fearful fangs. Some are caught between them, and their heads crushed into powder.

28. As roaring torrents of water rush forward into the ocean, so do these heroes of our mortal world rush into thy flaming mouths.

29. And as moths swiftly rushing enter a burning flame and die, so all these men rush to thy fire, rush fast to their own destruction.

30. The flames of thy mouths devour all the worlds. Thy glory fills the whole universe. But how terrible thy splendours burn!

31. Reveal thyself to me! Who art thou in this form of terror? I adore thee, O god supreme: be gracious unto me. I yearn to know thee, who are from the beginning: for I understand not thy mysterious works.

KRISHNA

32 I am all-powerful Time which destroys all things, and I have come here to slay these men. Even if thou dost not fight, all the warriors facing thee shall die.

33. Arise therefore! Win thy glory, conquer thine enemies, and enjoy thy kingdom. Through the fate of their Karma I have doomed them to die: be thou merely the means of my work.

34. Drona, Bhishma, Jayad-ratha and Karna, and other heroic warriors of this great war have already been slain by me: tremble not, fight and slay them. Thou shalt conquer thine enemies in battle.

SANJAYA

35. When Arjuna heard the words of Krishna he folded his hands trembling; and with a faltering voice, and bowing in adoration, he spoke.

ARJUNA

36. It is right, O God, that peoples sing thy praises, and that they are glad and rejoice in thee. All evil spirits fly away in fear; but the hosts of the saints bow down before thee.

37. How could they not bow down in love and adoration, before thee God of gods, Spirit Supreme? Thou creator of Brahma, the god of creation, thou infinite, eternal, refuge of the world! Thou who art all that is, and all that is not, and all that is Beyond.

38. Thou God from the beginning, God in man since man was. Thou Treasure supreme of this vast universe. Thou the One to be known and the Knower, the final resting place. Thou infinite Presence in whom all things are.

39. God of the winds and the waters, of fire and death! Lord of the solitary moon, the Creator, the Ancestor of all! Adoration unto thee, a thousand adorations; and again and again unto thee adoration.

40. Adoration unto thee who art before me and behind me: adoration unto thee who art on all sides, God of all. All-powerful God of immeasurable might. Thou art the consummation of all: thou art all.

41. If in careless presumption, or even in friendliness, I said 'Krishna! Son of Yadu! My friend!', this I did unconscious of thy greatness.

42. And if in irreverence I was disrespectful – when alone or with others – and made a jest of thee at games, or resting, or at a feast, forgive me in thy mercy, O thou Immeasurable!

43. Father of all. Master supreme. Power supreme in all the worlds. Who is like thee? Who is beyond thee?

44. I bow before thee, I prostrate in adoration; and I beg thy grace, O glorious Lord! As a father to his son, as a friend to his friend, as a lover to his beloved, be gracious unto me, O God.

45. In a vision I have seen what no man has seen before: I rejoice in exultation, and yet my heart trembles with fear. Have mercy upon me, Lord of gods, Refuge of the whole universe: show me again thine own human form.

46. I yearn to see thee again with thy crown and sceptre and circle. Show thyself to me again in thine own four-armed form, thou of arms infinite, Infinite Form.

KRISHNA

47. By my grace and my wondrous power I have shown to thee, Arjuna, this form supreme made of light, which is the Infinite, the All: mine own form from the beginning, never seen by man before.

48. Neither Vedas, nor sacrifices, not studies, nor benefactions, nor rituals, nor fearful austerities can give the vision of my Form Supreme. Thou alone hast seen this Form, thou the greatest of the Kurus.

49. Thou hast seen the tremendous form of my greatness, but fear not, and be not bewildered. Free from fear and with a glad heart see my friendly form again.

SANJAYA

50. Thus spoke Vasudeva to Arjuna, and revealed himself in his human form. The God of all gave peace to his fears and showed himself in his peaceful beauty.

ARJUNA

51. When I see thy gentle human face, Krishna, I return to my own nature, and my heart has peace.

KRISHNA

52. Thou hast seen now face to face my form divine so hard to see:
for even the gods in heaven ever long to see what thou hast seen.

53. Not by the Vedas, or an austere life, or gifts to the poor, or ritual
offerings can I be seen as thou hast seen me.

54. Only by love can men see me, and know me, and come unto me.

55. He who works for me, who loves me, whose End Supreme I am,
free from attachment to all things, and with love for all creation,
he in truth comes unto me.

Discipline of Threefold Faith

[17]

ARJUNA

1. Those who forsake the law of the Scriptures and yet offer sacrifice
full of faith – What is their condition, Krishna? Is it of Sattva,
Rajas, or Tamas – of light, of fire, or of darkness?

KRISHNA

2. The faith of men, born of their nature, is of three kinds: of light,
of fire and of darkness. Hear now of these.

3. The faith of a man follows his nature, Arjuna. Man is made of
faith: as his faith is so he is.

4. Men of light worship the gods of Light; men of fire worship the
gods of power and wealth; men of darkness worship ghosts and
spirits of night.

---

55. The celestial vision is not the final goal of man's search for Truth. The
fleeting glimpse must crystallize into a permanent experience and be trans-
muted into an abiding faith for future action in life. When once the reality of
the Supreme Self being the background for the never-ending procession of
finite things is realized, man should come to the point of acting without
attachments, as the mere instrument of the Supreme Self. In other words a
morally conscious individual who sees the Supreme in everything, and
everything in the Supreme, does not act selfishly.

5. There are men selfish and false who moved by their lusts and
6. passions perform terrible austerities not ordained by sacred books: fools who torture the powers of life in their bodies and me who dwells in them. Know that their mind is darkness.

7. Hear now of three kinds of food, the three kinds of sacrifice, the three kinds of harmony, and the three kinds of gifts.

8. Men who are pure like food which is pure: which gives health, mental power, strength and long life; which has taste, is soothing and nourishing, and which makes glad the heart of man.

9. Men of Rajas like food of Rajas: acid and sharp, and salty and dry, and which brings heaviness and sickness and pain.

10. Men of darkness eat food which is stale and tasteless, which is rotten and left overnight, impure, unfit for holy offerings.

11. A sacrifice is pure when it is an offering of adoration in harmony with the holy law, with no expectation of a reward, and with the heart saying 'it is my duty'.

12. But a sacrifice that is done for the sake of a reward, or for the sake of vainglory is an impure sacrifice of Rajas.

13. And a sacrifice done against the holy law, without faith, and sacred words, and the gifts of food, and the due offering, is a sacrifice of darkness.

14. Reverence for the gods of Light, for the twice-born, for the teachers of the Spirit and for the wise; and also purity, righteousness, chastity and non-violence: this is the harmony of the body.

15. Words which give peace, words which are good and beautiful and true, and also the reading of sacred books: this is the harmony of words.

16. Quietness of mind, silence, self-harmony, loving-kindness, and a pure heart: this is the harmony of the mind.

17. This threefold harmony is called pure when it is practised with supreme faith with no desire for a reward and with oneness of soul.

18. But false austerity, for the sake of reputation, honour and reverence, is impure: it belongs to Rajas and is unstable and uncertain.

19. When self-control is self-torture, due to dullness of the mind, or when it aims at hurting another, then self-control is of darkness.

20. A gift is pure when it is given from the heart to the right person at the right time and at the right place, and when we expect nothing in return.

21. But when it is given expecting something in return, or for the sake of a future reward, or when it is given unwillingly, the gift is of Rajas, impure.

22. And a gift given to the wrong person, at the wrong time and the wrong place, or a gift which comes not from the heart, and is given with proud contempt, is a gift of darkness.

23. OM, TAT, SAT. Each one of these three words is one word from Brahman, from whom came in the beginning the Brahmins, the Vedas and the Sacrifice.

24. Therefore with the word OM the lovers of Brahman begin all work of sacrifice, gift or self-harmony, done according to the Scriptures.

25. And with the word TAT, and with renunciation of all reward, this same work of sacrifice, gift or self-harmony is being done by seekers of Infinite Liberty.

26. SAT is what is good and what is true: when therefore a work is well done the end of that work is SAT.

27. Constant faithfulness in sacrifice, gift, or self-harmony is SAT; and also all work consecrated to Brahman.

28. But work done without faith is ASAT, is nothing: sacrifice, gift, or self-harmony done without faith are nothing, both in this world and in the world to come.

Discipline of Deliverance

[18]

ARJUNA

1. Speak to me, Krishna, of the essence of renunciation, and of the essence of surrender.

KRISHNA

2. The renunciation of selfish works is called renunciation; but the surrender of the reward of all work is called surrender.

3. Some say that there should be renunciation of action – since action disturbs contemplation; but others say that works of sacrifice, gift and self-harmony should not be renounced.

4. Hear my truth about the surrender of works, Arjuna. Surrender, O best of men, is of three kinds.

5. Works of sacrifice, gift, and self-harmony should not be abandoned, but should indeed be performed; for these are works of purification.

6. But even these works, Arjuna, should be done in the freedom of a pure offering, and without expectation of a reward. This is my final word.

7. It is not right to leave undone the holy work which ought to be done. Such a surrender of action would be a delusion of darkness.

8. And he who abandons his duty because he has fear of pain, his surrender is of Rajas, impure, and in truth he has no reward.

9. But he who does holy work, Arjuna, because it ought to be done, and surrenders selfishness and thought of reward, his work is pure, and is peace.

10. This man sees and has no doubts: he surrenders, he is pure and has peace. Work, pleasant or painful, is for him joy.

11. For there is no man on earth who can fully renounce living work, but he who renounces the reward of his work is in truth a man of renunciation.

12. When work is done for a reward, the work brings pleasure, or pain, or both, in its time; but when a man does work in Eternity, then Eternity is his reward.

13. Know now from me, Arjuna, the five causes of all actions as given in the Sankhya wisdom, wherein is found the end of all works.

14. The body, the lower 'I am', the means of perception, the means of action, and Fate. These are the five.

15. Whatever a man does, good or bad, in thought, word or deed, has these five sources of action.

16. If one thinks that his infinite Spirit does the finite work which nature does, he is a man of clouded vision and he does not see the truth.

17. He who is free from the chains of selfishness, and whose mind is

free from any ill-will, even if he kills all these warriors he kills them not and he is free.

18. In the idea of a work there is the knower, the knowing and the known. When the idea is work there is the doer, the doing and the thing done.

19. The knowing, the doer and the thing done are said in the science of the 'Gunas' to be of three kinds, according to their qualities. Hear of these three.

20. When one sees Eternity in things that pass away and Infinity in finite things, then one has pure knowledge.

21. But if one merely sees the diversity of things, with their divisions and limitations, then one has impure knowledge.

22. And if one selfishly sees a thing as if it were everything, independent of the ONE and the many, then one is in the darkness of ignorance.

23. When work is done as sacred work, unselfishly, with a peaceful mind, without lust or hate, with no desire for reward, then the work is pure.

24. But when work is done with selfish desire, or feeling it is an effort, or thinking it is a sacrifice, then the work is impure.

25. And that work which is done with a confused mind, without considering what may follow, or one's own powers, or the harm done to others, or one's own loss, is work of darkness.

26. A man free from the chains of selfish attachments, free from his lower 'I am', who has determination and perseverance, and whose inner peace is beyond victory or defeat – such a man has pure Sattva.

27. But a man who is a slave of his passions, who works for selfish ends, who is greedy, violent and impure, and who is moved by pleasure and pain, is a man of impure Rajas.

28. And a man without self-harmony, vulgar, arrogant and deceitful; malicious, indolent and despondent, and also procrastinating, is a man of the darkness of Tamas.

29. Hear now fully and in detail the threefold division of wisdom and steadiness, according to the three Gunas.

30. There is a wisdom which knows when to go and when to return, what is to be done and what is not to be done, what is fear and

what is courage, what is bondage and what is liberation – that is pure wisdom.

31. Impure wisdom has no clear vision of what is right and what is wrong, what should be done and what should not be done.

32. And there is a wisdom obscured in darkness when wrong is thought to be right, and when things are thought to be that which they are not.

33. When in the Yoga of holy contemplation the movements of the mind and of the breath of life are in a harmony of peace, there is steadiness, and that steadiness is pure.

34. But that steadiness which, with a desire for rewards, attaches itself to wealth, pleasure, and even religious ritual, is a steadiness of passion, impure.

35. And that steadiness whereby a fool does not surrender laziness, fear, self-pity, depression and lust, is indeed a steadiness of darkness.

36. Hear now, great Arjuna, of the three kinds of pleasure. There is the pleasure of following that right path which leads to the end of all pain.

37. What seems at first a cup of sorrow is found in the end immortal wine. That pleasure is pure: it is the joy which arises from a clear vision of the Spirit.

38. But the pleasure which comes from the craving of the senses with the objects of their desire, which seems at first a drink of sweetness but is found in the end a cup of poison, is the pleasure of passion, impure.

39. And that pleasure which both in the beginning and in the end is only a delusion of the soul, which comes from the dullness of sleep, laziness or carelessness, is the pleasure of darkness.

40. There is nothing on earth or in heaven which is free from these three powers of Nature.

41. The works of Brahmins, Kshatriyas, Vaisyas and Sudras are different, in harmony with the three powers of their born nature.

---

41. There are four broad types of nature and answering to them are four kinds of social living. The four classes are not determined by birth or colour but by psychological characteristics which fit the people for definite functions

42. The works of a Brahmin are peace; self-harmony, austerity and purity; loving-forgiveness and righteousness; vision and wisdom and faith.

43. These are the works of a Kshatriya: a heroic mind, inner fire, constancy, resourcefulness, courage in battle, generosity and noble leadership.

44. Trade, agriculture and the rearing of cattle is the work of a Vaisya. And the work of the Sudra is service.

45. They all attain perfection when they find joy in their work. Hear how a man attains perfection and finds joy in his work.

46. A man attains perfection when his work is worship of God, from whom all things come and who is in all.

47. Greater is thine own work, even if this be humble, than the work of another, even if this be great. When a man does the work God gives him, no sin can touch this man.

48. And a man should not abandon his work, even if he cannot achieve it in full perfection; because in all work there may be imperfection, even as in all fire there is smoke.

49. When a man has his reason in freedom from bondage, and his soul is in harmony, beyond desires, then renunciation leads him to a region supreme which is beyond earthly action.

50. Hear now how he then reaches Brahman, the highest vision of Light.

51. When the vision of reason is clear, and in steadiness the soul is in harmony; when the world of sound and other senses is gone, and the spirit has risen above passion and hate;

52. When a man dwells in the solitude of silence, and meditation and contemplation are ever with him; when too much food does not disturb his health, and his thoughts and words and body are in peace; when freedom from passion is his constant will;

---

in society. Cf. *Dhammapada*: 'Not by matted hair, nor by lineage, nor by birth is one a Brahmin. He is a Brahmin in whom there are truth and righteousness.' The *Gita* cannot be used to support the existing social order with its rigidity and confusion. The one Spirit of the universe has produced the multiplicity of selves, and the Divine is their essential nature. Each self can get its deliverance by expressing itself true to its nature.

53. And his selfishness and violence and pride are gone; when lust and anger and greediness are no more, and he is free from the thought 'this is mine'; then this man has risen on the mountain of the Highest: he is worthy to be one with Brahman, with God.

54. He is one with Brahman, with God, and beyond grief and desire his soul is in peace. His love is one for all creation, and he has supreme love for me.

55. By love he knows me in truth, who I am and what I am. And when he knows me in truth he enters into my Being.

56. In whatever work he does he can take refuge in me, and he attains then by my grace the imperishable home of Eternity.

57. Offer in thy heart all thy works to me, and see me as the End of thy love, take refuge in the Yoga of reason, and ever rest thy soul in me.

58. If thy soul finds rest in me, thou shalt overcome all dangers by my grace; but if thy thoughts are on thyself, and thou wilt not listen, thou shalt perish.

59. If thou wilt not fight thy battle of life because in selfishness thou art afraid of the battle, thy resolution is in vain: nature will compel thee.

60. Because thou art in the bondage of Karma, of the forces of thine own past life; and that which thou, in thy delusion, with a good will dost not want to do, unwillingly thou shalt have to do.

61. God dwells in the heart of all beings, Arjuna: thy God dwells in thy heart. And his power of wonder moves all things – puppets in a play of shadows – whirling them onwards on the stream of time.

62. Go to him for thy salvation with all thy soul, victorious man. By his grace thou shalt obtain the peace supreme, thy home of Eternity.

63. I have given thee words of vision and wisdom more secret than hidden mysteries. Ponder them in the silence of thy soul, and then in freedom do thy will.

64. Hear again my Word supreme, the deepest secret of silence. Because I love thee well, I will speak to thee words of salvation.

65. Give thy mind to me, and give me thy heart, and thy sacrifice, and thy adoration. This is my Word of promise: thou shalt in truth come to me, for thou art dear to me.

66. Leave all things behind, and come to me for thy salvation. I will make thee free from the bondage of sins. Fear no more.

67. These things must never be spoken to one who lacks self-discipline, or who has no love, or who does not want to hear or who argues against me.

68. But he who will teach this secret doctrine to those who have love for me, and who himself has supreme love, he in truth shall come unto me.

69. For there can be no man among men who does greater work for me, nor can there be a man on earth who is dearer to me than he is.

70. He who learns in contemplation the holy words of our discourse, the light of his vision is his adoration. This is my truth.

71. And he who only hears but has faith, and in his heart he has no doubts, he also attains liberation and the worlds of joy of righteous men.

72. Hast thou heard these words, Arjuna, in the silent communion of thy soul? Has the darkness of thy delusion been dispelled by thine inner Light?

ARJUNA

73. By thy grace I remember my Light, and now gone is my delusion. My doubts are no more, my faith is firm; and now I can say 'Thy will be done'.

SANJAYA

74. Thus I heard these words of glory between Arjuna and the God of all, and they fill my soul with awe and wonder.

75. By the grace of the poet Vyasa I heard these words of secret silence. I heard the mystery of Yoga, taught by Krishna the Master himself.

76. I remember, O king, I remember the words of holy wonder between Krishna and Arjuna, and again and again my soul feels joy.

---

73. To will what God wills is the secret of divine or spiritual life. Cf. Jesus: 'Father, all things are possible unto thee; take away this cup from me; nevertheless not what I will, but what thou wilt' (Mark 14.36); 'Thy will be done in earth, as it is in heaven' (Matthew 6.10).

77. And I remember, I ever remember, that vision of glory of the God of all, and again and again joy fills my soul.

78. Wherever is Krishna, the End of Yoga, wherever is Arjuna who masters the bow, there is beauty and victory, and joy and all righteousness. This is my faith.

I.8 VALMIKI
RAMAYANA
[THE EPIC OF RAMA]

(Sanskrit, *c.* 600–300 B.C.)

Valmiki's *Ramayana*, somewhat resembling Homer's *Odyssey* in regard to the kind of adventures it narrates and Vergil's *Aeneid* in its tone and pious intentions, is considered 'scriptural' within the Indian tradition in the same sense as the Hebrew epic has been regarded as 'sacred' within the Semitic spiritualities. Even though such works have deep religious significance, within their respective traditions, they can nevertheless be studied and read as literature.

Valmiki treats the story of Rama, mentioned in the Third Book of the *Mahabharata*, with epic grandeur in seven books, weaving into the work idealistic attitudes, domestic virtues, and Karma causality. The poet depicts ideal family relations wherein the son takes his father's word as his commandment; a wife, remaining faithful to her marriage vow, follows her husband from palace to forest, like a 'shadow to the substance'; the younger brothers, adhering to the tradition, instead of coveting the elder brother's throne, renounce their claims. Thus, the characters are continually forced to make moral choices in their actions. On another level, the poet demonstrates that the evil in society is brought not by any outside agency, but by human action motivated by excessive desire (as in the case of the maid Manthar), when an individual fails to distinguish between the right and the wrong choice of action. Consequently, deeds, be they sweet or be they bitter, like seeds growing into huge trees bring to fruition their own inevitable consequences.

The poem is also read as an allegory of Rama and Ravan, representing the forces of Light and Darkness, in which Light overcomes Darkness. In celebration of this victory, Indians observe annually the ten-day Festival of Lights, called Dasara.

With the supreme confidence of a master poet,* Valmiki states in the second chapter of Book I.: 'As long as the mountains and rivers shall continue on the surface of the earth, so long shall the story of *Ramayana* be current in the world.'

The selections included here are pp. 1–5, 9–11, 14–26, 29–37, 46–63 from the condensed translation by Romesh C. Dutt, *The Ramayana and the Mahabharata*, New York: E. P. Dutton, 1910; London: J. M. Dent, 1910 (Everyman's Library No. 403). (First published in Temple Classics, 1899.)

I.8   VALMIKI
RAMAYANA

[THE EPIC OF RAMA, PRINCE OF INDIA]

Book I
Sita-Swayamvara (The Bridal of Sita)

The epic relates to the ancient traditions of two powerful races, the Kosalas and the Videhas, who lived in Northern India between the twelfth and tenth centuries before Christ. The names Kosala and Videha in the singular number indicate the kingdoms – Oudh and North Behar – and in the plural number they mean the ancient races which inhabited those two countries.

According to the Epic, Dasa-ratha king of the Kosalas had four sons, the eldest of whom was Rama the hero of the poem. And Janak king of the Videhas had a daughter named Sita, who was miraculously born of a field furrow, and who is the heroine of the Epic.

Janak ordained a severe test for the hand of his daughter, and many a prince and warrior came and went away disappointed. Rama suc-

---

*Cf. Shakespeare, Sonnet XVIII:
         So long as men can breathe, or eyes can see,
         So long lives this, and this gives life to thee.

ceeded, and won Sita. The story of Rama's winning his bride, and of
the marriage of his three brothers with the sister and cousins of Sita,
forms the subject of this Book.

I

AYODHYA, THE RIGHTEOUS CITY

Rich in royal worth and valour, rich in holy Vedic lore,
Dasa-ratha ruled his empire in the happy days of yore.

Loved of men in fair Ayodhya, sprung of ancient Solar Race,
Royal *rishi* in his duty, saintly *rishi* in his grace.

Great as Indra in his prowess, bounteous as Kuvera kind,
Dauntless deeds subdued his foemen, lofty faith subdued his mind!

Like the ancient monarch Manu, father of the human race,
Dasa-ratha ruled his people with a father's loving grace.

Truth and Justice swayed each action and each baser motive quelled.
People's Love and Monarch's Duty every thought and deed impelled,

And his town like Indra's city – tower and dome and turret brave –
Rose in proud and peerless beauty on Sarayu's limpid wave!

Peaceful lived the righteous people, rich in wealth in merit high,
Envy dwelt not in their bosoms and their accents shaped no lie.

Fathers with their happy households owned their cattle, corn, and
 gold;
Galling penury and famine in Ayodhya had no hold.

Neighbours lived in mutual kindness, helpful with their ample wealth;
None who begged the wasted refuse, none who lived by fraud and
 stealth!

And they wore the gem and earring, wreath and fragrant sandal paste,
And their arms were decked with bracelets, and their necks with
 nishkas graced.

Cheat and braggart and deceiver lived not in the ancient town.
Proud despiser of the lowly wore not insults in their frown.

Poorer fed not on the richer, hireling friend upon the great,
None with low and lying accents did upon the proud man wait!

Men to plighted vows were faithful, faithful was each loving wife,
Impure thought and wandering fancy stained not holy wedded life.

Robed in gold and graceful garments, fair in form and fair in face,
Winsome were Ayodhya's daughters, rich in wit and woman's grace.

Twice-born men were free from passion, lust of gold and impure greed,
Faithful to their Rites and Scriptures, truthful in their word and deed.

Altars blazed in every mansion, from each home was bounty given,
Stooped no man to fulsome falsehood, questioned none the will of
    Heaven.

Kshatras bowed to holy Brahmans, Vaisyas to the Kshatras bowed,
Toiling Sudras lived by labour, of their honest duty proud.

To the Gods and to the Fathers, to each guest in virtue trained,
Rites were done with true devotion as by holy writ ordained.

Pure each caste in due observance, stainless was each ancient rite,
And the nation thrived and prospered by its old and matchless might,

And each man in truth abiding lived a long and peaceful life,
With his sons and with his grandsons, with his loved and honoured
    wife.

Thus was ruled the ancient city by her monarch true and bold,
As the earth was ruled by Manu in the misty days of old.

Troops who never turned in battle, fierce as fire and strong and brave,
Guarded well her lofty ramparts as the lions guard the cave.

Steeds like Indra's in their swiftness came from far Kamboja's land,
From Vanaya and Vahlika and from Sindhu's rock-bound strand,

Elephants of mighty stature from the Vindhya mountains came,
Or from deep and darksome forests round Himalay's peaks of fame,

Matchless in their mighty prowess, peerless in their wondrous speed,
Nobler than the noble tuskers sprung from high celestial breed.

Thus Ayodhya, 'virgin city' – faithful to her haughty name –
Ruled by righteous Dasa-ratha won a world-embracing fame.

Strong-barred gates and lofty arches, tower and dome and turret high
Decked the vast and peopled city fair as mansions of the sky.

Queens of proud and peerless beauty born of houses rich in fame,
Loved of royal Dasa-ratha to his happy mansion came,

Queen Kausalya blessed with virtue true and righteous Rama bore,
Queen Kaikeyi young and beauteous bore him Bharat rich in lore,

Queen Sumitra bore the bright twins, Lakshman and Satrughna bold,
Four brave princes served their father in the happy days of old!

II

MITHILA, AND THE BREAKING OF THE BOW

Janak monarch of Videha spake his message near and far, –
He shall win my peerless Sita who shall bend my bow of war, –

Suitors came from farthest regions, warlike princes known to fame,
Vainly strove to wield the weapon, left Videha in their shame.

Viswa-mitra royal *rishi*, Rama true and Lakshman bold,
Came to fair Mithila's city from Ayodhya famed of old,

Spake in pride the royal *rishi*: 'Monarch of Videha's throne,
Grant, the wondrous bow of Rudra be to princely Rama shown.'

Janak spake his royal mandate to his lords and warriors bold:
'Bring ye forth the bow of Rudra decked in garlands and in gold,'

And his peers and proud retainers, waiting on the monarch's call,
Brought the great and goodly weapon from the city's inner hall.

Stalwart men of ample stature pulled the mighty iron car
In which rested all-inviolate Janak's dreaded bow of war,

And where midst assembled monarchs sat Videha's godlike king,
With a mighty toil and effort did the eight-wheeled chariot bring.

'This the weapon of Videha,' proudly thus the peers begun,
'Be it shown to royal Rama, Dasa-ratha's righteous son.'

'This the bow,' then spake the monarch to the *rishi* famed of old,
To the true and righteous Rama and to Lakshman young and bold,

'This the weapon of my fathers prized by kings from age to age,
Mighty chiefs and sturdy warriors could not bend it, noble sage!

Gods before the bow of Rudra have in righteous terror quailed,
Rakshas fierce and stout *Asuras* have in futile effort failed,

Mortal man will struggle vainly Rudra's wondrous bow to bend,
Vainly strive to string the weapon and the shining dart to send.

Holy saint and royal *rishi*, here is Janak's ancient bow,
Shew it to Ayodhya's princes, speak to them my kingly vow!'

Viswa-mitra humbly listened to the words the monarch said,
To the brave and righteous Rama, Janak's mighty bow displayed,

Rama lifted high the cover of the pond'rous iron car,
Gazed with conscious pride and prowess on the mighty bow of war.

'Let me,' humbly spake the hero, 'on this bow my fingers place,
Let me lift and bend the weapon, help me with your loving grace.'

'Be it so,' the *rishi* answered, 'Be it so,' the monarch said,
Rama lifted high the weapon on his stalwart arms displayed.

Wond'ring gazed the kings assembled as the son of Raghu's race
Proudly raised the bow of Rudra with a warrior's stately grace,

Proudly strung the bow of Rudra which the kings had tried in vain,
Drew the cord with force resistless till the weapon snapped in twain!

Like the thunder's pealing accent rose the loud terrific clang,
And the firm earth shook and trembled and the hills in echoes rang,

And the chiefs and gathered monarchs fell and fainted in their fear,
And the men of many nations shook, the dreadful sound to hear!

Pale and white the startled monarchs slowly from their terror woke,
And with royal grace and greetings Janak to the *rishi* spoke:

'Now my ancient eyes have witnessed wond'rous deed by Rama done,
Deed surpassing thought or fancy wrought by Dasa-ratha's son,

And the proud and peerless princess, Sita glory of my house,
Sheds on me an added lustre as she weds a godlike spouse.

True shall be my plighted promise, Sita dearer than my life,
Won by worth and wond'rous valour shall be Rama's faithful wife!

Grant us leave, O royal *rishi*, grant us blessings kind and fair,
Envoys mounted on my chariot to Ayodhya shall repair,

They shall speak to Rama's father glorious feat by Rama done,
They shall speak to Dasa-ratha, Sita is by valour won,

They shall say the noble princes safely live within our walls,
They shall ask him by his presence to adorn our palace halls!'

Pleased at heart the sage assented, envoys by the monarch sent,
To Ayodhya's distant city with the royal message went.

VI

THE WEDDING

Sage Vasishtha skilled in duty placed Videha's honoured king,
Viswa-mitra, Sata-nanda, all within the sacred ring.

And he raised the holy altar as the ancient writs ordain,
Decked and graced with scented garlands grateful unto gods and men,

And he set the golden ladles, vases pierced by artists skilled,
Holy censers fresh and fragrant, cups with sacred honey filled,

Sanka bowls and shining salvers, *arghya* plates for honoured guest,
Parchèd rice arranged in dishes, corn unhusked that filled the rest,

And with careful hand Vasishtha grass around the altar flung,
Offered gift to lighted Agni and the sacred *mantra* sung!

Softly came the sweet-eyed Sita, – bridal blush upon her brow, –
Rama in his manly beauty came to take the sacred vow,

Janak placed his beauteous daughter facing Dasa-ratha's son,
Spake with father's fond emotion and the holy rite was done:

'This is Sita child of Janak, dearer unto him than life,
Henceforth sharer of thy virtue, be she, prince, thy faithful wife,

Of thy weal and woe partaker, be she thine in every land,
Cherish her in joy and sorrow, clasp her hand within thy hand,

As the shadow to the substance, to her lord is faithful wife,
And my Sita best of women follows thee in death or life!'

Tears bedew his ancient bosom, gods and men his wishes share,
And he sprinkles holy water on the blest and wedded pair.

Next he turned to Sita's sister, Urmila of beauty rare,
And to Lakshman young and valiant spake in accents soft and fair:

'Lakshman, dauntless in thy duty, loved of men and Gods above,
Take my dear devoted daughter, Urmila of stainless love,

Lakshman, fearless in thy virtue, take thy true and faithful wife,
Clasp her hand within thy fingers, be she thine in death or life!'

To his brother's child Mandavi, Janak turned with father's love,
Yielded her to righteous Bharat, prayed for blessings from above:

'Bharat, take the fair Mandavi, be she thine in death or life,
Clasp her hand within thy fingers as thy true and faithful wife!'

Last of all was Sruta-kriti, fair in form and fair in face,
And her gentle name was honoured for her acts of righteous grace,

'Take her by the hand, Satrughna, be she thine in death or life,
As the shadow to the substance, to her lord is faithful wife!'

Then the princes held the maidens, hand embraced in loving hand,
And Vasishtha spake the *mantra*, holiest priest in all the land,

And as ancient rite ordaineth, and as sacred laws require,
Stepped each bride and princely bridegroom round the altar's lighted
  fire,

Round Videha's ancient monarch, round the holy *rishis* all,
Lightly stepped the gentle maidens, proudly stepped the princes tall!

And a rain of flowers descended from the sky serene and fair,
And a soft celestial music filled the fresh and fragrant air.

Bright *Gandharvas* skilled in music waked the sweet celestial song,
Fair *Apsaras* in their beauty on the greensward tripped along!

As the flowery rain descended and the music rose in pride,
Thrice around the lighted altar every bridegroom led his bride,

And the nuptial rites were ended, princes took their brides away.
Janak followed with his courtiers, and the town was proud and gay!

Book II
Vana-Gamana-Adesa (The Banishment)

The events narrated in this Book occupy scarcely two days. The
description of Rama's princely virtues and the rejoicings at his pro-
posed coronation, with which the Book begins, contrast with much
dramatic force and effect with the dark intrigues which follow, and
which end in his cruel banishment for fourteen years.

I
THE COUNCIL CONVENED

Thus the young and brave Satrughna, Bharat ever true and bold,
Went to warlike western regions where Kaikeyas lived of old,

Where the ancient Aswa-pati ruled his kingdom broad and fair,
Hailed the sons of Dasa-ratha with a grandsire's loving care.

Tended with a fond affection, guarded with a gentle sway,
Still the princes of their father dreamt and thought by night and day,

And their father in Ayodhya, great of heart and stout of hand,
Thought of Bharat and Satrughna living in Kaikeyas' land.

For his great and gallant princes were to him his life and light,
Were a part of Dasa-ratha like his hands and arms of might,

But of all his righteous children righteous Rama won his heart,
As Swayambhu of all creatures, was his dearest, holiest part,

For his Rama strong and stately was his eldest and his best,
Void of every baser passion and with every virtue blest!

Soft in speech, sedate and peaceful, seeking still the holy path,
Calm in conscious worth and valour, taunt nor cavil waked his wrath

In the field of war excelling, boldest warrior midst the bold,
In the palace chambers musing on the tales by elders told,

Faithful to the wise and learned, truthful in his deed and word,
Rama dearly loved his people and his people loved their lord!

To the Brahmans pure and holy Rama due obeisance made,
To the poor and to the helpless deeper love and honour paid.

Spirit of his race and nation was to high-souled Rama given,
Thoughts that widen human glory, deeds that ope the gates of heaven.

Not intent on idle cavil Rama spake with purpose high,
And the God of speech might envy when he spake or made reply,

In the learning of the *Vedas* highest meed and glory won,
In the skill of arms the father scarcely matched the gallant son!

Taught by sages and by elders in the manners of his race,
Rama grew in social virtues and each soft endearing grace.

Taught by inborn pride and wisdom patient purpose to conceal,
Deep determined was his effort, dauntless was his silent will!

Peerless in his skill and valour steed and elephant to tame,
Dauntless leader of his forces, matchless in his warlike fame,

Higher thought and nobler duty did the righteous Rama move,
By his toil and by his virtues still he sought his people's love!

Dasa-ratha marked his Rama with each kingly virtue blest,
And from lifelong royal duties now he sought repose and rest:

'Shall I see my son anointed, seated on Kosala's throne,
In the evening of my lifetime ere my days on earth be done,

Shall I place my ancient empire in the youthful Rama's care,
Seek for me a higher duty and prepare for life more fair?'

Pondering thus within his bosom counsel from his courtiers sought,
And to crown his Rama, Regent, was his purpose and his thought,

For strange signs and diverse tokens now appeared on earth and sky,
And his failing strength and vigour spoke his end approaching nigh,

And he witnessed Rama's virtues filling all the world with love,
As the full-moon's radiant lustre fills the earth from skies above!

Dear to him appeared his purpose, Rama to his people dear,
Private wish and public duty made his path serene and clear.

Dasa-ratha called his Council, summoned chiefs from town and plain,
Welcomed too from distant regions monarchs and the kings of men,

Mansions meet for prince and chieftain to his guests the monarch gave,
Gracious as the Lord of Creatures held the gathering rich and brave!

Nathless to Kosala's Council nor Videha's monarch came,
Nor the warlike chief Kaikeya, Aswa-pati king of fame,

To those kings and near relations, ancient Dasa-ratha meant,
Message of the proud anointment with his greetings would be sent.

Brightly dawned the day of gathering; in the lofty Council Hall
Stately chiefs and ancient burghers came and mustered one and all,

And each prince and peer was seated on his cushion rich and high,
And on monarch Dasa-ratha eager turned his anxious eye,

Girt by crownèd kings and chieftains, burghers from the town and
plain,
Dasa-ratha shone like Indra girt by heaven's immortal train!

II

THE PEOPLE CONSULTED

With the voice of pealing thunder Dasa-ratha spake to all,
To the princes and the burghers gathered in Ayodha's hall:

'Known to all, the race of Raghu rules this empire broad and fair,
And hath ever loved and cherished subjects with a father's care.

In my fathers' footsteps treading I have sought the ancient path,
Nursed my people as my children, free from passion, pride and wrath,

Underneath this white umbrella, seated on this royal throne,
I have toiled to win their welfare and my task is almost done!

Years have passed of fruitful labour, years of work by fortune blest,
And the evening of my lifetime needs, my friends, the evening's rest.

Years have passed in watchful effort, Law and Duty to uphold,
Effort needing strength and prowess – and my feeble limbs are old!

Peers and burghers, let your monarch, now his lifelong labour done,
For the weal of loving subjects on his empire seat his son.

Indra-like in peerless valour, *rishi*-like in holy lore,
Rama follows Dasa-ratha, but in virtues stands before!

Throned in Pushya's constellation shines the moon with fuller light,
Throned to rule his father's empire Rama wins a loftier might,

He will be your gracious monarch favoured well by Fortune's Queen;
By his virtue and his valour lord of earth he might have been!

Speak your thoughts and from this bosom lift a load of toil and care,
On the proud throne of my fathers let me place a peerless heir.

Speak your thought, my chiefs and people, if this purpose please you
    well,
Or if wiser, better counsel in your wisdom ye can tell.

Speak your thoughts without compulsion, though this plan to me be
  dear,
If some middle course were wiser, if some other way were clear!'

Gathered chieftains hailed the mandate with applauses long and loud,
As the peafowls hail the thunder of the dark and laden cloud,

And the gathered subjects echoed loud and long the welcome sound,
Till the voices of the people shook the sky and solid ground!

Brahmans versed in laws of duty, chieftains in their warlike pride,
Countless men from town and hamlet heard the mandate far and wide,

And they met in consultation, joyously with one accord,
Freely and in measured accents, gave their answer to their lord:

'Years of toil and watchful labour weigh upon thee, king of men,
Young in years is righteous Rama, Heir and Regent let him reign,

We would see the princely Rama, Heir and Regent duly made,
Riding on the royal tusker in the white umbrella's shade!'

Searching still their secret purpose, seeking still their thought to know,
Spake again the ancient monarch in his measured words and slow:

'I would know your inner feelings, loyal thoughts and whispers kind,
For a doubt within me lingers and a shadow clouds my mind,

True to Law and true to Duty while I rule this kingdom fair,
Wherefore would you see my Rama seated as the Regent Heir?'

'We would see him Heir and Regent, Dasa-ratha, ancient lord,
For his heart is blessed with valour, virtue marks his deed and word.

Lives not man in all the wide earth who excels the stainless youth.
In his loyalty to Duty, in his love of righteous Truth,

Truth impels his thought and action, Truth inspires his soul with
  grace,
And his virtue fills the wide earth and exalts his ancient race!

Bright Immortals know his valour; with his brother Lakshman bold
He hath never failed to conquer hostile town or castled hold,

And returning from his battles, from the duties of the war,
Riding on his royal tusker or his all-resistless car,

As a father to his children to his loving men he came,
Blessed our homes and maids and matrons till our infants lisped his
name,

For our humble woes and troubles Rama hath the ready tear,
To our humble tales of suffering Rama lends his willing ear!

Happy is the royal father who hath such a righteous son,
For in town and mart and hamlet every heart hath Rama won,

Burghers and the toiling tillers tales of Rama's kindness say,
Man and infant, maid and matron, morn and eve for Rama pray,

To the Gods and bright Immortals we our inmost wishes send,
May the good and godlike Rama on his father's throne ascend,

Great in gifts and great in glory, Rama doth our homage own,
We would see the princely Rama seated on his father's throne!'

III
THE CITY DECORATED

With his consort pious Rama, pure in deed and pure in thought,
After evening's due ablutions Narayana's chamber sought,

Prayed unto the Lord of Creatures, Narayana Ancient Sire,
Placed his offering on his forehead, poured it on the lighted fire,

Piously partook the remnant, sought for Narayana's aid,
As he kept his fast and vigils on the grass of *kusa* spread.

With her lord the saintly Sita silent passed the sacred night,
Contemplating World's Preserver, Lord of Heaven's ethereal height.

And within the sacred chamber on the grass of *kusa* lay,
Till the crimson streaks of morning ushered in the festive day,

Till the royal bards and minstrels chanted forth the morning call,
Pealing through the holy chamber, echoing through the royal hall.

Past the night of sacred vigils, in his silken robes arrayed,
Message of the proud anointment Rama to the Brahmans said,

And the Brahmans spake to burghers that the festive day was come,
Till the mart and crowded pathway rang with note of pipe and drum,

And the townsmen heard rejoicing of the vigils of the night,
Kept by Rama and by Sita for the day's auspicious rite.

Rama shall be Heir and Regent, Rama shall be crowned today, –
Rapid flew the gladdening message with the morning's gladsome ray,

And the people of the city, maid and matron, man and boy,
Decorated fair Ayodhya in their wild tumultuous joy!

On the temple's lofty steeple high as cloud above the air,
On the crossing of the pathways, in the garden green and fair,

On the merchant's ample warehouse, on the shop with stores displayed,
On the mansion of the noble by the cunning artist made,

On the gay and bright pavilion, on the high and shady trees,
Banners rose and glittering streamers, flags that fluttered in the breeze!

Actors gay and nimble dancers, singers skilled in lightsome song,
With their antics and their music pleased the gay and gathered throng,

And the people met in conclaves, spake of Rama, Regent Heir,
And the children by the roadside lisped of Rama brave and fair!

Women wove the scented garland, merry maids the censer lit,
Men with broom and sprinkled water swept the spacious mart and
    street,

Rows of trees and posts they planted hung with lamps for coming
    night,
That the midnight dark might rival splendour of the noonday light!

Troops of men and merry children laboured with a loving care,
Woman's skill and woman's fancy made the city passing fair,

So that good and kindly Rama might his people's toil approve,
So that sweet and soft-eyed Sita might accept her people's love!

Groups of joyous townsmen gathered in the square or lofty hall,
Praised the monarch Dasa-ratha, regent Rama young and tall:

'Great and good is Dasa-ratha born of Raghu's royal race,
In the fullness of his lifetime on his son he grants his grace,

And we hail the rite auspicious for our prince of peerless might,
He will guard us by his valour, he will save our cherished right,

Dear unto his loving brothers in his father's palace hall,
As is Rama to his brothers dear is Rama to us all,

Long live ancient Dasa-ratha king of Raghu's royal race,
We shall see his son anointed by his father's righteous grace!'

Thus of Rama's consecration spake the burghers one and all,
And the men from distant hamlets poured within the city wall,

From the confines of the empire, north and south and west and east,
Came to see the consecration and to share the royal feast!

And the rolling tide of nations raised their voices loud and high,
Like the tide of sounding ocean when the full moon lights the sky,

And Ayodhya thronged by people from the hamlet, mart and lea,
Was tumultuous like the ocean thronged by creatures of the sea!

IV

INTRIGUE

In the inner palace chamber stood the proud and peerless queen,
With a mother's joy Kaikeyi gaily watched the festive scene,

But with deep and deadly hatred Manthara, her nurse and maid,
Marked the city bright with banners, and in scornful accents said:

'Take thy presents back, Kaikeyi, for they ill befit the day,
And when clouds of sorrow darken, ill beseems thee to be gay,

And thy folly moves my laughter though an anguish wakes my sigh,
For a gladness stirs thy bosom when thy greatest woe is nigh!

Who that hath a woman's wisdom, who that is a prudent wife,
Smiles in joy when prouder rival triumphs in the race of life,

How can hapless Queen Kaikeyi greet this deed of darkness done,
When the favoured Queen Kausalya wins the empire for her son?

Know the truth, O witless woman! Bharat is unmatched in fame,
Rama, deep and darkly jealous, dreads thy Bharat's rival claim,

Younger Lakshman with devotion doth on eldest Rama wait,
Young Satrughna with affection follows Bharat's lofty fate,

Rama dreads no rising danger from the twins, the youngest-born,
But thy Bharat's claims and virtues fill his jealous heart with scorn!

Trust me, queen, thy Bharat's merits are too well and widely known,
And he stands too near and closely by a rival brother's throne.

Rama hath a wolf-like wisdom and a fang to reach the foe,
And I tremble for thy Bharat, Heaven avert untimely woe!

Happy is the Queen Kausalya, they will soon anoint her son,
When on Pushya's constellation gaily rides tomorrow's moon,

Happy is the Queen Kausalya in her regal pomp and state,
And Kaikeyi like a bond-slave must upon her rival wait!

Wilt thou do her due obeisance as we humble women do,
Will thy proud and princely Bharat as his brother's henchman go,

Will thy Bharat's gentle consort, fairest princess in this land,
In her tears and in her anguish wait on Sita's proud command?'

With a woman's scornful anger Manthara proclaimed her grief,
With a mother's love for Rama thus Kaikeyi answered brief:

'What inspires thee, wicked woman, thus to rail in bitter tone,
Shall not Rama, best and eldest, fill his father's royal throne?

What alarms thee, crooked woman, in the happy rites begun,
Shall not Rama guard his brothers as a father guards his son?

And when Rama's reign is over, shall not Gods my Bharat speed,
And by law and ancient custom shall not younger son succeed,

In the present bliss of Rama and in Bharat's future hope,
What offends thee, senseless woman, wherefore dost thou idly mope?

Dear is Rama as my Bharat, ever duteous in his ways.
Rama honours Queen Kausalya, loftier honour to me pays,

Rama's realm is Bharat's kingdom, ruling partners they shall prove,
For himself than for his brothers Rama owns no deeper love!'

Scorn and anger shook her person and her bosom heaved a sigh,
As in wilder, fiercer accents Manthara thus made reply:

'What insensate rage or madness clouds thy heart and blinds thine eye,
Courting thus thy own disaster, courting danger dread and high,

What dark folly clouds thy vision to the workings of thy foe,
Heedless thus to seek destruction and to sink in gulf of woe?

Know, fair queen, by law and custom, son ascends the throne of pride,
Rama's son succeedeth Rama, luckless Bharat steps aside,

Brothers do not share a kingdom, nor can one by one succeed,
Mighty were the civil discord if such custom were decreed!

For to stop all war and tumult, thus the ancient laws ordain,
Eldest son succeeds his father, younger children may not reign,

Bharat barred from Rama's empire, vainly decked with royal grace,
Friendless, joyless, long shall wander, alien from his land and race!

Thou hast borne the princely Bharat, nursed him from thy gentle
   breast,
To a queen and to a mother need a prince's claims be pressed,

To a thoughtless heedless mother must I Bharat's virtues plead,
Must the Queen Kaikeyi witness Queen Kausalya's son succeed?

Trust thy old and faithful woman who hath nursed thee, youthful
   queen,
And in great and princely houses many darksome deeds hath seen,

Trust my word, the wily Rama for his spacious empire's good,
Soon will banish friendless Bharat and secure his peace with blood!

Thou hast sent the righteous Bharat to thy ancient father's land,
And Satrughna young and valiant doth beside his brother stand.

Young in years and generous-hearted, they will grow in mutual love,
As the love of elder Rama doth in Lakshman's bosom move.

Young companions grow in friendship, and our ancient legends tell,
Weeds protect a forest monarch which the woodman's axe would fell.

Crownèd Rama unto Lakshman will a loving brother prove,
But for Bharat and Satrughna, Rama's bosom owns no love,

And a danger thus ariseth if the elder wins the throne.
Haste thee, heedless Queen Kaikeyi, save the younger and thy son!

Speak thy mandate to thy husband, let thy Bharat rule at home,
In the deep and pathless jungle let the banished Rama roam.

This will please thy ancient father and thy father's kith and kin,
This will please the righteous people, Bharat knows no guile or sin!

Speak thy mandate to thy husband, win thy son a happy fate,
Doom him not to Rama's service or his unrelenting hate,

Let not Rama in his rancour shed a younger brother's blood,
As the lion slays the tiger in the deep and echoing wood!

With the magic of thy beauty thou hast won thy monarch's heart,
Queen Kausalya's bosom rankles with a woman's secret smart,

Let her not with woman's vengeance turn upon her prouder foe,
And as crownèd Rama's mother venge her in Kaikeyi's woe,

Mark my word, my child Kaikeyi, much these ancient eyes have seen,
Rama's rule is death to Bharat, insult to my honoured queen!'

Like a slow but deadly poison worked the ancient nurse's tears,
And a wife's undying impulse mingled with a mother's fears,

Deep within Kaikeyi's bosom worked a woman's jealous thought,
Speechless in her scorn and anger mourner's dark retreat she sought.

V

THE QUEEN'S DEMAND

Rama shall be crowned at sunrise, so did royal bards proclaim,
Every rite arranged and ordered, Dasa-ratha homeward came,

To the fairest of his consorts, dearest to his ancient heart,
Came the king with eager gladness joyful message to impart,

Radiant as the Lord of Midnight, ere the eclipse casts its gloom,
Came the old and ardent monarch heedless of his darksome doom!

Through the shady palace garden where the peacock wandered free,
Lute and lyre poured forth their music, parrot flew from tree to tree.

Through the corridor of creepers, painted rooms by artists done,
And the halls where scented *Champak* and the flaming *Asok* shone,

Through the portico of splendour graced by silver, tusk and gold,
Radiant with his thought of gladness walked the monarch proud and
   bold.

Through the lines of scented blossoms which by limpid waters shone,
And the rooms with seats of silver, ivory bench and golden throne,

Through the chamber of confection, where each viand wooed the taste,
Every object in profusion as in regions of the blest,

Through Kaikeyi's inner closet lighted with a softened sheen,
Walked the king with eager longing – but Kaikeyi was not seen!

Thoughts of love and gentle dalliance woke within his ancient heart,
And the magic of her beauty and the glamour of her art,

With a soft desire the monarch vainly searched the vanished fair,
Found her not in royal chamber, found her not in gay parterre!

Filled with love and longing languor loitered not the radiant queen,
In her soft voluptuous chamber, in the garden, grove or green,

And he asked the faithful warder of Kaikeyi loved and lost,
She who served him with devotion and his wishes never crost,

Spake the warder in his terror that the queen with rage distraught,
Weeping silent tears of anguish had the mourner's chamber sought!

Thither flew the stricken monarch; on the bare and unswept ground
Trembling with tumultuous passion was the Queen Kaikeyi found,

On the cold uncovered pavement sorrowing lay the weeping wife,
Young wife of an ancient husband, dearer than his heart and life!

Like a bright and blossoming creeper rudely severed from the earth,
Like a fallen fair *Apsara*, beauteous nymph of heavenly birth,

Like a female forest-ranger bleeding from the hunter's dart,
Whom her mate the forest-monarch soothes with soft endearing art,

Lay the queen in tears of anguish! And with sweet and gentle word
To the lotus-eyèd lady softly spake her loving lord:

'Wherefore thus, my Queen and Empress, sorrow-laden is thy heart?
Who with daring slight or insult seeks to cause thy bosom smart?

If some unknown ailment pains thee, evil spirit of the air,
Skilled physicians wait upon thee, priests with incantations fair,

If from human foe some insult, wipe thy tears and doom his fate,
Rich reward or royal vengeance shall upon thy mandate wait!

Wilt thou doom to death the guiltless, free whom direst sins debase,
Wilt thou lift the poor and lowly or the proud and great disgrace,

Speak, and I and all my courtiers Queen Kaikeyi's hest obey,
For thy might is boundless, Empress, limitless thy regal sway!

Rolls my chariot-wheel revolving from the sea to farthest sea,
And the wide earth is my empire, monarchs list my proud decree,

Nations of the eastern regions and of Sindhu's western wave,
Brave Saurashtras and the races who the ocean's dangers brave,

Vangas, Angas and Magadhas, warlike Matsyas of the west,
Kasis and the southern races, brave Kosalas first and best,

Nations of my world-wide empire, rich in corn and sheep and kine,
All shall serve my Queen Kaikeyi and their treasures all are thine,

Speak, command thy king's obedience, and thy wrath will melt away
Like the melting snow of winter 'neath the sun's reviving ray!'

Blinded was the ancient husband as he lifted up her head,
Heedless oath and word he plighted that her wish should be obeyed,

Scheming for a fatal purpose, inly then Kaikeyi smiled,
And by sacred oath and promise bound the monarch love-beguiled:

'Thou hast given, Dasa-ratha, troth and word and royal oath,
Three and thirty Gods be witness, watchers of the righteous truth,

Sun and Moon and Stars be witness, Sky and Day and sable Night,
Rolling Worlds and this our wide Earth, and each dark and unseen
   wight,

Witness Rangers of the forest, Household Gods that guard us both,
Mortal beings and Immortal, – witness ye the monarch's oath,

Ever faithful to his promise, ever truthful in his word,
Dasa-ratha grants my prayer, Spirits and the Gods have heard!

Call to mind, O righteous monarch, days when in a bygone strife,
Warring with thy foes immortal thou hadst almost lost thy life,

With a woman's loving tendance poor Kaikeyi cured thy wound,
Till from death and danger rescued, thou wert by a promise bound,

Two rewards my husband offered, what my loving heart might seek,
Long delayed their wished fulfilment, – now let poor Kaikeyi speak,

And if royal deeds redeem not what thy royal lips did say,
Victim to thy broken promise Queen Kaikeyi dies today!

By these rites ordained for Rama, – such the news my menials bring, –
Let my Bharat, and not Rama, be anointed Regent King,

Wearing skins and matted tresses, in the cave or hermit's cell,
Fourteen years in Dandak's forests let the elder Rama dwell,

These are Queen Kaikeyi's wishes, these are boons for which I pray.
I would see my son anointed, Rama banished on this day!'

VII

THE SENTENCE

Morning came and duteous Rama to the palace bent his way,
For to make his salutation and his due obeisance pay,

And he saw his aged father shorn of kingly pomp and pride,
And he saw the Queen Kaikeyi sitting by her consort's side.

Duteously the righteous Rama touched the ancient monarch's feet,
Touched the feet of Queen Kaikeyi with a son's obeisance meet.

'Rama!' cried the feeble monarch, but the tear bedimmed his eye,
Sorrow choked his failing utterance and his bosom heaved a sigh.

Rama started in his terror at his father's grief or wrath,
Like a traveller in the jungle crossed by serpent in his path!

Reft of sense appeared the monarch, crushed beneath a load of pain,
Heaving oft a sigh of sorrow as his heart would break in twain,

Like the ocean tempest-shaken, like the sun in eclipse pale,
Like a crushed repenting *rishi* when his truth and virtue fail!

Breathless mused the anxious Rama, – what foul action hath he done,
What strange anger fills his father, wherefore greets he not his son?

'Speak, my mother,' uttered Rama, 'what strange error on my part,
Unremembered sin or folly fills with grief my father's heart.

Gracious unto me is father with a father's boundless grace,
Wherefore clouds his altered visage, wherefore tears bedew his face?

Doth a piercing painful ailment rack his limbs with cruel smart,
Doth some secret silent anguish wring his torn and tortured heart?

Bharat lives with brave Satrughna in thy father's realms afar,
Hath some cloud of dark disaster crossed their bright auspicious star?

Duteously the royal consorts on the loving monarch wait,
Hath some woe or dire misfortune dimmed the lustre of their fate?

I would yield my life and fortune ere I wound my father's heart.
Hath my unknown crime or folly caused his ancient bosom smart?

Ever dear is Queen Kaikeyi to her consort and her king,
Hath some angry accent escaped thee thus his royal heart to wring?

Speak, my ever-loving mother, speak the truth, for thou must know,
What distress or deep disaster pains his heart and clouds his brow?'

Mother's love nor woman's pity moved the deep-determined queen
As in cold and cruel accents thus she spake her purpose keen:

'Grief nor woe nor sudden ailment pains thy father loved of old,
But he fears to speak his purpose to his Rama true and bold,

And his loving accents falter some unloving wish to tell,
Till you give your princely promise, you will serve his mandate well!

Listen more, in bygone seasons, – Rama thou wert then unborn, –
I had saved thy royal father, he a gracious boon had sworn,

But his feeble heart repenting is by pride and passion stirred,
He would break his royal promise as a caitiff breaks his word,

Years have passed and now the monarch would his ancient word
    forgo.
He would build a needless causeway when the waters ceased to flow!

Truth inspires each deed attempted and each word by monarchs spoke,
Not for thee, though loved and honoured, should a royal vow be broke,

If the true and righteous Rama binds him by his father's vow,
I will tell thee of the anguish which obscures his royal brow,

If thy feeble bosom falter and thy halting purpose fail,
Unredeemed is royal promise and unspoken is my tale!'

'Speak thy word,' exclaimed the hero, 'and my purpose shall not fail,
Rama serves his father's mandate and his bosom shall not quail,

Poisoned cup or death untimely, – what the cruel fates decree, –
To his king and to his father Rama yields obedience free,

Speak my father's royal promise, hold me by his promise tied,
Rama speaks and shall not palter, for his lips have never lied.'

Cold and clear Kaikeyi's accents fell as falls the hunter's knife,
'Listen then to word of promise and redeem it with thy life,

Wounded erst by foes immortal, saved by Queen Kaikeyi's care,
Two great boons your father plighted and his royal words were fair,

I have sought their due fulfilment, – brightly shines my Bharat's star,
Bharat shall be Heir and Regent, Rama shall be banished far!

If thy father's royal mandate thou wouldst list and honour still,
Fourteen years in Dandak's forest live and wander at thy will,

Seven long years and seven, my Rama, thou shalt in the jungle dwell,
Bark of trees shall be thy raiment and thy home the hermit's cell,

Over fair Kosala's empire let my princely Bharat reign,
With his cars and steeds and tuskers, wealth and gold and armèd men!

Tender-hearted is the monarch, age and sorrow dim his eye,
And the anguish of a father checks his speech and purpose high,

For the love he bears thee, Rama, cruel vow he may not speak,
I have spoke his will and mandate, and thy true obedience seek.'

Calmly Rama heard the mandate, grief nor anger touched his heart,
Calmly from his father's empire and his home prepared to part.

Book III
Dasa-Ratha-Viyoga (The Death of the King)

The first six days of Rama's wanderings are narrated in this Book. Sita
and the faithful Lakshman accompanied Rama in his exile, and the
loyal people of Ayodhya followed their exiled prince as far as the banks
of the Tamasa river, where they halted on the first night. Rama had to
steal away at night to escape the citizens, and his wanderings during
the following days give us beautiful glimpses of forest life in holy
hermitages. Thirty centuries have passed since the age of the Kosalas

and Videhas, but every step of the supposed journey of Rama is well known in India to this day, and is annually traversed by thousands of devoted pilgrims. The past is not dead and buried in India, it lives in the hearts of millions of faithful men and faithful women, and shall live for ever.

On the third day of their exile, Rama and his wife and brother crossed the Ganges; on the fourth day they came to the hermitage of Bharad-vaja, which stood where Allahabad now stands, on the confluence of the Ganges and the Jumna; on the fifth day they crossed the Jumna, the southern shores of which were then covered with woods; and on the sixth day they came to the hill of Chitra-kuta, where they met the saint Valmiki, the reputed author of this Epic. 'We have often looked,' says a writer in *Calcutta Review*, vol. xxii, 'on that green hill: it is the holiest spot of that sect of the Hindu faith who devote themselves to this incarnation of Vishnu. The whole neighbourhood is Rama's country. Every headland has some legend, every cavern is connected with his name, some of the wild fruits are still called Sita-phal, being the reputed food of the exile. Thousands and thousands annually visit the spot, and round the hill is raised a footpath on which the devotee, with naked feet, treads full of pious awe.'

Grief for the banished Rama pressed on the ancient heart of Dasa-ratha. The feeble old king pined away and died, remembering and recounting on his death-bed how in his youth he had caused sorrow and death to an old hermit by killing his son. Scarcely any passage in the Epic is more touching than this old sad story told by the dying monarch.

I

WOMAN'S LOVE

'Dearly loved, devoted Sita! daughter of a royal line,
Part we now, for years of wand'ring in the pathless woods is mine,

For my father, promise-fettered, to Kaikeyi yields the sway,
And she wills her son anointed, – fourteen years doth Rama stray,

But before I leave thee, Sita, in the wilderness to rove,
Yield me one more tender token of thy true and trustful love!

Serve my crownèd brother, Sita, as a faithful, duteous dame,
Tell him not of Rama's virtues, tell him not of Rama's claim,

Since my royal father willeth, – Bharat shall be regent-heir,
Serve him with a loyal duty, serve him with obeisance fair,

Since my royal father willeth, – years of banishment be mine,
Brave in sorrow and in suffering, woman's brightest fame be thine!

Keep thy fasts and vigils, Sita, while thy Rama is away,
Faith in Gods and faith in virtue on thy bosom hold their sway.

In the early watch of morning to the Gods for blessings pray,
To my father Dasa-ratha honour and obeisance pay.

To my mother, Queen Kausalya, is thy dearest tendance due,
Offer her thy consolation, be a daughter fond and true!

Queen Kaikeyi and Sumitra equal love and honour claim,
With a soothing soft endearment sweetly serve each royal dame,

Cherish Bharat and Satrughna with a sister's watchful love,
And a mother's true affection and a mother's kindness prove!

Listen, Sita, unto Bharat speak no heedless angry word,
He is monarch of Kosala and of Raghu's race is lord,

Crownèd kings our willing service and our faithful duty own,
Dearest sons they disinherit, cherish strangers near the throne!

Bharat's will with deep devotion and with faultless faith obey,
Truth and virtue on thy bosom ever hold their gentle sway.

And to please each dear relation, gentle Sita, be it thine,
Part we love! for years of wand'ring in the pathless woods is mine!'

Rama spake, and soft-eyed Sita, ever sweet in speech and word,
Stirred by loving woman's passion boldly answered thus her lord:

'Do I hear my husband rightly, are these words my Rama spake,
And her banished lord and husband will the wedded wife forsake?

Lightly I dismiss the counsel which my lord hath lightly said,
For it ill beseems a warrior and my husband's princely grade!

For the faithful woman follows where her wedded lord may lead,
In the banishment of Rama, Sita's exile is decreed,

Sire nor son nor loving brother rules the wedded woman's state,
With her lord she falls or rises, with her consort courts her fate.

If the righteous son of Raghu wends to forests dark and drear,
Sita steps before her husband wild and thorny paths to clear!

Like the tasted refuse water cast thy timid thoughts aside,
Take me to the pathless jungle, bid me by my lord abide.

Car and steed and gilded palace, vain are these to woman's life,
Dearer is her husband's shadow to the loved and loving wife!

For my mother often taught me and my father often spake,
That her home the wedded woman doth beside her husband make,

As the shadow to the substance, to her lord is faithful wife,
And she parts not from her consort till she parts with fleeting life!

Therefore bid me seek the jungle and in pathless forests roam,
Where the wild deer freely ranges and the tiger makes his home,

Happier than in father's mansions in the woods will Sita rove,
Waste no thought on home or kindred, nestling in her husband's love!

World-renowned is Rama's valour, fearless by her Rama's side,
Sita will still live and wander with a faithful woman's pride.

And the wild fruit she will gather from the fresh and fragrant wood,
And the food by Rama tasted shall be Sita's cherished food!

Bid me seek the sylvan greenwoods, wooded hills and plateaus high,
Limpid rills and crystal *nullas* as they softly ripple by,

And where in the lake of lotus tuneful ducks their plumage lave,
Let me with my loving Rama skim the cool translucent wave!

Years will pass in happy union, – happiest lot to woman given, –
Sita seeks not throne or empire, nor the brighter joys of heaven,

Heaven conceals not brighter mansions in its sunny fields of pride,
Where without her lord and husband faithful Sita would reside!

Therefore let me seek the jungle where the jungle-rangers rove,
Dearer than the royal palace, where I share my husband's love,

And my heart in sweet communion shall my Rama's wishes share,
And my wifely toil shall lighten Rama's load of woe and care!'

Vainly gentle Rama pleaded dangers of the jungle life,
Vainly spake of toil and trial to a true and tender wife!

II

BROTHER'S FAITHFULNESS

Tears bedewed the face of Lakshman as he heard what Sita said,
And he touched the feet of Rama and in gentle accents prayed:

'If my elder and his lady to the pathless forests wend,
Armed with bow and ample quiver Lakshman will on them attend,

Where the wild deer range the forest and the lordly tuskers roam,
And the bird of gorgeous plumage nestles in its jungle home,

Dearer far to me those woodlands where my elder Rama dwells,
Than the homes of bright Immortals where perennial bliss prevails!

Grant me then thy sweet permission, – faithful to thy glorious star,
Lakshman shall not wait and tarry when his Rama wanders far,

Grant me then thy loving mandate, – Lakshman hath no wish to stay,
None shall bar the faithful younger when the elder leads the way!'

'Ever true to deeds of virtue, duteous brother, faithful friend,
Dearer than his life to Rama, thou shall not to forests wend.

Who shall stay by Queen Kausalya, Lakshman, if we both depart,
Who shall stay by Queen Sumitra, she who nursed thee on her heart?

For the king our aged father, he who ruled the earth and main,
Is a captive to Kaikeyi, fettered by her silken chain.

Little help Kaikeyi renders to our mothers in her pride,
Little help can Bharat offer, standing by his mother's side.

Thou alone can'st serve Kausalya when for distant woods I part,
When the memory of my exile rankles in her sorrowing heart,

Thou alone can'st serve Sumitra, soothe her sorrows with thy love.
Stay by them, my faithful Lakshman, and thy filial virtues prove.

Be this then thy sacred duty, tend our mothers in their woe,
Little joy or consolation have they left on earth below!'

Spake the hero: 'Fear no evil, well is Rama's prowess known,
And to mighty Rama's mother Bharat will obeisance own,

Nathless if the pride of empire sways him from the righteous path,
Blood will venge the offered insult and will quench our filial wrath!

But a thousand peopled hamlets Queen Kausalya's hests obey,
And a thousand armed champions own her high and queenly sway,

Aye, a thousand village-centres Queen Sumitra's state maintain,
And a thousand swords like Lakshman's guard her proud and pros-
    perous reign!

All alone with gentle Sita thou shalt track thy darksome way,
Grant it, that thy faithful Lakshman shall protect her night and day,

Grant it, with his bow and quiver Lakshman shall the forests roam,
And his axe shall fell the jungle, and his hands shall rear the home!

Grant it, in the deepest woodlands he shall seek the forest fruit,
Berries dear to holy hermits and the sweet and luscious root,

And when with thy meek-eyed Sita thou shalt seek the mountain crests,
Grant it, Lakshman ever duteous watch and guard thy nightly rest!'

Words of brother's deep devotion Rama heard with grateful heart,
And with Sita and with Lakshman for the woods prepared to part:

'Part we then from loving kinsmen, arms and mighty weapons bring,
Bows of war which Lord Varuna rendered to Videha's king,

Coats of mail to sword impervious, quivers which can never fail,
And the rapiers bright as sunshine, golden-hilted, tempered well.

Safely rest these goodly weapons in our great preceptor's hall,
Seek and bring them, faithful brother, for methinks we need them
    all!'

Rama spake; his valiant brother then the wondrous weapons brought,
Wreathed with fresh and fragrant garlands and with gold and jewels
    wrought.

'Welcome, brother,' uttered Rama, 'stronger thus to woods we go.
Wealth and gold and useless treasure to the holy priests bestow,

To the son of saint Vasishtha, to each sage is honour due,
Then we leave our father's mansions, to our father's mandate true!'

VII
CROSSING THE JUMNA – VALMIKI'S HERMITAGE

Morning dawned, and faithful Sita with the brothers held her way,
Where the dark and eddying waters of the sacred Jumna stray,

Pondering by the rapid river long the thoughtful brothers stood,
Then with stalwart arms and axes felled the sturdy jungle wood,

Usira of strongest fibre, slender bamboo smooth and plain,
Jambu branches intertwining with the bent and twisting cane,

And a mighty raft constructed, and with creepers scented sweet,
Lakshman for the gentle Sita made a soft and pleasant seat.

Then the rustic bark was floated, framed with skill of woodman's craft,
By her loving lord supported Sita stepped upon the raft,

And her raiments and apparel Rama by his consort laid,
And the axes and the deerskins, bow and dart and shining blade.

Then with stalwart arms the brothers plied the bending bamboo oar,
And the strong raft gaily bounding left for Jumna's southern shore.

'Goddess of the glorious Jumna!' so the pious Sita prayed,
'Peaceful be my husband's exile in the forest's darksome shade,

May he safely reach Ayodhya, and a thousand fattened kine,
Hundred jars of sweet libation, mighty Jumna, shall be thine.

Grant that from the woods returning he may see his home again,
Grant that honoured by his kinsmen he may rule his loving men!'

On her breast her arms she folded while the princes plied the oar,
And the bright bark bravely bounding reached the wooded southern
  shore.

And the wanderers from Ayodhya on the river's margin stood,
Where the unknown realm extended mantled by unending wood.

Gallant Lakshman with his weapons went before the path to clear,
Soft-eyed Sita followed gently, Rama followed in the rear.

Oft from tree and darksome jungle, Lakshman ever true and brave,
Plucked the fruit or smiling blossom and to gentle Sita gave.

Oft to Rama turned his consort, pleased and curious evermore,
Asked the name of tree or creeper, fruit or flower unseen before.

Still with brotherly affection Lakshman brought each dewy spray,
Bud or blossom of wild beauty from the woodland bright and gay.

Still with eager joy and pleasure Sita turned her eye once more,
Where the tuneful swans and *saras* flocked on Jumna's sandy shore.

Two miles thus they walked and wandered and the belt of forest
  passed,
Slew the wild deer of the jungle, spread on leaves their rich repast.

Peacocks flew around them gaily, monkeys leaped on branches bent.
Fifth night of their endless wanderings in the forest thus they spent.

'Wake, my love, and list the warblings and the voices of the wood,'
Thus spake Rama when the morning on the eastern mountains stood.

Sita woke and gallant Lakshman, and they sipped the sacred wave.
To the hill of Chitra-kuta held their way serene and brave.

'Mark, my love,' so Rama uttered, 'every bush and tree and flower,
Tinged by radiant light of morning sparkles in a golden shower,

Mark the flaming flower of *Kinsuk* and the *Vilwa* in its pride,
Luscious fruits in wild profusion ample store of food provide,

Mark the honeycombs suspended from each tall and stately tree,
How from every virgin blossom steals her store the faithless bee!

Oft the lone and startled wild cock sounds its clarion full and clear,
And from flowering fragrant forests peacocks send the answering
   cheer,

Oft the elephant of jungle ranges in this darksome wood,
For yon peak is Chitra-kuta loved by saints and hermits good,

Oft the chanted songs of hermits echo through its sacred grove,
Peaceful on its shady uplands, Sita, we shall live and rove!'

Gently thus the princes wandered through the fair and woodland
   scene,
Fruits and blossoms lit the branches, feathered songsters filled the
   green,

Anchorites and ancient hermits lived in every sylvan grove,
And a sweet and sacred stillness filled the woods with peace and love!

Gently thus the princes wandered to the holy hermitage,
Where in lofty contemplation lived the mighty Saint and Sage.

Heaven inspired thy song, Valmiki! Ancient Bard of ancient day,
Deeds of virtue and of valour live in thy undying lay!

And the Bard received the princes with a father's greetings kind,
Bade them live in Chitra-kuta with a pure and peaceful mind.

To the true and faithful Lakshman, Rama then his purpose said,
And of leaf and forest timber Lakshman soon a cottage made.

'So our sacred *Sastras* sanction,' thus the righteous Rama spake,
'Holy offering we should render when our dwelling-home we make.

Slay the black buck, gallant Lakshman, and a sacrifice prepare,
For the moment is auspicious and the day is bright and fair.'

Lakshman slew a mighty black-buck, with the antlered trophy came,
Placed the carcass consecrated by the altar's blazing flame,

Radiant round the mighty offering tongues of red fire curling shone,
And the buck was duly roasted and the tender meat was done.

Pure from bath, with sacred *mantra* Rama did the holy rite,
And invoked the bright Immortals for to bless the dwelling site,

To the kindly Viswa-devas, and to Rudra fierce and strong,
And to Vishnu Lord of Creatures, Rama raised the sacred song.

Righteous rite was duly rendered for the forest-dwelling made,
And with true and deep devotion was the sacred *mantra* prayed,

And the worship of the Bright Ones purified each earthly stain,
Pure-souled Rama raised the altar and the *chaitya's* sacred fane.

Evening spread its holy stillness, bush and tree its magic felt,
As the Gods in Brahma's mansions, exiles in their cottage dwelt,

In the woods of Chitra-kuta where the Malyavati flows,
Sixth day of their weary wand'rings ended in a sweet repose.

VIII

TALE OF THE HERMIT'S SON

Wise Sumantra chariot-driver came from Ganga's sacred wave,
And unto Ayodhya's monarch, banished Rama's message gave.

Dasa-ratha's heart was shadowed by the deepening shade of night,
As the darkness of the eclipse glooms the sun's meridian light!

On the sixth night, – when his Rama slept in Chitra-kuta's bower, –
Memory of an ancient sorrow flung on him its fatal power,

Of an ancient crime and anguish, unforgotten, dark and dread,
Through the lapse of years and seasons casting back its death-like
　shade!

And the gloom of midnight deepened, Dasa-ratha sinking fast,
To Kausalya sad and sorrowing spake his memories of the past:

'Deeds we do in life, Kausalya, be they bitter, be they sweet,
Bring their fruit and retribution, rich reward or suffering meet.

Heedless child is he, Kausalya, in his fate who doth not scan
Retribution of his *karma*, sequence of a mighty plan!

Oft in madness and in folly we destroy the mango grove,
Plant the gorgeous gay *palasa* for the red flower that we love,

Fruitless as the red *palasa* is the *karma* I have sown,
And my barren lifetime withers through the deed which is my own!

Listen to my tale, Kausalya, in my days of youth renowned,
I was called a *sabda-bedhi*, archer prince who shot by sound.

I could hit the unseen target, by the sound my aim could tell, –
Blindly drinks a child the poison, blindly in my pride I fell!

I was then my father's Regent, thou a maid to me unknown.
Hunting by the fair Sarayu in my car I drove alone.

Buffalo or jungle tusker might frequent the river's brink,
Nimble deer or watchful tiger stealing for his nightly drink,

Stalking with a hunter's patience, loitering in the forests drear,
Sound of something in the water struck my keen and listening ear.

In the dark I stood and listened, some wild beast the water drunk,
'Tis some elephant, I pondered, lifting water with its trunk.

I was called a *sabda-bedhi*, archer prince who shot by sound,
On the unseen fancied tusker dealt a sure and deadly wound.

Ah! too deadly was my arrow and like hissing cobra fell,
On my startled ear and bosom smote a voice of human wail.

Dying voice of lamentation rose upon the midnight high,
Till my weapons fell in tremor and a darkness dimmed my eye!

Hastening with a nameless terror soon I reached Sarayu's shore,
Saw a boy with hermit's tresses, and his pitcher lay before,

Weltering in a pool of red blood, lying on a gory bed,
Feebly raised his voice the hermit, and in dying accents said:

"What offence, O mighty monarch, all-unknowning have I done,
That with quick and kingly justice slayest thus a hermit's son?

Old and feeble are my parents, sightless by the will of fate,
Thirsty in their humble cottage for their duteous boy they wait,

And thy shaft that kills me, monarch, bids my ancient parents die,
Helpless, friendless, they will perish, in their anguish deep and high!

Sacred lore and lifelong penance change not mortal's earthly state,
Wherefore else they sit unconscious when their son is doomed by fate,

Or if conscious of my danger, could they dying breath recall,
Can the tall tree save the sapling doomed by woodman's axe to fall?

Hasten to my parents, monarch, soothe their sorrow and their ire,
For the tears of good and righteous wither like the forest fire.

Short the pathway to the *asram*, soon the cottage thou shalt see,
Soothe their anger by entreaty, ask their grace and pardon free!

But before thou goest, monarch, take, O take thy torturing dart,
For it rankles in my bosom with a cruel burning smart,

And it eats into my young life as the river's rolling tide
By the rains of summer swollen eats into its yielding side."

Writhing in his pain and anguish thus the wounded hermit cried,
And I drew the fatal arrow, and the holy hermit died!

Darkly fell the thickening shadows, stars their feeble radiance lent,
As I filled the hermit's pitcher, to his sightless parents went,

Darkly fell the moonless midnight, deeper gloom my bosom rent,
As with faint and falt'ring footsteps to the hermits slow I went.

Like two birds bereft of plumage, void of strength, deprived of flight,
Were the stricken ancient hermits, friendless, helpless, void of sight,

Lisping in their feeble accents still they whispered of their child,
Of the stainless boy whose red blood Dasa-ratha's hands defiled!

And the father heard my footsteps, spake in accents soft and kind:
"Come, my son, to waiting parents, wherefore dost thou stay behind,

Sporting in the rippling water didst thou midnight's hour beguile,
But thy faint and thirsting mother anxious waits for thee the while,

Hath my heedless word or utterance caused thy boyish bosom smart,
But a feeble father's failings may not wound thy filial heart,

Help of helpless, sight of sightless, and thy parents' life and joy,
Wherefore art thou mute and voiceless, speak, my brave and beauteous boy!"

Thus the sightless father welcomed cruel slayer of his son,
And an anguish tore my bosom for the action I had done.

Scarce upon the sonless parents could I lift my aching eye,
Scarce in faint and faltering accents to the father make reply,

For a tremor shook my person and my spirit sank in dread.
Straining all my utmost prowess, thus in quavering voice I said:

"Not thy son, O holy hermit, but a Kshatra warrior born,
Dasa-ratha stands before thee by a cruel anguish torn,

For I came to slay the tusker by Sarayu's wooded brink,
Buffalo or deer of jungle stealing for his midnight drink,

And I heard a distant gurgle, some wild beast the water drunk, –
So I thought, – some jungle tusker lifting water with its trunk,

And I sent my fatal arrow on the unknown, unseen prey,
Speeding to the spot I witnessed, – there a dying hermit lay!

From his pierced and quivering bosom then the cruel dart I drew,
And he sorrowed for his parents as his spirit heavenward flew,

Thus unconscious, holy father, I have slayed thy stainless son,
Speak my penance, or in mercy pardon deed unknowing done!"

Slow and sadly by their bidding to the fatal spot I led,
Long and loud bewailed the parents by the cold unconscious dead,

And with hymns and holy water they performed the funeral rite,
Then with tears that burnt and withered, spake the hermit in his
   might:

"Sorrow for a son beloved is a father's direst woe,
Sorrow for a son beloved, Dasa-ratha, thou shalt know!

See the parents weep and perish, grieving for a slaughtered son,
Thou shalt weep and thou shalt perish for a loved and righteous son!

Distant is the expiation, – but in fullness of the time,
Dasa-ratha's death in anguish cleanses Dasa-ratha's crime!"

Spake the old and sightless prophet; then he made the funeral pyre,
And the father and the mother perished in the lighted fire,

Years have gone and many seasons, and in fullness of the time,
Comes the fruit of pride and folly and the harvest of my crime!

Rama eldest born and dearest, Lakshman true and faithful son,
Ah! forgive a dying father and a cruel action done,

Queen Kaikeyi, thou hast heedless brought on Raghu's race this stain.
Banished are the guiltless children and thy lord and king is slain!

Lay thy hands on mine, Kausalya, wipe thy unavailing tear,
Speak a wife's consoling accents to a dying husband's ear,

Lay thy hands on mine, Sumitra, vision fails my closing eyes,
And for brave and banished Rama wings my spirit to the skies!'

Hushed and silent passed the midnight, feebly still the monarch
   sighed,
Blessed Kausalya and Sumitra, blest his banished sons, and died.

Book IV
Rama-Bharata-Sambada (The Meeting of the Princes)

The scene of this Book is laid at Chitra-kuta. Bharat returning from
the kingdom of the Kaikeyas heard of his father's death and his
brother's exile, and refused the throne which had been reserved for
him. He wandered through the woods and jungle to Chitra-kuta, and
implored Rama to return to Ayodhya and seat himself on the throne of
his father. But Rama had given his word, and would not withdraw
from it.

Few passages in the Epic are more impressive than Rama's wise
and kindly advice to Bharat on the duties of a ruler, and his firm
refusal to Bharat's passionate appeal to seat himself on the throne.

Equally touching is the lament of Queen Kausalya when she meets Sita in the dress of an anchorite in the forest.

But one of the most curious passages in the whole Epic is the speech of Jabali the Sceptic, who denied heaven and a world hereafter. In ancient India as in ancient Greece there were different schools of philosophers, some of them orthodox and some of them extremely heterodox, and the greatest latitude of free thought was permitted. In Jabali, the poet depicts a free-thinker of the broadest type. He ridicules the ideas of Duty and of Future Life with a force of reasoning which a Greek sophist and philosopher could not have surpassed. But Rama answers with the fervour of a righteous, truth-loving, God-fearing man.

All persuasion was in vain, and Bharat returned to Ayodhya with Rama's sandals, and placed them on the throne, as an emblem of Rama's sovereignty during his voluntary exile. Rama himself then left Chitra-kuta and sought the deeper forests of Dandak, so that his friends and relations might not find him again during his exile. He visited the hermitage of the Saint Atri; and the ancient and venerable wife of Atri welcomed the young Sita, and robed her in rich raiments and jewels, on the eve of her departure for the unexplored wildernesses of the south.

I

THE MEETING OF THE BROTHERS

Sorrowing for his sire departed Bharat to Ayodhya came,
But the exile of his brother stung his noble heart to flame,

Scorning sin-polluted empire, travelling with each widowed queen,
Sought through wood and trackless jungle Chitra-kuta's peaceful scene.

Royal guards and Saint Vasishtha loitered with the dames behind.
Onward pressed the eager Bharat, Rama's hermit-home to find.

Nestled in a jungle thicket, Rama's cottage rose in sight,
Thatched with leaves and twining branches, reared by Lakshman's faithful might.

Faggots hewn of gnarlèd branches, blossoms culled from bush and
  tree,
Coats of bark and russet garments, *kusa* spread upon the lea,

Store of horns and branching antlers, fire-wood for the dewy night, –
Spake the dwelling of a hermit suited for a hermit's rite.

'May the scene,' so Bharat uttered, 'by the righteous *rishi* told,
Markalvati's rippling waters, Chitra-kuta's summit bold,

Mark the dark and trackless forest where the untamed tuskers roam,
And the deep and hollow caverns where the wild beasts make their
  home,

Mark the spacious wooded uplands, wreaths of smoke obscure the
  sky,
Hermits feed their flaming altars for their worship pure and high.

Done our weary work and wand'ring, righteous Rama here we meet,
Saint and king and honoured elder! Bharat bows unto his feet,

Born a king of many nations, he hath forest refuge sought,
Yielded throne and mighty kingdom for a hermit's humble cot,

Honour unto righteous Rama, unto Sita true and bold,
Theirs be fair Kosala's empire, crown and sceptre, wealth and gold!'

Stately *Sal* and feathered palm-tree on the cottage lent their shade
Strewn upon the sacred altar was the grass of *kusa* spread.

Gaily on the walls suspended hung two bows of ample height,
And their back with gold was pencilled, bright as Indra's bow of
  might.

Cased in broad unfailing quivers arrows shone like light of day,
And like flame-tongued fiery serpents cast a dread and lurid ray.

Resting in their golden scabbards lay the swords of warriors bold,
And the targets broad and ample bossed with rings of yellow gold.

Glove and gauntlet decked the cottage safe from fear of hostile men,
As from creatures of the forest is the lion's lordly den!

Calm in silent contemplation by the altar's sacred fire,
Holy in his pious purpose though begirt by weapons dire,

Clad in deer-skin pure and peaceful, poring on the sacred flame,
In his bark and hermit's tresses like an anchorite of fame,

Lion-shouldered, mighty-armèd, but with gentle lotus eye,
Lord of wide earth ocean-girdled, but intent on penance high,

Godlike as the holy Brahma, on a skin of dappled deer
Rama sat with meek-eyed Sita, faithful Lakshman loitered near!

'Is this he whom joyous nations called to fair Ayodhya's throne,
Now the friend of forest-rangers wandering in the woods alone,

Is this he who robed in purple made Ayodhya's mansions bright,
Now in jungle bark and deer-skin clad as holy anchorite,

Is this he whose wreathèd ringlets fresh and holy fragrance shed,
Now a hermit's matted tresses cluster round his royal head,

Is this he whose royal *yajnas* filled the earth with righteous fame,
Now inured to hermit's labour by the altar's sacred flame,

Is this he whose brow and forehead royal gem and jewel graced,
Heir to proud Kosala's empire, eldest, noblest, and the best?'

Thus lamented pious Bharat, for his heart was anguish-rent,
As before the feet of Rama he in loving homage bent,

'*Arya!*' in his choking accents this was all that Bharat said,
'*Arya!*' spake the young Satrughna and he bent his holy head!

Rama to his loving bosom raised his brothers from his feet.
Ah, too deep is love for utterance when divided brothers meet.

Faithful Guha, brave Sumantra, bowed to Rama's righteous feet,
And a joy and mingled sadness filled the hermit's calm retreat!

II
BHARAT'S ENTREATY AND RAMA'S REPLY

'Speak, my true, my faithful Bharat,' so the righteous Rama cried,
'Wherefore to this jungle dwelling hast thou from Ayodhya hied,

Speak, my fond and loving brother, if our father bade thee come,
Leaving throne and spacious empire in this wilderness to roam?

Heir and Regent of Kosala! Dost thou tend our father well,
And obey the lofty mandate from his royal lips that fell,

And the ancient Dasa-ratha, glorious still in regal might,
Doth he pass his bright life's evening in each pure and holy rite?

Doth my mother, Queen Kausalya, still for Rama wet her eye,
And the gentle Queen Sumitra for her banished Lakshman sigh,

Doth the peerless Queen Kaikeyi pass her days in duties fair,
Guard her Bharat's mighty empire, tend him with a mother's care?

Is each holy rite and homage to the Gods and Fathers done,
Is the honour due to elders rendered by each duteous son,

Do thy warriors guard thy kingdom as of yore with matchless skill,
And with counsel deep and duteous do thy min'sters serve thy will?

Rich thy fields in corn and produce fed by rivers broad and deep,
Rich thy green unending pastures with the kine and fattened sheep,

Tend the herdsman and his cattle, tend the tiller of the soil,
Watch and help with all thy bounty workmen in their peaceful toil,

For the monarch's highest duty is to serve his people's weal
And the ruler's richest glory is to labour and to heal!

Guard thy forts with sleepless caution with the engines of the war,
With the men who shoot the arrow and who drive the flying car,

Guard Kosala's royal treasure, make thy gifts of wealth and food,
Not to lords and proud retainers, but to worthy and the good!

Render justice pure and spotless as befits thy royal line,
And to save the good and guiltless, Bharat, be it ever thine,

For the tears of suffering virtue wither like the thunder levin,
And they slay our men and cattle like the wrath of righteous heaven.

Fruitful be thy lore of Veda, fruitful be each pious rite,
Be thy queen a fruitful mother, be thy empire full of might!'

Weeping, weeping, Bharat answered Dasa-ratha's eldest son,
'Dasa-ratha walks the bright sky, for his earthly task is done!

For impelled by Queen Kaikeyi to the woods he bade thee go,
And his spotless fame was clouded and his bosom sank in woe,

And my mother, late repenting, weeps her deed of deepest shame,
Weeps her wedded lord departed, and a woman's tarnished fame!

Thou alone canst wipe this insult by a deed of kindness done, –
Rule o'er Dasa-ratha's empire, Dasa-ratha's eldest son.

Weeping queens and loyal subjects supplicate thy noble grace, –
Rule o'er Raghu's ancient empire, son of Raghu's royal race!

For our ancient Law ordaineth and thy Duty makes it plain,
Eldest-born succeeds his father as the king of earth and main.

By the fair Earth loved and welcomed, Rama, be her wedded lord,
As by planet-jewelled Midnight is the radiant Moon adored!

And thy father's ancient min'sters and thy courtiers faithful still,
Wait to do thy righteous mandate and to serve thy royal will,

As a pupil, as a brother, as a slave, I seek thy grace, –
Come and rule thy father's empire, king of Raghu's royal race!'

Weeping, on the feet of Rama, Bharat placed his lowly head,
Weeping for his sire departed, tears of sorrow Rama shed,

Then he raised his loving brother with an elder's deathless love.
Sorrow wakes our deepest kindness and our holiest feelings prove!

'But I may not,' answered Rama, 'seek Ayodhya's ancient throne,
For a righteous father's mandate duteous son may not disown.

And I may not, gentle brother, break the word of promise given,
To a king and to a father who is now a saint in heaven!

Not on thee, nor on thy mother, rests the censure or the blame.
Faithful to his father's wishes Rama to the forest came.

For the son and duteous consort serve the father and the lord,
Higher than an empire's glory is a father's spoken word!

All inviolate is his mandate, – on Ayodhya's jewelled throne,
Or in pathless woods and jungle Rama shall his duty own,

All inviolate is the blessing by a loving mother given,
For she blessed my life in exile like a pitying saint of heaven!

Thou shalt rule the kingdom, Bharat, guard our loving people well,
Clad in wild bark and in deer-skin I shall in the forests dwell,

So spake saintly Dasa-ratha in Ayodhya's palace hall,
And a righteous father's mandate duteous son may not recall!'

III
KAUSALYA'S LAMENT AND RAMA'S REPLY

Slow and sad with Saint Vasishtha, with each widowed royal dame,
Unto Rama's hermit-cottage ancient Queen Kausalya came,

And she saw him clad in wild bark like a hermit stern and high,
And an anguish smote her bosom and a tear bedewed her eye.

Rama bowed unto his mother and each elder's blessings sought,
Held their feet in salutation with a holy reverence fraught.

And the queens with loving fingers, with a mother's tender care,
Swept the dust of wood and jungle from his head and bosom fair.

Lakshman too in loving homage bent before each royal dame,
And they blessed the faithful hero spotless in his righteous fame.

Lastly came the soft-eyed Sita with obeisance soft and sweet,
And with hands in meekness folded bent her tresses to their feet,

Pain and anguish smote their bosoms, round their Sita as they prest,
As a mother clasps a daughter, clasped her in their loving breast!

Torn from royal hall and mansions, ranger of the darksome wood,
Reft of home and kith and kindred by her forest hut she stood!

'Hast thou, daughter of Videha,' weeping thus Kausalya said,
'Dwelt in woods and leafy cottage and in pathless jungle strayed,

Hast thou, Rama's royal consort, lived a homeless anchorite,
Pale with rigid fast and penance, worn with toil of righteous rite?

But thy sweet face, gentle Sita, is like faded lotus dry,
And like lily parched by sunlight, lustreless thy beauteous eye,

Like the gold untimely tarnished is thy sorrow-shaded brow,
Like the moon by shadows darkened is thy form of beauty now!

And an anguish scathes my bosom like the withering forest fire,
Thus to see thee, duteous daughter, in misfortunes deep and dire,

Dark is wide Kosala's empire, dark is Raghu's royal house,
When in woods my Rama wanders and my Rama's royal spouse!'

Sweetly, gentle Sita answered, answered Rama fair and tall,
That a righteous father's mandate duteous son may not recall!

IV
JABALI'S REASONING AND RAMA'S REPLY

Jabali a learned Brahman and a Sophist skilled in word,
Questioned Faith and Law and Duty, spake to young Ayodhya's lord:

'Wherefore, Rama, idle maxims cloud thy heart and warp thy mind,
Maxims which mislead the simple and the thoughtless human kind?

Love nor friendship doth a mortal to his kith or kindred own,
Entering on his wide earth friendless, and departing all alone,

Foolishly upon the father and the mother dotes the son,
Kinship is an idle fancy, – save thyself thy kith is none!

In the wayside inn he halteth who in distant lands doth roam,
Leaves it with the dawning daylight for another transient home.

Thus on earth are kin and kindred, home and country, wealth and
    store,
We but meet them on our journey, leave them as we pass before!

Wherefore for a father's mandate leave thy empire and thy throne,
Pass thy days in trackless jungle sacrificing all thy own,

Wherefore to Ayodhya's city, as to longing wife's embrace,
Speed'st thou not to rule thy empire, lord of Raghu's royal race?

Dasa-ratha claims no duty, and this will is empty word.
View him as a foreign monarch, of thy realm thou art the lord,

Dasa-ratha is departed, gone where all the mortals go,
For a dead man's idle mandate wherefore lead this life of woe?

Ah! I weep for erring mortals who on erring duty bent
Sacrifice their dear enjoyment till their barren life is spent,

Who to Gods and to the Fathers vainly still their offerings make,
Waste of food! for God nor Father doth our pious homage take!

And the food by one partaken, can it nourish other men,
Food bestowed upon a Brahman, can it serve our Fathers then?

Crafty priests have forged these maxims and with selfish objects say,
Make thy gifts and do thy penance, leave thy worldly wealth and pray!

There is no Hereafter, Rama, vain the hope and creed of men,
Seek the pleasures of the present, spurn illusions poor and vain,

Take the course of sense and wisdom, cast all idle faith aside,
Take the kingdom Bharat offers, rule Ayodhya in thy pride!'

'Fair thy purpose,' answered Rama, 'false thy reason leads astray,
Tortuous wisdom brings no profit, virtue shuns the crooked way,

For the deed proclaims the hero from the man of spacious lies,
Marks the true and upright *Arya* from the scheming worldly-wise!

If assuming virtue's mantle I should seek the sinful path,
Gods who judge our secret motives curse me with their deepest
  wrath,

And thy counsel helps not, *rishi*, mansions of the sky to win,
And a king his subjects follow adding deeper sin to sin!

Sweep aside thy crafty reasoning, Truth is still our ancient way,
Truth sustains the earth and nations and a monarch's righteous sway,

Mighty Gods and holy sages find in Truth their haven shore,
Scorning death and dark destruction, Truth survives for evermore!

Deadlier than the serpent's venom is the venom of a lie,
From the false, than from the cobra, men with deeper terror fly.

Dearer than the food to mortals, Truth as nourishment is given,
Truth sustains the wide creation, Truth upholds the highest heaven.

Vain were gifts and sacrifices, rigid penances were vain,
Profitless the holy *Vedas* but for Truth which they sustain.

Gifts and rites and rigid penance have no aim or purpose high,
Save in Truth which rules the wide earth and the regions of the sky!

I have plighted troth and promise and my word may not unsay,
Fourteen years in pathless forests father's mandate I obey,

And I seek no spacious reasons my relinquished throne to win,
Gods nor Fathers nor the *Vedas* counsel tortuous paths of sin!

Pardon, *rishi*, still unchanging shall remain my promise given
To my mother Queen Kaikeyi, to my father now in heaven,

Pardon, *rishi*, still in jungle we shall seek the forest fare,
Worship Gods who watch our actions, and pervade the earth and air!

Unto Agni, unto Vayu, shall my constant prayers run,
I shall live like happy Indra, hundred sacrifices done,

And the deep and darksome jungle shall be Rama's royal hall,
For a righteous father's mandate duteous son may not recall!'

196

V

THE SANDALS

Tears nor sighs nor sad entreaty Rama's changeless purpose shook,
Till once more with hands conjoinèd Bharat to his elder spoke:

'Rama, true to royal mercy, true to duties of thy race,
Grant this favour to thy mother, to thy brother grant this grace.

Vain were my unaided efforts to protect our father's throne,
Town and hamlet, lord and tiller, turn to thee and thee alone!

Unto Rama, friends and kinsmen, chiefs and warriors, turn in pain,
And each city chief and elder, and each humble village swain.

Base thy empire strong, unshaken, on a loyal nation's will,
With thy worth and with thy valour serve thy faithful people still!'

Rama raised the prostrate Bharat to his ever-loving breast,
And in voice of tuneful *hansa* thus his gentle speech addrest:

'Trust me, Bharat, lofty virtue, strength and will to thee belong,
Thou could'st rule a worldwide empire in thy faith and purpose
   strong,

And our father's ancient min'sters, ever faithful, wise and deep,
They shall help thee with their counsel and thy ancient frontiers keep.

List! the Moon may lose his lustre, Himalaya lose his snow,
Heaving Ocean pass his confines surging from the caves below,

But the truth-abiding Rama will not move from promise given,
He hath spoke and will not palter, help him righteous Gods in heaven!'

Blazing like the Sun in splendour, beauteous like the Lord of Night,
Rama vowed his Vow of Duty, changeless in his holy might!

'Humble token,' answered Bharat, 'still I seek from Rama's hand,
Token of his love and kindness, token of his high command.

From thy feet cast forth those sandals, they shall decorate the throne,
They shall nerve my heart to duty and shall safely guard thy own,

They shall to a loyal nation absent monarch's will proclaim,
Watch the frontiers of the empire and the people's homage claim!'

Rama gave the loosened sandals as his younger humbly prayed,
Bharat bowed to them in homage and his parting purpose said:

'Not alone will banished Rama barks and matted tresses wear,
Fourteen years the crownèd Bharat will in hermit's dress appear.

Henceforth Bharat dwells in palace guised as hermit of the wood,
In the sumptuous hall of feasting wild fruit is his only food.

Fourteen years shall pass in waiting, weary toil and penance dire,
Then, if Rama comes not living, Bharat dies upon the pyre!'

With the sandals of his elder Bharat to Ayodhya went.
Rama sought for deeper forests on his arduous duty bent.

ILANGO ADIGAL
SHILAPPADIKARAM
[THE ANKLE BRACELET]
(Tamil, *c.* 200 B.C.–A.D. 200)

Among the Dravidian languages of India, only Tamil has preserved some of the ancient ways of life and culture in two epics (often called the 'Twin Epics'), namely Ilango Adigal's *Shilappadikaram* and its sequence, Kulavanigam Cattanar's *Manimekhalai*. These epics incorporate earlier Dravidian stories, songs, and learning surviving in oral transmission into the framework of a legend, and subordinate the material to an epic theme. The process of synthesizing the cultural experience of the people in a literary form probably took place during the period 200 B.C. to A.D. 200.

The epics reveal many contrasting attitudes to the northern kingdoms. They recall with fond memories the extent of the Dravidian dominion in the sub-continent and the time when their kings carved marks of the limits of their expeditions on the rocks of the Himalayas. Important centres of Dravidian culture and religious significance in the north, such as Benares where Lord Shiva still rules supreme, and Mathura (Southern Madurai) where Krishna, the dark-one, mandivine, first lived among the cowherds of Brindavan, and later played his divine role in the battle at Kurukshetra, seem to exist in close proximity in their mental landscape as a part of their inherited tradition. Even though accounts of such places and events are magnificently expressed in Sanskrit works, they do not deny the revealing fact that some of what has been so expressed in Sanskrit had non-Sanskrit origins, in the same sense as much of what is expressed in English (e.g. Shakespeare's *King Lear* or *Othello*, or Milton's *Paradise Lost*) had non-Teutonic sources.

The origin of literary works in Dravidian languages is clouded in fabulous antiquity, and perhaps will remain so until such time as the

Indus Valley script is more completely deciphered.* The tradition claims that the earliest works passed through three *Sangams* (Assemblies or Academies) of which only some works of the Third Sangam have survived. The Third Sangam, extending over a period of 1,850 years, ended about the second century A.D. The legend says that the seat of the First Sangam was now lost Madura (perhaps in the Indus Valley, or Mathura on the banks of the Ganges?), and that gods and sages participated in it. The Sangam lasted for 4,440 years. The Second Sangam was established at Kapatapuram, where it continued for 3,700 years, and in which sages participated. The Second Sangam came to an end when masses of water made inroads into the city and it had to be abandoned. The Third Sangam was established at modern Madurai in South India. Perhaps this legend, in its vague references, recollects the memories from the collective consciousness of the race in the Jungian sense, of cultural centres overtaken by natural calamities or prehistoric invasions.

Ilango Adigal's epic *Shilappadikaram* breathes the author's intense enthusiasm for Jainism, a religion that found re-expression of its teaching in its twenty-fourth *Thirthankara* (Prophet), Vardhamana Mahavir (599–527 B.C.). Mahavir, meaning 'great hero', was called the 'Jina' or the one who was victorious in achieving peace or blessedness. Consequently, the epic upholds the Jain principle of *ahimsa* (non-injury) as the highest law and emphasizes: (1) that Divine Law appears in the form of Death whenever human law allows a miscarriage of justice; (2) that the chaste and faithful wife by worshipping no other gods but her husband achieves a higher order of spirituality, bordering divinity: and (3) that actions done in one state of being or existence find their fulfilment in inevitable consequences in another state of being or existence, as per the law of cosmic causality, called Karma.

The epic is divided into three parts: I, Puhar; II, Madurai; and III, Vanji, the names of three towns in three Dravidian kingdoms of

---

*Cf. *Decipherment of the Proto-Dravidian Inscriptions of the Indus Civilization* by Asko Parpola, Seppo Koskenniemi, Simo Parpola, and Pentti Aalto, Special Publication Nos. 1 and 2. Copenhagen: The Scandinavian Institute of Asian Studies, 1969.

Chola, Pandya, and Chera. The story, beginning in Puhar on the seashore by the mouth of the river Kaveri, progresses to Madurai on the
plains, and ends in Vanji on the mountains, symbolically representing
the journey upstream backwards to the source, or what Lao Tzu calls
'returning to the roots'. This also provides for the portrayal of the
social, political, economic, and cultural life of the people of the time,
classified according to the geographical regions, with different occupations, sources of subsistences, and attitudes to life, namely
Peoples of the seashore; Peoples of the plains; Peoples of the hills; and
Peoples of the mountains.

The story of *Shilappadikaram* deals with the marriage, domestic life,
and trials of a young couple from Puhar, called Kovalan and Kannaki.
In the first part, the couple are married and happily established in a
home of their own. Soon, Kovalan leaves Kannaki in favour of a
charming courtesan Madhavi; after wasting the family fortune on the
courtesan, he returns to the uncomplaining Kannaki. The couple then
decide to leave Puhar and start a new life in Madurai. In this journey
Kovalan, without knowing, walks into his own tragic destiny, resulting
in tragedy and purification by the ordeal of fire. After Kovalan's death,
overtaken and disfigured by inconsolable sorrow, Kannaki leaves
Madurai and arrives at Vanji, where her story becomes mythified into
a legend. The Chera king Shenguttuvan, the brother of the poet, then
desiring to install the deified Kannaki's image, carved out of a rock from
the high Himalayas and bathed in the holy Ganges, leads an expedition
to the north and returns victorious. Finally Kannaki, the Lady of the
Ankle Bracelet, is honoured as the goddess of Faithfulness, and the
king is granted a beatific vision.

Kannaki, the heroine of the epic, and her sisters Sita in the epic
Ramayana and Savitri in the *Mahabharata*, symbolize the Indian ideal
of womanhood, who while exemplifying the traditional attitude of
wife being a 'shadow to the substance' somehow grow to be such overwhelming shadows that they almost redeem their erring men.

The portions included here relate the story of Kovalan and Kannaki
in Madurai, the Pandya capital. Canto 16 tells of their arrival on the
outskirts of the city, where they take shelter in the home of a cowherdess. After a pious meal, Kannaki gives one of her Ankle Bracelets
(representing something like a wedding ring) to Kovalan. Kovalan

then leaves for the city to sell the Ankle Bracelet and get some money; however, because of the villainy of the court goldsmith and a momentary lapse in the administration of justice by the king, Kovalan is put to death. On hearing the news, Kannaki goes to the Pandya king, demanding justice. When the king learns the truth and discovers the consequences of his injustice, he dies instantly from shock. The most virtuous wife, who worshipped no gods but her husband, disfigures herself, and the fire of righteousness burns the city of Madurai to purify it from its evil deed. The goddess of the city, afraid to come in front of the suffering chaste wife, approaches her from behind, and, explaining to her the cause of all causes, promises her eventual reunion with her husband in a state of blessedness.

The selections are taken from the translation by Alain Danielou, *Shilappadikaram* (The Ankle Bracelet), New York: New Directions, 1965, Cantos 16, 18–21, and 23.

I.9   ILANGO ADIGAL
SHILAPPADIKARAM
[THE ANKLE BRACELET]

Canto Sixteen
The Site of Agony

Madari the cowherdess had joyfully taken charge of the frail Kannaki. In the sheltered cottage to which she led her, cowgirls lived who wore shining bracelets. The cottage was dark red. In front was an open courtyard. Thorny hedges kept it private from other huts inhabited by the cowherds who sold buttermilk.

Madari prepared a cool bath for the stranger and paid her compliments:

'You have come here, adorned only by your beauty, to render ridiculous the cosmetics and costly jewelry of the city women. My daughter Aiyai will be at your service, and I shall protect you like a precious object. O girl with fragrant hair entrusted to my care, the virtuous saint has relieved you of the weariness of your journey, and led you to a safe retreat. Your man need not worry.' Turning toward the girls, she said: 'Her master observes all the rules of the pious Jains, who do not eat after sunset. Bring at once our best saucepans so that Kannaki may help Aiyai to prepare a good meal.'

The cowgirls brought new utensils, as is done for wealthy people, and some ripe fruit from the never-flowering breadfruit tree. There were also white-striped cucumbers, green pomegranates and mangoes, sweet bananas, good rice, and fresh cow's milk. The girls said:

'Lady with the round bracelets, accept these modest gifts.'

Kannaki sliced various vegetables with a short knife: her tender fingers grew red, her face was perspiring, tears came to her lovely eyes. She had to turn her face away from the oven. Over a straw fire lit by Aiyai, Kannaki began to prepare her husband's evening meal.

Kovalan seated himself on a small expertly woven palm-leaf mat. Then Kannaki, with her flower-hands, poured water from a jug to wash her master's feet. As if attempting to awaken our mother Earth from a swoon, she sprinkled water on the ground and lustrated the beaten soil with her palms. Then she placed before her husband a tender plantain leaf and said:

'Here is your food, my lord! May you be pleased to eat.'

Having performed with care the rites prescribed for the sons of merchants, they ate their dinner together. Aiyai and her mother looked at them with delight. They exclaimed:

'The noble lord, eating this simple food, must be Krishna himself, whose complexion is like newly open pepper flowers. Krishna too was fed in a cowherd's village, by Yashoda. Is not this lady of the many bracelets the beacon of our caste, who once rescued the god who is the colour of blue sapphire near the Jumna River? We cannot open our eyes wide enough to enjoy this rare sight!'

To tall Kovalan, pleased with his dinner, Kannaki of the gleaming black plaits then offered betel leaves and chopped betel nuts. He embraced her and said:

'My parents would never believe that such tender feet could have trodden paths littered with pebbles and hard stones. Would they not pity you if they knew that we had together crossed such vast and cruel country? It all seems to me like a dream, like a game played by fate. My mind is dull: I fail to understand. Is there any hope left for a man who wasted his youth in the pernicious company of debauched friends, laughing at vulgar deeds and scandals, seeking mischief, and neglectful of the warning words of his wise elders? I neglected all my duties toward my good parents. I was a source of shame to you, so young in years yet so rich in wisdom. I did not see the extent of my faults. I asked you not to leave our city, yet you came with me on this long journey. What sufferings have you not already borne for my sake!'

Kannaki answered:

'In my husband's absence, I could not distribute presents to good men, honour Brahmins, welcome saintly monks, or receive friends, as is done in all noble homes. After your desertion I tried to hide my tears from your respected mother and your renowned and proud father, whom the king holds in high esteem. Yet they understood my sorrow, showed me their affection, and spoke to me kindly. In spite of my efforts to smile, the feebleness of my body betrayed to them the anguish of my heart. You may have gone astray from the path of virtue, but I wished to do my duty, and so I followed you.'

Kovalan said:

'You left your old parents, your friends, your attendants, your nurse, and all your retinue, and kept at your service only your modesty, your faith, your virtue, and your loyalty. You came with me and relieved me of remorse. Precious as a golden liana, girl with the fragrant plaits! You are the incarnation of faithfulness, the beacon of the world, the tender bud of chastity, the store of all virtues. I must now go to the town, taking with me one of the gold circlets that grace your charming ankles. Having exchanged it for money, I shall soon return. Till then do not let your courage fail.'

After kissing the long black hair he loved, heartbroken to leave her all alone, and holding back the tears that filled his eyes, he walked heavily away. As a stranger to those parts, he could not know that the humped bull that stood before him as he passed the meeting place of the cowherds was a fearful omen.

Passing through the street of the courtesans, he reached the bazaar. There he saw a goldsmith in court dress, who was walking along, tweezers in hand, followed by a hundred jewellers all famous for their craftsmanship. Kovalan thought this must be the goldsmith of the Pandya monarch. So he approached him and inquired:

'Could you estimate the value of an ankle bracelet worthy of the consort of the great king who protects us?'

The goldsmith had the face of Death's dread messenger. He answered with obsequious politeness:

'I am a novice in this great art: I know only how to make diadems and a few royal ornaments.' Kovalan opened the packet containing the precious anklet. The perfidious goldsmith examined the fine workmanship of the chiselling in pure gold and the rare rubies and diamonds. After a pause he said: 'This circlet can be purchased only by the queen herself. I am going to the palace, and shall speak to the victorious king. You may wait with the anklet near my humble home till I return.'

Kovalan sat down in a small shrine that stood near the villain's cottage. When he saw him waiting in the narrow temple, the hard-hearted thief thought: Before anyone discovers that it was I who stole the [queen's] anklet, I shall accuse this foreigner before the king. He then walked on.

The great queen, resentful of the king's interest in Madurai's pretty dancers, who sing songs of all sorts and show in their movements their understanding of music, was disguising her jealousy under the mask of a friendly quarrel. Pretending a sudden headache, she left the royal presence. Later, when ministers and counsellors had gone, the king entered the inner apartment where the great queen lay surrounded by maids with long alluring eyes.

The goldsmith met the king near the innermost door, where guards had been posted. He bowed low, praising the monarch in a hundred ways. Then he said:

'The man who stole an anklet from this palace has been found. He apparently did not use heavy tools or crowbars, but just the power of magic words, with which he put to sleep the soldiers who were guarding the doors. He then quietly took away the handsomest ankle bracelet in the palace. He is now hiding near my humble house, fearing the guards that patrol the city.'

Now it befell that this was the moment when the actions of Kovalan's past lives had become ripe like a mature crop in the fields. The king, who wears the garland of margosa leaves, did not call for any inquiry. He simply summoned some town guards and ordered:

'Should you find, in the hands of a most clever thief, an ankle ornament resembling a wreath of flowers, which belongs to my consort, put the man to death and bring me the bracelet.'

When he heard the royal order, the infamous goldsmith, with mirth in his heart, thought: I've brought it off! He led the guards to Kovalan, whom a merciless fate had thrown into his net, and told him:

'On orders from the king, whose army has won all battles, these officers have come with me to look at your piece of jewelry.' He pointed out to them the details of the ankle bracelet's design. But they protested:

'The appearance of this good man is surely not that of a thief. We cannot put him to death.'

The astute goldsmith smiled contemptuously. He explained to these simple men that the people whose shameful trade is theft have invented eight ways to deceive their innocent victims: these are spells, bewitching, drugs, omens, and magic, as well as place, time, and devices.

'If you let yourselves become intoxicated by the drugs this man dares use, you expose yourselves to the anger of our great king.

'The thief who utters magic spells becomes invisible, like a child of the gods. When he calls for the help of celestial genii, he can carry away his stolen objects unseen. Stupefying his victims with his drugs, he renders them incapable of the slightest movement. Unless omens are good, a real thief abstains from any activity even when he sees before him objects of great value ready to fall into his hands. When he makes use of enchantments, he can despoil the king of the gods himself of the wreath that adorns his chest. If he has chosen in advance the place of his rapine, no one can see him there. When he has set the time, the gods themselves could not stop him from seizing the object he wants. If he uses his implements to steal things of great value, no one can find him out. If you should read in the thieves' sacred book, you would see that their art requires arduous study, and that it has almost no limits.

'It happened once that a clever thief, disguised as an ambassador, had stood a whole day before the door of the palace. At night he changed himself into a young woman, and, entering unnoticed, hid in the shadow cast by a lamp. He seized the rare diamond necklace, bright as the sun, that shone round the neck of the sleeping crown prince. Waking up, the prince felt that his necklace was not on his shoulders. He drew his sword, but the thief was able to grasp it and keep the prince from striking a blow. When he tired of this, the prince tried fighting with his hands, but the thief, expert in his profession, ran away, leaving the prince alone and fighting against a stone pillar studded with precious gems. There is no thief on earth equal to this villain. If one of you has a better one, then he may bring him to me.'

A young hangman who had been listening to the criminal goldsmith's words, spear in hand, said:

'In the season of rains, during a dark night when my village was fast asleep, a thief came armed with a ploughshare like those used in the fields. Dressed in black, searching for jewels, he seemed fiercer than a tiger. I drew my sword but he tore it away from me and vanished, never to be found. The deeds of thieves are amazing. If we do not obey the king, we shall surely be in trouble. Brave soldiers, let's do our duty.'

Thereupon one of these drunkards hurled his sword at Kovalan. It pierced his body. Blood gushing from the wound fell upon the Earth, mother of men, and she shuddered with grief. Defeated by his fate, Kovalan fell, and the virtuous sceptre of the Pandyas was bent.

CODA

And since the champion of justice
failed to safeguard Kannaki's beloved spouse,
the upright sceptre of the Pandya kings
became forever bent.
All these events had been foreseen,
for actions, be they good or evil,
bear their inexorable fruits.
This is the reason that wise men
make all their actions
accord with the great moral laws.

Canto Eighteen
The Wreath of Agony

Other hardy and shapely cowgirls had been bathing in the deep waters of the Vaigai. On their return they worshipped Vishnu, offering him flowers, incense, sandalwood, and fragrant wreaths. Toward the end of the love-dance, a girl who had heard some rumours in the city returned in haste. She stopped, silent and motionless, at some distance from Kannaki, who asked:

'Will you not speak to me, my friend? Tell me. My husband has not yet returned, and my heart feels oppressed. My breath is as hot as that from a blacksmith's bellows. Have you not brought some news from the city? Long may you live, my friend.

'Though the sun is still high, I am trembling. Why has my beloved not come back? My heart is becoming heavy with fear. Since you see that I am worried by his absence, please distract me with some gossip from town. May the gods bless you, friend.

'Shall I beg your help? My lord has not yet returned. I fear he may be in danger. My mind is bewildered, I feel anxious. Are you hiding something from me? Pray speak to me, my friend. Tell me what people who live in your city, strangers to me, have said.'

At last the cowgirl spoke:

'They abused him. They said he was a thief, come secretly to steal a wonderful ankle bracelet from the royal palace. They accused him, calling him a robber, mysterious in his behaviour. And the royal soldiers, those who wear noisy anklets, put him to death.'

On hearing this, Kannaki leaped up in her anger, then collapsed to the ground. It seemed as if the moon had risen in the sky; then fallen, shrouded with clouds. She wept, and her eyes became still redder. She clamoured, 'Where are you, beloved husband?' and fell in a swoon. When she came back to her senses, she lamented:

'And must I die of sorrow, like the wretched women who take fearful oaths upon the pyres of their beloved husbands? For I have lost the man who dearly loved me, by the fault of a king his own subjects must despise.

'Must I die of despair, like the lonely women who carry their grief from pilgrimage to pilgrimage, and bathe in holy rivers, after the death of husbands who wore fragrant flower-garlands on their broad chests?

'Must I die, an embodiment of meaningless virtue, through the fatal error of a ruler who bears the sceptre of injustice? Must I languish in loneliness, like the forlorn women who, after their tender husbands have vanished in the funeral pyre's smoke, remain, half-alive, in abject widowhood?

'Must I, with broken heart, suffer an endless agony, because in tragic error the sceptre of a Pandya king has gone astray from the path of right?

'Look at me! Hearken to my words, you honest cowgirls here assembled! It was with just foreboding that you danced the dance of love. Now hearken to my words! Listen to me, cowherds' daughters!

'Sun god, whose rays are flames! You, the eternal witness of all the deeds committed on the sea-encircled earth, speak! Could my husband be called a thief?'

A voice was heard, coming from the sky:

'He was never a thief! Woman of the carplike eyes, this city shall be purified by fire!'

Canto Nineteen
The Murmurs of the City

The Sun had given its verdict. The woman with the bright armlets stood up. Holding in her hand her remaining ankle bracelet, mate to the one she had given to Kovalan, Kannaki went to the city, and walked through it, crying:

'Virtuous women who live in this city ruled by a nefarious monarch, listen to me! Today I underwent unspeakable agony. What must nowise happen has happened. Never shall I accept this iniquitous injustice. Was my husband a thief? No, he was killed to avoid paying him the price of my ankle bracelet. Can there be a more flagrant denial of justice? Should I ever see the body of the man who dearly loved me, I shall not hear from him the words I need to hear, saying he is not at fault. Is that justice? He can no longer protect me, so why don't you come and accuse me too of some invented crime? Do you hear me?'

The people of the rich city of Madurai were dismayed at the sight of this distracted woman. In their stupefaction, they exclaimed:

'The just and virtuous sceptre of our king has been forever bent. A crime that nothing can undo has been committed against this innocent woman. What shall this lead us to? Tarnished is the honour of Tennavan, the king of kings, who inherited an infallible spear and a stainless white parasol. What are we to think? The parasol of our victorious king was protecting the land, keeping us cool under its shade; and now the fierce rays of the sun may devour us. What are we to expect?

'A new and mighty goddess has appeared to us. In her hand she carries an ankle bracelet made of gold. Is this a portent from heaven? From the desperate woman's eyes, red and running with black collyrium, tears are flowing. She seems possessed by a genie. What must we think?'

Thus bewildered, the people of Madurai gathered around her, showing their good will and attempting to console her. Everywhere indignant words could be heard. In the midst of this disorder, some-one showed Kannaki the body of her dear husband. The lianalike woman saw him; he could not see her.

The Sun was unable to bear this sight. Suddenly it extinguished its rays, hiding behind the hills. The veil of night covered the earth. In the evening dusk Kannaki, resembling a frail reed in bloom, lamented, and the whole city resounded with her cries. That very morning, be-tween two kisses, she had received from her husband a flower wreath he was wearing, and with it she had adorned her tresses. Now on the evening of the same day she looked down at him lying in a pool of blood that had flowed from his open wound. He could not even see her grief. She cried out in anger and despair:

'O witness of my grief, you cannot console me. Is it right that your body, fairer than pure gold, lie unwashed here in the dust? Will people not say that it was my ill luck that led a just king to a mistake that was the fruit of his ignorance? Is it just that in the red glow of the twilight your handsome chest, framed with a flower wreath, lies thrown down on the bare earth, while I remain alone, helpless and abandoned to despair? Shall people not be led to say that it was my own predestination that compelled the innocent Pandya to such an injustice when the whole world could easily see that he had committed an error?

'Is there no woman here? Is there no real woman, or only the sort of woman who would allow such an injustice to be done to her lawful husband? Are there such women here?

'Is there no man in this land? Is there no honest man, or only the sort of man who nourishes and protects only the sons of his own blood?

'Is there no god? Is there no god in this country? Can there be a god in a land where the sword of the king is used for the murder of innocent strangers? Is there no god, no god?'

Thus lamenting, Kannaki clasped her husband's chest that Fortune had so dearly cherished. Suddenly Kovalan arose and exclaimed, 'Your moonlike face appears tarnished.' With affectionate hands he wiped away the tears that burned her eyes. The lovely woman fell to the ground, weeping and moaning. With bracelet-laden hands she grasped the feet of her beloved husband. But he departed, rising into the air. Surrounded by hosts of angels, he shed his mortal frame and disappeared. His voice could still be heard, fading away:

'Beloved! Stay there, stay! Remain peacefully in life!'

She thought: Is this an illusion of my demented mind? What else could all this be? Is some spirit eager to deceive me? Where can I discover the truth? I shall not search for my husband before he is avenged. I shall meet this inhuman king and ask for his justice against himself.

She stood up, and then she remembered her vision. Tears fell from her long carp-shaped eyes. She stiffened, and recalled her anger. Wiping away her burning tears, she ran to the majestic gate of the royal palace.

Canto Twenty
The Call for Justice

The Pandya queen spoke:

'Alas! I saw, in a dream, a sceptre bent, a fallen parasol. The bell at the gate moved of itself and rang loudly. Alas! I also saw . . . I saw the eight directions of space wavering, the night devouring the sun. Alas! I also saw . . . I saw the rainbow shining in the night, a glittering star falling by day. Alas!'

THE OMENS

'The sceptre of justice and the white parasol fallen to the hard ground, the bell ringing alone at the gate of a victorious king's palace, my heart trembling with fear, the rainbow in the night, the star falling by day, the directions of space vacillating – all these are portents of a fearful danger at hand. I must inform the king.'

Adorned with resplendent jewels, she went to the king's apartments, followed by maids who carried her mirror and her various trifles. With her went her hunchbacks, dwarfs, deaf-mutes, and buffoons, carrying silks, betel, cosmetics, pastes, garlands, feather-fans, and incense. The ladies in waiting, with flowers in their hair, sang her praise:

'May the consort of the Pandya, who protects the vast universe, live many happy days.'

Thus the great queen, followed by her guards and maids singing her praises and bowing before her feet, went to King Tennavan, on whose chest Fortune rests. He was seated on the lion throne. She told him her sinister dream.

At the same moment cries were heard:

'Hoy, doorkeeper! Hoy, watchman! Hoy, palace guards of an irresponsible ruler whose vile heart lightly casts aside the kingly duty of rendering justice! Go! Tell how a woman, a widow, carrying a single ankle bracelet from a pair that once joyfully rang together, waits at the gate. Go! Announce me!'

The watchman bowed before the king and said:

'Long live the ruler of Korkai! Long live Tennavan, lord of the southern mountains, whose fair name calumny and scandal have never touched!

'A woman is waiting at the gate. She is not Korravai, the victorious goddess who carries in her hand a glorious spear and stands upon the neck of a defeated buffalo losing its blood through its fresh wounds. She is not Anangu, youngest of the seven virgins, for whom Shiva once danced; and she is not Kali, who dwells in the darkest forests inhabited by ghosts and imps. Neither is she the goddess who pierced the chest of the mighty Daruka. She seems filled with a mad fury, suffused with rage. She has lost someone dear to her, and stands at the gate clasping an ankle bracelet of gold in her hands.'

The king said:

'Let her come in. Bring her to me.' The gatekeeper let the woman enter, and brought her to the king. When she drew near the monarch, he said: 'Woman, your face is soiled from weeping. Who are you, young woman? What brings you before us?'

Kannaki answered sharply:

'Inconsiderate king! I have much to say. I was born in Puhar, that well-known capital, the names of whose kings remain unsullied. One of them, Shibi, in ancient times sacrificed his own life to save a dove, in the presence of all the gods. Another, Manunitikanda, when a cow with weeping eyes rang the palace bell in search of justice for her calf, crushed under a chariot wheel, sacrificed his own son, guilty of the act, under the same wheel. There in Puhar a man named Kovalan was born. He was the son of a wealthy merchant, Mashattuvan. His family is known and his name untarnished. Led by fate, O king, he entered your city, with ringing anklets, expecting to earn a living. When he tried to sell my ankle bracelet, he was murdered. I am his wife. My name is Kannaki.'

The king answered:

'Divine woman, there is no injustice in putting a robber to death. Do you not know that that is the duty of a king?'

The beautiful girl said:

'King of Korkai, you went astray from the path of duty. Remember that my ankle bracelet was filled with precious stones.'

'Woman,' the king answered, 'what you have said is pertinent. For ours was filled, not with gems, but with pearls. Let it be brought.' The ankle bracelet was brought and placed before the king. Kannaki seized it and broke it open. A gem sprang up into the king's face. When he saw the stone, he faltered. He felt his parasol fallen, his sceptre bent. He said: 'Is it right for a king to act upon the word of a miserable goldsmith? I am the thief. For the first time I have failed in my duty as protector of the southern kingdom. No way is left open to me save to give up my life.' And having spoken, the king swooned. The great queen fell near him. Trembling, she lamented:

'Never can a woman survive her husband's death.' And, placing the feet of her lord on her head, the unfortunate queen fainted away.

Kannaki said:

'Today we have seen evidence of the sage's warning: *The Divine Law appears in the form of death before the man who fails in his duty.* Consort of a victorious king who committed a deed both cruel and unjust! I too am guilty of great sins. Be witness to the cruel deed I perform.'

CODA

The poet speaks:

With terror I saw Kannaki, tears streaming from her blood-red eyes, holding in her hand her remaining ankle bracelet, her body lifeless, her undone hair resembling a dark forest.

I saw the sovereign of Kudal become a corpse. I must be guilty of great crimes to be witness to such fearful events.

The lord of the Vaigai saw Kannaki's body, soiled with dust, her black dishevelled hair, her tears, and the solitary ankle bracelet in her fair hand. Overwhelmed with sorrow, he listened to the words Kannaki had said in her rage. He could not bear to remain alive, and fell dead.

Canto Twenty-one
The Malediction

Kannaki then spoke to the dying Pandya queen:

'Wife of a great monarch! I too am a victim of fate. I have never wished to cause pain. But it is said that he who has wronged another in the morning must, before darkness falls, repay his debt.

'A woman with abundant hair one day asked and obtained that at midday her kitchen and the oven's fire should take human form to testify to her purity.

'Once, as a joke, her friends told a virtuous and naïve widow, whose pubis showed some stripes, that her husband was a sand effigy modelled on the bank of the Kaveri. The faithful woman stayed near the image. The rising tide, which had surrounded her, stayed aloof, not daring to approach.

214

'A daughter of the famous king, Karikala, once jumped into the sea that had carried away her husband Vanjikkon, calling to him, "Lord with shoulders like mountains!" The god of the Sea himself brought back her husband to her. Clasping him like a liana, she led him to their home.

'Another good woman changed herself into stone and remained in a garden near the shore gazing at the approaching ships. She recovered her human shape only on the day when her husband returned home.

'When the son of a co-wife fell into a well, a woman threw in her own son and succeeded in saving both.

'Because a stranger had glanced at her with lustful eyes, a chaste woman changed her moonlike face into that of a monkey. Only when her husband returned did this flowerlike woman, who treasured her body more than a jewel, take back her human face.

'There was also a girl, fair and lovely as a statue of gold. She heard her mother say to her father, "Women's settlements unsettle all things. Once, as a joke, I told my maid, 'When I have a daughter, and when you, maid with pretty bangles, have a son, my daughter shall be your son's bride.' The maid kept this in her memory, and today she asked me for the girl. I am at my wit's end, not knowing what to say. How unfortunate I am!" When she overheard this, the girl like a golden statue put on a silk dress, tied her hair, and came to the maid's son. She knelt before him and placed his foot upon her head.

'It was in Puhar, the city from which I come, that they all lived, these noble women with fragrant braids. If these stories are true, and if I am faithful, I cannot allow your city to survive. I must destroy it, together with its king. You shall soon see the meaning of my words.'

Kannaki then left the king's palace, shouting:

'Men and women of Madurai, city of the four temples! And you, gods of heaven! Listen to me! I curse this town whose ruler put to death the man I dearly loved. The blame is not mine.'

Suddenly, with her own hands, she twisted and tore her left breast from her body. Then she walked three times round the city, repeating her curse at each gate. In her despair she threw away her lovely breast, which fell in the dirt of the street. Then before her there appeared the god of Fire in the shape of a priest. His body was all blue and encircled with tongues of flames. His hair was as red as the evening sky, his milk-white teeth shone brightly. He said:

'Faithful woman! I have orders to destroy this city on the very day you suffered such great wrong. Is there someone that should be spared?'

Kannaki bade him:

'Spare Brahmins, good men, cows, truthful women, cripples, old men, children. Destroy evildoers.'

And the city of Madurai, capital of the Pandyas, whose chariots are invincible, was immediately hidden in flames and smoke.

CODA

When the glorious Pandya, his dancers and his palace,
his soldiers holding shining bows, even
his elephants, were all burnt down to ashes,
destroyed by the flames of virtue,
the wretched town's immortals went away,
for they are blameless.

Canto Twenty-Three
The Explanation

The great goddess of Madurai was the protector of the royal clan that rules over the cool port of Korkai, the Cape of the Virgin, and Mount Podiyil. Her power extends as far as the Himalaya.

The goddess wears the moon's crescent in her thick, tangled hair. Her eyes resemble lotuses. Her face is luminous. Her coral lips cover gleaming teeth. Her body is blue on the left side and golden on the right. She carries a gold lotus in her left hand, and in her right a sparkling and fearsome sword. The victors' circlet can be seen on her left ankle, another unrivalled anklet tinkles on her right.

Not daring to come too near the beautiful woman whom adversity had so cruelly smitten and who in her despair had torn away her own breast, the wise goddess approached her from behind and gently said:

'Blessed woman! Can you listen to my request?'

Kannaki, whose face was shrivelled with pain, turned toward her and said:

'Who are you? Why do you follow me? Can you fathom the depth of my sorrow?'

The goddess of Madurai replied:

'I know the immensity of your pain. Faultless woman! I am the tutelar deity of this vast city. Anxious for your husband's future, I wish to speak to you. Listen to what I say, woman with the golden bracelets. Noble woman! As a friend, I ask your attention to the great tragedy that is breaking my heart. Dear one! Listen to the sad tale of the misdeeds committed by our kings in their previous incarnations. Listen to your husband's past life, cause of all the evils that have overwhelmed us.

'Until this day my ears have heard only the chant of the *Vedas*, never the tolling of the bell of justice. We have seen the people mock at monarchs come to pay tribute and bow down before our king, whose edicts were never questioned by his subjects. It is true that young girls with timid looks inspire in him, on occasion, passions that he cannot control, like a young elephant that escapes from his mahout. But there can be no wrong in this for a young prince who is the scion of a noble and virtuous clan.

'Do you know the story of the Pandya monarch who with his own hands broke the diadem and glowing bracelets of heaven's king, though he was armed with thunderbolts? One day this Pandya was walking near the cottage of a man named Kirandai, whose life had no value for anyone. He heard the wife of this poor man say, 'You want to go away, leaving me in this open yard, and you say that no door can protect us better than the royal justice. Is our door rotten, then?' The king closed both his ears as if a red-hot iron had pierced him through and through. He shuddered with fear, his heart was afire. He cut off his own hand so that his sceptre might be strengthened. Since then the name of the whole dynasty has remained untarnished.

'Another king, who handled his polished spear with great art, and fed his soldiers generously after bringing peace and order to the land, one day assembled his subjects in the audience hall. A most learned Brahmin named Parashar had heard of the magnificence of this Chera, who, it was said, had with his sabre opened the gateway of heaven before a great Tamil poet of Brahmin blood. Parashar thought: I must go to meet this Chera, renowned for his valour and the power of his lance. This Brahmin was born in the peace-loving and fertile country of Puhar, whose kings bear a virtuous sceptre and a victorious sword. You know that one of them gave his own flesh to save a humble dove, and that another avenged a cow that had been wronged. Parashar set out on his journey. He passed through the hills of Malaya, deep jungles, countless villages and cities. He was a great master of dialectics, an art greatly appreciated by the twice-born, who, seeking unity with infinite good, light the three sacred fires ordained by the four *Vedas*, perform the five rituals of sacrifice, and never fail in the six duties of a priest.

'Parashar defeated all opponents in philosophical debates and thus won from the king the title of *Parpanavahai*, Sublime Scholar. As he was returning homeward, laden with gifts, he reached the village of Tangal, in the Pandya kingdom, where noble Brahmins lived. In this village there was a green *bodhi* tree. Tired, the traveller, with his staff, his bowl, his white parasol, his five sticks, his bundle, and his shoes, rested awhile. He said, "Long live the conqueror whose immaculate parasol so well protects his subjects and whose realm is secure! Long live the protector of men who dragged the *kadamba* tree from the sea! Long live the king who carved his name on the proud brow of the Himalaya! Long live the royal *Poraiyan* who rules over the plains where the cool and lovely Porunai flows. Long live the great King Mandaran Cheral!"

'Laughing children crowded about him. Some had long curls; others already had their hair in tufts. Several could still hardly speak with their coral lips. They all came to play on the road. Parashar said to them, "Young Brahmins! If you can faultlessly repeat after me the Vedic hymns I shall chant, you may take my bundle, which contains a treasure." Then Alamar Shelvan, young son of the renowned priest Varttikan, stood forth. His red lips still tasted of his mother's milk. Lisping, before all his playmates, he proudly repeated the sacred words without an error. Charmed by this child of the south, the old Brahmin gave him a string of pearls, brilliant gems, gold bracelets and earrings. Then he continued his journey.

'Some policeman of the town, jealous of Varttikan, whose son went decked in these ornaments, accused him: "This Brahmin appropriated some treasure that he found, which, by law, belongs to the king." They threw him into prison. Varttikan's wife Karttikai became mad with despair. In her sorrow, she wallowed in the dust, shrieking and cursing everybody. Seeing her, the goddess Durga, whose name is ever untarnished, refused to let the door of her temple be opened at prayer time. The king, whose sword is ever victorious, heard that the heavy door of the temple would not open. He was dismayed, and called his ministers: "Some injustice must have been done. Let me know if you have noticed some unconscious failure in the discharge of our duties toward the goddess who gives victory."

'His young messengers bowed before his feet and told him about Varttikan. "This is unfair!" cried the king in anger. Summoning Varttikan to him, he said, "Your duty is to forgive us. My virtuous rule has not yet ended, although, through the fault of my servants, I have been led astray from the path of justice." And the king gave him the country of Tangal, with its rice fields watered by irrigation channels from the lakes. He also offered him the town of Vayalur and its immense income. Then he lay prostrate at the feet of Karttikai's husband to pacify his anger.

'And the door of the temple, abode of the goddess who rides a deer, opened with a crash that echoed through all the ancient city's streets, lined by cliff-like mansions. Then the king sent a drummer on an elephant through the streets to proclaim his order: "All prisoners shall be reprieved, all unpaid taxes remitted. Those who discover a treasure may enjoy their fortune in peace."

'Now I shall explain how our king could be led to such injustice. It was predicted long ago that great Madurai would be burned and its king would be made destitute during the month of Adi, the eighth day after the full moon appeared on a Friday, at a time when the Pleiades and Aries should be in the ascendant.

'Listen, woman with the rich bracelets! Once the kings Vasu and Kumara, who with their shining swords and strong armies had justly ruled the richly forested Kalinga country, became enemies. One ruled over Singapuram in the plain, the other over Kapilapuram in the bamboo forest. They belonged to a great dynasty whose fortune appeared everlasting. While they were fighting, no one dared to approach within six miles of the battlefield.

'A young merchant named Sangaman, anxious to increase his wealth, came with his wife in the garb of a refugee. He carried a huge bale on his head and soon began to sell his precious wares in a bazaar in Singapuram.

'Woman with gold bracelets! Your husband Kovalan, in a previous incarnation, was known as Bharata. He was in the service of valorous King Vasu. He had renounced his vow of non-violence and was hated by all. He believed Sangaman to be a spy of the enemy king. He had him caught, brought him before the king of the victorious lance, and caused him to be beheaded. Nili, the wife of the unhappy Sangaman, found herself left alone. She ran through the streets and squares, creating great uproar and shouting, "King, is that your justice? Merchants, is that justice? Workmen, do you call that justice?" For fourteen days she wandered, taking no rest, then inspired by the thought that the day was auspicious, she climbed the high rocks to follow her husband in death. As she threw herself down into the valley, she shouted a curse: "He who inflicted a cruel death upon my husband shall share his fate." So today a destiny that no power could stop has brought you this ordeal.

'Hearken to what I say! Actions committed in past lives always bear fruit. No amount of austerity or virtue can loose the bonds of our actions. Woman with lovely hair! After fourteen days you shall see the man you love in his celestial garb, for never more can you behold his human form.'

When she had thus explained to Kannaki – soon herself to become a goddess – all the strange events of the day, the goddess of Madurai was able to control the flames that were devouring the city.

Then Kannaki told her:

'I wish neither to sit nor sleep nor stop, until I see the husband dear to my heart.' She went and broke all her bracelets, as widows do, in the temple of Durga. She cried, 'I entered this city through the eastern gate with a beloved husband. Today I leave it through the western portal, alone.' Unaware of light or darkness, she wandered, desolate, near the Vaigai in flood. Sad and distracted, unheeding when she fell in a ditch or climbed a cliff, she ascended the sacred hill where the god Neduvel resides, he whose fiery lance once tore through the entrails of the sea. There, under the *kinos* in bloom, Kannaki wept and lamented: 'Alas, I am guilty of a great crime.'

Fourteen days thus passed. Then heaven's king, with all his angels, thought the time had come to proclaim the saintliness of this woman, whose name men shall ever recall. He showered down a rain of never-fading flowers, then appeared and bowed at her feet.

On a divine chariot, seated beside Kovalan, who had been put to death in the royal city, Kannaki, with her hair profuse as a forest, ascended, happy, into heaven.

CODA

Even the gods pay honour to the wife
who worships no one save her husband.
Kannaki, pearl among all women of the earth,
is now a goddess, and is highly honoured
by all the gods who dwell in Paradise.

❧

Part Two

AGE OF GURUS
[TEACHERS]
600 B.C.–A.D. 500

❧

A. GAUTAMA SIDDHARTHA, THE BUDDHA

Tipitaka (Pali, 477 B.C.)

Saddharma-Pundarika (Sanskrit, *c.* A.D. 100)

B. TIRU-VALLUVAR

Gautama Siddhartha (563–483 B.C.), the prince of Sakyas (a kingdom on the foothills of the Himalayan mountains with its capital at Kapilavastu), leaving behind his wife and a son in the palace and abandoning his throne, embarked on a spiritual quest at the age of twenty-nine. Disassociating himself from historical tradition and ritual, he sought to reform society and its spiritual attitudes by reasserting the Upanishadic spirit of free inquiry into the sufferings of mankind. When he finally attained his enlightenment and became the Buddha at the age of thirty-five, he taught his way of life for the next forty-five years. After his death, his teachings established a new religion called Buddhism, which in its turn gave rise to a distinct body of literature.

Much of the Buddhist literature which has become scriptural or canonical has been classified as belonging to two of its great traditions, namely, the earlier Theravada (Way of the Elders), current in South Asia, and the later Mahayana (Great Vehicle), current in North Asia. The Theravada texts, written in Pali language (derived from Vedic Sanskrit), were collected in an anthology or 'Holy Book' called *Tipitaka* (Sanskrit, *tri-pitaka*), meaning Three Containers or Three Testaments. The various *Mahayana* texts, written in Classical Sanskrit (as distinct from Vedic Sanskrit), Tibetan, Chinese, and Japanese, are not so precisely collected into one anthology.

The *Tipitaka* contains Buddha's sermons, sayings, and rules of the Order, as recalled from the minds of men at the First Great Council of Elders and Disciples held at Rajagriha in 477 B.C., soon after the Buddha's death. Subsequently, these texts were perfected and canonized at the Second Great Council, held at Vaisali in 377 B.C., and the Third Great Council, held at Pataliputra in 247 B.C. under the patronage of Emperor Asoka. These texts were organized in three *Pitakas* or parts, called:

I. *Vinaya Pitaka,* containing rules of discipline concerning the *Sangha* or the Order of Disciples;

II. *Sutta Pitaka* (Sanskrit, *Sutra*), containing sermons and sayings of Buddha, arranged in five Nikayas (sections), according to the length of the sermons:

  (i) Digha Nikaya (Long Sermons)
 (ii) Majjhima Nikaya (Medium Sermons)
(iii) Smyutta Nikaya (Kindred Sayings)
 (iv) Anguttara Nikaya (Gradual Sayings)
  (v) Khuddaka Nikaya (Miscellaneous), containing, among other
      things, (a) *Dhammapada* (Way of Righteousness), consisting of
      423 couplets or sayings of Buddha on various occasions; and
      (b) *Jataka* (Birth-stories), consisting of 550 stories of Gautama
      Buddha's former lives.

III. *Abhidhamma Pitaka* (Beyond or Higher *Dhamma*; Sanskrit, *dharma*), containing commentaries on the *Sutta Pitaka* and philosophical analyses of the sermons.

When schism overtook Buddhism, the division came in slow stages. In the first two centuries after the establishment of the religion, differences arose among the followers on their views on the Order, on their interpretation of the teachings of Buddha, and on their attitude to metaphysical questions. By the time of the third century B.C., there were eighteen different schools, one of which was known as *Sarvasti-vadins*. It was from this sect that the school of *Maha-Sanghika* (Great Order) was first established in the first century B.C., which subsequently led to the growth of a distinct Buddhist tradition called *Mahayana* (Great Vehicle of Law), as opposed to *Theravada*. Under the *Mahayana* doctrine a number of other schools emerged, the most important of which are the *Madhyamika* (Middle Doctrine) school of Nagarjuna (first century A.D.), and *Vijnana-vada* or *Yoga-cara* (Mind, only, or Subjective Idealism) school of Vasubhandhu (A.D. 420–500).

At the Fifth Great Council held in A.D. 70 in Kashmir under the patronage of King Kanishka, the Council promulgated *Mahayana* doctrines, not recognized by *Theravada*. A number of new concepts were evolved to enlarge the scope of Buddha's teaching from individual salvation to universal salvation. The element of grace was introduced through the operation of *Bodhisattva* (a saint who having attained enlightenment renounces *Nirvana* (state of bliss), in order to help humanity on its spiritual pilgrimage). Thus the teaching of Buddha was made to appeal to the heart more than to the head. The verbal teachings were mystically interpreted to communicate meaning on a variety of levels to every type of mind on every level of spiritual sophistication. While the goal of *Theravada* remained the attainment of self-salvation or Arahatship, the *Mahayana* ideal became more and more identified with the attainment of the Bodhisattva-hood, the renouncing of Nirvana and the compassionate helping of mankind in its progress towards spiritual perfection.

(Pali, 477 B.C.)

Buddha's first sermon, given at Benares after seven years of spiritual quest and final enlightenment, contains the crystallized essence of his prolonged meditation on the human condition. In this sermon Buddha expresses his testament of faith, prescribing a necessary basis for a good way of life, and lays down the foundation of a just society on earth. Buddha's remarkably simple system has so influenced the spiritual sensibilities of so many people that it has become the religion of a large portion of the human race. In this sense, the first sermon somewhat parallels Chapter 20 of Exodus, in which Moses preached a way of life embodied in the Ten Commandments, or Chapter 5 of Matthew, in which Jesus explained his view of good life in the Sermon on the Mount. It would be illuminating to try to find out to whom the pre-Jesus Essenese preachers of Qumran monastery in Palestine were referring as the 'Prophet of Righteousness', three centuries after the establishment of Buddhism in India and its spread to other parts of Asia.

Rejecting metaphysical and theological dogmas, Buddha maintained that his system is based on human experience, and comprises Four Noble Truths and the Eight-fold Path; and that these would be sufficient to provide a humanistic basis for existential ethics. Buddha was not endeavouring to explain the inconceivable metaphysical principle underlying all manifested universe. To him what was real was the change, and the suffering caused by it was not an illusion. Therefore, he maintained that his main concern was to relieve man of his suffering in some way, just as a medical man would attend to relieve the misery of a wounded man, without first attempting to determine the legal or moral responsibilites for the accident. Consequently, Buddha argued that the assumptions or hypotheses that man makes in regard to the origin of the world, the creation of man, the destruction of the world and the nature of underlying Reality, being conceptual, are somewhat conjectural and of a dogmatic nature, and lead to contention. Such hypothetical here-before and here-after are not necessary for living a good life here on earth. What was necessary, from the Buddha's point of view, was that man should develop an attitude of compassionate understanding of the next man, for change, and the pain and suffering conditioned by it, are common to all men.

The Buddhists consider the occasion of the delivery of the First Sermon at Benares as being of prime historic importance, for it set into motion the 'Royal Chariot Wheel of the Supreme Dominion of the Dhamma', and thus inaugurated the 'Kingdom of Righteousness'. Commenting on this epoch-making sermon at Benares, Rhys-Davids, the translator, wrote: 'Never in the history of the world had a scheme of salvation been put forth so simple in its nature, so free from any superhuman agency, so independent of, so even antagonistic to the belief in a soul, the belief in God, and the hope of future life.'*

In the excerpt from his last sermon included here, Buddha denies any kind of divine authority or supernatural mystery about his teaching. Besides, he exhorts his disciples to comprehend the Four Noble Truths and practise the Eight-fold Path, and, becoming thus self-reliant, be lamps unto themselves, for he maintained: 'Only a lighted lamp could light another.'

The texts of the two sermons are taken from the translation of T. W. Rhys-Davids, *Buddhist Suttas*, Vol. XI of the Sacred Books of the East series, edited by F. Max Müller, Oxford: Clarendon Press, 1881; reprinted, Delhi: Motilal Banarsidass, 1965.

Selections: 'Kingdom of Righteousness' from *Dhamma-kakka-ppavattana-sutta* [The Foundation of the Kingdom of Righteousness], from *Anguttara Nikaya*, 4th section of *Sutta Pitaka: Buddhist Suttas*, Vol. XI, pp. 146–55. 'Lamp Unto Yourself' from *Maha-Parinibbana-sutta* [The Book of the Great Decease], from *Sutta Pitaka: Buddhist Suttas*, Vol. XI, pp. 34–9.

---

*T. W. Rhys-Davids, *Buddhist Suttas*, p. 142.

II.10   'KINGDOM OF RIGHTEOUSNESS'
BUDDHA'S FIRST SERMON

Reverence to the Blessed One, the Holy One, the Fully-Enlightened One.

1. Thus have I heard. The Blessed One was once staying at Benares, at the hermitage called Migadaya. And there the Blessed One addressed the company of the five Bhikkhus, and said:

2. 'There are two extremes, O Bhikkhus, which the man who has given up the world ought not to follow – the habitual practice, on the one hand, of those things whose attraction depends upon the passions; and especially of sensuality – a low and pagan way (of seeking satisfaction), unworthy, unprofitable, and fit only for the worldly-minded – and the habitual practice, on the other hand, of asceticism (or self-mortification), which is painful, unworthy, and unprofitable.

3. 'There is a middle path, O Bhikkhus, avoiding these two extremes, discovered by the Tathagata – a path which opens the eyes, and bestows understanding, which leads to peace of mind, to the higher wisdom, to full enlightenment, to Nirvana.

4. 'What is that middle path, O Bhikkhus, avoiding these two extremes, discovered by the Tathagata – that path which opens the eyes, and bestows understanding, which leads to peace of mind, to the higher wisdom, to full enlightenment, to Nirvana? Verily! it is this noble eightfold path; that is to say:

> 'Right views;
> Right aspirations;
> Right speech;
> Right conduct;
> Right livelihood;

---

1. *Five Bhikkhus:* five monks who had waited on the Buddha during his austerities, and became his first disciples: Kondanna, Vappa, Bhaddiya, Mahanama, and Assagi.

3. *Tathagata:* an epithet of Buddha, meaning one who has already gone through the Path.

Nirvana: state of blessedness, or Kingdom of Heaven.

> Right effort;
> Right mindfulness; and
> Right contemplation.

'This, O Bhikkhus, is that middle path, avoiding these two extremes, discovered by the Tathagata – that path which opens the eyes, and bestows understanding, which leads to peace of mind, to the higher wisdom, to full enlightenment, to Nirvana!

5. 'Now this, O Bhikkhus, is the noble truth concerning suffering.

'Birth is attended with pain, decay is painful, disease is painful, death is painful. Union with the unpleasant is painful, painful is separation from the pleasant; and any craving that is unsatisfied, that too is painful. In brief, the five aggregates which spring from attachment (the conditions of individuality and their cause) are painful.

'This then, O Bhikkhus, is the noble truth concerning suffering.

6. 'Now this, O Bhikkhus, is the noble truth concerning the origin of suffering.

'Verily, it is that thirst (or craving), causing the renewal of existence, accompanied by sensual delight, seeking satisfaction now here, now there – that is to say, the craving for the gratification of the passions, or the craving for (a future) life, or the craving for success (in this present life).

'This then, O Bhikkhus, is the noble truth concerning the origin of suffering.

7. 'Now this, O Bhikkhus, is the noble truth concerning the destruction of suffering.

'Verily; it is the destruction, in which no passion remains, of this very thirst; the laying aside of, the getting rid of, the being free from, the harbouring no longer of this thirst.

---

5. Cf. *Dhammapada*, XIV. 190–2.

Five aggregates: five *Skandhas* or factors which create the temporal continuity of individual personality, namely the body, feelings, ideas, volitions, and conscious awareness. Physical body is not dualistically separated from the mental factors, but the five elements are held together under the concept of 'momentariness' like the flame, or the river.

6. The Middle Path does not completely deny desire or body, but denies only lust or thirst or craving, or excessively selfish desire which causes pain or suffering.

'This then, O Bhikkhus, is the noble truth concerning the destruction of suffering.

8. 'Now this, O Bhikkhus, is the noble truth concerning the way which leads to the destruction of sorrow. Verily! it is this noble eightfold path; that is to say:

> 'Right views;
> Right aspirations;
> Right speech;
> Right conduct;
> Right livelihood;
> Right effort;
> Right mindfulness; and
> Right contemplation.

'This then, O Bhikkhus, is the noble truth concerning the destruction of sorrow.

9. 'That this was the noble truth concerning sorrow, was not, O Bhikkhus, among the doctrines handed down, but there arose within me the eye (to perceive it), there arose the knowledge (of its nature), there arose the understanding (of its cause), there arose the wisdom (to guide in the path of tranquillity), there arose the light (to dispel darkness from it).

10. 'And again, O Bhikkhus, that I should comprehend that this was the noble truth concerning sorrow, though it was not among the doctrines handed down, there arose within me the eye, there arose the knowledge, there arose the understanding, there arose the wisdom, there arose the light.

11. 'And again, O Bhikkhus, that I had comprehended that this was the noble truth concerning sorrow, though it was not among the doctrines handed down, there arose within me the eye, there arose the knowledge, there arose the understanding, there arose the wisdom, there arose the light.

9–20. Threefold realization of the meaning of each of the four Noble Truths, e.g. (1) the recognition of the Truth; (2) the need to comprehend it; (3) realization of it in practice.

9–11. First Noble Truth concerning Sorrow (*Dukkha*).

12. 'That this was the noble truth concerning the origin of sorrow, though it was not among the doctrines handed down, there arose within me the eye; but there arose within me the knowledge, there arose the understanding, there arose the wisdom, there arose the light.

13. 'And again, O Bhikkhus, that I should put away the origin of sorrow, though the noble truth concerning it was not among the doctrines handed down, there arose within me the eye, there arose the knowledge, there arose the understanding, there arose the wisdom, there arose the light.

14. 'And again, O Bhikkhus, that I had fully put away the origin of sorrow, though the noble truth concerning it was not among the doctrines handed down, there arose within me the eye, there arose the knowledge, there arose the understanding, there arose the wisdom, there arose the light.

15. 'That this, O Bhikkhus, was the noble truth concerning the destruction of sorrow, though it was not among the doctrines handed down; but there arose within me the eye, there arose the knowledge, there arose the understanding, there arose the wisdom, there arose the light.

16. 'And again, O Bhikkhus, that I should fully realize the destruction of sorrow though the noble truth concerning it was not among the doctrines handed down, there arose within me the eye, there arose the knowledge, there arose the understanding, there arose the wisdom, there arose the light.

17. 'And again, O Bhikkhus, that I had fully realized the destruction of sorrow though the noble truth concerning it was not among the doctrines handed down, there arose within me the eye, there arose the knowledge, there arose the understanding, there arose the wisdom, there arose the light.

18. 'That this was the noble truth concerning the way which leads to the destruction of sorrow, was not, O Bhikkhus, among the doctrines handed down; but there arose within me the eye, there arose the

---

12-14. Second Noble Truth concerning the origin of sorrow (*Tanha*).
15-17. Third Noble Truth concerning the destruction of sorrow (*Niroda*).
18-20. Fourth Noble Truths concerning the Middle Path (*Marga*).

knowledge, there arose the understanding, there arose the wisdom, there arose the light.

19. 'And again, O Bhikkhus, that I should become versed in the way which leads to the destruction of sorrow, though the noble truth concerning it was not among the doctrines handed down, there arose within me the eye, there arose the knowledge, there arose the understanding, there arose the wisdom, there arose the light.

20. 'And again, O Bhikkhus, that I had become versed in the way which leads to the destruction of sorrow, though the noble truth concerning it was not among the doctrines handed down, there arose within me the eye, there arose the knowledge, there arose the understanding, there arose the wisdom, there arose the light.

21. 'So long, O Bhikkhus, as my knowledge and insight were not quite clear, regarding each of these four noble truths in this triple order, in this twelvefold manner – so long was I uncertain whether I had attained to the full insight of that wisdom which is unsurpassed in the heavens or on earth, among the whole race of Samanas and Brahmans, or of gods or men.

22. 'But as soon, O Bhikkhus, as my knowledge and insight were quite clear regarding each of these four noble truths, in this triple order, in this twelvefold manner – then did I become certain that I had attained to the full insight of that wisdom which is unsurpassed in the heavens or on earth, among the whole race of Samanas and Brahmans, or of gods or men.

23. 'And now this knowledge and this insight has arisen within me. Immovable is the emancipation of my heart. This is my last existence. There will now be no rebirth for me!'

24. Thus spake the Blessed One. The company of the five Bhikkhus, glad at heart, exalted the words of the Blessed One. And when the discourse had been uttered, there arose within the venerable Kondanna the eye of truth, spotless, and without a stain, (and he saw that) whatsoever has an origin, in that is also inherent the necessity of coming to an end.

---

21. *Samanas and Brahmans:* practitioners of the Vedic religion.
24. *Kondanna:* one of the disciples.

25. And when the royal chariot wheel of the truth had thus been set rolling onwards by the Blessed One, the gods of the earth gave forth a shout, saying:

'In Benares, at the hermitage of the Migadaya, the supreme wheel of the empire of Truth has been set rolling by the Blessed One – that wheel which not by any Samana or Brahman, not by any god, not by any Brahma or Mara, not by any one in the universe, can ever be turned back!'

26. And when they heard the shout of the gods of the earth, the attendant gods of the four great kings (the guardian angels of the four quarters of the globe) gave forth a shout, saying:

'In Benares, at the hermitage of the Migadaya, the supreme wheel of the empire of Truth has been set rolling by the Blessed One – that wheel which not by any Samana or Brahman, not by any god, not by any Brahma or Mara, not by any one in the universe, can ever be turned back!'

27. [And thus as the gods in each of the heavens heard the shout of the inhabitants of the heaven beneath, they took up the cry until the gods in the highest heaven of heavens] gave forth the shout, saying:

'In Benares, at the hermitage of the Migadaya, the supreme wheel of the empire of Truth has been set rolling by the Blessed One – that wheel which not by any Samana or Brahman, not by any god, not by any Brahma or Mara, not by any one in the universe can ever be turned back!'

28. And thus, in an instant, a second, a moment, the sound went up even to the world of Brahma: and this great ten-thousand-world-system quaked and trembled and was shaken violently, and an immeasurable bright light appeared in the universe, beyond even the power of the gods!

29. Then did the Blessed One give utterance to this exclamation of joy: 'Kondanna hath realized it. Kondanna hath realized it!' And so

---

25. *Mara:* Evil One.

29. *The Maha Vagga* completes the narrative as follows: 'And then the venerable Annata-Kondanna having seen the truth, having arrived at the truth, having known the truth, having penetrated the truth, having passed beyond doubt, having laid aside uncertainty, having attained to confidence,

the venerable Kondanna acquired the name of Annata-Kondanna ('the Kondanna who realized').

II.11   'LAMP UNTO YOURSELF'
             BUDDHA'S LAST SERMON

26. Now when the Blessed One had remained as long as he wished at Ambapali's grove, he addressed Ananda, and said: 'Come, Ananda, let us go on to Beluva.'

'So be it, Lord,' said Ananda, in assent, to the Blessed One.

Then the Blessed One proceeded, with a great company of the brethren, to Beluva, and there the Blessed One stayed in the village itself.

27. Now the Blessed One there addressed the brethren, and said: 'O mendicants, do you take up your abode round about Vesali, each according to the place where his friends, intimates, and close companions may live, for the rainy season of vassa. I shall enter upon the rainy season here at Beluva.'

'So be it, Lord!' said those brethren, in assent, to the Blessed One. And they entered upon the rainy season round about Vesali, each according to the place where his friends or intimates or close companions lived: whilst the Blessed One stayed even there at Beluva.

28. Now when the Blessed One had thus entered upon the rainy

---

and being dependent on no one beside himself for knowledge of the religion of the teacher, spake thus to the Blessed One:

' "May I become, O my Lord, a novice under the Blessed One, may I receive full ordination!"

' "Welcome, O brother!" said the Blessed One, "the truth has been well laid down. Practise holiness to the complete suppression of sorrow!"

'And that was the ordination of the Venerable One.'

The other four, Vappa, Bhaddiya, Mahanama, and Assagi, were converted on the following days (Rhys-Davids).

26. *Ananda*: the cousin and the 'beloved disciple' of the Buddha (literally, 'joy' or 'bliss').

Beluva: a village on a slope at the foot of a hill near Vesali, says Buddhaghosa.

season, there fell upon him a dire sickness, and sharp pains came upon him, even unto death. But the Blessed One, mindful and self-possessed, bore them without complaint.

29. Then this thought occurred to the Blessed One, 'It would not be right for me to pass away from existence without addressing the disciples, without taking leave of the order. Let me now, by a strong effort of the will, bend this sickness down again, and keep my hold on life till the allotted time be come.'

30. And the Blessed One, by a strong effort of the will, bent that sickness down again, and kept his hold on life till the time he fixed upon should come. And the sickness abated upon him.

31. Now very soon after, the Blessed One began to recover; when he had quite got rid of the sickness, he went out from the monastery, and sat down behind the monastery on a seat spread out there. And the venerable Ananda went to the place where the Blessed One was, and saluted him, and took a seat respectfully on one side, and addressed the Blessed One, and said: 'I have beheld, Lord, how the Blessed One was in health, and I have beheld how the Blessed One had to suffer. And though at the sight of the sickness of the Blessed One my body became weak as a creeper, and the horizon became dim to me, and my faculties were no longer clear, yet notwithstanding I took some little comfort from the thought that the Blessed One would not pass away from existence until at least he had left instructions as touching the order.'

32. 'What, then, Ananda? Does the order expect that of me? I have preached the truth without making any distinction between exoteric and esoteric doctrine: for in respect of the truths, Ananda, the Tathagata has no such thing as the closed fist of a teacher, who keeps some things back. Surely, Ananda, should there be any one who harbours the thought, 'It is I who will lead the brotherhood,' or, 'The order is dependent upon me,' it is he who should lay down instructions in any matter concerning the order. Now the Tathagata, Ananda, thinks not that it is he who should lead the brotherhood, or that the order is dependent upon him. Why then should he leave instructions in any matter concerning the order! I too, O Ananda, am now grown old, and full of years, my journey is drawing to its close, I have reached my sum of days, I am turning eighty years of age; and just as a worn-out cart,

Ananda, can only with much additional care be made to move along, so, methinks, the body of the Tathagata can only be kept going with much additional care. It is only, Ananda, when the Tathagata, ceasing to attend to any outward thing, or to experience any sensation, becomes plunged in that devout meditation of heart which is concerned with no material object – it is only then that the body of the Tathagata is at ease.

33. 'Therefore, O Ananda, be ye lamps unto yourselves. Be ye a refuge to yourselves. Betake yourselves to no external refuge. Hold fast to the truth as a lamp. Hold fast as a refuge to the truth. Look not for refuge to any one besides yourselves. And how, Ananda, is a brother to be a lamp unto himself, a refuge to himself, betaking himself to no external refuge, holding fast to the truth as a lamp, holding fast as a refuge to the truth, looking not for refuge to any one besides himself?

34. 'Herein, O Ananda, let a brother, as he dwells in the body, so regard the body that he, being strenuous, thoughtful, and mindful, may, whilst in the world, overcome the grief which arises from bodily craving – while subject to sensations let him continue so to regard the sensations that he, being strenuous, thoughtful, and mindful, may, whilst in the world, overcome the grief which arises from the sensations – and so, also, as he thinks, or reasons, or feels, let him overcome the grief which arises from the craving due to ideas, or to reasoning, or to feeling.

35. 'And whosoever, Ananda, either now or after I am dead, shall be a lamp unto themselves, and a refuge unto themselves, shall betake themselves to no external refuge, but holding fast to the truth as their lamp, and holding fast as their refuge to the truth, shall look not for refuge to any one besides themselves – it is they, Ananda, among my Bhikkhus, who shall reach the very topmost Height! – but they must be anxious to learn.'

DHAMMAPADA

[THE WAY OF *Dhamma* OR RIGHTEOUSNESS]

(Pali, 477 B.C.)

Dhammapada (Sanskrit, *dharma*), the best-loved book and the fountainhead of faith in all the traditions of Buddhism, is unique among the literary masterpieces of the world. It consists of 423 verses, arranged in 26 chapters under different headings. These verses are the sayings of Buddha, uttered on various occasions during forty-five years of his life as the Enlightened Teacher; they breathe the spirit of moral earnestness characteristic of Buddha's life and compassionate attitude to mankind. Though these sayings communicate profound meanings through obvious nature imageries, the elegant simplicity of the verses is the simplicity of an inspired man with a large spirit and deep faith. One can easily perceive this distinctive quality of *Dhammapada* also in the refreshing simplicity of the *Analects* of Confucius, or the *Tao Teh Ching* of Lao Tzu, or the *Book of Isaiah* of the Hebrew prophet. If someone were to collect all the sayings of Jesus and put them together in one book under a thematic arrangement, such a book would be somewhat comparable to *Dhammapada*.* The period between the sixth and the first centuries B.C. seems to have been a great age of 'wisdom explosion' throughout the world, during which time enlightened men with moral earnestness preached ways of life based on universal principles, transcending tribal and national traditions.

Commenting on the spread of the 'way of life' of the *Dhammapada* in Asia, Lin Yutang states: 'Its [*Dhammapada's*] closeness to Confucian and Taoist teachings (e.g. advice on good friends, distinction between the wise and the fools, emphasis on self-examination, freedom

---

*Cf. Raja Rammogun Roy, ed., *The Precepts of Jesus: The Guide to Peace and Happiness*, Calcutta, 1820.

from fear, moral strength and inner repose) explains why Buddhism is so readily acceptable to the Chinese people.'*

The selections included here are taken from the translation of F. Max Müller, *The Dhammapada*, Vol. X of the Sacred Books of the East Series, Oxford: Clarendon Press, 1881.

II.12 *DHAMMAPADA*

[THE WAY OF *Dhamma* OR RIGHTEOUSNESS]

Chapter I: The Twin-verses

1. All that we are is the result of what we have thought: it is founded on our thoughts, it is made up of our thoughts. If a man speaks or acts with an evil thought, pain follows him, as the wheel follows the foot of the ox that draws the carriage.

2. All that we are is the result of what we have thought: it is founded on our thoughts, it is made up of our thoughts. If a man speaks or acts with a pure thought, happiness follows him, like a shadow that never leaves him.

3. 'He abused me, he beat me, he defeated me, he robbed me' – in those who harbour such thoughts hatred will never cease.

4. 'He abused me, he beat me, he defeated me, he robbed me' – in those who do not harbour such thoughts hatred will cease.

5. For hatred does not cease by hatred at any time: hatred ceases by love – this is an old rule.

6. The world does not know that we must all come to an end here; but those who know it, their quarrels cease at once.

7. He who lives looking for pleasures only, his senses uncontrolled, immoderate in his food, idle and weak, Mara (the tempter) will certainly overthrow him, as the wind throws down a weak tree.

8. He who lives without looking for pleasures, his senses well controlled, moderate in his food, faithful and strong, him Mara will

---

*Lin Yutang, ed., *The Wisdom of China and India*, New York: The Modern Library (G. 59), p. 326.

certainly not overthrow, any more than the wind throws down a rocky mountain.

9. He who wishes to put on the yellow dress without having cleansed himself from sin, who disregards also temperance and truth, is unworthy of the yellow dress.

10. But he who has cleansed himself from sin, is well grounded in all virtues, and endowed also with temperance and truth: he is indeed worthy of the yellow dress.

11. They who imagine truth in untruth, and see untruth in truth, never arrive at truth, but follow vain desires.

12. They who know truth in truth, and untruth in untruth, arrive at truth, and follow true desires.

13. As rain breaks through an ill-thatched house, passion will break through an unreflecting mind.

14. As rain does not break through a well-thatched house, passion will not break through a well-reflecting mind.

15. The evil-doer mourns in this world, and he mourns in the next; he mourns in both. He mourns and suffers when he sees the evil result of his own work.

16. The virtuous man delights in this world, and he delights in the next; he delights in both. He delights and rejoices, when he sees the purity of his own work.

17. The evil-doer suffers in this world, and he suffers in the next; he suffers in both. He suffers when he thinks of the evil he has done; he suffers more when going on the evil path.

18. The virtuous man is happy in this world, and he is happy in the next; he is happy in both. He is happy when he thinks of the good he has done; he is still more happy when going on the good path.

19. The thoughtless man, even if he can recite a large portion of the law, but is not a doer of it, has no share in the priesthood, but is like a cowherd counting the cows of others.

20. The follower of the law, even if he can recite only a small portion of the law, but, having forsaken passion and hatred and foolishness, possesses true knowledge and serenity of mind, he, caring for nothing in this world or that to come, has indeed a share in the priesthood.

Chapter II: On Earnestness

21. Earnestness is the path of immortality (Nirvana), thoughtlessness the path of death. Those who are in earnest do not die, those who are thoughtless are as if dead already.

22. Having understood this clearly, those who are advanced in earnestness delight in earnestness, and rejoice in the knowledge of the elect.

23. These wise people, meditative, steady, always possessed of strong powers attain to Nirvana, the highest happiness.

24. If an earnest person has roused himself, if he is not forgetful, if his deeds are pure, if he acts with consideration, if he restrains himself, and lives according to law – then his glory will increase.

25. By rousing himself, by earnestness, by restraint and control, the wise man may make for himself an island which no flood can overwhelm.

26. Fools follow after vanity. The wise man keeps earnestness as his best jewel.

27. Follow not after vanity, nor after the enjoyment of love and lust! He who is earnest and meditative, obtains ample joy.

28. When the learned man drives away vanity by earnestness, he, the wise, climbing the terraced heights of wisdom, looks down upon the fools: free from sorrow he looks upon the sorrowing crowd, as one that stands on a mountain looks down upon them that stand upon the plain.

29. Earnest among the thoughtless, awake among the sleepers, the wise man advances like a racer, leaving behind the hack.

30. By earnestness did Maghavan (Indra) rise to the lordship of the gods. People praise earnestness; thoughtlessness is always blamed.

31. A Bhikshu (mendicant) who delights in earnestness, who looks with fear on thoughtlessness, moves about like fire, burning all his fetters, small or large.

32. A Bhikshu (mendicant) who delights in reflection, who looks with fear on thoughtlessness, cannot fall away from his perfect state – he is close upon Nirvana.

Chapter III: Thought

33. As a fletcher makes straight his arrow, a wise man makes straight his trembling and unsteady thought, which is difficult to guard, difficult to hold back.

34. As a fish taken from his watery home and thrown on the dry ground, our thought trembles all over in order to escape the dominion of Mara, the tempter.

35. It is good to tame the mind, which is difficult to hold in and flighty, rushing wherever it listeth; a tamed mind brings happiness.

36. Let the wise man guard his thoughts, for they are difficult to perceive, very artful, and they rush wherever they list: thoughts well guarded bring happiness.

37. Those who bridle their mind which travels far, moves about alone, is without a body, and hides in the chamber of the heart, will be free from the bonds of Mara, the tempter.

38. If a man's faith is unsteady, if he does not know the true law, if his peace of mind is troubled, his knowledge will never be perfect.

39. If a man's thoughts are not dissipated, if his mind is not perplexed, if he has ceased to think of good or evil, then there is no fear for him while he is watchful.

40. Knowing that this body is fragile like a jar, and making his thought firm like a fortress, one should attack Mara, the tempter, with the weapon of knowledge, one should watch him when conquered, and should never rest.

41. Before long, alas! this body will lie on the earth, despised, without understanding, like a useless log.

42. Whatever a hater may do to a hater, or an enemy to an enemy, a wrongly-directed mind will do him greater mischief.

43. Not a mother, not a father, will do so much, nor any other relatives; a well-directed mind will do us greater service.

Chapter IV: Flowers

47. Death carries off a man who is gathering flowers, and whose mind is distracted, as a flood carries off a sleeping village.

48. Death subdues a man who is gathering flowers, and whose mind is distracted, before he is satiated in his pleasures.

49. As the bee collects nectar and departs without injuring the flower, or its colour or scent, so let a sage dwell in his village.

50. Not the perversities of others, not their sins of commission or omission but his own misdeeds and negligences should a sage take notice of.

51. Like a beautiful flower, full of colour, but without scent, are the fine but fruitless words of him who does not act accordingly.

52. But like a beautiful flower, full of colour and full of scent, are the fine and fruitful words of him who acts accordingly.

Chapter V: The Fool

60. Long is the night to him who is awake; long is a mile to him who is tired; long is life to the foolish who do not know the true law.

61. If a traveller does not meet with one who is his better, or his equal, let him firmly keep to his solitary journey; there is no companionship with a fool.

62. 'These sons belong to me, and this wealth belongs to me,' with such thoughts a fool is tormented. He himself does not belong to himself; how much less sons and wealth?

63. The fool who knows his foolishness, is wise at least so far. But a fool who thinks himself wise, he is called a fool indeed.

64. If a fool be associated with a wise man even all his life, he will perceive the truth as little as a spoon perceives the taste of soup.

65. If an intelligent man be associated for one minute only with a wise man, he will soon perceive the truth, as the tongue perceives the taste of soup.

66. Fools of poor understanding have themselves for their greatest enemies, for they do evil deeds which bear bitter fruits.

67. That deed is not well done of which a man must repent, and the reward of which he receives crying and with a tearful face.

68. No, that deed is well done of which a man does not repent, and the reward of which he receives gladly and cheerfully.

69. As long as the evil deed done does not bear fruit, the fool thinks it is like honey; but when it ripens, then the fool suffers grief.

Chapter VI: The Wise Man

76. If you see a man who shows you what is to be avoided, who administers reproofs, and is intelligent, follow that wise man as you would one who tells of hidden treasures; it will be better, not worse, for him who follows him.

77. Let him admonish, let him teach, let him forbid what is improper! – he will be beloved of the good, by the bad he will be hated.

78. Do not have evil-doers for friends, do not have low people for friends: have virtuous people for friends, have for friends the best of men.

79. He who drinks in the law lives happily with a serene mind: the sage rejoices always in the law, as preached by the elect.

80. Well-makers lead the water wherever they like; fletchers bend the arrow; carpenters bend a log of wood; wise people fashion themselves.

81. As a solid rock is not shaken by the wind, wise people falter not amidst blame and praise.

82. Wise people, after they have listened to the laws, become serene, like a deep, smooth, and still lake.

Chapter VII: The Venerable

92. Men who have no riches, who live on recognized food, who have perceived void and unconditioned freedom (Nirvana), their path is difficult to understand, like that of birds in the air.

93. He whose appetites are stilled, who is not absorbed in enjoyment, who has perceived void and unconditioned freedom (Nirvana), his path is difficult to understand, like that of birds in the air.

Chapter VIII: The Thousands

100. Even though a speech be a thousand (of words), but made up of senseless words, one word of sense is better, which if a man hears, he becomes quiet.

101. Even though a Gatha (poem) be a thousand (of words), but

made up of senseless words, one word of a Gatha is better, which if a man hears, he becomes quiet.

102. Though a man recite a hundred Gathas made up of senseless words, one word of the law is better, which if a man hears, he becomes quiet.

103. If one man conquer in battle a thousand times a thousand men, and if another conquer himself, he is the greatest of conquerors.

109. He who always greets and constantly reveres the aged, four things will increase to him: life, beauty, happiness, power.

115. And he who lives a hundred years, not seeing the highest law, a life of one day is better if a man sees the highest law.

Chapter IX: Evil

116. A man should hasten towards the good, and should keep his thought away from evil; if a man does what is good slothfully, his mind delights in evil.

117. If a man commits a sin, let him not do it again; let him not delight in sin: the accumulation of evil is painful.

118. If a man does what is good, let him do it again; let him delight in it: the accumulation of good is delightful.

119. Even an evil-doer sees happiness so long as his evil deed does not ripen; but when his evil deed ripens, then does the evil-doer see evil.

120. Even a good man sees evil days so long as his good deed does not ripen; but when his good deed ripens, then does the good man see good things.

121. Let no man think lightly of evil, saying in his heart, It will not come nigh unto me. Even by the falling of water-drops a water-pot is filled; the fool becomes full of evil, even if he gather it little by little.

122. Let no man think lightly of good, saying in his heart, It will not come nigh unto me. Even by the falling of water-drops a water-pot is filled; the wise man becomes full of good, even if he gather it little by little.

123. Let a man avoid evil deeds, as a merchant, if he has few

companions and carries much wealth, avoids a dangerous road; as a man who loves life avoids poison.

124. He who has no wound on his hand, may touch poison with his hands; poison does not affect one who has no wound; nor is there evil for one who does not commit evil.

125. If a man offend a harmless, pure, and innocent person, the evils falls back upon that fool, like light dust thrown up against the wind.

Chapter X: Punishment

129. All men tremble at punishment, all men fear death; remember that you are like unto them, and do not kill, nor cause slaughter.

130. All men tremble at punishment, all men love life; remember that thou are like unto them, and do not kill, nor cause slaughter.

131. He who, seeking his own happiness, punishes or kills beings who also long for happiness, will not find happiness after death.

132. He who, seeking his own happiness, does not punish or kill beings who also long for happiness, will find happiness after death.

133. Do not speak harshly to anyone; those who are spoken to will answer thee in the same way. Angry speech is painful: blows for blows will touch thee.

134. If, like a shattered metal plate (gong), thou utter nothing, then thou hast reached Nirvana; anger is not known to thee.

135. As a cowherd with his staff drives his cows into the stable, so do Age and Death drive the life of men.

141. Not nakedness, not plaited hair, not dirt, not fasting, or lying on the earth, not rubbing with dust, not sitting motionless, can purify a mortal who has not overcome desires.

142. He who, though dressed in fine apparel, exercises tranquillity, is quiet, subdued, restrained, chaste, and has ceased to find fault with all other beings, he indeed is a Brahmana, an ascetic (*sramana*), a friar (*bhikshu*).

143. Is there in this world any man so restrained by shame that he does not provoke reproof, as a noble horse the whip?

Chapter XI: Old Age

152. A man who has learnt little, grows old like an ox; his flesh grows, but his knowledge does not grow.

Chapter XII: Self

157. If a man hold himself dear, let him watch himself carefully; during one at least out of the three watches a wise man should be watchful.

158. Let each man direct himself first to what is proper, then let him teach others; thus a wise man will not suffer.

159. If a man make himself as he teaches others to be, then, being himself well subdued, he may subdue others; for one's own self is difficult to subdue.

160. Self is the lord of self, who else could be the lord? With self well subdued, a man finds a lord such as few can find.

161. The evil done by one's self, self-forgotten, self-bred, crushes the foolish, as a diamond breaks even a precious stone.

162. He whose wickedness is very great brings himself down to that state where his enemy wishes him to be, as a creeper does with the tree which it surrounds.

163. Bad deeds, and deeds hurtful to ourselves, are easy to do; what is beneficial and good, that is very difficult to do.

164. The foolish man who scorns the rule of the venerable (*Arhat*), of the elect (*Ariya*), of the virtuous, and follows a false doctrine, he bears fruit to his own destruction, like the fruits of the Katthaka reed.

165. By one's self the evil is done, by one's self one suffers; by one's self evil is left undone, by one's self one is purified. The pure and the impure stand and fall by themselves, no one can purify another.

166. Let no one forget his own duty for the sake of another's, however great; let a man, after he has discerned his own duty, be always attentive to his duty.

Chapter XIV: The Buddha – The Awakened

182. Difficult to obtain is the conception of men, difficult is the life of mortals, difficult is the hearing of the True Law, difficult is the birth of the Awakened (the attainment of Buddhahood).

183. Not to commit any sin, to do good, and to purify one's mind, that is the teaching of all the Awakened.

184. The Awakened call patience the highest penance, long-suffering the highest Nirvana; for he is not an anchorite (*pravragita*) who strikes others, he is not an ascetic (*sramana*) who insults others.

185. Not to blame, not to strike, to live restrained under the law, to be moderate in eating, to sleep and sit alone, and to dwell on the highest thoughts – this is the teaching of the Awakened.

186. There is no satisfying lusts, even by a shower of gold pieces; he

187. who knows that lusts have a short taste and cause pain, he is wise; even in heavenly pleasures he finds no satisfaction, the disciple who is fully awakened delights only in the destruction of all desires.

188. Men, driven by fear, go to many a refuge, to mountains and forests, to groves and sacred trees.

189. But that is not a safe refuge, that is not the best refuge; a man is not delivered from all pains after having gone to that refuge.

190-2. He who takes refuge with Buddha, the Law, and the Church; he who, with clear understanding, sees the four holy truths: pain, the origin of pain, the destruction of pain, and the eightfold holy way that leads to the quieting of pain; – that is the safe refuge, that is the best refuge; having gone to that refuge, a man is delivered from all pain.

193. A supernatural person (a Buddha) is not easily found: he is not born everywhere. Wherever such a sage is born, that race prospers.

194. Happy is the arising of the Awakened, happy is the teaching of True Law, happy is peace in the church, happy is the devotion of those who are at peace.

195. He who pays homage to those who deserve homage, whether

196. the awakened (Buddha) or their disciples, those who have overcome the host of evils, and crossed the flood of sorrow, he who pays homage to such as have found deliverance and know no fear, his merit can never be measured by anyone.

Chapter XV: Happiness

197. We live happily indeed, not hating those who hate us! among men who hate us we dwell free from hatred! We live happily indeed, free from ailments among the ailing! among men who are ailing let us dwell free from ailments!

198. We live happily indeed, free from greed among the greedy! among men who are greedy let us dwell free from greed!

199. We live happily indeed, though we call nothing our own! We shall be like the bright gods, feeding on happiness!

201. Victory breeds hatred, for the conquered is unhappy. He who has given up both victory and defeat, he, the contented, is happy.

202. There is no fire like passion; there is no losing throw like hatred; there is no pain like this body; there is no happiness higher than rest.

203. Hunger is the worst of diseases, the elements of the body the greatest evil; if one knows this truly, that is Nirvana, the highest happiness.

204. Health is the greatest of gifts, contentedness the best riches; trust is the best of relationships, Nirvana the highest happiness.

205. He who has tasted the sweetness of solitude and tranquillity, is free from fear and free from sin, while he tastes the sweetness of drinking in the law.

Chapter XVI: Pleasure

215. From lust comes grief, from lust comes fear; he who is free from lust knows neither grief nor fear.

216. From love comes grief, from love comes fear; he who is free from love knows neither grief nor fear.

217. From greed comes grief, from greed comes fear; he who is free from greed knows neither grief nor fear.

Chapter XVII: Anger

221. Let a man leave anger, let him forsake pride, let him overcome all bondage! No sufferings befall the man who is not attached to name and form, and who calls nothing his own.

222. He who holds back rising anger like a rolling chariot, him I call a real driver; other people are but holding the reins.

223. Let a man overcome anger by love, let him overcome evil by good; let him overcome the greedy by liberality, the liar by truth!

224. Speak the truth, do not yield to anger; give, if thou art asked for little; by these three steps thou wilt go near the gods.

225. The sages who injure nobody, and who always control their body, they will go to the unchangeable place (Nirvana), where, if they have gone, they will suffer no more.

231. Beware of bodily anger, and control thy body! Leave the sins of the body, and with thy body practise virtue!

232. Beware of the anger of the tongue, and control thy tongue! Leave the sins of the tongue, and practise virtue with thy tongue!

233. Beware of the anger of the mind, and control thy mind! Leave the sins of the mind, and practise virtue with thy mind!

234. The wise who control their body, who control their tongue, the wise who control their mind, are indeed well controlled.

Chapter XVIII: Impurity

238. Make thyself an island, work hard, be wise! When thy impurities are blown away, and thou art free from guilt, thou wilt not enter again into birth and decay.

239. Let a wise man blow off the impurities of himself, as a smith blows off the impurities of silver, one by one, little by little, and from time to time.

240. As the impurity which springs from the iron, when it springs from it, destroys it; thus do a transgressor's own works lead him to the evil path.

251. There is no fire like passion, there is no shark like hatred, there is no snare like folly, there is no torrent like greed.

252. The fault of others is easily perceived, but that of one's self is difficult to perceive; a man winnows his neighbour's faults like chaff, but his own fault he hides, as a cheat hides the bad die from the player.

253. If a man looks after the faults of others, and is always inclined to be offended, his own passions will grow, and he is far from the destruction of passions.

Chapter XIX: The Just

260. A man is not an elder because his head is grey; his age may be ripe, but he is called 'Old-in-vain'.

261. He in whom there is truth, virtue, pity, restraint, moderation, he who is free from impurity and is wise, he is called an elder.

266. A man is not a mendicant (*Bhikshu*) simply because he asks others for alms; he who adopts the whole law is a Bhikshu, not he who only begs.

267. He who is above good and evil, who is chaste, who with care passes through the world, he indeed is called a Bhikshu.

268. A man is not a Muni because he observes silence if he is foolish 269. and ignorant; but the wise who, as with the balance, chooses the good and avoids evil, he is a Muni, and is a Muni thereby; he who in this world weighs both sides is called a Muni.

270. A man is not an elect (*Ariya*) because he injures living creatures; because he has pity on all living creatures, therefore is a man called Ariya.

Chapter XX: The Way

273. The best of ways is the eightfold; the best of truths the four words; the best of virtues passionlessness; the best of men he who has eyes to see.

277. 'All created things perish': he who knows and sees this becomes passive in pain; this is the way to purity.

278. 'All created things are grief and pain': he who knows and sees this becomes passive in pain; this is the way that leads to purity.

279. 'All forms are unreal': he who knows and sees this becomes passive in pain; this is the way that leads to purity.

280. He who does not rouse himself when it is time to rise, who, though young and strong, is full of sloth, whose will and thought are weak, that lazy and idle man never finds the way to knowledge.

282. Through zeal knowledge is gained, through lack of zeal knowledge is lost; let a man who knows this double path of gain and loss thus place himself that knowledge may grow.

283. Cut down the whole forest of desires, not a tree only! Danger comes out of the forest of desires. When you have cut down both the forest of desires and its undergrowth, then, Bhikshus, you will be rid of the forest and of desires!

Chapter XXIV: Thirst

334. The thirst of a thoughtless man grows like a creeper; he runs from life to life, like a monkey seeking fruit in the forest.

335. Whomsoever this fierce poisonous thirst overcomes, in this world, his sufferings increase like the abounding Birana grass.

336. But from him who overcomes this fierce thirst, difficult to be conquered in this world, sufferings fall off, like water-drops from a lotus leaf.

337. This salutary word I tell you, 'Do ye, as many as are here assembled, dig up the root of thirst, as he who wants the sweet-scented Usira root must dig up the Birana grass, that Mara, the tempter, may not crush you again and again, as the stream crushes the reeds.'

338. As a tree, even though it has been cut down, is firm so long as its root is safe, and grows again, thus, unless the feeders of thirst are destroyed, this pain of life will return again and again.

339. He whose thirty-six streams are strongly flowing in the channels of pleasure, the waves – his desires which are set on passion – will carry away that misguided man.

340. The channels run everywhere, the creeper of passion stands sprouting; if you see the creeper springing up, cut its root by means of knowledge.

341. A creature's pleasures are extravagant and luxurious; given up to pleasure and deriving happiness, men undergo again and again birth and decay.

342. Beset with lust, men run about like a snared hare; held in fetters and bonds, they undergo pain for a long time, again and again.

343. Beset with lust, men run about like a snared hare; let therefore the mendicant drive out thirst, by striving after passionlessness for himself.

344. He who, having got rid of the forest of lust (after having reached Nirvana), gives himself over to forest-life (to lust), and who, when free from the forest (from lust), runs to the forest (to lust), look at that man! though free, he runs into bondage.

345. Wise people do not call that a strong fetter which is made of iron, wood, or hemp; passionately strong is the care for precious stones and rings, for sons and a wife.

346. That fetter wise people call strong which drags down, yields, but is difficult to undo; after having cut this at last, people leave the world, free from cares, and leaving the pleasures of love behind.

347. Those who are slaves to passions, run down the stream of desires, as a spider runs down the web which he has made himself; when they have cut this, at last, wise people go onwards, free from cares, leaving all pain behind.

348. Give up what is before, give up what is behind, give up what is between when thou goest to the other shore of existence; if thy mind is altogether free, thou will not again enter into birth and decay.

349. If a man is tossed about by doubts, full of strong passions, and yearning only for what is delightful, his thirst will grow more and more, and he will indeed make his fetters strong.

350. If a man delights in quieting doubts, and, always reflecting, dwells on what is not delightful, he certainly will remove, nay, he will cut the fetter of Mara.

351. He who has reached the consummation, who does not tremble, who is without thirst and without sin, he has broken all the thorns of life: this will be his last body.

352. He who is without thirst and without affection, who understands the words and their interpretation, who knows the order of letters (those which are before and which are after), he has received his last body, he is called the great sage, the great man.

353. 'I have conquered all, I know all, in all conditions of life I am free from taint; I have left all, and through the destruction of

thirst I am free; having learnt myself, whom should I indicate as my teacher?'

354. The gift of the law exceeds all gifts; the sweetness of the law exceeds all sweetness; the delight in the law exceeds all delights; the extinction of thirst overcomes all pain.

355. Riches destroy the foolish, if they look not for the other shore; the foolish by his thirst for riches destroys himself, as if he were destroying others.

356. The fields are damaged by weeds, mankind is damaged by passion: therefore a gift bestowed on the passionless brings great reward.

357. The fields are damaged by weeds, mankind is damaged by hatred: therefore a gift bestowed on those who do not hate brings great reward.

358. The fields are damaged by weeds, mankind is damaged by vanity: therefore a gift bestowed on those who are free from vanity brings great reward.

359. The fields are damaged by weeds, mankind is damaged by lust: therefore a gift bestowed on those who are free from lust brings great reward.

Chapter XXV: The Bhikshu

360. Restraint in the eye is good, good is restraint in the ear, in the nose restraint is good, good is restraint in the tongue.

361. In the body restraint is good, good is restraint in speech, in thought restraint is good, good is restraint in all things. A Bhikshu, restrained in all things, is free from all pain.

362. He who controls his hand, he who controls his feet, he who controls his speech, he who is well controlled, he who delights inwardly, who is collected, who is solitary and content, him they call Bhikshu.

363. The Bhikshu who controls his mouth, who speaks wisely and calmly, who teaches the meaning and the law, his word is sweet.

364. He who dwells in the law, delights in the law, meditates on the law, recollects the law: that Bhikshu will never fall away from the true law.

365. Let him not despise what he has received, nor ever envy others: a mendicant who envies others does not obtain peace of mind.

366. A Bhikshu who, though he receives little, does not despise what he has received, even the gods will praise him, if his life is pure, and if he is not slothful.

367. He who never identifies himself with name and form, and does not grieve over what is no more, he indeed is called a Bhikshu.

368. The Bhikshu who behaves with kindness, who is happy in the doctrine of Buddha, will reach the quiet place (Nirvana), happiness arising from the cessation of natural inclinations.

369. O Bhikshu, empty this boat! if emptied, it will go quickly; having cut off passion and hatred, thou wilt go to Nirvana.

370. Cut off the five fetters, leave the five, rise above the five. A Bhikshu, who has escaped from the five fetters, he is called Oghatinna – 'saved from the flood'.

371. Meditate, O Bhikshu, and be not heedless! Do not direct thy thought to what gives pleasure, that thou mayest not for thy heedlessness have to swallow the iron ball in hell, and that thou mayest not cry out when burning, 'This is pain.'

372. Without knowledge there is no meditation, without meditation there is no knowledge: he who has knowledge and meditation is near unto Nirvana.

373. A Bhikshu who has entered his empty house, and whose mind is tranquil, feels a more than human delight when he sees the law clearly.

374. As soon as he has considered the origin and destruction of the elements of the body, he finds happiness and joy which belong to those who know the immortal (Nirvana).

375. And this is the beginning here for a wise Bhikshu: watchfulness over the senses, contentedness, restraint under the law; keep noble friends whose life is pure, and who are not slothful.

376. Let him live in charity, let him be perfect in his duties; then in the fullness of delight he will make an end of suffering.

377. As the Vassika plant shed its withered flowers, men should shed passion and hatred, O ye Bhikshus!

378. The Bhikshu whose body and tongue and mind are quieted,

who is collected, and has rejected the baits of the world, he is called quiet.

379. Rouse thyself by thyself, examine thyself by thyself, thus self-protected and attentive wilt thou live happily, O Bhikshu!

380. For self is the lord of self, self is the refuge of self; therefore curb thyself as the merchant curbs a noble horse.

381. The Bhikshu, full of delight, who is happy in the doctrine of Buddha will reach the quiet place (Nirvana), happiness consisting in the cessation of natural inclinations.

382. He who, even as a young Bhikshu, applies himself to the doctrine of Buddha, brightens up this world, like the moon when free from clouds.

Chapter XXVI: The Brahmana

383. Stop the stream valiantly, drive away the desires, O Brahmana! When you have understood the destruction of all that was made, you will understand that which was not made.

384. If the Brahmana has reached the other shore in both laws, in restraint and contemplation, all bonds vanish from him who has obtained knowledge.

385. He for whom there is neither the hither nor the further shore, nor both, him, the fearless and unshackled, I call indeed a Brahmana.

386. He who is thoughtful, blameless, settled, dutiful, without passions, and who has attained the highest end, him I call indeed a Brahmana.

387. The sun is bright by day, the moon shines by night, the warrior is bright in his armour, the Brahmana is bright in his meditation; but Buddha, the Awakened, is bright with splendour day and night.

388. Because a man is rid of evil, therefore he is called Brahmana; because he walks quietly, therefore he is called Samana; because he has sent away his own impurities, therefore he is called Pravragita (*Pabbagita*, a pilgrim).

389. No one should attack a Brahmana, but no Brahmana, if attacked, should let himself fly at his aggressor! Woe to him who strikes a Brahmana, more woe to him who flies at his aggressor!

390. It advantages a Brahmana not a little if he holds his mind back from the pleasures of life; the more all wish to injure has vanished the more all pain will cease.

391. Him I call indeed a Brahmana who does not offend by body, word, or thought, and is controlled on these three points.

392. He from whom he may learn the law, as taught by the Well-awakened (Buddha), him let him worship assiduously, as the Brahmana worships the sacrificial fire.

393. A man does not become a Brahmana by his plaited hair, by his family, or by birth; in whom there is truth and righteousness, he is blessed, he is a Brahmana.

394. What is the use of plaited hair, O fool! what of the raiment of goatskins? Within thee there is ravening, but the outside thou makest clean.

395. The man who wears dirty raiments, who is emaciated and covered with veins, who meditates alone in the forest, him I call indeed a Brahmana.

396. I do not call a man a Brahmana because of his origin or of his mother. He is indeed arrogant, and he is wealthy: but the poor, who is free from all attachments, him I call indeed a Brahmana.

397. Him I call indeed a Brahmana who, after cutting all fetters, never trembles, is free from bonds and unshackled.

398. Him I call indeed a Brahmana who, after cutting the strap and the thong, the rope with all that pertains to it, has destroyed all obstacles, and is awakened.

399. Him I call indeed a Brahmana who, though he has committed no offence, endures reproach, stripes, and bonds: who has endurance for his force, and strength for his army.

400. Him I call indeed a Brahmana who is free from anger, dutiful, virtuous, without appetites, who is subdued and has received his last body.

401. Him I call indeed a Brahmana who does not cling to sensual pleasures like water on a lotus leaf, like a mustard seed on the point of a needle.

402. Him I call indeed a Brahmana who, even here, knows the end of his own suffering, has put down his burden, and is unshackled.

403. Him I call indeed a Brahmana whose knowledge is deep, who

possesses wisdom, who knows the right way and the wrong, and has attained the highest end.

404. Him I call indeed a Brahmana who keeps aloof both from laymen and from mendicants, who frequents no houses, and has but few desires.

405. Him I call indeed a Brahmana who without hurting any creatures, whether feeble or strong, does not kill nor cause slaughter.

406. Him I call indeed a Brahmana who is tolerant with the intolerant, mild with the violent, and free from greed among the greedy.

407. Him I call indeed a Brahmana from whom anger and hatred, pride and hypocrisy have dropped like a mustard seed from the point of a needle.

408. Him I call indeed a Brahmana who utters true speech, instructive and free from harshness, so that he offend no one.

409. Him I call indeed a Brahmana who takes nothing in the world that is not given him, be it long or short, small or large, good or bad.

410. Him I call indeed a Brahmana who fosters no desires for this world or for the next, has no inclinations, and is unshackled.

411. Him I call indeed a Brahmana who has no interests, and when he has understood the truth, does not say How, how? and who has reached the depth of the Immortal.

412. Him I call indeed a Brahmana who in this world has risen above both ties, good and evil, who is free from grief, from sin and from impurity.

413. Him I call indeed a Brahmana who is bright like the moon, pure, serene, undisturbed, and in whom all gaiety is extinct.

414. Him I call indeed a Brahmana who has traversed this miry road, the impassible world, difficult to pass, and its vanity, who has gone through, and reached the other shore, is thoughtful, steadfast, free from doubts, free from attachment, and content.

415. Him I call indeed a Brahmana who in this world, having abandoned all desires, travels about without a home, and in whom all concupiscence is extinct.

416. Him I call indeed a Brahmana who, having abandoned all longings, travels about without a home, and in whom all covetousness is extinct.

417. Him I call indeed a Brahmana who, after leaving all bondage

to men, has risen above all bondage to the gods, and is free from all and every bondage.

418. Him I call indeed a Brahmana who has left what gives pleasure and what gives pain, who is cold, and free from all germs of renewed life: the hero who has conquered all the worlds.

419. Him I call indeed a Brahmana who knows the destruction and the return of beings everywhere, who is free from bondage, welfaring (Sugata), and awakened (Buddha).

420. Him I call indeed a Brahmana whose path the gods do not know, nor spirits (Gandharvas), nor men, whose passions are extinct, and who is an Arhat.

421. Him I call indeed a Brahmana who calls nothing his own, whether it be before, behind, or between, who is poor, and free from the love of the world.

422. Him I call indeed a Brahmana, the manly, the noble, the hero, the great sage, the conqueror, the indifferent, the accomplished, the awakened.

423. Him I call indeed a Brahmana who knows his former abodes, who sees heaven and hell, has reached the end of births, is perfect in knowledge, a sage, and whose perfections are all perfect.

(Pali, 477 B.C.)

Spiritual leaders throughout the world have taught great moral truths by means of simple parables. In this simpler form, the visionary understanding of the Enlightened Ones has been communicated to ordinary mortals. Buddha also used a number of parables to communicate the meaning of his teaching to his followers. Two such parables are included here: (a) The Parable of Kisa Gotami, and (b) The Parable of Prince Dighavu.

In the Parable of Kisa Gotami (also called the Parable of the Mustard Seed), Buddha makes Kisa Gotami realize the meaning of death in terms of his fundamental teaching that phenomenal existence, being transitory, is subject to change, and there is no cure for death. Second, death being an essential part of life, there is a need for it to be accepted realistically and, consequently, a need for compassionate understanding of the pain it gives rise to, common to all living beings. Suffering leads to service – this is the implication of the parable, and therefore a life of service transcends death.

In the Parable of Prince Dighavu, Buddha tries to clarify the futility of hatred and vengeance, since hatred cannot be cured by hatred, neither by retaliation of one for one, nor even by massive retaliation. During his forty years of ministry, Buddha had to intervene often in the bitter disputes that arose among some of his followers, and on one such occasion he told the story of Prince Dighavu. By this parable, Buddha sought to emphasize the main point of his teaching, namely, that hatred can be cured only by non-hatred or love, and that each man needs to have a compassionate understanding of the next man.

The two parables included here are taken from the translation by E. W. Burlingame, *Buddhist Parables*, New Haven, Conn.: Yale University Press, 1922, pp. 92–4 and 20–8, respectively. The story of Prince Dighavu is slightly condensed from the original, omitting repetitive epithets and speeches, and minor incidents.

II.13   PARABLE: KISA GOTAMI

Gotami was her family name, but because she tired easily she was called Kisa Gotami, or Frail Gotami. She was reborn at Savatthi in a poverty-stricken house. When she grew up, she married, going to the house of her husband's family to live. There, because she was the daughter of a poverty-stricken house, they treated her with contempt. After a time she gave birth to a son. Then they accorded her respect.

But when that boy of hers was old enough to play and run hither and about, he died. Sorrow sprang up within her. Thought she: 'Since the birth of my son, I, who was once denied honour and respect in this very house, have received respect. These folk may even seek to cast my son away.' Taking her son on her hip, she went about from one house-door to another, saying: 'Give me medicine for my son!'

Wherever people encountered her, they said: 'Where did you ever meet with medicine for the dead?' So saying, they clapped their hands and laughed in derision. She had not the slightest idea what they meant.

Now a certain wise man saw her and thought: 'This woman must have been driven out of her mind by sorrow for her son. But medicine for her, – no one else is likely to know, – the Possessor of the Ten Forces alone is likely to know.' Said he: 'Woman, as for medicine for your son, – there is no one else who knows, – the Possessor of the Ten Forces, the foremost individual in the world of men and the Worlds of the Gods, resides at a neighbouring monastery. Go to him and ask.'

'The man speaks the truth,' thought she. Taking her son on her hip, when the Tathagata sat down in the Seat of the Buddhas, she took her stand in the outer circle of the congregation and said: 'O Exalted One, give me medicine for my son!'

The Teacher, seeing that she was ripe for conversion, said: 'You did well, Gotami, in coming hither for medicine. Go enter the city, make the rounds of the entire city, beginning at the beginning, and in whatever house no one has ever died, from that house fetch tiny grains of mustard seed.'

'Very well, Reverend Sir,' said she. Delighted in heart, she entered within the city, and at the very first house said: 'The Possessor of the

Ten Forces bids me fetch tiny grains of mustard seed for medicine for my son. Give me tiny grains of mustard seed.' 'Alas! Gotami,' said they, and brought and gave to her.

'This particular seed I cannot take. In this house one has died!'

'What say you, Gotami! Here it is impossible to count the dead!'

'Well then, enough! I'll not take it. The Possessor of the Ten Forces did not tell me to take mustard seed from a house where any one has ever died.'

In this same way she went to the second house, and to the third. Thought she: 'In the entire city this alone must be the way! This the Buddha, full of compassion for the welfare of mankind, must have seen!' Overcome with emotion, she went outside of the city, carried her son to the burning-ground, and holding him in her arms, said: 'Dear little son, I thought that you alone had been overtaken by this thing which men call death. But you are not the only one death has overtaken. This is a law common to all mankind.' So saying, she cast her son away in the burning-ground. Then she uttered the following stanza:

> No village-law, no law of market-town,
> No law of a single house is this, –
> Of all the world and all the Worlds of Gods
> This only is the law, that all things are impermanent.

Now when she had so said, she went to the Teacher. Said the Teacher to her: 'Gotami, did you get the tiny grains of mustard seed?' 'Done, Reverend Sir, is the business of the mustard seed! Only give me a refuge!' Then the Teacher recited to her the following stanza in the *Dhammapada*:

> That man who delights in children and cattle,
> That man whose heart adheres thereto,
> Death takes that man and goes his way,
> As sweeps away a mighty flood a sleeping village. (xx. 287)

> Though one should live a hundred years,
> Not seeing the Region of the Deathless,
> Better were it for one to live a single day,
> The Region of the Deathless seeing. (viii. 114)

At the conclusion of the stanza she attained Sainthood.

II.14   PARABLE: PRINCE DIGHAVU

In olden times at Benares, Brahmadatta king of Kasi was rich, possessed of great wealth, ample means of enjoyment, a mighty army, many vehicles, an extensive kingdom, and well-filled treasuries and store-houses. Dighiti king of Kosala was poor, possessed of meagre wealth, scanty means of enjoyment, a small army, few vehicles, a little kingdom, and unfilled treasuries and store-houses.

Now Brahmadatta drew up his fourfold army and went up against Dighiti. Then to Dighiti occurred the following thought: 'Brahmadatta king of Kasi is rich, possessed of great wealth, ample means of enjoyment, a mighty army, many vehicles, an extensive kingdom, and well-filled treasuries and store-houses. But I am poor, possessed of meagre wealth, scanty means of enjoyment, a small army, few vehicles, a little kingdom, and unfilled treasuries and store-houses. I am not strong enough to withstand even a single clash with Brahmadatta. Suppose I were merely to countermarch and slip out of the city!'

Accordingly Dighiti king of Kosala took his consort, merely countermarched, and slipped out of the city. Thereupon Brahmadatta king of Kasi conquered the army and vehicles and territory and treasuries and store-houses of Dighiti king of Kosala, and took possession. And Dighiti king of Kosala with his consort set out for Benares, and in due course arrived at Benares. And there, in a certain place on the outskirts of Benares, Dighiti resided with his consort, in a potter's dwelling, in disguise, in the guise of a wandering ascetic.

Now in no very long time the consort of Dighiti king of Kosala became pregnant. And when that unborn child had reached maturity, the consort of Dighiti king of Kosala brought forth a son, and they called his name Dighavu. And in no very long time Prince Dighavu reached the age of reason.

Now to Dighiti occurred the following thought: 'This Brahmadatta king of Kasi has done us much injury. He has robbed us of army and vehicles and territory and treasuries and store-houses. If he recognizes us, he will cause all three of us to be put to death. Suppose I were to cause Prince Dighavu to dwell outside of the city!' Accordingly Dighiti king of Kosala caused Prince Dighavu to dwell outside of the city. And Prince Dighavu, residing outside of the city, in no very long time acquired all the arts and crafts.

Now at that time the barber of Dighiti king of Kosala resided at the court of Brahmadatta king of Kasi. The barber saw Dighiti residing with his consort in a certain place on the outskirts of Benares, in a potter's dwelling, in disguise, in the guise of a wandering ascetic. When he saw him, he approached Brahmadatta king of Kasi, and said: 'O king, Dighiti king of Kosala is residing with his consort in a certain place on the outskirts of Benares, in a potter's dwelling, in disguise, in the guise of a wandering ascetic.'

Then Brahmadatta ordered his men: 'Now then, take Dighiti king of Kosala with his consort, bind their arms tight behind their backs with a stout rope, shave their heads, and to the loud beating of a drum lead them about from street to street, from crossing to crossing, conduct them out of the South gate, hack their bodies into four pieces south of the city, and throw the pieces in the four directions.'

'Yes, your majesty,' said those men to Brahmadatta king of Kasi; and in obedience to his command took Dighiti king of Kosala with his consort, bound their arms tight behind their backs with a stout rope, shaved their heads, and to the loud beating of a drum led them about from street to street, from crossing to crossing.

Now to Prince Dighavu occurred the following thought: 'It is a long time since I have seen my mother and father. Suppose I were to see my mother and father!' Accordingly Prince Dighavu entered Benares, and saw his mother and father, their arms bound tight behind their backs, their heads shaven, being led about, to the loud beating of a drum, from street to street, from crossing to crossing. When he saw this, he approached his mother and father.

Dighiti king of Kosala saw Prince Dighavu approaching even from afar. When he saw him, he said this to Prince Dighavu: 'Dear Dighavu, do not look long! Do not look short! For, dear Dighavu, hatreds are not quenched by hatred. Nay rather, dear Dighavu, hatreds are quenched by love.'

At these words those men said this to Dighiti: 'This Dighiti king of Kosala is stark mad, and talks gibberish. Who is Dighavu to him? To whom did he speak thus: "Dear Dighavu, do not look long! Do not look short! For, dear Dighavu, hatreds are not quenched by hatred. Nay rather, dear Dighāvu, hatreds are quenched by love"?' 'I am not stark mad, I assure you, nor do I talk gibberish. However, he that is intelligent will understand clearly.'

Then those men led Dighīti with his consort about from street to street, from crossing to crossing, conducted them out of the South gate, hacked their bodies into four pieces south of the city, threw the pieces in the four directions, posted a guard of soldiers, and departed.

Thereupon Prince Dighāvu entered Benares, procured liquor, and gave it to the soldiers to drink. When they were drunk and had fallen, he gathered sticks of wood, built a pyre, placed the bodies of his mother and father on the pyre, lighted it, and with joined hands upraised in reverent salutation thrice made sunwise circuit of the pyre.

Now at that time Brahmadatta king of Kāsi was on an upper floor of his splendid palace. When he saw this, the following thought occurred to him: 'Without doubt that man is a kinsman or blood-relative of Dighīti king of Kosala. Alas, my wretched misfortune, for no one will tell me the facts!'

Now Prince Dighāvu went to the forest, wailed and wept his fill, and wiped his tears away. Then he entered Benares, went to the elephant-stable adjoining the royal palace, and said this to the elephant-trainer: 'Trainer, I wish to learn your art.' 'Very well, young man, learn it.' Accordingly Prince Dighāvu rose at night, at time of dawn, and sang and played the lute with charming voice in the elephant-stable.

Brahmadatta king of Kāsi heard him as he rose at night, at time of dawn, and asked his men: 'Who was it, pray, that rose at night, at time of dawn, and sang and played the lute with charming voice in the elephant-stable?' 'Your majesty, it was a young man, the pupil of such-and-such an elephant-trainer.' 'Very well, bring that young man to me.' 'Yes, your majesty,' said those men to Brahmadatta king of Kāsi; and in obedience to his command brought Prince Dighāvu to him.

'Was it you, young man, who rose at night, at time of dawn, and sang, and played the lute with charming voice in the elephant-stable?' 'Yes, your majesty.' 'Very well, young man, sing and play the lute for me.' 'Yes, your majesty,' said Prince Dighāvu to Brahmadatta king of

Kasi; and in obedience to his command, desiring to win his favour, sang and played the lute with charming voice.

Thereupon Brahmadatta said this to Prince Dighavu: 'You, young man, may wait upon me.' 'Yes, your majesty,' said Prince Dighavu, and obeyed his command. And in no very long time Brahmadatta king of Kasi appointed Prince Dighavu to a highly confidential position.

Now Brahmadatta said this to Prince Dighavu: 'Now then, young man, harness the chariot; I wish to go a-hunting.' 'Yes, your majesty,' said Prince Dighavu. Thereupon Brahmadatta mounted the chariot: Prince Dighavu drove the chariot. In such wise did he drive the chariot that the army went one way, the chariot the other.

Now when he had gone a long way, Brahmadatta said: 'Now then, young man, unharness the chariot. I am tired: I wish to lie down.' 'Yes, your majesty,' said Prince Dighavu; and in obedience to his command unharnessed the chariot and sat down on the ground cross-legged. And Brahmadatta king of Kasi lay down, placing his head in Prince Dighavu's lap. So tired was he that in the mere fraction of a moment he fell asleep.

Thereupon to Prince Dighavu occurred the following thought: 'This Brahmadatta has done us much injury. He has robbed us of army and vehicles and territory and treasuries and store-houses. And he has killed my mother and father. This would be the very time for me to satisfy my hatred!' And he drew sword from sheath. Then to Prince Dighavu occurred the following thought: 'My father said to me in the hour of death: "Dear Dighavu, do not look long! Do not look short! For, dear Dighavu, hatreds are not quenched by hatred. Nay rather, dear Dighavu, hatreds are quenched by love." It is not fitting that I should transgress the command of my father.' And he returned sword to sheath. And this happened a second time, and a third time.

Suddenly Brahmadatta king of Kasi rose, frightened, agitated, alarmed, terrified. Thereupon Prince Dighavu said this to Brahmadatta king of Kasi: 'Why, your majesty, did you rise so suddenly, frightened, agitated, alarmed, terrified?' 'Right here, young man, Prince Dighavu, son of Dighiti king of Kosala, fell upon me with his sword in a dream. Therefore I rose suddenly, frightened, agitated, alarmed, terrified.'

Then Prince Dighavu, stroking the head of Brahmadatta king of

Kasi with his left hand, and drawing his sword with his right hand, said this to Brahmadatta: 'I, your majesty, am Prince Dighavu, son of Dighiti king of Kosala. You have done us much injury. You have robbed us of army and vehicles and territory and treasuries and store-houses. And you have killed my mother and father. This would be the very time for me to satisfy my hatred!'

Thereupon Brahmadatta king of Kasi prostrated himself on his face at the feet of Prince Dighavu, and said. 'Grant me my life, dear Dighavu! Grant me my life, dear Dighavu!' 'How have I the power to grant your majesty your life? Your majesty, however, might grant me my life.' 'Very well, dear Dighavu. You grant me my life, and I will grant you your life.' Then Brahmadatta king of Kasi and Prince Dighavu granted each other their lives and shook hands and swore an oath not to injure each other.

Then Brahmadatta king of Kasi entered Benares, caused the ministers of his council to be assembled, and said this: 'If, sirs, you were to see Prince Dighavu, son of Dighiti king of Kosala, what would you do to him?' Some spoke thus: 'We, your majesty, would cut off his hands.' Others spoke thus: 'We, your majesty, would cut off his feet.' 'We would cut off his hands and feet.' 'We would cut off his ears.' 'We would cut off his nose.' 'We would cut off his ears and nose.' 'We, your majesty, would cut off his head.' 'Sirs, this is Prince Dighavu, son of Dighiti king of Kosala; it is not permissible to do anything to him. He has granted me my life, and I have granted him his life.'

Then Brahmadatta said to Prince Dighavu: 'When, dear Dighavu, your father said to you in the hour of death: "Dear Dighavu, do not look long! Do not look short! For, dear Dighavu, hatreds are not quenched by hatred. Nay rather, dear Dighavu, hatreds are quenched by love," what did your father mean by that?' 'When, your majesty, my father said to me in the hour of death: "Not long," what he meant was: "Do not cherish hatred long." This, your majesty, is what my father meant when he said to me in the hour of death: "Not long." When, your majesty, my father said to me in the hour of death: "Not short," what he meant was: "Do not break with your friends quickly." This, your majesty, is what my father meant when he said to me in the hour of death: "Not short."

268

'When, your majesty, my father said to me in the hour of death: "For, dear Dighavu, hatreds are not quenched by hatred. Nay rather, dear Dighavu, hatreds are quenched by love," what he meant to have me understand was this: Your majesty has killed my mother and father. Were I to deprive your majesty of life, your majesty's well-wishers would deprive me of life, and my well-wishers would deprive yours of life. Thus that hatred would not be quenched by hatred. But as matters stand, your majesty has granted me my life, and I have granted your majesty, his life. Thus hatred has been quenched by love. This, your majesty, is what my father meant when he said to me in the hour of death: "For, dear Dighavu, hatreds are not quenched by hatred. Nay rather, dear Dighavu, hatreds are quenched by love." '

Thereupon Brahmadatta king of Kasi exclaimed: 'O how wonderful, O how marvellous, that this Prince Dighavu should understand in its fullness a matter which his father expressed so briefly!' And he restored to him the army and vehicles and territory and treasuries and store-houses of his fathers, and gave him his daughter in marriage.

'For, monks, of these kings who took the rod, who took the sword, such is said to have been the patience and gentleness. How much more, monks, should you, who have retired from the world under a Doctrine and Discipline so well taught, let your light so shine in this world as to be known of men as patient and gentle.' And for the third time the Exalted One said this to those monks: 'Enough, monks! No quarrelling! No brawling! No contending! No wrangling!'

Then the Exalted One recited the following Stanza:*

He abused me, he struck me, he defeated me, he robbed me:
If any cherish this thought, their hatred never ceases.

He abused me, he struck me, he defeated me, he robbed me:
If any cherish not this thought, their hatred ceases.

For never in this world do hatreds cease through hatred;
Through love alone do hatreds cease: this is an eternal law.

*See *Dhammapada*, I.3-5.

II.15   *MILINDAPANHA*
[THE QUESTIONS OF MILINDA]
(Pali, *c.* 200 B.C.)

Milindapanha, or The Questions of Milinda (Greek, Menander), an important supplement to the Buddhist Pali canon, is an account of the discussions between Thera Nagasena, a Buddhist monk, and the Greek King Menander who ruled Bactria in the middle of the second century B.C. Probably such confrontations between Greek and Indian scholars occurred after Alexander's campaign in the Punjab in 326 B.C., especially at the famous university which flourished about that time at Takshasila or Taxila. This also accounts for the rise of a distinctive school of art called Gandhara in that region.

According to *Milindapanha,* King Menander was finally converted to Buddhism but the process of conversion was not easy either for the Greek king or for the Buddhist monk, for in their encounter two cultures and traditions collided. The resultant synthesizing experience is most refreshing. To Milinda's innumerable questions on a wide range of subjects touching Buddhism, Nagasena responds with either counter-questions or subtle answers through a series of similes. In this process, Nagasena provides a metaphysical basis for the teachings of Buddha. Though the question-answer technique of *Milindapanha* somewhat resembles the Upanishadic dialogue, yet it has a distinct Buddhist flavour.

The text of *Milindapanha* was translated from Pali into English by T. W. Rhys-Davids, *The Questions of King Milinda,* Parts I and II, Vols. 35 and 36 of the Sacred Books of the East Series, edited by F. Max Müller, Oxford: Clarendon Press, 1890, 1894.

In the selections included here, taken from Part I, Nagasena explains the composite nature of the individual personality in terms of the simile of the chariot (Bk II.1.1, pp. 40–5). By a series of further similes, Nagasena demonstrates (a) that the composite personality is continually changing with the passage of time, while retaining only a spacious unity through the existential body (Bk II.2.1, pp. 63–5); (b) that rebirth is possible without any identifiable soul, substratum of personality, or hypothetical entity passing in its totality from one existential form to another (Bk III. 5.6, p. 111); (c) that in the process of death and simultaneous rebirth, while the essence continues, only the name-form changes to a new name-form, which remains accountable for the cumulative good or bad consequences of actions of the previous name-form (Bk II.2.6, pp. 71–5); and (d) that people are not alike because they spring from seeds of previous actions or Karma (Bk III. 4.2, pp. 100–1).

II.15   *MILINDAPANHA*
            [THE QUESTIONS OF MILINDA]

        Book II · Lakkhana Panha
    The distinguishing characteristics of ethical qualities

CHAPTER I

1. Now Milinda the king went up to where the venerable Nagasena was, and addressed him with the greetings and compliments of friendship and courtesy, and took his seat respectfully apart. And Nagasena reciprocated his courtesy, so that the heart of the king was propitiated.

And Milinda began by asking, 'How is your Reverence known, and what, Sir, is your name?'

'I am known as Nagasena, O king, and it is by that name that my brethren in the faith address me. But although parents, O king, give such a name as Nagasena, or Surasena, or Virasena, or Sihasena, yet this, Sire – Nagasena and so on – is only a generally understood term, a designation in common use. For there is no permanent individuality (no soul) involved in the matter.'

Then Milinda called upon the Yonakas and the brethren to witness: 'This Nagasena says there is no permanent individuality (no soul) implied in his name. Is it now even possible to approve him in that?' And turning to Nagasena, he said: 'If, most reverend Nagasena, there be no permanent individuality (no soul) involved in the matter, who is it, pray, who gives to you members of the Order your robes and food and lodging and necessaries for the sick? Who is it who enjoys such things when given? Who is it who lives a life of righteousness? Who is it who devotes himself to meditation? Who is it who attains to the goal of the Excellent Way, to the Nirvana of Arahatship? And who is it who destroys living creatures? who is it who takes what is not his own? who is it who lives an evil life of worldly lusts, who speaks lies, who drinks strong drink, who (in a word) commits any one of the five sins which work out their bitter fruit even in this life? If that be so there is neither merit nor demerit; there is neither doer nor causer of good or evil deeds; there is neither fruit nor result of good or evil Karma. If, most reverend Nagasena, we are to think that were a man to kill you there would be no murder, then it follows that there are no real masters or teachers in your Order, and that your ordinations are void. – You tell me that your brethren in the Order are in the habit of addressing you as Nagasena. Now what is that Nagasena? Do you mean to say that the hair is Nagasena?'

'I don't say that, great king.'

'Or the hairs on the body, perhaps?'

'Certainly not.'

'Or is it the nails, the teeth, the skin, the flesh, the nerves, the bones, the marrow, the kidneys, the heart, the liver, the abdomen, the spleen, the lungs, the larger intestines, the lower intestines, the stomach, the faeces, the bile, the phlegm, the pus, the blood, the sweat, the fat, the tears, the serum, the saliva, the mucus, the oil that lubricates the joints, the urine, or the brain, or any or all of these, that is Nagasena?'

And to each of these he answered no.

'Is it the outward form then (*Rupa*) that is Nagasena, or the sensations (*Vedana*), or the ideas (*Sanna*), or the confections (the constituent elements of character, *Samkhara*), or the consciousness (*Vinnana*), that is Nagasena?'

And to each of these also he answered no.

'Then is it all these Skandhas combined that are Nagasena?'

'No! great king.'

'But is there anything outside the five Skandhas that is Nagasena?'

And still he answered no.

'Then thus, ask as I may, I can discover no Nagasena. Nagasena is a mere empty sound. Who then is the Nagasena that we see before us? It is a falsehood that your reverence has spoken, an untruth!'

And the venerable Nagasena said to Milinda the king: 'You, Sire, have been brought up in great luxury, as beseems your noble birth. If you were to walk this dry weather on the hot and sandy ground, trampling under foot the gritty, gravelly grains of the hard sand, your feet would hurt you. And as your body would be in pain, your mind would be disturbed, and you would experience a sense of bodily suffering. How then did you come, on foot, or in a chariot?'

'I did not come, Sir, on foot. I came in a carriage.'

'Then if you came, Sire, in a carriage, explain to me what that is. Is it the pole that is the chariot?'

'I did not say that.'

'Is it the axle that is the chariot?'

'Certainly not.'

'Is it the wheels, or the framework, or the ropes, or the yoke, or the spokes of the wheels, or the goad, that are the chariot?'

And to all these he still answered no.

'Then is it all these parts of it that are the chariot?'

'No, Sir.'

'But is there anything outside them that is the chariot?'

And still he answered no.

'Then thus, ask as I may, I can discover no chariot. Chariot is a mere empty sound. What then is the chariot you say you came in? It is a falsehood that your Majesty has spoken, an untruth! There is no such thing as a chariot! You are king over all India, a mighty monarch. Of whom then are you afraid that you speak untruth?' And he called upon the Yonakas and the brethren to witness saying: 'Milinda the king here has said that he came by carriage. But when asked in that case to explain what the carriage was, he is unable to establish what he averred. Is it, forsooth, possible to approve him in that?'

When he had thus spoken the five hundred Yonakas shouted their applause, and said to the king: 'Now let your Majesty get out of that if you can!'

And Milinda the king replied to Nagasena, and said: 'I have spoken no untruth, reverend Sir. It is on account of its having all these things – the pole, and the axle, the wheels, and the framework, the ropes, the yoke, the spokes, and the goad – that it comes under the generally understood term, the designation in common use, of "chariot".'

'Very good! Your Majesty had rightly grasped the meaning of "chariot". And just even so it is on account of all those things you questioned me about – the thirty-two kinds of organic matter in a human body, and the five constituent elements of being – that I come under the generally understood term, the designation in common use, of "Nagasena". For it was said, Sire, by our Sister Vagira in the presence of the Blessed One:

' "Just as it is by the condition precedent of the co-existence of its various parts that the word 'chariot' is used, just so is it that when the Skandhas are there we talk of a 'being'." '

'Most wonderful, Nagasena, and most strange. Well has the puzzle put to you, most difficult though it was, been solved. Were the Buddha himself here he would approve your answer. Well done, well done, Nagasena!'

BOOK II. CHAPTER 2

1. The king said: 'He who is born, Nagasena, does he remain the same or become another?'

'Neither the same nor another.'

'Give me an illustration.'

'Now what do you think, O king? You were once a baby, a tender thing, and small in size, lying flat on your back. Was that the same as you who are now grown up?'

'No. That child was one, I am another.'

'If you are not that child, it will follow that you have had neither mother nor father, no! nor teacher. You cannot have been taught either learning, or behaviour, or wisdom. What, great king! is the mother of the embryo in the first stage different from the mother of the embryo in the second stage, or the third, or the fourth? Is the mother of the baby a different person from the mother of the grown-up man! Is the person who goes to school one, and the same when he has finished his schooling another? Is it one who commits a crime, another who is punished by having his hands or feet cut off?'

'Certainly not. But what would you, Sir, say to that?'

The Elder replied: 'I should say that I am the same person, now I am grown up, as I was when I was a tender tiny baby, flat on my back. For all these states are included in one by means of this body.'

'Give me an illustration.'

'Suppose a man, O king, were to light a lamp, would it burn the night through?'

'Yes, it might do so.'

'Now, is it the same flame that burns in the first watch of the night, Sir, and in the second?'

'No.'

'Or the same that burns in the second watch and in the third?'

'No.'

'Then is there one lamp in the first watch, and another in the second, and another in the third?'

'No. The light comes from the same lamp all the night through.'

'Just so, O king, is the continuity of a person or thing maintained. One comes into being, another passes away; and the rebirth is, as it were, simultaneous. Thus neither as the same nor as another does a man go on to the last phase of his self-consciousness.'

'Give me a further illustration.'

'It is like milk, which when once taken from the cow, turns, after a lapse of time, first to curds, and then from curds to butter, and then from butter to ghee. Now would it be right to say that the milk was the same thing as the curds, or the butter, or the ghee?'

'Certainly not; but they are produced out of it.'

'Just so, O king, is the continuity of a person or thing maintained. One comes into being, another passes away; and the rebirth is, as it were, simultaneous. Thus neither as the same nor as another does a man go on to the last phase of his self-consciousness.'

'Well put, Nagasena!'

6. The king said: 'What is it, Nagasena, that is reborn?'

'Name-and-form is reborn.'

'What, is it this same name-and-form that is reborn?'

'No: but by this name-and-form deeds are done, good or evil, and by these deeds (this Karma) another name-and-form is reborn.'

'If that be so, Sir, would not the new being be released from its evil Karma?'

The Elder replied: 'Yes, if it were not reborn. But just because it is reborn, O king, it is therefore not released from its evil Karma.'

'Give me an illustration.'

'Suppose, O king, some man were to steal a mango from another man, and the owner of the mango were to seize him and bring him before the king, and charge him with the crime. And the thief were to say: "Your Majesty! I have not taken away this man's mangoes. Those that he put in the ground are different from the ones I took. I do not deserve to be punished." How then? would he be guilty?'

'Certainly, Sir. He would deserve to be punished.'

'But on what ground?'

'Because, in spite of whatever he may say, he would be guilty in respect of the last mango which resulted from the first one (the owner set in the ground).'

'Just so, great king, deeds good or evil are done by this name-and-form and another is reborn. But that other is not thereby released from its deeds (its Karma).' . . .

'Give me a further illustration.'

'Suppose, O king, a man were to take a lamp and go up into the top storey of his house, and there eat his meal. And the lamp blazing up were to set the thatch on fire, and from that the house should catch fire, and that house having caught fire the whole village should be burnt. And they should seize him and ask: "What, you fellow, did you set our village on fire for?" And he should reply: "I've not set your village on fire! The flame of the lamp, by the light of which I was eating was one thing; the fire which burnt your village was another thing." Now if they, thus disputing, should go to law before you, O king, in whose favour would you decide the case?'

'In the villagers' favour.'

'But why?'

'Because, Sir, in spite of whatever the man might say, the one fire was produced from the other.'

'Just so, great king, it is one name-and-form which has its end in death, and another name-and-form which is reborn. But the second is the result of the first, and is therefore not set free from its evil deeds.'

'Give me a further illustration.'

'Suppose, O king, a man were to choose a young girl in marriage, and give a price for her and go away. And she in due course should grow up to full age, and then another man were to pay a price for her and marry her. And when the first one had come back he should say: "Why, you fellow, have you carried off my wife?" And the other were to reply: "It's not your wife I have carried off! The little girl, the mere child, whom you chose in marriage and paid a price for is one; the girl grown up to full age whom I chose in marriage and paid a price for, is another." Now if they, thus disputing, were to go to law about it before you, O king, in whose favour would you decide the case?'

'In favour of the first.'

'But why?'

'Because, in spite of whatever the second might say, the grown-up girl would have been derived from the other girl.'

'Just so, great king, it is one name-and-form which has its end in death, and another name-and-form which is reborn. But the second is the result of the first, and is therefore not set free from its evil deeds.'

'Give me a further illustration.'

'Suppose a man, O king, were to buy of a herdsman a vessel of milk, and go away leaving it in his charge, saying: "I will come for it to-morrow"; and the next day it were to become curds. And when the man should come and ask for it, then suppose the other were to offer him the curds, and he should say: "It was not curds I bought of you; give me my vessel of milk." And the other were to reply: "Without any fault of mine your milk has turned to curds." Now if they, thus disputing, were to go to law about it before you, O king, in whose favour would you decide the case?'

'In favour of the herdsman.'

'But why?'

'Because, in spite of whatever the other might say, the curds were derived from the milk.'

'Just so, great king, it is one name-and-form that finds its end in death, and another that is reborn. But that other is the result of the first, and is therefore not thereby released from its evil deeds (its bad Karma).'

'Very good, Nagasena!'

BOOK III.   CHAPTER 4

2. The king said: 'Why is it, Nagasena, that all men are not alike, but some are short-lived and some long-lived, some sickly and some healthy, some ugly and some beautiful, some without influence and some of great power, some poor and some wealthy, some low born and some high born, some stupid and some wise?'

The Elder replied: 'Why is it that all vegetables are not alike, but some sour, and some salt, and some pungent, and some acid, and some astringent, and some sweet?'

'I fancy, Sir, it is because they come from different kinds of seeds.'

'And just so, great king, are the differences you have mentioned among men to be explained. For it has been said by the Blessed One: "Beings, O brahmin, have each their own Karma, are inheritors of Karma, belong to the tribe of their Karma, are relatives by Karma, have each their Karma as their protecting overlord. It is Karma that divides them up into low and high and the like divisions."'

'Very good, Nagasena!'

CHAPTER 5

5. The king said: 'Where there is no transmigration, Nagasena, can there be rebirth?'

'Yes, there can.'

'But how can that be? Give me an illustration.'

'Suppose a man, O king, were to light a lamp from another lamp, can it be said that the one transmigrates from, or to, the other?'

'Certainly not.'

'Just so, great king, is rebirth without transmigration.'

'Give me a further illustration.'

'Do you recollect, great king, having learnt, when you were a boy, some verse or other from your teacher?'

'Yes, I recollect that.'

'Well then, did that verse transmigrate from your teacher?'

'Certainly not.'

'Just so, great king, is rebirth without transmigration.'

'Very good, Nagasena!'

[THE LOTUS OF THE TRUE LAW]

(Sanskrit, *c.* A.D. 100)

Saddharma-Pundarika (The Lotus of the True Law), written in Classical Sanskrit, is one of the most important Mahayana Buddhist Sutras. In this work the historical Buddha, the Tathagata, or Sakyamuni, presented in a transfiguration, teaches the larger law to the historical Sangh, as well as to all living creatures. The aim of the Buddha is to direct all living beings towards degrees of spiritual perfection attainable within the scope of their lives, and thus help them with the aid of Bodhisattvas, to progress gradually, in successive stages of growth, to higher levels of spirituality. To illustrate this principle Buddha relates the Parable of the Burning House. On gaining understanding of Buddha's law, the disciples then relate the Parable of the Prodigal Son.

The two parables are taken from the translation by H. Kern, *Saddharma Pundarika*, or *The Lotus of the True Law*, Vol. 21 of the Sacred Books of the East Series, edited by F. Max Müller, Oxford: Clarendon Press, 1884, Chapter III, pp. 72–82, and Chapter IV, pp. 99–108.

II.16   MAHAYANA PARABLE:
           THE BURNING HOUSE

Let us suppose the following case, Sariputra. In a certain village, town, borough, province, kingdom, or capital, there was a certain housekeeper, old, aged, decrepit, very advanced in years, rich, wealthy, opulent; he had a great house, high, spacious, built a long time ago and old, inhabited by some two, three, four, or five hundred living beings. The house had but one door, and a thatch; its terraces were tottering, the bases of its pillars rotten, the coverings and plaster of the walls loose. On a sudden the whole house was from every side put in conflagration by a mass of fire. Let us suppose that the man had many little boys, say five, or ten, or even twenty, and that he himself had come out of the house.

Now, Sariputra, that man, on seeing the house from every side wrapt in a blaze by a great mass of fire, got afraid, frightened, anxious in his mind, and made the following reflection: I myself am able to come out from the burning house through the door, quickly and safely, without being touched or scorched by that great mass of fire; but my children, those young boys, are staying in the burning house, playing, amusing, and diverting themselves with all sorts of sports. They do not perceive, nor know, nor understand, nor mind that the house is on fire, and do not get afraid. Though scorched by that great mass of fire, and affected with such a mass of pain, they do not mind the pain, nor do they conceive the idea of escaping.

The man, Sariputra, is strong, has powerful arms, and (so) he makes this reflection: I am strong, and have powerful arms; why, let me gather all my little boys and take them to my breast to effect their escape from the house. A second reflection then presented itself to his mind: This house has but one opening; the door is shut; and those boys, fickle, unsteady, and childlike as they are, will, it is to be feared, run hither and thither, and come to grief and disaster in this mass of fire. Therefore I will warn them. So resolved, he calls to the boys: Come, my children; the house is burning with a mass of fire; come, lest ye be burnt in that mass of fire, and come to grief and disaster. But the ignorant boys do not heed the words of him who is their well-wisher; they are not afraid, not alarmed, and feel no misgiving; they do not care, nor fly, nor even know nor understand the purport of the word 'burning'; on the contrary, they run hither and thither, walk about, and repeatedly look at their father; all, because they are so ignorant.

Then the man is going to reflect thus: The house is burning, is blazing by a mass of fire. It is to be feared that myself as well as my children will come to grief and disaster. Let me therefore by some skilful means get the boys out of the house. The man knows the disposition of the boys, and has a clear perception of their inclinations. Now these boys happen to have many and manifold toys to play with, pretty, nice, pleasant, dear, amusing, and precious. The man, knowing the disposition of the boys, says to them: My children, your toys, which are so pretty, precious, and admirable, which you are so loth to miss, which are so various and multifarious, (such as) bullock-carts, goat-carts, deer-carts, which are so pretty, nice, dear, and precious to you, have all been put by me outside the house-door for you to play with. Come, run out, leave the house; to each of you I shall give what he wants. Come soon; come out for the sake of these toys. And the boys on hearing the names mentioned of such playthings as they like and desire, so agreeable to their taste, so pretty, dear, and delightful, quickly rush out from the burning house, with eager effort and great alacrity, one having no time to wait for the other, and pushing each other on with the cry of 'Who shall arrive first, the very first?'

The man, seeing that his children have safely and happily escaped, and knowing that they are free from danger, goes and sits down in the open air on the square of the village, his heart filled with joy and delight, released from trouble and hindrance, quite at ease. The boys go up to the place where their father is sitting, and say: 'Father, give us those toys to play with, those bullock-carts, goat-carts, and deer-carts.' Then, Sariputra, the man gives to his sons, who run swift as the wind, bullock-carts only, made of seven precious substances, provided with benches, hung with a multitude of small bells, lofty, adorned with rare and wonderful jewels, embellished with jewel wreaths, decorated with garlands of flowers, carpeted with cotton mattresses and woollen coverlets, covered with white cloth and silk, having on both sides rosy cushions, yoked with white, very fair and fleet bullocks, led by a multitude of men. To each of his children he gives several bullock-carts of one appearance and one kind, provided with flags, and swift as the wind. That man does so, Sariputra, because being rich, wealthy, and in possession of many treasures and granaries, he rightly thinks: Why should I give these boys inferior carts, all these boys being my own children, dear and precious? I have got such great vehicles, and ought to treat all the boys equally and without partiality. As I own many treasures and granaries, I could give such great vehicles to all beings, how much more then to my own children. Meanwhile the boys are mounting the vehicles with feelings of astonishment and wonder. Now, Sariputra, what is thy opinion? Has that man made himself guilty of a falsehood by first holding out to his children the prospect of three vehicles and afterwards giving to each of them the greatest vehicles only, the most magnificent vehicles?

Sariputra answered: By no means, Lord; by no means, Sugata. That is not sufficient, O Lord, to qualify the man as a speaker of falsehood, since it only was a skilful device to persuade his children to go out of the burning house and save their lives. Nay, besides recovering their very body, O Lord, they have received all those toys. If that man, O Lord, had given no single cart, even then he would not have been a speaker of falsehood, for he had previously been meditating on saving the little boys from a great mass of pain by some able device. Even in this case, O Lord, the man would not have been guilty of falsehood, and far less now that he, considering his having plenty of treasures and prompted by no other motive but the love of his children, gives to all, to coax them, vehicles of one kind, and those the greatest vehicles. That man, Lord, is not guilty of falsehood.

The venerable Sariputra having thus spoken, the Lord said to him: Very well, very well, Sariputra, quite so; it is even as thou sayest. So, too, Sariputra, the Tathagata, is free from all dangers, wholly exempt from all misfortune, despondency, calamity, pain, grief, the thick enveloping dark mists of ignorance. He, the Tathagata, endowed with Buddha-knowledge, forces, absence of hesitation, uncommon properties, and mighty by magical power, is the father of the world, who has reached the highest perfection in the knowledge of skilful means, who is most merciful, long-suffering, benevolent, compassionate. He appears in this triple world, which is like a house the roof and shelter whereof are decayed, (a house) burning by a mass of misery, in order to deliver from affection, hatred, and delusion the beings subject to birth, old age, disease, death, grief, wailing, pain, melancholy, despondency, the dark enveloping mists of ignorance, in order to rouse them to supreme and perfect enlightenment. Once born, he sees how the creatures are burnt, tormented, vexed, distressed by birth, old age, disease, death, grief, wailing, pain, melancholy, despondency; how for the sake of enjoyments, and prompted by sensual desires, they severally suffer various pains. In consequence both of what in this world they are seeking and what they have acquired, they will in a future state suffer various pains, in hell, in the brute creation, in the realm of Yama; suffer such pains as poverty in the world of gods or men, union with hateful persons or things, and separation from the beloved ones. And whilst incessantly whirling in that mass of evils they are sporting, playing, diverting themselves; they do not fear, nor dread, nor are they seized with terror; they do not know, nor mind; they are not startled, do not try to escape, but are enjoying themselves in that triple world which is like unto a burning house, and run hither and thither. Though overwhelmed by that mass of evil, they do not conceive the idea that they must beware of it.

Under such circumstances, Sariputra, the Tathagata reflects thus: Verily, I am the father of these beings; I must save them from this mass of evil, and bestow on them the immense, inconceivable bliss of Buddha-knowledge, wherewith they shall sport, play, and divert themselves, wherein they shall find their rest.

Then, Sariputra, the Tathagata reflects thus: If, in the conviction of my possessing the power of knowledge and magical faculties, I manifest to these beings the knowledge, forces, and absence of hesitation of the Tathagata, without availing myself of some device, these beings will not escape. For they are attached to the pleasures of the five senses, to worldly pleasures; they will not be freed from birth, old age, disease, death, grief, wailing, pain, melancholy, despondency, by which they are burnt, tormented, vexed, distressed. Unless they are forced to leave the triple world which is like a house the shelter and roof whereof is in a blaze, how are they to get acquainted with Buddha-knowledge?

Now, Sariputra, even as that man with powerful arms, without using the strength of his arms, attracts his children out of the burning house by an able device, and afterwards gives them magnificent, great carts, so, Sariputra, the Tathagata, the Arhat, possessed of knowledge and freedom from all hesitation, without using them, in order to attract the creatures out of the triple world which is like a burning house with decayed roof and shelter, shows, by his knowledge of able devices, three vehicles, viz. the vehicle of the disciples, the vehicle of the Pratyekabuddhas, and the vehicle of the Bodhisattvas. By means of these three vehicles he attracts the creatures and speaks to them thus: Do not delight in this triple world, which is like a burning house, in these miserable forms, sounds, odours, flavours, and contacts. For in delighting in this triple world you are burnt, heated, inflamed with the thirst inseparable from the pleasures of the five senses. Fly from this triple world; betake yourselves to the three vehicles: the vehicle of the disciples, the vehicle of the Pratyekabuddhas, the vehicle of the Bodhisattvas. I give you my pledge for it, that I shall give you these three vehicles; make an effort to run out of this triple world. And to attract them I say: These vehicles are grand, praised by the Aryas, and provided with most pleasant things; with such you are to sport, play, and divert yourselves in a noble manner. You will feel the great delight of the faculties, powers, constituents of Bodhi, meditations, the (eight) degrees of emancipation, self-concentration, and the results of self-concentration, and you will become greatly happy and cheerful.

Now, Sariputra, the beings who have become wise have faith in the Tathagata, the father of the world, and consequently apply themselves to his commandments. Amongst them there are some who, wishing to follow the dictate of an authoritative voice, apply themselves to the commandment of the Tathagata to acquire the knowledge of the four great truths, for the sake of their own complete Nirvana. These one may say to be those who, coveting the vehicle of the disciples, fly from the triple world, just as some of the boys will fly from that burning house, prompted by a desire of getting a cart yoked with deer. Other beings desirous of the science without a master, of self-restraint and tranquillity, apply themselves to the commandment of the Tathagata to learn to understand causes and effects, for the sake of their own complete Nirvana. These one may say to be those who, coveting the vehicle of the Pratyekabuddhas, fly from the triple world, just as some of the boys fly from the burning house, prompted by the desire of getting a cart yoked with goats. Others again desirous of the knowledge of the all-knowing, the knowledge of Buddha, the knowledge of the self-born one, the science without a master, apply themselves to the commandment of the Tathagata to learn to understand the knowledge, powers, and freedom from hesitation of the Tathagata, for the sake of the common weal and happiness, out of compassion to the world, for the benefit, weal, and happiness of the world at large, both gods and men, for the sake of the complete Nirvana of all beings. These one may say to be those who, coveting the great vehicle, fly from the triple world. Therefore they are called Bodhisattvas Mahasattvas. They may be likened to those among the boys who have fled from the burning house prompted by the desire of getting a cart yoked with bullocks.

In the same manner, Sariputra, as that man, on seeing his children escaped from the burning house and knowing them safely and happily rescued and out of danger, in the consciousness of his great wealth, gives the boys one single grand cart; so, too, Sariputra, the Tathagata, the Arhat, on seeing many kotis of beings recovered from the triple world, released from sorrow, fear, terror, and calamity, having escaped owing to the command of the Tathagata, delivered from all fears, calamities, and difficulties, and having reached the bliss of Nirvana, so, too, Sariputra, the Tathagata, the Arhat, considering that he possesses great wealth of knowledge, power, and absence of hesitation, and that all beings are his children, leads them by no other vehicle but the Buddha-vehicle to full development. But he does not teach a particular Nirvana for each being; he causes all beings to reach complete Nirvana by means of the complete Nirvana of the Tathagata. And those beings, Sariputra, who are delivered from the triple world, to them the Tathagata gives as toys to amuse themselves with the lofty pleasures of the Aryas, the pleasures of meditation, emancipation, self-concentration, and its results; (toys) all of the same kind. Even as that man, Sariputra, cannot be said to have told a falsehood for having held out to those boys the prospect of three vehicles and given to all of them but one great vehicle, a magnificent vehicle made of seven precious substances, decorated with all sorts of ornaments, a vehicle of one kind, the most egregious of all, so, too, Sariputra, the Tathagata, the Arhat, tells no falsehood when by an able device he first holds forth three vehicles and afterwards leads all to complete Nirvana by one great vehicle. For the Tathagata, Sariputra, who is rich in treasures and store-houses of abundant knowledge, powers, and absence of hesitation, is able to teach all beings the law which is connected with the knowledge of the all-knowing. In this way, Sariputra, one has to understand how the Tathagata by an able device and direction shows but one vehicle, the great vehicle.

II.17   MAHAYANA PARABLE:
               THE PRODIGAL SON

It is a case, O Lord, as if a certain man went away from his father and
betook himself to some other place. He lives there in foreign parts for
many years, twenty or thirty or forty or fifty. In course of time the
one (the father) becomes a great man; the other (the son) is poor; in
seeking a livelihood for the sake of food and clothing he roams in all
directions and goes to some place, whereas his father removes to
another country. The latter has much wealth, gold, corn, treasures,
and granaries; possesses much (wrought) gold and silver, many gems,
pearls, lapis lazuli, conch shells, and stones, corals, gold and silver;
many slaves male and female, servants for menial work and journey-
men; is rich in elephants, horses, carriages, cows, and sheep. He keeps
a large retinue; has his money invested in great territories, and does
great things in business, money-lending, agriculture, and commerce.

In course of time, Lord, that poor man, in quest of food and clothing, roaming through villages, towns, boroughs, provinces, kingdoms,
and royal capitals, reaches the place where his father, the owner of
much wealth and gold, treasures and granaries, is residing. Now the
poor man's father, Lord, the owner of much wealth and gold, treasures
and granaries, who was residing in that town, had always and ever
been thinking of the son he had lost fifty years ago, but he gave no
utterance to his thoughts before others, and was only pining in
himself and thinking: I am old, aged, advanced in years, and possess
abundance of bullion, gold, money and corn, treasures and granaries,
but have no son. It is to be feared lest death shall overtake me and all
this perish unused. Repeatedly he was thinking of that son: O how
happy should I be, were my son to enjoy this mass of wealth!

Meanwhile, Lord, the poor man in search of food and clothing was
gradually approaching the house of the rich man, the owner of
abundant bullion, gold, money and corn, treasures and granaries.
And the father of the poor man happened to sit at the door of his
house, surrounded and waited upon by a great crowd of Brahmans,
Kshatriyas, Vaisyas, and Sudras; he was sitting on a magnificent
throne with a footstool decorated with gold and silver, while dealing

with hundred thousands of kotis of gold-pieces, and fanned with a chowrie, on a spot under an extended awning inlaid with pearls and flowers and adorned with hanging garlands of jewels; sitting (in short) in great pomp. The poor man, Lord, saw his own father in such pomp sitting at the door of the house, surrounded with a great crowd of people and doing a householder's business. The poor man frightened, terrified, alarmed, seized with a feeling of horripilation all over the body, and agitated in mind, reflects thus: Unexpectedly have I here fallen in with a king or grandee. People like me have nothing to do here; let me go; in the street of the poor I am likely to find food and clothing without much difficulty. Let me no longer tarry at this place, lest I be taken to do forced labour or incur some other injury.

Thereupon, Lord, the poor man quickly departs, runs off, does not tarry from fear of a series of supposed dangers. But the rich man, sitting on the throne at the door of his mansion, has recognized his son at first sight, in consequence whereof he is content, in high spirits, charmed, delighted, filled with joy and cheerfulness. He thinks: Wonderful! he who is to enjoy this plenty of bullion, gold, money and corn, treasures and granaries, has been found! He of whom I have been thinking again and again, is here now that I am old, aged, advanced in years.

At the same time, moment, and instant, Lord, he dispatches couriers, to whom he says: Go, sirs, and quickly fetch me that man. The fellows thereon all run forth in full speed and overtake the poor man, who, frightened, terrified, alarmed, seized with a feeling of horripilation all over his body, agitated in mind, utters a lamentable cry of distress, screams, and exclaims: I have given you no offence. But the fellows drag the poor man, however lamenting, violently with them. He, frightened, terrified, alarmed, seized with a feeling of horripilation all over his body, and agitated in mind, thinks by himself: I fear lest I shall be punished with capital punishment; I am lost. He faints away, and falls on the earth. His father dismayed and near despondency says to those fellows: Do not carry the man in that manner. With these words he sprinkles him with cold water without addressing him any further. For that householder knows the poor man's humble disposition and his own elevated position; yet he feels that the man is his son.

The householder, Lord, skilfully conceals from everyone that it is his son. He calls one of his servants and says to him: Go, sirrah, and tell that poor man: Go, sirrah, whither thou likest; thou art free. The servant obeys, approaches the poor man and tells him: Go, sirrah, whither thou likest; thou art free. The poor man is astonished and amazed at hearing these words; he leaves that spot and wanders to the street of the poor in search of food and clothing. In order to attract him the householder practises an able device. He employs for it two men ill-favoured and of little splendour. Go, says he, go to the man you saw in this place; hire him in your own name for a double daily fee, and order him to do work here in my house. And if he asks: What work shall I have to do? tell him: Help us in clearing the heap of dirt. The two fellows go and seek the poor man and engage him for such work as mentioned. Thereupon the two fellows conjointly with the poor man clear the heap of dirt in the house for the daily pay they receive from the rich man, while they take up their abode in a hovel of straw in the neighbourhood of the rich man's dwelling. And that rich man beholds through a window his own son clearing the heap of dirt, at which sight he is anew struck with wonder and astonishment.

Then the householder descends from his mansion, lays off his wreath and ornaments, parts with his soft, clean, and gorgeous attire, puts on dirty raiment, takes a basket in his right hand, smears his body with dust, and goes to his son, whom he greets from afar, and thus addresses: Please, take the baskets and without delay remove the dust. By this device he manages to speak to his son, to have a talk with him and say: Do, sirrah, remain here in my service; do not go again to another place; I will give thee extra pay, and whatever thou wantest thou mayst confidently ask me, be it the price of a pot, a smaller pot, a boiler or wood, or be it the price of salt, food, or clothing. I have got an old cloak, man; if thou shouldst want it, ask me for it, I will give it. Any utensil of such sort, when thou wantest to have it, I will give thee. Be at ease, fellow; look upon me as if I were thy father, for I am older and thou art younger, and thou hast rendered me much service by clearing this heap of dirt, and as long as thou hast been in my service thou hast never shown nor art showing wickedness, crookedness, arrogance, or hypocrisy; I have discovered in thee no vice at all of such as are commonly seen in other man-servants. From henceforward thou art to me like my own son.

From that time, Lord, the householder addresses the poor man by the name of son, and the latter feels in presence of the householder as a son to his father. In this manner, Lord, the householder affected with longing for his son employs him for the clearing of the heap of dirt during twenty years, at the end of which the poor man feels quite at ease in the mansion to go in and out, though he continues taking his abode in the hovel of straw.

After a while, Lord, the householder falls sick, and feels that the time of his death is near at hand. He says to the poor man: Come hither, man, I possess abundant bullion, gold, money and corn, treasures and granaries. I am very sick, and wish to have one upon whom to bestow (my wealth); by whom it is to be received, and with whom it is to be deposited. Accept it. For in the same manner as I am the owner of it, so art thou, but thou shalt not suffer anything of it to be wasted.

And so, Lord, the poor man accepts the abundant bullion, gold, money and corn, treasures and granaries of the rich man, but for himself he is quite indifferent to it, and requires nothing from it, not even so much as the price of a prastha of flour; he continues living in the same hovel of straw and considers himself as poor as before.

After a while, Lord, the householder perceives that his son is able to save, mature and mentally developed; that in the consciousness of his nobility he feels abashed, ashamed, disgusted, when thinking of his former poverty. The time of his death approaching, he sends for the poor man, presents him to a gathering of his relations, and before the king or king's peer and in the presence of citizens and country-people makes the following speech: Hear, gentlemen! this is my own son, by me begotten. It is now fifty years that he disappeared from such and such a town. He is called so and so, and myself am called so and so. In searching after him I have from that town come hither. He is my son, I am his father. To him I leave all my revenues, and all my personal (or private) wealth shall he acknowledge (his own).

The poor man, Lord, hearing this speech was astonished and amazed; he thought by himself: Unexpectedly have I obtained this bullion, gold, money and corn, treasures and granaries.

Even so, O Lord, do we represent the sons of the Tathagata, and the Tathagata says to us: Ye are my sons, as the householder did. We were oppressed, O Lord, with three difficulties, viz. the difficulty of pain, the difficulty of conceptions, the difficulty of transition (or evolution); and in the worldly whirl we were disposed to what is low. Then have we been prompted by the Lord to ponder on the numerous inferior laws (or conditions, things) that are similar to a heap of dirt. Once directed to them we have been practising, making efforts, and seeking for nothing but Nirvana as our fee. We were content, O Lord, with the Nirvana obtained, and thought to have gained much at the hands of the Tathagata because of our having applied ourselves to these laws, practised, and made efforts. But the Lord takes no notice of us, does not mix with us, nor tell us that this treasure of the Tathagata's knowledge shall belong to us, though the Lord skilfully appoints us as heirs to this treasure of the knowledge of the Tathagata. And we, O Lord, are not (impatiently) longing to enjoy it, because we deem it a great gain already to receive from the Lord, Nirvana as our fee. We preach to the Bodhisattvas Mahasattvas a sublime sermon about the knowledge of the Tathagata; we explain, show, demonstrate the knowledge of the Tathagata, O Lord, without longing. For the Tathagata by his skilfulness knows our disposition, whereas we ourselves do not know, nor apprehend. It is for this very reason that the Lord just now tells us that we are to him as sons, and that he reminds us of being heirs to the Tathagata. For the case stands thus: we are as sons to the Tathagata, but low (or humble) of disposition; the Lord perceives the strength of our disposition and applies to us the denomination of Bodhisattvas; we are, however, charged with a double office in so far as in presence of Bodhisattvas we are called persons of low disposition and at the same time have to rouse them to Buddha-enlightment. Knowing the strength of our disposition the Lord has thus spoken, and in this way, O Lord, do we say that we have obtained unexpectedly and without longing the jewel of omniscience, which we did not desire, nor seek, nor search after, nor expect, nor require; and that inasmuch as we are the sons of the Tathagata.

TIRU-VALLUVAR
TIRU-KURAL

(Tamil, *c.* 100 B.C.)

Tiru-Valluvar's *Tiru-Kural* (Tamil *tiru*, 'sacred' or 'holy'), affectionately called by the people 'The Tamil Veda', gives in terse and vivid couplets the moral wisdom and practical philosophy of the venerable sage of Tamilnad, on matters relating to householders, ascetics, princes, councillors, ambassadors, state officials, subjects, and lovers. The work deals mainly with the conduct and character of people as private and public persons, in various orders of the society of the time.

The *Kural*, consisting of 133 chapters of ten couplets each, is arranged in three parts with an Introduction (Chapters 1–4), namely: I. *Aram* or Righteousness (5–38); II. *Porul* or Wealth (39–108); and III. *Inbam* or Love (109–33). These categories can roughly be compared to the 'Aims of Man' (Sanskrit, *Purushartha*): *Dharma, Artha,* and *Kama.* Apparently, Tiru-Valluvar felt, as did the Chinese sage Confucius, that if a man were to live a good life on earth according to the teaching then he would inevitably arrive at the door of deliverance (Sanskrit, *Moksha*), and, therefore, there is no need to dwell on that hypothetical subject in practical terms.

In the first section of the *Kural, Aram,* Valluvar speaks of man in relation to his family. 'The chiefest blessing,' declares the sage, 'is an honourable home, and its crowning glory is worthy offspring' (verse 60). Such a home is made by a woman who worships not the gods but her husband (verse 55), a maxim magnificently exemplified in their lives and actions by Kannaki, the heroine of the Tamil epic *Shilappadikaram,* and Sita, the heroine of the Sanskrit epic *Ramayana.* Tiru-Valluvar upholds the law of hospitality as being of great value, in the same manner as classical Greek civilization. Valluvar seems to have held that only the virtuous are free, for he says: 'They alone live who live without blemish; and they alone die who have lived without glory' (verse 240). The true renunciation, according to the sage, who worked all his life at the loom, is not renunciation of life, but of excessive desire: 'If you want joy, renounce early; for many are the delights that you shall enjoy after renouncing' (verse 342).

Valluvar places as much, if not greater, emphasis on political and social life and its organization, as on domestic and ascetic life: for he devotes seven hundred couplets to the second section, called *Porul*, or wealth of all kinds – of mind, body, family, and goods. He says that such wealth cannot be pursued, enjoyed, or maintained with justice except under a stable, well-ordered, benevolent government. In a country where people starve, there is something wrong with its government, and consequently, like the Chinese philosopher Mencius, Valluvar maintains that a bad government 'is worse than an assassin' (verse 551); it should be eliminated and have another government put in its place. Though most of Valluvar's sayings in this section refer to the body politic, namely the prince, minister, councillor, ambassador, public official, often they have a much more general application: for example 'Worse than excessive rage is the unguardedness that comes from overweening self-complacency' (verse 531).

In the last section, entitled *Inbam* or Love, the sage speaks of love between a couple before and after marriage, and of their separation and reunion. These couplets could be broadly classified under two headings, dealing with (a) *Kalavu*, or furtive or secret love – a spontaneous union of man and maid in the nature of 'Gandharva marriage', one of the ordinary customs among ancient social practices, and recognized as a prelude to a binding union; and (b) *Karpu*, or married love, portraying the joys of love between husband and wife, the pangs of separation, and the bliss of reunion. Some commentators have classified these chapters as treating of lovers in relation to (i) *Kurunji*, or meeting (109–13); (ii) *Palai*, or separation (114–18); (iii) *Mullai*, or loneliness (119–23); (iv) *Neidal*, or complaints (124–8); and (v) *Marudam*, or sulking (129–33). However, each verse can be considered as describing one of the innumerable moods of lovers.

Tiru-Valluvar's approach to life is based on realistic human experience. He may have been somewhat influenced by Jain teaching in as much as he upholds '*ahimsa*' (non-injury, or non-killing) as the highest virtue (verse 321). But what is unusual in his maxims is his view that work by one's own hands is worthy of any man of virtue (103), and that laziness and beggary, practised by an individual, a group, or a nation, are the result of lack of energy and enterprise (105–7). For he feels that 'even though the gods be against, Industry is bound to pay the wages of labour' (verse 619). Valluvar does not believe that the Creator intended man to live in beggary of any kind; and if it should be otherwise, the sage who 'uttered nothing false' declares daringly that such a creator should 'wander about the world and perish' (verse 1062). For, he says, 'The fair one called Earth laughs to herself when she sees the sluggard cry, saying: Alas, I have nothing to eat!' (verse 1040). Tiru-Valluvar's teaching becomes all the more important when considered in relation to present-day India, where colonial and caste snobberies have made sophisticated country-men of the sage look down upon manual labour, and resort to beggary, individual or national, as the easiest solution or way of life. For Valluvar says it is only that nation which has energy, and mobilizes it, that can be truly called rich (verse 591).

Among the many commentators on *Kural*, Parimelalakar, who lived and taught at Kanchi in the thirteenth century, appears to have explored the heart and mind of Tiru-Valluvar, and brought out the beauty of his sayings. Parimelalakar's Commentary is preserved with devout religious care. The *Kural* and the Commentary have been a source of inspiration to the rulers and the ruled alike in the land of their birth.

The word 'kural' means the short rhymed couplet in which the sayings of Valluvar are composed. The first line of the couplet is of four feet, and the second line is of three. The first foot of each line rhymes, for example:

> *Kamam vekuli mayakkam ivaimundrin*
> *Namam kedakkedum noy.*
> When he has conquered utterly desire, anger, and delusion,
> All suffering ceases for man. (Verse 360)*

though sometimes the last foot of the first line also rhymes with the first foot.

The 300 couplets (out of 1,330) included here are from the trans-

---

* V. V. S. Aiyar, *The Kural*, or *The Maxims of Tiru-Valluvar*. Tiruchirapalli, 1952. p. xlv.

lation by V. V. S. Aiyar, *The Kural* or *The Maxims of Tiru-Valluvar*.
Tiruchirapalli: V. V. S. Krishnamurthy, 1952.

II.18   TIRU-VALLUVAR
TIRU-KURAL

Introduction

GOD

1. A is the starting-point of the world of sound; even so is the Ancient One Supreme the starting-point of all that exists.
2. Of what avail is all your learning if you worship not the holy feet of Him of the perfect intelligence?
10. They alone cross the ocean of births and deaths who take refuge in the feet of the Lord: the others traverse it not.

RAIN

11. It is the unfailing fall of rain that sustains the earth; therefore, look upon it as very *amrita* – the drink of immortality.
12. Every food that is sweet to the taste is the gift of rain to man; and rain itself is the food for the thirsty.

ASCETIC

23. Behold the men who have weighed this life with the next and have renounced the world; the earth is made radiant by their greatness.
24. Behold the man whose firm will controls his five senses even as the goading hook controls the elephant; he is a seed fit for the fields of heaven.
26. The great ones are they who can achieve the impossible (control of their senses); the feeble ones are those who cannot.

RIGHTEOUSNESS

32. There is no greater good than Righteousness, nor no greater ill than the forgetting of it.

34. Be pure in heart: all righteousness is contained in this one commandment; all other things are nought but empty sound.

35. Avoid envy and greed, anger and harsh words: that is the way to acquire righteousness.

39. They alone are joys which flow from a virtuous life; all other pleasures end but in disgrace and sorrow.

Part I: *ARAM* [Righteousness] (Sanskrit, *Dharma*)

FAMILY LIFE

41. The householder is the mainstay of all who follow the other paths of life.

43. Five are the duties of the householder, namely, the offering of oblations to the *pitris* (spirit of ancestors), the performance of sacrifices to the gods, the offering of hospitality, the rendering of help to others, and the looking after one's own self.

45. If love abounds in the home and righteousness does prevail, the home is perfect and its end is all fulfilled.

47. Among those that seek after salvation, the greatest are they who lead a virtuous family life, performing aright all the duties that belong to it.

48. Behold the householder who helps others in the observance of their vows and who leads a virtuous life himself. He is a greater saint than those who betake themselves to a life of fasting and prayer.

49. Righteousness belongs especially to the married life, and a good name is its ornament.

HOME'S HELPMATE

51. She is the good helpmate who possesses every wifely virtue and spends not above her husband's means.

52. All other blessings turn to nought if the wife fails in wifely virtues.

54. What is there that is grander than woman, when she is strong in the strength of her chastity?

55. Behold the woman who worships not the gods but worships her husband even as she rises from bed; the rain cloud obeys her commands.

56. She is the good housewife who guards her virtue and her reputation, and tends her husband with loving care.

60. The chiefest blessing is an honourable home; and its crowning glory is worthy offspring.

OFFSPRING

61. We know of no blessing so great as the begetting of children that are endowed with understanding.

62. Behold the man whose children bear an unstained character; no evil will touch him up to his seventh reincarnation.

64. Sweeter verily than ambrosia is the gruel soused and spattered by the tender hands of one's own children.

65. The touch of children is the delight of the body; the delight of the ear is the hearing of their speech.

66. The flute is sweet and the guitar dulcet; so say they who have not heard the babbling speech of their little ones.

67. Great is the joy of the mother when a man child is born unto her but greater far is her delight when she hears him called worthy.

LOVE

71. Where is the bar that can close in the gates of love? The gentle tear drops that form themselves in the eyes of lovers are sure to proclaim its presence.

72. Those that love not live only for themselves; as to those that love, they will give their very bones for helping others.

73. They say it is to taste again of love that the soul has consented once more to be encased in bone.

74. Love makes the heart tender towards all; and tenderness yields that priceless treasure called friendship.

76. They are fools who say that love is for the righteous alone; for even against the evil-minded love is the only ally for a man.

79. Of what avail is a lovely outside, if love, the soul's ornament, has no place in the heart?

80. The seat of life is in Love; the man who has it not is only a mass of skin-encased bone.

HOSPITALITY

81. What for do the wise toil and set up homes? It is to feed the guest and help the pilgrim.
82. Were it even the draught of immortality, it shall not be tasted alone when the guest is in the hall.
83. No evil can befall the man who never fails to honour the incoming guest.
84. Behold the man who receives the worthy guest with his best smile; Lakshmi [goddess of wealth] delights to abide in his home.
85. Behold the man who has tended the outgoing guest and waits for the incoming one; he is a welcome guest to the gods.

KIND SPEECH

92. Better even than a generous gift is sweet speech and a kind and gracious look.
95. Modesty and loving speech, these alone are ornaments to a man, and none other.

GRATITUDE

101. Behold the kindness done without any obligation; even the heavens and the earth are too poor to repay it.
102. A kindness done in the hour of need may look small; but it outweighs the whole world.
103. Behold the kindness done without thought of recompense; the ocean will look small when compared with its worth.
108. It is ignoble to forget a kindness; but an injury received, it is the part of nobility to forget at once.

UPRIGHT HEART

115. Evil and good come unto all; but his upright heart is the glory of the man of worth.

116. When your heart swerves from the right and turns unto evil, know that your destruction is near at hand.

120. Behold the business man that looks after the interests of others as his own; his business will expand.

SELF-CONTROL

121. Self-control leads unto heaven, but uncontrolled passion is the royal road to endless darkness.

125. Humility is beautiful in all men: but on the rich it shines in all its splendour.

126. Behold the man who can draw in into himself his five senses even as the tortoise does its limbs; he hath laid up for himself a treasure that will last even unto his seventh reincarnation.

128. If even one word of yours causes pain to another, all your virtue is lost.

129. The burn caused by fire heals in its time; but the wound burned in by the tongue remains a running sore for ever.

PURE CONDUCT

131. The man whose conduct is pure is honoured by all; purity of conduct is, therefore, to be prized even above life.

138. Purity of conduct sows the seed of prosperity; but an evil course is the mother of endless ills.

ADULTERY

146. The adulterer knows no respite from four things: hatred, sin, fear, and shame.

147. He is the righteous householder whose heart is not attracted by the charms of his neighbour's wife.

FORGIVENESS

151. The earth supports even those that dig into her entrails; even so bear with those that traduce you: for that is greatness.

152. Forgive always the injuries that others may do; but if you forget them, it were even better.

153. The most shameful poverty is the refusal of hospitality; and the greatest strength is to bear with the dullness of fools.

156. The joy of revenge lasts but a day; but the glory of him who forgives endures for ever.

158. Conquer by your nobility those that in their pride have injured you.

NON-ENVYING

161. Know that your heart is inclining towards virtue when you find that it is free from all feelings of envy.

162. No blessing is so great as a nature that is free from all envy.

NON-COVETING

174. Behold the men that have mastered their senses and enlarged their vision; they covet not saying, Lo, we are in want.

175. Of what avail is a mind that is subtle and comprehending, if it yields to greed and consents to insensate deeds?

177. Covet not the wealth that greed gathers; for its fruit is bitter in the day of enjoyment.

NON-SLANDER

182. It is wrong to turn away from good and do evil; but it is far worse to smile before and vilify behind.

190. If a man can scan his own faults as he does those of his enemies, can evil ever come to him?

VAIN SPEAKING

193. He that multiplies empty words declares loud his want of worth.

EVIL DOING

201. The evil fear not the folly called sin; but the worthy flee from it.

202. Evil brings forth evil; evil therefore is to be feared even more than fire.

203. The chiefest wisdom, they say, is to abstain from injury even to an enemy.

204. Let not a man compass another's ruin even unthinkingly; for Justice will compass the ruin of him that plots evil.
207. There is a way of escape for every other enemy; but ill deeds never die but pursue and destroy their author.
208. As the shadow leaves not a man but follows his footsteps wherever he goes, even so do evil deeds pursue their author and work his destruction.

COMPLAISANCE

211. The gracious expect no return when they oblige; how can the world ever repay the rain-cloud?
214. He alone lives who knows what is proper; he who knows not what is fitting shall be classed with the dead.

CHARITY

221. Giving to the poor is alone charity; all other giving is of the nature of loan.

GLORY

231. Give to the poor and add glory unto your name; there is no greater profit for man than this.
240. They alone live who live without blemish; and they alone die who have lived without glory.

MERCY

241. The chiefest wealth is a heart that overflows with mercy; for material wealth is found even in the hands of vile men.
247. The other world is not for those whose heart is incapable of pity, even as this world is not for them that are without riches.
248. The poor in substance may one day thrive and prosper; but they that lack pity are poor indeed, and their day comes never.
249. It is as easy for the hard of heart to do deeds of righteousness as for the confused in mind to see the Truth.
251. How can he feel pity, who eats other flesh in order to fatten his own?

253. The heart of the man that tastes flesh turns not towards good, even as the heart of him that is armed with steel.

AUSTERITIES

261. Patient endurance of suffering and non-injuring of life, in these is contained the whole of *tapas* [austerities].

266. It is the men that do *tapas* that look after their own interests; the rest are caught in the snares of desire and only do themselves harm.

268. Behold the man who has attained mastery over himself; all other men worship him.

IMPOSTURE

272. Of what avail is an imposing presence when evil is in the heart and the heart is conscious thereof?

278. Many there be whose heart is impure but who bathe in holy streams and prowl about.

279. The arrow is straight but thirsts for blood, while the lute that has a bend radiates harmony around; judge men by their acts and not by their appearance.

FRAUD

283. The fortune that is built up by fraud may appear to thrive, but it is doomed for ever.

284. The thirst for plunder leads in its season to endless grief.

TRUTHFULNESS

291. What is truthfulness? It is the speaking of that which is free from even the slightest taint of injury.

292. Even non-truth is of the nature of truth if it brings forth unmixed good.

293. Hold not forth as truth what you know to be false; for your own conscience will burn you when you have lied.

297. If a man can live without ever uttering a falsehood, all other virtues are superfluous to him.

298. Water cleans but the outward form; but the purity of the heart is proved by truthfulness.

299. The worthy regard not all other light as light; it is only the light of truth that they look upon as a veritable illumination.

ANGER

304. Anger kills the smile and destroys cheer. Has man a crueller foe than anger?

NON-INJURY

312. Even when another has injured him in his hate, the man who is pure in heart returns not the injury.

314. How shall man punish them that have injured him? Let him do them a good turn and make them ashamed in their hearts.

315. Of what avail is intelligence to a man if he does not feel as his very own the pain suffered by other beings, and so feeling does not abstain from injuring any?

319. If a man injures his neighbour in the forenoon, evil will come to him in the afternoon of its own accord.

NON-KILLING

321. The greatest of virtue is non-killing (*ahimsa*); killing brings in its train every other evil.

322. To divide one's bread with the needy and to abstain from killing: these are the greatest of all the commandments of all the prophets.

327. Take not away from any living thing the life that is sweet unto all, even if it be to save your own.

VANITY

331. There is no greater folly than the infatuation that looks upon the transient as if it were everlasting.

334. Time looks like an innocent thing; but verily it is a saw that is continually sawing away the life of man.

336. By yesterday a man was and today he is not. That is the wonder of wonders in this world.

340. Has the soul no fixed home of its own, that it seeks a lodging in this worthless body?

RENUNCIATION

342. If you want joy, renounce early; for many are the delights that you shall enjoy after renouncing.

353. Behold the man who has freed himself from doubts and who has realized the Truth; heaven is nearer to him than earth.

365. It is those that have conquered their desire that are called the liberated ones; the others appear to be free but they are verily in bondage.

368. He that has no desires has no grief; but ills on ills descend on the man that hankers after things.

371. Resolution comes to a man when Fortune is about to smile on him; but Indolence appears when Fortune is about to leave.

372. Evil fate dulls the faculties; but when Fortune is about to smile on a man, she first expands his intelligence.

379. They that rejoice when good comes, why should they fret when they encounter evil?

Part II: *PORUL* [Wealth] (Sanskrit, *Artha*)

THE PRINCE

381. He is a lion among princes who is well endowed in respect of the six things, to wit, troops, population, substance, council, alliances, and fortifications.

382. Four qualities should never be wanting in the prince, namely, courage, liberality, sagacity, and energy.

LEARNING

392. Two are the eyes of living kind: the one is called Numbers, and the other, Letters.

393. The learned alone can be said to possess eyes; the unlettered have but two sores in their heads.

395. Though you have to humble yourself before the teacher even as a beggar before a man of wealth, yet you acquire learning; it is those that refuse to learn that are the lowest among men.

403. Even a fool will be counted wise if he could hold his peace before the learned.

411. The most precious of treasures is the treasure of the ear; verily it is the crown of all kinds of wealth.

419. Humility of speech is hard to be attained by those who have not listened to the subtle words of the wise.

426. It is a part of wisdom to conform to the ways of the world.

427. The man of understanding knows what is coming; but the fool foresees not what is before.

428. It is folly to rush headlong into danger; it is the part of the wise to fear what ought to be feared.

COMPANY

449. Profit is not for those that have no capital; even so stability is not for them that repose not on the firm support of the wise.

450. It is foolish to make a multitude of foes; but it is ten times worse to give up the intimacy of the good.

452. Water alters and takes the character of the soil through which it flows; even so the mind takes the colour of the company with which it consorts.

455. Purity of heart and purity of action depend upon the purity of a man's company.

OPPORTUNITY

484. You can conquer even the whole world if you choose the proper time and the proper objectives.

490. When the tide is against you feign inaction like the stork; but when the tide is on, strike with the swiftness of its souse.

494. It is an immense advantage even to the powerful and the strong to be based on fortified places.

495. All-powerful is the crocodile in deep water; but out of it, it is the plaything of its foes.

496. The strong-wheeled chariot runs not on the sea; nor sails the ocean-going ship on dry land.

499. Even if they have no proper defences and other advantages, it is hard to beat a people on their own soil.

TESTING OF MEN

505. Do you want to find out whether a man is noble or little-minded? Know that conduct is the touchstone of character.

506. Beware of trusting men that have no kindred; for their hearts will be without attachment and they will be callous to shame.

510. To trust a man whom you have not tried and to suspect a man whom you have found worthy lead alike to endless ills.

513. Let him alone be selected for service who is well endowed with kindness and intelligence and decision, and who is free from greed.

537. Nothing is impossible to the man who can bring unto his work a mind that is ever wakeful and cautious.

GOVERNMENT

542. The world looks up to the rain-cloud for life; even so do men look up to the sceptre of the prince for protection.

549. Behold the prince that guards his subjects from enemies both within and without; if he punish them when they go wrong it is not a blemish: it is his duty.

551. Behold the prince who oppresses his subjects and does iniquity; he is worse than an assassin.

578. Behold the man who can be considerate towards others without derogating from any of his duties; he will inherit the earth.

581. Let the prince understand that Political Science and his Intelligence Corps are the eyes wherewith he sees.

ENERGY

591. Those that possess energy are alone to be called rich; as to those that possess it not, do they really possess what they own?

592. Energy alone can be called a man's wealth; for riches endure not for ever and will depart from him one day.

593. Behold the men that hold in their hands the resource called unremitting energy; they will never despair, saying: Alas, we are ruined!

595. The water with which a plant is watered is the measure of the luxuriance of its flower; even so, the spirit of a man is the measure of his fortunes.

596. Let all your purposes be grand; for then, even if they fail, your glory will tarnish never.

600. Exuberance of spirit, that alone is strength; those that have it not are mere stocks; their human bodies alone make the difference.

613. The proud pleasure of being able to serve all men belongs only to the greatness that shrinks not from any exertion.

616. Industry is the mother of Prosperity; but Indolence only brings forth Penury and Destitution.

619. Even though the gods be against, Industry is bound to pay the wages of labour.

621. When you meet with Misfortune face it with your best smile; for there is nothing like a smile to enable a man to hold his own against it.

623. Troubles they send away troubled who trouble not themselves at the sight of troubles.

COUNCILLOR

631. Behold the man who can judge aright the ways and means of achieving great enterprises and the proper season to commence them; he is the proper man for the Council.

632. Study, resolution, manly exertion, and loving attention to the welfare of the people, these make, along with the last [631], the five qualifications of the councillor.

671. The end of all deliberation is to arrive at a decision; and when a decision is come to, it is wrong to delay the execution thereof.

678. Men decoy one elephant by means of another; even so make one enterprise the means of achieving a second.

687. He is the fittest ambassador who has a just eye for time and place, who knows his duty, and who weighs his words before uttering them.

740. Even if a country has all the blessings it is worth nothing if it is not blessed in its ruler.

FRIENDSHIP

784. The object of friendship is not merry-making; but the restraining and reproving of oneself when one goes astray.

787. That man alone is your friend who turns you aside from wrong, directs you toward the right, and bears you company in misfortune.

796. There is a virtue even in misfortune; for misfortune is the rod wherewith one can measure the loyalty of friends.

797. What is the greatest profit that can accrue to a man? It is a release from the friendship of fools.

816. The enmity of the wise is ten million times better than the intimacy of fools.

819. Behold the men whose acts belie their spoken words; it is bitter to recall their fellowship even in dreams.

827. Trust not an enemy though he bends low in his speech; for the bending of the bow forebodes nothing but harm.

FOLLY

837. If the fool should come by a great fortune it is strangers that will feast and his kindred will only starve.

841. The veritable poverty is the poverty of sense; the world regards not other poverty as poverty.

843. The troubles that a fool brings down on his head, it is hard even for his enemies to cause him.

844. Do you want to know what is shallowness of wit? It is the conceit that says to itself, I am wise.

TRAITOR

882. Fear not the foe that is like the naked sword; but beware of the enemy that comes as a friend.

INFLUENCE OF WOMEN

905. The man who fears his wife will never have the courage to do the worthy [action].

920. Women of two hearts, drink, and the dice-table, these are the delights of men whom fortune has forsaken.

DRINKING

923. The sight of the man who is intoxicated is an abomination even unto the mother that bore him; what must it be then to the worthy?

GAMBLING

931. Take not to gambling even if you win; for your wins are even as the baited hook that the fish swallows.

MEDICINE

942. The body requires no medicine if new food is eaten only after the old food is fully digested.

943. Eat with moderation and after the food that you have taken is digested; that is the way to prolong your days.

GENTLEMAN

953. Four are the attributes of the true gentleman: a smiling face, a liberal hand, sweetness of speech, and condescension.

959. The nature of a soil is known by the seedling that grows therein; even so is the family of a man known by the words that come out of his mouth.

HONOUR

967. It is better for a man to die at once than to maintain himself by hanging on to those that scorn him.

GREATNESS

974. Even as chastity in a woman, greatness can be maintained only by being true to one's own self.

984. The virtue of the saint is non-killing; the virtue of the worthy man is the abstaining from scandalous speech.

999. Behold the men who cannot smile; in all the wide, wide world they will see nothing but darkness even during the day!

SHAME

1012. Food, clothing, and progeny are common to all men; it is in the sensibility to shame that they differ from one another.

1015. Behold the men that blush for others' disgrace as if it were their own; they will be called the very dwelling place of delicacy.

1020. The men that are dead to shame live not; they merely sham life even as wooden marionettes that are moved by strings.

FAMILY

1021. Nothing advances a man's family so much as his determination never to weary in labouring with his hands.

1022. Manly exertion and a sound understanding – it is the fullness of these two that exalts the family.

1023. When a man sets out saying, I shall advance my house, the very gods gird up their loins and march before him.

1028. There is no season for them that desire the advancement of their family; if they take things easy or stand upon their dignity, their house will be brought low.

HUSBANDRY

1031. Roam where they will, men must at last stand behind the plough for their food; in spite of every hardship, therefore, husbandry is the chiefest industry.

1033. They alone live who live by tilling the ground; all others but follow in their train and eat only the bread of dependence.

1038. Manuring profits more than the ploughing; and when the land is weeded, guarding it profits more than irrigation.

1040. The fair one called Earth laughs to herself when she sees the sluggard cry, saying: Alas, I have nothing to eat!

PENURY

1044. Want will drive even men of high family to forget their dignity and to speak the language of abject servility.

1045. There are a thousand mortifications concealed underneath this one curse called poverty.

1049. It is possible to go to sleep even in the midst of flames; but it is impossible to get even a wink of sleep in the midst of poverty.

BEGGING

1055. If men take freely to begging as a means of livelihood, it is because there are men in the world that refuse not alms.

1062. If HE that made the earth intended that man should continue to live even when he is reduced to beg for his food, may HE wander about the world and perish.

1064. Behold the dignity that consents not to beg even when reduced to utter destitution: even the whole universe is too small to hold it.

1065. Though it is only gruel thin as water, nothing is more savoury than the food that is earned by the labour of one's hands.

DEBASED

1073. Like unto very gods are the base ones on earth! For they too are a law unto themselves.

Part III: INBAM [Love] (Sanskrit, *Kama*)

FURTIVE LOVE

1083. I never knew Death before: I know it now: it wears the form of a woman and has large and battling eyes.

1084. She is simple and gracious, but yet her eyes are versed in the ways of waging war: for they drink the lives of those that look on her.

1090. Wine gives joy, but only to him that tastes it; it can never delight at the mere seeing as does love.

1093. She looked, and then she bowed: that was the watering of the young plant of love that was springing up between us.

1094. When I look at her, she looks at the ground: but when I look away, she looks on me and softly smiles.

1098. The slender-shaped maid melts to see my imploring look and softly smiles; and the gentle smile gives her an added grace.

1100. When eyes speak their consent to eyes, the words of the mouth are quite superfluous.

1102. The cure of all disease does always lie in some other thing than that which causes it; but the pang that this damsel causes, she alone can heal.

1103. Is the world of the lotus-eyed God sweeter than the tender arms of her that one loves?

1108. Joyous to the loving pair is the embrace that allows not even the air to come between.

1110. Even as a man feels his ignorance the more keenly the more wise he grows, even so do I love her the more ardently, the more I enjoy her company.

1113. Her arm is as the bamboo; her body is as the tender leaf; her smile is a very pear; the sweetest of odours is in her breath; and her painted eye is piercing as the lance.

1124. It is as life when she is near; but it is as very death when she leaves my side.

1126. He will not go from my eyes, neither will he be hurt when I wink; so subtle is the form of my beloved.

MARRIED LOVE

1152. His mere look was once a delight to me; but now even his embrace saddens, for that I fear that he is to part.

1158. Bitter is life in a place where there are no bosom friends; but bitterer far is separation from the beloved one.

1159. Has fire, which burns only when it is touched, the power, like love, to burn when it is far away?

1170. If my eyes can run, even as my heart runs, to where he is, they need not now be swimming in a sea of tears.

1192. What the rain is to all the world, that is the tenderness of the beloved to her that loves.

1193. They alone can pride themselves on their happiness who are loved in return by those whom they love.

1201. Even in the recollection love is sweet with endless delights; Love is, therefore, sweeter than wine.

1251. The door that is bolted with the bolt of modesty will yet yield to the axe of an overpowering love.

1266. When he is before me I can see no faults in him; but when I see him not, I can see nothing in him but faults.

1302. Sulkiness is the salt of love: to lengthen it unduly, however, is like adding too much of salt to food.

1309. Water is pleasant only in shady groves; and pettishness has a charm only in one who loves ardently.

1324. In my very quarrel with my beloved lies the engine that storms the defences of my heart.

1326. Sweeter is digestion than the meal: even so is the lover's quarrel sweeter than the embrace.

1327. It is the one who yields first who is the winner in lovers' quarrels; you cannot see it indeed at the hour of reconciliation.

1330. Sulkiness is the charm of love; and the charm of that again is the sweet embrace at its close.

Part Three

AGE OF ACHARYAS
[SCHOLARS]
400 B.C.–A.D. 1000

19. Vishnu Sarma, *Pancha-tantra* [Fables] (Sanskrit, *c.* 200 B.C.)
20. Chanakya Kautilya, *Artha Sastra* [Polity] (Sanskrit, *c.* 321–300 B.C.)
21. Patanjali, *Yoga Sutra* [Psychology] (Sanskrit, *c.* 300 B.C.)
22. Sankara, *Vedanta Sutra Bhashya* [Philosophy] (Sanskrit, *c.* A.D. 800)
23. Bhasa, *Svapna Vasavadattam* [Drama] (Sanskrit, *c.* A.D. 300)
24. Kalidasa, *Megha Duuta* [Elegy] (Sanskrit, *c.* A.D. 400)
25. Dandin, *Dasa-Kumara-Carita* [Novel] (Sanskrit, *c.* A.D. 600)
26. *Kuruntokai* [Anthology of Love Poems] (Tamil, *c.* A.D. 100–300)
27. Bhartrihari, *Satakas* [Lyrics] (Sanskrit, *c.* A.D. 650)

VISHNU SARMA
PANCHA-TANTRA
[FIVE TREATISES]

(Sanskrit, *c.* 200 B.C.)

It was perhaps inevitable that Indian people living in close proximity
to nature and wild life should use fables to explain partly human nature
and certain behavioural attitudes. The epics contain a number of such
animal stories, but a collection of fables does not appear until the
beginning of the rise of Buddhism, when a number of fables were
employed to demonstrate Buddhist teachings and the doctrine of
transmigration. Through these stories the spiritual progress of
Bodhisattva (Buddha-to-be) by virtuous actions in earlier incarnations
was illustrated. Thus, animal stories acquired a definite religious
significance when they were clustered around the large symbol of
Buddha in numerous cycles of existence. This collection of 547 stories,
called *Jatakas* or Birth Stories (Pali, *c.* 400 B.C.), was included in the
Tipitaka, the Buddhist 'Holy Books'.

In the post-Pali era, when classical Sanskrit emerged as the dominant
language of culture in North India, some of the earlier fables, divorced
from their didacticism, and many others revealing intellectual subtlety
and a shrewd understanding of political necessity, were rearranged
under the title *Pancha-tantra* or Five Treatises. This composition, containing chains of stories within frame-stories, is not merely an anthology
but an artistic triumph.

The Introduction to *Pancha-tantra* explains the occasion which
caused the venerable Vishnu Sarma to accept from King Amara-sakti
the task of awakening the intelligence in his three unteachable block-
head sons and making them 'incomparable masters of the art of
practical life' within six months. The old Brahman achieved his
objective by skilfully telling the moron princes stories under five
headings, each heading representing the title of one of the five
Books.

MIGRATION OF INDIAN FABLES*

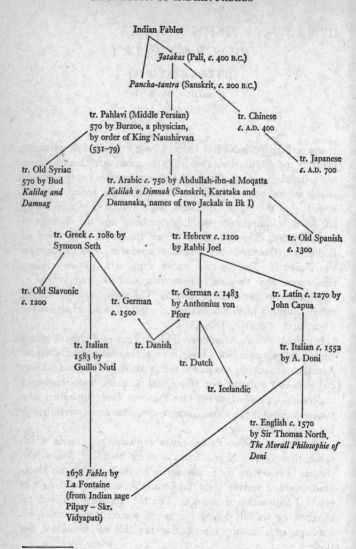

Indian Fables

Jatakas (Pali, *c.* 400 B.C.)

Pancha-tantra (Sanskrit, *c.* 200 B.C.)

tr. Pahlavi (Middle Persian) 570 by Burzoe, a physician, by order of King Naushirvan (531–79)

tr. Chinese *c.* A.D. 400

tr. Japanese *c.* A.D. 700

tr. Old Syriac 570 by Bud *Kalilag and Damnag*

tr. Arabic *c.* 750 by Abdullah-ibn-al Moqatta *Kalilah o Dimnah* (Sanskrit, Karataka and Damanaka, names of two Jackals in Bk I)

tr. Greek *c.* 1080 by Symeon Seth

tr. Hebrew *c.* 1100 by Rabbi Joel

tr. Old Spanish *c.* 1300

tr. Old Slavonic *c.* 1200

tr. German *c.* 1500

tr. German *c.* 1483 by Anthonius von Pforr

tr. Latin *c.* 1270 by John Capua

tr. Italian 1583 by Guillo Nuti

tr. Danish

tr. Dutch

tr. Icelandic

tr. Italian *c.* 1552 by A. Doni

tr. English *c.* 1570 by Sir Thomas North, *The Morall Philosophie of Doni*

1678 *Fables* by La Fontaine (from Indian sage Pilpay – Skr. Vidyapati)

---

*For a detailed account see A. B. Keith, *A History of Sanskrit Literature*. London: Oxford University Press, 1961, pp. 357–9.

The First Book, entitled 'The Loss of Friends', relates in seventeen interrelated stories how two cunning jackals, Victor and Cheek (Sanskrit, Karataka and Damanaka), succeed in separating two inseparable and good friends, namely Rusty the Lion and Lively the Bull. The Second Book, 'The Winning of Friends', explains by means of five stories how great and mighty ones may at times need the friendship and aid of even their apparently small and insignificant friends. Book Three, under the heading 'War and Peace' (or 'Crows and Owls'), demonstrates the kinds of conflict which necessarily arise from contrary natures and attitudes. Books Four and Five each have two tales, discussing the 'Loss of Gains' and 'Ill-considered Action'.

The stories are narrated in prose with an inlay of gnomic verses. The leading characters are animals, and they move freely among human beings. By using animals as the main characters in the stories, the author has been able to portray vividly, under the mask of general animality, the fundamental humanity common to all races of men, and by holding as it were concave and convex mirrors to human life and society, he has drawn, with gentle humour and good-natured satire, diminutive and enlarged portraits of the weaknesses, follies and foibles of mankind.

Fables from the *Jatakas* and *Pancha-tantra* have been retold time and again throughout the centuries, both inside India and outside. They have migrated from India to all corners of the world with the spread of spiritualities, and through the art of story-tellers and translators. Consequently, stories from these collections have been included (either in direct translation or unwittingly borrowing from earlier transmissions) in many great works, such as *The Arabian Nights* and innumerable European cycles of fables and stories of the medieval and Renaissance periods (*Decameron, Canterbury Tales, Reineke Fuchs, Fabliaux, Fables* of La Fontaine, etc.), including tales by the Brothers Grimm and Andersen. The universal appeal of these fables lies perhaps in the particular art of capsuling practical wisdom in obviously simple stories.

The selections included here are taken from the translation by Arthur W. Ryder, *The Pancha-tantra*, Chicago: The University of Chicago Press, 1956 (first published 1925).

Selections:

III.19   VISHNU SARMA
               PANCHA-TANTRA

                 [FIVE TREATISES]

                   Introduction

          One Vishnusharman, shrewdly gleaning
          All worldly wisdom's inner meaning,
          In these five books the charm compresses
          Of all such books the world possesses.

And this is how it happened.

In the southern country is a city called Maidens' Delight. There lived a king named Immortal-Power. He was familiar with all the works treating of the wise conduct of life. His feet were made dazzling by the tangle of rays of light from jewels in the diadems of mighty kings who knelt before him. He had reached the far shore of all the arts that embellish life. This king had three sons. Their names were Rich-Power, Fierce-Power, Endless-Power, and they were supreme block-heads.

Now when the king perceived that they were hostile to education, he summoned his counsellors and said: 'Gentlemen, it is known to you that these sons of mine, being hostile to education, are lacking in discernment. So when I behold them, my kingdom brings me no happiness, though all external thorns are drawn. For there is wisdom in the proverb:

> Of sons unborn, or dead, or fools,
> Unborn or dead will do:
> They cause a little grief, no doubt;
> But fools, a long life through.

And again:

> To what good purpose can a cow
> That brings no calf nor milk, be bent?
> Or why beget a son who proves
> A dunce and disobedient?

Some means must therefore be devised to awaken their intelligence.'

And they, one after another, replied: 'O King, first one learns grammar, in twelve years. If this subject has somehow been mastered, then one masters the books on religion and practical life. Then the intelligence awakens.'

But one of their number, a counsellor named Keen, said: 'O King, the duration of life is limited, and the verbal sciences require much time for mastery. Therefore let some kind of epitome be devised to wake their intelligence. There is a proverb that says:

> Since verbal science has no final end,
> Since life is short, and obstacles impend,
> Let central facts be picked and firmly fixed,
> As swans extract the milk with water mixed.

'Now there is a Brahman here named Vishnusharman, with a reputation for competence in numerous sciences. Entrust the princes to him. He will certainly make them intelligent in a twinkling.'

When the king had listened to this, he summoned Vishnusharman and said: 'Holy sir, as a favour to me you must make these princes incomparable masters of the art of practical life. In return, I will bestow upon you a hundred land-grants.'

And Vishnusharman made answer to the king: 'O King, listen. Here is the plain truth. I am not the man to sell good learning for a hundred land-grants. But if I do not, in six months' time, make the boys acquainted with the art of intelligent living, I will give up my own name. Let us cut the matter short. Listen to my lion-roar. My boasting arises from no greed for cash. Besides, I have no use for money; I am eighty years old, and all the objects of sensual desire have lost their charm. But in order that your request may be granted, I will show a sporting spirit in reference to artistic matters. Make a note of the date. If I fail to render your sons, in six months' time, incomparable masters of the art of intelligent living, then His Majesty is at liberty to show me His Majestic bare bottom.'

When the king, surrounded by his counsellors, had listened to the Brahman's highly unconventional promise, he was penetrated with wonder, entrusted the princes to him, and experienced supreme content.

Meanwhile, Vishnusharman took the boys, went home, and made them learn by heart five books which he composed and called: (I) 'The Loss of Friends', (II) 'The Winning of Friends', (III) 'Crows and Owls', (IV) 'Loss of Gains', (V) 'Ill-considered Action'.

These the princes learned, and in six months' time they answered the prescription. Since that day this work on the art of intelligent living, *Pancha-tantra*, or the 'Five Books', has travelled the world, aiming at the awakening of intelligence in the young. To sum the matter up:

> Whoever learns the work by heart,
> Or through the story-teller's art
>   Becomes acquainted,
> His life by sad defeat – although
> The king of heaven be his foe –
>   Is never tainted.

Book I *The Loss of Friends*

I(I) HOW THE CROW-HEN KILLED THE BLACK SNAKE

In a certain region grew a great banyan tree. In it lived a crow and his wife, occupying the nest which they had built. But a black snake crawled through the hollow trunk and ate their chicks as fast as they were born, even before baptism. Yet for all his sorrow over this violence, the poor crow could not desert the old familiar banyan and seek another tree. For

> Three cannot be induced to go –
> The deer, the cowardly man, the crow:
> Three go when insult makes them pant –
> The lion, hero, elephant.

At last the crow-hen fell at her husband's feet and said: 'My dear lord, a great many children of mine have been eaten by that awful snake. And grief for my loved and lost haunts me until I think of moving. Let us make our home in some other tree. For

> No friend like health abounding;
>   And like disease, no foe;
> No love like love of children;
>   Like hunger-pangs, no woe.

And again:

> With fields o'erhanging rivers,
>   With wife on flirting bent,
> Or in a house with serpents,
>   No man can be content.

We are living in deadly peril.'

At this the crow was dreadfully depressed, and he said: 'We have lived in this tree a long time, my dear. We cannot desert it. For

> Where water may be sipped, and grass
> Be cropped, a deer might live content;
> Yet insult will not drive him from
> The wood where all his life was spent.

321

Moreover, by some shrewd device I will bring death upon this villainous and mighty foe.'

'But,' said the wife, 'this is a terribly venomous snake. How will you hurt him?' And he replied: 'My dear, even if I have not the power to hurt him, still I have friends who possess learning, who have mastered the works on ethics. I will go and get from them some shrewd device of such nature that the villain – curse him! – will soon meet his doom.'

After this indignant speech he went at once to another tree, under which lived a dear friend, a jackal. He courteously called the jackal forth, related all his sorrow, then said: 'My friend, what do you consider opportune under the circumstances? The killing of our children is sheer death to my wife and me.'

'My friend,' said the jackal, 'I have thought the matter through. You need not put yourself out. That villainous black snake is near his doom by reason of his heartless cruelty. For

> Of means to injure brutal foes
>   You do not need to think,
> Since of themselves they fall, like trees
>   Upon the river's brink.

And there is a story:

> A heron ate what fish he could,
>   The bad, indifferent, and good;
> His greed was never satisfied
>   Till, strangled by a crab, he died.'

'How was that?' asked the crow. And the jackal told the story of

THE HERON THAT LIKED CRAB-MEAT

There was once a heron in a certain place on the edge of a pond. Being old, he sought an easy way of catching fish on which to live. He began by lingering at the edge of his pond, pretending to be quite irresolute, not eating even the fish within his reach.

Now among the fish lived a crab. He drew near and said: 'Uncle, why do you neglect today your usual meals and amusements?' And the heron replied: 'So long as I kept fat and flourishing by eating fish, I spent my time pleasantly, enjoying the taste of you. But a great disaster will soon befall you. And as I am old, this will cut short the pleasant course of my life. For this reason I feel depressed.'

'Uncle,' said the crab, 'of what nature is the disaster?' And the heron continued: 'Today I overheard the talk of a number of fishermen as they passed near the pond. "This is a big pond," they were saying, "full of fish. We will try a cast of the net tomorrow or the day after. But today we will go to the lake near the city." This being so, you are lost, my food supply is cut off, I too am lost, and in grief at the thought, I am indifferent to food today.'

Now when the water-dwellers heard the trickster's report, they all feared for their lives and implored the heron, saying: 'Uncle! Father! Brother! Friend! Thinker! Since you are informed of the calamity, you also know the remedy. Pray save us from the jaws of this death.'

Then the heron said: 'I am a bird, not competent to contend with men. This, however, I can do. I can transfer you from this pond to another, a bottomless one.' By this artful speech they were so led astray that they said: 'Uncle! Friend! Unselfish kinsman! Take me first! Me first! Did you never hear this?

> Stout hearts delight to pay the price
> Of merciful self-sacrifice,
> Count life as nothing, if it end
> In gentle service to a friend.'

Then the old rascal laughed in his heart, and took counsel with his mind, thus: 'My shrewdness has brought these fishes into my power. They ought to be eaten very comfortably.' Having thus thought it through, he promised what the thronging fish implored, lifted some in his bill, carried them a certain distance to a slab of stone, and ate them there. Day after day he made the trip with supreme delight and satisfaction, and meeting the fish, kept their confidence by ever new inventions.

One day the crab, disturbed by the fear of death, importuned him with the words: 'Uncle, pray save me, too, from the jaws of death.' And the heron reflected: 'I am quite tired of this unvarying fish diet. I should like to taste him. He is different, and choice.' So he picked up the crab and flew through the air.

But since he avoided all bodies of water and seemed planning to alight on the sun-scorched rock, the crab asked him: 'Uncle, where is that pond without any bottom?' And the heron laughed and said: 'Do you see that broad, sun-scorched rock? All the water-dwellers have found repose there. Your turn has now come to find repose.'

Then the crab looked down and saw a great rock of sacrifice, made horrible by heaps of fish-skeletons. And he thought: 'Ah me!

> Friends are foes and foes are friends
> As they mar or serve your ends;
> Few discern where profit tends.

Again:

> If you will, with serpents play;
> Dwell with foemen who betray:
> Shun your false and foolish friends,
> Fickle, seeking vicious ends.

Why, he has already eaten these fish whose skeletons are scattered in heaps. So what might be an opportune course of action for me? Yet why do I need to consider?

> Man is bidden to chastise
> Even elders who devise
> Devious courses, arrogant,
> Of their duty ignorant.

Again:

> Fear fearful things, while yet
>   No fearful thing appears;
> When danger must be met,
>   Strike, and forget your fears.

So, before he drops me there, I will catch his neck with all four claws.'

When he did so, the heron tried to escape, but being a fool, he found no parry to the grip of the crab's nippers, and had his head cut off.

Then the crab painfully made his way back to the pond, dragging the heron's neck as if it had been a lotus-stalk. And when he came among the fish, they said: 'Brother, why come back?' Thereupon he showed the head as his credentials and said: 'He enticed the water-dwellers from every quarter, deceived them with his prevarications, dropped them on a slab of rock not far away, and ate them. But I – further life being predestined – perceived that he destroyed the trustful, and I have brought back his neck. Forget your worries. All the water-dwellers shall live in peace.'

'And that is why I say:

A heron ate what fish he could, ...

and the rest of it.'

'My friend,' said the crow, 'tell me how this villainous snake is to meet his doom.' And the jackal answered: 'Go to some spot frequented by a great monarch. There seize a golden chain or a necklace from some wealthy man who guards it carelessly. Deposit this in such a place that when it is recovered, the snake may be killed.'

So the crow and his wife straightway flew off at random, and the wife came upon a certain pond. As she looked about, she saw the women of a king's court playing in the water, and on the bank they had laid golden chains, pearl necklaces, garments, and gems. One chain of gold the crow-hen seized and started for the tree where she lived.

But when the chamberlains and the eunuchs saw the theft, they picked up clubs and ran in pursuit. Meanwhile, the crow-hen dropped the golden chain in the snake's hole and waited at a safe distance.

Now when the king's men climbed the tree, they found a hole and in it a black snake with swelling hood. So they killed him with their clubs, recovered the golden chain, and went their way. Thereafter the crow and his wife lived in peace.

That is why I say:

In case where brute force would fail,
A shrewd device may still prevail.

I(2)   LEAP AND CREEP

In the palace of a certain king stood an incomparable bed, blessed with every cubiculary virtue. In a corner of its coverlet lived a female louse named Creep. Surrounded by a thriving family of sons and daughters, with the sons and daughters of sons and daughters, and with more remote descendants, she drank the king's blood as he slept. On this diet she grew plump and handsome.

While she was living there in this manner, a flea named Leap drifted in on the wind and dropped on the bed. This flea felt supreme satisfaction on examining the bed – the wonderful delicacy of its coverlet, its double pillow, its exceptional softness like that of a broad, Gangetic sand-bank, its delicious perfume. Charmed by the sheer delight of touching it, he hopped this way and that until – fate willed it so – he chanced to meet Creep, who said to him: 'Where do *you* come from? This is a dwelling fit for a king. Begone, and lose no time about it.' 'Madam,' said he, 'you should not say such things. For

> The Brahman reverences fire,
> Himself the lower castes' desire;
> The wife reveres her husband dear;
> But all the world must guests revere.

Now I am your guest. I have of late sampled the various blood of Brahmans, warriors, business men, and serfs, but found it acid, slimy, quite unwholesome. On the contrary, he who reposes on this bed must have a delightful vital fluid, just like nectar. It must be free from morbidity, since wind, bile, and phlegm are kept in harmony by constant and heedful use of potions prepared by physicians. It must be enriched by viands unctuous, tender, melting in the mouth; viands prepared from the flesh of the choicest creatures of land, water, and air, seasoned furthermore with sugar, pomegranate, ginger, and pepper. To me it seems an elixir of life. Therefore, with your kind permission, I plan to taste this sweet and fragrant substance, thus combining pleasure and profit.'

'No,' said she. 'For fiery-mouthed stingers like you, it is out of the question. Leave this bed. You know the proverb:

> The fool who does not know
> His own resource, his foe,
> His duty, time, and place,
> Who sets a reckless pace,
> Will by the wayside fall,
> Will reap no fruit at all.'

Thereupon he fell at her feet, repeating his request. And she agreed, since courtesy was her hobby, and since, when the story of that prince of sharpers, Muladeva, was being repeated to the king while she lay on a corner of the coverlet, she had heard how Muladeva quoted this verse in answer to the question of a certain damsel:

> Whoever, angry though he be,
> Has spurned a suppliant enemy,
> In Shiva, Vishnu, Brahma, he
> Has scorned the Holy Trinity.

Recalling this, she agreed, but added: 'However, you must not come to dinner at a wrong place or time.' 'What is the right place and what is the right time?' he asked. 'Being a newcomer, I am not *au courant*.' And she replied: 'When the king's body is mastered by wine, fatigue, or sleep, then you may quietly bite him on the feet. This is the right place and the right time.' To these conditions he gave his assent.

In spite of this arrangement, the famished bungler, when the king had just dozed off in the early evening, bit him on the back. And the poor king, as if burned by a firebrand, as if stung by a scorpion, as if touched by a torch, bounded to his feet, scratched his back, and cried to a servant: 'Rascal! Somebody bit me. You must hunt through this bed until you find the insect.'

Now Leap heard the king's command and in terrified haste crept into a crevice in the bed. Then the king's servants entered, and following their master's orders, brought a lamp and made a minute inspection. As fate would have it, they came upon Creep as she crouched in the nap of the fabric, and killed her with her family.

And that is why I say:

> With no stranger share your house. . . .

I(3)   THE BLUE JACKAL

There was once a jackal named Fierce-Howl, who lived in a cave near the suburbs of a city. One day he was hunting for food, his throat pinched with hunger, and wandered into the city after nightfall. There the city dogs snapped at his limbs with their sharp-pointed teeth, and terrified his heart with their dreadful barking, so that he stumbled this way and that in his efforts to escape and happened into the house of a dyer. There he tumbled into a tremendous indigo vat, and all the dogs went home.

Presently the jackal – further life being predestined – managed to crawl out of the indigo vat and escaped into the forest. There all the thronging animals in his vicinity caught a glimpse of his body dyed with the juice of indigo, and crying out: 'What is this creature enriched with that unprecedented colour?' they fled, their eyes dancing with terror, and spread the report: 'Oh, oh! Here is an exotic creature that has dropped from somewhere. Nobody knows what his conduct might be, or his energy. We are going to vamoose. For the proverb says:

> Where you do not know
> Conduct, stock, and pluck,
> 'Tis not wise to trust,
> If you wish for luck.'

Now Fierce-Howl perceived their dismay, and called to them: 'Come, come, you wild things! Why do you flee in terror at sight of me? For Indra, realizing that the forest creatures have no monarch, anointed me – my name is Fierce-Howl – as your king. Rest in safety within the cage formed by my resistless paws.'

On hearing this, the lions, tigers, leopards, monkeys, rabbits, gazelles, jackals, and other species of wild life bowed humbly, saying: 'Master, prescribe to us our duties.' Thereupon he appointed the lion prime minister and the tiger lord of the bedchamber, while the leopard was made custodian of the king's betel, the elephant doorkeeper, and the monkey the bearer of the royal parasol. But to all the jackals, his own kindred, he administered a cuffing, and drove them away. Thus he enjoyed the kingly glory, while lions and others killed food-animals and laid them before him. These he divided and distributed to all after the manner of kings.

While time passed in this fashion, he was sitting one day in his court when he heard the sound made by a pack of jackals howling near by. At this his body thrilled, his eyes filled with tears of joy, he leaped to his feet, and began to howl in a piercing tone. When the lions and others heard this, they perceived that he was a jackal, and stood for a moment shamefaced and downcast, then they said: 'Look! We have been deceived by this jackal. Let the fellow be killed.' And when he heard this, he endeavoured to flee, but was torn to bits by a tiger and died.

And that is why I say:

> Whoever leaves his friends,
>   Strange folk to cherish,
> Like foolish Fierce-Howl, will
>   Untimely perish.

I(4)   SHELL-NECK, SLIM, AND GRIM

In a certain lake lived a turtle named Shell-Neck. He had as friends two ganders whose names were Slim and Grim. Now in the vicissitudes of time there came a twelve-year drought, which begot ideas of this nature in the two ganders: 'This lake has gone dry. Let us seek another body of water. However, we must first say farewell to Shell-Neck, our dear and long-proved friend.'

When they did so, the turtle said: 'Why do you bid me farewell? I am a water-dweller, and here I should perish very quickly from the scant supply of water and from grief at loss of you. Therefore, if you feel any affection for me, please rescue me from the jaws of this death. Besides, as the water dries in this lake, you two suffer nothing beyond a restricted diet, while to me it means immediate death. Consider which is more serious, loss of food or loss of life.'

But they replied: 'We are unable to take you with us since you are a water-creature without wings.' Yet the turtle continued: 'There is a possible device. Bring a stick of wood.' This they did, whereupon the turtle gripped the middle of the stick between his teeth, and said: 'Now take firm hold with your bills, one on each side, fly up, and travel with even flight through the sky until we discover another desirable body of water.'

But they objected: 'There is a hitch in this fine plan. If you happen to indulge in the smallest conversation, then you will lose your hold on the stick, will fall from a great height, and will be dashed to bits.'

'Oh', said the turtle, 'from this moment I take a vow of silence, to last as long as we are in heaven.' So they carried out the plan, but while the two ganders were painfully carrying the turtle over a neighbouring city, the people below noticed the spectacle, and there arose a confused buzz of talk as they asked: 'What is this cartlike object that two birds are carrying through the atmosphere?'

Hearing this, the doomed turtle was heedless enough to ask: 'What are these people chattering about?' The moment he spoke, the poor simpleton lost his grip and fell to the ground. And persons who wanted meat cut him to bits in a moment with sharp knives.

And that is why I say:

> To take advice from kindly friends, ...
>> Be ever satisfied:
> The stupid turtle lost his grip
>> Upon the stick, and died.

I(5)   THE DUAL BETWEEN ELEPHANT AND SPARROW

In a dense bit of jungle lived a sparrow and his wife, who had built their nest on the branch of a tamal tree, and in course of time a family appeared.

Now one day a jungle elephant with the spring fever was distressed by the heat, and came beneath that tamal tree in search of shade. Blinded by his fever, he pulled with the tip of his trunk at the branch where the sparrows had their nest, and broke it. In the process the sparrows' eggs were crushed, though the parent-birds – further life being predestined – barely escaped death.

Then the hen-sparrow lamented, desolate with grief at the death of her chicks. And presently, hearing her lamentation, a woodpecker bird, a great friend of hers, came grieved at her grief, and said: 'My dear friend, why lament in vain? For the Scripture says:

> For lost and dead and past
>> The wise have no laments:
> Between the wise and fools
>> Is just this difference.

And again:

> No life deserves lament;
>> Fools borrow trouble,
> Add sadness to the sad,
>> So make it double.

And yet again:

> Since kinsmen's sticky tears
>> Clog the departed,
> Bury them decently,
>> Tearless, whole-hearted.'

'That is good doctrine,' said the hen-sparrow, 'but what of it? This elephant – curse his spring fever! – killed my babies. So if you are my friend, think of some plan to kill this big elephant. If that were done, I should feel less grief at the death of my children. You know the saying:

> While one brings comfort in distress,
>> Another jeers at pain;
> By paying both as they deserve,
>> A man is born again.'

'Madam,' said the woodpecker, 'your remark is very true. For the proverb says:

> A friend in need is a friend indeed,
>> Although of different caste;
> The whole world is your eager friend
>> So long as riches last.

And again:

> A friend in need is a friend indeed;
> Fathers indeed are those who feed;
> True comrades they, and wives indeed,
> Whence trust and sweet content proceed.

'Now see what my wit can devise. But you must know that I, too, have a friend, a gnat called Lute-Buzz. I will return with her, so that this villainous beast of an elephant may be killed.'

So he went with the hen-sparrow, found the gnat, and said: 'Dear madam, this is my friend the hen-sparrow. She is mourning because a villainous elephant smashed her eggs. So you must lend your assistance while I work out a plan for killing him.'

'My good friend,' said the gnat, 'there is only one possible answer. But I also have a very intimate friend, a frog named Cloud-Messenger. Let us do the right thing by calling him into consultation. For the proverb says:

A wise companion find,
Shrewd, learned, righteous, kind;
For plans by him designed
Are never undermined.'

So all three went together and told Cloud-Messenger the entire story. And the frog said: 'How feeble a thing is that wretched elephant when pitted against a great throng enraged! Gnat, you must go and buzz in his fevered ear, so that he may shut his eyes in delight at hearing your music. Then the woodpecker's bill will peck out his eyes. After that I will sit on the edge of a pit and croak. And he, being thirsty, will hear me, and will approach expecting to find a body of water. When he comes to the pit, he will fall in and perish.'

When they carried out the plan, the fevered elephant shut his eyes in delight at the song of the gnat, was blinded by the woodpecker, wandered thirst-smitten at noonday, followed the croak of a frog, came to a great pit, fell in, and died.

Book II *The Winning of Friends*

II(6)   THE MICE THAT SET ELEPHANTS FREE

There was once a region where people, houses, and temples had fallen into decay. So the mice, who were old settlers there, occupied the chinks in the floors of stately dwellings with sons, grandsons (both in the male and female line), and further descendants as they were born, until their holes formed a dense tangle. They found uncommon happiness in a variety of festivals, dramatic performances (with plots of their own invention), wedding-feasts, eating-parties, drinking-bouts, and similar diversions. And so the time passed.

But into this scene burst an elephant-king, whose retinue numbered thousands. He, with his herd, had started for the lake upon information that there was water there. As he marched through the mouse community, he crushed faces, eyes, heads, and necks of such mice as he encountered.

Then the survivors held a convention. 'We are being killed,' they said, 'by these lumbering elephants – curse them! If they come this way again, there will not be mice enough for seed. Besides:

> An elephant will kill you, if
> He touch; a serpent if he sniff;
> King's laughter has a deadly sting;
> A rascal kills by honouring.

Therefore let us devise a remedy effective in this crisis.'

When they had done so, a certain number went to the lake, bowed before the elephant-king, and said respectfully. 'O King, not far from here is our community, inherited from a long line of ancestors. There we have prospered through a long succession of sons and grandsons. Now you gentlemen, while coming here to water, have destroyed us by the thousand. Furthermore, if you travel that way again, there will not be enough of us for seed. If then you feel compassion toward us, pray travel another path. Consider the fact that even creatures of our size will some day prove of some service.'

And the elephant-king turned over in his mind what he had heard, decided that the statement of the mice was entirely logical, and granted their request.

Now in the course of time a certain king commanded his elephant-trappers to trap elephants. And they constructed a so-called water-trap, caught the king with his herd, three days later dragged him out with a great tackle made of ropes and things, and tied him to stout trees in that very bit of forest.

When the trappers had gone, the elephant-king reflected thus: 'In what manner, or through whose assistance, shall I be delivered?' Then it occurred to him: 'We have no means of deliverance except those mice.'

So the king sent the mice an exact description of his disastrous position in the trap through one of his personal retinue, an elephant-cow who had not ventured into the trap, and who had previous information of the mouse community.

When the mice learned the matter, they gathered by the thousand, eager to return the favour shown them, and visited the elephant herd. And seeing king and herd fettered, they gnawed the guy-ropes where they stood, then swarmed up the branches, and by cutting the ropes aloft, set their friends free.

Book III Crows and Owls

III(7) THE BRAHMAN'S GOAT

In a certain town lived a Brahman named Friendly who had undertaken the labour of maintaining the sacred fire. One day in the month
of February, when a gentle breeze was blowing, when the sky was veiled
in clouds and a drizzling rain was falling, he went to another village to
beg a victim for the sacrifice, and said to a certain man: 'O sacrificer,
I wish to make an offering on the approaching day of the new moon.
Pray give me a victim.' And the man gave him a plump goat, as
prescribed in Scripture. This he put through its paces, found it sound,
placed it on his shoulder, and started in haste for his own city.

Now on the road he was met by three rogues whose throats were
pinched with hunger. These, spying the plump creature on his shoulder,
whispered together: 'Come now! If we could eat that creature, we
should have the laugh on this sleety weather. Let us fool him, get the
goat, and ward off the cold.'

So the first of them changed his dress, issued from a by-path to
meet the Brahman, and thus addressed that man of pious life: 'O pious
Brahman, why are you doing a thing so unconventional and so ridiculous? You are carrying an unclean animal, a dog, on your shoulder.
Are you ignorant of the verse:

> The dog and the rooster,
>   The hangman, the ass,
> The camel, defile you:
>   Don't touch them, but pass.'

At that the Brahman was mastered by anger, and he said: 'Are you
blind, man, that you impute doghood to a goat?' 'O Brahman,' said
the rogue, 'do not be angry. Go wither you will.'

But when he had travelled a little farther, the second rogue met him
and said: 'Alas, holy sir, alas! Even if this dead calf was a pet, still you
should not put it on your shoulder. For the proverb says:

> Touch not unwisely man or beast
>   That lifeless lie;
> Else, gifts of milk and lunar fast
>   Must purify.'

Then the Brahman spoke in anger: 'Are you blind, man? You call a goat a calf.' And the rogue said: 'Holy sir, do not be angry. I spoke in ignorance. Do as you will.'

But when he had walked only a little farther through the forest, the third rogue, changing his dress, met him and said: 'Sir, this is most improper. You are carrying a donkey on your shoulder. Yet the proverb tells you:

> If you should touch an ass – be it
> In ignorance or not –
> You needs must wash your clothes and bathe,
> To cleanse the sinful spot.

Pray drop this thing, before another sees you.'

So the Brahman concluded that it was a goblin in quadruped form, threw it on the ground, and made for home, terrified. Meanwhile, the three rogues met, caught the goat, and carried out their plan.

III(8)   THE FROGS THAT RODE SNAKEBACK

There was once an elderly black snake in a certain spot, and his name was Slow-Poison. He considered the situation from this point of view: 'How in the world can I get along without overtaxing my energies?' Then he went to a pond containing many frogs, and behaved as if very dejected.

As he waited thus, a frog came to the edge of the water and asked: 'Uncle, why don't you bustle about today for food as usual?'

'My dear friend,' said Slow-Poison, 'I am afflicted. Why should I wish for food? For this evening, as I was bustling about for food, I saw a frog and made ready to catch him. But he saw me and, fearing death, he escaped among some Brahmans intent upon holy recitation, nor did I perceive which way he went. But in the water at the edge of the pond was the great toe of a Brahman boy, and stupidly deceived by its resemblance to a frog, I bit it, and the boy died immediately. Then the sorrowing father cursed me in these terms: "Monster! Since you bit my harmless son, you shall for this sin become a vehicle for frogs, and shall subsist on whatever they choose to allow you." Consequently, I have come here to serve as your vehicle.'

Now the frog reported this to all the others. And every last one of them, in extreme delight, went and reported to the frog-king, whose name was Water-Foot. He in turn, accompanied by his counsellors, rose hurriedly from the pond – for he thought it an extraordinary occurrence – and climbed upon Slow-Poison's hood. The others also, in order of age, climbed on his back. Yet others, finding no vacant spot, hopped along behind the snake. Now Slow-Poison, with an eye to making his living, showed them fancy turns in great variety. And Water-Foot, enjoying contact with his body, said to him:

> I'd rather ride Slow-Poison than
> The finest horse I've seen,
> Or elephant, or chariot,
> Or man-borne palanquin.

The next day, Slow-Poison was wily enough to move very slowly. So Water-Foot said: 'My dear Slow-Poison, why don't you carry us nicely, as you did before?'

And Slow-Poison said: 'O King, I have no carrying power today because of lack of food.' 'My dear fellow,' said the king, 'eat the plebeian frogs.'

When Slow-Poison heard this, he quivered with joy in every member and made haste to say: 'Why, that is a part of the curse laid on me by the Brahman. For that reason I am greatly pleased at your command.' So he ate frogs uninterruptedly, and in a very few days he grew strong. And with delight and inner laughter he said:

> The trick was good. All sorts of frogs
> Within my power have passed.
> The only question that remains,
> Is: How long will they last?

Water-Foot, for his part, was befooled by Slow-Poison's plausibilities, and did not notice a thing.

Book IV Loss of Gains

IV(9)   THE ASS IN THE TIGER-SKIN

There was once a laundryman named Clean-Cloth in a certain town.
He had a single donkey who had grown very feeble from lack of fodder.

As the laundryman wandered in the forest, he saw a dead tiger, and
he thought: 'Ah, this is lucky. I will put this tiger-skin on the donkey
and let him loose in the barley fields at night. For the farmers will
think him a tiger and will not drive him out.'

When this was done, the donkey ate barley to his heart's content.
And at dawn the laundryman took him back to the barn. So as time
passed, he grew plump. He could hardly squeeze into the stall.

But one day the donkey heard the bray of a she-donkey in the
distance. At the mere sound he himself began to bray. Then the farmers
perceived that he was a donkey in disguise, and killed him with blows
from clubs and stones and arrows.

Book V Ill-Considered Action

V(10)   THE LOYAL MONGOOSE

There was once a Brahman named Godly in a certain town. His wife
mothered a single son and a mongoose. And as she loved little ones,
she cared for the mongoose also like a son, giving him milk from her
breast, and salves, and baths, and so on. But she did not trust him, for
she thought: 'A mongoose is a nasty kind of creature. He might hurt
my boy.' Yes, there is sense in the proverb:

> A son will ever bring delight,
> Though bent on folly, passion, spite,
> Though shabby, naughty, and a fright.

One day she tucked her son in bed, took a water-jar, and said to her
husband: 'Now, Professor, I am going for water. You must protect the
boy from the mongoose.' But when she was gone, the Brahman went
off somewhere himself to beg food, leaving the house empty.

While he was gone, a black snake issued from his hole and, as fate
would have it, crawled toward the baby's cradle. But the mongoose,

feeling him to be a natural enemy, and fearing for the life of his baby brother, fell upon the vicious serpent halfway, joined battle with him, tore him to bits, and tossed the pieces far and wide. Then, delighted with his own heroism, he ran, blood trickling from his mouth, to meet the mother; for he wished to show what he had done.

But when the mother saw him coming, saw his bloody mouth and his excitement, she feared that the villain must have eaten her baby boy, and without thinking twice, she angrily dropped the water-jar upon him, which killed him the moment that it struck. There she left him without a second thought, and hurried home, where she found the baby safe and sound, and near the cradle a great black snake, torn to bits. Then, overwhelmed with sorrow because she had thoughtlessly killed her benefactor, her son, she beat her head and breast.

V(11)   THE LION-MAKERS

In a certain town were four Brahmans who lived in friendship. Three of them had reached the far shore of all scholarship, but lacked sense. The other found scholarship distasteful; he had nothing but sense.

One day they met for consultation. 'What is the use of attainments,' said they, 'if one does not travel, win the favour of kings and acquire money? Whatever we do, let us all travel.'

But when they had gone a little way, the eldest of them said: 'One of us, the fourth, is a dullard, having nothing but sense. Now nobody gains the favourable attention of kings by simple sense without scholarship. Therefore we will not share our earnings with him. Let him turn back and go home.'

Then the second said: 'My intelligent friend, you lack scholarship. Please go home.' But the third said: 'No, no. This is no way to behave. For we have played together since we were little boys. Come along, my noble friend. You shall have a share of the money we earn.'

With this agreement they continued their journey, and in a forest they found the bones of a dead lion. Thereupon one of them said: 'A good opportunity to test the ripeness of our scholarship. Here lies some kind of creature, dead. Let us bring it to life by means of the scholarship we have honestly won.'

Then the first said: 'I know how to assemble the skeleton.' The second said: 'I can supply skin, flesh, and blood.' The third said: 'I can give it life.'

So the first assembled the skeleton, the second provided skin, flesh, and blood. But while the third was intent on giving the breath of life, the man of sense advised against it, remarking: 'This is a lion. If you bring him to life, he will kill every one of us.'

'You simpleton!' said the other, 'it is not I who will reduce scholarship to a nullity.' 'In that case,' came the reply, 'wait a moment, while I climb this convenient tree.'

When this had been done, the lion was brought to life, rose up, and killed all three. But the man of sense, after the lion had gone elsewhere, climbed down and went home.

V(12)   THE BRAHMAN'S DREAM

In a certain town lived a Brahman named Seedy, who got some barley-meal by begging, ate a portion, and filled a jar with the remainder. This jar he hung on a peg one night, placed his cot beneath it, and fixing his gaze on the jar, fell into a hypnotic reverie.

'Well, here is a jar full of barley-meal,' he thought. 'Now if famine comes, a hundred rupees will come out of it. With that sum I will get two she-goats. Every six months they will bear two more she-goats. After goats, cows. When the cows calve, I will sell the calves. After cows, buffaloes; after buffaloes, mares. From the mares I shall get plenty of horses. The sale of these will mean plenty of gold. The gold will buy a great house with an inner court. Then someone will come to my house and offer his lovely daughter with a dowry. She will bear a son, whom I shall name Moon-Lord. When he is old enough to ride on my knee, I will take a book, sit on the stable roof, and think. Just then Moon-Lord will see me, will jump from his mother's lap in his eagerness to ride on my knee, and will go too near the horses. Then I shall get angry and tell my wife to take the boy. But she will be busy with her chores and will not pay attention to what I say. Then I will get up and kick her.'

Being sunk in his hypnotic dream, he let fly such a kick that he smashed the jar. And the barley-meal which it contained turned him white all over.

III(20) CHANAKYA KAUTILYA
ARTHA SASTRA
[SCIENCE OF POLITY]

(Sanskrit, *c.* 321–300 B.C.)

Chanakya Kautilya (also called Vishnugupta) was a celebrated scholar from Kerala, who, after distinguishing himself from the University of Taxila (Takshashila), took a leading part in the overthrow of the corrupt Nanda king and, placing Chandragupta on the throne at Pataliputra in 321 B.C., established the Maurya Dynasty. Thereafter, as Chandragupta's prime minister Kautilya excelled as a statesman and the greatest exponent of the art of government and the science of diplomacy. His political exploits were dramatized by the classical playwright Vishakadatta in his play *Mudra-rakshasa* or The Signet Ring of Rakshasa (Sanskrit, *c.* A.D. 860). In recent years, the Indian government named the diplomatic enclave in New Delhi 'Chanakya-puri' (Chanakya town), in honour of this outstanding Indian political scientist.

Kautilya crystallized his life's experience and capsuled his shrewd observations on the political, economic, and social life of his time in his work *Artha Sastra* (Science of Well-being), composed almost 2,000 years before Machiavelli's *The Prince* (1513) or Adam Smith's *The Wealth of Nations* (1776). Kautilya defines 'artha' as 'the subsistence of mankind, or wealth; and that science which treats of the means of acquiring and maintaining "artha" as *Artha Sastra*, Science of Polity' (Bk XV, Ch. I). However, Kautilya says in the opening paragraph that his work 'is made as a compendium of almost all the *Artha Sastras*, which, in view of acquisition and maintenance of "artha", have been composed by ancient teachers' (Bk I, Ch. I).

In his book, Kautilya discusses in 150 chapters, arranged in 15 books, important aspects of the art of government, namely: I. Concerning Discipline and the End of Sciences; II. The Duties of Government; III. Concerning Law; IV. The Removal of Thorns; V. The Conduct of Courtiers; VI. The Source of Sovereign States;

VII. The Ends of Sixfold Policy; VIII. Concerning Vices and Calamities; IX. The Work of the Invader; X. The Art of War; XI. The Conduct of Corporations; XII. Concerning a Powerful Enemy; XIII. Strategic Means; XIV. Secret Means; and XV. The Plan of the Treatise.

Kautilya maintains that the end of all sciences is to explain the operation of the social forces, and to discipline and enlighten the rulers and administrators who have to contend with such forces, so as to enable them to carry out the functions of government under a proper system of *Danda* (punishments). For, when rulers under the influence of greed, anger, or ignorance impose punishments that are severe, they become repulsive to the people; if they are mild, they become contemptible. When a government loses the sense of proportion of *Danda*, it gives rise to such disorder as is implied in the *Matsta-nyaya* (Law of the Fish), where a greater fish swallows the smaller fishes (Bk I, Ch. IV). It is only in the proper exercise of *Danda-niti* (law of punishments) that a just government could be established and maintained over a society in which the weak can resist the strong, the people can follow their legitimate occupations and perform their respective duties, adhere to righteousness, and devote themselves to works of production and enjoyment of the fruits thereof. For it is 'a means to make acquisitions, to keep them secure, to improve them, and to distribute, among the deserved, the profits of improvement. It is on this science of government that the course of progress of the world depends' (Bk I, Ch. IV).

Some of the details of government mentioned by Kautilya in his work, such as the duties of various organs of the State (king, ministers, councillors, magistrates, officials, subjects, allies), the nature of statecraft, the end of policy, concern for national well-being and security, internal administration, methods of diplomacy, and the need for international relations, are to some extent corroborated by the writings of the Greek ambassador, Megasthenese, who arrived at the court of Chandragupta in Pataliputra in 302 B.C. as a representative of the Greek king of Alexander's eastern dominion, Seleucos Nikator. Though Nikator attempted to re-establish Greek authority in the Punjab during 305–302 B.C., in the manner of Alexander's incursions during 327–326 B.C., he finally made peace with Chandragupta, and, entering into a matrimonial alliance, exchanged ambassadors. As a privileged individual at the Mauryan court, Megasthenese travelled widely in north India during 302–291 B.C., and wrote his impressions in his book *Indika*, accounts of which have been preserved by later classical European historians like Arrian and Diodorus. Whether Megasthenese, a contemporary of Kautilya, knew of *Artha Sastra* or its political views, or whether a text of it surviving among Greek books influenced the political thoughts of Machiavelli during the Renaissance in Italy when Greek learning was revived, are still unresolved questions.

In the excerpts from *Artha Sastra* given below, Kautilya, showing a humane and realistic understanding of the problems of life in its varied complexity, as well as recognizing the need for cultural continuity, deals undogmatically with (a) law concerning marriage and sons (Bk III, chs. II, VII); (b) the source of sovereign states: the elements of sovereignty, and concerning peace and exertion (Bk VI, chs. I, II); and (c) the ends of the sixfold policy: the determination of deterioration, stagnation, and progress, and the nature of alliance (Bk VII, chs. I, II).

The selections are taken from the translation by R. Shama Sastry, *Kautilya's Artha Sastra*, Mysore: Mysore Printing and Publishing House, 1915: 8th edn 1967, Bk III, Chapter II, pp. 174–7; Chapter VII, pp. 188–90; Bk VI, Chapters I and II, pp. 289–94; Bk VII, Chapters I and II, pp. 295–9.

CHANAKYA KAUTILYA
ARTHA SASTRA
[SCIENCE OF POLITY]

Book III Concerning Law

CHAPTER II

CONCERNING MARRIAGE. THE DUTY OF MARRIAGE, THE PROPERTY OF A WOMAN, AND COMPENSATIONS FOR REMARRIAGE

Marriage is the basis of all disputes (*vyavahara*).

The giving in marriage of a maiden well adorned is called Brahma-marriage. The joint performance of sacred duties (by a man and a woman) is known as a prajapatya marriage.

(The giving in marriage of a maiden) for a couple of cows is called Arsha. (The giving in marriage of a maiden) to an officiating priest in a sacrifice is called Daiva. The voluntary union of a maiden with her lover is called Gandharva. Giving a maiden after receiving plenty of wealth (*sulka*) is termed Asura. The abduction of a maiden is called Rakshasa. The abduction of a maiden while she is asleep and in intoxication is called Paisacha marriage.

Of these, the first four are ancestral customs of old and are valid on their being approved of by the father. The rest are to be sanctioned by both the father and the mother; for it is they that receive the money (*sulka*) paid by the bridegroom for their daughter. In case of the absence by death of either the father or the mother, the survivor will receive the sulka. If both of them are dead, the maiden herself shall receive it. Any kind of marriage is approvable, provided it pleases all those (that are concerned in it).

(PROPERTY OF WOMEN)

Means of subsistence (*vrtti*) or jewellery (*abadhya*) constitute what is called the property of a woman. Means of subsistence valued at above two thousand shall be endowed (in her name). There is no limit to jewellery. It is no guilt for the wife to make use of this property in maintaining her son, her daughter-in-law, or herself, whenever her absent husband has made no provision for her maintenance. In calamities, disease and famine, in warding off dangers and in charitable acts, the husband, too, may make use of this property. Neither shall there be any complaint against the enjoyment of this property by mutual consent by a couple who háve brought forth a twin. Nor shall there be any complaint if this property has been enjoyed for three years by those who are wedded in accordance with the customs of the first four kinds of marriage. But the enjoyment of this property in the cases of Gandharva and Asura marriages shall be liable to be restored, together with interest on it. In the cases of such marriages as are called Rakshasa and Paisacha, the use of this property shall be dealt with as theft. Thus the duty of marriage is dealt with.

On the death of her husband, a woman desirous to lead a pious life shall at once receive not only an endowment and jewellery but also the balance of sulka due to her. If after obtaining these two things she remarries another, she shall be caused to pay them back together with interest (on their value). If she is desirous of a second marriage (*kutumbakama*), she shall be given on the occasion of her remarriage (*nivesakale*) whatever either her father-in-law or her husband or both had given to her. The time at which women can remarry shall be explained in connexion with the subject of long sojourn of husbands.

If a widow marries any man other than of her father-in-law's selection, she shall forfeit whatever had been given to her by her father-in-law and her deceased husband.

The kinsman (*gnatis*) of a woman shall return to her old father-in-law whatever property of her own she had taken with her while remarrying a kinsman. Whoever justly takes a woman under his protection shall equally protect her property. No woman shall succeed in her attempt to establish her title to the property of her deceased husband, after she remarries.

If she lives a pious life, she may enjoy it. No woman with a son or sons shall (after remarriage) be at liberty to make free use of her own property (*stridhana*); for that property of hers, her sons shall receive.

If a woman after remarriage attempts to take possession of her own property under the plea of maintaining her sons by her former husband, she shall be made to endow it in their name. If a woman has many male children by many husbands, then she shall conserve her property in the same condition as she had received it from her husbands. Even that property which has been given her with full powers of enjoyment and disposal, a remarried woman shall endow in the name of her sons.

A barren widow who is faithful to the bed of her dead husband may, under the protection of her teacher, enjoy her property as long as she lives: for it is to ward off calamities that women are endowed with property. On her death, her property shall pass into the hands of kinsmen (*Dayada*). If the husband is alive and the wife is dead, then her sons and daughters shall divide her property among themselves. If there are no sons, her daughters shall divide her property among themselves. If there are no sons, her daughters shall have it. In their absence her husband shall take that amount of money (*sulka*) which he had given her, and her relatives shall retake whatever in the shape of gift or dowry they had presented to her. Thus the determination of the property of a woman is dealt with.

(REMARRIAGE OF MALES)

If a woman either brings forth no (live) children, or has no male issue, or is barren, her husband shall wait for eight years before marrying another. If she bears only a dead child, he has to wait for ten years. If she brings forth only females, he has to wait for twelve years. Then if he is desirous to have sons, he may marry another. In case of violating this rule, he shall be made to pay her not only sulka, her property (*stridhana*) and an adequate monetary compensation (*adhivedani-kamartham*), but also a fine of 24 panas to the government. Having given the necessary amount of sulka and property even to those women who have not received such things on the occasion of their marriage with him, and also having given his wives the proportionate compensation and an adequate subsistence (*vrtti*), he may marry any number of women; for women are created for the sake of sons. If many or all of them are at the same time in menses, he shall lie with that woman among them whom he married earlier or who has a living son. In case of his concealing the fact of her being in menses, or neglecting to lie with any of them after her menses, he shall pay a fine of 96 panas.

Of women who either have sons or are pious or barren, or bring forth only a dead child or are beyond the age of menstruation, none shall be associated with against her liking. If a man has no inclination, he may not lie with his wife who is either afflicted with leprosy or is a lunatic. But if a woman is desirous of having sons, she may lie with men suffering from such disease.

If a husband either is of bad character, or is long gone abroad, or has become a traitor to his king, or is likely to endanger the life of his wife, or has fallen from his caste, or has lost virility, he may be adandoned by his wife.

CHAPTER VII

DISTINCTION BETWEEN SONS

My preceptor says that the seed sown in the field of another shall belong to the owner of that field. Others hold that the mother being only the receptacle for the seed (*mata bhastra*), the child must belong to him from whose seed it is born. Kautilya says that it must belong to both the living parents.

The son begotten by a man on his wife who has gone through all the required ceremonials is called aurasa, natural son; equal to him is the son of an appointed daughter (*putrikaputra*); the son begotten on a wife by another man, appointed for the purpose, and of the same gotra as that of the husband, or of a different gotra, is called kshetraja; on the death of the begetter, the kshetraja son will be the son to both the fathers, follow the gotras of both, offer funeral libations to both, and take possession of the property (*riktha*) of both of them; of the same status as the kshetraja is he who is secretly begotten in the house of relatives and is called gudhaja, secretly born; the son cast off by his natural parents is called apaviddha, and will belong to that man who performs necessary religious ceremonials to him; the son born of a maiden (before wedlock) is called kanina; the son born of a woman married while carrying is called sahodha; the son of a remarried woman (*punarbhutayah*) is called punarbhava. A natural son can claim relationship with both his father and his father's relatives; but a son born to another man can have relationship only with his adopter.

Of the same status as the latter is he who is given in adoption with water by both the father and mother and is called datta. The son who, either of his own accord or following the intention of his relatives, offers himself to be the son of another, is called upagata. He who is appointed as a son is called krtaka; and he who is purchased is called krita.

On the birth of a natural son, savarna sons shall have one third of inheritance; while asavarna sons shall have only food and clothing.

Sons begotten by Brahmans or Kshatriyas on women of the same caste (*anantaraputrah*) are called savarnas; but on women of lower castes are called asavarnas. (Of such asavarna sons), the son begotten by a Brahman on a Vaisya woman is called Ambhashtha; on a Sudra woman is called Nishada or Parasava. The son begotten by a Kshatriya on a Sudra woman is known as Ugra; the son begotten by a Vaisya on a Sudra woman is no other than a Sudra. Sons begotten by men of impure life of any of the four castes on women of same castes are called Vratyas. The above kinds of sons are called anuloma, sons begotten by men of higher on women of lower castes.

Sons begotten by a Sudra on women of higher castes are Ayogava, Kshatta, and Chandala; by a Vaisya, Magadha, and Vaidehaka; and by a Kshatriya, Suta. But men of the names Suta and Magadha, celebrated in the Puranas, are quite different and of greater merit than either Brahmans or Kshatriyas. – The above kinds of sons are pratiloma, sons begotten by men of lower on women of higher castes, and originate on account of kings violating all dharmas.

The son begotten by an Ugra on a Nishada woman is called Kukkutaka, and the same is called Pulkasa if begotten in the inverse order. The son begotten by an Ambhashtha on a Vaidehaka woman is named Vainya; the same in the reverse order is called Kusilava. An Ugra begets on a Kshatta woman a Svapaka. These and other sons are of mixed castes (*Antaralas*).

A Vainya becomes a Rathakara, chariot-maker, by profession. Members of this caste shall marry among themselves. Both in customs and avocations they shall follow their ancestors. They may either become Sudras, if they are not born as Chandalas.

The king who guides his subjects in accordance with the above rules will attain to heaven; otherwise he will fall into the hell.

Offsprings of mixed castes (*Antaralas*) shall have equal divisions of inheritance.

Partition of inheritance shall be made in accordance with the customs prevalent in the country, caste, guild (*sangha*), or the village of the inheritors.

Book VI The Source of Sovereign States

CHAPTER I

THE ELEMENTS OF SOVEREIGNTY

The king, the minister, the country, the fort, the treasury, the army and the friend, and the enemy are the elements of sovereignty.

Of these, the best qualities of the king are:

Born of a high family, godly, possessed of valour, seeing through the medium of aged persons, virtuous, truthful, not of a contradictory nature, grateful, having large aims, highly enthusiastic, not addicted to procrastination, powerful to control his neighbouring kings, of resolute mind, having an assembly of ministers of no mean quality, and possessed of a taste for discipline – these are the qualities of an inviting nature.

Inquiry, hearing, perception, retention in memory, reflection, deliberation, inference and steadfast adherence to conclusions are the qualities of intellect.

Valour, determination of purpose, quickness, and probity are the aspects of enthusiasm.

Possessed of a sharp intellect, strong memory, and keen mind, energetic, powerful, trained in all kinds of arts, free from vice, capable of paying in the same coin by way of awarding punishments or rewards, possessed of dignity; capable of taking remedial measures against dangers, possessed of foresight, ready to avail himself of opportunities when afforded in respect of place, time, and manly efforts, clever enough to discern the causes necessitating the cessation of treaty or war with an enemy, or to lie in wait keeping treaties, obligations and pledges, or to avail himself of his enemy's weak points, making jokes with no loss of dignity or secrecy, never browbeating and casting haughty and stern looks, free from passion, anger, greed, obstinacy, fickleness, haste and back-biting habits, talking to others with a smiling face, and observing customs as taught by aged persons – such is the nature of self-possession.

The qualifications of a minister have been described in the beginning, middle, and at the close of the work.

Possessed of capital cities both in the centres and the extremities of the kingdom, productive of subsistence not only to its own people, but also to outsiders on occasions of calamities, repulsive to enemies, powerful enough to put down neighbouring kings, free from miry, rocky, uneven, and desert tracts, as well as from conspirators, tigers, wild beasts, and large tracts of wilderness, beautiful to look at, containing fertile lands, mines, timber and elephant forests, and pasture grounds, artistic, containing hidden passages, full of cattle, not depending upon rain for water, possessed of land and waterways, rich in various kinds of commercial articles, capable of bearing the burden of a vast army and heavy taxation, inhabited by agriculturists of good and active character, full of intelligent masters and servants, and with a population noted for its loyalty and good character – these are the qualities of a good country.

The excellent qualities of forts have been already described.

Justly obtained either by inheritance or by self-acquisition, rich in gold and silver, filled with an abundance of big gems of various colours and of gold coins, and capable to withstand calamities of long duration, is the best treasury.

Coming down directly from father and grandfather (of the king), ever strong, obedient, happy in keeping their sons and wives well contented, not averse to making a long sojourn, ever and everywhere invincible, endowed with the power of endurance, trained in fighting various kinds of battles, skilful in handling various forms of weapons, ready to share in the weal or woe of the king, and consequently not falling foul with him, and purely composed of soldiers of Kshatriya caste, is the best army.

Coming down directly from father and grandfather, long-standing, open to conviction, never falling foul; and capable of making preparations for war quickly and on a large scale, is the best friend.

Not born of a royal family, greedy, possessed of a mean assembly of ministers, with disloyal subjects, ever doing unrighteous acts, of loose character, addicted to mean pleasures, devoid of enthusiasm, trusting to fate, indiscreet in action, powerless, helpless, impotent and ever injurious, is the worst enemy. Such an enemy is easily uprooted.

Excepting the enemy, these seven elements, possessed of their excellent characteristics are said to be the limb-like elements of sovereignty.

A wise king can make even the poor and miserable elements of his sovereignty happy and prosperous; but a wicked king will surely destroy the most prosperous and loyal elements of his kingdom.

Hence a king of unrighteous character and of vicious habits will, though he is an emperor, fall a prey either to the fury of his own subjects or to that of his enemies.

But a wise king, trained in politics, will, though he possesses a small territory, conquer the whole earth with the help of the best fitted elements of his sovereignty, and will never be defeated.

CHAPTER II

CONCERNING PEACE AND EXERTION

Acquisition and security (of property) are dependent upon peace and industry.

Effort to achieve the results of works undertaken is industry (*vyayama*).

Absence of disturbance to the enjoyment of the results achieved from works is peace.

The application of the sixfold royal policy is the source of peace and industry.

Deterioration, stagnation, and progress are the three aspects of position.

Those causes of human make which affect position are policy and impolicy (*naya* and *apanaya*); fortune and misfortune (*aya* and *anaya*) are providential causes. Causes, both human and providential, govern the world and its affairs.

What is unforeseen is providential; here, the attainment of that desired end which seemed almost lost is (termed) fortune.

What is anticipated is human; and the attainment of a desired end as anticipated is (due to policy).

What produces unfavourable results is impolicy. This can be foreseen; but misfortune due to providence cannot be known.

The king who, being possessed of good character and best-fitted elements of sovereignty, is the fountain of policy, is termed the conqueror.

The king who is situated anywhere immediately on the circumference of the conqueror's territory is termed the enemy.

The king who is likewise situated close to the enemy, but separated from the conqueror only by the enemy, is termed the friend (of the conqueror).

A neighbouring foe of considerable power is styled an enemy; and when he is involved in calamities or has taken himself to evil ways, he becomes assailable; and when he has little or no help, he becomes destructible; otherwise (i.e. when he is provided with some help), he deserves to be harassed or reduced. Such are the aspects of an enemy.

In front of the conqueror and close to his enemy, there happen to be situated kings such as the conqueror's friend, next to him the enemy's friend, and next to the last, the conqueror's friend's friend, and next, the enemy's friend's friend.

In the rear of the conqueror, there happen to be situated a rearward enemy (*parshnigraha*), a rearward friend (*akranda*), an ally of the rearward enemy (*parshnigrahasara*), and an ally of the rearward friend (*akrandasara*).

That foe who is equally of high birth and occupies a territory close to that of the conqueror is a natural enemy; while he who is merely antagonistic and creates enemies to the conqueror is a factitious enemy.

He whose friendship is derived from father and grandfather, and who is situated close to the territory of the immediate enemy of the conqueror is a natural friend; while he whose friendship is courted for self-maintenance is an acquired friend.

The king who occupies a territory close to both the conqueror and his immediate enemy in front and who is capable of helping both the kings, whether united or disunited, or of resisting either of them individually is termed a Madhyama (mediatory) king.

He who is situated beyond the territory of any of the above kings, and who is very powerful and capable of helping the enemy, the conqueror, and the Madhyama king, together or individually, or of resisting any of them individually, is a neutral king (*udasina*) – these are the (twelve) primary kings.

The conqueror, his friend, and his friend's friend are the three primary kings constituting a circle of states. As each of these three kings possesses the five elements of sovereignty, such as the minister, the country, the fort, the treasury, and the army, a circle of states consists of eighteen elements. Thus, it needs no commentary to understand that the (three) Circles of States having the enemy (of the conqueror), the Madhyama king, or the neutral king at the centre of each of the three circles are different from that of the conqueror. Thus there are four primary Circles of States, twelve kings, sixty elements of sovereignty, and seventy-two elements of states.*

Each of the twelve primary kings shall have their elements of sovereignty, power and end. *Strength is power, and happiness is the end.*

Strength is of three kinds: power of deliberation is intellectual strength; the possession of a prosperous treasury and a strong army is the strength of sovereignty; and martial power is physical strength.

The end is also of three kinds: that which is attainable by deliberation is the end of deliberation; that which is attainable by the strength of sovereignty is the end of sovereignty; and that which is to be secured by perseverance is the end of martial power.

The possession of power and happiness in a greater degree makes a king superior to another; in a less degree, inferior; and in equal degree, equal. Hence a king shall always endeavour to augment his power and elevate his happiness.

A king who is equal to his enemy in the matter of his sovereign elements shall, in virtue of his own righteous conduct or with the help of those who are hostile or conspiring against his enemy, endeavour to throw his enemy's power into the shade; or if he thinks:

---

*(1) The conqueror's circle of states; (2) the enemy's circle of states; (3) the Madhyama king's circle of states; (4) the neutral king's circle of states. As each of the twelve primary kings has five elements of sovereignty, the total number of elements is sixty. These sixty elements with the twelve kings amount to seventy-two elements.

'That my enemy, possessed as he is of immense power, will yet in the near future hurt the elements of his own sovereignty, by using contumelious language, by inflicting severe punishments, and by squandering his wealth; that though attaining success for a time, yet he will blindly take himself to hunting, gambling, drinking and women; that as his subjects are disaffected, himself powerless haughty, I can overthrow him; that when attacked, he will take shelter with all his paraphernalia into a fort or elsewhere; that possessed as he is of a strong army, he will yet fall into my hands, as he has neither a friend nor a fort to help him; that a distant king is desirous to put down his own enemy, and also inclined to help me to put down my own assailable enemy when my resources are poor, or that I may be invited as Madhyama king' – for these reasons the conqueror may allow his enemy to grow in strength and to attain success for the time being.

Throwing the circumference of the Circle of States beyond his friends' territory, and making the kings of those states as the spokes of that circle, the conqueror shall make himself as the nave of that circle.

A reducible or a conquerable enemy will, when placed between a conqueror and the conqueror's friend, appear to be growing in strength.

Book VII: The Ends of the Sixfold Policy

CHAPTER I

THE SIXFOLD POLICY, AND DETERMINATION OF DETERIORATION, STAGNATION AND PROGRESS

The Circle of States is the source of the sixfold policy.

My teacher says that peace (*sandhi*), war (*vigraha*), observance of neutrality (*asana*), marching (*yana*), alliance (*samsraya*), and making peace with one and waging war with another are the six forms of state policy.

But Vatavyadhi holds that there are only two forms of policy, peace and war, in as much as the six forms result from these two primary forms of policy.

While Kautilya holds that, as their respective conditions differ, the forms of policy are six.

Of these, agreement with pledges is peace; offensive operation is war; indifference is neutrality; making preparations is marching; seeking the protection of another is alliance; and making peace with one and waging war with another, is termed a double policy (*dvaidhibhava*). These are the six forms.

Whoever is inferior to another shall make peace with him; whoever is superior in power shall wage war; whoever thinks 'No enemy can hurt me, nor am I strong enough to destroy my enemy' shall observe neutrality; whoever is possessed of necessary means shall march against his enemy; whoever is devoid of necessary strength to defend himself shall seek the protection of another; whoever thinks that help is necessary to work out an end shall make peace with one and wage war with another. Such is the aspect of the six forms of policy.

Of those, a wise king shall observe that form of policy which, in his opinion, enables him to build forts, to construct buildings and commercial roads, to open new plantations and villages, to exploit mines and timber and elephant forests and at the same time to harass similar works of his enemy.

Whoever thinks himself to be growing in power more rapidly both in quality and quantity (than his enemy), and the reverse of his enemy, may neglect his enemy's progress for the time.

If any two kings, hostile to each other, find the time of achieving the results of their respective works to be equal, they shall make peace with each other.

No king shall keep that form of policy, which causes him the loss of profit from his own works, but which entails no such loss on the enemy; for it is deterioration.

Whoever thinks that in the course of time his loss will be less than his acquisition as contrasted with that of his enemy, may neglect his temporary deterioration.

If any two kings, hostile to each other, and deteriorating, expect to acquire equal amount of wealth in equal time, they shall make peace with each other.

That position in which neither progress nor retrogression is seen is stagnation.

Whoever thinks his stagnancy to be of a shorter duration and his prosperity in the long run to be greater than his enemy's, may neglect his temporary stagnation.

My teacher says that if any two kings, who are hostile to each other, and are in a stationary condition, expect to acquire equal amount of wealth and power in equal time, they shall make peace with each other.

'Of course,' says Kautilya, 'there is no other alternative.' Or if a king thinks:

'That keeping the agreement of peace, I can undertake productive works of considerable importance and destroy at the same time those of my enemy; or apart from enjoying the results of my own works, I shall also enjoy those of my enemy in virtue of the agreement of peace; or I can destroy the works of my enemy by employing spies and other secret means; or by holding out such inducements as a happy dwelling, rewards, remission of taxes, little work and large profits and wages, I can empty my enemy's country of its population, with which he has been able to carry his own works; or being allied with a king of considerable power, my enemy will have his own work destroyed; or I can prolong my enemy's hostility with another king whose threats have driven my enemy to seek my protection; or being allied with me, my enemy can harass the country of another king who hates me; or oppressed by another king, the subjects of my enemy will immigrate into my country, and I can, therefore, achieve the results of my own works very easily; or being in a precarious condition due to the destruction of his works, my enemy will not be so powerful as to attack me; or by exploiting my own resources in alliance with any two (friendly) kings, I can augment my resources; or if a Circle of States is formed by my enemy as one of its members, I can divide them and combine with the others; or by threats or favour I can catch hold of my enemy, and when he desires to be a member of my own Circle of States, I can make him incur the displeasures of the other members and fall a victim to their own fury' – if a king thinks thus, then he may increase his resources by keeping peace.

Or if a king thinks:

'That as my country is full of born soldiers and of corporations of fighting men, and as it possesses such natural defensive positions as mountains, forests, rivers, and forts with only one entrance, it can easily repel the attack of my enemy; or having taken my stand in my impregnable fortress at the border of my country, I can harass the works of my enemy; or owing to internal troubles and loss of energy, my enemy will early suffer from the destruction of his works; or when my enemy is attacked by another king, I can induce his subjects to immigrate into my country', then he may augment his own resources by keeping open hostility with such an enemy.

Or if a king thinks:

'That neither is my enemy strong enough to destroy my works, nor am I his; or if he comes to fight with me like a dog with a boar, I can increase his afflictions without incurring any loss in my own works,' then he may observe neutrality and augment his own resources.

Or if a king thinks:

'That by marching my troops it is possible to destroy the works of my enemy; and as for myself, I have made proper arrangements to safeguard my own works,' then he may increase his resources by marching.

Or if a king thinks:

'That I am strong enough neither to harass my enemy's works nor to defend my own against my enemy's attack,' then he shall seek protection from a king of superior power, and endeavour to pass from the stage of deterioration to that of stagnancy and from the latter to that of progress.

Or if a king thinks:

'That by making peace with one, I can work out my own resources, and by waging war with another, I can destroy the works of my enemy,' then he may adopt that double policy and improve his resources.

Thus, a king in the circle of sovereign states shall, by adopting the sixfold policy, endeavour to pass from the state of deterioration to that of stagnation, and from the latter to that of progress.

CHAPTER II

THE NATURE OF ALLIANCE

When the advantages derivable from peace and war are of equal character, one should prefer peace; for disadvantages, such as the loss of power and wealth, sojourning, and sin, are ever attending upon war.

The same holds good in the case of neutrality and war.

Of the two (forms of policy), double policy and alliance, double policy (i.e. making peace with one and waging war with another) is preferable; for whoever adopts the double policy enriches himself, being ever attentive to his own works, whereas an allied king has to help his ally at his own expense.

One shall make an alliance with a king who is stronger than one's neighbouring enemy; in the absence of such a king, one should ingratiate oneself with one's neighbouring enemy, either by supplying money or army or by ceding a part of one's territory and by keeping oneself aloof; for there can be no greater evil to kings than alliance with a king of considerable power, unless one is actually attacked by one's enemy.

A powerless king should behave as a conquered king (towards his immediate enemy); but when he finds that the time of his own ascendancy is at head, due to a fatal disease, internal troubles, increase of enemies, or a friend's calamities that are vexing his enemy, then under the pretence of performing some expiatory rites to avert the danger of his enemy, he may get out (of the enemy's court); or if he is in his own territory, he should not go to see his suffering enemy; or if he is near to his enemy he may murder the enemy when opportunity affords itself.

A king who is situated between two powerful kings shall seek protection from the stronger of the two; or from one of them on whom he can rely; or he may make peace with both of them on equal terms. Then he may begin to set one of them against the other by telling each that the other is a tyrant causing utter ruin to himself, and thus cause dissension between them. When they are divided, he may put down each separately by secret or covert means. Or, throwing himself under the protection of any two immediate kings of considerable power, he may defend himself against an immediate enemy. Or, having made an alliance with a chief in a stronghold, he may adopt the double policy (i.e. make peace with one of the two kings and wage war with another). Or, he may adapt himself to circumstances, depending upon the causes of peace and war in order. Or, he may make friendship with traitors, enemies, and wild chiefs who are conspiring against both the kings. Or, pretending to be a close friend of one of them, he may strike the other at the latter's weak point by employing enemies and wild tribes. Or, having made friendship with both, he may form a Circle of States. Or, he may make an alliance with the Madhayama or the neutral king; and with this help he may put down one of them or both. Or when hurt by both, he may seek protection from a king of righteous character among the Madhyama king, the neutral king, and their friends or equals, or from any other king whose subjects are so disposed as to increase his happiness and peace, with whose help he may be able to recover his last position, with whom his ancestors were in close intimacy or blood relationship and in whose kingdom he can find a number of powerful friends.

Of two powerful kings who are on amicable terms with each other, a king shall make alliance with one of them who likes him and whom he likes; this is the best way of making alliance.

The most outstanding Indian contribution to world culture, which has become widely known as of distinctively Indian origin, is the philosophy and practice of yoga. Though India contributed, among other things, the revolutionary concept of zero to the world of mathematics, and Upanishadic thought to philosophy, it is the mystery and metaphysics of yoga which have drawn the world's curiosity and serious attention, particularly since the studies of Freud and Jung and researches in parapsychology.

The word *yoga* has come to mean a variety of things. In the same way as the English word 'art' (fine arts, performing arts, bachelor of arts, art object, painting as an art, cooking as an art, or even the art of telling a lie!), the Sanskrit word *yoga* evokes a number of ideas, from the popularly known body exercises, intended to develop general health and keep the waist line, to the exotic and incredible practices of *yogis*, such as levitation and the rope-trick. In this confusion the deeper significance and profounder purposes of yoga are lost. Etymologically, yoga means 'to yoke', that is, to yoke the body-apparatus to a particular purpose, such as action, devotion, meditation, or identification of self (*atman*) with the Supreme Self (*Brahman*).

In Indian civilization, yoga is one of the oldest concepts, generally associated with the Supreme Yogi, Shiva. Its methods of practice and philosophy appear to have evolved during long periods of time, under the rigorous and austere discipline of the *rishis*. In this process, the sages discovered a number of means, some external and some internal, to discipline the energies of the body and the powers of the mind. Though this cumulative knowledge was transmitted from *guru* (master) to *sishya* (pupil) orally from age to age, discussions on yoga are to be found in a number of *Upanishads** and in the *Bhagavad Gita.*†

---

* Yoga Chudamani Upanishad, Yoga Tatva Upanishad, Nada Bindu Upanishad, Yoga Kundali Upanishad, Akshi Upanishad; references to yoga are to be found in *Brihad-Aranyaka Upanishad* and *Katha Upanishad*.

† Chapter 6.

However, the main elements of this discipline were systematized and codified by Patanjali (third century B.C.) in his concise and extremely cryptic text the *Yoga Sutra*. This text became the basis of *Yoga Darsana* (yoga method of apprehension of reality), included in the Six Darsanas, or popularly known as the Six Systems of Indian Philosophy.*

The *Yoga Sutra* assumes much of the metaphysics flowing from the *Upanishads*. Since the universe is pervaded by *Purusha*, or the Supreme Self, there are no aspects of the universe which cannot be used for the purpose of attaining reintegration or realization of the unity of *atman* and *Brahman*. Consequently, yoga practices vary according to the needs in the life of an individual. For example, the *Bhagavad Gita* mentions a number of such yogas or approaches to the Ultimate: *Karma* or *Kriya* yoga, the yoga of action; *Jnana* yoga, yoga of knowledge; *Dhyana* yoga, the yoga of meditation; *Bhakti* yoga, the yoga of loving-faith or devotion. These distinctions are mostly a matter of emphasis. In practice, they often merge with one another. For example, a Karma Yogi (man of active life) may also blend in his life a certain amount of *Jnana* yoga and *Bhakti* yoga, as did Mahatma Gandhi.

Apart from the above differences in emphasis, five main types of yoga have traditionally been distinguished. Though all of them basically follow the Eight Stages of the pattern for psychic progress mentioned in the *Yoga Sutra*, each one of them has come to acquire a specific name and meaning. They are:

Hatha Yoga, the path of physical energy. Hatha Yoga brings the body and its vital energies under control through a process of disciplined exercises. This yoga is considered basic to all other yogas, and is often called the 'ladder' to *Raja Yoga*.

Mantra Yoga, the path of prayer. This is practised in the form of rhythmic repetition of certain *mantra* or prayer formula, e.g. *Gayatri*, or *Om*. The secret power of the sound leads the *Mantra Yogi* to the reintegration of his self with the Supreme Self.

Laya Yoga, the path of mergence. Since the microcosm and the

---

* The Six Darsanas (Systems) are: *Nyaya, Vaisesika, Samkhya, Yoga, Mimamsa,* and *Vedanta*.

macrocosm are, in essence, the same, the macrocosm is potentially present in the microcosm, in the form of a lotus of a thousand petals. Consequently, the nature-energy which pervades the universe lies at the centre of an individual, as if in a coiled sleep (*kundalini*). *Laya Yogi* arouses this latent energy in him and merges his self with the Supreme Self by contemplating on the inner sound and inner light.

Raja Yoga, the royal path, or yoga *par excellence*. This is the highest form of yoga, all other forms being preparatory to it. The *Raja Yogi* harmonizes dualities and multiplicities, and achieves complete reintegration of *atman* and *Brahman*.

Rajadhiraja Yoga, the path of king of kings, or the path of Lord of Sleep, Shiva. Having acquired supreme mastery over the body, outer and inner senses, the *Rajadhiraja Yogi*, contemplating the Supreme Yogi (Shiva), liberates his self and completely dissolves his *atman* in *Brahman* in a prolonged peace. This yoga (also called *Maha Yoga*) is sometimes identified with *Raja Yoga*.

Patanjali's *Yoga Sutra*, consisting of about 200 aphorisms in four chapters, deals with (I) the nature of mental concentration or yoking for identification (*Samadhi*); (II) the pathway to it (*Sadhana*), including the Eight Yoga Steps; (III) the supernatural powers that may be acquired through it (*Vibhuti*); (IV) the nature of the goal of life, consisting in the isolation of the self (*Kaivalya*). The disciplining of the body and the mind through the Eight Steps to the highest possible peak of perfect health and energy is achieved in two stages. First, the 'Outer Stage', consisting of the first four steps: abstinences (*Yama*), observances (*Niyama*), postures (*Asanas*), and breath control (*Pranayama*). Second, the 'Inner Stage', consisting of the last four steps: withdrawal of senses (*Pratyahara*), concentration (*Dharana*), meditation (*Dhyana*), and identification or super consciousness (*Samadhi*). These stages are technically helped by some body gestures (*Mudras*), muscular contracts (*Bandhas*), and internal purifications (*Shat-karma*). The transition from the Outer to the Inner Stage is made through the most important gateway of breath control. Since Patanjali's aphorisms are in a very condensed form they can hardly be understood fully (like swimming instructions) without lengthy commentaries, guidance from a *guru*, and actual practice.

The *Yoga Sutra* mentions the possibility of attaining supernatural powers through yogic practices. However, classical authors do not encourage the acquisition of such powers because they are only incidental to the attainment of the true goal of spiritual freedom.

The text is taken from the translation by Swami Vivekananda, *Raja Yoga*, or *Conquering the Internal Nature*, Calcutta: Swami Trigunatita, 1901; London: Luzac, 1937.

PATANJALI
YOGA SUTRA

(Sanskrit, *c.* 300 B.C.)

Chapter I: Concentration (Samadhi)

NATURE OF YOGA

1. Now concentration is explained.

2. Yoga is restraining the mind-stuff (*Chitta*) from taking various forms (*Vrittis*).

3. At that time (the time of concentration) the seer (*Purusha*) rests in his own (unmodified) state.

4. At other times (other than that of concentration) the seer is identified with the modifications.

FORMS OF MIND-STUFF MODIFICATIONS

5. There are five classes of modifications, (some) painful and (others) not painful.

6. (These are) right knowledge, indiscrimination, verbal delusion, sleep and memory.

7. Direct perception, inference, and competent evidence, are proofs.

8. Indiscrimination is false knowledge not established in real nature.

9. Verbal delusion follows from words having no (corresponding) reality.

10. Sleep is a *Vritti* which embraces the feeling of voidness.

1.2. The mind is possessed of the three 'gunas', showing as it does the nature of illumination (*sattva*), activity (*rajas*), and inertia (*tamas*). That particular state of mind in which the manifestations of real cognition etc. have been restrained is the state of yoga (Radhakrishnan).

1.6. Real cognition, unreal cognition, imagination, deep sleep, and memory (Radhakrishnan).

11. Memory is when (*Vrittis* of) perceived subjects do not slip away (and through impressions come back to consciousness).

12. Their control is by practice and non-attachment.

NATURE OF CONTROL

13. Continuous struggle to keep them (the *Vrittis*) perfectly restrained in practice.

14. It becomes firmly grounded by long constant efforts with great love (for the end to be attained).

15. That effect which comes to those who have given up their thirst after objects either seen or heard, and which wills to control the objects, is non-attachment.

16. That is extreme non-attachment which gives up even the qualities, and comes from the knowledge of (the real nature of) the *Purusha*.

NATURE OF SAMADHI

17. The concentration called right knowledge is that which is followed by reasoning, discrimination, bliss, unqualified egoism.

18. There is another *Samadhi* which is attained by the constant practice of cessation of all mental activity, in which the *Chitta* retains only the unmanifested impressions.

19. (This *Samadhi* when not followed by extreme non-attachment) becomes the cause of the re-manifestation of the gods and of those that become merged in nature.

20. To others (this *Samadhi*) comes through faith, energy, memory, concentration, and discrimination of the real.

21. Success is speedy for the extremely energetic.

1.16. Cf. *Bhagavad Gita*, 7.12; Ch. 17.

Purusha: the Self. According to yoga philosophy, the whole of nature is conditioned by three *gunas* (*sattva*, *rajas*, and *tamas*). All manifestations are combinations and recombinations of these three forces. But the individual self, being a part of the Universal Self, is beyond these three *gunas*; it is effulgent, pure, and perfect. Whatever intelligence is seen in Nature is but the reflection of this Self upon Nature (Vivekananda).

ISVARA AND THE OM

22. The success of *Yogis* differs according as the means they adopt are mild, medium or intense.

23. Or by devotion to *Isvara*.

24. *Isvara* (the Supreme Ruler) is a special *Purusha*, untouched by misery, actions, their results and desires.

25. In Him becomes infinite that all-knowingness which in others is (only) a germ.

26. He is the Teacher of even the ancient teachers, being not limited by time.

27. His manifesting word is *Om*.

28. The repetition of this (*Om*) and meditating on its meaning (is the way).

29. From that is gained (the knowledge of) introspection, and the destruction of obstacles.

MAIN OBSTACLES

30. Disease, mental laziness, doubt, lack of enthusiasm, lethargy, clinging to sense-enjoyments, false perception, non-attaining concentration, and falling away from the state when obtained, are the obstructing distractions.

31. Grief, mental distress, tremor of the body, irregular breathing, accompany non-retention of concentration.

32. To remedy this, the practice of one subject (should be made).

PACIFICATION OF MIND-STUFF

33. Friendship, mercy, gladness and indifference, being thought of in regard to subjects, happy, unhappy, good and evil respectively, pacify the *Chitta*.

34. By throwing out and restraining the Breath.

35. Those forms of concentration that bring extraordinary sense perceptions cause perseverance of the mind.

36. Or (by the meditation on) the Effulgent Light, which is beyond all sorrow.

37. Or (by meditation on) the heart that has given up all attachment to sense-objects.

38. Or by meditating on the knowledge that comes in sleep.

39. Or by the meditation on anything that appeals to one as good.

40. The *Yogi*'s mind thus meditating, becomes unobstructed from the atomic to the infinite.

KINDS OF SAMADHI

41. The *Yogi* whose *Vrittis* have thus become powerless (controlled) obtains in the receiver, (the instrument of) receiving, and the received (the Self, the mind, and external objects), concentratedness and sameness, like the crystal (before different coloured objects).

42. Sound, meaning, and resulting knowledge, being mixed up, is (called) *Samadhi* with-question.

43. *Samadhi* called 'without-question' (comes) when the memory is purified, or devoid of qualities, expressing only the meaning (of the meditated object).

44. By this process (the concentrations) with discrimination and without discrimination, whose objects are finer, are (also) explained.

45. The finer objects end with the *Pradhana*.

46. These concentrations are with seed.

47. The concentration 'without discrimination' being purified, the *Chitta* becomes firmly fixed.

48. The knowledge in that is called 'filled with Truth'.

49. The knowledge that is gained from testimony and inference is about common objects. That from the *Samadhi* just mentioned is of a much higher order, being able to penetrate where inference and testimony cannot go.

50. The resulting impression from this *Samadhi* obstructs all other impressions.

51. By the restraint of even this (impression, which obstructs all other impressions), all being restrained, comes the 'seedless' *Samadhi*.

I.41. Becoming like a transparent crystal on the modifications disappearing, the mind acquires the power of thought-transformation (*samapatti*), the power of appearing in the shape of whatever object is presented to it, be it the knower, the knowable, or the act of knowing (Radhakrishnan).

I.45. *Pradhana*: noumenal.

Chapter II: Methods (Sadhana)

YOGA OF ACTION

1. Mortification, study, and surrendering fruits of work to God are called *Kriya-yoga*.

2. (It is for) the practice of *Samadhi* and minimizing the pain-bearing obstructions.

3. The pain-bearing obstructions are – ignorance, egoism, attachment, aversion, and clinging to life.

4. Ignorance is the productive field of all these that follow, whether they are dormant, attenuated, overpowered, or expanded.

5. Ignorance is taking the non-eternal, the impure, the painful, and the non-Self, as the eternal, the pure, the happy, and the Atman or Self (respectively).

6. Egoism is the identification of the seer with the instrument of seeing.

7. Attachment is that which dwells on pleasure.

8. Aversion is that which dwells on pain.

9. Flowing through its own nature, and established even in the learned, is the clinging to life.

10. The five *Samskaras* are to be conquered by resolving them into their causal state.

11. By meditation, their (gross) modifications are to be rejected.

NATURE OF ACTION

12. The 'receptacle of works' has its root in these pain-bearing obstructions, and their experience is in this visible life, or in the unseen life.

II.1. *Kriya-yoga*: yoga of action.

II.10. *Samskaras*, Pain-bearing obstructions (II.3 above), are the subtle impressions that manifest themselves into gross forms later on (Vivekananda).

II.12. The Vehicle of action has its origin in afflictions (lust, avarice, forgetfulness, and anger), and is experienced in visible and invisible life (Radhakrishnan).

13. The root being there, the fruition comes (in the form of) species, life, and experience of pleasure and pain.

14. They bear fruit as pleasure or pain, caused by virtue or vice.

15. To the discriminating, all is, as it were, painful on account of everything bringing pain, either as consequence, or as anticipation of loss of happiness or as fresh craving arising from impressions of happiness, and also as counter-action of qualities.

16. The misery which is not yet come is to be avoided.

THE INDEPENDENCE OF THE SOUL AS SEER

17. The cause of that which is to be avoided is the junction of the seer and the seen.

18. The experienced is composed of elements and organs, is of the nature of illumination, action, and inertia, and is for the purpose of experience and release (of the experiencer).

19. The states of the qualities are the defined, the undefined, the indicated only, and the signless.

20. The seer is intelligence only, and though pure, sees through the colouring of the intellect.

21. The nature of the experienced is for him.

22. Though destroyed for him whose goal has been gained, yet it is not destroyed, being common to others.

23. Junction is the cause of the realization of the nature of both the powers, the experienced and its Lord.

24. Ignorance is its cause.

25. There being absence of that (ignorance) there is absence of junction, which is the thing-to-be-avoided; that is the independence of the seer.

26. The means of destruction of ignorance is unbroken practice of discrimination.

27. His knowledge is of the sevenfold highest ground.

THE EIGHT STAGES

28. By the practice of the different parts of *Yoga* the impurities being destroyed, knowledge becomes effulgent up to discrimination.

29. *Yama, Niyama, Asana, Pranayama, Pratyahara, Dharana, Dhyana,* and *Samadhi,* are the eight limbs of *Yoga.*

1. FIVE RESTRAINTS (*Yama*)

30. Non-killing, truthfulness, non-stealing, continence, and non-receiving, are called *Yama.*

31. These, unbroken by time, place, purpose and caste-rules, are (universal) great vows.

2. FIVE OBSERVANCES (*Niyama*)

32. Internal and external purification, contentment, mortification, study, and worship of God, are the *Niyamas.*

33. To obstruct thoughts which are inimical to *Yoga,* contrary thoughts should be brought.

34. The obstructions to *Yoga* are killing, falsehood, etc., whether committed, caused, or approved; either through avarice, or anger or ignorance; whether slight, middling, or great; and result in infinite ignorance and misery. This is (the method of) thinking the contrary.

35. Non-killing being established, in his presence all enmities cease (in others).

36. By the establishment of truthfulness the *Yogi* gets the power of attaining for himself and others the fruits of work without the works.

37. By the establishment of non-stealing all wealth comes to the *Yogi.*

38. By the establishment of continence energy is gained.

39. When he is fixed in non-receiving he gets the memory of past life.

II.29. Abstinences, observances, postures, breath control, withdrawal of senses, concentration, meditation, identification (or trance).

II.30. *Ahimsa, Satya, Asteya, Brahmacharya, Aparigrapha* (non-accumulation).

II.32. *Saucha* (purity), *Santosh* (joyful satisfaction), *Tapa* (austerity), *Svadhvaya* (self-development), *Isvara Pranidhana* (constant thought of divinity).

40. Internal and external cleanliness being established, arises disgust for one's own body, and non-intercourse with others.

41. There also arises purification of the *Sattva*, cheerfulness of the mind, concentration, conquest of the organs, and fitness for the realization of the Self.

42. From contentment comes superlative happiness.

43. The result of mortification is bringing powers to the organs and the body, by destroying the impurity.

44. By repetition of the *Mantra* comes the realization of the intended deity.

45. By sacrificing all to *Isvara* comes *Samadhi*.

3. POSTURE (*Asana*)

46. Posture is that which is firm and pleasant.

47. By lessening the natural tendency (for restlessness) and meditating on the unlimited (posture becomes firm and pleasant).

48. Seat being conquered, the dualities do not obstruct.

4. BREATH CONTROL (*Pranayama*)

49. Controlling the motion of the exhalation and the inhalation follows after this.

II.44. *Mantra*: prayer.

II.46. To yoke the body and stabilize the mind 84 *asanas* (postures) are prescribed, of which four are generally considered ideal for identification, namely: *Siddha-asana* (posture of attainment); *Padma-asana* (lotus posture); *Svastika-asana* (auspicious posture); *Simha-asana* (lion posture), or sometimes *Bhadra-asana* (prosperity posture). The best yogi is he who ever sits without effort in *Siddha-asana*. Cf. *Bhagavad Gita*. 6.11-12.

II.48. When posture has been mastered the yogi is not disturbed by the pairs of opposites, such as heat and cold.

Besides postures, three types of muscle contractions (*bandhas*), twenty-five gestures (*mudras*), and six purificatory acts (*shat-karma*) are also prescribed.

II.49. Breath control is practised at three stages: in-breathing (*puraka*), out-breathing (*rechaka*), and holding the breath (*kumbhaka*). Though there are many varieties of breath control, nine distinctive types, each having different effects, are mentioned.

50. Its modifications are either external or internal, or motionless, regulated by place, time, and number, either long or short.

51. The fourth is restraining the *Prana* by reflecting on external or internal objects.

52. From that, the covering to the light of the *Chitta* is attenuated.

53. The mind becomes fit for *Dharana*.

5. WITHDRAWAL OF SENSES (*Pratyahara*)

54. The drawing in of the organs is by their giving up their own objects and taking the form of the mind-stuff, as it were.

55. Thence arises supreme control of the organs.

Chapter III: Powers (Vibhuti)

We have now come to the chapter in which the *Yoga* powers are described.

6. CONCENTRATION (*Dharana*)

1. *Dharana* is holding the mind on to some particular object.

7. MEDITATION (*Dhyana*)

2. An unbroken flow of knowledge in that object is *Dhyana*.

8. SUPERCONSCIOUSNESS (*Samadhi*)

3. When that, giving up all forms, reflects only the meaning, it is *Samadhi*.

INNER DISCIPLINE

4. (These) three (when practised) in regard to one object is *Samyama*.

5. By the conquest of that comes light of knowledge.

III.1. Concentration on anything, gross or subtle.
III.2. Meditation on material, luminous or subtle.
III.4. *Samyama:* 'Inner discipline' (Radhakrishnan).

6. That should be employed in stages.

7. These three are more internal than those that precede.

8. But even they are external to the seedless (*Samadhi*).

9. By the suppression of the disturbed impressions of the mind, and by the rise of impressions of control, the mind, which persists in that moment of control, is said to attain the controlling modifications.

10. Its flow becomes steady by habit.

11. Taking in all sorts of objects, and concentrating upon one object, these two powers being destroyed and manifested respectively, the *Chitta* gets the modification called *Samadhi*.

12. The one-pointedness of the *Chitta* is when the impression that is past and that which is present are similar.

13. By this is explained the threefold transformation of form, time and state, in fine or gross matter, and in the organs.

14. That which is acted upon by transformations, either past, present or yet to be manifested, is the qualified.

15. The succession of changes is the cause of manifold evolution.

THE TRANSFORMATION OF MENTAL POWERS

16. By making *Samyama* on the three sorts of changes comes the knowledge of past and future.

17. By making *Samyama* on word, meaning, and knowledge, which are ordinarily confused, comes the knowledge of all animal sounds.

18. By perceiving the impressions, (comes) the knowledge of past life.

19. By making *Samyama* on the signs in another's body, knowledge of his mind comes.

20. But not its contents, that not being the object of the *Samyama*.

21. By making *Samyama* on the form of the body, the perceptibility of the form being obstructed, and the power of manifestation in the eye being separated, the *Yogi's* body becomes unseen.

22. By this the disappearance or concealment of words which are being spoken and such other things, are also explained.

23. *Karma* is of two kinds, soon to be fructified, and late to be fructified. By making *Samyama* on these, or by the signs called

Arishta, portents, the *Yogis* know the exact time of separation from their bodies.

24. By making *Samyama* on friendship, mercy, etc. (I. 33), the *Yogi* excels in respective qualities.

25. By making *Samyama* on the strength of the elephant, and others, their respective strength comes to the *Yogi*.

26. By making *Samyama* on the effulgent light (I. 36) comes the knowledge of the fine, the obstructed and the remote.

27. By making *Samyama* on the sun, (comes) the knowledge of the world.

28. On the moon, (comes) the knowledge of the cluster of stars.

29. On the pole-star, (comes) the knowledge of the motion of the stars.

30. On the navel circle, (comes) the knowledge of the constitution of the body.

31. On the hollow of the throat, (comes) cessation of hunger.

32. On the nerve called *Kurma* (comes) fixity of the body.

33. On the light emanating from the top of the head, sight of the *Siddhas*.

34. Or by the power of *Pratibha* all knowledge.

35. In the heart, knowledge of minds.

36. Enjoyment comes by the non-discrimination of the Soul and *Sattva* which are totally different. The latter whose actions are for another is separate from the self-centred one. *Samyama* on the self-centred one gives knowledge of the *Purusha*.

37. From that arises the knowledge belonging to *Pratibha* and (supernatural) hearing, touching, seeing, tasting, and smelling.

38. These are obstacles to *Samadhi*: but they are powers in the worldly state.

SUPERNATURAL POWERS

39. When the cause of bondage of the *Chitta* has become loosened, the *Yogi*, by his knowledge of its channels of activity (the nerves), enters another's body.

III.33. *Siddhas:* perfected ones, little above ghosts (Vivekananda).

III.34. *Pratibha:* prescience: spontaneous enlightenment from purity (Vivekananda).

40. By conquering the current called *Udana* the Yogi does not sink in water, or in swamps, he can walk on thorns, etc., and can die at will.

41. By the conquest of the current *Samana* he is surrounded by a blaze of light.

42. By making *Samyama* on the relation between the ear and the *Akasa* comes divine hearing.

43. By making *Samyama* on the relation between the *Akasa* and the body and becoming light as cotton wool, etc., through meditation on them, the *Yogi* goes through the skies.

44. By making *Samyama* on the 'real modifications' of the mind, outside of the body, called great disembodiedness, comes disappearance of the covering to light.

45. By making *Samyama* on the gross and fine forms of the elements, their essential traits, the inherence of the *Gunas* in them and on their contributing to the experience of the soul, comes mastery of the elements.

46. From that comes minuteness, and the rest of the powers, 'glorification of the body,' and indestructibleness of the bodily qualities.

47. The 'glorification of the body' is beauty, complexion, strength, adamantine hardness.

48. By making *Samyama* on the objectivity and power of illumination of the organs, on egoism, the inherence of the *Gunas* in them and on their contributing to the experience of the soul, comes the conquest of the organs.

49. From that comes to the body the power of rapid movement like the mind, power of the organs independently of the body, and conquest of nature.

50. By making *Samyama* on the discrimination between *Sattva* and the *Purusha* come omnipotence and omniscience.

III.40. Life manifesting in all the powers of sensation and action is conceived as acting in fivefold. The *prana* (vital breath) moves through the mouth and the nose, and manifests itself within the chest. The *samana* manifests up to the navel. Manifesting down to the soles of the feet is *apana*. Manifesting up to the head is the *udana*. The *vyana* pervades the whole body in every direction. Of these, the *prana* is the chief (Radhakrishnan).

III.42. *Akasa:* the ether.

ISOLATION OR COMPLETE FREEDOM

51. By giving up even these powers comes the destruction of the very seed of evil, which leads to *Kaivalya*.

52. The *Yogi* should not feel allured or flattered by the overtures of celestial beings, for fear of evil again.

53. By making *Samyama* on a particle of time and its precession and succession comes discrimination.

54. Those things which cannot be differentiated by species, sign and place, even they will be discriminated by the above *Samyama*.

55. The saving knowledge is that knowledge of discrimination which simultaneously covers all objects, in all their variations.

56. By the similarity of purity between the *Sattva* and the *Purusha* comes *Kaivalya*.

Chapter IV: Independence (Kaivalya)

DESIRES AND OBJECTS OF THE MIND

1. The *Siddhis* (powers) are attained by birth, chemical means, power of words, mortification or concentration.

2. The change into another species is by the filling in of nature.

3. Good and bad deeds are not the direct causes in the transformations of nature, but they act as breakers of obstacles to the evolutions of nature: as a farmer breaks the obstacles to the course of water, which then runs down by its own nature.

4. From egoism alone proceed the created minds.

5. Though the activities of the different created minds are various, the one original mind is the controller of them all.

6. Among the various *Chittas* that which is attained by *Samadhi* is desireless.

7. Works are neither black nor white for the *Yogis*; for others they are threefold – black, white, and mixed.

8. From these threefold works are manifested in each state only

---

III.51. *Kaivalya:* complete isolation or independence.

those desires (which are) fitting to that state alone. (The others are held in abeyance for the time being.)

9. There is consecutiveness in desires, even though separated by species, space and time, there being identification of memory and impressions.

10. Thirst for happiness being eternal desires are without beginning.

11. Being held together by cause, effect, support, and objects, in the absence of these is its absence.

12. The past and future exist in their own nature, qualities having different ways.

13. They are manifested or fine, being of the nature of the *Gunas*.

14. The unity in things is from the unity in changes.

15. Since perception and desire vary with regard to the same object, mind and object are of different nature.

16. Things are known or unknown to the mind, being dependent on the colouring which they give to the mind.

17. The states of the mind are always known because the lord of the mind, the *Purusha*, is unchangeable.

18. The mind is not self-luminous, being an object.

19. From its being unable to cognize both at the same time.

20. Another cognizing mind being assumed there will be no end to such assumptions and confusion of memory will be the result.

21. The essence of knowledge (the *Purusha*) being unchangeable, when the mind takes its form, it becomes conscious.

22. Coloured by the seer and the seen the mind is able to understand everything.

23. The mind though variegated by innumerable desires acts for another (the *Purusha*), because it acts in combination.

COMPLETE ISOLATION

24. For the discriminating the perception of the mind as Atman ceases.

25. Then bent on discriminating, the mind attains the previous state of *Kaivalya* (isolation).

26. The thoughts that arise as obstructions to that are from impressions.

27. Their destruction is in the same manner as of ignorance, egoism. etc., as said before (II.10).

28. Even when arriving at the right discriminating knowledge of the essences, he who gives up the fruits, unto him comes as the result of perfect discrimination, the *Samadhi* called the cloud of virtue.

29. From that comes cessation of pains and works.

30. Then knowledge, bereft of covering and impurities, becoming infinite, the knowable becomes small.

31. Then are finished the successive transformations of the qualities, they having attained the end.

32. The changes that exist in relation to moments, and which are perceived at the other end (at the end of a series) are succession.

33. The resolution in the inverse order of the qualities, bereft of any motive of action for the *Purusha*, is *Kaivalya*, or it is the establishment of the power of knowledge in its own nature.

SANKARA
VEDANTA SUTRA BHASHYA
[VEDANTA SUTRA COMMENTARY]

(Sanskrit, *c.* A.D. 800)

In the long and continuous evolution and re-expression of philosophic thought in India, the *Vedas* have always remained the fountainhead from which all other streams and rivers have flown. Yet the manner in which generations of thinkers have expounded the visions of Vedic *rishis* has differed from age to age. In the first instance, the seminal ideas in the *Vedas* were developed in the earliest metaphysical dialogues of the *Upanishads*, also called the *Vedanta*. In subsequent centuries a vast body of literature grew out of these sources, examining various phases of human activity, and these writings were classified as *Sastras* (Sciences). It soon became necessary to systematize and codify the ever-increasing knowledge and capsule the essential thoughts in concise statements, and hold them together like beads in a string. Such cryptic aphorisms were called *Sutras*. Thus Upanishadic thought, after centuries of scholarly elaboration, was crystallized in Badarayana's *Vedanta Sutra* (Sanskrit. *c.* 500 B.C.), consisting of 555 sutras. This is also called *Brahma Sutra*, since it deals with the doctrine of Brahman.

The *Sutras* remained meaningful in their compressed form for a long time, but, as time passed, subsequent generations found them more and more difficult to understand. Consequently, there was need to explain them, which in turn gave rise to an ever-growing stream of commentaries. Thus the *Sutras* came to occupy a central position in the Indian stream of thought: on the one hand they summarized earlier investigations and inquiries, and, on the other, they supported endless interpretations and explanations. It is at this stage of development that a number of outstanding commentators wrote their scholarly works and established schools of philosophy. The profoundest and the most influential among them is Sankara (A.D. 788–820), also called Sankar-acharya.

In his writings, Sankara expounded the well-known *Advaita* (nondualistic) philosophy, unrivalled for its boldness, depth, and subtlety of speculation. If Vedanta continues to be the dominant philosophical thought not only in India but even among contemporary Existentialist thinkers, the credit is mainly due to the genius of Sankara and his illuminating exposition of the innermost core of India's most ancient spirito-philosophic heritage. His brilliant *Bhashya* had the one avowed aim of explicating the Truth as revealed in the *Upanishads* by demonstrating that whatever is, is in reality One, and that there is cosmic unity in universal diversity. The notions of multiplicity that an individual confronts are due to the central fact that *atman*, which in essence is *Brahman*, allows itself to be superimposed on by a concept of existential individuality and thus creates subject–object relations. Because of this superimposition, an individual's perception of many aspects of the Truth (*Saguna-Brahman*) are confused with the Truth itself, which is non-conceptual (*Nirguna-Brahman*). The non-discrimination between relative and absolute Truth resulting from the superimposition of individuality on the *atman* is called the *Maya*.

Consequently, an unenlightened individual is unable to look through and beyond this veil of *Maya* (a kind of mental fog!); because the *atman*, instead of recognizing itself to be *Brahman*, blindly identifies itself with its adjuncts, and seeks its self in the body and its organs, thus becoming subject to duality. The liberation (*Moksha*) from such *Maya* could come only through unitive knowledge in the realization of the Truth (*sat*) that the *atman* is *Brahman*, that underlying the diversity of the universe is a non-dual unitary principle. If one lives and acts in this simultaneous apprehension of one's universal and existential relation, one will achieve the peace (*shanti*) that passes beyond understanding. Sankara's *advaita* (monistic) philosophy thus calls for visionary comprehension of Reality simultaneously on two levels, the relative and the existential, and the Absolute and the Eternal.

The extract included here is Sankara's Introduction to his *Bhashya* or Commentary on Badarayana's *Vedanta Sutra*. The text is taken from the translation by George Thibaut, *The Vedanta Sutras of Badarayana with the Commentary by Sankara*, Vols. 34 and 38 in the Sacred Books of the East Series, Oxford: Clarendon Press, 1890 and 1896; reprinted New York: Dover Publications, 1962 (T.994 and T.995). The Introduction is in Vol. 34, pp. 3–9.

III.22   SANKARA
VEDANTA SUTRA BHASHYA
[VEDANTA SUTRA COMMENTARY]

Sankara's Introduction

—

FIRST ADHYAYA

FIRST PADA

REVERENCE TO THE AUGUST VASUDEVA!

It is a matter not requiring any proof that the object and the subject whose respective spheres are the notion of the 'Thou' (the Non-Ego) and the 'Ego', and which are opposed to each other as much as darkness and light are, cannot be identified. All the less can their respective attributes be identified. Hence it follows that it is wrong to super-impose upon the subject – whose Self is intelligence, and which has for its sphere the notion of the Ego – the object whose sphere is the notion of the Non-Ego, and the attributes of the object, and vice versa to superimpose the subject and the attributes of the subject on the object. In spite of this it is on the part of man a natural procedure – which has its cause in wrong knowledge – not to distinguish the two entities (object and subject) and their respective attributes, although they are absolutely distinct, but to superimpose upon each the charac-teristic nature and the attributes of the other, and thus, coupling the Real and the Unreal, to make use of expressions such as 'That am I', 'That is mine'. – But what have we to understand by the term 'superimposition'? – The apparent presentation, in the form of remembrance, to consciousness of something previously observed, in some other thing.

Some indeed define the term 'superimposition' as the super-imposition of the attributes of one thing on another thing. Others, again, define superimposition as the error founded on the non-apprehension of the difference of that which is superimposed from that on which it is superimposed. Others, again, define it as the fictitious assumption of attributes contrary to the nature of that thing on which something else is superimposed. But all these definitions agree in so far as they represent superimposition as the apparent presentation of the attributes of one thing in another thing. And therewith agrees also the popular view which is exemplified by expressions such as the following: 'Mother-of-pearl appears like silver', 'The moon although one only appears as if she were double'. But how is it possible that on the interior Self which itself is not an object there should be superimposed objects and their attributes? For every one superimposes an object only on such other objects as are placed before him (i.e. in contact with his sense-organs), and you have said before that the interior Self which is entirely disconnected from the idea of the Thou (the Non-Ego) is never an object. It is not, we reply, non-object in the absolute sense. For it is the object of the notion of the Ego, and the interior Self is well known to exist on account of its immediate (intuitive) presentation. Nor is it an exceptionless rule that objects can be superimposed only on such other objects as are before us, i.e. in contact with our sense-organs; for non-discerning men superimpose on the ether, which is not the object of sensuous perception, dark-blue colour.

Hence it follows that the assumption of the Non-Self being superimposed on the interior Self is not unreasonable.

This superimposition thus defined, learned men consider to be Nescience (*avidya*), and the ascertainment of the true nature of that which is (the Self) by means of the discrimination of that (which is superimposed on the Self), they call knowledge (*vidya*). There being such knowledge (neither the Self nor the Non-Self) are affected in the least by any blemish or (good) quality produced by their mutual superimposition. The mutual superimposition of the Self and the Non-Self, which is termed Nescience, is the presupposition on which they base all the practical distinctions – those made in ordinary life as well as those laid down by the Veda – between means of knowledge, objects of knowledge (and knowing persons), and all scriptural texts, whether they are concerned with injunctions and prohibitions (of meritorious and non-meritorious actions), or with final release. – But how can the means of right knowledge such as perception, inference, etc., and scriptural texts have for their object that which is dependent on Nescience? – Because, we reply, the means of right knowledge cannot operate unless there be a knowing personality, and because the existence of the latter depends on the erroneous notion that the body, the senses, and so on, are identical with, or belong to, the Self of the knowing person. For without the employment of the senses, perception and the other means of right knowledge cannot operate. And without a basis (i.e. the body) the senses cannot act. Nor does anybody act by means of a body on which the nature of the Self is not superimposed. Nor can, in the absence of all that, the Self which, in its own nature is free from all contact, become a knowing agent. And if there is no knowing agent, the means of right knowledge cannot operate (as said above). Hence perception and the other means of right knowledge, and the Vedic texts have for their object that which is dependent on Nescience. (That human cognitional activity has for its presupposition the superimposition described above), follows also from the non-difference in that respect of men from animals. Animals, when sounds or other sensible qualities affect their sense of hearing or other senses, recede or advance according as the idea derived from the sensation is a comforting or disquieting one. A cow, for instance, when she sees a man approaching with a raised stick in his hand, thinks that he wants to beat her, and therefore moves away; while she walks up to a man who advances with some fresh grass in his hand. Thus men also – who possess a higher intelligence – run away when they see strong fierce-looking fellows drawing near with shouts and brandishing swords; while they confidently approach persons of contrary appearance and behaviour. We thus see that men and animals follow the same course of procedure with reference to the means and objects of knowledge. Now it is well known that the procedure of animals bases on the non-distinction (of Self and Non-Self); we therefore conclude that, as they present the same appearances, men also – although distinguished by superior intelligence – proceed with regard to perception and so on, in the same way as animals do; as long, that is to say, as the mutual superimposition of Self and Non-Self lasts. With reference again to that kind of activity which is founded on the Veda (sacrifices and the like), it is true indeed that the reflecting man who is qualified to enter on it, does so not without knowing that the Self has a relation to another world; yet that qualification does not depend on the knowledge, derivable from the Vedanta-texts, of the true nature of the Self as free from all wants, raised above the distinctions of the Brahmana and Kshatriya-classes and so on, transcending transmigratory existence. For such knowledge is useless and even contradictory to the claim (on the part of sacrificers, etc., to perform certain actions and enjoy their fruits). And before such knowledge of the Self has arisen, the Vedic texts continue in their operation, to have for their object that which is dependent on Nescience. For such texts as the following, 'A Brahmana is to sacrifice', are operative only on the supposition that on the Self are superimposed particular conditions such as caste, stage of life, age, outward circumstances, and so on. That by superimposition we have to understand the notion of something in some other thing we have already explained. (The superimposition of the Non-Self will be understood more definitely from the following examples.) Extra-personal attributes are superimposed on the Self, if a man considers himself sound and entire, or the contrary, as long as his wife, children, and so on are sound and entire or not. Attributes of the body are superimposed on the Self, if a man thinks of himself (his Self) as stout, lean, fair, as standing, walking, or jumping. Attributes of the sense-organs, if he thinks 'I am mute, or deaf, or one-eyed, or blind.' Attributes of the internal organ when he considers himself subject to desire, intention, doubt, determination, and so on. Thus the producer of the notion of the Ego (i.e. the internal organ) is superimposed on the interior Self, which, in reality, is the witness of all the modifications of the internal organ, and vice versa the interior Self, which is the witness of everything, is superimposed on the internal organ, the senses, and so on. In this way there goes on this natural beginning – and endless superimposition, which appears in the form of wrong conception, is the cause of individual souls appearing as agents and enjoyers (of the results of their actions), and is observed by every one.

With a view to freeing one's self from that wrong notion which is the cause of all evil and attaining thereby the knowledge of the absolute unity of the Self the study of the Vedanta-texts is begun. That all the Vedanta-texts have the mentioned purport we shall show in this so-called Sariraka-mimamsa.

Indian drama, like any other world drama, had its origins in ancient
religious ceremonies and gradually became secular entertainment in the
classical period. During this evolution, theatrical presentations were
basically confined to themes derived from Vedic myths and epic
legends, with considerable emphasis placed on their religious over-
tones. At the beginning of the classical period, however, Bhasa (third
century A.D.) attempted to adopt for dramatic purposes material from
recent history and contemporary society, in addition to the traditional
sources. Thus, his plays *The Minister's Vows* (*Pratijna Yaugandha-
rayanam*) and *The Vision of Vasavadatta* (*Svapna Vasavadattam*) were
based on stories relating to King Udayana of Vatsa, while another
play, *Charudatta in Poverty* (*Daridra Carudattam*), portrayed the life
of his time. Of these, *The Vision of Vasavadatta* is an outstanding play
in which the author skilfully blends dramatic conventions and poetic
embellishments, and delineates delicate sentiment.

By the time Bhasa wrote the plays, theatrical tradition had evolved
techniques and established dramatic conventions which were systematized in Bharata's *Natya Sastra* (*c*. second century B.C.), a treatise on
dramaturgy. According to this work, the purpose of dramatic presentation was to achieve aesthetic bliss. Consequently, the dramatist was
supposed so to construct his plot and present his characters and actions
first to arouse various emotions in the spectators and then to blend
those emotions into a delightful flavour or sentiment, technically called
rasa. This aesthetic sentiment would then balance the onlooker's
emotions (not purge them, as in accordance with the theory of
katharsis) and harmonize his being from within, resulting in his ex-
periencing an unalloyed joy.

The classical dramatists were obviously writing their plays with this
theory of *rasa* in mind. As a result, the presentation of actions depicting violent or excessive emotions (e.g. killing or love-making), or
of actions which would disturb or destroy the harmonious blending of
the emotions, was avoided. For this reason, the Indian theatre never
developed tragedy of the Greek or Renaissance type, for that would be

too disturbing, and, in fact, luxuriating in one emotion to unreasonable excess.

The plot of *The Vision of Vasavadatta* was derived from stories and legends that had become current about the king of Vatsa, a kingdom in the Gangetic valley, with the powerful kingdoms of Magadha to the east and Ujjain to the south. The Vatsa kingdom, with its capital at Kausambi (modern Kosam, near Allahabad), was ruled by Udayana, a perfection of chivalry, and skilful master of the lute. Hearing his reputation, Vasavadatta, the princess of Ujjain (daughter of King Pradyota Mahasena and Queen Angaravati), saw Udayana in a dream and fell in love with him. Mahasena decoyed Udayana to Ujjain and kept him in prison, where he became music teacher to Vasavadatta. When Udayana was set at liberty by the minister, he carried off Vasavadatta from her parents and other suitors and made her his queen.

So devotedly did Udayana come to love Vasavadatta that he neglected the affairs of his state, and spent his days in a village called Lavanaka. When the kingdom was threatened, the faithful Vatsa minister Yaugandharayana decided on a strategy to secure political alliance with the powerful neighbouring King Darsaka of Magadha and at the same time fulfil the prediction of soothsayers that Darsaka's sister, Princess Padmavati, would marry Udayana. The difficulty was that Udayana was hopelessly in love with his own wife. With the consent of Vasavadatta, the minister then played a trick on Udayana. While the king was hunting one day, the royal pavilion was set on fire, and the news was given out that Vasavadatta, who was inside, and minister Yaugandharayana, who allegedly attempted to rescue her, were both consumed by fire. Disguised as a Brahmin, Yaugandharayana then took Vasavadatta (disguised as the Lady of Avanti) to Magadha and left her in the charge of Princess Padmavati. Though Udayana was unconsolable for a time, finally he was persuaded by other ministers to seek Magadha's alliance, since his kingdom was taken over by the usurper Aruni. Darsaka received Udayana kindly and offered him assistance, as well as his sister Padmavati in marriage. Vasavadatta saw her husband betrothed and married to Padmavati. After the marriage, with the help of the king of Magadha, Udayana recovered his Vatsa kingdom and returned to his capital at Kausambi, where the identity of the Lady of Avanti was revealed, the stratagem of Yaugandharayana was explained, and the king and his two wives were happily reconciled to each other and to King Mahasena of Ujjain.

Bhasa's first play, *The Minister's Vow*, deals with Udayana's adventures in Ujjain and his elopement with Vasavadatta. His second play, *The Dream of Vasavadatta*, deals with Udayana's adventures in Magadha. In the second play Bhasa treats of the emotion of love with extraordinary delicacy. The play has some resemblance to Shakespeare's *As You Like It*, in which Rosalind, disguised as Ganymede, sees herself wooed by her lover Orlando and enjoys her situation. Vasavadatta, on the other hand, disguised as the Lady of Avanti, has to live through a situation in which she is required to help another lady to get betrothed and married to her own husband. The Indian attitude to the plurality of wives, instead of leading the characters to a tragic love-triangle, allows the triangle to be comfortably accommodating, and makes it possible for Vasavadatta to have a double vision and double-edged comments in the play.

Commenting on the play, Henry Wells states that *The Dream of Vasavadatta* is a 'highly idealistic work' depicting two women 'who by virtue of their situation are potentially rivals but by virtue of their goodness of heart are true friends. . . . While honouring one queen whom he has newly married, he [Udayana] is haunted by the memory of the other, whom he mistakenly believes to be dead. The play is thus a study in time, memory, reality, and illusion, with a temper at times Proustian.'*

The translation is by A. C. Woolner and Lakshman Sarup, *Thirteen Trivandrum Plays Attributed to Bhasa*, Vol. I, Punjab University Oriental Publication No. 13, London: Oxford University Press, 1930, pp. 39–70.

---

* Henry W. Wells, ed., *Six Sanskrit Plays*, in English translation, Bombay: Asia Publishing House, 1964, p. 4.

BHASA

SVAPNA VASAVADATTAM

[THE VISION OF VASAVADATTA]

(Sanskrit, *c.* A.D. 300)

A DRAMA IN SIX ACTS

Dramatis Personae

(in order of appearance)

Stage-manager, SUTRADHARA – in Prologue only

Two guards in the retinue of Princess Padmavati

YAUGANDHARAYANA, chief minister of Udayana, king of the Vatsas

VASAVADATTA, princess of Ujjain, daughter of King Pradyota-Mahasena and Queen Angaravati, and the first queen of Udayana, supposed to have been burnt alive and brought to Magadha in disguise as the Lady of Avanti

Chamberlain⎱ from Magadha with Princess Padmavati
Maid⎰

PADMAVATI, princess of Magadha, sister of King Darsaka. In the last three acts the second queen of Udayana

Lady hermit

Student of theology

Nurse of the princess of Magadha

Second maid, of the princess of Magadha

Jester (Vasantaka) of King Udayana

UDAYANA, king of the Vatsas

Padminika⎱ maids in attendance on the princess of Magadha
Madhukarika⎰

Chamberlain of the Vatsa king at Kausambi

Vijaya, portress at Kausambi palace

Raibhya, chamberlain from the Avanti court at Ujjain

Vasundhara, nurse of Vasavadatta from Ujjain

PROLOGUE

At the end of the Opening Ceremony,* enter the stage-manager.

STAGE-MANAGER: May the arms of Balarama† protect thee, arms as
fair as the young moon at its rising, given their full vigour by wine,
full of Beauty incarnate, and lovely as Spring.

> [*By paronomasia this verse introduces the names of Udayana,
> Vasavadatta, Padmavati, and Vasantaka.*]

With these words, my lords and gentlemen, I have to announce to
you . . . But what is that? I thought I heard a noise, just as I was
to make my announcement. Well, I must see what it is.

> *Voice behind the scene.*

VOICE: Out of the way, there! Away, sirs, out of the way.

STAGE-MANAGER: So be it. I understand.

> The devoted servitors of the king of Magadha, escorting their
> princess, are sternly driving aside everybody they meet in the
> Grove of Penance. [*Exit.*]

END OF PROLOGUE

ACT I

Forest road near a hermitage. Enter two guards.

GUARDS: Out of the way! Away, sirs, out of the way!

> *Enter Yaugandharayana, disguised as a religious mendicant, and
> Vasavadatta in the garb of a lady of Avanti.*

YAUGANDHARAYANA [*listening*]: What? Even here are people driven
aside? For,

> These grave seniors, dwellers in the hermitage, content with
> woodland fruits and clad in bark, worthy of all respect, are
> being terrified.

> Who is this insolent fellow, this lack-courtesy, made arrogant

---

**Opening Ceremony.* Sanskrit plays usually begin with a benedictory stanza
called *Nandi*, at the end of which the stage-manager enters.

† *Balarama* or *Baladeva:* elder brother of Krishna. He was fair, and a great
lover of wine and merriment.

by fickle fortune, who by his rough commands is turning a
peaceful penance-grove into a village street?*

VASAVADATTA: Who is it, sir, that turns us aside?

YAUGANDHARAYANA: One who turns aside his own soul from
righteousness.

VASAVADATTA: Nay, sir, that is not what I would say.† Am I to be
driven aside?

YAUGANDHARAYANA: Even the gods, lady, are rejected unawares.

VASAVADATTA: Ah! sir, fatigue is not so distressing as this humiliation.

YAUGANDHARAYANA: This is something your Highness has enjoyed
and then given up. It should not trouble you. For,

Aforetime thou also didst obtain thy heart's desire; with the
victory of thy lord thou wilt once more attain an exalted state.
The series of worldly fortunes revolves with the march of time
like the spokes in a wheel.

GUARDS: Out of the way, sirs, out of the way!

Enter the Chamberlain.

CHAMBERLAIN: No, Sambhashaka, no, you must not drive these
people aside. Look you,

Bring no reproach on the King. Show no harshness to the
inmates of a hermitage. These high-minded men make their
home in the forest to escape from the brutalities of a town.

GUARDS: Very well, sir. [*Exeunt.*]

YAUGANDHARAYANA: Why, he seems to be an enlightened person.
[*To Vasavadatta*] Come, child, let us approach him.

VASAVADATTA: As you please, sir.

YAUGANDHARAYANA [*approaching*]: Oh, sir, what is the reason of
this hustling?

---

* Turning a peaceful penance-grove into a village street. Cf. the opening
scene in Kalidasa's *Shakuntala*, where the peaceful Kanwa's hermitage is
disturbed by the coming of King Dushyanta, representing the transition of
gunas from *Sattva* to *Rajas*, leading to *Tamas*.

† *That is not what I would say.* Vasavadatta subtly suggests that both of
them are, in fact, turning their souls from righteousness because of their false
appearance in disguise.

CHAMBERLAIN: Ah! good hermit.

YAUGANDHARAYANA [*aside*]: 'Hermit', of course, is an honourable form of address, but as I am not used to it, it does not please me.

CHAMBERLAIN: Hearken, good sir. Padmavati is here, sister to our great king, named by his parents Darsaka. She has been to visit the queenmother, Mahadevi, who has made her home in a hermitage, and having taken leave of that noble lady, is on her way to Rajagriha.* So today she is pleased to stay in this hermitage. Therefore,

You may fetch from the forest, at your sweet will, holy water, fuel, flowers, and sacred grass. The king's daughter is a friend of piety, she would not wish your pious duties to be hindered. Such is the tradition of her family.

YAUGANDHARAYANA [*aside*]: So this is the Padmavati, princess of Magadha, who, the soothsayers Pushpaka, Bhadraka, and others have predicted, is destined to become the consort of my royal master.

Aversion or respect arise from one's purpose. Because I am so eager to see her wedded to my master, I am inspired with great devotion.

VASAVADATTA [*aside*]: Hearing that she is a princess, I too feel for her a sisterly affection.

Enter Padmavati with her retinue and a maid.

MAID: Come this way, please, princess. Here is the hermitage. Be pleased to enter.

A lady-hermit is discovered, seated.

LADY-HERMIT: Princess, you are most welcome.

VASAVADATTA [*aside*]: This is the princess. Her beauty proclaims indeed her noble birth.

PADMAVATI: Reverend lady, I salute you.

LADY-HERMIT: Long may you live. Come in, my child, come in. A hermitage is indeed the guest's own home.

PADMAVATI: So it is, your reverence. I feel quite at home, and grateful to you for your kind words.

VASAVADATTA [*aside*]: Her words are as sweet as her looks.

---

* *Rajagriha:* capital of Magadha.

LADY-HERMIT [*to the maid*]: My good girl, has no king as yet sought the hand of your blessed sovereign's sister?

MAID: Yes, there is King Pradyota of Ujjain. He has sent an ambassador on behalf of his son.

VASAVADATTA [*aside*]: I am glad to hear it. And now she has become one of my own dear people.

LADY-HERMIT: Such loveliness well deserves this honour. We have heard that both are mighty royal families.

PADMAVATI [*to the Chamberlain*]: Sir, have you found any hermits that will do us the favour of accepting our gifts? Distribute according to their heart's desire and demand by proclamation, what any man would have.

CHAMBERLAIN: As your ladyship desires. Hearken, ye saintly men, dwelling in the hermitage, hearken to my words. Her Highness, the Princess of Magadha, is gratified by your cordial welcome, and invites you to accept her gifts that she may gain religious merit.

Who, then, needs a beggar's bowl? Who requires a robe? Some student whose studies are complete, according to the Rule, what fee would he have to offer his preceptor? The princess, devoted to those that delight in law, requests you as a favour to herself, whatever any one desires let him declare it, what shall be given today and to whom?

YAUGANDHARAYANA [*aside*]: Ah, I see my opportunity.

[*Aloud*] Sir, I ask a boon.

PADMAVATI: Happily my visit to this penance-grove is fruitful.

LADY-HERMIT: Everybody in this hermitage is contented. This must be some stranger.

CHAMBERLAIN: Well, sir, what can we do for you?

YAUGANDHARAYANA: This is my sister. Her husband has gone abroad. My wish is that her Highness would take my sister under her protection for some time. For,

No need have I of wealth, or of worldly joys, or of fine raiment, nor have I donned the orange robe to gain a livelihood. The royal maid is wise and knoweth well the path of duty. She can well protect the virtue of my sister.

VASAVADATTA [*aside*]: So! the noble Yaugandharayana is determined to leave me here. Be it so, he will not act without reflection.

CHAMBERLAIN: Lady! His expectation is great indeed. How can we consent? For,

> Wealth it would be easy to give, or one's life, or the fruit of austerity. Anything else would be easy, but hard is the guarding of a pledge.

PADMAVATI: My lord, after first making our proclamation – what would any one have? – it is improper to hesitate. Whatever he says, must be done.

CHAMBERLAIN: These words are worthy of your Highness.

MAID: Long live the princess, who keeps her word.

LADY-HERMIT: Long life to you, blessed lady!

CHAMBERLAIN: Very well, my lady. [*Approaching Yaugandharayana*] Reverend sir, her Highness accepts the guardianship of your sister.

YAUGANDHARAYANA: I am much indebted to her Highness.

[*To Vasavadatta*] My child! Approach her Highness.

VASAVADATTA [*aside*]: There is no escape. I will go, unfortunate that I am.

PADMAVATI: Yes, come hither. Now you belong to me.

LADY-HERMIT: She looks to me like the daughter of a king.

MAID: You are right, reverend mother. I, too, can see that she has known better days.

YAUGANDHARAYANA [*aside*]: Ah! half my task is ended. Things are turning out just as it was arranged with the other ministers. When my royal master is reinstalled and Vasavadatta is restored to him, her Highness, the princess of Magadha, will be my surety for her. For, indeed,

> Those who first predicted our troubles, foretold that Padmavati was destined to become the consort of my king. On that prophecy I have relied in acting as I did, for fate does not transgress the words of well-tried oracles.

Enter a Student of Theology.

STUDENT [*looking upwards*]: It is midday and I am tired out. Where shall I take a rest? [*Turning about*] Good, there must be a penance-grove nearby, because

> The deer are quietly grazing, free from fear, in a place where they feel safe. All the trees, tended with loving care, have their

branches loaded with fruit and blossom. There is a great wealth of tawny kine, but no fields are tilled on any side. Undoubtedly it is a penance-grove, for this smoke arises from many an altar. I will go in. [*Entering*] Hallo! This person is out of keeping with a hermitage. [*Looking in another direction*] But there are also hermits. There is no harm in proceeding further. Oh! ladies!

CHAMBERLAIN: Come in, sir, with perfect freedom, sir. A hermitage is indeed common to all.

VASAVADATTA: How now!

PADMAVATI: Oho! this lady shuns the sight of strangers. Very well, I must take good care of my ward.

CHAMBERLAIN: Sir, we were here first. Please accept our hospitality to a guest.

STUDENT [*drinks*]: Thank you. Now I am refreshed.

YAUGANDHARAYANA: Sir, whence have you come, whither are you going, and where is your abode?

STUDENT: I will tell you, sir. I am from Rajagriha. In order to specialize in Vedic studies, I took up my abode in Lavanaka; it's a village in the Vatsa country.

VASAVADATTA [*aside*]: Ah! Lavanaka! At the mention of that name my anguish seems renewed.

YAUGANDHARAYANA: And have you completed your studies?

STUDENT: No, not yet.

YAUGANDHARAYANA: If you have not finished your studies, why have you returned?

STUDENT: A terrible catastrophe has happened there.

YAUGANDHARAYANA: What was that?

STUDENT: There was a king there named Udayana.

YAUGANDHARAYANA: I have heard of his Highness. What about him?

STUDENT: He was passionately enamoured of his queen, Vasavadatta, a princess of Avanti.

YAUGANDHARAYANA: Quite possible. What then?

STUDENT: When the king had gone out hunting the village took fire, and she was burnt alive.

VASAVADATTA [*aside*]: Untrue, untrue, I am living still, poor wretch!

YAUGANDHARAYANA: Well, go on.

STUDENT: Then in attempting to rescue her a minister named Yaugandharayana fell into the flames himself.

YAUGANDHARAYANA: Did he really? Well, what then?

STUDENT: Then the king came back, and when he heard the news he
was distracted with grief at their separation, and wanted to end his
life in that very fire. It was all the ministers could do to hold him
back.

VASAVADATTA [*aside*]: Yes, I know my lord's tender feelings for me.

YAUGANDHARAYANA: And then?

STUDENT: The king clasped to his breast the half-burnt ornaments
that had adorned her person and fell down unconscious.

ALL: Alas!

VASAVADATTA [*aside*]: And now I hope the noble Yaugandharayana
is satisfied.

MAID: Princess, this noble lady is in tears.

PADMAVATI: She must be very tender-hearted.

YAUGANDHARAYANA: Quite so, quite so. My sister is tender-hearted
by nature. What happened then?

STUDENT: Then, by degrees, he regained consciousness.

PADMAVATI: Thank goodness, he is alive. The words 'fell down unconscious' took my breath away.

YAUGANDHARAYANA: Well, proceed.

STUDENT: Then the king suddenly got up, his body stained with dust
from rolling on the ground, and burst into lamentation after lamentation. 'Oh! Vasavadatta – Princess of Avanti – Alas, my beloved –
my darling pupil – oh!' and so on and so on. In short,
   No love birds so lament their loss, nor even those that are bereft
   of fairy brides.* Happy the woman who is thus loved by her
   lord: consumed by fire, but by reason of her husband's love not
   consumed by woe.

YAUGANDHARAYANA: But tell me, sir, was none of his ministers at
pains to comfort him?

---

*King Pururava inconsolably lamented the loss of his bride, Nymph
Urvasi. This Vedic legend was made into a play by Kalidasa, *Vikramorvacie*,
or *The Hero and the Nymph*, tr. Sri Aurobindo.

STUDENT: Yes, there was a minister named Rumanvan who did his
very best to console him.
> Like the king he will touch no food, his face is wasted by ceaseless
> weeping. Depressed by sorrow like his lord, he neglects the care
> of his person. Day and night he attends untiring on the king.
> Should the king suddenly depart this life, he also will expire.

VASAVADATTA [*aside*]: Happily my lord is in good hands.

YAUGANDHARAYANA [*aside*]: What a heavy responsibility Rumanvan
has to bear! For,
> My burden has been lightened, his toil is constant. Everything
> depends on him, on whom the king himself depends.

[*Aloud*] Well, sir, by this time is the king consoled?

STUDENT: That I do not know. The ministers left the village, taking
with them – after great difficulty – the king, who was pouring out a
piteous tale. 'Here it was that I laughed with her, here I talked with
her, here I sat with her, here we fell out, and here I passed the night
with her', and so forth. With the departure of the king the village
became desolate like the sky when the moon and stars have set. Then,
I, too, came away.

LADY-HERMIT: He must indeed be a noble king who is praised like
this even by a stranger.

MAID: What think you, princess, will he offer his hand to another
woman?

PADMAVATI [*aside*]: My heart was asking that very question.

STUDENT: Let me take leave of you. I must be going.

BOTH: Go, and fare you well.

STUDENT: Thank you. [*Exit.*]

YAUGANDHARAYANA: Good. I too wish to go if her Highness per-
mits.

CHAMBERLAIN: The holy hermit wishes to depart with your Highness's permission.

PADMAVATI: This gentleman's sister will feel lonely in his absence.

YAUGANDHARAYANA: She is in good hands, she will not repine.
[*To the Chamberlain*] Pray let me go.

CHAMBERLAIN: Very well, we shall meet again.

YAUGANDHARAYANA: I hope so. [*Exit.*]

CHAMBERLAIN: It is time now to go within.

PADMAVATI: Reverend lady, I salute you.

LADY-HERMIT: My child, may you get a husband as good as yourself.

VASAVADATTA: Reverend lady, I too salute you.

LADY-HERMIT: And you also, may you soon find your husband.

VASAVADATTA: I thank you.

CHAMBERLAIN: Come, please, this way. This way, my lady. For now,
The birds have returned to their nests. The hermits have
plunged into the stream. Fires have been lit and are burning
brightly, smoke is spreading in the penance-grove. The sun has
dropped a long way down, gathering his rays together he turns
his chariot and slowly descends on the summit of the western
mountain.

Exeunt omnes.

END OF THE FIRST ACT

ACT II

INTERLUDE

Palace garden at Magadha. Enter a Maid.

MAID: Kunjarika, Kunjarika! Where, oh where is the Princess Padmavati?
What do you say? 'The princess is playing at ball near the jasmine
bower.'* Very good, I shall go to her.   [*Turning and looking around*]
Ah! here comes the princess playing with a ball. The jewels in her
ears are turned upwards; the exertion has spangled her brow with
tiny drops of perspiration, so that fatigue lends a charm to her face.
I will go and meet her.   [*Exit.*]

END OF THE INTERLUDE

---

*She hears a voice off the stage.

Enter Padmavati, playing with a ball accompanied by her retinue and Vasavadatta.

VASAVADATTA: Here is your ball, my dear.

PADMAVATI: Dear lady! Now that is enough.

VASAVADATTA: You have played over long with your ball, my dear. Your hands are quite red, they might belong to somebody else.*

MAID: Play on, princess, play on. Enjoy these charming days of girlhood while you may.

PADMAVATI: What's in your thoughts, dear lady? I think you are laughing at me.

VASAVADATTA: No, no, my dear. You are looking more beautiful than ever today. I am getting a full view as it were of your pretty face.†

PADMAVATI: Away with you! Don't you make fun of me.

VASAVADATTA: Well, I am mute – O daughter-in-law elect of Mahasena!

PADMAVATI: Who, pray, is this Mahasena?

VASAVADATTA: There is a king of Ujjain, named Pradyota, who is called Mahasena on account of the vast size of his army.

MAID: It is not with that king the princess wishes to be related.

VASAVADATTA: Whom does she want, then?

MAID: There is a king of the Vatsas named Udayana. It is of his virtues that the princess is enamoured.

VASAVADATTA [*aside*]: She wants my noble lord as her husband. [*Aloud*] For what reason?

MAID: He is so tender-hearted – that's why.

VASAVADATTA [*aside*]: I know, I know. I, too, fell in love with him like that.

MAID: But, princess, suppose the king is ugly.

VASAVADATTA: No, no. He is very handsome.

PADMAVATI: How do you know that, dear lady?

VASAVADATTA [*aside*]: Partiality to my lord has made me transgress the bounds of propriety. What shall I do now? Yes, I see – [*aloud*] That is what everybody says in Ujjain, my dear.

---

* Suggesting the palms dyed for marriage.

† There is a *double entendre*, suggesting 'a husband's face'.

PADMAVATI: Quite so. He is not, of course, inaccessible to the people of Ujjain, and beauty fascinates the hearts of all.

Enter a Nurse.

NURSE: Victory to the princess! Princess, you are betrothed.

VASAVADATTA: To whom, good lady?

NURSE: To Udayana, the king of the Vatsas.

VASAVADATTA: Is he in good health, that king?

NURSE: He arrived here quite well, and the princess is betrothed to him.

VASAVADATTA: Alack-a-day!

NURSE: Alack-a-day! Why, what's the matter?

VASAVADATTA: Oh, nothing. His grief was so great, and now he is indifferent.

NURSE: Madam, the hearts of great men are ruled by the Sacred Scriptures, and are therefore easy to console.

VASAVADATTA: Good lady, tell me, did he choose her himself?

NURSE: Oh, no. He came here on some other business; when our king observed his nobility, wisdom, youth, and beauty, he offered her hand of his own accord.

VASAVADATTA [*aside*]: Just so. Thus my lord is without reproach.

Enter another Maid.

SECOND MAID: Make haste, madam. Our queen declares that the conjunction of stars is auspicious today, and the nuptial celebrations must take place this very day.

VASAVADATTA [*aside*]: The more they hasten, the deeper the gloom in my heart.

NURSE: Come, your Highness, come.

Exeunt omnes.

END OF THE SECOND ACT

ACT III

Palace Garden. Enter Vasavadatta, deep in thought.

VASAVADATTA: I have left Padmavati in the ladies' court, with its festive wedding crowd of women, and have come here alone to this pleasure garden. Here I can give vent to the sorrow which fate has laid upon me. [*Walking about*] Alas! I am undone. Even my noble lord now belongs to another woman. Let me sit down. [*Sits down*] Blessed indeed is the Love-bird.* Parted from her mate she ceases to live. But I cannot escape from life. Miserable that I am, I live on in the hope of seeing him again.

    Enter a Maid carrying flowers.

MAID: Where has the noble lady of Avanti gone? [*Turning and looking around*] Ah, there she is, sitting on a stone bench under the *priyangu* creeper. There she sits, wearing a graceful garment unadorned, her mind intent on distant thoughts, looking like a digit of the moon obscured by mist. I will go up to her. [*Approaching*] Noble lady of Avanti, I have been seeking you for ever so long.

VASAVADATTA: What for?

MAID: What our queen says is this: 'The lady comes from a noble family, she is kind and skilful. So let her plait this wedding garland.'

VASAVADATTA: And for whom is it to be made?

MAID: For our princess.

VASAVADATTA [*aside*]: Must I do even this? The gods are indeed cruel.

MAID: Madam, there is not time now to think of other things. The bridegroom is taking his bath in the inlaid room, so please plait the garland quickly.

VASAVADATTA [*aside*]: I can think of nothing else. [*Aloud*] My good girl, have you seen the bridegroom?

MAID: Yes, I have seen him. That was through affection for the princess and my own curiosity.

VASAVADATTA: What is he like?

MAID: Oh, madam, I tell you, I never saw any one like him.

VASAVADATTA: Well, tell me, tell me, my dear, is he handsome?

MAID: One might say the god of Love himself, without the bow and arrows.

VASAVADATTA: Thanks, that will do.

MAID: Why do you stop me?

VASAVADATTA: It is improper to listen to any one singing the praises of another woman's husband.

---

*Lit. female 'cakravaka', symbol of conjugal fidelity.

399

MAID: Then please finish the garland as quickly as you can.

VASAVADATTA: I shall do it at once. Give me the flowers.

MAID: Here they are. Please take them.

VASAVADATTA [*turns out the basket and examines the flowers*]: What is the name of this plant?

MAID: It is called 'Lords and Ladies'.*

VASAVADATTA [*aside*]: I must work in lots of this for myself and Padmavati. [*Aloud*] What do you call this flower?

MAID: Oh, that is 'Old Wife's Bane'.†

VASAVADATTA: We needn't use that one.

MAID: Why not?

VASAVADATTA: His wife is dead, so it wouldn't be any use.
  Enter another Maid.

SECOND MAID: Please make haste, madam. The ladies of living lords are conducting the bridegroom to the ladies' court.

VASAVADATTA: There, it's ready, I tell you. Take it.

FIRST MAID: How beautiful! Madam, I must be off.
  Exeunt the two Maids.

VASAVADATTA: She is gone. Alas! All is over.
  My noble lord is now another's. Heaven help me! I'll to bed; it
  may soothe my pain, if I can sleep. [*Exit.*]

END OF THE THIRD ACT

ACT IV

INTERLUDE

Palace at Magadha. Enter the Jester.

JESTER [*joyfully*]: Ha! ha! How good to see the delightful time of the auspicious and welcome marriage of His Highness the king of the Vatsas. Who could have known that after being hurled into such a whirlpool of misfortune we should rise again to the surface? Now we live in palaces, we bathe in the tanks of the inner court, we eat

---

*Lit. 'antidote to widowhood'. † Lit. 'co-wife's ruin'.

dainty and delicious dishes of sweetmeats – in short, I feel myself to be in Paradise, except that there are no nymphs to keep me company. But there is one great drawback. I do not digest my food at all well. Even on the downiest couches I cannot sleep, for I seem to see the Wind and Blood disease circling round. Bah! there is no happiness in life, if you are full of ailments, or without a good breakfast.

   Enter a Maid.

MAID: Wherever has the worthy Vasantaka got to?

   [*Turning and looking around*] Why, here he is! [*Going up to him*] Oh, Master Vasantaka, what a search I have had looking for you!

JESTER [*with a leer*]: And why were you searching for me, my dear?

MAID: Our queen says, 'hasn't the bridegroom finished his bath?'

JESTER: Why does she want to know?

MAID: So that I may bring him a garland and unguents, of course.

JESTER: His Highness has bathed. You may bring everything except food.

MAID: Why do you bar food?

JESTER: Unfortunate that I am, like the rolling of cuckoo's eyes ... my stomach is like that.

MAID: May you ever be as you are!

JESTER: Off with you! I will go and attend on his Highness.

   Exeunt.

END OF INTERLUDE

Palace garden.
   Enter Padmavati with her retinue and Vasavadatta dressed as a lady of Avanti.

MAID: What has brought your ladyship to this pleasure-garden?

PADMAVATI: My dear, I want to see if the *seoli** clusters have flowered or not.

MAID: Yes, princess, they have, with blossoms like pendants of pearls interset with coral.

PADMAVATI: If that is so, my dear, why do you delay?

---

* *Seoli*, a modern form of *Sephalika*, is Nyctanthes Arbor Tristis – with a white and orange flower which falls in the morning (A. C. Woolner).

MAID: Won't your ladyship sit on this stone bench for a moment while I gather some flowers?

PADMAVATI: Shall we sit here, dear lady?

VASAVADATTA: Let us do so.

Both sit down.

MAID [*after gathering some flowers*]: Oh, look, princess, look! My hands are full of the *seoli* blossoms, with their half-way hose of *realgar.**

PADMAVATI [*looking at the flowers*]: See, lady, how brilliant are the colours of these flowers!

VASAVADATTA: Yes, how beautiful they are.

MAID: Princess, shall I pick any more?

PADMAVATI: No, no, my dear, no more.

VASAVADATTA: Why do you stop her, my dear?

PADMAVATI: If my noble lord should come here and see this abundance of blossom, I should be so honoured.

VASAVADATTA: Why, my dear, are you so much in love with your husband?

PADMAVATI: I don't know, lady, but when he is away from me I feel wretched.

VASAVADATTA [*aside*]: How difficult it is for me. Even she speaks in this strain.

MAID: How delicately the princess has told us that she loves her husband.

PADMAVATI: I have just one doubt.

VASAVADATTA: And what is that?

PADMAVATI: Was my noble lord as much to Vasavadatta as he is to me?

VASAVADATTA: Nay, more.

PADMAVATI: How do you know?

VASAVADATTA [*aside*]: Ah! Partiality to my noble lord has made me transgress the bounds of propriety. I know what I will say. [*Aloud*] Had her love been less, she would not have forsaken her own people.

PADMAVATI: Possibly not.

---

*The blossoms have orange stems, which are compared to puttees the colour of red arsenic.

MAID: Princess, you might gently suggest to your husband, that you too would like to learn to play the lute.*

PADMAVATI: I did speak to him about it.

VASAVADATTA: And what did he say?

PADMAVATI: He said nothing. He heaved a deep sigh, and became silent.

VASAVADATTA: What did that mean, do you think?

PADMAVATI: I think the memory of the noble Vasavadatta's virtues came over him, but out of courtesy he restrained his tears in my presence.

VASAVADATTA [*aside*]: How happy I should be if that were true!
    Enter the King and the Jester.

JESTER: Aha! how pretty the garden looks with a thin sprinkling of *bandhujiva* flowers, fallen while they were being gathered. This way, my lord.

KING: Very well, my dear Vasantaka, here I come.

Once in Ujjain, when the unimpeded vision of Avanti's princess brought me to that condition that you know of, the God of Love let fly at me with all his five arrows. Of those I still bear the pain in my heart, and now I am wounded again. If Cupid has only five arrows, what is this sixth dart he has discharged at me?

JESTER: Where has Lady Padmavati gone? Has she gone to the creeper-bower? Or perhaps to the stone seat called the 'Crest of the Hill', which is so strewn with *asana* flowers that it looks as if it were covered with a tiger's skin. Or could she have entered the wood of the Seven-leaved Trees with their powerful pungent scent? Or perhaps she has gone into the wooden pavilion with crowds of birds and beasts painted on the walls. [*Looking up*] Oh, look, your Highness! Do you see this line of cranes advancing steadily along the clear autumn sky, as beautiful as the long white arms of the adored Baladeva?

KING: Yes, comrade, I see it.

Now stretched in an even line, now wide apart; now soaring high, now sinking low, crooked in its twists and turns, as the

---

* Udayana was a master player on the lute. When in captivity he gave lessons to the princess Vasavadatta (see page 385).

group of Seven Rishis.* Bright as a serpent's belly just slipped
from its slough, like a boundary line it cuts the sky in two.

MAID: Look, princess, look at this flock of cranes advancing steadily
in line, as delicately tinted as a garland of pink water-lilies. Oh! the
King!

PADMAVATI: Ah! 'tis my noble lord. Lady, for your sake I shall avoid
seeing my husband. So let us go into this bower of *madhavi* creepers.

VASAVADATTA: Very well.

They do so.

JESTER: Lady Padmavati came here and went away again.

KING: How do you know that?

JESTER: Just look at these *seoli* clusters from which the flowers have
been picked.

KING: Oh, Vasantaka! What a gorgeous flower it is!

VASAVADATTA [*aside*]: That name 'Vasantaka' makes me feel as if I
were at Ujjain again.

KING: Let us sit down, Vasantaka, on this stone seat and wait for
Padmavati.

JESTER: Very well, sir. [*Sits down and gets up again*] The heat of the
scorching autumn sun is unbearable. So let us go into this bower of
madhavi creepers.

KING: All right. Lead the way.

JESTER: Very well. [*Both walk round*]

PADMAVATI: The worthy Vasantaka is bent on spoiling everything.
What shall we do now?

MAID: Princess, shall I keep his Highness away by shaking this hanging creeper swarming with black bees?

PADMAVATI: Yes, do.

Maid does so.

JESTER: Help! help! Keep away, your Highness, keep away!

KING: What is the matter?

JESTER: I am being stung by these damnable bees.

KING: No, no, do not do that. One should never frighten the bees.
Look,

Drowsy with drafts of honey, the bees are humming softly in the

_____
*The constellation of the Great Bear.

close embraces of their love-sick queens. Should our footsteps startle them, like us, they will be parted from their darlings. So let us stay here.

JESTER: Very well.

Both sit down.

MAID: Princess, we are in truth made prisoners.

PADMAVATI: Happily it is my noble lord who sits there.

VASAVADATTA [*aside*]: I am glad to see my noble lord looking so well.

MAID: Princess, the lady's eyes are filled with tears.

VASAVADATTA: The moringa pollen has got into my eyes because of the naughty bees, and made them water.

PADMAVATI: Quite so.

JESTER: Well, now, there is nobody in this pleasure-garden. There is something I want to ask. May I ask you a question?

KING: Yes, if you like.

JESTER: Which do you love best, the lady Vasavadatta that was, or Padmavati of today?

KING: Now why do you put me in such a very difficult position?

PADMAVATI: Oh, my dear; what a difficult position for my noble lord!

VASAVADATTA [*aside*]: And for me, too, unfortunate that I am.

JESTER: Now you must speak frankly. One is dead, the other is nowhere near.

KING: No, my dear fellow, no, I am not going to say anything. You are a chatterer.

PADMAVATI: By so much he has said enough.

JESTER: Oh, I swear truly, I won't tell a soul. My lips are sealed.

KING: No, my friend, I dare not speak.

PADMAVATI: How stupidly indiscreet he is. Even after that he cannot read his heart.

JESTER: What, you won't tell me? If you don't, you shall not stir a single step from the stone seat. Your Highness is now my prisoner.

KING: What, by force?

JESTER: Yes, by force.

KING: We shall see.

JESTER: Forgive me, your Highness. I conjure you in the name of our friendship to tell me the truth.

KING: No escape. Well listen,
Padmavati I much admire for her beauty, charm, and virtue, and yet she has not won my heart still bound to Vasavadatta.

VASAVADATTA [*aside*]: So may it ever be. This is my reward for all my suffering. My living here unknown is beginning to be delightful.

MAID: Oh, princess, his Highness is very discourteous.

PADMAVATI: My dear, don't say that. My noble lord is courteous indeed, for even now he remembers the virtues of the noble Vasavadatta.

VASAVADATTA: My dear child, your words are worthy of your birth.

KING: Well, I have spoken. Now you must tell me, which is your favourite: Vasavadatta that was, or Padmavati of today?

PADMAVATI: My noble lord is mimicking Vasantaka.

JESTER: What is the use of my chatter! I have the greatest admiration for both their ladyships.

KING: Idiot. You made me tell, and now you are afraid to speak.

JESTER: What, would you force me?

KING: Why, yes, of course.

JESTER: Then you will never hear it.

KING: Forgive me, mighty brahman, speak of your own free will.

JESTER: Now you shall hear. Lady Vasavadatta I greatly admired. Lady Padmavati is young, beautiful, gentle, free from pride, gently spoken, and very courteous. But there is one other great virtue. Vasavadatta used to come to me with delicious dishes, saying, 'Where has the good Vasantaka got to?'

VASAVADATTA [*aside*]: Bravo, Vasantaka. You must remember this.

KING: Very well, Vasantaka. I shall tell all this to Queen Vasavadatta.

JESTER: Alas, Vasavadatta! Where is Vasavadatta? She is dead long
ago.

KING [*sadly*]: It is true, Vasavadatta is no more.
By your raillery you confused my mind, and by force of former
usage those words slipped out.

PADMAVATI: This was a delightful conversation, but now the
wretch has spoiled it all.

VASAVADATTA [*aside*]: Well, well, I am consoled. How sweet it is to
hear these words without being seen.

JESTER: Be of good cheer, your Highness. Fate cannot be gainsaid.
It is so, and that's all about it.

KING: My dear fellow, you do not understand my condition. For,
A deeply-rooted passion it is hard to abandon, by constant
recollection the pain is renewed. This is the way of the world that
the mind must cancel its debt with tears to gain tranquillity.

JESTER: His Highness's face is wet with tears. I will get some water
to wash it.

PADMAVATI: Madam, my lord's face is hidden in a veil of tears. Let
us slip away.

VASAVADATTA: Yes, let us go. Nay, you stay here. It is not right
for you to go and leave your husband unhappy. I will go alone.

MAID: The lady is right. You should go to him, Princess.

PADMAVATI: What do you say? Shall I go?

VASAVADATTA: Yes, dear, do. [*Exit.*]
    Enter the Jester.

JESTER [*with water in a lotus leaf*]: Why, here is Lady Padmavati.

PADMAVATI: What is it, my good Vasantaka?

JESTER: This is that, that is this.

PADMAVATI: Speak out, sir, speak.

JESTER: Lady, the pollen of the moringa flowers, carried by the wind,
has got into his Highness's eyes, and his face is wet with tears.
Please take him this water to wash his face.

PADMAVATI: [*aside*]: Oho! like master, like man, how courteous he is. [*Approaching the king*] Greeting, my lord. Here is some water for your face.

KING: Eh, what, Padmavati? [*Aside to Jester*] What's this, Vasantaka?

JESTER: It's like this. [*Whispers in his ear*]

KING: Bravo, Vasantaka, bravo. [*Sipping water*] Padmavati, pray be seated.

PADMAVATI: As my lord commands. [*Sits down*]

KING: Padmavati,

> The motes of the moringa blossoms, agitated by the breeze, fair lady, have bathed my face in tears.

[*Aside*]

> She's but a girl and newly wed, should she learn the truth it would distress her. Courage she has, it is true, but women are by nature easily alarmed.

JESTER: This afternoon his Majesty the King of Magadha will, as usual, receive his friends, giving yourself the place of honour. Courtesy reciprocating courtesy engenders affection. So it is time for your Highness to make a move.

KING: Yes, indeed. It is a good suggestion. [*Rises*]

> Men of eminent virtues are easily found in this world, as those whose hospitable treatment is unfailing, but it is difficult to find men who duly appreciate these qualities.

Exeunt omnes.

END OF THE FOURTH ACT

ACT V

At Magadha

INTERLUDE

Enter Padminika.

PADMINIKA: Madhukarika, oh, Madhukarika, come here quick.
  Enter Madhukarika.

MADHUKARIKA: Here I am, my dear, what do you want me to do?

PADMINIKA: Don't you know, my dear, that Princess Padmavati is ill with a bad headache?

MADHUKARIKA: Alas!

PADMINIKA: Run quick, my dear, and call Madam Avantika. Only tell her the princess has a headache, and she will come of her own accord.

MADHUKARIKA: But, my dear, what good can she do?

PADMINIKA: Why, she will tell the princess pleasant stories and drive away the pain.

MADHUKARIKA: Very likely. Where have you made up the princess's bed?

PADMINIKA: It is spread in the sea-room.*
Now you go. I shall look for the good Vasantaka, to inform his Highness.

MADHUKARIKA: Very well. [*Exit*]

PADMINIKA: Now I will look for the good Vasantaka.
Enter the Jester.

JESTER: The heart of the illustrious king of the Vatsas was depressed by separation from his queen, but now on this auspicious and extremely joyful occasion, fanned as it were by this marriage with Padmavati, it burns the more fiercely with the flame of the fire of love. [*Observing Padminika*] Hallo! here's Padminika. Well, Padminika, what's the news?

PADMINIKA: My good Vasantaka, don't you know that Princess Padmavati has a bad headache?

JESTER: Truly, lady, I did not know.

PADMINIKA: Well, let his Highness know about it. Meanwhile, I will hurry up with the ointment for her forehead.

JESTER: Where has Padmavati's bed been made up?

PADMINIKA: It is spread in the sea-room.

JESTER: Well, you had better be off. I will tell his Highness.
Exeunt ambo.

END OF THE INTERLUDE

---

*Samudra-grha. Perhaps a room built out into a lake, or a room with jets of water.

Enter the King.

KING: Once again, with the lapse of time, I have taken up the burden of wedlock, but my thoughts fly back to Avanti's daughter,
worthy daughter of a worthy sire; to her, whose slender frame
was consumed by the fire at Lavanaka, like a lotus-plant blasted
by the frost.

Enter the Jester.

JESTER: Quick, your Highness, quick.

KING: What is the matter?

JESTER: Lady Padmavati has a bad headache.

KING: Who told you?

JESTER: Padminika told me.

KING: Alas!
Now that I have won another bride, endowed with grace and
beauty, and possessed of all the virtues, my grief is somewhat
dulled, yet after my experience of woe, still sick with the former
pain, I anticipate the like for Padmavati.

Where is Padmavati?

JESTER: They put her bed in the sea-room.

KING: Then show me the way.

JESTER: Come this way, your Highness. [*Both walk round*] This is the
sea-room. Be pleased to enter.

KING: You go in first.

JESTER: Very well, sir. [*Enters*] Help, help. Back, your Highness,
stand back.

KING: What is the matter?

JESTER: Here's a snake wriggling on the floor. Its body is visible in
the light of the lamp.

KING [*entering, has a look round, and smiles*]:
Ha! the idiot thinks he sees a snake,*

---

*Snake and *garland:* Indian philosophers use the imagery of rope being
mistaken for a snake in dim light as an example of superimposing one idea
over the other, thus causing illusion or *Maya.* In such an illusion, man
generally takes the manifested world to be real. The dramatist skilfully
prepares for the 'double vision' of the king in this scene.

For the dangling garland dropped from the portal arch, and lying stretched along the ground, thou dost suppose, poor fool, to be a serpent. Turned over by the light evening breeze it does move somewhat like a snake.

JESTER [*looking closely*]: Your Highness is right. It is not a snake. [*Entering and looking round*] Lady Padmavati must have been here and gone away.

KING: She cannot have come, comrade.

JESTER: How do you know that?

KING: What need of knowing? Look,

The bed has not been pressed, it is as smooth as when made. There is no crinkle in the counterpane, the pillow is not rumpled nor stained with medicines for an aching head. There is no decoration to divert a patient's gaze. Those who are brought to bed by illness are not likely to leave it so soon.

JESTER: Then you might sit down on the bed for a while and wait for her ladyship.

KING: Very well. [*Sits down*] I feel dreadfully sleepy, old fellow. Tell me a story.

JESTER: I will tell you a story, but your Highness must say 'Oh!' or something to show you are listening.

KING: Very well.

JESTER: There is a town called Ujjain. There there are most delightful swimming baths.

KING: What, Ujjain did you say?

JESTER: If you do not like this story, I will tell you another.

KING: Comrade, it is not that I do not like it. But

I remember the daughter of Avanti's king. At the moment of leaving she thought of her kinsfolk, and through affection a tear welled up, which, after clinging to the corner of her eye, fell on my breast.

Moreover,

Time and again during her lessons she would fix her gaze on me and, dropping the quill, her hand would go on playing in the air.

JESTER: All right. I will tell you another.

There is a town called Brahmadatta, where there was a king named Kampilya.

KING: What's that? What did you say?

   Jester repeats what he has just said.

KING: Idiot! You should say King Brahmadatta and Kampilya City.

JESTER: Is Brahmadatta the king and Kampilya the city?

KING: Yes, that's right.

JESTER: Well, then, just wait a moment, while I get it pat. 'King
   Brahmadatta, Kampilya City.' [*Repeats this several times*]
   Now listen.
   Why, his Highness is fast asleep. It is very chilly at this hour. I
   will go and fetch my cloak. [*Exit*]

   Enter Vasavadatta in Avanti dress and a Maid.

MAID: Come this way, lady. The princess is suffering from a severe
   headache.

VASAVADATTA: I am so sorry. Where has her bed been made up?

MAID: It is spread in the sea-room.

VASAVADATTA: Well, do you lead the way.

   Both walk round.

MAID: This is the sea-room. Go in, madam, I will hurry up the
   ointments for her forehead. [*Exit*]

VASAVADATTA: Oh, how cruel are the gods to me.
   Padmavati, who was a source of comfort to my lord in the agony of
   his bereavement, has now fallen ill herself. I will go in. [*Entering
   and looking round*] Ah! how careless the servants are. Padmavati
   is ill and they have left her alone with only a lamp to keep her company. So, she is asleep. I shall sit down. But if I sit elsewhere it
   might look as if I had but little love for her. So I shall sit on this
   same bed. [*Sits down*] Why is it that now I am sitting beside her,
   my heart seems to thrill with joy? Happily her breathing is easy
   and regular. Her headache must have gone. And by leaving me one
   side of the bed she seems to invite me to clasp her in my arms. I
   will lie by her side. [*Proceeds to lie down*]

KING [*talking in his sleep*]: O Vasavadatta.

VASAVADATTA [*starting up*]: Ah! It is my lord and not Padmavati.
   Has he seen me? If so, the elaborate scheme of the noble Yaugandharayana will come to naught.

KING: O daughter of Avanti's king.

VASAVADATTA: Happily my lord is only dreaming. There is no one about. I shall stay a little while and gladden my eyes and my heart.

KING: Dear one, my darling pupil, answer me.

VASAVADATTA: I am speaking, my lord, I am speaking.

KING: Are you displeased?

VASAVADATTA: Oh no! Oh no! Only very miserable.

KING: If you are not displeased, why do you wear no jewels?

VASAVADATTA: What could be better than this?

KING: Are you thinking of Viracika?*

VASAVADATTA [angrily]: O fie. Even here, Viracika!

KING: Then I entreat forgiveness for Viracika.

Stretches out his hands.

VASAVADATTA: I have stayed too long. Some one might see me. I will go. But first I will put back on the bed that hand of his hanging down. [*She does so and exit*]

KING [rising suddenly]: Stay! Vasavadatta, stay! Alas!

Rushing out in my confusion, I struck against a panel of the door and now I have no clear idea whether or no this was really my heart's desire.

Enter the Jester.

JESTER: Ah! Your Highness is awake.

KING: Delightful news! Vasavadatta is alive.

JESTER: Oh, help us! What's this about Vasavadatta? Why she died long ago.

KING: Say not so, my friend,

As I lay sleeping on this couch she wakened me and disappeared. Rumanvan deceived me when he said she perished in the fire.

JESTER: Goodness gracious! but it's impossible, isn't it? I was talking about the swimming baths and you have been thinking of her ladyship, and you must have seen her in a dream.

KING: So then it was only a dream.

If that was a dream, how glorious never to wake again, if this be illusion, long may that illusion last.

JESTER: There is a sylph dwelling in this city named Avantisundari. That's what you must have seen, my dear fellow.

---

*Probably referring to the king's suspected indiscretion with a court lady.

KING: No, no.

At the end of my dream I awoke and saw her face; the eyes strangers to collyrium and the long unbraided locks were those of a lady guarding her virtue.

Beside, see, comrade, see

This arm of mine was closely clasped by the agitated queen. Even now it has not ceased to thrill with joy though it felt her touch only in a dream.

JESTER: Come, now, no futile fancies. Come along, let us go to the ladies' court.

Enter the Chamberlain.

CHAMBERLAIN: Greeting to my noble lord.

King Darsaka, our sovereign lord, sends you these tidings: Rumanvan, the minister of your Highness, has arrived in the vicinity with a large force to attack Aruni.* Likewise my own victorious army, elephants, cavalry, chariots, and infantry, is equipped and ready. Arise, therefore. Moreover,

Your foes are divided. Your subjects, devoted to you by reason of your virtues, have gained confidence. Arrangements are completed to protect your rear when you advance. Whatever is needed to crush the foe, I have provided. Forces have crossed the Ganges, the Vatsa kingdom is in the hollow of your hand.

KING [*rising*]: Very good. Now.

I shall see that Aruni, adept in dreadful deeds and in the battlefield, surging like a mighty ocean with huge elephants and horses, with a lashing spray of arrows on the wing. I will destroy him.

END OF THE FIFTH ACT

---

*Aruni: usurper of Vatsa kingdom.

ACT VI

INTERLUDE

The Palace at Kausambi, capital of Vatsa.

Enter a Chamberlain.

CHAMBERLAIN: What ho, there! Who is on duty at the door of the golden arch?

    Enter Portress.

PORTRESS: Sir, it is I, Vijaya. What do you want me to do?

CHAMBERLAIN: Good woman, to take a message to Udayana, whose glory has increased by the capture of the Vatsa kingdom. Tell him that a chamberlain of the Raibhya clan has come here from the court of Mahasena. Also Vasavadatta's nurse, named Vasundhara, sent by Queen Angaravati. They are both waiting at the gate.

PORTRESS: Sir, this is not the place or time for a porter's message.

CHAMBERLAIN: Not the place or time – how's that?

PORTRESS: Listen, sir. Today some one in the sun-faced* palace was playing on the lute. When my lord heard it he said, 'I seem to hear the notes of Ghoshavati'.†

CHAMBERLAIN: And then?

PORTRESS: Then somebody went and asked where he got that lute. He said he had found it lying in a thicket of reeds on the banks of the Narmada. If it was any use, they could take it to the king. So they brought it, and my lord pressed it to his side and went off in a swoon. When he came to himself, with the tears running down his face, he said, 'Thou art found, Ghoshavati, but her we cannot see.' That, sir, is why the occasion is unsuitable. How can I take your message?

CHAMBERLAIN: My good woman, you must really let him know, for this as it were hangs on to that.

---

  * Perhaps the palace or wing facing the sun.

  † 'Sonorous', the name of his lute.

PORTRESS: I will let him know, sir. Why, here is my lord coming down from the sun-faced palace. I shall tell him here.

CHAMBERLAIN: Yes, do, good woman.

Exeunt.

END OF INTERLUDE

Enter the King and the Jester.

KING: Oh, my lute, whose notes are so sweet to the ear, after reposing in the lap of the queen and resting against her twin bosoms, how camest thou to dwell in that dreadful abode in the wilds, where flocks of birds have fouled thy strings?

How heartless art thou, Ghoshavati, with no memory of thy unhappy mistress:

How she pressed thee to her side as she bore thee on her hip; how when weary she tucked thee softly between her breasts; how she bewailed the loss of me when we were parted; how she smiled and chatted in the intervals of playing.

JESTER: Enough now, don't torment yourself beyond measure.

KING: Say not so, dear friend.

My passion, for a long time dormant, has been awakened by the lute, but the queen, who loved this lute, I cannot see.

Vasantaka, have Ghoshavati refitted with new strings by some skilful artist and bring it back to me at once.

JESTER: As your Highness commands.

Exit, taking the lute.

Enter Portress.

PORTRESS: Greeting, my lord. There has arrived here from the court of Mahasena a chamberlain of the Raibhya clan and also Vasavadatta's nurse, Dame Vasundhara, sent by the Queen Angaravati. They are waiting at the entrance.

KING: Then go and call Padmavati.

PORTRESS: As my lord commands.

KING: Can Mahasena have learned this news so soon?

Enter Padmavati and the Portress.

PORTRESS: This way, Princess.

PADMAVATI: Greeting, my noble lord.

KING: Padmavati, did they tell you? A chamberlain named Raibhya has come from Mahasena with Dame Vasundhara, Vasavadatta's nurse, from Queen Angaravati, and they are waiting outside.

PADMAVATI: My noble lord, I shall be glad to have good news of my relative's family.

KING: It is worthy of you to speak of Vasavadatta's relatives as your own. Padmavati, be seated. Now why do you not sit down?

PADMAVATI: My noble lord, would you have me seated at your side when you receive these people?

KING: What harm is there in that?

PADMAVATI: That your lordship has married again may seem like indifference.

KING: To hide my wife from the view of people who should see her would create a great scandal. So please be seated.

PADMAVATI: As my noble lord commands.
[*Sits down*] My lord, I am rather uneasy as to what the dear parent will say.

KING: Quite so, Padmavati.
My heart is full of misgivings as to what he will say. I stole away his daughter, and I have not kept her safe. Through fickle fortune I have greatly injured my fair name and I am afraid, like a son who has roused his father's wrath.

PADMAVATI: Nothing can be preserved when its time has come.

PORTRESS: The chamberlain and the nurse are waiting at the door.

KING: Bring them in at once.

PORTRESS: As my lord commands. [*Exit*]
Enter the Chamberlain, the Nurse, and the Portress.

CHAMBERLAIN: To visit this kingdom, allied to ours by marriage ties, is a great joy, but when I remember the death of our princess I am filled with sorrow. O Destiny, was it not enough for thee that the kingdom should be seized by foes if the welfare of the queen remained?

PORTRESS: Here is my lord. Approach him, sir.

CHAMBERLAIN [*approaching the king*]: Greeting to your Highness.

NURSE: Greeting, your Highness.

KING [*respectfully*]: Sir,
That king who regulates the rise and fall of royal dynasties on

this earth, that king with whom I craved alliance, tell me, is he well?

CHAMBERLAIN: Why, yes. Mahasena is very well, and he would be informed of the health of everybody here.

KING [*rising from his seat*]: What are the commands of Mahasena?

CHAMBERLAIN: This is worthy of Vaidehi's son. Now pray be seated and listen to Mahasena's message.

KING: As Mahasena commands. [*Sits down*]

CHAMBERLAIN: 'Congratulations on the recovery of your kingdom seized by enemies, for,

There is no energy in those that are weak and faint-hearted – while the glory of kingship is enjoyed as a rule only by those that have energy.'

KING: Sir, it is all due to the might of Mahasena.
For,

Aforetime when he had vanquished me he cherished me with his own sons. His daughter I stole away by force, but have not kept her safe. Now, learning of her decease, he shows me the same affection, for the king is the cause of my regaining the land of the Vatsas, my lawful subjects.

CHAMBERLAIN: That is the message of Mahasena.

The queen's message will be delivered by this lady.

KING: Ah! tell me, nurse.

The holy goddess of the city, chief among the sixteen queens, my mother – so afflicted with grief at my departure – is she in good health?

NURSE: The queen is well, and sends inquiries for the health of your lordship and all that are yours.

KING: The health of all that are mine? Ah, nurse, what sort of health is that?

NURSE: Nay, now, my lord, do not torment yourself beyond measure.

CHAMBERLAIN: Compose yourself, my noble lord.

Though Mahasena's daughter has passed away, she has not ceased to exist, while she is so mourned by her noble lord. But verily whom can any one protect in the hour of death? When the rope breaks, who can hold the pitcher? It is the same law for men and trees: now they grow, and anon they are cut down.

KING: Nay, sir, say not so.

> Mahasena's daughter was my pupil and my beloved queen.
> How could I forget her, even in births to come?

NURSE: Thus saith the queen: 'Vasavadatta has passed away. To me and to Mahasena you are as dear as our Gopala and Palaka, for from the very first we intended you to be our son-in-law. That is why you were brought to Ujjain. Under the pretext of learning the lute we gave her to you, with no ritual fire as witness. In your impetuosity, you carried her off without the celebration of the auspicious nuptial rites. So then we had portraits painted of you and of Vasavadatta on a panel and therewith celebrated the marriage. We send you the portraits,* and hope the sight of them will give you satisfaction.

KING: Ah, how loving and how noble is the message of her Majesty!

> Those words I hold more precious than the conquest of a hundred
> realms. For I am not forgotten in her love, in spite of all my
> transgressions.

PADMAVATI: My lord, I would like to see the portrait of my eldest sister and salute her.

NURSE: Look, princess, look.   [*Shows her the picture.*]

PADMAVATI [*aside*]: Why! It is very much like the Lady Avantika.
[*Aloud*] My lord, is this a good likeness of her ladyship?

KING: Likeness? No, I think it is herself. Oh, alas!

> How could cruel calamity befall this charming loveliness?
> How could fire ravage the sweetness of this face?

PADMAVATI: By looking at my lord's portrait I can tell whether her ladyship's is a good likeness or not.

NURSE: See here, princess.

PADMAVATI [*looking*]: My lord's portrait is so good, I am sure her ladyship's must be a good likeness too.

KING: My queen, ever since you looked at the picture I see you are delighted but perplexed. Why is that?

---

*The text gives but one picture-board for the two portraits. For the mock marriage and the action of this scene two separate pictures would be more convenient.

PADMAVATI: My noble lord, there is a lady living here who is exactly like this portrait.

KING: What, of Vasavadatta?

PADMAVATI: Yes.

KING: Then send for her at once.

PADMAVATI: My noble lord, a certain brahman left her with me as a ward, before my marriage, saying that she was his sister. Her husband is away, and she shuns the sight of other men. So when you see her in my company you will know who it is.

KING: If she be a brahman's sister, it is manifest she must be another. Identity of form occurs in life as of very doubles.

Enter Portress.

PORTRESS: Greetings to my noble lord.

Here is a brahman from Ujjain who says he placed his sister as a ward in the hands of the princess. He wants to take her back, and he is waiting at the door.

KING: Padmavati, is this the brahman you spoke of?

PADMAVATI: It must be.

KING: Let the brahman be introduced at once with the formalities proper to the inner court.

PORTRESS: As my lord commands. [*Exit.*]

KING: Padmavati, do you bring the lady.

PADMAVATI: As my noble lord commands. [*Exit.*]

Enter Yaugandharayana and the Portress.

YAUGANDHARAYANA: Ah! [*Aside*]

Though it was in the king's interest that I concealed the Queen Consort, though I can see that what I've done is to his benefit, yet even when my work is done my heart misgives me as to what my royal master will say.

PORTRESS: Here is my lord. Approach him, sir.

YAUGANDHARAYANA: Greeting to your Highness, greeting!

KING: I seem to have heard that voice before.

Sir Brahman, did you leave your sister as a ward in the hands of Padmavati?

YAUGANDHARAYANA: Certainly I did.

KING: Then let his sister come here at once without delay.

PORTRESS: As my lord commands. [*Exit.*]

Enter Padmavati, Avantika, and Portress.

PADMAVATI: Come, lady. I have pleasant news for you.

AVANTIKA: What is it?

PADMAVATI: Your brother has come.

AVANTIKA: Happily he still remembers me.

PADMAVATI [*approaching*]: Greeting, my noble lord. Here is my ward.

KING: Make a formal restitution, Padmavati. A deposit should be returned in the presence of witnesses. The worthy Raibhya here and this good lady will act as recorders.

PADMAVATI: Now, sir, resume your charge of this lady.

NURSE [*looking closely at Avantika*]: Oh, but this is the princess Vasavadatta.

KING: What, Mahasena's daughter? Oh, my queen, go into the ladies' court with Padmavati.

YAUGANDHARAYANA: No, no, she must not go in there. This lady, I tell you, is my sister.

KING: What are you saying? This is the daughter of Mahasena.

YAUGANDHARAYANA: O king,

Born in the Bharata clan, you are self-controlled, enlightened, and pure. To take her by force were unworthy of you, a model of kingly duty.

KING: Very well, but let us just see this similarity of form. Draw the curtain aside.*

YAUGANDHARAYANA: Greeting to my royal master.

VASAVADATTA: Greeting to my noble lord.

KING: Heavens! This is Yaugandharayana, and this Mahasena's daughter.

This time is it true, or do I see the vision again? I saw her before just like this, but was deceived.

YAUGANDHARAYANA: Sire, by concealing the queen I am guilty of a grave offence. Please, pardon me, my royal master.

Falls at his feet.

KING [*raising him*]: You are certainly Yaugandharayana.

By feigning madness, by battles and by plans worked out accord-

---

*Perhaps idiomatic – 'unveil'.

ing to the codes of polity – you, by your exertions, raised me up when I was sinking.

YAUGANDHARAYANA: I do but follow the fortunes of my royal master.

PADMAVATI: So then this is her Majesty the Queen. Lady, in treating you as a companion, I have unwillingly transgressed the bounds of propriety. I bow my head and beg your forgiveness.

VASAVADATTA: Rise, rise, happy lady of a living lord, rise, I say. If anything offends it is your suppliant form.

PADMAVATI: I thank you!

KING: Tell me, my dear Yaugandharayana, what was your object in concealing the queen?

YAUGANDHARAYANA: My one idea was to save Kausambi.

KING: What was your reason for putting her in the hands of Padmavati as a ward?

YAUGANDHARAYANA: The soothsayers, Pushpaka and Bhadraka, had predicted that she was destined to become your queen.

KING: Did Rumanvan know of this?

YAUGANDHARAYANA: Sire, they all knew.

KING: Oho! what a rogue he is – Rumanvan!

YAUGANDHARAYANA: Sire, let the worthy Raibhya and this good lady return this very day to announce the news of the safety of the queen.

KING: No, no. We will all go together, taking Queen Padmavati.

YAUGANDHARAYANA: As your Majesty commands.

EPILOGUE

This earth, that extends to the ocean, with the Himalaya and Vindhya mountains as ear-drops – may our Lion King rule over her, marked with the symbol of a single sovereign sway.

KALIDASA
MEGHA DUUTA
[THE CLOUD MESSENGER]
(Sanskrit, *c*. A.D. 400)

Kalidasa, the greatest Indian poet and dramatist, often compared to Shakespeare, flourished in the Golden Age of Guptas. He was one of the 'Nava-ratna' (Nine Jewels) that adorned the court of Emperor Chandra Gupta II (also called Vikramaditya). Chandra Gupta ruled from Ujjain in west central India from A.D. 375 to 413. During this time the city of Ujjain rose to prominence as the centre for culture and international commerce, like Florence in Renaissance Italy.

Though not much is known about Kalidasa's life, his fame has prospered, based on his unsurpassed works, which include: *Megha Duuta* [The Cloud Messenger], an elegy; *Rtu-samhara* [The Seasons], a lyric poem; *Raghu-vamsa* [The Dynasty of Raghu] and *Kumara-sambhava* [The Birth of the War God], literary epics; *Abhijnana-Shakuntala* [Shakuntala Recognized by a Token], *Malavikagnimitra* [Malavika and Agnimitra], and *Vikramorvasiya* [Urvasi Won by Valour], dramas. Of these works perhaps the best known and most often translated are the play *Shakuntala* and the poem *Megha Duuta*.

Megha Duuta is divided into two parts, the *Purva-megha* [The Former Cloud] containing 63 stanzas, and the *Uttara-megha* [The Latter Cloud] containing 52 stanzas. It is in the form of an elegy in which an exiled Yaksha, pining for his beloved, sends her a message through a cloud. In the first half of the poem the Yaksha describes the long journey of the cloud; the second half contains the description of the beloved and the message. The poem thus combines, on the one hand, a poetic travelogue describing Nature's beautiful spots and historical places *en route* a journey, like Byron's *Childe Harold* (1812), and on the other, elegiac form expressing a separated lover's lament, somewhat different from the elegies of Catullus or Ovid, or the pastoral elegies of Spenser's November Eclogue in *Shepherd's Calendar* (1579), Milton's *Lycidas* (1632), or Shelley's *Adonais* (1821).

The unique form and technique of *Megha Duuta* so fascinated poets in subsequent centuries that they imitated this work, often unsuccessfully, leaving behind 'no less than fifty Duuta-poems' modelled on Kalidasa's work.* This accounts for the unusual popularity of the poem. Commenting on the uniqueness of Kalidasa's masterpiece, A. B. Keith concludes:

It is difficult to praise too highly either the brilliance of the description of the cloud's progress or the pathos of the picture of the wife sorrowful and alone. Indian criticism has ranked it highest among Kalidasa's poems for brevity of expression, richness of content, and power to elicit sentiment, and the praise is not undeserved.†

Kalidasa was first introduced to European readers through William Jone's translation of *Shakuntala* in 1789. Goethe was so overcome by the beauty of Shakuntala that he wrote a poem to express his admiration. Schiller was inspired to adopt Kalidasa's technique of sending a message through a cloud in his play *Maria Stuart* (1800).

The poem, composed with much subtlety, contains 115 stanzas of 4 lines each, each line consisting of 17 syllables. It is written in Mandakranta metre, or 'the slow-stepper', echoing the majestic roar of the rain cloud, and blending descriptive imagery with expressive emotion. Though the English translation has five lines to the stanza, the translater assures us that 'it contains fewer syllables, a constant check on the temptation of padding'. The notes appended to each stanza are not reproduced here because they distract the attention from the reading of the poem; their content is included in the summary of the poem given below.

I. FORMER CLOUD

A Yaksha, because he neglected his duty as a divine attendant on Kubera (the god of Wealth), is exiled for a year from his home in the heavenly city of Alaka in the Himalayas, to the Vindya mountains in

---

* Gaurinath Sastri, *A Concise History of Classical Sanskrit Literature*, Calcutta: Oxford University Press, 1960, p. 120.

† Arthur Berriedale Keith, *A History of Sanskrit Literature*, London: Oxford University Press, 1961, p. 86.

Central India. Thus separated from his young bride, the Yaksha pines for his love on the Ramagiri peak for eight months, unable to send her tidings of his health and unchanging love. When the rain clouds approach the peak, he begs a passing cloud to carry his message to his beloved in the remote Himalayas (I–IV). He assures the cloud that its kindly labours will not only be richly rewarded by the pleasures on the way, but it will also find his beloved neither dead nor faithless in the Yaksha city (V–XII).

Thereafter the Yaksha describes, with much power and extra-ordinary beauty, the various scenes on the airy pathway along the northward course, *en route* to Lake Manasa: first the Ramagiri peak itself with dense forests, the dwelling place of Siddhas, divine beings of great sanctity; the Mala plateau and the loving glances of farmers' wives; the Mango Peak; the Amrakuta on whose peak the cloud will rest a while; the Nerbudda river foaming against mountain slopes from whose currents it will refresh itself; then on forward journey, visit Dasharna country with all its flora, fauna, and fruits: the royal city of Vidish on the bank of Reed river, where city youths fondly gloat over unbridled pleasures (XIII–XXVI).

Then the cloud will journey towards fair Ujjain (the home of the poet) in the land of Avanti, on the bank of the river Vetravati, which, stretching like a lover, tells her love in gestures first. The cloud will then pass through the finest city of Ujjain, as if fallen from heaven, including the famous shrine of Shiva, called Mahakala, where it will partake in the evening sacrifice and repose that night in that glamorous city (XXVII–XXXVII).

The next day morning the cloud is besought to travel over Deep River and thence to the Holy Peak, the dwelling place of Skanda, the god of Wars, seed of Siva and Gauri; to Skin River, whose name recalls the sacrifice of pious emperor Rantideva (XXXVIII–XLVII); next over Kurukshetra, the hallowed land where Arjuna discharged his arrowy showers on Kauravas; after refreshing itself from the Saraswati whose waters Balaram preferred in place of wine, it will proceed to mingle with the holy stream of Ganga and go up the mountain from which she descends (XLVIII–LVI). After passing through the Snow-gate, carved by Parasurama on the snowy slopes, and refreshing itself on the waters of Lake Manasa, it will seek the

hospitable care of Kailasa wherein is the Yaksha city of Alaka
(LVII–LXIII).

II THE LATTER CLOUD

In the second half of the poem the Yaksha first describes the beauties
of the splendid heavenly city of Alaka, where flowers bloom in all
seasons, the magic trees yield whatever is desired, enchanting gardens
with nymphs ever young echo love-impassioned songs, and the
loveliness of maidens is ever sweetened (I–XI). Then the unhappy
Yaksha describes his own home by the side of his master's palace, hill
of sport, and pool of lotus, where blue-necked peacocks dance
(XII–XVIII). He bids the cloud to rest where gems enhance the
glory of the hill beside his home, and peep into the house and observe
the superb woman of matchless beauty, passing through the ten stages
of passion of love, on account of the long separation from her lover
(XIX–XXII) – namely, longing glances, wishfulness, meandering
desire, sleeplessness, emaciation, loss of interest in ordinary delights,
loss of bashfulness, absentmindedness in lovely madness, and pros-
tration in wretchedness – all of which should bring a rain-drop tear
from soft breasts that are pitiful of others' woes (XXII–XXX).

The Yaksha assures the cloud that on seeing the suffering of his
bride it will soon believe her sorrow and also discover in her omens of
speedy reunion with her beloved, in the quivering of her eyelids and
the trembling of her limbs (XXII–XXXIII). If she is asleep, he bids
the cloud not to thunder but let her keep the dreaming vision of her
lover's face; then awakening her gently like jasmine budding in
wonder, the cloud is instructed how to announce itself in such a way
as to win her favour and then with words of thunder speak boldly the
message of her lover: 'Thy lover lives', with only four lover's solaces
available in separation – looking at objects that remind him of her,
painting a picture of her, dreaming of her, and touching something
which she has touched (XXXIII–XLIV). The bride is besought not
to lose heart but to remember that the period of exile has its end. Thus
consoling her, the Yaksha begs the cloud to return to him with a
message of comfort and a tender token from his wife. Finally the
Yaksha dismisses the passing cloud with a prayer for its welfare
(XLV–LII).

The text of *Megha Duuta* included here is taken from the translation by Arthur W. Ryder, *Kalidasa: Shakuntala and Other Writings*,
New York: E. P. Dutton & Co., 1912; London: J. M. Dent, 1912;
reprinted, New York: Dutton Paperback (D.40), 1959, pp. 185–
208.

III.24   KALIDASA
                             MEGHA DUUTA
                          [THE CLOUD MESSENGER]

                            I. Former Cloud

                                    1

        On Rama's shady peak where hermits roam,
      Mid streams by Sita's bathing sanctified,
          An erring Yaksha made his hapless home,
      Doomed by his master humbly to abide,
      And spend a long, long year of absence from his bride.

                                    2

        Some months were gone; the lonely lover's pain
      Had loosed his golden bracelet day by day
          Ere he beheld the harbinger of rain,
      A cloud that charged the peak in mimic fray,
      As an elephant attacks a bank of earth in play.

                                    3

        Before this cause of lovers' hopes and fears
      Long time Kubera's bondman sadly bowed
          In meditation, choking down his tears –
      Even happy hearts thrill strangely to the cloud;
      To him, poor wretch, the loved embrace was disallowed.

4

Longing to save his darling's life, unblest
With joyous tidings, through the rainy days,
    He plucked fresh blossoms for his cloudy guest,
Such homage as a welcoming comrade pays,
And bravely spoke brave words of greeting and of praise.

5

Nor did it pass the lovelorn Yaksha's mind
How all unfitly might his message mate
    With a cloud, mere fire and water, smoke and wind –
Ne'er yet was lover could discriminate
'Twixt life and lifeless things, in his love-blinded state.

6

I know, he said, thy far-famed princely line,
Thy state, in heaven's imperial council chief,
    Thy changing forms; to thee, such fate is mine,
I come a suppliant in my widowed grief –
Better thy lordly 'no' than meaner souls' relief.

7

O cloud, the parching spirit stirs thy pity;
My bride is far, through royal wrath and might;
    Bring her my message to the Yaksha city,
Rich-gardened Alaka, where radiance bright
From Shiva's crescent bathes the palaces in light.

8

When thou art risen to airy paths of heaven,
Through lifted curls the wanderer's love shall peep
    And bless the sight of thee for comfort given;
Who leaves his bride through cloudy days to weep
Except he be like me, whom chains of bondage keep?

9

While favouring breezes waft thee gently forth,
And while upon thy left the plover sings
His proud, sweet song, the cranes who know thy worth
Will meet thee in the sky on joyful wings
And for delights anticipated join their rings.

10

Yet hasten, O my brother, till thou see –
Counting the days that bring the lonely smart –
The faithful wife who only lives for me:
A drooping flower is woman's loving heart,
Upheld by the stem of hope when two true lovers part.

11

And when they hear thy welcome thunders break,
When mushrooms sprout to greet thy fertile weeks,
The swans who long for the Himalayan lake
Will be thy comrades to Kailasa's peaks,
With juicy bits of lotus-fibre in their beaks.

12

One last embrace upon this mount bestow
Whose flanks were pressed by Rama's holy feet,
Who yearly strives his love for thee to show,
Warmly his well-belovèd friend to greet
With the tear of welcome shed when two long-parted meet.

13

Learn first, O cloud, the road that thou must go,
Then hear my message ere thou speed away;
Before thee mountains rise and rivers flow:
When thou art weary, on the mountains stay,
And when exhausted, drink the rivers' driven spray.

14

Elude the heavenly elephants' clumsy spite;
Fly from this peak in richest jungle dressed;
    And Siddha maids who view thy northward flight
Will upward gaze in simple terror, lest
The wind be carrying quite away the mountain crest.

15

Bright as a heap of flashing gems, there shines
Before thee on the ant-hill, Indra's bow;
    Matched with that dazzling rainbow's glittering lines,
Thy sombre form shall find its beauties grow,
Like the dark herdsman Vishnu, with peacock-plumes aglow.

16

The farmers' wives in Mala's lofty lea,
Though innocent of all coquettish art,
    Will give thee loving glances; for on thee
Depends the fragrant furrow's fruitful part;
Thence, barely westering, with lightened burden start.

17

The Mango Peak whose forest fires were laid
By streams of thine, will soothe thy weariness;
    In memory of a former service paid,
Even meaner souls spurn not in time of stress
A suppliant friend; a soul so lofty, much the less.

18

With ripened mango-fruits his margins teem;
And thou, like wetted braids, art blackness quite;
    When resting on the mountain, thou wilt seem
Like the dark nipple on Earth's bosom white,
For mating gods and goddesses a thrilling sight.

19

His bowers are sweet to forest maidens ever;
Do thou upon his crest a moment bide,
    Then fly, rain-quickened, to the Reva river
Which gaily breaks on Vindhya's rocky side,
Like painted streaks upon an elephant's dingy hide.

20

Where thick rose-apples make the current slow,
Refresh thyself from thine exhausted state
    With ichor-pungent drops that fragrant flow;
Thou shalt not then to every wind vibrate –
Empty means ever light, and full means added weight.

21

Spying the madder on the banks, half brown,
Half green with shoots that struggle to the birth,
    Nibbling where early plantain-buds hang down,
Scenting the sweet, sweet smell of forest earth,
The deer will trace thy misty track that ends the dearth.

22

Though thou be pledged to ease my darling's pain,
Yet I foresee delay on every hill
    Where jasmines blow, and where the peacock-train
Cries forth with joyful tears a welcome shrill;
Thy sacrifice is great, but haste thy journey still.

23

At thine approach, Dasharna land is blest
With hedgerows where gay buds are all aglow,
    With village trees alive with many a nest
Abuilding by the old familiar crow,
With lingering swans, with ripe rose-apples' darker show.

24

There shalt thou see the royal city, known
Afar, and win the lover's fee complete,
   If thou subdue thy thunders to a tone
Of murmurous gentleness, and taste the sweet,
Love-rippling features of the river at thy feet.

25

A moment rest on Nichais' mountain then,
Where madder-bushes don their blossom coat
   As thrilling to thy touch; where city men
O'er youth's unbridled pleasures fondly gloat
In caverns whence the perfumes of gay women float.

26

Fly on refreshed; and sprinkle buds that fade
On jasmine-vines in gardens wild and rare
   By forest rivers; and with loving shade
Caress the flower-girls' heated faces fair,
Whereon the lotuses droop withering from their hair.

27

Swerve from thy northern path; for westward rise
The palace balconies thou mayst not slight
   In fair Ujjain; and if bewitching eyes
That flutter at thy gleams should not delight
Thine amorous bosom, useless were thy gift of sight.

28

The neighbouring mountain stream that gliding grants
A glimpse of charms in whirling eddies pursed,
   While noisy swans accompany her dance
Like a tinkling zone, will slake thy loving thirst –
A woman always tells her love in gestures first.

29

Thou only, happy lover! canst repair
The desolation that thine absence made:
   Her shrinking current seems the careless hair
That brides deserted wear in single braid,
And dead leaves falling give her face a paler shade.

30

Oh, fine Ujjain! Gem to Avanti given,
Where village ancients tell their tales of mirth
   And old romance! Oh, radiant bit of heaven,
Home of a blest celestial band whose worth
Sufficed, though fallen from heaven, to bring down heaven
     on earth!

31

Where the river-breeze at dawn, with fragrant gain
From friendly lotus-blossoms, lengthens out
   The clear, sweet passion-warbling of the crane,
To cure the women's languishing, and flout
With a lover's coaxing all their hesitating doubt.

32

Enriched with odours through the windows drifting
From perfumed hair, and greeted as a friend
   By peacock pets their wings in dances lifting,
On flower-sweet balconies thy labour end,
Where prints of dear pink feet an added glory lend.

33

Black as the neck of Shiva, very God,
Dear therefore to his hosts, thou mayest go
   To his dread shrine, round which the gardens nod
When breezes rich with lotus-pollen blow
And ointments that the gaily bathing maidens know.

34

Reaching that temple at another time,
Wait till the sun is lost to human eyes;
   For if thou mayest play the part sublime
Of Shiva's drum at evening sacrifice,
Then hast thou in thy thunders grave a priceless prize.

35

The women there, whose girdles long have tinkled
In answer to the dance, whose hands yet seize
   And wave their fans with lustrous gems besprinkled,
Will feel thine early drops that soothe and please,
And recompense thee from black eyes like clustering bees.

36

Clothing thyself in twilight's rose-red glory,
Embrace the dancing Shiva's tree-like arm;
   He will prefer thee to his mantle gory
And spare his grateful goddess-bride's alarm,
Whose eager gaze will manifest no fear of harm.

37

Where women steal to rendezvous by night
Through darkness that a needle might divide,
   Show them the road with lightning-flashes bright
As golden streaks upon the touchstone's side –
But rain and thunder not, lest they be terrified.

38

On some rich balcony where sleep the doves,
Through the dark night with thy belovèd stay,
   The lightning weary with the sport she loves;
But with the sunrise journey on thy way –
For they that labour for a friend do not delay.

39

The gallant dries his mistress' tears that stream
When he returns at dawn to her embrace –
  Prevent thou not the sun's bright-fingered beam
That wipes the tear-dew from the lotus' face;
His anger else were great, and great were thy disgrace.

40

Thy winsome shadow-soul will surely find
An entrance in Deep River's current bright,
  As thoughts find entrance in a placid mind;
Then let no rudeness of thine own affright
The darting fish that seem her glances lotus-white.

41

But steal her sombre veil of mist away,
Although her reeds seem hands that clutch the dress
  To hide her charms; thou hast not time to stay,
Yet who that once has known a dear caress
Could bear to leave a woman's unveiled loveliness?

42

The breeze 'neath which the breathing acre grants
New odours, and the forest figs hang sleek,
  With pleasant whistlings drunk by elephants
Through long and hollow trunks, will gently seek
To waft thee onward fragrantly to Holy Peak.

43

There change thy form; become a cloud of flowers
With heavenly moisture wet, and pay the meed
  Of praise to Skanda with thy blossom showers;
That sun-outshining god is Shiva's seed,
Fire-born to save the heavenly hosts in direst need.

44

God Skanda's peacock – he whose eyeballs shine
By Shiva's moon, whose flashing fallen plume
   The god's fond mother wears, a gleaming line
Over her ear beside the lotus bloom –
Will dance to thunders echoing in the caverns' room.

45

Adore the reed-born god and speed away,
While Siddhas flee, lest rain should put to shame
   The lutes which they devoutly love to play;
But pause to glorify the stream whose name
Recalls the sacrificing emperor's blessèd fame.

46

Narrow the river seems from heaven's blue;
And gods above, who see her dainty line
   Matched, when thou drinkest, with thy darker hue,
Will think they see a pearly necklace twine
Round Earth, with one great sapphire in its midst ashine.

47

Beyond, the province of Ten Cities lies,
Whose women, charming with their glances rash,
   Will view thine image with bright, eager eyes,
Dark eyes that dance beneath the lifted lash,
As when black bees round nodding jasmine-blossoms flash.

48

Then veil the Hallowed Land in cloudy shade;
Visit the field where to this very hour
   Lie bones that sank beneath the soldier's blade,
Where Arjuna discharged his arrowy shower
On men, as thou thy rain-jets on the lotus-flower.

49

Sweet friend, drink where those holy waters shine
Which the plough-bearing hero – loath to fight
   His kinsmen – rather drank than sweetest wine
With loving bride's reflected eyes alight;
Then, though thy form be black, thine inner soul is bright.

50

Fly then where Ganges o'er the king of mountains
Falls like a flight of stairs from heaven let down
   For the sons of men; she hurls her billowy fountains
Like hands to grasp the moon on Shiva's crown
And laughs her foamy laugh at Gauri's jealous frown.

51

If thou, like some great elephant of the sky,
Shouldst wish from heaven's eminence to bend
   And taste the crystal stream, her beauties high –
As thy dark shadows with her whiteness blend –
Would be what Jumna's waters at Prayaga lend.

52

Her birth-place is Himalaya's rocky crest
Whereon the scent of musk is never lost,
   For deer rest ever there where thou wilt rest
Sombre against the peak with whiteness glossed,
Like dark earth by the snow-white bull of Shiva tossed.

53

If, born from friction of the deodars,
A scudding fire should prove the mountain's bane,
   Singeing the tails of yaks with fiery stars,
Quench thou the flame with countless streams of rain –
The great have power that they may soothe distress and
    pain.

54

If mountain monsters should assail thy path
With angry leaps that of their object fail,
　　Only to hurt themselves in helpless wrath,
Scatter the creatures with thy pelting hail –
For who is not despised that strives without avail?

55

Bend lowly down and move in reverent state
Round Shiva's footprint on the rocky plate
　　With offerings laden by the saintly great;
The sight means heaven as their eternal fate
When death and sin are past, for them that faithful wait.

56

The breeze is piping on the bamboo-tree;
And choirs of heaven sing in union sweet
　　O'er demon foe of Shiva's victory;
If thunders in the caverns drumlike beat,
Then surely Shiva's symphony will be complete.

57

Pass by the wonders of the snowy slope:
Through the Swan-gate, through mountain masses rent
　　To make his fame a path by Bhrigu's hope
In long, dark beauty fly, still northward bent,
Like Vishnu's foot, when he sought the demon's chastisement.

58

Seek then Kailasa's hospitable care,
With peaks by magic arms asunder riven,
　　To whom, as mirror, goddesses repair,
So lotus-bright his summits cloud the heaven,
Like form and substance to God's daily laughter given.

59

Like powder black and soft I seem to see
Thine outline on the mountain slope as bright
   As new-sawn tusks of stainless ivory;
No eye could wink before as fair a sight
As dark-blue robes upon the Ploughman's shoulder white.

60

Should Shiva throw his serpent-ring aside
And give Gauri his hand, go thou before
   Upon the mount of joy to be their guide;
Conceal within thee all thy watery store
And seem a terraced stairway to the jewelled floor.

61

I doubt not that celestial maidens sweet
With pointed bracelet gems will prick thee there
   To make of thee a shower-bath in the heat;
Frighten the playful girls if they should dare
To keep thee longer, friend, with thunder's harshest blare.

62

Drink where the golden lotus dots the lake;
Serve Indra's elephant as a veil to hide
   His drinking; then the tree of wishing shake,
Whose branches like silk garments flutter wide:
With sports like these, O cloud, enjoy the mountain side.

63

Then, in familiar Alaka find rest,
Down whom the Ganges' silken river swirls,
   Whose towers cling to her mountain lover's breast,
While clouds adorn her face like glossy curls
And streams of rain like strings of close-inwoven pearls.

II. Latter Cloud

1

Where palaces in much may rival thee –
Their ladies gay, thy lightning's dazzling powers –
  Symphonic drums, thy thunder's melody –
Their bright mosaic floors, thy silver showers –
Thy rainbow, paintings, and thy height, cloud-licking towers.

2

Where the autumn lotus in dear fingers shines,
And lodh-flowers' April dust on faces rare,
  Spring amaranth with winter jasmine twines
In women's braids, and summer siris fair,
The rainy madder in the parting of their hair.

3

Where men with maids whose charm no blemish mars
Climb to the open crystal balcony
  Inlaid with flower-like sparkling of the stars,
And drink the love-wine from the wishing-tree,
And listen to the drums' deep-thundering dignity.

4

Where maidens whom the gods would gladly wed
Are fanned by breezes cool with Ganges' spray
  In shadows that the trees of heaven spread;
In golden sands at hunt-the-pearl they play,
Bury their little fists, and draw them void away.

5

Where lovers' passion-trembling fingers cling
To silken robes whose sashes flutter wide,
    The knots undone; and red-lipped women fling,
Silly with shame, their rouge from side to side,
Hoping in vain the flash of jewelled lamps to hide.

6

Where, brought to balconies' palatial tops
By ever-blowing guides, were clouds before
    Like thee who spotted paintings with their drops;
Then, touched with guilty fear, were seen no more,
But scattered smoke-like through the lattice' grated door.

7

Where from the moonstones hung in nets of thread
Great drops of water trickle in the night –
    When the moon shines clear and thou, O cloud, art fled –
To ease the languors of the women's plight
Who lie relaxed and tired in love's embraces tight.

8

Where lovers, rich with hidden wealth untold,
Wander each day with nymphs for ever young,
    Enjoy the wonders that the gardens hold,
The Shining Gardens, where the praise is sung
Of the god of wealth by choirs with love-impassioned tongue.

9

Where sweet nocturnal journeys are betrayed
At sunrise by the fallen flowers from curls
    That fluttered as they stole along afraid,
By leaves, by golden lotuses, by pearls,
By broken necklaces that slipped from winsome girls.

10

Where the god of love neglects his bee-strung bow,
Since Shiva's friendship decks Kubera's reign;
   His task is done by clever maids, for lo!
Their frowning missile glances, darting plain
At lover-targets, never pass the mark in vain.

11

Where the wishing-tree yields all that might enhance
The loveliness of maidens young and sweet:
   Bright garments, wine that teaches eyes to dance,
And flowering twigs, and rarest gems discrete,
And lac-dye fit to stain their pretty lotus-feet.

12

There, northward from the master's palace, see
Our home, whose rainbow-gateway shines afar;
   And near it grows a little coral-tree,
Bending 'neath many a blossom's clustered star,
Loved by my bride as children of adoption are.

13

A pool is near, to which an emerald stair
Leads down, with blooming lotuses of gold
   Whose stalks are polished beryl; resting there,
The wistful swans are glad when they behold
Thine image, and forget the lake they loved of old.

14

And on the bank, a sapphire-crested hill,
Round which the golden plantain-hedges fit;
   She loves the spot; and while I marvel still
At thee, my friend, as flashing lightnings flit
About thine edge, with restless rapture I remember it.

15

The ashoka-tree, with sweetly dancing lines,
The favourite bakul-tree, are near the bower
   Of amaranth-engirdled jasmine-vines;
Like me, they wait to feel the winning power
Of her persuasion, ere they blossom into flower.

16

A golden pole is set between the pair,
With crystal perch above its emerald bands
   As green as young bamboo; at sunset there
Thy friend, the blue-necked peacock, rises, stands,
And dances when she claps her bracelet-tinkling hands.

17

These are the signs – recall them o'er and o'er,
My clever friend – by which the house is known,
   And the Conch and Lotus painted by the door:
Alas! when I am far, the charm is gone –
The lotus' loveliness is lost with set of sun.

18

Small as the elephant cub thou must become
For easy entrance; rest where gems enhance
   The glory of the hill beside my home,
And peep into the house with lightning-glance,
But make its brightness dim as fireflies' twinkling dance.

19

The supremest woman from God's workshop gone –
Young, slender; little teeth and red, red lips,
   Slight waist and gentle eyes of timid fawn,
An idly graceful movement, generous hips,
Fair bosom into which the sloping shoulder slips –

20

Like a bird that mourns her absent mate anew
Passing these heavy days in longings keen.
   My girlish wife whose words are sweet and few,
My second life, shall there of thee be seen –
But changed like winter-blighted lotus-blooms, I ween.

21

Her eyes are swoll'n with tears that stream unchidden;
Her lips turn pale with sorrow's burning sighs;
   The face that rests upon her hand is hidden
By hanging curls, as when the glory dies
Of the suffering moon pursued by thee through nightly skies.

22

Thou first wilt see her when she seeks relief
In worship; or, half fancying, half recalling,
   She draws mine image worn by absent grief;
Or asks the cagèd, sweetly-singing starling:
'Do you remember, dear, our lord? You were his darling.'

23

Or holds a lute on her neglected skirt,
And tries to sing of me, and tries in vain;
   For she dries the tear-wet string with hands inert,
And e'er begins, and e'er forgets again,
Though she herself composed it once, the loving strain.

24

Or counts the months of absence yet remaining
With flowers laid near the threshold on the floor,
   Or tastes the bliss of hours when love was gaining
The memories recollected o'er and o'er –
A woman's comforts when her lonely heart is sore.

25

Such daytime labours doubtless ease the ache
Which doubly hurts her in the helpless dark;
  With news from me a keener joy to wake,
Stand by her window in the night, and mark
My sleepless darling on her pallet hard and stark.

26

Resting one side upon that widowed bed,
Like the slender moon upon the Eastern height,
  So slender she, now worn with anguish dread,
Passing with stifling tears the long, sad night
Which, spent in love with me, seemed but a moment's flight.

27

On the cool, sweet moon that through the lattice flashes
She looks with the old delight, then turns away
  And veils her eyes with water-weighted lashes,
Sad as the flower that blooms in sunlight gay,
But cannot wake nor slumber on a cloudy day.

28

One unanointed curl still frets her cheek
When tossed by sighs that burn her blossom-lip;
  And still she yearns, and still her yearnings seek
That we might be united though in sleep –
Ah! Happy dreams come not to brides that ever weep.

29

Her single tight-bound braid she pushes oft –
With a hand uncared for in her lonely madness –
  So rough it seems, from the cheek that is so soft:
That braid ungarlanded since the first day's sadness,
Which I shall loose again when troubles end in gladness.

30

The delicate body, weak and suffering,
Quite unadorned and tossing to and fro
   In oft-renewing wretchedness, will wring
Even from thee a raindrop-tear, I know –
Soft breasts like thine are pitiful to others' woe.

31

I know her bosom full of love for me,
And therefore fancy how her soul doth grieve
   In this our first divorce; it cannot be
Self-flattery that idle boastings weave –
Soon shalt thou see it all, and seeing, shalt believe.

32

Her hanging hair prevents the twinkling shine
Of fawn-eyes that forget their glances sly,
   Lost to the friendly aid of rouge and wine –
Yet the eyelids quiver when thou drawest nigh
As water-lilies do when fish go scurrying by.

33

And limbs that thrill to thee thy welcome prove,
Limbs fair as stems in some rich plantain-bower,
   No longer showing marks of my rough love,
Robbed of their cooling pearls by fatal power,
The limbs which I was wont to soothe in passion's hour.

34

But if she should be lost in happy sleep,
Wait, bear with her, grant her but three hours' grace,
   And thunder not, O cloud, but let her keep
The dreaming vision of her lover's face –
Loose not too soon the imagined knot of that embrace.

35

As thou wouldst wake the jasmine's budding wonder,
Wake her with breezes blowing mistily;
  Conceal thy lightnings, and with words of thunder
Speak boldly, though she answer haughtily
With eyes that fasten on the lattice and on thee.

36

'Thou art no widow; for thy husband's friend
Is come to tell thee what himself did say –
  A cloud with low, sweet thunder-tones that send
All weary wanderers hastening on their way,
Eager to loose the braids of wives that lonely stay.'

37

Say this, and she will welcome thee indeed,
Sweet friend, with a yearning heart's tumultuous beating
  And joy-uplifted eyes; and she will heed
The after message: such a friendly greeting
Is hardly less to woman's heart than lovers' meeting.

38

Thus too, my king, I pray of thee to speak,
Remembering kindness is its own reward;
  'Thy lover lives, and from the holy peak
Asks if these absent days good health afford –
Those born to pain must ever use this opening word.

39

With body worn as thine, with pain as deep,
With tears and ceaseless longings answering thine,
  With sighs more burning than the sighs that keep
Thy lips ascorch – doomed far from thee to pine,
He too doth weave the fancies that thy soul entwine.

40

He used to love, when women friends were near,
To whisper things he might have said aloud
   That he might touch thy face and kiss thine ear;
Unheard and even unseen, no longer proud,
He now must send this yearning message by a cloud.

41

"I see thy limbs in graceful-creeping vines,
Thy glances in the eyes of gentle deer,
   Thine eyebrows in the ripple's dancing lines,
Thy locks in plumes, thy face in moonlight clear –
Ah, jealous! But the whole sweet image is not here.

42

And when I paint that loving jealousy
With chalk upon the rock, and my caress
   As at thy feet I lie, I cannot see
Through tears that to mine eyes unbidden press –
So stern a fate denies a painted happiness.

43

And when I toss mine arms to clasp thee tight,
Mine own though but in visions of a dream –
   They who behold the oft-repeated sight,
The kind divinities of wood and stream,
Let fall great pearly tears that on the blossoms gleam.

44

Himalaya's breeze blows gently from the north,
Unsheathing twigs upon the deodar
   And sweet with sap that it entices forth –
I embrace it lovingly; it came so far,
Perhaps it touched thee first, my life's unchanging star!

45

Oh, might the long, long night seem short to me!
Oh, might the day his hourly tortures hide!
   Such longings for the things that cannot be,
Consume my helpless heart, sweet-glancing bride,
In burning agonies of absence from thy side.

46

Yet much reflection, dearest, makes me strong,
Strong with an inner strength; nor shouldst thou feel
   Despair at which has come to us of wrong;
Who has unending woe or lasting weal?
Our fates move up and down upon a circling wheel.

47

When Vishnu rises from his serpent bed
The curse is ended; close thine eyelids tight
   And wait till only four months more are sped;
Then we shall taste each long-desired delight
Through nights that the full autumn moon illumines bright.

48

And one thing more: thou layest once asleep,
Clasping my neck, then wakening with a scream;
   And when I wondered why, thou couldst but weep
A while, and then a smile began to beam:
'Rogue! Rogue! I saw thee with another girl in dream.'

49

This memory shows me cheerful, gentle wife;
Then let no gossip thy suspicions move:
   They say the affections strangely forfeit life
In separation, but in truth they prove
Toward the absent dear, a growing bulk of tenderest love." '

50

Console her patient heart, to breaking full
In our first separation; having spoken,
  Fly from the mountain ploughed by Shiva's bull;
Make strong with message and with tender token
My life, so easily, like morning jasmines, broken.

51

I hope, sweet friend, thou grantest all my suit,
Nor read refusal in thy solemn air;
  When thirsty birds complain, thou givest mute
The rain from heaven: such simple hearts are rare,
Whose only answer is fulfilment of the prayer.

52

Thus, though I pray unworthy, answer me
For friendship's sake, or pity's, magnified
  By the sight of my distress; then wander free
In rainy loveliness, and ne'er abide
One moment's separation from thy lightning bride.

III.25   DANDIN
DASA-KUMARA-CARITA
[THE STORY OF TEN YOUNG MEN]
(Sanskrit, c. A.D. 600)

Like poetry, literary prose developed in India from the Vedic period onward. The earliest specimens of elegant and simple prose are to be found in the *Krishna Yajur Veda* and the *Atharva Veda*, and the ritual gloss contained in the manuals attached to the *Vedas*, called the *Brahmanas*. In the following centuries prose achieved precise terseness in Sastra and Sutra literature, culminating in the grand expository form in the *Bhashyas* or Commentaries, notable examples of which are Sankara's *Bhashyas*. As well as literary prose, prose fiction also evolved in India, as in any other 'hydraulic civilization', from fabulous antiquity in various stages, such as myth, legend, fable, story, romance, and the novel proper in the sixth and seventh centuries A.D.

There is a popular misconception that the novel form is of European origin, transplanted to Asia after the colonial adventures. If one examines the world literary scene, one finds that the first major novels appeared in Asia – in the sixth and seventh centuries in India, the tenth and eleventh centuries in Japan, and the thirteenth and fifteenth centuries in China, before the novel began to take shape in Europe in the seventeenth century.* When the Asian novelists were writing their great prose works in their peak days, the fiction writers in Europe were exploiting narrative in verse in such works as the *Chansons de geste* and the later medieval romances. It was only at the beginning of the Renaissance, in the fourteenth century, that prose narratives

---

*Dandin's *Dasa-Kumara-Carita* (Sanskrit, c. A.D. 600), translated as *The Ten Princes*; Murasaki Shikibu's *Genji Monogatari* (Japanese, A.D. 1000–1015), translated as *The Tale of Genji*; Shui Mai-an's *Shi Hu Chuan* (Chinese, c. A.D. 1300) translated as *The Water Margin*, or *All Men Are Brothers*; and Wu Cheng-en's *Hsi Yu Chi* (Chinese, c. A.D. 1500), translated as *Journey to the West*, or *Monkey*.

became popular in the form of tales or '*Novellen*', of which the most famous example is Boccaccio's *Decameron* (Italian, 1348–53). The nearest European approach to an outstanding Asian novel like Murasaki's *Genji Monogatari* could be Madame de Lafayette's *La Princesse de Cleves* (French, 1678). It is obvious that the Asian novel did not begin with the start of European influence over Asia, from the seventeenth century onwards, but had its own independent existence through a cycle of a thousand years of growth and decay. The Asian novel was helped in some way in its reappearance or intensification in the nineteenth and twentieth centuries, when this literary form was popularized with the importation of the processes of publishing and marketing literary products, perfected in Europe and America, and to some extent with the development of a systematic study of such forms.

The evolution of the Indian novel from earlier prose fiction took place in three stages. (1) The Cluster Stories: a collection of stories which creates and enlarges a significant character, who is not completely developed in any one of the stories, but is suggested by them cumulatively and collectively; for example *Jatakas* (Pali, *c.* 400 B.C.) deals with the Bodhisattva (Buddha-to-be) in a series of existences before the birth of the historical Gautama Siddhartha. (2) The Chain Stories: a number of stories subtly knit into one another in the framework of one main story, thus prolonging the action of this main story, for example *Pancha-tantra* (Sanskrit, *c.* 200 B.C.). There were besides a number of collections of stories which did not develop in this way into a cohesive whole, but remained merely anthologies, e.g. Gunadhya's *Brhat-Katha* (Paisaci Prakrit, *c.* A.D. 200). (3) The novel proper, combining the techniques of *Akhayayika* (fiction with a historical basis) and *Katha* (fiction created purely from the imagination), and composed in superb poetic prose, portraying, in great detail, social conditions of the time; for example Subandhu's *Vasavadatta* (Sanskrit, *c.* A.D. 600), Dandin's *Dasa-Kumara-Carita,* and Bana Bhatta's *Harsa-Carita* and *Kadambari* (Sanskrit, *c.* A.D. 700).

Dandin's novel deals with the adventures of Prince Rajavahana, son of the exiled Magadha king, Rajahansa, and his queen, Vasumati, and the nine former companions of the prince, mostly the sons of ministers and officials. Having grown up in the forest, as they come of age they go into the world, seeking adventure. When the prince is lost, the other nine young men go in search of him in different directions till each gets involved in his own individual adventures. However, the prince meets his companions one by one, sometimes by accident and sometimes in the course of their adventures, and each young man tells the story of his particular encounter. These tales are not just ten separate stories, loosely put together, but are intricately woven into the plot structure of the novel, and are related at different times in different situations, during which time the main story of Prince Rajavahana advances.

In telling the Story of Ten Young Men in a comic imitation of the grandiose epic expeditions, Dandin mingles the picaresque and the scandalous with subtle moralizing passages, at the same time providing realistic descriptions of various peoples, their customs, manners, and morals, and even the kind of education they were exposed to. For example, the princes and courtiers were instructed not only in the so-called liberal arts, such as writing, reading, poetry, drama, romance, novels, mythology; fine arts, such as music, singing, rhetoric; the art of warfare and diplomacy; but also in such illiberal arts as 'scientific skill in thievery, gambling, and the arts of deception in general'. A young society woman would be instructed in the graceful arts of dance, song, instrumental music, acting, painting, judgement in foods, perfumes, flowers, and graceful speech, but also in 'the art of flirtation, both major and minor'. In other words, the author suggests that the people believed in 'three things worth living for: virtue, money, and love'.

In Chapter V, selected here, Prince Rajavahana meets and recognizes one of his lost companions coming out of the city of Ujjaini, and learns from him of his adventures and marriage to a court lady, but also hears of the beauty of the princess of Avanti, the daughter of King Manasara, enemy of Rajavahana's father. Nevertheless, the two young men decide to enter the city and see the princess in a garden. An example of Dandin's rich imagery and vivid description can be seen in the passage where Rajavahana suddenly stands face to face with slender-waisted Avantisundari, the daughter of Malwa's Monarch. The novelist compares her creation with the process of the creation of Woman herself – but very much unlike the creation of Eve!

The passage is taken from the translation by Arthur W. Ryder, *Dandin's Dasha-Kumara-Carita: The Ten Princes*, Chicago: University of Chicago Press, 1927.

III.25   DANDIN
DASA-KUMARA-CARITA
[THE STORY OF TEN YOUNG MEN]

Chapter V
The Marriage of the Belle of Avanti

Then came the spring. In separated hearts the season fanned the flame of fondness with southern breezes (leading Love's marshalled army) that blew dilute as if subtilized by the snapping of serpents crowding tree-cavities on Malabar Mountain, that travelled tranquilly as if balanced by their sandal's perfumed burden. It made the horizon's circle vocal with coo and hum of bees and cuckoos whose throats were thrilling to the flavour of the mango blossoms' honey. In minds of self-sufficing maids it caused fantasies to flower, and flowers to flare on mango, vitex, red *ashoka*, dhak, and sesamum. It spurred the spirit of sensitive taste toward love's great festival.

In this entrancing season the belle of Avanti, Manasara's daughter Avantisundari, with her favourite friend Balachandrika who loved a frolic in a lovely country garden, surrounded too by a bevy of the city's sweetest maidens, piled sand in the cool shade of a baby mango tree and there paid playful worship to the love-god with a varied heap of fragrant offerings, among them perfumes, blossoms, turmeric powder, and strips of Chinese silk.

In this wooden garden, like Love with spring, came Rajavahana attended by Pushpodbhava; for he longed to behold the belle of Avanti, the image of the goddess Charm. From time to time, from spot to spot, he listened to polylogies of cuckoo companies and parrot parties and swarms of bees amid mangoes gay with crowding twig and flower and fruit on branches swaying to the southern breezes. He gazed from time to time at lakes winsome with clear, cool waters tunefully troubled by serried swans and cranes and ducks and sheldrakes that gaily played where lotus clusters – blue and bright and white – began to open into flower. So, with unhesitating grace, he drew near the lovely ladies. Then Balachandrika waved a hand that said: 'No shyness! Come!' And summoned thus, surpassing heaven's king in majesty, Rajavahana stood face to face with slender-waisted Avantisundari.

She shone, a creation of Love. Yes, Love had fashioned a paragon of women, as if he wished, in wistful memory of Charm, to image forth this duplicate. He formed her feet from the sweetness of two autumn lilies in his own pleasure pool; the languid grace of her gait from the course of a wanton swan down a long lake in a planted garden; her calves from a quiver's curve; her comely thighs from the shapeliness of two plantain stems by the door of a summer-house; her generous hips from the sweep of conquering chariots; her navel (which seemed an eddy in Ganges' stream) from the semblance of an early-flowing ornamental lotus bud; her three plicatures from the ordered rise of a palace stairway; her capillation from the lovely sheen of bees that, clinging, form Love's bowstring; her breasts from the beauty of two full golden bowls; her arms from the delicacy of vines in a bower; her neck from the symmetry of a conch of victory; her lip, like a *bimba* fruit, from the redness of mango flowers that maidens fondly wear above the ear; her sweet smile from the splendour of Love's flower-arrows; her every word from the witchery of the soft song of Love's first messenger, the cuckoo; the breath of her sigh from the gentleness of the southern breeze, leader of all Love's soldiers; her eyes from the pride of two fishes figured on a conquering banner; her brows from the curve of a bow; her face from the spotless enchantment of Love's first friend, the moon; her hair from the similitude of a pet peacock's fan. Then he bathed the image in sandal perfume, mingled with essence of honey and musk, and polished it with camphor dust.

Like the embodied goddess of beauty, the daughter of Malwa's monarch gazed at one who seemed the love-god, incarnate, self-propitiate, self-revealed to grant her heart's desire; and such emotion filled her that she trembled like a vine swaying to soft breezes. Hence she relied on a demure deportment and turned aside, making shy trial of this demeanour now, and now of that.

With passionate wonder he gazed at her and murmured: 'Surely, when God created his host of lovely women, *she* was a marvellous accident, as when (to quote the homely proverb) a worm traces a perfect letter while boring in a book. Else, why did he, possessed of such creative skill, fashion no rival loveliness?' And she, unable for shame to face him, withdrew half-hidden among her friends, still gazing at Rajavahana from under arching eyebrows with sidelong glances of eyes half-closed yet seeking his. His beauty was the snare, and she the deer.

He also felt his heart the target of bitter shafts that sapped his strength with the sum of graces which she then revealed. Meantime she wondered: 'No rival vies with him in charm. In what city does he make holiday for the eyes of blissful maidens? Among all matrons blest in husband and in son, what mother, through possession of this gem, becomes herself the central pearl of honour's diadem? Who is his goddess? What his errand here? Since I discovered that he mocks the love-god's beauty, the jealous god tortures me cruelly, makes me a disembodied spirit like himself. What shall I do? How can I know him?'

Now Balachandrika, interpreting their secret feelings by research of their manners, felt that a full recital of the prince's story would not be etiquette before a company of young ladies, so introduced him in more general terms: 'Princess, this is a gentleman of lofty birth, proficient in all gracious arts, a dangerous enemy, one who draws near to the divine. He is a judge of gems and charms and balms. He merits attention and should receive your homage.'

The princess, serenely greeting this echo of her own desire, gently ruffled by rapture as a wave by a zephyr, provided a decorous throne for the prince who transcended the love-god's deadly beauty. Then, by the skilful hand of her friend, she paid him homage with abundant, varied offerings, including perfumes, flowers, rice, camphor, and betel leaves.

Meanwhile Rajavahana was thinking: 'Surely, in a former life she was Yajnavati, my bride. Not otherwise could such love for her rise in my heart. In the hour when the curse was fulfilled, the holy hermit did indeed grant us a common memory of that life; yet when occasion offers, I will awaken her remembrance by hinting the details.' At this moment a beautiful swan moved gaily toward him. And seeing Balachandrika, at the princess' eager instigation, prepared to catch it, he thought: 'The time to speak has come.' Thereupon Rajavahana, an artist in narration, related this graceful tale:

'Dear friend, in days long past there was a king named Shamba. With his heart's dearest he thought to spend a happy hour beside a lotus pond. There in a cluster of red water lilies lay a swan that slept inert. He crept upon it, caught it, and bound its feet with a cord of lotus fibre. Then, gazing at his beloved's loving countenance, while a slow smile bloomed upon his cheek, he said: "My moon-faced bride, the swan is bound and lies calm as a peaceful saint. Go with him where you will." Then the swan pronounced a curse on Shamba: "O King, I *am* a saint, vowed to lifelong poverty and chastity. I lay in this lotus cluster, deep in devotion, sunk in bliss, when you brought shame upon me for no cause beyond your kingly pride. For this sin endure the torment of separation from your love." And Shamba's face grew sad, for he could not suffer separation from the mistress of his life. He fell stiffly to the ground and spoke imploringly: "Master, forgive a deed inspired by ignorance." Then pity entered the holy heart, and these words were spoken: "O King, throughout your present life the curse shall be remitted. Yet my words may not be frustrate. In a life to be, when this flower-eyed lady's soul has entered another body, you shall love her with devotion. Then, because you have bound my feet for two moments, for two months your feet shall be fettered, while you endure the sadness of separation from your love. Yet you shall live long thereafter with your bride, in kingly happiness." He also granted both a memory continuing from life to life. Therefore – you must not bind a swan.'

When the princess heard this tale, she regained remembrance of her own former life. Her memory whispered that this was indeed her soul's delight; and the stem of devotion put forth blossoms as she said with a tender smile: 'Dear sir, in days long past Shamba thus bound the swan in deference to the appeal of Yajnavati. Thus in the world even discerning men do wrong for gallant reasons.' In this fashion maiden and prince, by hints revealing each to each a common knowledge of life and names recalled from long ago, felt their hearts fill with a passion of love.

At this moment the queen of Malwa, with her retinue, approached the spot to witness her daughter's holiday. But Balachandrika, seeing her from afar and fearing disclosure of the secret, waved an agitated hand that sent Rajavahana with Pushpodbhava into the cover of a group of trees. Manasara's queen remained but a moment to enjoy her daughter's gay and graceful play with her friends; then wished to conduct the princess to the palace.

As the belle of Avanti followed her mother, she spoke these words, ambiguous between swan and prince: 'O splendid royal creature, you come to me in the garden to share my holiday, and I send you away untimely. I follow my mother, for such is my duty. Love me no less for this.' She added courteous nothings, but more than once her wistful eyes turned back to seek his face, as she moved toward the palace.

There, introducing the subject of her longing, she learned from Balachandrika his name and lineage, while Love's bewildering arrows pierced her heart. In the anguish of separation she faded daily like the crescent of the waning moon. Food and all occupation grew distasteful; in a quiet chamber her slender body tossed on a couch of flower clusters and single blossoms sprinkled with sandal perfume. Her girl friends, grieved to see their dainty princess so tortured by the flame of love, devised and used many refrigerant remedies – water for sprinkling gathered in golden bowls, with infusions of sandal, cuscus, and camphor; garments made of softest fibres; lotus-leaf fans. Yet this cooling service of her person, like water in boiling oil, turned to universal heat.

On Balachandrika, distressed and at her wits' end, the maiden turned a tear-dimmed, peeping glance from half-closed eyes, and with lips parched by hot sighs of absent love, she slowly sobbed: 'They say, my dear, Love has five arrows, made of flowers. It is not true. He strikes me with countless shafts, and they are iron. My dear, I find the moon more fierce than the fire beneath the sea. For though the ocean dries when entered by the fire, it swells again at the moment when the fire departs. But how can I describe the cruelty of the ruthless moon, who kills the lotus, home and birthplace of his own sister, Beauty? The southern breeze blows thin, scorched, doubtless, by contact with a heart that shrivels in the flame of absence. This couch of new-plucked blossoms burns my body, as if turfed with flames of desire. Even this sandal sears my limbs, as if thick with clotted venom from the dripping fangs of serpents that coiled round its mother-tree. Give over your toil to cool and heal. The prince whose beauty beats the deadly love-god, is the only physician for the sickness of love. And him I cannot win. What shall I do?'

Now Balachandrika perceived that the delicate princess was reduced to the last extremity of love's fever, with no salvation other than the handsome Rajavahana to whom her heart was subject; and she thought: 'I must bring the prince at once. If not, Love will lead her down the path of memory. Well, when prince and princess met in the garden, the archer-god shot simultaneous shafts. Therefore, it should be easy to bring the prince.' She then left the belle of Avanti in the care of friends deft in necessary service, and visited the prince's dwelling.

She found Rajavahana (whose heart seemed a quiver to hold the flower-arrows of the archer) reclining on a couch strewn with blossoms that withered at the touch of his fevered limbs, and conversing with Pushpodbhava concerning the mistress of his life. When he saw that mistress's favoured friend draw near, he thrilled with joy to find before him in Balachandrika the very simple that he sought. And when her gracefully joined hands were lifted, seeming a lovely lotus bud against the background of her brow, he offered her a decorous seat, received a gracious gift of betel leaves and camphor from Avanti-sundari, and begged for tidings of his love.

This was the flattering reply: 'Your Majesty, since seeing you in the garden, she is racked by love and finds no peace on beds of flower. She seeks the unattainable, as a dwarf the fruit on a lofty tree: love-blinded, she seeks the bliss of resting on your bosom. Unurged, she has written a letter and bade me deliver it to her beloved.' The prince took the letter and read:

> Your body, like a tender flower,
> Shows matchless love-compelling power;
> Dear friend, you must not let me find
> A hardened heart, to love unkind.

When he had read, he said with reverence: 'Dear friend, you are at once the beloved bride of Pushpodbhava, who follows me like a shadow, and, so to speak, the projected life of that fawn-eyed maiden. Your wit watered the vine of this enterprise. I will do anything. The fawn-eyed lady accuses me of carrying a hard heart. When she met my gaze in the garden, she straightway stole my heart and took it home with her. Let her judge whether it be soft or hard. It is no light matter to enter a maid's chamber. Yet in one day or two at most, I will contrive a proper method to be united with her. Give her this word from me, and let it be your care that no harm befall one delicate as a siris flower.' And Balachandrika, joyful at receiving his love-laden message, departed for the palace.

Rajavahana also withdrew with Pushpodbhava, to console the woe of absence in the garden where he had experienced the blissful vision of his soul's chosen. There he found the grove of trees whose twigs had yielded flower clusters to the maid with partridge eyes; the spot where she, her face entrancing as the autumn moon, had offered worship to the love-god; the cool bank of sand that preserved her footprints; the remnant of the meal untasted by his sweet-smiling lady; the blossom couch within the bower of jasmine vines. Ever recalling beginnings half-completed when he met the perfect princess, ever beholding with alarm – for they seemed the tufted flame-points of passion – the young mango twigs that trembled in the gentle breeze, ever hearing the coo and cry and hum of love's whisperers, cuckoo, parrot, and bee, he moved from spot to spot, for emotion forbade repose.

At this juncture a Brahman chanced to appear, attended by a fellow with shaven pate. The Brahman charmed by his taste in costume, for his robe was gay and finely woven, while showy gems hung sparkling from his ears. Observing that Rajavahana was source and centre of a circle of majesty, he pronounced a benediction. And when the prince courteously inquired: 'Who sir, are you? In what branch of scholarship are you eminent?' he announced: 'I am Vidyeshvara, the scientist. My special field is legerdemain. I travel widely, providing diversion for princes, and have today reached Ujjain in my rounds.' Then, regarding Rajavahana more narrowly, he laughed and asked with meaning: 'Why so pale in this pleasure-garden?'

To this question Pushpodbhava felt it incumbent on himself to give respectful answer: 'Surely, sir, your first words came to us from lips friendly to goodness. Your chaste benediction made you at once a dear friend of ours. And what secret is kept from friends? When the princess of Malwa came to this garden to celebrate the spring festival and chanced to meet this prince, a passion came to birth, mutual and overwhelming. His present melancholy results from the lack of means to bring about a firm and happy union.'

Then Vidyeshvara, remarking the sweet embarrassment of the prince's countenance, said with a quizzical smile: 'Your Majesty, what ambition of yours is unattainable while I am at your service? I will perplex the mind of the monarch of Malwa by scientific jugglery, will celebrate his daughter's wedding in the very presence of the populace, and will introduce you into her chamber. This proposal should be conveyed before-hand to the princess through the agency of her friend.' And the prince, delighted to find unselfish friendship, witnessed a display of Vidyeshvara's dexterity in jugglery, tested his judgement of deception, of pretended affection, of genuine devotion, and parted with high esteem.

So Rajavahana, deeming his desire as good as granted through Vidyeshvara's scientific skill, returned with Pushpodbhava to his dwelling, whence he sent to his darling, by the mouth of Balachandrika, an account of the plan for their union undertaken by the Brahman; then, torn by impatience, he tried to fight the night.

When morning dawned, the scientist Vidyeshvara, correct in taste, style, deportment, and gait, with numerous attendants equally correct, came to the palace entrance, briskly presenting his credentials to the doorkeepers, who obsequiously informed the king of the arrival of a conjurer. The king of Malwa, himself desirous of witnessing the spectacle spurred furthermore by curious ladies, summoned the scientist into a special chamber, where he pronounced a formal benediction and was bidden to begin. Then amid the blare of the banging band, while warbling women cooed like mating cuckoos, while waving peacock feather-dusters fascinated the spectator's spirits to a pitch of passion, while the whirl of attendants gyrated about him, he stood for a moment with squinting eyes. Straightway hooded serpents, with violent venting of vehement vemon, dazzling the palace with the jewels on their crests, crawled horribly forth. But numerous vultures seized the monstrous snakes in their beaks, and paraded the sky. Next, the Brahman astonished the king with a spectacle of Man-lion tearing the devil chieftain Hiranyakashipu, then said: 'Your Majesty, as our concluding number it is proper that you witness a scene of happy omen. We are therefore to present a wedding, initiating a long life of felicity, between a maiden personating your daughter and a prince marked with all marks of royalty.'

Receiving the permission of the expectant monarch, his face blossoming at the quaint conception of success in such a stratagem, he smeared his eyes with a most mystifying lotion and peered about him. And while all the spellbound spectators cried: 'This *is* magic!' at the appearance of Rajavahana, his heart aflower with bliss, and of Avantisundari, forewarned and richly decked with splendid gems, the prestidigitator showed his perfect familiarity with every text of the marriage service by uniting them before the sacred fire.

At the conclusion of the ceremony, the Brahman cried aloud: 'All creatures of magic, begone!' and all the phantom forms obediently vanished. Rajavahana also, previously instructed in the mechanics of disappearance, floated like a spectre into the maiden's apartments. The king of Malwa, for his part, considering this a superior exhibition, gave the Brahman scientist a munificent fee, dismissed him, and with-drew to the inner palace.

Meanwhile, the belle of Avanti, with her best friends as brides-maids, conducted her husband to a splendid chamber. Thus Rajava-hana, tasting fruition of his wishes through powers human and super-human, systematically conquered the shyness of his fawn-eyed bride by tastefully tender attentions, taught her the bliss of abandon, awakened an intimate confidence. Finally, eager for the heavenly delight of hearing a beloved woman repeat his own words, he related the complication and exciting history of the fourteen divisions of the universe.

[A.D. 100–800]

The classical Indian poets excelled in exquisite lyrics, often epigrammatic, chiselled with artful care. These 'brilliant poems in miniature' display a subtle play of fancy, graceful tender feelings, and worldly wisdom. They contain condensed poetic imagery and compact meaning.

Most of the short poems were collected and preserved in anthologies. The earliest of such collections are the Tamil *Sangam* anthologies, composed during the first and third centuries A.D. Some of the Sanskrit lyrics, on the other hand, are preserved in groups of one or more *Sataka* (Hundred Stanzas), thematically arranged, and attributed to individual authors, such as Armaru's *Sataka* (c. A.D. 700), containing about a hundred verses on love, or Bhartrihari's *Satakas* (c. A.D. 650), containing over three hundred poems, arranged under three headings: On Conduct, On Love, and On Renunciation. However, the later Sanskrit anthologies of short verses, called *Subhasita* (literally 'that which is well said'), contain from 2,000 to 4,000 poems, including selections from *Satakas* as well as from well-known and unknown poets.

The selections included in this section are from *Kuruntokai*, one of the earliest of the eight Tamil *Sangam* anthologies, and Bhartrihari's *Satakas*, an outstanding collection of Sanskrit *Subhasita* verse.

KURUNTOKAI

[ANTHOLOGY OF LOVE POEMS]

(Tamil, *c.* A.D. 100–300)

Tamil, one of the three classical languages – the other two being Sanskrit and Pali – is the 'only language of contemporary India which is recognizably continuous with a classical past'.* Consequently, this Dravidian language occupies a unique place in the literary history of South Asia.

It is only in this century, after the growth of awareness of the existence of a highly sophisticated pre-Aryan Indus Valley empire, that scholars are beginning to revise earlier hypotheses and attitudes to Sanskrit culture, and are attempting to trace the Indus Valley script to a proto-Dravidian language. In the previous two centuries, enthusiastic Orientalists, in an attempt to find a common identity, examined the relation between Sanskrit and other Indo-European languages. However, Indologists today have come to recognize that a closer examination of all that is expressed in Sanskrit in relation to the Dravidian culture is more relevant. It would seem that much of the ancient Dravidian literature surviving in oral transmission was perhaps lost during cataclysmic prehistoric changes, while some found re-expression in Vedic and classical Sanskrit, and some is preserved in classical Tamil, what is now known as *Sangam* literature. The central importance of this body of thought and culture, irrespective of the medium of its re-expression, has yet to be determined and properly placed in the continuing and composite Indian tradition.

The Tamil tradition recognizes the existence of three *Sangams* (or *Sankam*, literally meaning 'Academy' or 'fraternity' of poets), lasting for long periods of time, and dating back to prehistory. But all that is known of the *Sangam* literature today is a few remnants from these rich periods, namely *Tolkappiyam*, a manual of grammar and prosody

---

* A. K. Ramanujan, tr., *The Interior Landscape*, Bloomington and London: Indiana University Press, 1967, p. 97.

belonging to the Second *Sangam*; and eight anthologies of lyrics and ten long poems belonging to the Third *Sangam*. Though the anthologies were compiled during the years A.D. 100–300, the poems included were obviously composed in a much earlier period.

Kuruntokai, the earliest of the eight anthologies, contains 400 love lyrics, attributed to about 200 poets. These subjective lyrics are called *Akam* or poems giving expression to the inner being of the person, as contrasted with *Puram* in which the poet describes the outside world. In *Akam* verses, the poet explores the individual's experience as if carving out an 'interior landscape'. In such exploration the love theme lends itself to a variety of expressions, such as love at first sight, love before and after marriage, love in union and separation, and unrequited and mismatched love. Each phase of love is associated with a particular landscape – flowers, birds, dances, the seasons – and the stylized imagery thus suggests an appropriate emotion. Lovers' union is associated with mountains, and separation with the desert; patient waiting with the forests, and anxious waiting with the seashore; lovers' fidelity and the beloved's resentment with pastoral regions.* The poetic design and convention limit the situations and characters to a minimum – a lover, a beloved, a friend, a messenger, a foster parent, a concubine, or a passer-by. The reader, so to say, overhears the poem. Thus, the lyric in this tradition 'implies, evokes, enacts a drama in a monologue'.†

The poems included here are taken from the translation by A. K. Ramanujan, *The Interior Landscape*, Bloomington and London: Indiana University Press, 1967, *Kuruntokai* 3, 6, 16, 17, 18, 32, 40, 42, 95, 138, 142, 176, 226, 234, 235, 324, 378.

---

*ibid., pp. 105–8; the author provides a detailed chart of the interior landscape.

† ibid., p. 112.

III.26   *KURUNTOKAI*

[ANTHOLOGY OF LOVE POEMS]

Dramatis Personae

He	Her Foster-Mother
She	Concubine
Her Friend	Passers-by

1. What She Said

Bigger than earth, certainly,
higher than the sky,
more unfathomable than the waters
is this love for this man

> of the mountain slopes
> where bees make rich honey
> from the flowers of the *kurinci*
> that has such black stalks.   Tevakulattar [3]

2. What She Said

The still drone of the time
past midnight.
All words put out,
men are sunk into the sweetness
of sleep. Even the far-flung world
has put aside its rages
for sleep.

> Only I
am awake.   Patumanar [6]

3. *What Her Friend Said*

Will he not really think of us
when he passes the clumps of milk-hedge
with their fragrant trunks
and hears the red-legged lizard call
to his mate
in cluckings that sound like
the highway robber's fingernail
testing the point of his iron arrow,
will he not really think of us, friend?

Palaipatiya Perunkatunko [16]

4. *What He Said*

When love is ripe beyond bearing
and goes to seed,
men will ride even palmyra stems
like horses; will wear on their heads
the reeking cones of the *erukkam* bud
like flowers; will draw to themselves
the gossip of the streets;

and will do worse.

Pereyin Muruvalar [17]

5. *What Her Friend Said to Him*

O man of the mountain slopes
where the jackfruit tree has fruit almost on its roots
with the small live bamboo for its fences,
be of good thoughts and think of marriage.
No one knows of her state.

467

She's like those other trees on the slopes,
their giant jacks hanging
from slender boughs:
her breath is short,
and her love great beyond bearing.   Kapilar [18]

6. *What He Said*

If one can tell morning
from noon from listless evening,
the night of sleeping towns from dawn,
then one's love
is a lie.

   If I should lose her
I could proclaim my misery in the streets
riding mock horses on palmyra stems in my wildness:
but that seems such a shame.
            But then, even living
away from her, seems such a shame.
                              Allur Nanmullaiyar [32]

7. *What He Said*

What could my mother be
to yours? What kin is my father
to yours anyway? And how
did you and I meet ever?

         But in love our hearts are as red
earth and pouring rain:
         mingled
beyond parting.   Cempulappeyanirar [40]

8. *What Her Friend Said to Him*

Even if passion should pass,
    O man of the hills
    where
        after the long tempestuous rains
        of night
    the morning's waterfalls
    make music in the caverns,
would our love also pass
with the passion?   Kapilar [42]

9. *What He Said*

Where the white waters from the peak
crash through the mountain caves,
it flowers on the slopes;

    and there, the little hill-town chieftain
    has a younger daughter, a girl
    with great arms, and she is tender as water;

    fancy her quelling my fire!   Kapilar [95]

10. *What Her Friend Said*

The great city fell asleep
but we did not sleep.
Clearly we heard, all night,
from the hillock next to our house
the tender branches of the flower-clustered tree
with leaves like peacock feet
let fall
their blue-sapphire flowers.   Kollan Arici [138]

11. What He Said

Does that girl,
      eyes like flowers, gathering flowers
from pools for her garlands, driving away the parrots
from the millet fields,
      does that girl know at all
or doesn't she,
      that my heart is still there with her
      bellowing sighs
      like a drowsy midnight elephant?   Kapilar [142]

12. What Her Friend Said

He did not come just one day: he did not come
  just two days.
But many days he came and softened my good heart
with many modest words said many times. And
      like a honey comb ripening on the hills
      suddenly falling
      he went.

Where is our man, good as a father, on whom we leaned?

      As from rainstorms pouring
      on a distant green land
my heart runs muddy.   Varumulaiyaritti [176]

13. What She Said

Before I laughed with him
   nightly,

   the slow waves beating
   on his wide shores
   and the palmyra
   bringing forth hero–like flowers
   near the waters,

my eyes were like the lotus
my arms had the grace of the bamboo
my forehead was mistaken for the moon.

   But now
                Maturai Eruttalan Centamputan [226]

14. What She Said

Only the dim-witted say it's evening
   when the sun goes down
   and the sky reddens,
   when misery deepens,
   and the *mullai* begins to bloom
   in the dusk.

But even when the tufted cock
   calls in the long city
   and the long night
   breaks into dawn,
   it is evening:
        even noon
   is evening,
   to the companionless.   Milaipperun Kantan [234]

15. *What He said*

Be good to her, O North Wind,
and may you prosper!

There, among thin silver rills
that look like hanging snake skins,

high on the hill

where herds of elk
plunder the gooseberry
in the courtyards,
there
lies my good woman's village
of grass-thatched cottages.   Mayentan [235]

16. *What Her Girl-Friend Said to Him*
when he wanted to come by night

Man-eaters, male crocodiles with crooked legs,
cut off the traffic on these waterways.
               But you
in your love, will come to her swimming
through the shoals of fish in the black salt marshes.
               And she,
she will suffer in her simpleness.
               And I,
what can I do but shudder in my heart
like a woman watching her poisoned twins?

                    Kavaimakan [324]

17. What Her Foster-Mother Said

Let no sun burn
may trees shade the little ways on the hill
may the paths be covered with sand
may cool rain
cool the desert roads

> for that simple girl
> her face the colour of the new mango leaf
> who left us
> for a man
> with the long bright spear!   Kaymanar [378]

BHARTRIHARI
SATAKAS
[HUNDRED STANZAS]

(Sanskrit, *c.* A.D. 650)

Bhartrihari (d. A.D. 651) has been credited with three collections of short verses in varied metres, theoretically arranged under three headings: *Niti Sataka* (Hundred Stanzas on Conduct), *Sringara Sataka* (Hundred Stanzas on Love), and *Vairagya Sataka* (Hundred Stanzas on Renunciation). In these lyrics Bhartrihari, apparently a prince, an exiled courtier, a grammarian, a lover, and a philosopher, capsules his varied experiences, and presents his views on life. According to the Indian tradition, it is legitimate for a man to pursue the four recognized 'Aims of Life', namely *Dharma* (righteousness), *Artha* (material gains), *Kama* (beauty, including love), and *Moksha* (renunciation of worldly activity for spiritual quest). The poet broadly expresses himself on these human pursuits.

Each of Bhartrihari's stanzas, standing independently, conveys with dramatic brevity one idea through a single sentiment or *Rasa*, be it of policy, of love, or of resignation. Commenting on this expressive power, A. B. Keith observes:

> The extraordinary power of compression which Sanskrit possesses is seen here at its best; the effect on the mind is that of a perfect whole in which the parts coalesce by inner necessity, and the impression thus created on the mind cannot be reproduced in an analytical speech like English, in which it is necessary to convey the same content, not in a single sentence syntactically merged into a whole, like the idea which it expresses, but in a series of loosely connected predications. The effect which the best stanzas of the lyric poets achieve is essentially synthetic.*

The selections included here are taken from the translation by John Brough, *Poems From the Sanskrit*, Harmondsworth, England:

---

*A. B. Keith, *A History of Sanskrit Literature*, London: Oxford University Press, 1961, p. 178.

Penguin Books, 1968. The number in brackets at the end of each stanza refers to the source, namely Bhartrihari, *Satakatrayadi Subhasita-samgraha:* The Epigrams attributed to Bhartrihari, ed. D. D. Kosambi, Bombay, 1948.

Selections: B. 8, 9, 32, 82, 84, 88, 108, 120, 124, 169, 200, 221, 235, 237, 301, 311, 312.

III.27   BHARTRIHARI
                SATAKAS

            [HUNDRED STANZAS]

1

The ignorant are quickly satisfied,
And argument will soon convince the wise;
But Heaven's own wisdom scarcely will suffice
To contradict a half-baked scholar's pride.   [8]

2

If you can snatch the jewel a crocodile
    Holds in its teeth,
If you can swim across the ocean, while
    The tempest roars,
If round your head, unruffled, you can wind
    A poison snake,
You still can't hope to change the stubborn mind
    of a born fool.   [9]

3

Deer and fish and good men live
On grass and water and content:
No cause for hatred do they ever give
To hunters, fishers, or to men malevolent.   [32]

475

4

She needs no instruction in the art
Of using woman's wiles to win man's heart:
The lily's scarlet stamens grew untaught,
The bee came freely, wishing to be caught   [82]

5

No more evasions, please. Consider well
The facts, and tell where best to seek for rest:
At court, or exiled where flanked mountains swell?
Or in her smile, reclining on her breast?   [84]

6

In this vain fleeting universe, a man
Of wisdom has two courses: first, he can
Direct his time to pray, to save his soul,
And wallow in religion's nectar-bowl;
But, if he cannot, it is surely best
To touch and hold a lovely woman's breast,
And to caress her warm round hips, and thighs,
And to possess that which between them lies.   [88]

7

Her face is not the moon, nor are her eyes
Twin lotuses, nor are her arms pure gold:
She's flesh and bone. What lies the poets told!
Ah, but we love her, we believe the lies.   [108]

8

You cheat yourself and others with your lies,
      Philosopher, so foolish-wise,
        In that you state
          A celibate
      Has greater grace to win the prize.
Are there not heavenly nymphs beyond the skies?   [120]

9

'No! don't!' she says at first, while she despises
The very thought of love; then she reveals
A small desire; and passion soon arises,
Shyly at first, but in the end she yields.
With confidence then playing without measure
Love's secret game, at last no more afraid
She spreads her legs wide in her boundless pleasure.
Ah! love is lovely with a lovely maid!   [124]

10

In former days we'd both agree
That you were me, and I was you.
What has now happened to us two,
That you are you, and I am me?   [312]

11

She who is always in my thoughts prefers
Another man, and does not think of me.
Yet he seeks for another's love, not hers;
And some poor girl is grieving for my sake.
  Why then, the devil take
Both her and him; and love; and her; and me.   [311]

12

A man lives long who lives a hundred years:
Yet half is sleep, and half the rest again
Old age and childhood. For the rest, a man
Lives close companion to disease and tears,
Losing his love, working for other men.
Where can joy find a space in this short span?   [200]

13

The pleasant city and its mighty king,
The tributary princes at his side,
The learned men that were the kingdom's pride,
The minstrels with a ready song to sing,
The gracious ladies of the court, the ring
Of haughty nobles, arrogant of birth,
Are conquered by the Lord of all the earth,
Time, who makes memories of everything.   [169]

14

The noble man works for another's good,
Sacrificing his own. Most common men
Will help another, if it's understood
That nothing of their own is thereby lost.
Devils incarnate we can comprehend,
Those who wax fat while others bear the cost.
But are there wretches who would harm a friend
And neighbour without any hope of gain?   [221]

15

Patience, better than armour, guards from harm.
And why seek enemies, if you have anger?
With friends, you need no medicine for danger.
With kinsmen, why ask fire to keep you warm?
What use are snakes when slander sharper stings?
What use is wealth where wisdom brings content?
With modesty, what need for ornament?
With poetry's Muse, why should we envy kings?   [237]

16

For one short act, a child; next act, a boy
In love; then poor; a short act to enjoy
Status and wealth; till in the last act, Man,

Painted with wrinkles, body bent with age,
Ending the comedy which birth began,
Withdraws behind the curtain of life's stage.   [235]

17

Earth, my own mother; father Air; and Fire,
My friend; and Water, well-beloved cousin;
And Ether, brother mine; to all of you
This is my last farewell. I give you thanks
For all the benefits you have conferred
During my sojourn with you. Now my soul
Has won clear, certain knowledge, and returns
To the great Absolute from whence it came.   [301]

❧

Part Four

AGE OF BHAKTAS
[MYSTICS]
A.D. 700–1800

❧

A. SAIVISM

28. Manikka Vasahar, *Tiru Vasaham* (Tamil, *c.* A.D. 700)
29. Basavanna, *Vachana* (Kannada, *c.* A.D. 1168)
30. Lalla, *Vakyani* (Kashmiri, *c.* A.D. 1300)

B. SAKTISM

31. Ramprasad (1718–1775), *Kirtan* (Bengali)

C. VAISHNAVISM

32. Jayadeva, *Gita Govinda* (Sanskrit, *c.* A.D. 1200)
33. Mira-bai, *Bhajan* (Gujarati, Hindi, *c.* A.D. 1400)
34. Tulsi Das (1532–1623), *Vinaya Patrika* (Hindi)
35. Tukaram (1598–1649), *Abhang* (Marathi)

D. SUFISM

36. Kabir (1440–1518), *Poems* (Hindi)
37. Mir (*c.* 1723–82), *Ghazal* (Urdu)

E. SIKHISM

38. Nanak (1469–1538), *Adi Granth* (Gurmukhi, 1604)

Towards the end of the age of Acharyas [Scholars], though the South Indian Kingdoms of Pallavas, Cholas, and later Vijayanagara were becoming more powerful, the increasing waves of foreign invasions in the north from the eleventh century onwards, first by the Afghans and later by the Moghuls, caused the gradual disintegration of the mainsprings of sophisticated classical culture. In the general violence that usually follows the fury of conquests not only was the framework of the society in the north destroyed, but more specifically, the blind dogmatism with which the invaders interpreted the Semitic religion of Peace (Islam) justified, to them, the intolerable destruction of Indian temples. This vandalism was somehow fatal to the continuity of Indian culture because the destruction of the temples led to the destruction of schools of learning and institutions of professional skill in arts attached to such temples. With the collapse of the establishment and the imposition of foreign rule, traditional Indian learning, having become submerged under layers of foreign language, religion, and culture, was driven into comparative obscurity for survival. Though some kind of synthesis was attempted under the Moghul rule, the real spiritual ferment of the time gave birth to generations of local saints and mystics who taught the people by their own examples of fervent devotion or *Bhakti* (loving faith) to a personalized concept of God. The *Bhaktas* (devotees) gave expression to their ecstasy in inspired poetry in the regional languages, namely, Tamil, Kannada, Telugu, and Malayalam in the south; Bengali, Assamese, and Oriya in the east; Hindi in the centre; Marathi, Gujarati, and Sindi in the west; and Punjabi and Kashmiri in the north. Thus, the poet-saints gave to the various Dravidian and Sanskrit dialects a literary respectability similar to that given by Dante and Petrarch in Italy, and Chaucer in Britain, to the dialects of Latin and Anglo-Saxon in Europe at about the same time.

The *Bhakti* movement was beginning to take shape in South India from the seventh century A.D., under royal patronage, as an opposition to the rising popularity of Buddhism and Jainism, and in an attempt to resurrect devotion to the most ancient Indian deity, Siva. Hitherto, Siva had been worshipped in the abstract form, a symbol of cosmic creative energy, namely *Lingam*; and some of the devotees of Siva who continued to worship him in such a form were known as *Lingayats*. However, the worship of Siva, having become more elaborate in form and ritual, soon established itself as a movement of *Saiva Bhakti*, or *Saivism*. On the other hand, another attitude to Siva worship also developed in India in which the devotee, conceiving Siva's cosmic energy (*Sakti*) as a feminine principle, and objectifying it as Siva's consort, worshipped her as a goddess under various names, such as *Durga* (the terrible one), *Kali* (the dark one, or one that overcomes *Kala*, time), *Chandi* (the wild one), *Tara* (the star), *Parvati* (the daughter of the mountain, Himalaya), *Uma* (the gracious one), or *Sati* (the faithful one), generally signifying the protective goddess or Mother. Such devotees were called the *Saktas*.

As a parallel movement to Saiva Bhakti, there also emerged the worship of Vishnu, especially in the name of his more popular incarnations, namely, Rama and Krishna. This devotional attitude, known as *Vaishnava Bhakti*, or *Vaishnavism*, gave rise to a tremendous need for the re-expression of the epics – the *Ramayana* and the *Mahabharata* – in the local languages of the time. Consequently, instead of translating the epics accurately, the Bhaktas made various attempts to retell them with considerable imaginative freedom to suit the needs of the *Bhakti* movement, giving rise to a number of local versions of the epics, the most famous of which are Kamban's Tamil *Ramayanam* (*c.* A.D. 1000) and Tulsi Das's Hindi *Rama-Carita-Manasa* (*c.* 1575). Besides, Rama-bhakti and Krishna-bhakti also introduced new literary forms to India in the shape of *Lilas* or Plays, called *Rama-lila* and *Krishna-lila*, in which incidents relating to Rama and Krishna were dramatized in a ballet-cum-opera in the manner of the mystery or morality plays or passion plays of medieval Europe. However, the crowning glory of literary creation from *Vaishnava Bhakti* is the famous last great poem in classical Sanskrit, namely, Jayadeva's *Gita Govinda*.

The Bhakti movement produced two other significant innovations. First, in softening the dogmatism of religious orthodoxy and formal rituals, and as a synthesis of Hinduism and Islam, a new mystic movement emerged in which the immediacy of a personal god was recognized outside theology and ritual. This movement gave rise to the growth of Sufism, an outstanding spokesman of which was Kabir. Second, there was the growth of a new spirituality in the Punjab under the Bhaktaship of Nanak, called Sikhism.

The hymns included here are taken from various schools of Bhaktas from different parts of India, expressed in the regional languages.

A. Saivism – Manikka Vasahar (Tamil), Basavanna (Kannada), Lalla Devi (Kashmiri)

B. Saktism – Ramprasad (Bengali)

C. Vaishnavism – Jayadeva (Sanskrit), Mira-bai (Gujarati), Tulsi Das (Hindi), Tukaram (Marathi)

D. Sufism – Kabir (Hindi), Mir (Urdu)

E. Sikhism – Nanak (Gurmukhi)

MANIKKA VASAHAR
             TIRU VASAHAM
           [SACRED UTTERANCES]
            (Tamil, *c.* A.D. 700)

Manikka Vasahar, the prime minister of the Pandyan court, on a
visit to the Siva shrine at Perundurai in Tanjore District suddenly
came under a religious spell and devotedly sang his 'Sacred Utterances' (*Tiru Vasaham*). He was named 'utterer of jewels' (*Manikka*).
Thereafter renouncing public life, he became a Saiva Bhakta. Among
Tamil Saiva poet-saints, none makes a stronger devotional appeal than
Manikka Vasahar, 'one who can melt the hearts of men'.

    The translations are by F. Kingsbury and G. E. Phillips, *Hymns of
the Tamil Saivite Saints*, The Heritage of India Series, London:
Oxford University Press, 1921, pp. 121–7 (Songs 126–38).

IV.28   MANIKKA VASAHAR
             TIRU VASAHAM
           [SACRED UTTERANCES]

Life's Consuming

126. Myself I cannot understand, nor what is day nor night;
    He who both word and thought transcends has reft my senses
      quite,
    He who for bull has Vishnu, and in Perundurai dwells,
    O Light supreme, in Brahman guise has cast on me strange spells.

127. I ask not fame, wealth, earth or heav'n. No birth, no death for me.
    None will I touch who love not Siva. Now 'tis mine to see
    Abiding Perundurai, wear the King's foot as my crown;
    Never will I leave this His shrine, nor let Him leave His own.

128. Art Thou like honey on the branch too high for me to climb?
    Or art Thou nectar ocean-churned? O Hara, King sublime,
    In Perundurai, circled with moist fields, I can see Thee
    With form ash-smeared, the spotless. Can I bear my ecstasy?

129. Many in this great earth who live do penance; I alone
    Bearing this frame of flesh, a barren jungle-tree have grown.
    Dweller in Perundurai old where blooms the kondai tree,
    May I the sinner cry 'Wilt Thou not grant Thyself to me'?

Pious Fear

130. I fear not serpents lurking smooth;
    I fear no liars' feigned truth;
    But when I see fools venturing
    E'en to the foot of him our king,
    Our three-eyed Lord with matted hair,
    Of His great godhead unaware,
    Fools thinking other gods can be,
    Terror such sight inspires in me.

131. I fear no javelin's gory blade;
    Nor sidelong glance of bangled maid;
    But when I see men void of grace
    Drinking no sweetness from the praise
    Of my unchiselled Gem, whose dance
    In Tillai's hall is seen, whose glance
    Melts men's whole frame in ecstasy,
    Terror such sight inspires in me.

I Cling to Thee

132. King of the heavenly ones! All-filling Excellence!
E'en to vile me Thou Thy wonders hast shown;
Balm of true bliss, ending false earthly bliss of sense,
Thou my whole household did'st take for Thine own.
Meaning of holy writ! Wondrous Thy glory!
True wealth, our Siva, to Thee, Lord, I cling.
Never to loose my hold, firmly I cling to Thee;
Where canst Thou go, leaving me sorrowing?

133. King of celestial ones, ever with bull for steed,
Evil am I, yet my riches art Thou;
Lest I should rot in my foul flesh, and die indeed,
Thou hast preserved me, and Thine am I now.
Thou art our God; Thou of grace art a boundless sea,
Saved from my flesh, now to Thee, Lord, I cling.
Never to let Thee loose, firmly I cling to Thee;
Where can'st Thou go, leaving me sorrowing?

134. Thou did'st come into my vile fleshly body,
E'en as 'twere into some great golden shrine
Soft'ning and melting it all, Thou hast savèd me,
Lord condescending, Thou gem all divine!
Sorrow and birth, death, all ties that deceivèd me,
Thou did'st remove, all my bonds severing;
True bliss, our kindly Light, firmly I cling to Thee;
Where canst Thou go leaving me sorrowing?

Naught but Thy Love

135. I ask not kin, nor name, nor place,
Nor learnèd men's society.
Men's lore for me no value has;
Kuttalam's lord, I come to Thee.
Wilt thou one boon on me bestow,
A heart to melt in longing sweet,
As yearns o'er new-born calf the cow,
In yearning for Thy sacred feet?

Longing for Union

136. I had no virtue, penance, knowledge, self-control.
     A doll to turn
   At others' will, I danced, whirled, fell. But me
       He filled in every limb
   With love's mad longing, and that I might climb
       there whence is no return,
     He shewed His beauty, made me His. Ah me,
       when shall I go to Him?

The Wonder of Grace

137. Fool's friend was I, none such may know
     The way of freedom; yet to me
   He shew'd the path of love, that so
     Fruit of past deeds might ended be.
       Cleansing my mind so foul, He made me like
         a god.
       Ah who could win that which the Father hath
         bestowed?

138. Thinking it right, sin's path I trod.
     But, so that I such paths might leave,
   And find His grace, the dancing God,
     Who far beyond our thought doth live,
       O wonder passing great! – to me His dancing
         shewed.
       Ah who could win that which the Father hath
         bestowed?

BASAVANNA
VACHANA
[SAYINGS]

(Kannada, *c.* A.D. 1168)

Basavanna (A.D. 1106–67) was a devotee of Siva from his early child-hood. At the age of sixteen, he broke his brahmanic sacred thread in disgust at the prevailing injustice of the caste system, left home 'raging for the Lord's love', and found a guru at Kappadi-sangama, the meeting-place of three rivers. Some time later, he saw a vision in which the Lord asked him to leave the place and seek King Bijjala. So he went to Kalyana where his uncle Baladeva was Bijjala's minister, married his uncle's daughter, Gangambika, and became a courtier. After Baladeva's death, Basavanna became the minister.

While Basavanna held the office of the State, he also matured as a minister of Lord Siva, and used his powers to further the Saiva-bhakti movement. His followers, disregarding all the barriers of caste, class, sex, lived together as a new community, and were called Vira-Saiva (Heroic Saiva). The growth of this new dynamic community based on egalitarian principles aroused the hostility of the orthodoxy. Finally, King Bijjala was prevailed upon to put a stop to the revo-lutionary erosion of caste-structured society. The king took his chance when a marriage took place in the Vira-Saiva community between an ex-outcaste and an ex-brahmin. The fathers of the bride and the bridegroom were put to death disgracefully by the king's order. The outraged community then rose against the 'State and Society', in spite of Basavanna's attempts to stop the popular fury. Finally Basavanna resigned his office and returned to Kappadi-sangam, where he died soon after. Meanwhile King Bijjala was assassinated by extremist youths.

Basavanna's devotional and inspired utterances on various occasions laid the foundation for a new spirituality of Vira-Saivism, 'based on the rejection of inequality of every kind, rejection of rituals and taboos and exultation of work in the name of the Lord'. His *Vachanas*, numbering about a thousand, were collected and arranged in six phases of development of the Bhakta. However, the most intense of Basavanna's utterances are in the 'first phase of man's struggling with the world and its ills and temptations'. Basavanna often uses the refrain 'the Lord of the Meeting Rivers' as his signature line, referring to the place where he became Siva Bhakta.

The above biographical account is condensed from the Introduction by A. K. Ramanujan to his translation of Basavanna's *Vachanas* in *Speaking of Siva: the Poems*. The selections included here are taken from this unpublished manuscript, through the courtesy of Mrs Bonnie Crown, Director of the Asian Literature Programme, Asia Society Inc., New York.

IV.29   BASAVANNA
VACHANA
[SAYINGS]

I

Look, the world, in a swell
of waves, is beating upon my face.

Why should it rise to my heart,
tell me.
O tell me, why is it
rising now to my throat?
Lord,
how can I tell you anything
when it is risen high

over my head
lord lord
listen to my cries
O lord of the meeting rivers
listen.   [8]

2

Does it matter how long
a rock soaks in the water:
will it ever grow soft?

Does it matter how long
I've spent in worship,
when the heart is fickle?

Futile as a ghost
I stand guard over hidden gold,
O lord of the meeting rivers.   [99]

3

The crookedness of the serpent
is straight enough for the snake-hole.

The crookedness of the river
is straight enough for the sea.

And the crookedness of our Lord's men
is straight enough for our Lord!   [144]

4

Before
          the grey reaches the cheek,
          the wrinkle and rounded chin
          and the body becomes a cage of bones:

before
          with fallen teeth
          and bent back
          you are someone else's ward:

before
          you drop your hand to the knee
          and clutch a staff:

before
>   age corrodes
>   your form:

before
>   death touches you:
>   worship
>   our lord
>   of the meeting rivers!   [161]

5

Make of my body the beam of a lute
>   of my head the sounding gourd
>   of my nerves the strings
>   of my fingers the plucking rods.

Clutch me close
>   and play your thirty-two songs
>   O lord of the meeting rivers!   [500]

6

The pot is a god. The winnowing
fan is a god. The stone in the
street is a god. The comb is a
god. The bowstring is also a
god. The bushel is a god and the
spouted cup is a god.

Gods, gods, there are so many
there's no place left
for a foot.

>   There is only
one god. He is our Lord
of the Meeting Rivers.   [563]

7

They plunge
wherever they see water.

They circumambulate
every tree they see.

How can they know you
O Lord
who adore
waters that run dry,
trees that wither?   [581]

8

The rich
will make temples for Siva.
What shall I,
a poor man,
do?

My legs are pillars,
the body the shrine,
the head a cupola
of gold.

Listen, O lord of the meeting rivers,
things standing shall fall,
but the moving ever shall stay.   [820]

9

I'm no worshipper;
I'm no giver;
I'm not even beggar,

           O lord
           without your grace.

494

Do it all yourself, my lord of meeting rivers,
as a mistress would
when maids are sick. [831]

10

Milk is left over
from the calves.
Water is left over
from the fishes,
flowers from the bees.

How can I worship you,
O Siva, with such offal?
But it's not for me
to despise left-overs,
so take what comes,

lord of the meeting rivers. [885]

LALLA
VAKYANI
[SAYINGS]

(Kashmiri, *c.* A.D. 1300)

In her Sayings, Lalla (sometimes also called Lalleshvari, or Lalla-devi), the Saiva mystic, expresses her intense longings for her beloved (Siva), and gives expression to her heart's desire and spiritual experiences.

The translations are by G. Grierson and L. D. Barnett, *Lalla-Vakyani*, London: Royal Asiatic Society, 1920, and quoted in Margaret Macnicol, *Poems by Indian Women*, The Heritage of India series, London: Oxford University Press, 1923, pp. 45–57. Vakyani 1–9.

LALLA
VAKYANI
[SAYINGS]

1. Put thou thy thoughts upon the path of immortality.
   If thou leave them without guidance, into evil state will they fall.
   There, be thou not fearful, but be thou very courageous.
   For they are like unto a suckling child, that tosseth restless on its
   mother's bosom.

2. He who hath deemed another and himself as the same,
   He who hath deemed the day (of joy) and the night (of sorrow) to
   be alike,
   He whose mind hath become free from duality,
   He, and he alone, hath seen the Lord of the chiefest of gods.

3. For a moment saw I a river flowing.
   For a moment saw I no bridge or means of crossing.
   For a moment saw I a bush all flowers.
   For a moment saw I nor rose nor thorn.

For a moment saw I a cooking hearth ablaze.
For a moment saw I nor hearth nor smoke.
For a moment saw I the mother of all the Pandavas.
For a moment saw I an aunt of a potter's wife.

4. Some, though they be sound asleep, are yet awake;
On others, though they be awake, hath slumber fallen.
Some, though they bathe in sacred pools, are yet unclean;
Others, though they be full of household cares, are yet free from
    action.

5. By a way I came, but I went not by the way.
While I was yet on the midst of the embankment, with its crazy
    bridges, the day failed for me.
I looked within my poke and not a cowry was there.
What shall I give for the ferry fee?

6. O heedless one! speedily lift up thy foot:
Now it is dawn: seek thou for the Friend.
Make to thyself wings: lift thou up the winged (feet);
Now it is dawn: seek thou for the Friend.

7. With a rope of untwisted thread am I towing a boat upon the ocean.
Where will my God hear? Will He carry even me over?
Like water in goblets of unbaked clay do I slowly waste away.
My soul is in a dizzy whirl. Fain would I reach my home.

8. Ah, restless mind! have no fear within thy heart.
The Beginningless One Himself taketh thought for thee.
(And considereth) how thy hunger may fall from thee.
Utter, therefore, to Him alone the cry of salvation.

9. I, Lalla, wearied myself seeking for him and searching.
I laboured and strove even beyond my strength.
I began to look for him, and lo, I saw that bolts were on his door;
And even in me, as I was, did longing for him become fixed;
And there, where I was, I gazed upon Him.

RAMPRASAD
KIRTAN
[SONGS]

(Bengali)

Ramprasad (1718–75), born in Halisahar in Bengal, after obtaining some education secured a post in Calcutta as a copyist in a private estate office. He found the office work dull and irksome and scribbled verses here and there on the office papers. When the employer noticed these verses, though he was annoyed, he introduced the young poet to a patron. Thereafter Ramprasad excelled as a poet and established his fame during his lifetime. His poems are addressed to *Sakti*, or creative energy, under various names as the consort of Siva.

The translation is by Edward J. Thompson and Arthur Marshman Spencer, *Bengali Religious Lyrics; Sakta*, Calcutta: YMCA Association Press, 1923; The Heritage of India Series. Songs X, XI, XIX, XXVII, XXIX, XLVII.

RAMPRASAD
KIRTAN
[SONGS]

*X. The Vanity of Life After Life**

It is just the hope of hope, this coming into the world, and it all ends in coming, the black bee's mistake when he falls on the pictured lotus. You have fed me with *nim*-leaves, calling them sugar, deceiving me

---

*A famous song. The 'hope of hope' recalls the Greek σκιᾶς ὄναρ. Birth after birth, and all is vanity and disappointment (Thompson and Spencer).

with words. Mother, in my greed for sweets, I have spent my whole day with wry, embittered lips.

Mother, you brought me down into the world, saying, 'Let us play.' You cheated me, and in the game that you have played my hope has not found fulfilment.

Ramprasad says: In the world-play, what was to be has been. Now at eventide, taking your child in your bosom, go home.

XI. He Trusts Kali Though she Neglects Him

Mother, you are in my heart.

Dark Goddess, who says you are in my heart? You are a stony-hearted girl, a harmful delusion. Through how much trouble you make me pass! In the difference of worship, all the Five Forms become yours. He that knows the Five are but One, from him, Mother, how will you escape? He that knows, and rests all on you, him you will not help! But will the man who knows the worth of gold accept glass? Prasad says: My heart is of the right tint of the lotus. You, building those five into one, dance and dwell in my mind!

XIX. The Soul's Sleep of Death

Drowsy with desire, you wake not. Excellent is this bed of time that you have found! Think you there will never be any dawn from this night of happiness? Desire sits in your lap like a harlot, and you will not turn from her. You have drawn the sheet of hope over your body; muffling up your face, you refuse to uncover. Winter and summer alike, you remain thus, and your filthy cloth you never send to the wash. You have drunk the wine of worldly possessions and the stupor of that wine holds you down. Day and night a drunkard, even in absent-mindedness, you do not utter Kali's name.

O you foolish Prasad, foolish beyond conception, even thus your sleep hunger is not appeased. In this your sleep the great sleep will come, when you will not wake, though we call and call.

XXVII. The Worshipper's Heart is Kali's Home

The Happy One is in my heart; ever is she playing there. I meditate on thoughts that come to me, but never do I forget her name. Though both my eyes are closed, yet in my heart I see her, garlanded with heads of men.

Possessions, understanding, all are gone, and men say I am mad. Let them say what they will; but at last, I pray thee, spurn me not.

Ramprasad says: Present art thou within my lotus-heart. Spurn me not at the last, Mother, me who have found refuge at thy Feet.

XXIX. The Tyranny of Rebirth

Mother, how often will you drive me round and round the Wheel of Being, like a blindfold ox that grinds the oil? Binding me to the log of the world, you urge me round incessantly. For what guilt have you subjected me to six oilmen?* After wandering through eighty *lakhs*† of rebirths, in form of beast and bird, still the door of the womb is not closed to me, but sorely hurt I come again. When the child weeps, uttering the dear name of Mother, then the mother takes it in her lap. Throughout the whole world I see this comes to pass, I alone am excepted. Crying Durga, many sinners have attained to pardon.

Take this binding from my eyes, that I may see the Feet which banish fear. Countless are the evil children, but who ever heard of an evil mother?

Mother, this is the hope of Ramprasad, that at the end I may find station at your Feet.

Six oilmen: six passions.
† *Lakhs:* 100,000.

XLVII. Kali the only Refuge

Mind, worship her who saves on the other side of the Ocean of the World. Know once for all what worth is in the trash of wealth. Vain is hope in men or money, this was said of old time. Where wast thou, whence hast thou come, and whither, O whither, wilt thou go?

The world is glass, and ever amid its snares delusion makes men dance. Thou art in the lap of an enchantress, held fast in thy prison. Pride, malice, anger, attachment to thy lovers, by what wisdom of judgement was it that thou didst divide the kingdom of thy body among these? The day is nearly done: think therefore in thy heart, the resting-place of Kali, that island filled with jewels, think upon the things that day has brought thee.

Prasad says: The name of Durga is my promised Land of Salvation, fields flowing with nectar. Tell thy tongue evermore to utter her name.

JAYADEVA
GITA GOVINDA
[SONG OF GOVINDA]

(Sanskrit, *c*. A.D. 1200)

Jayadeva's celebrated poem *Gita Govinda*, translated as 'Song of
Govinda', or 'The Indian Song of Songs' (having some resemblance
to the Hebrew Song of Solomon), has been more often misread than
read with enthusiasm, excitement, embarrassment, or ecstasy. Edwin
Arnold found while translating this 'Oriental Opera' that 'much has
had to be modified, and the last canto omitted, in order to comply
with canons of Western [Victorian!] propriety. An English dress
cannot – alas! – fail to destroy something of the Asiatic grace of Radha;
but in her own she is radiant, fascinating, and angelic.'* While some
critics have used the epithet 'profane' to describe this poem, others
have declared it to be 'divine'. However this poem may be read and
understood in the rest of the world, in the Indian tradition it is
certainly a religious poem, and stands at the very centre of the great
spiritual movement, Bhakti (Loving-faith), which swept across the
sub-continent for over six centuries, and also influenced the Sufi
mysticism of Persia.

Jayadeva, a poet in the court of King Laksmansea of Bengal, has
expressed in his poem another aspect of the Indian view of life in its
fullness, namely, that Love, being an essential part of life, has to be
lived through and not denied, and that on the basis of such experience
of physical love man can rise to understand the experience of metaphysical love in the union of *atman* and *Brahman*. Thus the intellectual
vigour of Upanishadic thought becomes re-expressed in the vocabulary
of human love through the thread of Krishna (man-divine, Narayana)

---

*Edwin Arnold, *Light of Asia* and *The Indian Song of Songs* [Gita Govinda].
Boston 1875. Reprinted. Bombay: Jaico Publishing House, Introduction to
Gita Govinda, p. 156.

of the *Bhagavad Gita*. While the *Bhagavad Gita* gives the message of Krishna as a gospel of action in an attitude of sacrifice, *Gita Govinda* celebrates Krishna as *Govinda* (cowherd), the Universal Lover, and *gopis* (cowherdesses) as individual seekers.

Whether one conceives the formless, nameless One, That, Ultimate Power, as father, mother, king, emperor, shepherd, cowherd, friend, or lover, man basically extends human relationship to the unknown in order to establish a spiritual balance for his being in an existential situation. The most noble among such relations is the love relation, devoid of social taboos and prudery, that force which holds all creations in its magnetic fold. The celebration of such love in terms of human proportions, easily understood by man, is, from the Indian point of view, as spiritual as celebrating the socio-political or para-military conquering king emperor–subject, ruler–ruled, master–servant relations accepted in some other cultures. This Lover–Beloved relation is not the allegorical dualism of Greek *agape* or *eros*, or Spenserian Earthly and Heavenly Love,* but rather a union of the two and a simultaneous recognition of the divine in the human in which *atman* consciousness transcends to *Brahman* superconsciousness.

The *Gita Govinda* in translation, like the libretto of an opera, provides us with only the bare text, without its symphonic music and mystic ecstasy. Nevertheless, through the wealth of poetic imagery and imagination human emotions are aroused and blended and dissolved with various moods of nature, demonstrating once again that man is not necessarily 'the measure of all things', but, being a part of the larger Nature, can easily dissolve like salt in water. Thus the woods, the river, the birds, the rain, the thunder, and the moon and stars all enlarge and extend the throbbing and palpitations of the human heart to the universal rhythm of Love. In addition, the poem has, with its haunting theme and vivid imagery, given rise to a distinct school of miniature painting in India.

The complete poem has a prelude, invoking the grace of Hari (Krishna, incarnation of Vishnu), and twelve cantos in which the themes of lovers' separation, reconciliation, and reunion are developed. There are only three characters: Radha, a *gopi* (cowherdess); another

---

*Edmund Spenser, *Fowre Hymnes* (1596).

gopi, her friend and confidante; and Krishna as Govinda (cowherd).*
The story progresses through the opening stanza of the canto, while
the rest of the canto is devoted to the expression of a particular mood
or emotion arising out of the situation.

The first canto opens with the friend and confidante of Radha telling
estranged Radha, estranged from Krishna, how hard it is to endure
being separated from the lover in the spring. She describes how
Krishna is sporting, within sight, with other *gopis* (I). Overcome by
pride and jealousy, Radha goes to a thicket of creepers and describes,
lamenting, how Krishna sported with her, and how she longs for him,
and urges her friend to make Krishna enjoy Radha (II). Abandoning
the *gopis*, and placing Radha deep in his heart, Krishna goes in search
of her, but not finding her, he goes to a bower on the banks of Jamna
river (III). Radha's friend comes to Krishna and tells him how Radha
is wasting away, yearning for him, and suffering deep sorrow at her
separation from her beloved (IV). Krishna tells the friend: 'I stay
here; you go to Radha; conciliate her with my words, and bring her
here.' The friend goes to Radha and urges her to be reconciled to
Krishna (V). Unable to move Radha from the bower where she sits
maddened with longing, the friend goes to Krishna and tells him of
Radha's delirium (VI).

In the evening, when the moon rises, Radha's love for Krishna
increases and she becomes most wretched in her anguish. She assumes
that Krishna is false, because he delays coming to her. She thinks
Death would be a blessing. Seeing her friend return alone, Radha
imagines that some other woman is sporting with Krishna. Radha
envies the girl who may be enjoying Krishna and thinks that the
other woman is not suffering the anguish of separation (VII). The
night has passed with the lovers still estranged. Then the friend goes
to Krishna and urges him to go to Radha and not expect her to come
to him (VIII). The friend urges Radha, putting aside her wounded
pride, to go to her lover, and allow him to speak to her in tender
words (IX). Then towards the end of the day, when Radha, softened
in her anger, weakened in restraint against her sighs, and expecting a

---

*In this poem, Krishna is referred to by various names: Hari, Kesava,
Kamsa's enemy, Madhava, Nanda's son, Mura's slayer, Narayana, etc.

message through her friend, Krishna secretly comes to her and speaks of his longing for her. He urges her to abandon her fears, and be loving to him (X).

At night fall, after soothing Radha, Krishna goes to the woods. When Radha is dressed and ornamented, and is cheerful again, the friend urges her to follow Krishna to the woods. Leading Radha to the hut in the woods, the friend coaxes shy Radha to go in and sport with Krishna. Radha enters the abode of love and beholds Krishna there, overwhelmed with joy, desiring her. Tears of delight overcome Radha as she meets her lover, who takes her in his arms (XI). Relieved of her heavy load of shame, she surrenders to Krishna on a couch of flowers. To her Krishna sings: 'To me who am Narayana (Man-divine), oh be attached, now always yours. Oh follow me, my little Radha.' The love play becomes delightful, and the lovers lie 'exhausted through the pleasures of love'. In the morning, 'her tender loveliness ravished, she continued to please'. Then Radha asks Krishna to make designs on her breasts, decorate her with ornaments and flowers, and adorn her with her clothes (XII).

The poet concludes by extolling his devotion to Vishnu and by stating that any love and beauty perceived through the music and the poetic form in his work is but the reflection of Vishnu's divine radiance.* He invokes blessings on all those who sing or read 'this poem of Jayadeva, the son of Ramadevi and Sri Bhojadeva' that they may achieve the same pure and unclouded joy which comes from the movements of hands of the Best of Men in amorous love play with Radha beside the Jamna river in Vrindavana, the forest of joy.

The selections included here, namely Cantos I–III, V, VIII, and X–XII, are taken from the translation by the artist George Kyt, *Sri Jayadeva's Gita Govinda: The Loves of Krsna and Radha*, Bombay: Kutub-Popular, 1940.

---

*Bhagavad Gita. X.41: 'Know thou that whatever is beautiful and good, whatever has glory and power is only a portion of my own radiance.'

IV.32   JAYADEVA
                       GITA GOVINDA
                     [SONG OF GOVINDA]

Canto I

In spring to Radha who walked the forest, given to following Krishna,
Radha whose limbs were tender like flowers in spring,
Whom torture of maddening thoughts through the fever of love
Hindered in movement, a friend thus tastefully said:

1. TO THE MELODY VASANTA AND THE
ACCOMPANIMENT YATI

In spring when tender Malayan breezes fondle the beautiful creepers
    of clove
And huts and bowers resound with the mingled noise of bees and
    kokila birds
Hari here in the forest dwells, in eager dance with the women folk –
It is hard to endure being parted in spring, my friend!

In spring when the women of absent traders wail and lament, distracted
    with love,
When swarms of bees on the tidy *bakula* branches fill the clustering
    flowers
Hari here in the forest dwells, in eager dance with the women folk –
It is hard to endure being parted in spring, my friend!

In spring when the violent odour of musk is the scent of the tender
    tamala sprout,
When the colour of *kimsuka* flowers, the nails of the love god's fingers,
    tears young hearts,
Hari here in the forest dwells, in eager dance with the women folk –
It is hard to endure being parted in spring, my friend!

In spring when the love lord's golden staff is seen in the colour of
   kesara flowers,
When bees which come to the clustering *patala* make that flower the
   quiver of love,
Hari here in the forest dwells, in eager dance with the women folk –
It is hard to endure being parted in spring, my friend!

In spring when youthful *karuna* trees look laughing at those who lose
   their shame,
When spear-shaped boughs are studding the quarters, piercing those
   who are parted from love,
Hari here in the forest dwells, in eager dance with the women folk –
It is hard to endure being parted in spring, my friend!

In spring – the natural friend of the young – charming with fragrance
   of *madhavika*,
And the jasmine scent, overpowering, swaying with folly the minds of
   even the sages,
Hari here in the forest dwells, in eager dance with the women folk –
It is hard to endure being parted in spring, my friend!

In spring when blossoming mangoes thrill to the clasp of the tremulous
   vernal creepers,
When the Vrindavana forest is cleansed by the water of Jamna mean-
   dering through the wood,
Hari here in the forest dwells, in eager dance with the women folk –
It is hard to endure being parted in spring, my friend!

This, the description – the forest in springtime, delightful – threaded
   with phases of passion,
The purpose of which is to recollect Hari, wells up in utterance of Sri
   Jayadeva.
Hari here in the forest dwells, in eager dance with the women folk –
It is hard to endure being parted in spring, my friend!

*

Attended by scent of opening *ketaki* flowers, clothing the forest with
　robes of silk –
Pollen of clove vines – the wind here burns the heart like the gushing
　forth of the love god's life.

These days – when fevered ears re-echo with low-toned *kokilas*,
　crying of pigeons
In play on mango sprouts shaken by bees gone greedily for the smell
　of the honey –
These days the travelling traders somehow spend, whose religious hour
　of thought
Is given to memoried feelings of union with absent women dear as
　their lives.

To Radha this friend who was close to her spoke again pointing out
　Krishna who stood within sight,
Agitated through clasping so many women, eager for rapturous love.

＊

Sandal and garment of yellow and lotus garlands upon his body of
　blue,
In his dance the jewels of his ears in movement dangling over his
　smiling cheeks.
Hari here disports himself with charming women given to love!

The wife of a certain herdsman sings as Hari sounds a tune of love
Embracing him the while with all the force of her full and swelling
　breasts.
Hari here disports himself with charming women given to love!

Another artless woman looks with ardour on Krishna's lotus face
Where passion arose through restless motion of playful eyes with side-
　long glances.
Hari here disports himself with charming women given to love!

Another comes with beautiful hips, making as if to whisper a word,
And drawing close to his ear the adorable Krishna she kisses upon the
　cheek.
Hari here disports himself with charming women given to love!

Another on the bank of the Jamna, when Krishna goes to a bamboo
thicket,
Pulls at his garment to draw him back, so eager is she for amorous
play.
Hari here disports himself with charming women given to love!

Hari praises another woman, lost with him in the dance of love,
The dance where the sweet low flute is heard in the clamour of
bangles on hands that clap.
Hari here disports himself with charming women given to love!

He embraces one woman, he kisses another, and fondles another
beautiful one,
He looks at another one lovely with smiles, and starts in pursuit of
another woman.
Hari here disports himself with charming women given to love!

May all prosperity spread from this, Sri Jayadeva's famed and
delightful
Song of wonderful Kesava's secret play in the forest of Vrindavana!
Hari here disports himself with charming women given to love!

*

With his limbs, tender and dark like rows of clumps of blue lotus
flowers,
By herd-girls surrounded, who embrace at pleasure any part of his
body,
Friend, in spring beautiful Hari plays like Love's own self
Conducting the love sport, with love for all, bringing delight into
being.

The wind from the Malayan range seeks Siva's mountain, to plunge in
its coolness,
As if tortured by heat from the coils of the serpents dwelling there in
its caves*
And the voices, low-toned and loud, of the *kokilas* 'kuhuh, kuhuh',
Delightedly crying at sight of the buds on smooth mango-summits.

---

*By reason of the sandal trees, among the roots of which snakes live.

May the smiling captivating Hari protect you, whom Radha, blinded by love,
Violently kissed as she made as if singing a song of welcome saying,
'Your face is nectar, excellent,' ardently clasping his bosom
In the presence of the fair-browed herd-girls dazed in the sport of love!

Canto II

Radha's Lament

In careless love with any among the herd-girls when Hari dwelt in the forest,
Radha, gone elsewhere, through broken pride and jealousy, gone to a thicket of creepers
Noisy above with the humming of swarms of bees encircling over,
Radha, hidden away and wasted in body, secretly said to her friend:

1. TO THE MELODY GURJARI AND THE ACCOMPANIMENT YATI

I remember Hari, the jests he made, who placed his sport in the pastoral dance,
The sweet of whose nectar of lips kept flowing with notes of his luring melodious flute,
With the play of whose eyes and the toss of whose head the earrings kept dangling upon his cheeks.

I remember Hari, the jests he made, who placed his sport in the pastoral dance,
Whose hair was encircled above with a circle of peacock feathers with moonlike eyes,
Whose beautiful form was a heavy cloud with a perfect rainbow coloured above.

I remember Hari, the jests he made, who placed his sport in the
pastoral dance,
Who had a desire for kissing the mouths of the *gopi* women with
ample hips,
Hari whose sprout-like lips were flowers of *bandhujiva*, fair with his
smile.

I remember Hari, the jests he made, who placed his sport in the
pastoral dance,
Whose thrilled and sprout-like arms with their hairs upstanding
resembled the thousands of girls
Around him, Hari who smote the night with the many gems on his
hands and feet.

I remember Hari, the jests he made, who placed his sport in the
pastoral dance,
Whose brow had a perfect sandal spot, as among dark clouds the disc
of the moon,
Whose door-like heart was without pity when crushing the bosoms of
swelling breasts.

I remember Hari, the jests he made, who placed his sport in the
pastoral dance,
Allaying their fear of sin who gathered together under the Kadamba
tree,
Pleasing me with his mind, with quivering looks as of bodiless Love*
embodied.

I remember Hari, the jests he made, who placed his sport in the
pastoral dance,
To whom recollection among the good the song now of Sri Jayadeva
induces,
Recollection devout, Hari with Vishnu's deluding and charmingly
lovely form.

*

---

*When Kama the love god was reduced to ashes by Siva he was known
as Ananga, bodiless.

Desire even now in my foolish mind for Krishna,
For Krishna – without me – lusting still for the herd-girls!
Seeing only the good in his nature, what shall I do?
Agitated, I feel no anger! Pleased without cause, I acquit him!

2. TO THE MELODY MALAVAGAUDA AND THE ACCOMPANIMENT EKATALI

O make him enjoy me, my friend, that haughty destroyer of Kesi, that
    Krishna so fickle,
Me who in darkness, unseen, to a thicket for house, departed with him,
Dwelling concealed in a secret place with him, only to lose him there-
    after
And wander in anxious quest all over for him who laughs out his love.

O make him enjoy me, my friend, that haughty destroyer of Kesi, that
    Krishna so fickle,
I who am shy like a girl on her way to the first of her trysts of love,
He who is charming with flattering words, I who am tender
In speech and smiling, he on whose hip the garment lies loosely worn.

O make him enjoy me, my friend, that haughty destroyer of Kesi, that
    Krishna so fickle,
He whose couch was of tender shoots beneath me, my bosom itself
For long which served as a bed for him, for Krishna the lips of whose
    mouth
Resembled a drink in kissing me, clasped while we were in each other's
    embrace.

O make him enjoy me, my friend, that haughty destroyer of Kesi, that
    Krishna so fickle,
Me who sweated and moistened all over my body with love's exertion,
That Krishna whose cheeks were lovely with down all standing on
    end as he thrilled,
Whose half-closed eyes were languid, and restless who was in his
    brimming desire.

O make him enjoy me, my friend, that haughty destroyer of Kesi, that
    Krishna so fickle,
Me whose masses of curls were like loose-slipping flowers, whose
    amorous words
Were vague as of doves and *kokila* birds, that Krishna whose bosom is
    marked
With scratches, surpassing all in his love that science of love could
    teach.

O make him enjoy me, my friend, that haughty destroyer of Kesi, that
    Krishna so fickle,
To whose act of desire accomplished the anklets upon my feet be-
    jewelled
Vibrated sounding, who gave his kisses seizing the hair of the head,
And to whom in his passionate love my girdle sounded in eloquence
    sweet.

O make him enjoy me, my friend, that haughty destroyer of Kesi, that
    Krishna so fickle,
Whose lotus eyes had closed a little, and who had drowsily grown –
Having tasted in bodily pleasure with me the shattering thrill in the
    end,
With me whose vine-like body collapsed, unable to bear any more.

O make him enjoy me, my friend, that haughty destroyer of Kesi,
    that Krishna so fickle,
And may he playfully make more pleasure, sung here by Sri Jayadeva
Describing his many and endless amours with amorous *gopi* women.

*

In the forest I see – I am thrilled – Govinda surrounded by herd-girls,
    his love-flute fallen;
At the girls with their arched eyebrows glancing, Govinda moist with
    sweat on his cheeks,
At seeing me an embarrassed nectar of a smile on his sweet face.

In the distance, my friend, the sight of the clustering buds of *asoka*
  creepers distresses,
And the wind from over the gardens and lakes, and the opening of buds
  on the mango tops
Alive with the humming of bees; so pleasant, no pleasure to me.

May Krishna in this his unusual aspect, gazing a long while into the
  mind,
Cleanse you of that sin which is seen in the pleasure of infatuated
  hearts
And in the meaning smiles and loosening dishevelled hair, in the
  gleam of the surging of herd-girls,
In their wanton raising of arms above their arm-pits to display their
  breasts.

Canto III

Krishna's Lament

Kamsa's enemy, abandoning the herd-girls, placed Radha in his heart,
Radha as a chain through relation to the robe of the world, Shri
  Krishna.

Krishna repentant, his heart scarred by shafts of the love god, went
  about looking for Radha,
Searching all over, full of dejection, he went to a bower on the banks of
  the Jamna.

I. TO THE MELODY GURJARI AND THE
ACCOMPANIMENT YATI

Radha so deeply wronged, troubled to see me surrounded by women,
She went, and I, in the fear of my guilt, made no attempt to stop her.
Alas, alas, she is gone in anger, her love destroyed!

Parted so long, now what will she do if I see her? What will she say?
What of wealth any more? What use of the herd-girls? Why continue
  to live?
Alas, alas, she is gone in anger, her love destroyed!

I think of that face of hers, wrathful, eyebrows crooked, knitted in
  anger,
A crimson lotus clouded beneath the bees which keep hovering over
  it!
Alas, alas, she is gone in anger, her love destroyed!

She who has come to my heart, I sport her always with warmth and
  fervour.
Why follow her here in the forest now? Why mourn in vain and
  lament?
Alas, alas, she is gone in anger, her love destroyed!

O my slender one, I imagine your heart is dejected through anger of
  me –
I cannot console you kneeling in homage, I know not where to find
  you!
Alas, alas, she is gone in anger, her love destroyed!

As if inconstant, coming and going, so you appear before me.
The ardent embrace you used to give me, oh why not give it again?
Alas, alas, she is gone in anger, her love destroyed!

If you pardon me now I shall never repeat this neglect of you ever –
O beautiful, give me your pleasure again, I burn with desire!
Alas, alas, she is gone in anger, her love destroyed!

This of Hari alone is a song by the famed Jayadeva,
Who arose, as out of the ocean the moon, from the village of Kindu-
  bilva,
Alas, alas, she is gone in anger, her love destroyed!

*

Not the king of serpents this lotus necklace upon my bosom,
Not the gleam of poison upon my neck this chain of blue lotus,
Not ash this unguent of sandal dust upon me;
Mistake me not for Siva,* O love god, assail not me!

---

*Allusion to Kama's assault on the ascetic god in order to influence him
with love for Parvati.

O love god, you who won conquering all through play,
Oh not in your bow place your arrow, this mango sprout, not in your
    hand!
What valour destroying the weakened?

My mind – through the pain of those other arrows of Love, the looks
    of the deer-eyed Radha –
I assure you, smarts me still!

On Radha, embodying his victory, Love, who conquers all things
Placed his bow, her sprout-like eyebrows; his arrows, her fluttering
    glances;
His bow-string, the tips of the curves of her ears; – the weapons of
    Love.

So your arrow of eye-play placed on your bow of an eyebrow wounds
    me;
Death's work is done too, my slender one, by your curly black tresses;
Your lip, like a *bimba* fruit, but infatuates further;
And your bosom, so chaste, how it ravages playing with my life!

These are with her the pleasures of being intimate:
The charms vibrant and moist of her eyes and the scent of her lotus
    mouth,
The ambiguous sweet nectar-dripping of her words and the sweetness
    of her *bimba* lips;
On these the mind dwelling attached, even so is increased the pain of
    being parted.

May welfare befall you from waves of sidelong glances
The love god's looks in Radha's moon of a face
Artlessly sweet, and of nectar, disclosed by the signs of the women who
    send their devotion
To the shining place of his flute, of him with his swaying head, whose
    earrings keep dangling across his neck!

*

Canto V
Maid tells Radha of Krishna's plight

'I stay here; you go to Radha; conciliate her with my words, and
   bring her!'
So himself did Madhu's enemy say to the friend; and she came to
Radha and said:

I. TO THE MELODY DESIVARADI AND THE
ACCOMPANIMENT RUPAKA

When breezes blow from the Malayan mountain, longing grows and
   increases;
When clusters of flowers open in bloom, torn are the hearts that are
   parted.
He droops, separated from you, O friend, the wearer of garlands!

When he appears to be dead, at the time, even then, when the cold
   moon is burning,
He wails in dejection beneath the falling of shafts from the god of
   desire.
He droops, separated from you, O friend, the wearer of garlands!

When he hears the noise of the swarms of bees, he covers his ears
   from their humming;
Pain he feels, night after night, of a heart in love that is parted.
He droops, separated from you, O friend, the wearer of garlands!

He dwells beneath the roof of the forest, discards his lovely garland;
He tosses in bed, on the floor of the forest, repeating your name in
   murmurs.
He droops, separated from you, O friend, the wearer of garlands!

Give his place in your heart to Hari, when the poet Jayadeva has
  spoken,
Your heart full of passion because of this poem which sings of love's
  separation.
He droops, separated from you, O friend, the wearer of garlands!

*

Again in the grove of the love-god, Madhava dwells on the past events
  of his amours –
His amours with you – and ceaselessly mutters, repeating the talks
  between you;
And yearns for that nectar again, the embrace of your breasts like
  pitchers.

2. TO THE MELODY GURJARI AND THE
ACCOMPANIMENT EKATALI

He has gone into the trysting place, full of all desired bliss, O you of
  lovely hips, delay no more!
Oh go forth now and seek him out, him the master of your heart, him
  endowed with passion's lovely form.
He dwells, the garland wearer, in the forest by the Jamna, in the
  gentle breezes there,
The swelling breasts of *gopi* girls who crushes ever with his restless
  hands.

Softly on his flute he plays, calling to the meeting place, naming it
  with notes and saying where;
And the pollen by the breezes borne, the breezes which have been on
  you, that pollen in his sight has high esteem.
He dwells, the garland wearer, in the forest by the Jamna, in the gentle
  breezes there,
The swelling breasts of *gopi* girls who crushes ever with his restless
  hands.

On fallen feathers of the birds, on leaves about the forest floor, he lies
  excited making there his bed,
And he gazes out upon the path, looks about with trembling eyes,
  anxious, looking out for your approach.
He dwells, the garland wearer, in the forest by the Jamna, in the gentle
  breezes there,
The swelling breasts of *gopi* girls who crushes ever with his restless
  hands.

Depart, my friend, now to that grove, impenetrable in its dark, and
  put upon your cloak of black;
Discard the anklets on your feet, betraying – noisy timid foes – which
  dance with clatter in the sport of love!
He dwells, the garland wearer, in the forest by the Jamna, in the gentle
  breezes there,
The swelling breasts of *gopi* girls who crushes ever with his restless
  hands.

O you with your complexion fair, Hari's breast will make you shine,
  that cloud with necklace as of fluttering cranes,
And there where merit-fruit is eaten, lightning you will seem in radiance, Krishna then in love-play lying beneath you!
He dwells, the garland wearer, in the forest by the Jamna, in the gentle
  breezes there,
The swelling breasts of *gopi* girls who crushes ever with his restless
  hands.

There on that bed of tender leaves, O lotus-eyed, embrace his hips,
  his naked hips from whence the girdle drops.
Those hips from whence the garment falls, those loins which are a
  treasure heap, the fountain and the source of all delight!
He dwells, the garland wearer, in the forest by the Jamna, in the gentle
  breezes there,
The swelling breasts of *gopi* girls who crushes ever with his restless
  hands.

Oh act according to my words, and satisfy with no delay the longing in
the love of Hari now!
Or otherwise now, like the ceasing of this night close on its end, that
haughty one's desire will cease for you.
He dwells, the garland wearer, in the forest by the Jamna, in the gentle
breezes there,
The swelling breasts of *gopi* girls who crushes ever with his restless
hands.

O worship Hari, to be welcomed in resembling merit, and who shows
so much of mercy to
His devotee, the poet Sri Jayadeva, who now makes his utterance of a
very lovely song!
He dwells, the garland wearer, in the forest by the Jamna, in the gentle
breezes there,
The swelling breasts of *gopi* girls who crushes ever with his restless
hands.

*

Among couples drunken with lust and gone with adulterous intent,
attained to confusion, indulging in talk,
What shameless delights are there not in the darkness, after embracing
and scratching and rousing desire and kissing,
After excitement, and starting the actions fulfilling desire!

O lovely face, the adorable one after seeing how you cast your trembling and fearful glances along the darkened road,
Pausing at every tree, tardily walking, arriving in secret, your limbs in
motion like waves of Love,
May he then realize his desire!

On the sweet and lotus-like face of Radha, he who resembles a bee,
Devaki's son, as a blue gem fit for the crests of the lords of the triple
world,
He who is death to the lords of the earth,
And among the herd-girls whenever he wishes a source of pleasure-
disturbance,
And to Kamsa the star of destruction; may he protect you!

*

Canto VIII

Krishna Urged to go to Radha

Then having somehow passed the night, and withered by the arrow
of love,
She reproachfully said to her lover at dawn, though he bowed in her
presence imploring with soothing words:

1. TO THE MELODY BHAIRAVI AND THE
ACCOMPANIMENT YATI

By breaking so much rest at night, his eyes today look very reddened,
and resemble passion in their colour,
His eyes the abode of drowsiness, and showing his addiction to
desire that so readily awakens.
Alas! Alas! Go, Madhava! Go, Kesava! Desist from uttering these
deceitful words!
Follow her, you lotus-eyed, she who can dispel your trouble, go to her!

Your mouth, O Krishna, darkened, enhances – making beautiful – the
crimson beauty of your lovely body,
Enhances with a darkness, a blackness that arises from the kissing of
eyes coloured with black unguent.
Alas! Alas! Go Madhava! Go, Kesava! Desist from uttering these
deceitful words!
Follow her, you lotus-eyed, she who can dispel your trouble, go to her!

Like a letter that declares the victory of love, and done in silver and in
gold and set with gems,
So your body now assumes the look – with scars of love-war marked
upon it, scratches made there by her fingernails.
Alas! Alas! Go Madhava! Go, Kesava! Desist from uttering these
deceitful words!
Follow her, you lotus-eyed, she who can dispel your trouble, go to her!

As if upon the tree of love, its foliage, the patches there, the coverings
of the tender leaves and sprouts,

So on this haughty breast of yours the patches here, the markings from
the red of lac made by her lotus foot.

Alas! Alas! Go, Madhava! Go, Kesava! Desist from uttering these
deceitful words!

Follow her you lotus-eyed, she who can dispel your trouble, go to her!

Made by her tooth the bruise, an imprint, on your lip I see, makes
pain for me, gives anguish to my mind;

And your body – does it not proclaim that you are no more mine, that
you have parted now from me, that you have changed?

Alas! Alas! Go, Madhava! Go, Kesava! Desist from uttering these
deceitful words!

Follow her, you lotus-eyed, she who can dispel your trouble, go to her!

I who follow you devoted – how can you deceive me, so tortured by
love's fever as I am!

O Krishna, like the look of you, your body which appears so black,
that heart of yours a blackness shall assume!

Alas! Alas! Go, Madhava! Go, Kesava! Desist from uttering these
deceitful words!

Follow her, you lotus-eyed, she who can dispel your trouble, go to her!

In your wanderings through the forest the way you ravish women, O
what is there so wonderful in that?

The Putanika yaksi proclaims to all your feat of youth – in your
pitiless destruction of the women!

Alas! Alas! Go, Madhava! Go, Kesava! Desist from uttering these
deceitful words!

Follow her, you lotus-eyed, she who can dispel your trouble, go to her!

Let those who understand give ear to this – the lamentation, the wail
of women destitute in love,

The grief of being neglected, sung by Sri Jayadeva, in heaven even
rare and sweet as nectar.

Alas! Alas! Go, Madhava! Go, Kesava! Desist from uttering these
deceitful words!

Follow her, you lotus-eyed, she who can dispel your trouble, go to her!

The sight of your flow of a love of a bosom aglow with patches of lac
from the foot of your sweetheart
Causes my shame to take the place of my sorrow born of my great
love being destroyed.

May blessings be bestowed by the sound of the flute of Kamsa's foe,
The sound of the flute removing the difficult grief of the gods by the
danavas humbled,
The sound of the flute, the great invitation to the deer-eyed women,
stirring, delighting, and making them bold,
The sound bringing down from the crests of the dwellers of heaven,
swaying with pleasure, the mandara flowers!

*

Canto X

Krishna Pleads for a Reconciliation

Then in the day's decline when Radha – softened in anger, weak in
restraint against her ceaseless sighs –
Was awaiting the message her friend would bring, Hari with faltering
steps of joy, shyly went to that beautiful one and said:

I. TO THE MELODY DESAVARADI AND THE
ACCOMPANIMENT ASTA

If you speak but a little the moon-like gleam of your teeth will destroy
the darkness frightful, so very terrible, come over me;
Your moon of a face which glitters upon my eye, the moonbird's eye,
now makes me long for the sweet of your lips.
O loved one, O beautiful, give up that baseless pride against me!
My heart is burnt by the fire of longing; give me that drink so sweet
of your lotus face!

O you with beautiful teeth, if you are in anger against me, strike me
then with your fingernails, sharp and like arrows,

Bind me, entwining, with the cords of your arms, and bite me then
with your teeth, and feel happy punishing!

O loved one, O beautiful, give up that baseless pride against me!

My heart is burnt by the fire of longing; give me that drink so sweet
of your lotus face!

You are my life, and you are my ornament, you are the jewel, the gem,
in the depth of the ocean of all my being,

So be gracious to me, and thus continue to be, and my heart shall
always endeavour to be most worthy of you!

O loved one, O beautiful, give up that baseless pride against me!

My heart is burnt by the fire of longing; give me that drink so sweet
of your lotus face!

O slender one, in your anger today even your eye, a blue lotus, assumes
now the look of a crimson lotus;

But if through the power of the flower-arrowed one, the love-god, you
make the blue Krishna crimson that action is only right!

O loved one, O beautiful, give up that baseless pride against me!

My heart is burnt by the fire of longing; give me that drink so sweet
of your lotus face!

Let the radiant cluster of gems that glitter upon your jar-shaped
breast make bright the region of your heart!

Let your girdle upon the swelling curve of your hips so firm make a
tinkling sound, proclaiming Love's command!

O loved one, O beautiful, give up that baseless pride against me!

My heart is burnt by the fire of longing; give me that drink so sweet
of your lotus face!

O you with your gentle voice, but speak! With lac I shall redden the
soles of your feet and make them glisten with oil,

Your pair of feet surpassing hibiscus flowers, delighting my heart, your
feet unrivalled in amorous play.

O loved one, O beautiful, give up that baseless pride against me!

My heart is burnt by the fire of longing; give me that drink so sweet
of your lotus face!

As an ornament place upon my head your proud and stalk-like feet,
as a cure for the venom of desire!

O let your feet remove the change now made by the pitiless fire of
love, which burns and which destroys!

O loved one, O beautiful, give up that baseless pride against me!

My heart is burnt by the fire of longing; give me that drink so sweet
of your lotus face!

All this song with these words of Mura's foe, adorned with the beautiful
speech of the poet Jayadeva,

Tender and skilful and full of delight, prevails, having won over
Radha and flattering haughty women.

O loved one, O beautiful, give up that baseless pride against me!

My heart is burnt by the fire of longing; give me that drink so sweet
of your lotus face!

*

Abandon your fears, O anxious one, but for the love god – that bodiless
one – none is so blest as to enter my heart, tenanted ever by you
with your hips and breasts so firm.

When you embrace me, my sweetheart, inflict upon me then, as a
penalty, all the things that result in the bondage of that embrace!

Pressing upon me your breasts so hard, entwining me with your vine-
like arms, biting me with your merciless teeth, inflict upon me,
foolish one, the suitable penalty!

Then through the blows of Love – that base one, the five-arrowed –
my life will depart from me, your rogue, and you shall be happy!

A cure unfailing, O moon-face one, is the nectar of your lips,

A cure for destroying the fear in the hearts of the young men who see
in their infatuation your eyebrow-curve as a deadly serpent.

To no purpose, O slender one, you pain me with silence! Make
music, O you of sweet notes, and dispel my heat with your glances!

O you of the beautiful face, but give up aversion to me, to me your
lover, sweet one, so tenderly waiting on you; elude not me!

Your lips are one with the colour of *bandhuka* blossoms, and the
tender skin of your cheek, you rogue, gleams pale like the *madhuka*
flower;
The beautiful blue of the lotus is shown in your eyes; your nose
resembles the sesamum flower;
And altogether, O loved one, with you, O you with your teeth of
jasmine, the god whose weapons are flowers conquers the world
with the hosts of your face!

With your languorous eyes, your glistening mouth like the moon, your
gait the delight of the people, your thighs excelling the trunk of
the plantain;
With your skilful amorous play, with the sweet and beautiful streaks
of your eyebrows;
How wonderful, slender one, though on earth, the way you bear in
your person the nymphs of heaven!

May that Hari bestow more happiness, that Hari who met the
Kuvalayapida demon in battle and saw in the jar-shaped hands of the
demon the likeness of Radha's breasts, and sweated and closed his
eyes a moment;
So that Kamsa, deluded, began to cry, 'Subdued! He is conquered!
He is overcome.'

Canto XI

Maid Urges Radha to be reconciled with Krishna

At nightfall, which robs one of sight, when Kesava, suitably clothed,
after soothing the deer-eyed one, and gone to the thicket,
A certain young woman said to Radha – who was cheerful now and
had put on her jewels and looked like the sun:

I. TO THE MELODY VASANTA AND THE
ACCOMPANIMENT YATI

Who made a song of coaxing words, bowing at your feet in homage,
And gone now to the lovely clump of bamboos, to the bed of passion,
O foolish woman, follow him who looks with favour now, O Radha,
Madhu's slayer!

O you who bear the weight of heavy thighs and heavy breasts, come
    hither
With tardy tread that shames the goose and with your jewelled anklets
    tinkling,
O foolish woman, follow him who looks with favour now, O Radha,
    Madhu's slayer!

Listen to his lovely noise, infatuating, end your yearning
Where the flocks of cuckoos praise the reign of him whose bow is
    flowers!
O foolish woman, follow him who looks with favour now, O Radha,
    Madhu's slayer!

O you with thighs like elephant trunks, these creepers with their
    hands aflutter,
Their tendrils waving in the wind, appear to ask you to the meeting!
O foolish woman, follow him who looks with favour now, O Radha,
    Madhu's slayer!

Consult your jar-shaped breast on which are spotless streams of
    necklaces,
Which quivers undulating on the waves, the surging force of passion!
O foolish woman, follow him who looks with favour now, O Radha,
    Madhu's slayer!

Your friends are all aware, you rogue, that you are ready for love's
    conflict,
Go, your belt aloud with bells, shameless, amorous, to the meeting!
O foolish woman, follow him who looks with favour now, O Radha,
    Madhu's slayer!

O you with arrows of Love for nails, leaning on your friend, seductive
Go to Hari, his ways are known, and know him by his bracelets'
    tinkling!
O foolish woman, follow him who looks with favour now, O Radha,
    Madhu's slayer!

May this song of Jayadeva dwell upon the necks of people
Given to Hari, necks the beauty of their necklaces surpassing.
O foolish woman, follow him who looks with favour now, O Radha,
    Madhu's slayer!

*

She will see me, her speech that of love, herself in the bliss of a close
    embrace, intimate, limb to limb, sporting in dalliance, O friend,
    having come!
Full of this thought the lover he sees her, imagining, in the grove in
    a mass of deep darkness,
And he trembles, thrilled, feels glad, perspires, and attempts to step
    forward, and swoons.

Beautiful, a robe of black, the darkness which has caused them to
    smear on their eyelids black unguent,
And wreaths of clusters of *tapiccha* blossoms over their ears and
    garlands of dark coloured lotuses over their heads and streaks of
    musk across their bosoms, O friend,
The darkness embracing the limbs of those beautiful rogues, the herd-
    girls, excited, in haste to go to the tryst.

Dark like tender *tamala* leaves the darkness shaped with an outline
    everywhere by the flashing clusters of jewels of the women gone to
    the tryst,
The women whose bodies are yellow with saffron,
The darkness the touchstone, the test of the gold of his love.

Then in the entrance to his hut in the thicket, lit by the central gems
    of his gold belt's pendant and the gems of his garland and on his
    anklets and earrings,
She pointed out Hari to Radha her friend, Radha so shy, and said:

2. TO THE MELODY VARADI AND THE ACCOMPANIMENT RUPAKA

O you who bear on your face the smile that comes of the ardour of
    passion,
Sport with him whose love-abode is the floor of the beautiful bower!
O Radha, go to Madhava, go in here!

O you whose necklaces tremble upon your breast resembling a pitcher,
Sport there where the bed of lustrous *asoka* sprouts is a treasure!
O Radha, go to Madhava, go in here!

O you whose body, tender and soft, resembles tender blossoms,
Sport there in that beautiful place, an abode made of heaps of flowers!
O Radha, go to Madhava, go in here!

O you who fear in alarm the shafts of desire falling in showers,
Sport in that place which is lovely and cool with Malayan breezes
    blowing!
O Radha, go to Madhava, go in here!

O you the curves of whose lovely hips are heavy and full of languor,
Sport long in that place so dense with sprouts of many wide-spreading
    creepers!
O Radha, go to Madhava, go in here!

O you whose heart is full of the longings of him whose arrows are
    flowers,
Sport in that place which is filled with the sound of bees who delight
    in sweetness!
O Radha, go to Madhava, go in here!

O Mura's foe bestow a hundred blessings on Jayadeva,
The king of the kings of poets, who sang your praises and made for
    Padmavati a happy circle!
O Radha, go to Madhava, go in here!

*

He is tired, having borne you so long in his heart, he is burnt by Love,
    and desires to drink of your lips contracted with nectar;
So adorn his lap for a moment here in this place that was given in fear
    to your slave, your slave who was bought with a little part of the
    wealth of a frown,
Your slave who has worshipped your lotus foot.

Her eyes to Govinda turning desirous, anxious and with delight
She entered the abode of Love, her beautiful anklets tinkling.

3. TO THE MELODY VARADI AND THE
ACCOMPANIMENT YATI

She looked on Hari who desired only her, on him who for long wanted
dalliance,
Whose face with his pleasure was overwhelmed and who was possessed
with Desire,
Hari on whose body the waves of many changes appeared at the sight
of her face
Like the ocean in dance with its waves ascending when seeing the
face of the moon.

She looked on Hari who desired only her, on him who for long wanted
dalliance,
Whose face with his pleasure was overwhelmed and who was possessed
with Desire,
After embracing her long and ardently, Hari with his necklace of pearls,
Hari like the Jamna in a mighty flood with its necklace of specks of
foam.

She looked on Hari who desired only her, on him who for long wanted
dalliance,
Whose face with his pleasure was overwhelmed and who was possessed
with Desire,
On Hari whose body was dark and tender, clothed in a garment of
yellow,
Like a lotus blue-coloured whose centre is circled around by a mass of
pollen.

She looked on Hari who desired only her, on him who for long wanted
dalliance,
Whose face with his pleasure was overwhelmed and who was possessed
with Desire,
Who engendered passion with his face made lovely through tremblings
of glancing eyes,
Like a pond in autumn with a pair of wagtails at play in a fullblown
lotus.

She looked on Hari who desired only her, on him who for long wanted
dalliance,

Whose face with his pleasure was overwhelmed, and who was possessed with Desire,

Who was adorned with earrings like suns come to clasp his lotus of a
face,

And who for her lips – with a sweet smile gleaming, lovely, like
sprouts – felt a longing.

She looked on Hari who desired only her, on him who for long wanted
dalliance,

Whose face with his pleasure was overwhelmed, and who was possessed with Desire,

Whose hair had beautiful flowers, like a cloud with moonbeams
studded within,

And whose brow had the sandal spot unblemished, like the disc of the
moon in the dark.

She looked on Hari who desired only her, on him who for long wanted
dalliance,

Whose face with his pleasure was overwhelmed, and who was possessed with Desire,

Whose body was thrilling all over, restless, because of his skill in love,

Whose body was lovely because of the ornaments, flashings of many
gems.

She looked on Hari who desired only her, on him who for long wanted
dalliance,

Whose face with his pleasure was overwhelmed, and who was possessed with Desire.

O people, place Hari for ever in your hearts, Hari the source of all
merit,

By whom, in the wealth of Jayadeva's poem, all beauty of art has been
doubled!

*

Like the gushing of the shower of sweat in the effort of her travel to
    come to his hearing,
Radha's eyes let fall a shower of tears when she met her beloved,
Tears of delight which went to the ends of her eyes and fell on her
    flawless necklace.

When she went near the couch and her friends left the bower, scratch-
    ing their faces to hide their smiles,
And she looked on the mouth of her loved one, lovely with longing,
    under the power of love,
The modest shame of that deer-eyed one departed.

May Nanda's son be happy to show you infinite joy,
Nanda's son laying gentle hands on Radha, and placing her in his
    arms, and suddenly stirred and embracing her close,
And looking round over his back, craning his neck, and fearing, 'May
    her firm high breasts not pierce and break through my body!'

The rod-like punishing arm of Mura's slayer prevails,
That arm which drips with the blood of the demon, playfully killed,
Kuvalayapida, elephant-like, that arm upon which the goddess of
    victory scattered the *mandara* flowers,
That arm self-marked, as it were, with lac, the blood, the sign of the
    joy of fighting the demon.

Canto XII

Reconciliation, Union, Realization

When the group of her friends had departed, Hari looked on his
    sweetheart Radha, she who was amorous, her eyes on the couch of
    flowers, a smile of desire on her lip,
Radha released of her heavy load of shame, and he said:

I. TO THE MELODY VIBHASA AND THE
ACCOMPANIMENT EKATALI

O you woman with desire, place upon this patch of flower-strewn floor
 your lotus foot, upon this bed of sprouts,
And let your foot through beauty win, contending with the bed's
 appearance, this bed of sprouts which is so fair to see!
To me who am Narayana,* oh be attached, now always yours! Oh
 follow me, my little Radha!

You came here journeying from afar, enduring much, so with my lotus
 flowers of hands I shall adore your feet;
Use me always on the bed, me, valiant in being attached, as if I were
 an anklet for your use!
To me who am Narayana, oh be attached, now always yours! Oh
 follow me, my little Radha!

Make pleasant conversation now and make complacent speech like
 drops of nectar falling from your face, the moon;
As if it were the garment on your bosom which conceals your breasts,
 I shall remove the pain of being parted!
To me who am Narayana, oh be attached, now always yours! Oh
 follow me, my little Radha!

To extinguish now my fire of passion lay your breast upon my
 bosom, place your jar-shaped breast against my breast,
Which seemed so hard for me to have, your lovely breast, elusive, and
 impatient for the pleasures of embrace!
To me who am Narayana, oh be attached, now always yours! Oh
 follow me, my little Radha!

O lovely woman, give me now the nectar of your lips, infuse new life
 into this slave of yours, so dead,
This slave whose heart is placed in you, whose body burned in
 separation, this slave denied the pleasures of your love!
To me who am Narayana, oh be attached, now always yours! Oh
 follow me, my little Radha!

_____
*Vishnu.

O moon-face woman, make the bells upon your jewelled girdle tinkle,
mimicking the noises of your throat,

And now at last destroy that pain of those from loved ones severed –
the agony of listening to the cuckoos!

To me who am Narayana, oh be attached, now always yours! Oh
follow me, my little Radha!

Your eye now looked upon by me extinguishes that me which was
embodiment of very shame itself,

Me made unhappy by your anger undeserved, me made to feel so
uselessly the agony of longing!

To me who am Narayana, oh be attached, now always yours! Oh
follow me, my little Radha!

Among all tasteful people may this song of Jayadeva create a state of
passionate delight,

This poem which in every verse proclaims the satisfaction in the
pleasure of the love of Madhu's slayer.

To me who am Narayana, oh be attached, now always yours! Oh
follow me, my little Radha!

*

Their love play grown great was very delightful, the low play where
thrills were a hindrance to firm embraces,

Where their helpless closing of eyes was a hindrance to longing looks
at each other, and their secret talk to their drinking of each the
other's nectar of lips, and where the skill of their love was hindered
by boundless delight.

She performed as never before throughout the course of the conflict
of love, to win, lying over his beautiful body, to triumph over her
lover;

And so through taking the active part her thighs grew lifeless, and
languid her vine-like arms, and her heart beat fast, and her eyes
grew heavy and closed;

For how may women prevail in the male performance!

In the morning most wondrous, the heart of her lord was smitten with
arrows of Love, arrows which went through his eyes,

Arrows which were her nailed-scratched bosom, her reddened sleep-
denied eyes, her crimson lips from a bath of kisses, her hair dis-
arranged with the flowers awry, and her girdle all loose and slipping.

With hair knot loosened and stray locks waving, her cheeks perspiring,
her glitter of *bimba* lips impaired,

And the necklace of pearls not appearing fair because of her jar-
shaped breast being denuded,

And her belt, her glittering girdle dimmed in beauty,

And all of a sudden placing her hands on her naked breasts, and over
her naked loins, to hide them, and looking embarrassed;

Even so, with her tender loveliness ravaged, she continued to please!

The happy one drank of the face where the lips were washed with the
juice of his mouth,

His mouth half open uttering amorous noises, vague and delirious, the
rows of teeth in the breath of an indrawn sigh delightedly chattering.

Drank of the face of that deer-eyed woman whose body lay helpless,
released of excessive delight, the thrilling delight of embraces
making the breasts both flaccid and firm.

Then Radha – free of love's obstacles, Radha whose lover lay prone
in her power, exhausted through pleasure of love –

Said with a wish for adornment:

2. TO THE MELODY RAMAKARI AND THE
ACCOMPANIMENT YATI

She said to the joy of her heart, the delight of the Yadus,

O delight of the Yadus, depict here and make a design, a pattern, with
musk on my breast,

My breast the twin of the festal pitcher of love, depict with your hand
which is cool!

She said to the joy of her heart, the delight of the Yadus,

O loved one, renew the kohl on my eyelids, shaming a cluster of bees, being blacker,

The kohl you have smudged with your kisses, the black on my eyelids releasing the arrows of Love!

She said to the joy of her heart, the delight of the Yadus,

O you apparelled so lovely, wear on the lobes of your ears earrings which shame.

Your dancing deer-eyes on the lobes of your ears which bear the noose of the play of Desire!

She said to the joy of her heart, the delight of the Yadus,

Adorn the curl on my brow which puts the lotus to shame, my spotless brow,

The curl which brings about laughter, which makes on my beautiful forehead a cluster of bees!

She said to the joy of her heart, the delight of the Yadus,

O lotus face, make a beautiful spot on my forehead, a spot with the paste of the sandal.

Like a digit of the hare-marked moon, make on the moon of my brow, which is sweating no more!

She said to the joy of her heart, the delight of the Yadus,

O giver of pride, on my tresses, untidy now on account of desire, place flowers,

My curls, excelling the feathers of peacocks, in which the whisk is the banner of Love!

She said to the joy of her heart, the delight of the Yadus,

O you with a beautiful heart, place on my hips the girdle, the clothes, and the jewels –

Cover my beautiful loins, luscious and firm, the cavern of Love to be feared!

She said to the joy of her heart, the delight of the Yadus,
Full of compassion, O place your heart in the words of the song of
    Sri Jayadeva
Ridding with nectar this sinful age of its fever recalling the feet of
    Hari!

*

Make a pattern upon my breasts and a picture on my cheeks and fasten
    over my loins a girdle,
Bind my masses of hair with a beautiful garland and place many brace-
    lets upon my hands and jewelled anklets upon my feet!
And he so who wore the yellow garment did as she told him.

*

Whatever is of the condition of love's discernment shown with beauty
    in poetic form, and all skill in the art of heaven's musicians, and all
    of reflection on Vishnu,
All such you may joyfully see, wise people, in this the song of the Lord
    of Herds, made by the poet devoted to him, the wise Jayadeva.

May the art of poetry seen in this poem be in the mouths of those who
    are dear to Parasara and the others,
This poem of Sri Jayadeva the son of Ramadevi and Sri Bhojadeva.
Jayadeva's words of insight wherever known, like love's own glorious
    flavour,
There, O drink, not pleasant is the thought of you any more; and hardly
    sweet you become, O sugar; and who, O wine, would want to look
    on you?
O nectar, you are no more immortal; and like water you taste, O milk;
    and you have to lament, O mango; and cease to compare, O beautiful
    lip.

May pure and unclouded joy and prosperity come from the movements
    of hands of the Best of Men, amorous hands delighting in breasts
    resembling the *prayaga* fruit,
Hands in performance of many forms of amorous play with Radha
    beside the Jamna.

On the bank where coquettish tresses were waving, at the tryst where his black hair mixed with her necklace of pearls, where the dark Jamna meets the Ganges' white stream at Prayaga.

MIRA-BAI

BHAJAN

[HYMNS]

(Gujarati, Hindi, *c.* A.D. 1400)

Mira-bai was a princess of Rajaputana, married to the son of Maharana
of Mewar, but widowed by the untimely death of her husband. When
her relatives persecuted her for her devotion to Krishna, she fled from
Chitor and became a Bhakta. By pouring forth her heart through the
love theme of Radha-Krishna in rapturous and melodious hymns,
Mira-bai popularized Krishna worship. In her devotion, she reached
a high degree of ecstasy, and became (like St Theresa), in her spiritual
life, the bride of Lord Krishna.

The translations from Gujarati are by Mrs Taylor and Mrs Ramanbai
M. Nilkanth (Bhajan XLIV, XLVII, XLIX), and from Hindi by Mrs
Keay (Bhajan LI, LIII, LIV, LVI), quoted in Margaret Macnicol,
ed., *Poems by Indian Women*, The Heritage of India Series, London:
Oxford University Press, 1923, pp. 60–6.

IV.33   MIRA-BAI

BHAJAN

[HYMNS]

XLIV. The Name Radha Krishna

Utter not, utter not, utter not any word but Radha Krishna.
Do not forsake the sweet taste of sugar and sugar cane and mix it with
 the bitter lime.
Do not forsake the light of the moon and the sun and set your affection
 on a glow-worm.
Do not give up diamonds, rubies and jewels, nor weigh real gems against
 pewter.
Miran says, 'The Lord who holds up the mountain has given you an
 equipoised body.'

XLVII. *Govind is my Life*

Govind is my life; the world tastes bitter to me.
I love Rama and Rama alone; let my eyes see no other.
In Miran's palace dwell Hari's saints; Hari dwells far from intrigue
   with his saints.

XLIX. *The Jewels of the Saint*

I, a woman, have a vast estate; true jewels are my portion.
I fashion my nose-ring of Vitthal and the wreath of Hari is on my heart.
My thoughts are a string of pearls and my bangles are Vishnu. Why
   should I go to the goldsmith?
My fetters are of the Lord of Life, Krishna my gold and silver anklets.
My silver ornaments are Rama and Narayan; my *anvat* is the one who
   discerns the heart.
Let me make Purushottam my casket; Trikam the name of the padlock.
Let me make the key of compassion and joy, and in it keep my jewels.

LI. *The Beloved*

I am fascinated by the beauty of Mohan:
In the bazaar and by the way he teases me.
I have not learned the sweet desire of my beloved.

His body is beautiful and his eyes are like lotus flowers.
His glance is very pleasing, and his smile is very sweet.

Near the bank of the river Jumna he is grazing the cows,
And sings a sweet song to the flute.

I surrender myself, body and soul and wealth, to the Mountain-holder.
Mira clasps his lotus feet.

LIII. *Separation*

The clouds, driven to and fro, have come,
But they have not brought any news of Hari.
The frog, the peacock and the sparrow hawk utter their cries,
And the cuckoo calls aloud.
In the black darkness the lightning is flashing,
And terrifies the women whose husbands are away.

The pleasant wind produces a sound like music,
And the rain is streaming down continually.
The coil of separation is like that of the cobra with its hissing sound,
But Mira's heart is set on Hari.

For lack of the vision of him my eyes are aching.

Ah, my Lord, ever since thou hast been separated from me my heart
     has found no rest.

Hearing thy voice, my heart begins to tremble.
Thy words are very sweet to me.

My eyes are fixed on the way of thy coming.
One night seems to me like six months.

O my companions, to whom shall I tell the pain of separation?
The whole night is passed by Mira in restlessness.

O my Lord, when shall I find thee,
So that thou mayst remove my pain and give me happiness?

LIV. *The Restlessness of Love*

I am true to my lord.
O my companions, there is nothing to be ashamed of now,
Since I have been seen dancing openly.

In the day I have no hunger.
I am always restless and sleep does not come in the night.
Leaving troubles behind, I shall go to the other side,
Because hidden knowledge has taken hold of me.

All my relations have come and surrounded me like bees.
But Mira is the servant of her beloved, the Mountain-holder.
And she cares not though the people mock her.

LVI. *Loneliness*

Apart from Rama, sleep does not come to me.
Through the sufferings of separation no sleep comes,
And the fire of love is kindled.
Without the light of my beloved, the temple is dark;
The lamp does not please me.
Apart from my beloved, I feel very lonely;
The night is passed in waking.
When will my beloved come home?

The frog, the peacock and the sparrow hawk utter their cries,
And the cuckoo calls aloud,
The clouds gather together,
And the flash of the lightning terrifies me.
My eyes are burning to see him.

O, my companions, what shall I do and where shall I go?
The pain of my heart is in no wise removed.
The pang of separation has stung me like a cobra.
My life ebbs away like a wave.
Prepare the herb and bring it to me.

Who will bring my beloved back to me, O, my companions?
O, my lord, when wilt thou come to see Mira?
Thou art pleasing to my heart.
When wilt thou come and talk and laugh with me?

TULSI DAS
VINAYA PATRIKA
[LETTERS OF PETITION]

(Hindi)

Tulsi Das (1532–1623) is the author of the greatest modern book of devotion in Hindi, the rendering of Valmiki's *Ramayana* under the title *Rama-carita-manasa* (The Holy Lake of the Acts of Rama), which Gandhi used to read at his prayer meetings. Tulsi Das's *Vinaya Patrika* contains devotional hymns intended for singing, and are addressed to Rama or Krishna.

The translation is by F. R. Allchin, *Tulsi Das: The Petition to Rama*, London: George Allen and Unwin, 1966, Part II pp. 134–5, 164–5.

TULSI DAS
VINAYA PATRIKA
[LETTERS OF PETITION]

65

1. Murmur 'Ram, Ram', repeat 'Ram, Ram', pray 'Ram, Ram', O my tongue!
   Be as stubborn as the rain-bird for the fresh cloud of love for Ram's name, O my mind!
2. And as all wells, rivers, lakes, oceans, and waters are useless for the love-thirsty *bird*.
   So for you are all the fruits of religious exercises unless you thirst for the pure ambrosial *svati*-drop of Ram's Name.
3. The cloud thunders, rumbles, rains hailstones and thunderbolts, and with these trials it tests the love within the bird's heart,
   Yet more and more affection swells within its breast for it recognizes the very limit *of love*.

4. With Ram's Name as the goal, Ram's Name in the mind, and Ram's
   Name as the object of love,
   Whoever has been, is, or will be, in the three worlds is most blessed;
5. This road of one-sided love is difficult to travel, *so* don't delay an
   instant for shade,
   Tulsi, your good lies in fulfilling on your own side this vow with
   undistracted persistence!

66

1. O mad one! repeat 'Ram', repeat 'Ram', repeat 'Ram',
   For that Name will be your ship across the terrible ocean of existence,
2. From endeavouring with this one method gain all wealth and all
   accomplishments,
   For the disease of the Dark Age has enveloped *such ways as* yoga,
   restraint and trance.
3. Be he good or evil, right or left,
   Yet in the end the Name of Ram will work for all;
4. This world is but a flowery, fruitful garden on the air,
   Seeing its pinnacles of smoke, be not deceived!
5. Says Tulsi, he who, abandoning Ram's Name, puts his trust elsewhere,
   Is like a fool who leaves the food served at his own table and goes
   begging for the scraps of others!

67

1. Repeat 'Ram, Ram', O my heart, ever with affection!
   In this Dark Age there is neither dispassion, yoga, sacrifice, nor
   renunciation;
2. Remembrance of Ram is the king of all observances,
   And to forget Ram is the crowning omission.
3. The Name of Ram is a great jewel, and the meshes of this world are
   a snake,
   If the jewel be taken, the serpent becomes perplexed and troubled;
4. The Name of Ram is a wishing-tree granting the four fruits *of life*,
   This the Vedas and Puranas, pandits and Purari all declare;

5. The love of the Name of Ram is the highest spiritual attainment,
   The Name of Ram is the basis of Tulsi's life!

121

1. O Hari, this is the surfeit of delusion
   That even while seeing, hearing, telling and understanding, these
     doubts and uncertainties do not depart,
2. 'But if this world is illusory, then say for what reason do we ex-
     perience the three types of burning?'
   – *Just as* the water of a mirage cannot be called true, and yet so long
     as the delusion lasts one suffers genuine pains;
3. As one who sleeps upon a comely bed dreams he is drowning in the
     ocean and is set upon by fear,
   Yet until he wakes up hundreds of thousands of boats will not carry
     him to shore.
4. This most terrible world ever appears delightful through the absence
     of discernment,
   But indeed for those whose conduct is with poise, joy, mercy and
     discrimination it is a source of happiness.
5. O Tulsi Das, though the scriptures sing that all this creation of the
     world is false
   Yet without devotion to Raghupati and association with saints, who
     can blot out the terrors of existence?

122

1. Hari, I know not how to perform spiritual exercises,
   As the ailment was, so was not the medicine given: what fault is then
     the physician's?
2. Or as in a dream a king may chance to be a Brahman-killer, and
     desperate he wanders with the sin attached to him,
   And though he perform a million Ashvamedhas, yet unless he
     wakes he is not purified *of the crime*;
3. Or as without discrimination one sees in a garland a great and awful
     serpent,
   And though he strikes it with many weapons and exhausts endless
     force, yet that does not kill it;

4. Or as from one's own delusion the watery mirage caused by the sun's rays creates great terror,
   So that a man sinking in it, though he mount a ship or boat, can never reach the other side.

5. Tulsi Das says, till this world, along with 'I', is rooted out,
   For so long, brother, though you perform religious vows and exercises for ten million aeons, you will die and you will not cross over!

123

1. This much do I understand, O Raghuraya,
   That without your grace, O merciful, O weal of your slave, neither infatuation nor Maya can be eradicated.

2. Excessive skill in spoken-knowledge has never carried anyone across existence,
   Just as talking of a lamp within a house at night time does not expel the darkness;

3. Or just as someone is wretched and sorrowful being quite with out food and gets only sorrows,
   And if any draw a picture of the wish-granting tree or desire-fulfilling cow, it does not wipe away his misery;

4. Or just as someone by night and day describes many sorts of foods, of the six flavours,
   Yet he only knows the happiness that comes from satiation who has eaten, – even without talking!

5. As long as there is no radiant light *of true knowledge* in the heart, and yearnings for sensual objects are there in the mind,
   For so long, Tulsi Das, one must wander through the wombs of existence and even in dreams is there no comfort.

TUKARAM
ABHANG
[SONGS]

(Marathi)

Tukaram (1598–1649), a grain merchant who lived near Poon, became the greatest of Maratha Bhaktas with his devotion to Vishnu under the name Vithoba at his shrine in Pandhalpur. After he gave up his worldly life, Tukaram sang his devotion in countless *Abhangs*, of which 4,600 are collected. By his religious enthusiasm, he drew together all classes of communities and contributed a strong unifying basis for the rise of Maratha power under the national hero, Shivaji, thus enabling the Marathas to resist the encroaching Moghul rule.

The translation is by Nicol Macnicol, *Psalms of Maratha Saints*, The Heritage of India Series, London: Oxford University Press, 1921, pp. 56–7, 62–3.

IV.35

TUKARAM
ABHANG
[SONGS]

XXXIII. The Mother's House

As the bride looks back to her mother's house,
    And goes, but with dragging feet;
So my soul looks up unto thee and longs,
    That thou and I may meet.

As a child cries out and is sore distressed,
    When its mother it cannot see,
As a fish that is taken from out the wave,
    So 'tis, says Tuka, with me.

XXXIV. *The Suppliant*

How can I know the right, –
　　So helpless I –
Since thou thy face hast hid from me,
　　Oh thou most high!

I call and call again
　　At thy high gate.
None hears me; empty is the house
　　And desolate.

If but before thy door
　　A guest appear,
Thou'lt speak to him some fitting word,
　　Some word of cheer.

Such courtesy, O Lord,
　　Becometh thee,
And we, – ah, we're not lost to sense
　　So utterly.

XXXV. *A Beggar for Love*

A beggar at thy door,
　　Pleading I stand;
Give me an alms, O God,
　　Love from thy loving hand.

Spare me the barren task,
　　To come, and come for nought.
A gift poor Tuka craves,
　　Unmerited, unbought.

XXXVI. *'God who is our Home'*

To the child how dull the Fair
If his mother be not there!

So my heart apart from thee,
O thou Lord of Pandhari!*

Chatak† turns from stream and lake,
Only rain his thirst can slake.

How the lotus all the night
Dreameth, dreameth of the light!

XLIII. Mother Vithoba

Ah, Pandurang, if, as men say,
  A sea of love thou art,
Then wherefore dost thou so delay?
  O take me to thy heart!

I cry for thee as for the hind
  The faun makes sore lament.
Nowhere its mother it can find,
  With thirst and hunger spent.

With milk of love, ah, suckle me
  At thy abounding breast,
O Mother, haste. – In thee, in thee
  My sad heart findeth rest.

XLIV. Me Miserable

Since little wit have I,
O hear my mournful cry.

Grant now, O grant to me
That I thy feet may see.

---

* *Lord of Pandhari*: that is, Vithoba, whose central shrine is at Pandharpur.

† *Chatak*: a species of cuckoo, often called the brain-fever bird. It is popularly believed to be able to drink only rain water, and hence its agonized cry for rain.

I have no steadfastness,
Narayan, I confess.

Have mercy, Tuka prays,
On my unhappy case.

XLV. *Within my Heart*

I know no way by which
My faith thy feet can reach
  Nor e'er depart.
How, how can I attain
That thou, O Lord, shalt reign
  Within my heart?

Lord, I beseech thee, hear
And grant to faith sincere,
  My heart within,
Thy gracious face to see,
Driving afar from me
  Deceit and sin.

O come, I, Tuka, pray,
And ever with me stay,
  Mine, mine to be.
Thy mighty hand outstretch
And save a fallen wretch,
  Yea, even me.

XLVI. *The Restless Heart*

As on the bank the poor fish lies,
  And gasps and writhes in pain,
Or as a man with anxious eyes
  Seeks hidden gold in vain, –
So is my heart distressed and cries
  To come to thee again.

Thou knowest, Lord, the agony
    Of the lost infant's wail,
Yearning his mother's face to see.
    (How oft I tell this tale!)
O at thy feet the mystery
    Of the dark world unveil!

The fire of this harassing thought
    Upon my bosom preys.
Why is it I am thus forgot?
    (O, who can know thy ways?)
Nay, Lord, thou seest my hapless lot;
    Have mercy, Tuka says.

KABIR
                POEMS

                    (Hindi)

Kabir (1440–1518), a Muhammadan by birth and Hindu in spirit,
lived as a weaver at Benares, weaving mystic visions in his songs. He
attempted to synthesize the religious spirit underlying Islam and
Hinduism by discarding the gloss of theology, ritual, and religious
exclusivism. His poems display an amazing boldness in attacking the
orthodoxy of his time. Borrowing freely from Sanskrit and Persian
vocabularies, Kabir expressed in his poems folk-wisdom as well as
mystic whisperings of love.

   The translation is by Rabindranath Tagore, assisted by Evelyn
Underhill, *Songs of Kabir*, New York: The Macmillan Co., 1915.
Songs 1, 2, 9, 11, 14, 22, 34, 39, 42, 43, 51, 52, 54, 67, 69, 79, 80.

IV.36   KABIR
                    POEMS

                     I

O servant, where dost thou seek Me?
Lo! I am beside thee.
I am neither in temple nor in mosque: I am neither in Kaaba nor in
   Kailash:
Neither am I in rites and ceremonies, nor in Yoga and renunciation.
If thou art a true seeker, thou shalt at once see Me: thou shalt meet Me
   in a moment of time.
Kabir says, 'O Sadhu! God is the breath of all breath.'

2

It is needless to ask of a saint the caste to which he belongs;
For the priest, the warrior, the tradesman, and all the thirty-six castes,
    alike are seeking for God.
It is but folly to ask what the caste of a saint may be;
The barber has sought God, the washerwoman, and the carpenter –
Even Raidas was a seeker after God.
The Rishi Swapacha was a tanner by caste.
Hindus and Moslems alike have achieved that End, where remains no
    mark of distinction.

9

O how may I ever express that secret word?
O how can I say He is not like this, and He is like that?
If I say that He is within me, the universe is ashamed:
If I say that He is without me, it is falsehood.
He makes the inner and the outer worlds to be indivisibly one;
The conscious and the unconscious, both are His footstools.
He is neither manifest nor hidden, He is neither revealed nor un-
    revealed:
There are no words to tell that which He is.

11

I played day and night with my comrades, and now I am greatly afraid.
So high is my Lord's palace, my heart trembles to mount its stairs:
    yet I must not be shy, if I would enjoy His love.
My heart must cleave to my Lover; I must withdraw my veil, and
    meet Him with all my body:
Mine eyes must perform the ceremony of the lamps of love.
Kabir says: 'Listen to me, friend: he understands who loves. If you
    feel not love's longing for your Beloved One, it is vain to adorn your
    body, vain to put unguent on your eyelids.'

14

The river and its waves are one surf: where is the difference between
the river and its waves?
When the wave rises, it is the water; and when it falls, it is the same
water again. Tell me, Sir, where is the distinction?
Because it has been named as wave, shall it no longer be considered as
water?

Within the Supreme Brahma, the worlds are being told like beads:
Look upon that rosary with the eyes of wisdom.

22

O brother, my heart yearns for that true Guru, who fills the cup of true
love, and drinks of it himself, and offers it then to me.
He removes the veil from the eyes, and gives the true Vision of Brahma:
He reveals the worlds in Him, and makes me to hear the Unstruck
Music:
He shows joy and sorrow to be one:
He fills all utterance with love.
Kabir says: 'Verily he has no fear, who has such a Guru to lead him
to the shelter of safety!'

34

How could the love between Thee and me sever?
As the leaf of the lotus abides on the water: so thou art my Lord, and
I am Thy servant.
As the night-bird Chakor gazes all night at the moon: so Thou art my
Lord and I am Thy servant.
From the beginning until the ending of time, there is love between
Thee and me; and how shall such love be extinguished?
Kabir says: 'As the river enters into the ocean, so my heart touches
Thee.'

39

O friend! this body is His lyre;
He tightens its strings, and draws from it the melody of Brahma.
If the strings snap and the keys slacken, then to dust must this instrument of dust return:
Kabir says: 'None but Brahma can evoke its melodies.'

42

There is nothing but water at the holy bathing places; and I know that they are useless, for I have bathed in them.
The images are all lifeless, they cannot speak; I know, for I have cried aloud to them.
The Purana and the Koran are mere words; lifting up the curtain, I have seen.
Kabir gives utterance to the words of experience; and he knows very well that all other things are untrue.

43

I laugh when I hear that the fish in the water is thirsty:
You do not see that the Real is in your home, and you wander from forest to forest listlessly!
Here is the truth! Go where you will, to Benares or to Mathura; if you do not find your soul, the world is unreal to you.

51

Dear friend, I am eager to meet my Beloved! My youth has flowered, and the pain of separation from Him troubles my breast.
I am wandering yet in the alleys of knowledge without purpose, but I have received His news in these alleys of knowledge.
I have a letter from my Beloved: in this letter is an unutterable message, and now my fear of death is done away.
Kabir says: 'O my loving friend! I have got for my gift the Deathless One.'

52

When I am parted from my Beloved, my heart is full of misery: I have
no comfort in the day, I have no sleep in the night. To whom shall
I tell my sorrow?

The night is dark; the hours slip by. Because my Lord is absent, I start
up and tremble with fear.

Kabir says: 'Listen, my friend! there is no other satisfaction, save in
the encounter with the Beloved.'

54

Have you not heard the tune which the Unstruck Music is playing?
In the midst of the chamber the harp of joy is gently and sweetly
played; and where is the need of going without to hear it?

If you have not drunk of the nectar of that One Love, what boots it
though you should purge yourself of all stains?

The Kazi is searching the words of the Koran, and instructing others:
but if his heart be not steeped in that love, what does it avail, though
he be a teacher of men?

The Yogi dyes his garments with red: but if he knows naught of that
colour of love, what does it avail though his garments be tinted?

Kabir says: 'Whether I be in the temple or the balcony, in the camp
or in the flower garden, I tell you truly that every moment my Lord
is taking His delight in me.'

67

I do not know what manner of God is mine.

The Mullah cries aloud to Him: and why? Is your Lord deaf? The
subtle anklets that ring on the feet of an insect when it moves are
heard of Him.

Tell your beads, paint your forehead with the mark of your God, and
wear matted locks long and showy: but a deadly weapon is in your
heart, and how shall you have God?

69

If God be within the mosque, then to whom does this world belong?

If Ram be within the image which you find upon your pilgrimage,
then who is there to know what happens without?

Hari is in the East: Allah is in the West. Look within your heart, for
there you will find both Karim and Ram;

All the men and women of the world are His living forms.

Kabir is the child of Allah and of Ram: He is my Guru, He is my Pir.

79

I am neither pious nor ungodly,

I live neither by law nor by sense,

I am neither a speaker nor hearer,

I am neither a servant nor master,

I am neither bond nor free,

I am neither detached nor attached.

I am far from none: I am near to none.

I shall go neither to hell nor to heaven.

I do all works; yet I am apart from all works.

Few comprehend my meaning: he who can comprehend it, he sits
unmoved.

Kabir seeks neither to establish nor to destroy.

80

The true Name is like none other name!

The distinction of the Conditioned from the Unconditioned is but a
word:

The Unconditioned is the seed, the Conditioned is the flower and the
fruit.

Knowledge is the branch, and the Name is the root.

Look, and see where the root is: happiness shall be yours when you
come to the root.

The root will lead you to the branch, the leaf, the flower, and the fruit:

It is the encounter with the Lord, it is the attainment of bliss, it is the
reconciliation of the Conditioned and the Unconditioned.

MIR (*c.* 1723–82)
GHAZAL
[CONVERSATION IN COUPLETS]
(Urdu)

In the sixteenth century, India was invaded by the Moghuls from the north and the Europeans from the south. During the next four centuries the Moghuls and the British imposed their imperial rule in succession on the peoples of the sub-continent. However, with the inevitable process of time, as the empires were dissolved, they left behind, as their legacies, two languages, namely Urdu and English, which the peoples of the region used with considerable skill and ingenuity for literary expression.

The establishment of Moghul rule in Delhi by Babur in 1526, and the stationing of his Persian army in the capital, gave rise to a mongrel speech in the military encampment, out of the local dialect spoken by the people, namely Brajbash, and the Persian used by the soldiers. This mixed dialect became in the course of the century the language of a larger group of the people and was called 'Urdu', meaning literally the language of the military camp. In the next century, while Persian remained the court language of the Moghuls Urdu gradually developed from a spoken language to a written language, borrowing heavily from the Persian court vocabulary and using persianized Arabic script. Having acquired respectability and produced its own literature in imitation of Persian models, Urdu finally replaced Persian as the court language of the later Moghul period. This development corresponds somewhat with the development after the Norman conquest of the Anglo-Saxon dialect, which borrowed from the Norman French court vocabulary, and finally became respectable with Chaucer's use of it.

Mir, an outstanding Urdu poet of the eighteenth century and a poetic chronicler of his time, was born at Agra, but spent the rest of his life in Delhi, the Moghul capital. When he was sixteen, in 1739, he saw the sack of Delhi by the Persian general Nadir Shah. The Moghul authority had already begun to decline at the centre, and the pro-

vincial governors were establishing their own local dynasties in
Panjab, Bengal, Oudh, and Deccan. While some poets found shelter
and patronage in the provincial courts, Mir remained in the capital,
witnessing the slow decay, decline, and destruction of the luxurious
Moghul city he had seen in his youth. The rise of the Maratha empire
in the west and the Afghan invasion in 1761 completed the destruction of the Moghul glory. Though the poet left the city in misery in
1761, he returned to it in 1772 and remained there until his end in
about 1782.

While most of the Indian poets in different regions of the country
were experimenting with literary forms partly derived from classical
Sanskrit, Pali, or Tamil, and partly invented locally, the Urdu poets
imported from the Persian and Arabic tradition literary forms, techniques, and even moods and themes. Among the significant poetic
forms introduced to India are the *Ghazal* (couplets or short lyrics),
Quasida (ode), and *Masnavi* (longer narrative poems), of which the
Ghazal became very popular and very highly developed.

Ghazal means literally conversation, most often between lovers. It
has a strict form bound by rules, containing from a minimum of five to
a maximum of seventeen couplets. Though each couplet expresses a
complete unit of thought, a series of them are usually grouped
together; thus 'the unity of the poem is one not of content but of form,
and is achieved by a common meter for all the couplets and a strict
rhyme scheme, AA, BA, CA, DA, etc.'*

Mir is one of the outstanding exponents of the *Ghazal* in Urdu in
the eighteenth century, writing mainly on the theme of love. In his
youth he had fallen in love with a beautiful girl, a close relative married
to another man. Though she returned his love occasionally in secret,
his beloved explained herself whenever she had to leave: 'I too grieve
at this parting. But what can I do? My honour must be my first
concern.'† Mir's youthful love remained with him all his life as a kind
of burning passion, even though later he married and had children.
Because of this love he suffered much social persecution. Some of the

---

*Ralph Russell and Khurshidul Islam, *Three Mughal Poets: Mir, Sauda,
Mir Hasan*, p. 8.
  † ibid., pp. 96–7.

couplets included here express his feelings for his mistress, using the basic conventions of poetic imagery and mood typical of south-west Asian tradition. In other couplets, Mir's love theme transcends physical love and can be interpreted as mystic.

With the growing awareness that the rituals of religion were more shackles than aids to spiritual growth, a reformation movement in Islam had emerged, spear-headed by the great Persian mystic Jalaluddin Rumi (A.D. 1207–73). Rumi was influenced by Upanishadic thought and attitudes, and by the boldness of his vision he had carved out a separate world for the Sufis within the Islamic tradition. Rumi's powerful influence was filtering back to the land of the *Upanishads* via Persian poetry. The Indian Moslem mystics, discarding the 'kafir-non-karif' theology, had come to see the underlying oneness of all religious experiences, and Kabir had already sung in Hindi about this synthesis. Mir was carrying forward this tradition in his Urdu *Ghazals*.

The selections included here are from the translation by Ralph Russell and Khurshidul Islam, *Three Mughal Poets: Mir, Sauda, Mir Hasan,* Cambridge, Mass.: Harvard University Press, 1968, pp. 99–270, 274–7.

IV.37   MIR
GHAZAL
[CONVERSATION]

I

1

I caught a glimpse of you with hair dishevelled
And my distracted heart was yours for life.   [I.40.25]

2

Much have I suffered in my love for you –
Cruelty, persecution, and much more
And lifelong deprivation of the joys
I spent the years in endless yearning for,
        Yet from my heart I pity any man
        Who never stood a suppliant at your door.   [I.54.7–10]

3

It was love's strength that brought me to her lane;
Where shall I find the strength to go back home?   [I.84.5]

4

I do not ask you not to favour others,
But only to remember me sometimes.   [I.130.14]

5

I ask you for a kiss and you get angry.
Why should a little thing like this upset you?   [II.216.4]

6

Morning and night mean nothing any more
To him whose eyes have seen her hair and face.   [II.278.8]

7

I nurse a wounded heart; she laughs and turns away.
Such is my heavy grief; so light she makes of it.   [II.305.5]

8

'Don't stand there all alone. Come and sit down.'
These words you could have said, but never did.   [II.308.19]

9

For love of you I count my life as nothing.
Is nothing in return then due from you?   [II.316.22]

10

On my side, love and loyalty: on hers, vindictive cruelty.
And this they know: yet it is I must bear the brand of
   infamy.   [II.342.9]

A.I.L. – 26

11

Until you see her walk you will not know
What grace and poise and matchless beauty are.   [II.357.12]

12

Her body yields such joy, I know no longer
Whether it is her body or my soul.   [II.360.12]

13

For you I live – whose tightly-clad, firm body
Teaches my soul what joy it is to live.   [III.392.12]

14

Mir, give her up before your life is forfeit –
That way you'll live to love another day.   [V.621.18]

15

True, you have said, 'And I love you too, Mir,'
But who would trust a lovely woman's love?   [VI.643.9]

*

II

16

Mir, quit the company of Shaikh and Brahmin
And mosque and temple too – leave them behind.
Lay one stone on another in the desert:
Worship your Love at your own humble shrine.   [I.39.8–10]

17

Tell me, what else exists but He?
To him who has the eyes to see
The day, the sun, the night, the moon
Show forth His forms, His Majesty.
Manifest, hidden, first and last
Is He, is He, is He, is He!   [I.138.8–11]

18

I grant you, sir, the preacher is an angel,
To be a man, now – that's more difficult.   [II.306.6]

19

What does it mean to me? Call me 'believer', call me
'infidel',
I seek His threshold, be it in the temple or the mosque. [II.366.3]

20

It is the power of His beauty fills the world with light
Be it the Ka'ba's candle or the lamp that lights Somnath. [II.210.7]

21

Houris and boys and palaces and streams of Paradise –
Cast every one of them to Hell, and I will love my love. [III.407.24]

22

To save their souls they kill themselves with care.
A Paradise like that can go to Hell!   [III.419.7]

23

True Musalman am I, for to these idols
I pledge my love. 'There is no god but God.'   [III.432.20]

24

I went to Mecca, and Medina, and to Karbala –
And what I was, I still remain now that I have returned. [IV.464.14]

---

20. *Somnath*. One of the most famous Indian temples destroyed by
Mohamud of Ghazna in 1025.

A Complete Ghazal of Mir*

1. All my plans have been overturned, and no medicine has had any effect. You see? This sickness of the heart (love) has killed me in the end (as I told you it would).

2. I passed the days of my youth in weeping, and in old age I closed my eyes. That is, I passed many nights in wakefulness, and when morning came I rested.

3. I do not question her life-giving power. It is just the excellence of my fortune that the first message that she sent me was my sentence of death.

4. We act under constraint, and you slander us when you say we have free will. It is your will that is done, and we are blamed without cause.

5. All the rakes and profligates of the whole world bow down before you. The proud, the perverse, the awkward, the independent – all have acknowledged you their leader.

6. If even in my distracted state I have been guilty of any want of respect [in daring to approach her], then it was little enough. For mile after mile as I made my way towards her, I fell down to worship her at every step.

7. What do we care for the Ka'ba and the direction in which we should turn to pray, and the holy places and the robes of Pilgrimage? We who live in her lane have said farewell to all these things.

---

*'The ghazal is from Mir's first *Diwan* [collected poems]. It has fifteen couplets, and its themes include among others, the lifelong suffering which the lover must bear (1, 2), God's injustice to man (4, 10), the poet's acknowledged pre-eminence among rakes and profligates – i.e. among mystics (5), the mystic's contempt for religious formalities and for those who uphold them (7, 8, 15), the great beauty of the beloved (11), and the beloved's timidity, elusiveness, fickleness, and inaccessibility (12, 13, 14). Thus there is no unity of theme in the ghazal as a whole; nor are the couplets on similar themes always grouped together.' Ralph Russell and Khurshidul Islam, op. cit., p. 272.

8. If the Shaikh stands naked in the mosque today it is because he spent the night drinking in the tavern, and in his drunkenness gave his cloak and gown and shirt and hat away.

9. If only she would lift the veil from her face now. What will it profit me if when my eyes are closed (in death) she unveils herself for all to see?

10. What can we do with the black and white of this world? If anything, then only this, that we can see the (black) night out with constant weeping, and bear the toil of the (white) day until evening comes.

11. At morning in the garden she walked out to take the air. Her cheek made the rose her slave, and her graceful stature made the cypress her thrall.

12. I held her silver-white wrists in my hands, but she swore (that she would come to me later), and I let them go. How raw and inexperienced I was to trust her word!

13. Every moment I beseeched her, and this has brought all my efforts to nothing. Her proud indifference increased fourfold with every time I importuned her.

14. Such a timid, fleet gazelle does not easily lose her fear of man. Those who have tamed you have performed a wonder, as though by magic power.

15. Why do you ask at this late hour what Mir's religion is? He has drawn the caste mark on his forehead and sat down in the temple. He abandoned Islam long ago.

NANAK
ADI GRANTH
[FIRST BOOK]

(Gurmukhi, 1604)

Nanak (1469–1538), the founder of Sikhism, originally a Kshatriya, was born at Talwandi, near Lahore (now in Pakistan). As he grew up he soon found interdependence in Hindu and Muslim life in Punjab during the time of the Afghan Sultanate in Delhi. His interest in the search for spirituality made him travel to many places and countries. He met Kabir and was influenced by his teachings. Some of Kabir's songs were included in the *Granth*.

Towards the end of his life, Nanak settled down at Kartarpur and preached his understanding of one God, whose Being is beyond man's capacity to know, relate or understand, but whose glory is manifest in His creation. His disciples (Sanskrit, *Shishyas*) became the *Sikhs* (the Punjabi version of the Sanskrit word).

Nanak's teachings are set out in vigorous verses. Their essence is contained in *Japji*, a collection of verses arranged for daily use in prayer. There are 974 hymns by Guru Nanak in the *Adi Granth* (also called the *Granth Sahib*, the Holy Book of the Sikhs).

The translations are by Trilochan Singh *et al.*, *Selections from the Sacred Writings of the Sikhs*, London: George Allen and Unwin, 1960, pp. 28–39.

NANAK
ADI GRANTH
[FIRST BOOK]

I. *The Japji*
or, The Meditation (Morning Prayer)

PROEM

There is one God,
Eternal Truth is His Name;
Maker of all things,
Fearing nothing and at enmity with nothing,
Timeless is His Image;
Not begotten, being of His own Being:
By the grace of the Guru, made known to men.

JAP: THE MEDITATION

AS HE WAS IN THE BEGINNING: THE TRUTH,
SO THROUGHOUT THE AGES,
HE NEVER HAS BEEN: THE TRUTH,
SO EVEN NOW HE IS TRUTH IMMANENT,
SO FOR EVER AND EVER HE SHALL BE
   TRUTH ETERNAL.

I

It is not through thought that He is to be comprehended
Though we strive to grasp Him a hundred thousand times;
Nor by outer silence and long deep meditation
Can the inner silence be reached;
Nor is man's hunger for God appeasable
By piling up world-loads of wealth.
All the innumerable devices of worldly wisdom
Leave a man disappointed; not one avails.

How then shall we know the Truth?
How shall we rend the veils of untruth away?
Abide thou by His Will, and make thine own,
His will, O Nanak, that is written in thy heart.

2

Through His Will He creates all the forms of things,
But what the form of His Will is, who can express?
All life is shaped by His ordering,
By His ordering some are high, some of low estate,
Pleasure and pain are bestowed as His Writ ordaineth.

Some through His Will are graciously rewarded,
Others must grope through births and deaths;
Nothing at all, outside His Will, is abiding.
O Nanak, he who is aware of the Supreme Will
Never in his selfhood utters the boast: 'It is I.'

3

Those who believe in power,
Sing of His power;
Others chant of His gifts
As His messages and emblems;
Some sing of His greatness,
And His gracious acts;
Some sing of His wisdom
Hard to understand;
Some sing of Him as the fashioner of the body;
Destroying what He has fashioned.
Others praise Him for taking away life
And restoring it anew.

Some proclaim His Existence
To be far, desperately far, from us;
Others sing of Him
As here and there a Presence
Meeting us face to face.

To sing truly of the transcendent Lord
Would exhaust all vocabularies, all human powers of
    expression.
Myriads have sung of Him in innumerable strains.
His gifts to us flow in such plentitude
That man wearies of receiving what God bestows;
Age on unending age, man lives on His bounty;
Carefree, O Nanak, the Glorious Lord smiles.

4

The Lord is the Truth Absolute,
True is His Name,
His language is love infinite;
His creatures ever cry to Him;
'Give us more, O Lord, give more';
The Bounteous One gives unwearyingly.

What then should we offer
That we might see His Kingdom?
With what language
Might we His love attain?

In the ambrosial hours of fragrant dawn
Think upon and glorify
His Name and greatness.
Our own past actions
Have put this garment on us,
But salvation comes only through His Grace.

O Nanak, this alone need we know,
That God, being Truth, is the one Light of all.

18

There is no counting fools, the morally blind,
No counting thieves and the crooked,
No counting the shedders of the innocent blood;
No counting the sinners who go on sinning;

No counting the liars who take pleasure in lies;
No counting the dirty wretches who live on filth;
No counting the calumniators
Who carry about on their heads their loads of sin.

Thus saith Nanak, lowliest of the lowly:
I am too petty to have anything to offer Thee;
I cannot, even once, be a sacrifice unto Thee.
To abide by Thy Will, O Lord, is man's best offering;
Thou who art Eternal, abiding in Thy Peace.

19

Countless are Thy Names, countless Thine abodes;
Completely beyond the grasp of the imagination
Are Thy myriad realms;
Even to call them myriad is foolish.

Yet through words and through letters
Is Thy Name uttered and Thy praise expressed;
In words we praise Thee,
In words we sing of Thy virtues.

It is in the words that we write and speak about Thee,
In words on man's forehead
Is written man's destiny,
But God who writes that destiny
Is free from the bondage of words.

As God ordaineth, so man receiveth.
All creation is His Word made manifest;
Except in the Light of His Word
There is no way.

How can an insignificant creature like myself
Express the vastness and wonder of Thy creation?
I am too petty to have anything to offer Thee;
I cannot, even once, be a sacrifice unto Thee.
To abide by Thy Will, O Lord, is man's best offering;
Thou who art Eternal, abiding in Thy Peace.

Part Five

AGE OF MAHATMA
[GREAT SOUL]
A.D. 1800 to the present

39. Rabindranath Tagore, *Gitanjali* (Bengali, 1912)
40. Mohandas Karamchand Gandhi, *The Mind of Mahatma Gandhi* (Indo-English, 1946)
41. Khushwant Singh, *Karma* (Indo-English).

RABINDRANATH TAGORE
GITANJALI
[SONG OFFERINGS]
(Bengali, 1912)

Rabindranath Tagore (1861–1941), the venerated *Gurudev* of modern India, through his actions and aesthetic expression during his long lifetime synthesized Indian culture, and accelerated the Indian renaissance. For he was truly a multi-purpose artist, expressing himself as a poet, dramatist, critic, singer, musician, and painter. In addition, Tagore was an educator, a world traveller, a politician of vision, and a true internationalist even while he remained very much an Indian. Above all, he was a sage in the tradition of the ancient *rishis*. When Gandhi (to whom the whole nation bowed in homage) bowed to Tagore, acknowledging him as '*Gurudev*' (spiritual director), the kindred spirit received Gandhi in his arms, calling him the '*Mahatma*' (Great Soul). So spiritually profound and deeply personal was the understanding of these two contrasting men of thought and action that, even when they disagreed on details of technique or methods of approach to India or international situations, they invariably felt oneness of spirit on every occasion of crisis or moment of Truth.

By the time Tagore was fifty-two years of age, he had won renown as a man of letters in Bengal, and as a national leader throughout India. But his fame became suddenly internationalized when he was awarded the Nobel Prize for Literature in 1913 for the English translation of his 'Song Offerings', entitled *Gitanjali*; for it was the first time that an Asian writer was so honoured.

The incidents relating to the publication of *Gitanjali* were somewhat accidental inasmuch as, first Tagore undertook to translate his Bengali poems into English himself in an attempt to find relaxation 'in a weak state of health', because he felt 'the urge to recapture, through the medium of another language, the feelings and sentiments which had created such a feast of joy' within him in past

573

days.* Secondly, Tagore's friend, William Rothenstein, English artist and author, showed the manuscript translations to W. B. Yeats in London. Commenting on the poems, Yeats wrote in the Introduction to *Gitanjali*, 'These lyrics ... display in their thought a world I have dreamed of all my life long. The work of a supreme culture, they yet appear as much the growth of the common soil as the grass and the rushes.'† Yeats seems to have been profoundly agitated by reading the poems, for he states that he carried the manuscript with him for days, reading it in trains, on the top of omnibuses, and in restaurants, and he had 'to close it lest some stranger would see how much it moved me.'‡

As a synthesizer of various Indian traditions, Tagore echoes many of the traditional attitudes in his songs. For example, he expresses the Vedic joyous exuberance (XLV), as well as the Upanishadic search for and realization of the endlessness of the self (I), and its attempt to reach out for oneness with Brahman (V, XII). At the same time, he adopts this unitive understanding to express the double-vision of the Bhakti poets in the theme of Radha-Krishna (beloved and divine lover), through the imagery of physical love and mystical ecstasy (XVII, XVIII). Challenging the conventional and orthodox attitudes to work and liberation, Tagore re-echoes the sublime and universal message of *Bhagavad Gita*, emphasizing the nobility of work by hands, which the so-called Indian intelligentsia had come to look down upon, partly because of the fossilized caste system and partly on account of inherited colonial snobbery (XI, LXXIII). The plurality of *nama-rupa* (name-form) for conceiving the Universal Self, the most characteristic Indian attitude to God, becomes manifest in a number of songs in which Tagore calls the Ultimate Power Master Singer (III), Master Poet (VII), Master Worker (XI), Master Potter (XCVI); also in the conventional and popularly accepted human relations to identify 'That nameless One' as Father (XXXV), Mother (LXXXIII),

---

*Letter to Indira Devi, dated London, 6 May 1913, in *A Tagore Reader*, ed. Amiya Chakravarty, New York: Beacon Press (BP 234), 1961, p. 21.

† W. B. Yeats, Introduction to *Gitanjali*, London: The Macmillan Company, 1912; reprinted, Boston: International Pocket Library, p. 8.

‡ ibid., p. 7.

Friend (II), Lover (LXXXVI), as well as in abstract imagery as Death (LXXXVI, XC, XCI), Time (LXXXII), or Energy (LXIX).

In all these songs, breathing a deep simplicity and joyous spontaneity, Tagore seems to accept with a measure of satisfaction life in all its vicissitudes, including the last and final fulfilment, death, and sets the reader vibrating to a larger rhythm beyond the rhythm of the words of the poems. In Tagore's art, Poetry becomes prayerful whisperings of Love.

The selections included here are taken from 'Gitanjali' in the *Collected Poems and Plays* of Tagore, New York: Macmillan Co., 1958.

V.39 RABINDRANATH TAGORE
GITANJALI
[SONG OFFERINGS]

I

Thou hast made me endless, such is thy pleasure. This frail vessel thou emptiest again and again, and fillest it ever with fresh life.

This little flute of a reed thou hast carried over hills and dales, and has breathed through it melodies eternally new.

At the immortal touch of thy hands my little heart loses its limits in joy, and gives birth to utterance ineffable.

Thy infinite gifts come to me only on these very small hands of mine. Ages pass, and still thou pourest, and still there is room to fill.

II

When thou commandest me to sing, it seems that my heart would break with pride; and I look to thy face, and tears come to my eyes.

All that is harsh and dissonant in my life melts into one sweet harmony – and my adoration spreads wings like a glad bird on its flight across the sea.

I know thou takest pleasure in my singing. I know that only as a singer I come before thy presence.

I touch by the edge of the far-spreading wing of my song thy feet which I could never aspire to reach.

Drunk with the joy of singing I forget myself and call thee friend who art my lord.

III

I know not how thou singest, my master! I ever listen in silent amazement.

The light of thy music illumines the world. The life-breath of thy music runs from sky to sky. The holy stream of thy music breaks through all stony obstacles and rushes on.

My heart longs to join in thy song, but vainly struggles for a voice.

I would speak, but speech breaks not into song, and I cry out baffled. Ah, thou hast made my heart captive in the endless meshes of thy music, my master!

IV

Life of my life, I shall ever try to keep my body pure, knowing that thy living touch is upon all my limbs.

I shall ever try to keep all untruths out from my thoughts, knowing that thou art that truth which has kindled the light of reason in my mind.

I shall ever try to drive all evils away from my heart and keep my love in flower, knowing that thou hast thy seat in the inmost shrine of my heart.

And it shall be my endeavour to reveal thee in my actions, knowing it is thy power gives me strength to act.

V

I ask for a moment's indulgence to sit by thy side. The works that I have in hand I will finish afterwards.

Away from the sight of thy face my heart knows no rest nor respite, and my work becomes an endless toil in a shoreless sea of toil.

Today the summer has come at my window with its sighs and murmurs; and the bees are plying their minstrelsy at the court of the flowering grove.

Now it is time to sit quiet, face to face with thee, and to sing dedication of life in this silent and overflowing leisure.

VII

My song has put off her adornments. She has no pride of dress and decoration. Ornaments would mar our union; they would come between thee and me; their jingling would drown thy whispers.

My poet's vanity dies in shame before thy sight. O master poet, I have sat down at thy feet. Only let me make my life simple and straight, like a flute of reed for thee to fill with music.

X

Here is thy footstool and there rest thy feet where live the poorest, and lowliest, and lost.

When I try to bow to thee, my obeisance cannot reach down to the depth where thy feet rest among the poorest, and lowliest, and lost.

Pride can never approach to where thou walkest in the clothes of the humble among the poorest, and lowliest, and lost.

My heart can never find its way to where thou keepest company with the companionless among the poorest, the lowliest, and the lost.

XI

Leave this chanting and singing and telling of beads! Whom dost thou worship in this lonely dark corner of a temple with doors all shut? Open thine eyes and see thy God is not before thee!

He is there where the tiller is tilling the hard ground and where the pathmaker is breaking stones. He is with them in sun and in shower, and his garment is covered with dust. Put off thy holy mantle and even like him come down on the dusty soil!

Deliverance? Where is this deliverance to be found? Our master himself has joyfully taken upon him the bonds of creation; he is bound with us all for ever.

Come out of thy meditations and leave aside thy flowers and incense! What harm is there if thy clothes become tattered and stained? Meet him and stand by him in toil and in sweat of thy brow.

XII

The time that my journey takes is long and the way of it long.

I came out on the chariot of the first gleam of light, and pursued my voyage through the wildernesses of worlds leaving my track on many a star and planet.

It is the most distant course that comes nearest to thyself, and that training is the most intricate which leads to the utter simplicity of a tune.

The traveller has to knock at every alien door to come to his own, and one has to wander through all the outer worlds to reach the innermost shrine at the end.

My eyes strayed far and wide before I shut them and said, 'Here art thou!'

The question and the cry, 'Oh, where?' melt into tears of a thousand streams and deluge the world with the flood of the assurance, 'I am!'

XIII

The song that I came to sing remains unsung to this day.

I have spent my days in stringing and in unstringing my instrument.

The time has not come true, the words have not been rightly set; only there is the agony of wishing in my heart.

The blossom has not opened; only the wind is sighing by.

I have not seen his face, nor have I listened to his voice; only I have heard his gentle footsteps from the road before my house.

The livelong day has passed in spreading his seat on the floor; but the lamp has not been lit and I cannot ask him into my house.

I live in the hope of meeting with him; but this meeting is not yet.

XIV

My desires are many and my cry is pitiful, but ever didst thou save me by hard refusals; and this strong mercy has been wrought into my life through and through.

Day by day thou art making me worthy of the simple, great gifts that thou gavest to me unasked – this sky and the light, this body and the life and the mind – saving me from perils of overmuch desire.

There are times when I languidly linger and times when I awaken and hurry in search of my goal; but cruelly thou hidest thyself from before me.

Day by day thou art making me worthy of thy full acceptance by refusing me ever and anon, saving me from perils of weak, uncertain desire.

XV

I am here to sing thee songs. In this hall of thine I have a corner seat.

In thy world I have no work to do; my useless life can only break out in tunes without a purpose.

When the hour strikes for thy silent worship at the dark temple of midnight, command me, my master, to stand before thee to sing.

When in the morning air the golden harp is tuned, honour me, commanding my presence.

XVI

I have had my invitation to this world's festival, and thus my life has been blessed. My eyes have seen and my ears have heard.

It was my part at this feast to play upon my instrument, and I have done all I could.

Now I ask, has the time come at last when I may go in and see thy face and offer thee my silent salutation?

XVII

I am only waiting for love to give myself up at last into his hands. That is why it is so late and why I have been guilty of such omissions.

They come with their laws and their codes to bind me fast; but I evade them ever, for I am only waiting for love to give myself up at last into his hands.

People blame me and call me heedless; I doubt not they are right in their blame.

The market day is over and work is all done for the busy. Those who came to call me in vain have gone back in anger. I am only waiting for love to give myself up at last into his hands.

XVIII

Clouds heap upon clouds and it darkens. Ah, love, why dost thou let me wait outside at the door all alone?

In the busy moments of the noontide work I am with the crowd, but on this dark lonely day it is only for thee that I hope.

If thou showest me not thy face, if thou leavest me wholly aside, I know not how I am to pass these long, rainy hours.

I keep gazing on the far-away gloom of the sky, and my heart wanders wailing with the restless wind.

XIX

If thou speakest not I will fill my heart with thy silence and endure it. I will keep still and wait like the night with starry vigil and its head bent low with patience.

The morning will surely come, the darkness will vanish, and thy voice pour down in golden streams breaking through the sky.

Then thy words will take wings in songs for every one of my birds' nests, and thy melodies will break forth in flowers in all my forest groves.

XXIII

Art thou abroad on this stormy night on thy journey of love, my friend? The sky groans like one in despair.

I have no sleep tonight. Ever and again I open my door and look out on the darkness, my friend!

I can see nothing before me. I wonder where lies thy path!

By what dim shore of the ink-black river, by what far edge of the frowning forest, through what mazy depth of gloom art thou threading thy course to come to me, my friend?

XXIV

If the day is done, if birds sing no more, if the wind has flagged tired, then draw the veil of darkness, thick upon me, even as thou hast wrapt the earth with the coverlet of sleep and tenderly closed the petals of the drooping lotus at dusk.

From the traveller, whose sack of provisions is empty before the voyage is ended, whose garment is torn and dust-laden, whose strength is exhausted, remove shame and poverty, and renew his life like a flower under the cover of thy kindly night.

XXV

In the night of weariness let me give myself up to sleep without struggle, resting my trust upon thee.

Let me not force my flagging spirit into a poor preparation for thy worship.

It is thou who drawest the veil of night upon the tired eyes of the day to renew its sight in a fresher gladness of awakening.

XXVI

He came and sat by my side but I woke not. What a cursed sleep it was, O miserable me!

He came when the night was still; he had his harp in his hands, and my dreams became resonant with its melodies.

Alas, why are my nights all thus lost? Ah, why do I ever miss his sight whose breath touches my sleep?

XXXIII

When it was day they came into my house and said, 'We shall only take the smallest room here.'

They said, 'We shall help you in the worship of your God and humbly accept only our own share of his grace'; and then they took their seat in a corner and they sat quiet and meek.

But in the darkness of night I find they break into my sacred shrine, strong and turbulent, and snatch with unholy greed the offerings from God's altar.

XXXV

Where the mind is without fear and the head is held high;

Where knowledge is free;

Where the world has not been broken up into fragments by narrow domestic walls;

Where words come out from the depth of truth;

Where tireless striving stretches its arms towards perfection;

Where the clear stream of reason has not lost its way into the dreary desert sand of dead habit;

Where the mind is led forward by thee into ever-widening thought and action –

Into that heaven of freedom, my Father, let my country awake.

XLV

Have you not heard his silent steps? He comes, comes, ever comes.

Every moment and every age, every day and every night he comes, comes, ever comes.

Many a song have I sung in many a mood of mind, but all their notes have always proclaimed, 'He comes, comes, ever comes.'

In the fragrant days of sunny April through the forest path he comes, comes, ever comes.

In the rainy gloom of July nights on the thundering chariot of clouds he comes, comes, ever comes.

In sorrow after sorrow it is his steps that press upon my heart, and it is the golden touch of his feet that makes my joy to shine.

XLVI

I know not from what distant time thou art ever coming nearer to meet me. Thy sun and stars can never keep thee hidden from me for aye.

In many a morning and eve thy footsteps have been heard and thy messenger has come within my heart and called me in secret.

I know not why today my life is all astir, and a feeling of tremulous joy is passing through my heart.

It is as if the time were come to wind up my work, and I feel in the air a faint smell of thy sweet presence.

XLVII

The night is nearly spent waiting for him in vain. I fear lest in the morning he suddenly come to my door when I have fallen asleep wearied out. Oh, friends, leave the way open to him – forbid him not.

If the sound of his steps does not wake me, do not try to rouse me, I pray. I wish not to be called from my sleep by the clamorous choir of birds, by the riot of wind at the festival of morning light. Let me sleep undisturbed even if my lord comes of a sudden to my door.

XLVIII

The morning sea of silence broke into ripples of bird songs; and the flowers were all merry by the roadside; and the wealth of gold was scattered through the rift of the clouds while we busily went on our way and paid no heed.

We sang no glad songs nor played; we went not to the village for barter; we spoke not a word nor smiled; we lingered not on the way. We quickened our pace more and more as the time sped by.

The sun rose to the mid sky and doves cooed in the shade. Withered leaves danced and whirled in the hot air of noon. The shepherd boy drowsed and dreamed in the shadow of the banyan tree, and I laid myself down by the water and stretched my tired limbs on the grass.

My companions laughed at me in scorn; they held their heads high and hurried on; they never looked back nor rested; they vanished in the distant blue haze. They crossed many meadows and hills, and passed through strange, far-away countries. All honour to you, heroic host of the interminable path! Mockery and reproach pricked me to rise, but found no response in me. I gave myself up for lost in the depth of a glad humiliation – in the shadow of a dim delight.

The repose of the sun-embroidered green gloom slowly spread over my heart. I forgot for what I had travelled, and I surrendered my mind without struggle to the maze of shadows and songs.

At last, when I woke from my slumber and opened my eyes, I saw thee standing by me, flooding my sleep with thy smile. How I had feared that the path was long and wearisome, and the struggle to reach thee was hard!

LVIII

Let all the strains of joy mingle in my last song – the joy that makes the earth flow over in the riotous excess of the grass, the joy that sets the twin brothers, life and death, dancing over the wide world, the joy that sweeps in with the tempest, shaking and waking all life with laughter, the joy that sits still with its tears on the open red lotus of pain, and the joy that throws everything it has upon the dust, and knows not a word.

LIX

Yes, I know, this is nothing but thy love, O beloved of my heart – this golden light that dances upon the leaves, these idle clouds sailing across the sky, this passing breeze leaving its coolness upon my forehead.

The morning light has flooded my eyes – this is thy message to my heart. Thy face is bent from above, thy eyes look down on my eyes, and my heart has touched thy feet.

LXIII

Thou hast made me known to friends whom I knew not. Thou hast given me seats in homes not my own. Thou hast brought the distant near and made a brother of the stranger.

I am uneasy at heart when I have to leave my accustomed shelter; I forget that there abides the old in the new, and that there also thou abidest.

Through birth and death, in this world or in others, wherever thou leadest me it is thou, the same, the one companion of my endless life who ever linkest my heart with bonds of joy to the unfamiliar.

When one knows thee, then alien there is none, then no door is shut. Oh, grant me my prayer that I may never lose the bliss of the touch of the one in the play of the many.

LXIX

The same stream of life that runs through my veins night and day runs through the world and dances in rhythmic measures.

It is the same life that shoots in joy through the dust of the earth in numberless blades of grass and breaks into tumultuous waves of leaves and flowers.

It is the same life that is rocked in the ocean-cradle of birth and of death, in ebb and in flow.

I feel my limbs are made glorious by the touch of this world of life. And my pride is from the life-throb of ages dancing in my blood this moment.

LXX

Is it beyond thee to be glad with the gladness of this rhythm? to be tossed and lost and broken in the whirl of this fearful joy?

All things rush on, they stop not, they look not behind, no power can hold them back, they rush on.

Keeping steps with that restless, rapid music, seasons come dancing and pass away – colours, tunes, and perfumes pour in endless cascades in the abounding joy that scatters and gives up and dies every moment.

LXXII

He it is, the innermost one, who awakens my being with his deep hidden touches.

He it is who puts his enchantment upon these eyes and joyfully plays on the chords of my heart in varied cadence of pleasure and pain.

He it is who weaves the web of this *maya* in evanescent hues of gold and silver, blue and green, and lets peep out through the folds his feet, at whose touch I forget myself.

Days come and ages pass, and it is ever he who moves my heart in many a name, in many a guise, in many a rapture of joy and of sorrow.

LXXIII

Deliverance is not for me in renunciation. I feel the embrace of freedom in a thousand bonds of delight.

Thou ever pourest for me the fresh draught of thy wine of various colours and fragrance, filling this earthen vessel to the brim.

My world will light its hundred different lamps with thy flame and place them before the altar of thy temple.

No, I will never shut the doors of my senses. The delights of sight and hearing and touch will bear thy delight.

Yes, all my illusions will burn into illumination of joy, and all my desires ripen into fruits of love.

LXXIV

The day is no more, the shadow is upon the earth. It is time that I go to the stream to fill my pitcher.

The evening air is eager with the sad music of the water. Ah, it calls me out into the dusk. In the lonely lane there is no passer-by, the wind is up, the ripples are rampant in the river.

I know not if I shall come back home. I know not whom I shall chance to meet. There at the fording in the little boat the unknown man plays upon his lute.

LXXV

Thy gifts to us mortals fulfil all our needs and yet run back to thee undiminished.

The river has its everyday work to do and hastens through fields and hamlets; yet its incessant stream winds towards the washing of thy feet.

The flower sweetens the air with its perfume; yet its last service is to offer itself to thee.

Thy worship does not impoverish the world.

From the words of the poet men take what meanings please them; yet their last meaning points to thee.

LXXVI

Day after day, O lord of my life, shall I stand before thee face to face? With folded hands, O lord of all worlds, shall I stand before thee face to face?

Under thy great sky in solitude and silence, with humble heart shall I stand before thee face to face?

In this laborious world of thine, tumultuous with toil and with struggle, among hurrying crowds shall I stand before thee face to face?

And when my work shall be done in this world, O King of kings, alone and speechless shall I stand before thee face to face?

LXXVII

I know thee as my God and stand apart – I do not know thee as my own and come closer. I know thee as my father and bow before thy feet – I do not grasp thy hand as my friend's.

I stand not where thou comest down and ownest thyself as mine, there to clasp thee to my heart and take thee as my comrade.

Thou art the Brother amongst my brothers, but I heed them not, I divide not my earnings with them, thus sharing my all with thee.

In pleasure and in pain I stand not by the side of men, and thus stand by thee. I shrink to give up my life, and thus do not plunge into the great waters of life.

LXXX

I am like a remnant of a cloud of autumn uselessly roaming in the sky, O my sun ever-glorious! Thy touch has not yet melted my vapour, making me one with thy light, and thus I count months and years separated from thee.

If this be thy wish and if this be thy play, then take this fleeting emptiness of mine, paint it with colours, gild it with gold, float in on the wanton wind and spread it in varied wonders.

And again when it shall be thy wish to end this play at night, I shall melt and vanish away in the dark, or it may be in a smile of the white morning, in a coolness of purity transparent.

LXXXI

On many an idle day have I grieved over lost time. But it is never lost, my lord. Thou hast taken every moment of my life in thine own hands.

Hidden in the heart of things thou art nourishing seeds into sprouts, buds into blossoms, and ripening flowers into fruitfulness.

I was tired and sleeping on my idle bed and imagined all work had ceased. In the morning I woke up and found my garden full with wonders of flowers.

LXXXII

Time is endless in thy hands, my lord. There is none to count thy minutes.

Days and nights pass and ages bloom and fade like flowers. Thou knowest how to wait.

Thy centuries follow each other perfecting a small wild flower.

We have no time to lose, and having no time we must scramble for our chances. We are too poor to be late.

And thus it is that time goes by while I give it to every querulous man who claims it, and thine altar is empty of all offerings to the last.

At the end of the day I hasten in fear lest thy gate be shut; but I find that yet there is time.

LXXIII

Mother, I shall weave a chain of pearls for thy neck with my tears of sorrow.

The stars have wrought their anklets of lights to deck thy feet, but mine will hang upon thy breast.

Wealth and fame come from thee and it is for thee to give or to withhold them. But this my sorrow is absolutely mine own, and when I bring it to thee as my offering thou rewardest me with thy grace.

LXXXIV

It is the pang of separation that spreads throughout the world and gives birth to shapes innumerable in the infinite sky.

It is this sorrow of separation that gazes in silence all night from star to star and becomes lyric among rustling leaves in rainy darkness of July.

It is this overspreading pain that deepens into loves and desires, into sufferings and joys in human homes; and this it is that ever melts and flows in songs through my poet's heart.

LXXXV

When the warriors came out first from their master's hall, where had they hid their power? Where were their armour and their arms?

They looked poor and helpless, and the arrows were showered upon them on the day they came out from their master's hall.

When the warriors marched back again to their master's hall, where did they hide their power?

They had dropped the sword and dropped the bow and the arrow; peace was on their foreheads, and they had left the fruits of their life behind them on the day they marched back again to their master's hall.

LXXXVI

Death, thy servant, is at my door. He has crossed the unknown sea and brought thy call to my home.

The night is dark and my heart is fearful – yet I will take up the lamp, open my gates and bow to him my welcome. It is thy messenger who stands at my door.

I will worship him with folded hands, and with tears. I will worship him placing at his feet the treasure of my heart.

He will go back with his errand done, leaving a dark shadow on my morning; and in my desolate home only my forlorn self will remain as my last offering to thee.

LXXXIX

No more noisy, loud words from me – such is my master's will. Henceforth I deal in whispers. The speech of my heart will be carried on in murmurings of a song.

Men hasten to the King's market. All the buyers and sellers are there. But I have my untimely leave in the middle of the day, in the thick of work.

Let then the flowers come out in my garden, though it is not their time; and let the midday bees strike up their lazy hum.

Full many an hour have I spent in the strife of the good and the evil, but now it is the pleasure of my playmate of the empty days to draw my heart on to him; and I know not why is this sudden call to what useless inconsequence!

XC

On the day when death will knock at thy door what wilt thou offer to him?

Oh, I will set before my guest the full vessel of my life – I will never let him go with empty hands.

All the sweet vintage of all my autumn days and summer nights, all the earnings and gleanings of my busy life will I place before him at the close of my days when death will knock at my door.

XCI

O thou the last fulfilment of life, Death, my death, come and whisper to me!

Day after day have I kept watch for thee; for thee have I borne the joys and pangs of life.

All that I am, that I have, that I hope, and all my love have ever flowed towards thee in depth of secrecy. One final glance from thine eyes and my life will be ever thine own.

The flowers have been woven and the garland is ready for the bridegroom. After the wedding the bride shall leave her home and meet her lord alone in the solitude of the night.

XCV

I was not aware of the moment when I first crossed the threshold of this life.

What was the power that made me open out into this vast mystery like a bud in the forest at midnight?

When in the morning I looked upon the light I felt in a moment that I was no stranger in this world, that the inscrutable without name and form had taken me in its arms in the form of my own mother.

Even so, in death the same unknown will appear as ever known to me. And because I love this life, I know I shall love death as well.

The child cries out when from the right breast the mother takes it away, in the very next moment to find in the left one its consolation.

XCVI

When I go from hence let this be my parting word, that what I have seen is unsurpassable.

I have tasted of the hidden honey of this lotus that expands on the ocean of light, and thus am I blessed – let this be my parting word.

In this playhouse of infinite forms I have had my play and here have I caught sight of him that is formless.

My whole body and my limbs have thrilled with his touch who is beyond touch; and if the end comes here, let it come – let this be my parting word.

XCVII

When my play was with thee I never questioned who thou wert. I knew no shyness nor fear, my life was boisterous.

In the early morning thou wouldst call me from my sleep like my own comrade and lead me running from glade to glade.

On those days I never cared to know the meaning of songs thou sangest to me. Only my voice took up the tunes, and my heart danced in their cadence.

Now, when the playtime is over, what is this sudden sight that is come upon me? The world with eyes bent upon thy feet stands in awe with all its silent stars.

CII

I boasted among men that I had known you. They see your pictures in all works of mine. They come and ask me, 'Who is he?' I know not how to answer them. I say, 'Indeed, I cannot tell.' They blame me and they go away in scorn. And you sit there smiling.

I put my tales of you into lasting songs. The secret gushes out from my heart. They come and ask me, 'Tell me all your meanings.' I know not how to answer them. I say, 'Ah, who knows what they mean!' They smile and go away in utter scorn. And you sit there smiling.

CIII

In one salutation to thee, my God, let all my senses spread out and touch this world at thy feet.

Like a rain-cloud of July hung low with its burden of unshed showers let all my mind bend down at thy door in one salutation to thee.

Let all my songs gather together their diverse strains into a single current and flow to a sea of silence in one salutation to thee.

Like a flock of homesick cranes flying night and day back to their mountain nests let all my life take its voyage to its eternal home in one salutation to thee.

V.40   MOHANDAS KARAMCHAND
GANDHI
THE MIND OF MAHATMA GANDHI
[SAYINGS AND THOUGHTS]
(Indo-English, 1946)

Mohandas Karamchand Gandhi (1869–1948), affectionately known in India as *Bapuji* (Father), and throughout the world as the *Mahatma* (Great Soul), needs no introduction to contemporary readers; for the picture of a frail man with an austere frame and compassionate smile, wrapped in a white cloth, is still fresh in the memory of mankind. During his meteoric life, he left no aspect of Indian life, including literature, untouched by the genius of his extraordinary personality.

Though Gandhi used his mother tongue, Gujarati, to write his famous autobiography (1925–7), later translated into English by his secretary Mahadev Desai under the title *The Story of My Experiments with Truth* (1929), he used Hindi and English with masterly skill and ease. As he lived through a phenomenal life among his people, who were attempting to liberate themselves from moral decadence, social lethargy, political degradation, economic exploitation, and cultural subordination, Gandhi wrote, day and night, in and out of prisons, for his two journals, *Young India* (1919–32) and *Harijan* (1933–42). In some rare moments of trial and confrontation, he saw, perhaps more clearly than anyone else, glimpses of Truth which he tried to explain in terms of his passionate commitment to his avowed principles of *Ahimsa* (least violence, or non-violence) and *Satyagraha* (truth force). In a vision of clarity, touching almost spirituality, he saw that what had seemed impossible to achieve was indeed within the reach of human endeavour. His perceptions, as recorded in his writing, sanctified the language. Thus, by writing in a language not his own, Gandhi not only enriched English but also contributed to the multifoliate modern Indian literature flowering in two dozen languages, including Indo-English.

Together with Tagore, Gandhi represents the Indian tradition at its best from two different points of view. Jawaharlal Nehru, who admired both, and synthesized in his own person the idealism of Tagore and the practical attitudes to action of Gandhi, viewed the two great souls with considerable affection and understanding, and wrote about them in his book *The Discovery of India* (Indo-English, 1946):

Tagore and Gandhi have undoubtedly been the two outstanding and dominating figures of India in this first half of the twentieth century. It is instructive to compare and contrast them. No two persons could be so different from one another in their make-up or temperaments. Tagore, the aristocratic artist, turned democrat with proletarian sympathies, represented essentially the cultural tradition of India, the tradition of accepting life in the fullness thereof and going through it with song and dance. Gandhi, more a man of the people, almost the embodiment of the Indian peasant, represented the other ancient tradition of India, that of renunciation and asceticism. And yet Tagore was primarily the man of thought, Gandhi of concentrated and ceaseless activity. Both, in their different ways, had a world outlook, and both were at the same time wholly Indian. They seemed to represent different but harmonious aspects of India and to complement one another.*

The thoughts of the Mahatma are taken from an anthology compiled by R. K. Prabhu and U. R. Rao, *The Mind of Mahatma Gandhi*, Madras: Oxford University Press, 1946 (with the permission of Navjivan Trust). The editors state that 'the proofs of this work were submitted to and read by Gandhiji', thus giving a tone of authenticity to the text. Some significant excerpts from the anthology are selected here to give some idea of Gandhi's way of thinking about India and the world and looking at life generally.

BC   *The Bombay Chronicle,* daily newspaper, Bombay
ER   *Ethical Religion,* by Mahatma Gandhi, Madras: S. Ganesan, 1930
H   *Harijan,* weekly journal, ed. M. K. Gandhi and also by others occasionally; started on 11 February 1933, and published from

---

*Jawaharlal Nehru, *The Discovery of India*, Calcutta: The Signet Press, 1946, p. 405.

Poona and later from Ahmedabad; ceased publication on 16 August 1942; revived on 10 February 1946

HS   *Hind Swaraj*, or *Indian Home Rule*, by Mahatma Gandhi, Ahmedabad: Navajivan Press; revised new edition 1928.

P   *The Pioneer*, daily paper published in Lucknow

SW   *Speeches and Writings of Mahatma Gandhi*, Madras: G. A. Natesan, 4th ed., 1933

WGC   *With Gandhiji in Ceylon*, by Mahadev Desai, Madras: S. Ganesan, 1928

YI   *Young India*, weekly journal, ed. Mahatma Gandhi from 8 October 1919, and published at Ahmedabad; ceased publication February 1932

V.40 MOHANDAS KARAMCHAND GANDHI
THE MIND OF MAHATMA GANDHI

I. *Gospel of Love*

(1) Scientists tell us that, without the presence of the cohesive force amongst the atoms that comprise this globe of ours, it would crumble to pieces and we would cease to exist; and even as there is cohesive force in blind matter, so must there be in all things animate, and the name for that cohesive force among animate beings is Love. We notice it between father and son, between brother and sister, friend and friend. But we have to learn to use that force among all that lives, and in the use of it consists our knowledge of God. Where there is love there is life; hatred leads to destruction.   [YI, 5 May 1920, p. 7]

(2) I have found that life persists in the midst of destruction and, therefore, there must be a higher law than that of destruction. Only under that law would a well-ordered society be intelligible and life worth living. And if that is the law of life, we have to work it out in daily life. Wherever there are jars, wherever you are confronted with an opponent, conquer him with love. In this crude manner, I have

worked it out in my life. That does not mean that all my difficulties are solved. Only I have found that this law of love has answered as the law of destruction has never done.   [YI, 1 October 1931, p. 286]

(3) I believe that the sum total of the energy of mankind is not to bring us down but to lift us up, and that is the result of the definite, if unconscious, working of the law of love. The fact that mankind persists shows that the cohesive force is greater than the disruptive force, centripetal force greater than centrifugal.

[YI, 12 November 1931, p. 355]

(4) All the teachers that ever lived have preached that law with more or less vigour. If Love was not the law of life, life would not have persisted in the midst of death. Life is a perpetual triumph over the grave. If there is a fundamental distinction between man and beast, it is the former's progressive recognition of the law and its application in practice to his own personal life. All the saints of the world, ancient and modern, were each according to his light and capacity a living illustration of that supreme Law of our Being. That the brute in us seems so often to gain an easy triumph is true enough. That, however, does not disprove the law. It shows the difficulty of practice. How should it be otherwise with a law which is as high as truth itself?

[H, 26 September 1936, p. 260]

(5) The safest rule of conduct is to claim kinship when we want to do service and not to insist on kinship when we want to assert a right.

[YI, 8 December 1927, p. 47]

(6) We must widen the circle of our love till it embraces the whole village; the village in its turn must take into its fold the district, the district the province, and so on till the scope of our love becomes co-terminous with the world.   [YI, 27 June 1929, p. 214]

(7) I have no weapon but love to wield authority over anyone.

[BC, 9 August 1942]

(8) I refuse to suspect human nature. It will, is bound to, respond to any noble and friendly action.   [YI, 4 August 1920, p. 5]

(9) Where I cannot help, I must resolutely refuse to hinder.

[YI, 25 June 1925, p. 222]

(10) Love never claims, it ever gives. Love ever suffers, never resents, never revenges itself.   [YI, 9 July 1925, p. 240]

(11) There is a real and substantial unity in all the variety that we see around us. The word 'inequality' has a bad odour about it, and it has led to arrogance and inhumanities, both in the East and the West. What is true about men is also true about nations, which are but groups of men. The false and rigid doctrine of inequality has led to the insolent exploitation of the nations of Asia and Africa. Who knows that the present ability of the West to prey upon the East is a sign of Western superiority and Eastern inferiority?

[YI, 11 August 1927, p. 253]

(12) The forms are many, but the informing spirit is one. How can there be room for distinctions of high and low where there is this all-embracing fundamental unity underlying the outward diversity? For that is a fact meeting you at every step in daily life. The final goal of all religions is to realize this essential oneness.

[H, 15 December 1933, p. 3]

(13) The golden rule of conduct . . . is mutual toleration, seeing that we will never all think alike and we shall always see Truth in fragment and from different angles of vision. Conscience is not the same thing for all. Whilst, therefore, it is a good guide for individual conduct, imposition of that conduct upon all will be an insufferable interference with everybody's freedom of conscience. . . . Even amongst the most conscientious persons, there will be room enough for honest differences of opinion. The only possible rule of conduct in any civilized society is, therefore, mutual toleration.

[YI, 23 September 1926, p. 334]

(14) In trying to explore the hidden treasures of ancient culture, I have come upon this inestimable boon that all that is permanent in ancient Hindu culture is also to be found in the teachings of Jesus, Buddha, Muhammad, and Zoroaster.   [WGC, p. 131]

(15) I believe in the fundamental truth of all great religions of the world. I believe that they are all God-given, and I believe that they were necessary for the people to whom these religions were revealed. And I believe that if only we could all of us read the scriptures of the different faiths from the standpoint of the followers of those faiths, we should find that they were at the bottom all one and were all helpful to one another.   [H, 2 February 1934, p. 8]

II. *Gospel of Labour*

(1) To a people famishing and idle, the only acceptable form in which God can dare appear is work and promise of food and wages.

[YI, 13 October 1921, p. 325]

(2) God created man to work for his food, and said that those who ate without work were thieves.   [YI, 13 October 1921, p. 325]

(3) There can never be too much emphasis placed on work. I am simply repeating the gospel taught by the *Gita*, where the Lord says, 'If I did not remain ever at work sleeplessly, I should set a wrong example to mankind.'   [H, 2 November 1935, p. 298]

(4) I do not fight shy of capital. I fight capitalism. ... Capital and labour need not be antagonistic to each other. I cannot picture to myself a time when no man shall be richer than another. But I do picture to myself a time when the rich will spurn to enrich themselves at the expense of the poor and the poor will cease to envy the rich. Even in a most perfect world, we shall fail to avoid inequalities, but we can and must avoid strife and bitterness.   [YI, 7 October 1926, p. 48]

(5) By the non-violent method, we seek not to destroy the capitalist, we seek to destroy Capitalism. We invite the capitalist to regard himself as a trustee for those on whom he depends for the making, retention, and the increase of his capital. ... If capital is power, so is work. Either power can be used destructively or creatively.

[YI, 26 March 1931, p. 49]

(6) It is impossible for one to be internationalist without being a nationalist. Internationalism is possible only when nationalism becomes a fact, i.e. when peoples belonging to different countries have organized themselves and are able to act as one man. It is not nationalism that is evil, it is the narrowness, selfishness, exclusiveness which is the bane of modern nations which is evil. . . . God having cast my lot in the midst of the people of India, I should be untrue to my Maker if I failed to serve them. If I do not know how to serve them I shall never know how to serve humanity. And I cannot possibly go wrong so long as I do not harm other nations in the act of serving my country.

[YI, 18 June 1925, p. 121]

(7) It is demoralizing for men and women who have strong arms and legs and who are otherwise physically fit to subsist on charity. They must find out some occupation for themselves. The idea is that no person, man or woman, who is physically fit should live on charity. There must be always enough occupation in a well-ordered state for all who are willing to work. [YI, 12 February 1925, p. 56]

III. *Gospel of Ahimsa* (Non-Violence or least violence)

(1) Non-violence is the law of our species as violence is the law of the brute. The spirit lies dormant in the brute and he knows no law but that of physical might. The dignity of man requires obedience to a higher law – to the strength of the spirit. [YI, 11 August 1920, p. 3]

(2) I have, therefore, ventured to place before India the ancient law of self-sacrifice. For *Satyagraha* and its off-shoots, non-cooperation and civil resistance are nothing but new names for the law of suffering. The *rishis*, who discovered the law of non-violence in the midst of violence, were greater geniuses than Newton. They were themselves greater warriors than Wellington. Having themselves known the use of arms, they realized their uselessness and taught a weary world that its salvation lay not through violence but through non-violence.

[YI, 11 August 1920, p. 3]

(3) I want India to recognize that she has a soul that cannot perish and that can rise triumphant above every physical weakness and defy the physical combination of a whole world.   [YI, 11 August 1920, p. 3]

(4) Non-violence is the first article of my faith. It is also the last article of my creed.   [YI, 23 March 1922, p. 166]

(5) Non-violence is an active force of the highest order. It is soul-force or the power of godhead within us.   [H, 12 November 1938, p. 326]

(6) The world is not entirely governed by logic. Life itself involves some kind of violence, and we have to choose the path of least violence.   [H, 28 September 1934, p. 259]

(7) The strength to kill is not essential for self-defence; one ought to have the strength to die. When a man is fully ready to die, he will not even desire to offer violence. Indeed, I may put it down as a self-evident proposition that the desire to kill is in inverse proportion to the desire to die. And history is replete with instances of men who by dying with courage and compassion on their lips converted the hearts of their violent opponents.   [YI, 23 January 1930, p. 27]

(8) My creed of non-violence is an extremely active force. It has no room for cowardice or even weakness. There is hope for a violent man to be some day non-violent, but there is none for a coward. I have, therefore, said more than once . . . that if we do not know how to defend ourselves, our women and our places of worship by the force of suffering, i.e. non-violence, we must, if we are men, be at least able to defend all these by fighting.   [YI, 16 June 1927, p. 196]

(9) It has become the fashion these days to say that society cannot be organized or run on non-violent lines. I join issue on that point. In a family, when a father slaps his delinquent child, the latter does not think of retaliating. He obeys his father not because of the deterrent effect of the slap but because of the offended love which he senses behind it. That, in my opinion, is an epitome of the way in which

society is or should be governed. What is true of the family must be true of society which is but a larger family.

[H, 3 December 1938, p. 358]

(10) National independence is not a fiction. It is as necessary as individual independence. But neither, if it is based on non-violence, may ever be a menace to the equal independence of the nation or the individual as the case may be. As with individual and national independence, so with the international. The legal maxim is equally moral. *Sic utere tuo ut alienum non laedas* (So use your own property as not to injure the rights of another). It has been well said that the universe is compressed in the atom. There is not one law for the atom and another for the universe. [YI, 31 December 1931, p. 426]

(11) Like opium production, the world manufacture of swords [armament] needs to be restricted. The sword is probably responsible for more misery in the world than opium.

[YI, 19 November 1925, p. 397]

IV. *Gospel of Satyagraha* [Force of Truth]

(1) A satyagrahi is nothing if not instinctively law-abiding, and it is his law-abiding nature which exacts from him implicit obedience to the highest law, that is the voice of conscience which overrides all other laws [legislated]. [SW, p. 465]

(2) Civil Disobedience is the inherent right of a citizen. He dare not give it up without ceasing to be a man. Civil Disobedience is never followed by anarchy. Criminal Disobedience can lead to it. Every state puts down Criminal Disobedience by force. It perishes, if it does not. But to put down Civil Disobedience is to attempt to imprison conscience. [YI, 5 January 1922, p. 5]

(3) Jesus Christ, Daniel, and Socrates represented the purest form of passive resistance or soul force. All these teachers counted their bodies as nothing in comparison to their soul. Tolstoy was the best and brightest [modern] exponent of the doctrine. He not only expounded

it, but lived according to it. In India, the doctrine was understood and commonly practised long before it came into vogue in Europe. It is easy to see that soul force is infinitely superior to body force. If people in order to secure redress of wrongs resort to soul force, much of the present suffering will be avoided. [sw, p. 165]

(4) In any case, the wielding of the force [Satyagraha] never causes suffering to others. So that whenever it is misused it only injures the users and not those against whom it is used. [sw, p. 165]

(5) Non-cooperation is a protest against an unwitting and unwilling participation in evil. Non-cooperation with evil is as much a duty as cooperation with good. [yi, 1 June 1921, p. 172]

(6) My non-cooperation, though it is part of my creed, is a prelude to cooperation. My non-cooperation is with methods and systems, never with men. . . . I regard ill-will as beneath the dignity of man.

[yi, 12 September 1929, p. 300]

(7) My non-cooperation has its root not in hatred, but in love. My personal religion peremptorily forbids me to hate anybody.

[yi, 6 August 1925, p. 272]

(8) It is not that I harbour disloyalty towards anything whatsoever, but I do so against all untruth, all that is unjust, all that is evil. . . . I remain loyal to an institution so long as that institution conduces to my growth, to the growth of the nation. Immediately I find that the institution instead of conducing to its growth impedes it, I hold it to be my bounden duty to be disloyal to it. [yi, 13 August 1925, p. 277]

V. *Gospel of Simple Life*

DRESS

(1) I wear the national dress because it is the most natural and the most becoming for an Indian. I believe that our copying of the European dress is a sign of our degradation, humiliation and our weakness, and

that we are committing a national sin in discarding a dress which is best suited to the Indian climate and which for its simplicity, art, and cheapness is not to be beaten on the face of the earth and which answers hygienic requirements. Had it not been for a false pride and equally false notions of prestige, Englishmen here would long ago have adopted the Indian costume. [P, 4 July 1917]

DUTY OF A LAWYER

(2) The duty of a lawyer is always to place before the judges, and to help them to arrive at the truth, never to prove the guilty as innocent.
[YI, 22 December 1927, p. 428]

MEANS AND ENDS

(3) Means and Ends are convertible in my philosophy of life.
[YI, 26 December 1924, p. 435]

(4) They say 'means are after all means'. I would say 'means are after all everything'. As the means, so the end. Violent means will give violent *swaraj* [self-rule]. . . . There is no wall of separation between means and end. Indeed, the Creator has given us control (and that too very limited) over means, none over the end. Realization of the goal is in exact proportion to that of the means.
[YI, 17 July 1924, pp. 236–7]

MORALITY

(5) True morality consists, not in following the beaten track, but in finding out the true path for ourselves and in fearlessly following it.
[ER, p. 36]

SECRECY

(6) All sins are committed in secrecy. The moment we realize that God witnesses even our thoughts we shall be free.
[YI, 5 June 1924, p. 186]

(7) A patient can ill afford to conceal his disease. If he does so he becomes his own enemy. [YI, 2 February 1928, p. 37]

(8) Confession of error is like a broom that sweeps away dirt and leaves the surface cleaner than before.   [YI, 16 February 1922, p. 102]

MEDICATION

(9) We want healers of souls rather than of bodies. The multiplicity of hospitals and medical men is no sign of true civilization.

[YI, September 1927, p. 327]

(10) The fact remains that the doctors induce us to indulge, and the result is that we have become deprived of self-control.   [HS, p. 83]

(11) I do not despise all medical treatment. . . . We can learn a good deal from the West. But the West attaches an exaggerated importance to prolonging man's earthly existence. Until man's last moment on earth you go on drugging him even by injecting. That, I think, is inconsistent with the recklessness with which they will shed their lives in war.   [H, 3 July 1937, p. 165]

(12) There is a great deal of truth in the saying that man becomes what he eats. The grosser the food the grosser the body.

[H, 5 August 1933, p. 4]

UNTOUCHABILITY

(13) There is an ineffaceable blot that Hinduism today carries with it. I have declined to believe that it has been handed down to us from immemorial times. I think that this miserable, wretched, enslaving spirit of 'untouchableness' must have come to us when we were at our lowest ebb. This evil has stuck to us and still remains with us. It is, to my mind, a curse that has come to us; and as long as that curse remains with us, so long I think we are bound to consider that every affliction in this sacred land is a proper punishment for the indelible crime that we are committing. That any person should be considered untouchable because of his calling passes my comprehension; that you, the student world, who receive all this modern education, if you become a party to this crime, it were better that you received no education whatsoever.

[Address at YMCA, Madras, 16 February 1916]

SWARAJ (Self-rule)

(14) Surely *Swaraj* will not drop from the clouds. It will be the fruit of patience, perseverance, ceaseless toil, courage and intelligent appreciation of the environment.   [YI, 27 August 1925, p. 297]

(15) *Swaraj* for me means freedom for the meanest of our countrymen. I am not interested in freeing India merely from the English yoke. I am bent upon freeing India from any yoke whatsoever. I have no desire to exchange 'king log for king stork'.   [YI, 12 June 1924, p. 195]

(16) Real *Swaraj* will come not by the acquisition of authority by a few but by the acquisition of the capacity by all to resist authority when it is abused. In other words, *Swaraj* is to be attained by educating the masses to a sense of their capacity to regulate and control authority.
[YI, 29 January 1925, p. 40]

(17) One sometimes hears it said: 'Let us get the Government of India in our own hands and everything will be all right.' There could be no greater superstition than this. No nation has thus gained its independence. The splendour of the spring is reflected in every tree.
[SW, p. 416]

(18) Finite human beings shall never know in its fulness Truth and Love which is in itself infinite. But we do know enough for our guidance. We shall err, and sometimes grievously, in our application. But man is a self-governing being, and self-government necessarily includes the power as much to commit errors as to set them right as often as they are made.   [YI, 21 April 1927, p. 128]

PRAYER

(19) I started with disbelief in God and prayer, and until at a late stage in life I did not feel anything like a void in life. But at that stage I felt that as food was indispensable for the body, so was prayer indispensable for the soul. In fact food for the body is not so necessary as prayer for the soul. For starvation is often necessary in order to keep

the body in health, but there is no such thing as prayer-starvation. . . . I am indifferent as to the form. Every one is a law unto himself in that respect. But there are some well-marked roads, and it is safe to walk along the beaten tracks, trod by the ancient teachers.

[Y I, 24 September 1931, p. 274]

(20) It is better in prayer to have a heart without words than words without a heart.   [Y I, 23 January 1930, p. 25]

The short story was a recognized literary form in India centuries before its popularization in modern times. Most of the ancient stories have come down to our day, originally through oral transmission, and subsequently by their inclusion in various literary devices, such as the cluster-stories, chain-stories, and frame-stories, or in plain and simple anthologies. However, with the popularization of literature through printing and publishing, and with the emergence of periodicals, journals, and little magazines in the last two centuries, there has been a steady growth of this particular genre in almost all the Indian languages.

The characteristic feature of the modern short story is its capacity to present a slice of life in terms of contemporary social realities. In a society gradually transforming itself from a traditional feudal outlook to modern industrial ways, attitudes to established values undergo changes or generate conflict. The shifting political and economic power under Moghul and British imperial rule, and the rising expectations of a reformed and renascent India, variously restratified mental attitudes to social and cultural values. Thus, the human condition in India provides rich and colourful material for creative writers and artists.

While some writers portray Indian life in a changing society with idealistic values in view, others vigorously depict human characters and actions against the background of stark social realism. It is only a few gifted ones who have been able to see contemporary life with all its foibles with a comic vision and to write in a satirical tone. Among them are a number of writers who have beautifully illustrated modern India's acutest problem, the 'English-educated' Indian, alienated from his tradition and mentally subordinated to European culture, whether deliberately by the educational machinery under the British rule or not so deliberately in independent India.

In the story *Karma*, Khushwant Singh (*b.* 1915), a contemporary Indian short storiest and novelist, writes about an anglicized Indian, very appropriately in Indo-English. The story is taken from his book, *The Voice of God and Other Stories*, published by Jaico Publishing House, Bombay, 1950.

KHUSHWANT SINGH
KARMA
(Indo-English)

Sir Mohan Lal looked at himself in the mirror of a first-class waiting room at the railway station. The mirror was obviously made in India. The red oxide at its back had come off at several places and long lines of translucent glass cut across its surface. Sir Mohan smiled at the mirror with an air of pity and patronage.

'You are so very much like everything else in this country – inefficient, dirty, indifferent,' he murmured.

The mirror smiled back at Sir Mohan.

'You are a bit of all right, old chap,' it said. 'Distinguished, efficient – even handsome. That neatly trimmed moustache, the suit from Savile Row with the carnation in the buttonhole, the aroma of eau de cologne, talcum powder, and scented soap all about you! Yes, old fellow, you are a bit of all right.'

Sir Mohan threw out his chest, smoothed his Balliol tie for the umpteenth time, and waved a good-bye to the mirror.

He glanced at his watch. There was still time for a quick one.

'*Koi hai?*'

A bearer in white livery appeared through a wire-gauze door.

'*Ek chota,*' ordered Sir Mohan, and sank into a large cane chair to drink and ruminate.

Outside the waiting room Sir Mohan Lal's luggage lay piled along the wall. On a small grey steel trunk, Lachmi, Lady Mohan Lal, sat chewing a betel leaf and fanning herself with a newspaper. She was short and fat and in her middle forties. She wore a dirty white sari with a red border. On one side of her nose glistened a diamond nose ring, and she had several gold bangles on her arms. She had been talking to the bearer until Sir Mohan had summoned him inside. As soon as he had gone, she hailed a passing railway coolie.

Koi hai? (Hindi) Anybody here?
Ek chota. (Hindi) One short peg.

'Where does the *zenana* stop?'

'Right at the end of the platform.'

The coolie flattened his turban to make a cushion, hoisted the steel trunk on his head, and moved down the platform. Lady Lal picked up her brass tiffin carrier and ambled along behind him. On the way she stopped by a hawker's stall to replenish her silver betel-leaf case, and then joined the coolie. She sat down on her steel trunk (which the coolie had put down) and started talking to him.

'Are the trains very crowded on these lines?'

'These days all trains are crowded, but you'll find room in the *zenana*.'

'Then I might as well get over the bother of eating.'

Lady Lal opened the brass carrier and took out a bundle of cramped chapatties and some mango pickle. While she ate, the coolie sat opposite her on his haunches, drawing lines in the gravel with his finger.

'Are you travelling alone, sister?'

'No, I am with my master, brother. He is in the waiting room. He travels first class. He is a vizier and a barrister, and meets so many officers and Englishmen in the trains – and I am only a native woman. I can't understand English and don't know their ways, so I keep to my *zenana* interclass.'

Lachmi chatted away merrily. She was fond of a little gossip and had no one to talk to at home. Her husband never had any time to spare for her. She lived in the upper story of the house and he on the ground floor. He did not like her poor, illiterate relatives hanging about his bungalow, so they never came. He came up to her once in a while at night and stayed for a few minutes. He just ordered her about in anglicized Hindustani, and she obeyed passively. These nocturnal visits had, however, borne no fruit.

The signal came down and the clanging of the bell announced the approaching train. Lady Lal hurriedly finished off her meal. She got up, still licking the stone of the pickled mango. She emitted a long, loud belch as she went to the public tap to rinse her mouth and wash her hands. After washing, she dried her mouth and hands with the loose

---

Zenana. Ladies' compartment.

end of her sari, and walked back to her steel trunk, belching and thanking the gods for the favour of a filling meal.

The train steamed in. Lachmi found herself facing an almost empty interclass *zenana* compartment next to the guard's van, at the tail end of the train. The rest of the train was packed. She heaved her squat, bulky frame through the door and found a seat by the window. She produced a two-anna bit from a knot in her sari and dismissed the coolie. She then opened her betel case and made herself two betel leaves charged with a red-and-white paste, minced betel-nuts, and cardamoms. These she thrust into her mouth till her cheeks bulged on both sides. Then she rested her chin on her hands and sat gazing idly at the jostling crowd on the platform.

The arrival of the train did not disturb Sir Mohan Lal's *sang-froid*. He continued to sip his Scotch and ordered the bearer to tell him when he had moved the luggage to a first-class compartment. Excitement, bustle, and hurry were exhibitions of bad breeding, and Sir Mohan was eminently well-bred. He wanted everything 'tickety-boo' and orderly. In his five years abroad, Sir Mohan had acquired the manners and attitudes of the upper classes. He rarely spoke Hindustani. When he did it was like an Englishman's – only the very necessary words and properly anglicized. But he fancied his English, finished and refined at no less a place than the University of Oxford. He was fond of conversation, and, like a cultured Englishman, he could talk on almost any subject – books, politics, people. How frequently had he heard English people say that he spoke like an Englishman!

Sir Mohan wondered if he would be travelling alone. It was a cantonment, and some English officers might be on the train. His heart warmed at the prospect of an impressive conversation. He never showed any sign of eagerness to talk to the English, as most Indians did. Nor was he loud, aggressive, and opinionated like them. He went about his business with an expressionless matter-of-factness. He would retire to his corner by the window and get out a copy of *The Times*. He would fold it in a way in which the name of the paper was visible to others while he did the crossword puzzle. *The Times* always attracted attention. Someone would like to borrow it when he put it aside with a gesture signifying 'I've finished with it.' Perhaps someone would recognize his Balliol tie, which he always wore while travelling. That would open a vista leading to a fairyland of Oxford colleges, masters, dons, tutors, boat races, and rugger matches. If both *The Times* and the tie failed, Sir Mohan would '*Koi hai*' his bearer to get the Scotch out. Whisky never failed with Englishmen. Then followed Sir Mohan's handsome gold cigarette case filled with English cigarettes. English cigarettes in India? How on earth did he get them? Sure he didn't mind? And Sir Mohan's understanding smile – of course he didn't. But could he use the Englishman as a medium to commune with his dear old England? Those five years of grey bags and gowns, of sports blazers and mixed doubles, of dinners at the Inns of Court and nights with Piccadilly prostitutes. Five years of a crowded, glorious life. Worth far more than the forty-five in India with his dirty, vulgar countrymen, with sordid details of the road to success, of nocturnal visits to the upper story and all-too-brief sexual acts with obese old Lachmi, smelling of sweat and raw onions.

Sir Mohan's thoughts were disturbed by the bearer's announcing the installation of the sahib's luggage in a first-class coupe next to the engine. Sir Mohan walked to his coupe with a studied gait. He was dismayed. The compartment was empty. With a sigh, he sat down in a corner and opened the copy of *The Times* he had read several times before.

Sir Mohan looked out of the window down the crowded platform. His face lit up as he saw two English soldiers trudging along, looking in all the compartments for room. They had their haversacks slung behind their backs, and walked unsteadily. Sir Mohan decided to welcome them, even though they were entitled to travel only second class. He would speak to the guard.

One of the soldiers came up to the last compartment and stuck his face through the window. He surveyed the compartment and noticed the unoccupied berth.

''Ere, Bill,' he shouted. 'One 'ere.'

His companion came up, also looked in, and looked at Sir Mohan.

'Get the nigger out,' he muttered to his companion.

They opened the door, and turned to the half-smiling, half-protesting Sir Mohan.

'Reserved!' yelled Bill.

'*Janta* – reserved. Army – *fauj*,' exclaimed Jim, pointing to his khaki shirt.

'*Ek dum jao* – get out!'

'I say, I say, surely,' protested Sir Mohan in his Oxford accent.

The soldiers paused. It almost sounded like English, but they knew better than to trust their inebriated ears. The engine whistled and the guard waved his green flag.

They picked up Sir Mohan's suitcase and flung it onto the platform. Then followed his thermos flask, bedding, and *The Times*. Sir Mohan was livid with rage.

'Preposterous, preposterous,' he shouted, hoarse with anger. 'I'll have you arrested. Guard, guard!'

Bill and Jim paused again. It did sound like English, but it was too much of the King's for them.

'Keep yer ruddy mouth shut!' And Jim struck Sir Mohan flat on the face.

The engine gave another short whistle and the train began to move. The soldiers caught Sir Mohan by the arms and flung him out of the train. He reeled backward, tripped on his bedding, and landed on the suitcase.

'Toodle-oo!'

Sir Mohan's feet were glued to the earth and he lost his speech. He stared at the lighted windows of the train going past him in quickening tempo. The tail-end of the train appeared with a red light and the guard, standing in the open doorway with the flags in his hands.

In the interclass *zenana* compartment was Lachmi, fair and fat, on whose nose the diamond nose ring glistened against the station lights. Her mouth was bloated with betel saliva that she had been storing up to spit as soon as the train had cleared the station. As the train sped past the lighted part of the platform, Lady Lal spat and sent a jet of red dribble flying across like a dart.

APPENDIXES

APPENDIX A

List of Texts for Comparative Study

The selections for the *Anthology of Indian Literature* were made, among other considerations, for their appropriateness (a) as a unit for reading, discussion, and understanding, and (b) for comparison and contrast with other texts in the tradition, and in world literature.

Genre	*Texts Chosen*	*Other Texts in World Literature*
I. Hymns	1. *Rig Veda*	Hebrew: *Psalms*, for imagery and myths
Dialogues	2–5. *Upanishads Katha Upanishad*	Greek: Plato, *Dialogues* Hebrew: *The Book of Job*
Heroic epic	6–7. *Mahabharata* 'Savitri'	Greek: *Iliad*; Orpheus-Euridyce and Alcestis legends; Euripides, *Alcestis*
	'Bhagavad Gita'	Greek: Achilles (like Arjuna) – conflict of an epic hero: refusal to fight
Literary epic	8. *Ramayana*	Greek: *Odyssey*; Latin: *Aeneid* Problems of a moral hero: Moses in Hebrew epic; Vainamoinen in Finnish epic
	9. *Shilappadikaram*	Theme of love and attitude of women in Indian literature: Savitri, Sita, Kannaki, and Radha (6, 8, 9, 32)
II. Prose/Poetry Sermons Parables	10–17. *Tipitaka*	Greek: *Gospels*; Chinese: *Chuang Tzu*; *Revelation to John*
Couplets	12. *Dhammapada* 15. *Milindapanha*	Chinese: *Tao Teh Ching* Greek: Plato, *Dialogues*
Visionary writing	16. *Saddharma-Pundarika*	Italian: Dante, *Divine Comedy* Chinese: Wu Cheng-en, *Monkey*
Aphorisms	18. *Tiru-Kural*	Chinese: Confucius, *Analects*

III. Fable	19. *Pancha-tantra*	Greek: Aesop, *Fables*
Prose: Polity	20. *Artha Sastra*	Italian: Machiavelli, *The Prince*
Psychology	21. *Yoga Sutra*	German: Freud and Jung
Philosophy	22. *V. S. Bhashya*	German: Kant, *Critique*
Drama	23. *Vasavadatta*	English: Shakespeare, *As You Like It*
Elegy	24. *Megha Duuta*	English: Gray, *Elegy*
Novel	25. *Dasa-Kumara-Carita*	Evolution of novel form in India
Lyrics	26. *Kuruntokai*	Italian: Petrarch, *Sonnets*
Couplets	27. *Satakas*	English: Pope, *Essay on Man*
		Japanese: Haiku

IV. Short verses expressing love theme, mysticism, piety, and worldly wisdom	28. *Tiru Vasaham*	English: metaphysical poets
	29. *Vachana*	
	30. *Vakyani*	Persian: Rumi, *Diwani*
	31. *Kirtan*	
	32. *Gita Govinda*	Hebrew: *Song of Solomon*
		English: Spenser, *Four Hymns*
	33. *Bhajan*	Spanish: Saint Theresa Saint John of the Cross
	34. *Vinaya Patrika*	
	35. *Abhang*	
	36. *Kabir, Songs*	Persian: Rumi, *Diwani*
	37. *Ghazal*	
	38. *Adi Granth*	

V. Songs	39. *Gitanjali*	India's three *Gitas* – of action (7), love (32), resurrection (39)
Prose: essays	40. Thoughts of Mahatma	French: Montaigne, *Essays*
short story	41. 'Karma'	Compare Dasaratha's karma in *Ramayana*

APPENDIX B

Select Bibliography

A. BIBLIOGRAPHIES

De Bary, William Theodore, ed. *A Guide to Oriental Classics* (Arabian, Persian, Indian, Chinese, and Japanese). New York: Columbia University Press, 1964.

Emeneau, Murray Barnson, ed. *A Union List of Printed Indic Texts and Translations in American Libraries*. American Oriental Series, Vol. 7. New Haven, Con.: American Oriental Society, 1935.

Nayagam, Xavier S. Thani. *A Reference Guide to Tamil Studies*. Kuala Lumpur: University of Malaya Press, 1966.

B. REFERENCE WORKS, HISTORY AND CRITICISM

Archer, William George. *The Loves of Krishna in Indian Painting and Poetry*. London: Allen and Unwin, 1957; New York: Macmillan, 1957; New York: Glove (Evergreen) Paperback, 1958.

Basham, Arthur Llewellyn. *The Wonder That Was India: A Survey of the Culture of the Indian Sub-Continent Before the Coming of the Muslims*. London: Sidgwick and Jackson, 1954; New York: Grove (Evergreen) Paperback, 1959.

Bhandarkar, R. G. *Vaisnavism, Saivism, and Minor Religious Systems*. Strassburg: Trübner, 1913.

Bharata. *Natya Sastra*, ed. Joanny Grosset. Paris: Ernest Leroux, 1898.

Bhave, Vinoba. *Talks on the Gita*. New York: Macmillan and Co., 1960; London: Allen and Unwin, 1960.

Bloomfield, Maurice. *The Religion of the Veda: The Ancient Religion of India*. London and New York: Putnam, 1908.

Bondurant, Joan. *The Conquest of Violence*. Princeton, N.J.: University Press, 1958; London: Oxford University Press, 1958.

Brown, William Norman, ed. *India, Pakistan, Ceylon*. Ithaca, N.Y.; Cornell University Press, 1950.

Burtt, E. A. *Teachings of the Compassionate Buddha*. New York: New American Library (Mentor), 1955.

Carpenter, Joseph. *Theism in Medieval India*. London: Williams and Norgate, 1921.

Chaitanya, Krishna. *A New History of Sanskrit Literature*. New York: Asia Publishing Co., 1962.

Dasgupta, Surendra Nath. *Yoga as Philosophy and Religion*. London: Kegan Paul, Trench, Trübner, 1924; New York: Dutton, 1924.

    Hindu Mysticism. Chicago: The Open Court Publishing Co., 1927.

    Indian Idealism. Cambridge, England: University Press, 1933.

    A History of Classical Sanskrit Literature. Calcutta: University Press, 1947.

    A History of Indian Philosophy. Vols. I–V. Cambridge, England: University Press, 1922, 1932, 1940, 1949, 1955.

Davies, Cuthbert Collin. *An Historical Atlas of the Indian Peninsula*. Bombay: Oxford University Press, 1949; 2nd ed. Madras, 1959.

Dayal, Har. *The Bodhisattva Doctrine in Buddhist and Sanskrit Literature*. London: Routledge, 1931.

De, S. K. *History of Sanskrit Literature*. Calcutta: University, 1947.

    Sanskrit Poetics as a Study of Aesthetic. Berkeley, Calif.: University of California Press, 1963.

De Barry, William Theodore, *et al. Sources of Indian Tradition*. New York: Columbia University Press, 1958; paperback ed. 2 vols., 1964.

    Approaches to the Oriental Classics: Asian Literature and Thought in General Education. New York: Columbia University Press, 1959.

Desai, Mahadev. *The Gospel of Selfless Action*, or *The Gita According to Gandhi*. Ahmedabad: Navajivan Publishing House, 1956.

Deussen, Paul. *The Philosophy of the Upanishads*, translated from the German by A. S. Geden. Edinburgh: Clark, 1906.

    The System of Vedanta, translated from the German by Charles Johnston. Chicago: Open Court, 1912.

Dowson, John. *A Classical Dictionary of Hindu Mythology and Religion, Geography, History, and Literature*. London: Routledge and Kegan Paul Ltd, 1950.

Fischer, Louis. *The Life of Mahatma Gandhi*. New York: Harper, 1950: London: Cape, 1951; New York: Collier (paperback), 1962.

Foucher, A. *The Life of the Buddha According to the Ancient Texts and Monuments of India*, abridged translation by Simone Brangier Boas. Middletown, Conn.: Wesleyan University Press, 1963.

Frazer, R. W. *A Literary History of India*. New York: Charles Scribner's Sons, 1898.

Ghose, Aurobindo (Sri Aurobindo). *Essays on Gita*. New York: Dutton, 1950.

Goshal, Upendra Nath. *A History of Hindu Political Theories*. London: Oxford University Press, 1927.

Gowen, Herbert. *A History of Indian Literature*. New York: D. Appleton, 1931.

Haas, George C. O., tr. *The Dasarupa*: A Treatise on Hindu Dramaturgy by Dhanamjaya. New York: Columbia University Press, 1912; republished Delhi: Motilal Banarsidass, 1962.

Harris, Mary B. *Kalidasa, Poet of Nature*. Boston: Meador Press, 1936.

Hastings, James, ed. *Encyclopaedia of Religion and Ethics*. 13 vols. Edinburgh: Clark, 1908–26; New York: Scribner's, 1913–27; 13 vols. in 7, New York: Scribner's, 1951.

Hiriyana, Mysore. *The Essentials of Indian Philosophy*. London: Allen and Unwin, 1932; New York: Macmillan, 1949.

    Outlines of Indian Philosophy. London: Allen and Unwin, 1932.

    Art Experience (Indian Aesthetics). Mysore: Kavyalaya Publishers, 1954.

Hopkins, E. Washburn. *Epics of India*. New Haven, Conn.: Yale University Press, 1924.

    The Great Epic of India. New York: Scribner's, 1901.

    Epic Mythology. Strassburg: Trübner, 1915.

    Legends of India. New Haven, Conn.: Yale University Press, 1928.

Jacobi, Hermann, *The Ramayana*, translated from German by S. N. Ghosal. Baroda: Oriental Institute, 1960.

Jha, Bechan. *Concept of Poetic Blemishes in Sanskrit Poetics*. Varanasi: Chowkamba Sanskrit Series Office, 1965.

Jhala, G. C. *Kalidasa, a Study*. Bombay: Padma Publications, 1943.

Kaegi, Adolf. *The Rigveda: The Oldest Literature of the Indians,* translated from German by R. Arrowsmith. Boston: Ginn & Co., 1886. Reprinted as *Life in Ancient India: Studies in Rig Vedic India*. Calcutta: Gupta, 1950.

Keith, Arthur Berriedale. *Buddhist Philosophy in India and in Ceylon*. Oxford: Clarendon Press, 1923.

    The Sanskrit Drama: Its Origin, Development, Theory and Practice. Oxford: Clarendon Press, 1924.

    The Religion and Philosophy of the Veda and Upanishads. Harvard Oriental Series, Vols. 31, 32. Cambridge, Mass.; Harvard University Press, 1925; London: Oxford University Press, 1925.

    A History of Sanskrit Literature. Oxford: Clarendon Press, 1928.

Kripalani, Krishna. *Rabindranath Tagore: A Biography*. New York: Grove Press, 1962; London: Oxford University Press, 1962.

Levi, Sylvain. *Le Théâtre indien*. Paris: Bouillon, 1890.

Macdonell, Arthur Anthony. *Vedic Mythology*. Strassburg: Trübner, 1897.

A History of Sanskrit Literature. New York: Appleton, 1900; London: Heinemann, 1900; reprint, Delhi: Banarsidass, 1956.

India's Past: A Survey of Her Literatures, Religions, Languages, and Antiquities. Oxford: Clarendon Press, 1927.

Majumdar, R. C., ed. *The History and Culture of the Indian People*. 10 vols. Bombay: Bharatiya Vidya Bhavan, 1951–; London: Allen and Unwin, 1951–.

Max Müller, Friedrich. *The Vedanta Philosophy*. Calcutta: Susil Gupta, 1955.

Monier-Williams, M. *Indian Epic Poetry*. London: Williams and Norgate, 1863.

Mukerjee, Radhakamal. *The Lord of the Autumn Moons*. Bombay: Asia Publishing House, 1957.

Murti, T. R. V. *The Central Philosophy of Buddhism: A Study of the Madhyamika System*. London: Allen and Unwin, 1955.

Nivedita, Sister (Margaret E. Noble), and Ananda Coomaraswamy. *Myths of the Hindus and Buddhists*. London: Harrap, 1913; New York: Holt, 1914; New York: Farrar and Rhinehart, 1934.

Oldenburg, Hermann. *Buddha: His Life, His Doctrine, His Order*, translated from the German by William Hoey. London: Williams and Norgate, 1882; Calcutta: Book Co., 1927; London: Luzac, 1928.

Radhakrishnan, Sarvepalli. *The Philosophy of the Upanishads*. London: Allen and Unwin, 1935.

The Brahma Sutra, the Philosophy of Spiritual Life. New York: Harper, 1960: London: Allen and Unwin, 1960.

Radhakrishnan, Sarvepalli, and Charles A. Moore, eds. *A Source Book in Indian Philosophy*. London: Oxford University Press, 1957; Princeton, N.J.: University Press, 1957.

Ranade, Ramchandra Dattatraya. *Indian Mysticism: Mysticism in Maharashtra*. Poona: Bilvakunja Publishing House, 1933.

Rawlinson, Hugh George. *India: A Short Cultural History*. London: Cresset Press, 1937; New York: Praeger, 1952.

Renou, Louis. *Religions of Ancient India*. London: Athlone Press, 1953.

Rhys-Davids, Caroline A. F. *The Milinda-Questions: An Inquiry into its Place in the History of Buddhism*. London: George Routledge, 1930.

Rhys-Davids, Thomas William. *Buddhism: Its History and Literature*. 3rd ed. rev., New York and London: Putnam, 1896.

Thomas, Edward J. *The History of Buddhist Thought*. New York: Knopf, 1933.

Rabindranath Tagore, Poet and Dramatist. London and New York: Oxford University Press, 1926; 2nd ed. rev., New York, 1948.

The Quest of Enlightenment: A Selection of Buddhist Scriptures. London: John Murray, 1956.

Wells, Henry Willis. *The Classical Drama of India: Studies in Its Value for the Literature and Theatre of the World.* Bombay: Asian Publishing House, 1963.

Westcott, G. H. *Kabir and the Kabir Panth.* Cawnpore: Christ Church Mission Press, 1907; Calcutta: S. Gupta, 1953.

Winternitz, Moriz. *A History of Indian Literature*, translated from the German by S. Ketkar and A. Kohn. Calcutta: University, Vols. I and II, 1927–33; Vol. III, part I, Delhi: Motilal Banarsidass, 1963.

Wood, Ernest. *Yoga.* Baltimore and Harmondsworth: Penguin Books, 1959.

Woodroffe, John G. (Arthur Avalon, pseud.). *The Serpent Power.* London: Luzac, 1919; 2nd ed. rev., Madras: Ganesh, 1924.

Zimmer, Heinrich. *Philosophies of India*, ed. by Joseph Campbell [Bollingen Series XXVI]. New York: Pantheon Books, 1951: London: Routledge and Kegan Paul, 1951; New York: Noonday Press (Meridian), 1956.

C. TRANSLATIONS

Aiyar, V. V. S. *The Kural, or The Maxims of Tiru-Valluvar.* Woriur, Tiruchirapalli: V. V. S. Krishnamurthy, 1952. (First published 1915.)

Allchin, F. R. *Tulsi Das: The Petition to Rama.* London: Allen and Unwin, 1966. [UNESCO]

Apte, Vasudeo Mahadeo. *Brahma Sutra Shankara Bhashya.* Bombay: Popular Book Depot, 1960.

Arnold, Edwin. *Light of Asia and the Indian Song of Songs.* Boston, 1875; *The Light of Asia* (A Poetic Life of Buddha). London: Kegan Paul, 1891.

    The Song Celestial, or Bhagavad Gita. 2nd ed., London: Kegan Paul, 1886. Also in Franklin Edgerton, *The Bhagavad Gita* (Harvard Oriental Series, Vol. 39). Cambridge, Mass.: Harvard University Press, 1944; London: Oxford University Press, 1944.

    The Indian Song of Songs, or Gita Govinda. 6th ed., London: Kegan Paul, Trench, Trübner, 1891.

    Indian Idylls. London: Trübner & Co., 1883.

Atkins, A. G. *The Ramayana of Tulsidas with Hindi Text.* 3 vols. New Delhi: Hindustan Times Press, 1954.

Babbitt, Irving. *Dhammapada.* New York and London: Oxford University Press, 1936.

Balasubramaniam, K. M. *Tiru-vachakam of Saint Manickavachar.* Madras: The Chenna-malleswarar and Chenna-kesa-Perumal Devasthanam, 1958.

Barnett, Lionel D. *Bhagavad Gita, or The Lord's Song.* London: Dent. 1905.
  The Path of Light. London: John Murray, 1909; New York; Dutton, 1909.

Brough, John. *The Gandara Dharmapada.* London: Oxford University Press, 1962.
  Poems from the Sanskrit. Harmondsworth: Penguin Books, 1968.

Burlingame, Eugene Watson. *Buddhist Parables.* New Haven, Conn.: Yale University Press, 1922.
  Buddhist Legends. (Harvard Oriental Series, vols. 28–30.) Cambridge, Mass.: Harvard University Press, 1921; London: Oxford University Press, 1922.

Chatterji, Mohini M. *The Bhagavad Gita, or The Lord's Lay.* London: Trübner, 1887; Boston: Tricknor, 1887.

Chelliah, J. V. *Pattu-pattu.* Ten Tamil Idylls. Colombo: General Publishers 1946.

Conze, Edward. *Buddhist Scriptures.* Baltimore and Harmondsworth: Penguin Books, 1959.
  Asta-sahasrika Prajna-paramita. Calcutta: Asiatic Society, 1958.
  Buddhist Wisdom Books: Containing the Diamond Sutra and the Heart Sutra. London: Allen and Unwin, 1958.
  Selected Sayings from the Perfection of Wisdom. London: Buddhist Society, 1955.

Danielou, Alain. *Shilappadikaram* (The Ankle Bracelet), by Prince Ilango Adigal. New York: New Directions, 1965 (ND 162).

Dutt, Manmatha Nath. *A Prose English Translation of the Mahabharata.* 8 vols. Calcutta: H. C. Dass, 1895–1905; reprint, New Delhi, 1960.

Dutt, Romesh C. *The Ramayana and the Mahabharata.* (Abridgements in verse.) Everyman's Library No. 403. London: Dent, 1910; New York: Dutton, 1910. Originally published: London: Temple Classics, 1899.

Edgerton, Franklin. *The Bhagavad Gita.* (Translation and interpretation.) 2 vols. Cambridge, Mass.: Harvard University Press, 1944. Harper Torchbook, 1964.
  The Pancha-tantra Reconstructed. American Oriental Series, Vol. 3. New Haven, Conn.: American Oriental Society, 1924.

Emeneau, M. B. *Abijnana Sakuntala.* Berkeley, Calif.: University of California Press (paperback), 1962.

Francis, H. T., and E. W. Thomas. *Jataka Tales.* Cambridge, England: University Press, 1916.

Gandhi, Mohandas Karamchand (Mahatma). *An Autobiography: The Story of My Experiments with Truth,* translated from the Gujarati by Mahadev Desai. 2 vols. Ahmedabad: Navajivan Press, 1926–7; 2nd ed.,

1940; London: Phoenix Press, 1949; Washington: Public Affairs Press, 1954; Boston: Beacon Press paperback, 1957.

The Mind of Mahatma Gandhi, compiled by R. K. Prabhu and U. R. Rao. Bombay: Oxford University Press, 1945.

Selected Writings of Mahatma Gandhi. Boston: Beacon Press, 1951; London: Faber, 1951.

Ganguli, Kisari Mohan, and Protap Chandra Roy. *The Mahabharata of Krishna Dwaipayana Vyasa*. 11 vols. Calcutta: Bharata Press, 1883–96. Calcutta: Datta Bose, 1919–30; Calcutta: Oriental Publishing Co., 1956.

Gopalachariar, A. V. *Bhartrihari's Sringara Sataka and Vairagya Sataka*. (Bound with Swetaranyam Narayana Sastriar's *Neetisataka*) Madras: V. Ramaswamy Sastrulu & Sons, 1954.

Gopinath, Purohit. *The Niti-sataka, Sringara-sataka, and Vairagya-sataka of Bhartrihari*. 2nd ed. Bombay: Venkateshwar Press, 1914.

Grierson G., and L. D. Barnett. *Lalla-Vakyani*. London: Royal Asiatic Society, 1920.

Griffith, Ralph Thomas Hotchin. *The Hymns of the Rig Veda*. 2 vols. First published 1889, 1896; 3rd ed., Benares: E. J. Lazarus, 1920–6; republished, Varanasi: Chowkamba Sanskrit Series, Vol. xxxv (parts I and II), 1963.

The Ramayan of Valmiki. 5 vols. London: Trübner, 1870–4; Benares: E. J. Lazarus and Co., 1870–4; reprinted, London: Luzac, 1895; Benares: Lazarus, 1895; reprinted in one vol., Varanasi: Chowkamba Sanskrit Series, 1963.

Growse, F. S. *The Ramayana of Tulsi Das*. Allahabad: Government Press, 1889; 7th ed. revised and corrected, Allahabad: Ram Narain Lal, 1957.

Gurner, C. W. *A Century of Passion; Being a Rendering into English Verse of the 'Sringara Satakam'*. Calcutta: Thacker, Spink, 1927.

Hass, George C. O. *The Dasa-rupa: A Treatise on Hindu Dramaturgy by Dhanamjaya*. New York: Columbia University Press, 1912; republished, Delhi: Motilal Banarsidass, 1962.

Hill, W. Doughlas P. *The Holy Lake of Acts of Rama*. Bombay: Oxford University Press, 1952.

Horner, J. B. *King Milinda's Questions* (Milinda-panha). Sacred Books of the Buddhists, Vols. 22 and 23. London: Luzac, 1963, in one volume.

Hume, Robert E. *The Thirteen Principal Upanishads*. London: Milford, 1921.

Iyer, V. V. S. *Thiru-valluvar, The Kural; or The Maxims of Thiruvalluvar*. New Delhi: Jupiter Press, 1915; 4th ed., Madras Amudha Nilaya, Teynampet, 1961.

Kale, M. R., and M. B. Gurjar. *The Niti-sataka and Vairagya-sataka of Bhartrhari*. Bombay: Gopal Narayan, 1898; 4th ed., 1913.

Kanagasabhai, V. *The Great Twin Epics of Tamil.* Madras: Saiva Siddhanta Works Publishing Society, 1956.

Kennedy, J. M. *The Satakas, or Wise Sayings of Bhartrihari.* London: Werner Laurie, 1913.

Kern, H. *Saddharma Pundarika, or The Lotus of the True Law.* The Sacred Books of the East, Vol. 21. Oxford: Clarendon Press, 1884; reprinted, New York: Dover, T. 1065, 1963.

Kingsbury, F., and G. E. Phillips. *Hymns of the Tamil Saivite Saints.* Calcutta: Association Press, 1921; London: Oxford University Press, 1921. The Heritage of India Series.

Krishnaswami Aiyangar, S. *Manimekhalai in its Historical Setting.* London: Luzac, 1928. Introduction and Summary.

Kyt, George. *Sri Jayadeva's Gita Govinda: The Loves of Krsna and Radha.* Bombay: Kutub-Popular, 1940.

Macauliffe, Max Arther. *The Sikh Religion: Its Gurus, Sacred Writings, and Authors.* 6 vols. Oxford: Clarendon Press, 1909.

Macdonnel, A. A. *Hymns from the Rigveda.* London: Oxford University Press, 1922. The Heritage of India Series.

Macfie, J. M. *The Mahabharata: A Summary.* Madras: Christian Literature Society for India, 1921.

   The Ramayan of Tulsidas, or The Bible of Northern India. Edinburgh: Clark, 1930.

Macnicol, Margaret, ed. *Poems by Indian Women.* Calcutta: YMCA Association Press, 1923. The Heritage of India Series.

Macnicol, Nicol. *Psalms of Maratha Saints.* Calcutta: YMCA Association Press, 1919. London: Oxford University Press, 1921. The Heritage of India Series.

Mascaró, Juan. *The Bhagavad Gita.* Baltimore and Harmondsworth: Penguin Books, 1962.

   The Upanishads. Baltimore and Harmondsworth: Penguin Books, 1965.

Max Müller, Friedrich. *Vedic Hymns.* Sacred Books of the East, Vol. 32. Oxford: Clarendon Press, 1891.

   The Upanishads. Sacred Books of the East, Vols. I, XV. Oxford: Clarendon Press, 1879, 1884; reprinted, New York: Dover Publications (T. 992, T. 993).

   The Dhammapada, A Collection of Verse. Sacred Books of the East, Vol. X. Oxford: Clarendon Press, 1881.

   Buddhist Mahayana Texts. Sacred Books of the East, Vol. 49. London: Oxford University Press, 1894.

Meenakshi-sundram, T. P. *Mullai-p-pattu. The Idyll of the Jasmine.* Calcutta: Orient Longmans, 1958.

Monier-Williams, M. *Sakuntala*. Hertford; Madden, 1853; 2nd ed., Oxford: Clarendon Press, 1876.

Narada, Thera. *The Dhammapada*. London: John Murray, 1954. Wisdom of the East Series.

Narasimhan, C. V. *The Mahabharata*. New York: Columbia University Press, 1964.

Nott, S. C. *The Mahabharata of Vyasa Krishna Dwaipayana*. New York: Philosophical Library, 1956; London: James Press, 1956.

Oldenburg, Hermann. *Vedic Hymns*. Sacred Books of the East, Vol. 46. Oxford: Clarendon Press, 1897.

Oliver, Rvilo Pendleton. *Mrccha-katika; The Little Clay Cart*. Urbana, Ill.: University of Illinois Press, 1938.

Pope, George Uglow. *The Naladiyar, or Four Hundred Quatrains in Tamil*. Oxford: Clarendon Press, 1893.

    The Sacred Kural of Tiruvalluvar Nayanar. London: Oxford University Press, 1886.

    Manimekalai. Madras: Meykandan, 1911.

Popley, H. A. *The Sacred Kural, or The Tamil Veda of Tiru-Valluvar*. Calcutta: YMCA Publishing House, 1931, 1958. The Heritage of India Series.

Prasad, Rama. *The Yoga Sutra of Patanjali*. The Sacred Books of the Hindus, Vol. 4. Allahabad: The Panini Office, 3rd ed., 1924.

Radhakrishnan, Sarvepalli. *The Principal Upanishads*. London: Allen and Unwin, 1953; New York: Harper, 1953.

    The Bhagavad Gita. London: Allen and Unwin, 1948; New York: Harper, 1948.

    The Dhammapada. London: Oxford University Press, 1950.

Ramachandra Dikshitar, V. R. *The Silappadikaram*. Madras: Oxford University Press, 1939.

Ramanujan, A. K. *The Interior Landscape*. Bloomington: Indiana University Press, 1967.

Rhys-Davids, Thomas William. *Buddhist Suttas*. Sacred Books of the East, Vol. XI. Oxford: Clarendon Press, 1881. Reprinted Delhi: Motilal Banarsidass, 1965.

    The Questions of King Milinda (Milindapanha). Sacred Books of the East, Vols. 35, 36. Oxford: Clarendon Press, 1890, 1894; reprinted, New York: Dover, 1963 (T.1063, T.1064).

Roy, Pratap Chandra. *The Mahabharata*. Calcutta: Bharata Press, 1890, 11 vols.; 2nd ed., Calcutta: Oriental Publishing, 1956.

Russell, Ralph, and Khurshidul Islam. *Three Mughal Poets: Mir, Sauda, Mir Hasan*. Cambridge, Mass.: Harvard University Press, 1968.

Ryder, Arthur W. *Kalidasa: Translations of Shakuntala and Other Works.* London: Dent, 1912; also under the title: *Shakuntala and Other Writings by Kalidasa,* New York: Dutton (Everyman paperback), 1959.

    The Pancha-tantra. Chicago: University Press, 1925, 1956.

    The Little Clay Cart by Shudraka. Cambridge, Mass.: Harvard University Press, 1905.

    The Ten Princes by Dandin. Chicago: University Press, 1927.

Sastry, R. Shama. *Kautilya's Artha Sastra.* Mysore: Mysore Printing and Publishing House, 1915, 8th ed., 1967.

Scott, Dixon. *Bhartrihari Says.* London: Frederick Muller, 1940.

Seeger, Elizabeth. *The Five Brothers: The Story of Mahabharata.* (A prose adaptation.) New York: John Day, 1948.

Shastri, Hari Prasad. *The Ramayana of Valmiki.* 3 vols. Prose English translation. London: Shanti Sadan, 1952–9.

Singh, Trilochan, *et al. Selections from the Sacred Writings of the Sikhs.* London: Allen and Unwin, 1960 (UNESCO)

Soma-sundaram Pillai, J. M. *Five Tamil Idylls of Pattu-pattu.* Madras: Solden and Co., 1947.

Tagore, Rabindranath, assisted by Evelyn Underhill. *Songs of Kabir.* New York: Macmillan Co., 1915.

Tagore, Rabindranath. *My Reminiscences.* New York and London: Macmillan, 1917.

    Collected Poems and Plays of Rabindranath Tagore. London and New York: Macmillan, 1937.

Tawney, C. H. *Two Centuries of Bhartihari.* Calcutta: Thacker, Spink, 1877.

Thibaut, George. *The Vedanta Sutras of Badarayana with the Commentary by Sankara.* Sacred Books of the East, Vols. 34, 38. Oxford: Clarendon Press, 1890, 1896; reprinted, New York: Dover, 1962 (T.994, T.995).

    The Vedanta Sutras with the Commentary of Ramanuja. Sacred Books of the East, Vol. 48. Oxford: Clarendon Press, 1907.

Thompson, Edward J., and Arthur Marshman Spencer. *Bengali Religious Lyrics; Sakta.* Calcutta: YMCA Association Press, 1923. The Heritage of India Series.

Vivekananda, Swami. *Raja Yoga, or Conquering the Internal Nature.* Calcutta: Swami Trigunatita, 1901; London: Luzac, 1937; 2nd ed., revised, New York: Ramakrishna Vivekananda Center, 1956.

Warren, Henry Clarke. *Buddhism in Translation.* Harvard Oriental Series, Vol. 3. Cambridge, Mass.: Harvard University Press, 1896; reprinted, New York: Atheneum, 1963.

Wilson, Horace Hayman. *The Mrichchhakati, or The Toy Cart.* Calcutta: V. Holcroft, 1826.

Woods, James Haughton. *The Yoga System of Patanjali; or the Ancient Hindu Doctrine of Concentration of Mind, Embracing the Mnemonic Rules, called Yoga Sutra of Patanjali.* Harvard Oriental Series, Vol. 17. 2nd ed., Cambridge, Mass.: Harvard University Press, 1927.

Woolner, A. C., and Lakshman Sarup. *Thirteen Trivandrum Plays Attributed to Bhasa.* Vol. 1. Punjab University Oriental Publication No. 13. London: Oxford University Press, 1930.

Zaehner, R. C. *Hindu Scriptures.* Selections from the *Vedas, Upanishads,* and *Bhagavad Gita.* Everyman's Library 944. London: Dent, 1966; New York: Dutton, 1966.

ACKNOWLEDGEMENTS

To Jaico Publishing House for permission to use 'Karma' taken from *The Voice of God and Other Stories* by Khushwant Singh.

To the Trustees of the Tagore Estate, Macmillan & Co. Ltd., and The Macmillan Co. for permission to use selections from 'The Gitanjali Songs' taken from *Collected Poems and Plays of Tagore*. © 1914 by The Macmillan Company, renewed 1942 by Rabindranath Tagore.

To the Trustees of the Tagore Estate, Macmillan & Co. Ltd, and The Macmillan Co. for permission to use selections from *The Songs of Kabir*, translated by Rabindranath Tagore. © 1915 by The Macmillan Company, renewed 1943 by Rabindranath Tagore.

To Kutub-Popular Ltd for permission to use extracts from *Sri Jayadeva's Gita Govinda*, translated by George Kyt.

To the Navajivan Trust for permission to use extracts from *The Mind of Mahatma Gandhi*, compiled by R. K. Prabhu and U. R. Rao.

To Routledge & Kegan Paul Ltd for permission to use extracts from *Mahabharata* by Krishna Dwaipayana Vyasa.

To Dr V. V. S. Krishnamurthy for permission to use extracts from 'Tiru-Kural', taken from *The Kural or The Maxims of Tiruvalluvar*, translated by V. V. S. Aiyar.

To Clarendon Press Ltd for permission, and Dover Publications Inc. for acknowledgement, to use extracts from *The Sacred Books of the East Series* edited by F. Max. Müller.

To George Allen & Unwin Ltd and Harvard University Press for permission to use extracts from *Three Mughal Poets* by Ralph Russell and Khurshidul Islam. © 1963 by The President and Fellows of Harvard College.

To George Allen & Unwin Ltd for permission to use extracts from *Tulsi Das: The Petition to Rama*, translated by F. R. Allchin; and from *The Sacred Writings of the Sikhs*, translated by Trilochan Singh *et al*.

To M. S. Srinivas for permission to use extracts from *Kautilya's Artha Sastra*, translated by R. Shama Sastry.

To Punjab University, Lahore, for permission to use extracts from the translation of Bhasa's Sanskrit play, *The Vision of Vasavadatta*.

To New Directions Publishing Co. for permission to use extracts from the *Shilappadikaram* by Prince Ilango Adigal, translated by Alain Danielou. © 1965 by Alain Danielou.

To the University of Chicago Press for permission to use extracts from the *Pancha-Tantra of Vishnu Sarma*, translated by Arthur W. Ryder.

To J. M. Dent & Sons Ltd and E. P. Dutton & Co. Inc. for permission to use extracts from Kalidasa's works from *Shakuntala and Other Writings*, translated by Arthur W. Ryder.

To E. P. Dutton & Co. Inc. for permission to use extracts from Valmiki's works from *The Ramayana and the Mahabharata* translated by Romesh C. Dutt, in Everyman's Library text.

To the Asia Society for permission to use extracts from *Speaking of Siva: the Poems* by Basavanna, translated by A. K. Ramanujan.

To Indiana University Press for permission to use extracts from *The Interior Landscape* translated by A. K. Ramanujan.

To the Ramakrishna-Vivekananda Center for permission to use the 'Yoga Sutra' of Patanjali from *Raja Yoga* translated by Swami Vivekananda.

To Yale University Press for permission to use extracts from *Buddhist Parables* translated by Eugene Watson Burlingame. © 1922 by Yale University Press.

To the Estate of Winifred M. Ryder for permission to use selections from *Dandin's Dasha-Kumara-Charita: The Ten Princes* translated by Arthur W. Ryder.

MORE ABOUT PENGUINS
AND PELICANS

Penguinews, which appears every month, contains details of all the new books issued by Penguins as they are published. From time to time it is supplemented by *Penguins in Print*, which is a complete list of all available books published by Penguins. (There are well over three thousand of these.)

A specimen copy of *Penguinews* will be sent to you free on request, and you can become a subscriber for the price of the postage. For a year's issues (including the complete lists) please send 30p if you live in the United Kingdom, or 60p if you live elsewhere. Just write to Dept EP, Penguin Books Ltd, Harmondsworth, Middlesex, enclosing a cheque or postal order, and your name will be added to the mailing list.

Note: *Penguinews* and *Penguins in Print* are not available in the U.S.A. or Canada

A HISTORY OF INDIA

Volume 1

ROMILA THAPAR

The first volume of this new history traces the evolution of India
before contact with modern Europe was established in the sixteenth
century. Romila Thapar is the Reader in History at the University
of Delhi: her account of the development of India's social and
economic structure is arranged within a framework of the principal political and dynastic events. Her narrative covers some 2,500
years of India's history, from the establishment of Aryan culture
in about 1000 B.C. to the coming of the Mughals in A.D. 1526
and the first appearance of European trading companies. In
particular she deals interestingly with the many manifestations of
Indian culture, as seen in religion, art, and literature, in ideas and
institutions.

Volume 2

PERCIVAL SPEAR

It is the aim of this book to relate the history of the Indian people
as a whole, and to make plain the unity of texture in the development of Indian society from the Mughal period to the reign of
Mrs Indira Gandhi.

Dr Spear, a specialist in Indian history, makes the unusual and
illuminating approach of dealing with the Mughal and British
periods together in one volume, on the principle of continuity. He
views the Mughal rule as a preparation and precondition for the
modern age ushered in by the British, and the British Raj as a
harbinger to India of western civilization, which precipitated the
transformation of India that is still in progress.